Grainger County
Tennessee

MINUTES OF COURT OF PLEAS
AND QUARTER SESSIONS

1802–1812

VOLUME 2

WPA RECORDS

Heritage Books
2024

HERITAGE BOOKS

AN IMPRINT OF HERITAGE BOOKS, INC.

Books, CDs, and more—Worldwide

For our listing of thousands of titles see our website
at
www.HeritageBooks.com

A Facsimile Reprint
Published 2024 by
HERITAGE BOOKS, INC.
Publishing Division
5810 Ruatan Street
Berwyn Heights, MD 20740

Originally published 1939

International Standard Book Number
Paperbound: 978-0-7884-9052-1

TENNESSEE

RECORDS OF GRAINGER COUNTY

MINUTES OF COURT OF PLEAS & QUARTER SESSIONS VOL. 2
1802 - 1812

Prepared By
The Historical Records Survey
Transcription Unit
Division of Women's and Professional Projects
Works Progress Administration

Mrs. John Trotwood Moore
State Librarian and Archivist, Sponsor

T. Marshall Jones
State Director

Mrs. Penelope Johnson Allen
State Supervisor

Mrs. Margaret Helms Richardson
District Supervisor

. . . . .

Nashville, Tennessee
The Historical Records Survey
March 9, 1939

Prepared By

Everett E. Holder
Mrs. Lillian C. Ewing

Indexed By

Mrs. Lillian C. Ewing
Everett E. Holder

Typed By

Mrs. Lillian C. Ewing

The Historical Records Survey

Luther H. Evans, National Director
T. Marshall Jones, State Director

Division of Women's and Professional Projects

Florence S. Kerr, Assistant Administrator
Elizabeth D. Coppedge, State Director

WORKS PROGRESS ADMINISTRATION

F. C. Harrington, Administrator
Harry S. Berry, State Administrator

GRAINGER COUNTY

COURT OF PLEAS & QUARTER SESSION
1802-1812   Vol. 2-

INDEX

Note: -

Page numbers in this index refer to those of the original volume
from which this copy was made. These numbers are carried throughout the
copy within parentheses, as: (p 124)

A

C

Campbell, (lawyer)- 245
Campbell, Major, 165,174
Campbell & Martin, 262,293,314
Campbell, Mathew, 16,31,32,33,42,
        48,63,64,56,60,65,68,70
        71,73,79,89,103,104,111
        116,119,126,145,146,147
        182,184,219,230,235,236
        245,250,260,277,278,282,
        287,288,289,295,297,300
        305,319,321,327,334,336
        337,341,349,353,358,372
        374,383,-389,391,395,396
        397,401,402,403,407,410
        412,414,420
Campbell, Patrick, 108
Campbell, Peter, 253,254
Campbell, Uri, 122
Campbell, Wsley, 25
Campbell, William, 122
Caney Creek, 10,208,209
Cannon, John, 104,111,114,133,
        173,176,181,184,188,192
        193,194,217
Cantril, John, 23
Capps, Jacob, 33,238
Capps, Mathew, 95
Capps, William, 238
Cariger, Godfrey, 170,375
Carley, George, 180
Carmack, Edward, 121
Carmichael,Company-10,91
Carmichael, Duncan,(Dunkin) -41,45,
        50,53,56,60,61,62,68,69,71,
        78,84,87,89,97,100,104,111,175
        176,181,184,188,195,222,227,
        252,259,265,267,268,270,295
Carmichael, James, 13,41,45,56,89,93
        104,111,115,119,124,129,141,174
        175,181,182,194,222,227,252,259
        262,281,287,290,295,299,303,313
        314,326,340,376,
Carmichael, Joseph, 401
Carmichael, Rachel, 249
Carney, Thomas, 150,289
Carns, Nicholas, 90
Carrell, Tarlton, 351,363
Carrick, Hugh, 228,229
Carrick, Montgomery,& Co. 106
Carrick, Samuel, D. 95,101,133,143
        144,135,167
Carrothers, John, 351
Carson, Anna, 61,221

Carson, Samuel, 27,61,221
Carwile, John, 45,76,89
Caseys Place, 264
Cathcart, John, 127
Cave Springs, 11,99, 168
Center, Elizabeth, 28
Chambers, Joseph, 351
Chamberlain, Andrew, 312
Chamberlain, Edward, 218
Chamberlain, Elizabeth, 313
Chamberlain, Jeremiah, 10,13,51,87,
        210,219,235,266,274,298,299,300
        302,313,350
Chamberlain, Mary, 63,218
Chamberlain, Ninian, 201,235
Chandler, Daniel, 287,295,349,351,370
        413
Chandler, James, 345
Chandler, Joseph, 355
Chandler, Richard, 108
Chandler, Robert, 290, 291
Chandler, William, 355
Chaney, John, 251,340,341
Charles, James, 335,345,357,377
Cheeks Cross Road, 114,175,185,216,371
Cheek,Dawson, 48,56,60,79,86,97,100
        104,111,119,164,365,366
Cheek,Dodson, 116
Cheek, Jesse, 5,6,41,42,48,56,60,69
        75,89,93,104,111,116,119,143,
        154,158,159,168,169,214,231,
        241,245,249,250,262,270,279
        280,281,287,292,293,294,297
        299,301,302, 303,308,326,339
        342,355,360,361,368,371,373
        374,375
Cheraher (Chisher) Thornton, 338,349
Childress, Elizabeth, 43
Chinn, James, 8,23,28,50,250
Chinn, Thomas, 7,8,14,33,140
Chilton, Richard, 20,26
Christian, Allen, 56,60,120,157,177
Christian, Jesse, 120
Christian, William, 17,20,26,45,46,57
        65,68,75,91,93,95,96
Churchman, Edward, 10,13,17,37,38,41
        45,69,75,88,116,119,126,141,
        250,260,273,275,279,287,293
        294,295,299,303,310,312,314
        326,349,376,415,427,
Churchman, Elizabeth, 142
Churchman, John, 277,287,297

Crocket, Patience, 82,
Cross, Gibbons, 247,288
Crow, John, 93,98,164,231,260,262
 263,273,278,284
Crozier, John, 52
Crump, William, 153,356
Cunningham, Thomas, 102
Cyrus, Mathew, 276
Cyrus, Nimrod, 93,253,265,267,299
 303,312,313,316

D

Dale, Abel, 79,223,231,296,324,371
 376
Dale, Jonathan, 223
Dalton, Rubin, 89,93,95,219,222,231,
 241,252,259,263,275,376,383,
 389,389
Damewood, Henry, 427
Daniel, (Dannel) Edward, 73,78,82,87,89
 93,116,119,129,133,174,
 198,210,219,278,284
Daniel (Dannel) Francis, 31,37,48,50,53
 56,73,78,82,84,87,95,103,104,
 111,124,129,137,185,210,211,
 219,220,222,227,231,240,244,
 265,278,284,301,352,359,361
 363,371,395,400,403,427
Daniel, James, 32,38,56,245,333,340,
 356
Daniel, John, 20,25,26,34,35,38,50,53
 74,78,84,87,90,176,181,182,
 220,260,263,273,325,363,371
Daniel, Joseph, 240
Dardis, Thomas, 65,83,84,88,121,127
 132,135,142,151,164,180,210
 233,241,246,273,278,284,311
David, Razor, 243
Davidson, David, 54
Davidson, Edward, 3,290
Davidson, Golder, 248,252,259,265
 267,268,270
Davidson, Samuel, 123
Davidson, William, 81,167,168,169
 187,210,222,227,293
Davis, Benjamin, 273,277,294
Davis, David, 20,26,56,60,65,68,70
 71,72,78,84,89,93,117
Davis, John, 225
Davis, Nancy, 124,172,220,221
Davis, Nathaniel, 65,71,91,105,179
Davis, Samuel, 363
Davis, Thomas, 46

Davis, William, 8,48,56,64,180
Deadrick, David, 344,402
Dedrick & Conway, 35
Deen, John, 17, 18,22,39,44,71,78,88,
 100,114,139,219,225,357
Defoe, Michjah, 182
Dennis, John, 153,166,222,223,227,
 239,260,274,277,279,282,325
 333,403
Dennis, John Jr. 136,145
Dennis, Joseph, 10,13,42,48,56,60,116
 119,121,125,126,142,173,195,197
 217,234,385
Dennis, Sarah, 403
Dennis, Thomas, 22,42,56,69,75,78,89
 93,104,111,114,115,140,141
 142,173,200,223,252,259,368
 385,412
Denson, Elizabeth, 173,184
Denson, Susannah, 428
Dickinson, James, 235
Dishan, Aaron, 111,112
District of Hamilton,12,15,21,24,25,
 40,59,68,71,74,77,87-91,97,98
 103,104,108,109,127,135,139,
 153,163,165,177,192,193,221,225
 237,255,259,285,286,291,293,297
 300,306,307,316,322,333,337,348
 350,354,355,367,372,398,423,428
 District of Washington, 74,97,108,109
 153,165,285,291,297,306,316,322
 333,348,350,354,355,367,372,
 298,423,428
Dixon, Benjamin, 356
Dixon, Jeremiah, 330,331
Dixon, Robert, 376
Dixon, Rubin, 116,122,135,166,176,
 181,194,196,210,218,219,220
 222,223,225,230,241,247,311
 316,327,329,330,355,416,417
Dodson, Company, 91,98,128,132
Dodson, James, 28
Dodson, John, 114,121,123,125,144,
 178,187,199,201,236
Dodson, Jesse, 101
Dodson, Nimrod, 5,39
Dodson, Samuel, 101,142,180,263,275
 325,370,376,363,386,388,389
Dodson, Thomas, 51,101,142,180
Dodson, Valentine, 366
Dodson, William, 180,223,330,331,338
 363,368,371,373,374,375,385
Doggett, Miller, 46
Doghart, Thomas, 180

Donaldson,(Donaldson) Andrew, 232,233,234-
Donaldson, John, 234
Donaldson, Stockley, 35
Donahoe, Patrick, 172
Donathan, Elijah, 6,39,48,69,83,90,102
    113,120,123,141,146,189
Donner, John, 356
Dorah, John, 5,7,23,51,169,258
Dorough (Dorah) John, 202
Dorset, Thomas, 253
Douglass, Fanney, 374
Douglass, Joseph, 260,377,372,374
Douglass, Nancy, 374
Douglass, Samuel, 374
Douglass, Younger, 374,405
Driver, William, 185
Dug Hill, 218
Duke, John, 56,105,188,205,223,301
    305,393,395,396,406,407
Duke, Pleasant, 5,10,13,17,22,30,31
    32,33,34,43,44,49,51,61,77
    80,83,88,89,96,99,104,106,
    111,126,136,139,142,145,150
    155,158,173,174,178,180,188
    191,192,193,255,301,305,393
    395,406,407
Dunville (Dunville) Richard, 161,
    221,223,257,258,282,291,294
    298,302,313
Dunville, Robert, 27,32,130,147,
    210
Duncan, John, 224
Duncan, William, 76
Dunham Harlin, 85
Dunlap, Hugh, 184
Dunlap, Josiah, 286
Dunlap, Samuel, 166,290,302,304,
Dunn, Thomas, 40,42,79,94,116,119
Duratt, Jacob, 253
Dyer, Abner, 99,103
Dyer, Benjamin, 90
Dyer, Elisha, 185
Dyer, George, 411
Dyer, Jacob, 183
Dyer, James, 11,29,44,54,59,61,63
    65,70,71,-75,81,82,84,90,97
    98,108,121,124,134,144,150
    183,186,192,197,218,219,229
    276,311,318,327,329,330,359
Dyer, Joseph, 68,69,158,182,224,235
Dyer, Josiah, 12,56,60,61,68,69,70
    71,72,76,80,84,91,94,99,101
    103,124,128,132,141,146,156
    160,170,171,175

Dyer, Spilsby, 223
Dyer, Thomas, 57,219
Dyer, William, 29,43,44,51,90,121
    125,126,137,183,185,221,
    235,260,268,269,377,420

E

Easley, Miller, 8,10,13,29,31,32
    41,46,54,63,72,87,89,90
    95,98,101,136,143,145,154
    169,176,178,180,182,209,
    210,219,221,222,224,225,
    228,230,239,241,246,252,
    253,269,287,295,297,345
    361,398,404,415
Eaton, Jenney, 235,350
Eaton, Joseph, 10,13,17,31,37,48
    131,154,159,235
Eaton, Robert D. 50,53,54,58,63
    64,65,95,103,104,111,
    116,119,136,145,146,
    150,223,235,252,259
    261,286,290,295,312,314
    327,329,338,341,376,383
    391,393,407,410,427
Eaton, (Eatan) William, 235
Eddins, Samuel, 82
Edington, Thomas, 153,155,158,224
Edward, Brown, 321
Edward, Lewis, 210,219,229,231
    267
Edward, Peter, 179,230
Elder, Andrew, 241,363,369
Elkins, David, 223,363,369,371
    373,374,379
Elkins, James, 286,363,379,382
Elliot, Abraham, 7,9,10,14,15,31
    37,39,40,55,56,60,63,73,
    77,80,81,96,117,135,140
    153,162,170,173,186,200
Elliot, Benjamin, 18,20,26,43,
    44,48,56,60,65,68,70,71
    104,111,124,129,141
Elliot, Israel, 88,112
Elliot, Jacob, 39,56,71,73,80,99
    116,119,153,173,181,182
    183,197,200,222,227,
Elliot, Mathew, 88
Elliot, William, 88,112,
Ellis, Robert, 17
Ellison, James, 204,286,333,379
Elsey, John, 21,39,49,78,90

Emerson, Thomas, 45
English, William, 161
English, Wilson, 112,173
Epps, Edward, 30,42,68,70
Erwine, David, 367
Erwine, John, 76,400,403
Estis, John, 4,41,45,51,56,60
        78,84,87,89,93,104,111,
        112,115,136,145,146,147
        154,159,175,180,188,210
        219,222,224,227,241,244
        247,255,262,278,281,294
        299,303,311,313,315,341
        343,349
Estis, Thomas, 31,37
Evans, Andrew, 13,33,76
Evans, David, 58,236
Evans, Eliah, 263,275
Evans, George, 29,54,77,88,119
        183,232,236,260,262
        279,292,293,294,297
        301,308,321,322,323
        326,339,360,361,362
        375,377,406,412
Evans, Jesse, 277
Evans, John, 58,89
Evans, Joseph, 13,14
Evans, Walter, 6
Evans, William, 57,58
Ewing, William, 248
Ezell, James, 393

F

Fears, James, 71,79,224
Fenn, Richard, 17,19,22,357
Ferguson, James, 87,95,161,188,311
Ferguson, John, 414
Ferguson, William, 161

Ferries-
Ferry, Circles, 139,158 (Circle's)
        Bullers, 266
        Evans, 262
        Hodges, 223
        Marshall, 39,73,112
        Moore's, 48,56,64,65,78,192
                216,217,238,249,299
        Nances, 89
        Peeters, 84
        Robertsons, 51,304
        Smith, 116,122
Fields, David, 3,17,56,60,68,69,71,
        154,159,167,168,169

Fields, Edward, 22
Fields, Joseph, 69,75,85,89,93,99,136
        137,139,153,154,159,161,166,173
        175,182,196,201,223,229,232,234
        241,247,278,284,412
Fields, Littler, 129
Fields, Robert, 196,197,210,217,218,
        219,223,231,241,247,252,259,286
        299,303,325,336,385
Finley, George, 157
Finley, John, 38,49,51,163,306
Fisher, Joseph, 248
Floyd, Allison, 106
Floyd, David, 50,51
Floyd, James, 49
Fords-
        Bullers, 185,205
        Circles, 173
        Dodson Creek, 374
        Hankins, 195
        Hodges, 173,200
        Island, 175,238,286
        Marshall, 15,114,222,411
        Hays, 220,239,252,363
Ford, Ralph, 123,232,233,239,340,341
Ford, Shelton, 175,185,194,195,198
        203,216,264,315,341
Fowlers Gap, 421
Fowler, James, 300,364,413
Franklin, Edward, 241
Frazier, Samuel, 18
Free, Moses, 257
Free, Philip, 77,154,166,176,194,228,229
Fry, Gabriel, 192,193,205,212,213,222
                224,229,243,282
Fulcher, William, 214,221

G

Gaines, James, 165
Gaines, Robert, 27,56,60,65,68,70,71
        72,122,174,187,196,201,241
        247,376,404
Gallion, Isaiah, 252
Gallion, Jacob, 131
Gallion, John, 313,326,388
Gallion (Gallyan) Lewis, 229
Gallion, (Galleyan) Thomas, 102
Garrett, Absolem, 183,184,186,211,220,224
Garrett, William, 65,85
Gaw, John, 278,284,285,289
Gentry, Joseph, 108
German Creek, 102,186
Gibson, Archelus, 10,13,84,88,90,112

Gibson, Archibald, 78
Gibson, Bryan, 338,348
Gibson, Isaac, 51
Gibson, Jacob, 151,154
Gibson, James, 165
Gibson, William, 112
Gilbert, Charles, 38,78,84,85,120
Gilbreath, James, 50
Gill, Thomas, 315,342,345,347,348
    350,355,359,361,362,363,372
    374,375,379,382,401,411,416
Gilliton, Charles, 422
Gillem, Derieux, 184
Gillentine, John, 3,23,40,43,47
Gillentine, Nicholas, 50,51,52,
    57,58,59,60,82,83,85,92
    98,99
Gillmore, Ann, 225
Gillmore, John, 85,103
Gillmore, Peter, 85,235,427
Glosset, Sairah, 204
Goard, Stephen, 238,263,285
Going, Caleb, 154
Going, Clayborn, 130,172,220
Going, Daniel, 89,93,131,222,
    232,278,284
Going, James, 154
Going, Sarah, 130,137,172
Gold, John, 105,121,160
Golden, William, 94,136,154
Golder, William, 145
Golding, William, 84
Gordon, George, 345
Gordon, Robert C. 10,17,21,22,24,
    28,31,36,39,40,54,59,80,81
    83,105,121,135,160,171
Gowing (Going) Clos, 220,222
Gowing, (Going) Daniel, 64,80,219,221
Gowing, John, 51
Gowing, Pricilla, 221
Graham (Grayham) James, 80
Graham, Thomas, 49
Graham, William, 42,123
Grannot, John Bactor, 124
Grantham, Richard, 180,222,227,240,257,
    361,367
Grassey Point, 264
Gray, John, 102
Gray, Thomas, 32,385,389,425,429
Grayson, James, 27,40,41,42,100,305
    213,221,225,230,275
Green, John, 107,120,121,123,136,137
    158,162,167,175,280,288,
    289,345

Green, Joseph, 120,153
Green, Farnifold, 56,85
Griffey, John, 342
Griffin, Spencer, 5,6,8,14,33,39,41
    50,51,52,57,58,59,60,78,82
    83,85,88,90,92,98,99,110,113
    115,132,135,143,144,187
Griffitts, Elijah, 362
Griffitts, Griffey, 141,264
Griffitts, John, 17,19,141,224,241
    247,304,373,374,401,412,428
Griffords (Griffards) George, 252
Griffords Company, 273,310
Grigsby, Simeon, B. 39
Grimes, David, 101
Grimes, Elizabeth, 101
Grimes, Thomas, 28,147,202
Grove, Benjamin, 380
Grove Holley, 380
Grove, Reubin, 174,183,196,233,371
    373,420
Grubb, Jesse, 298
Grubb, Joseph, 298
Grusham (Grisson) 276,292
Guinn, James, 43,47
Guinn, (Gwynn) William, 8,79,112,
    165,239,252,253,351,414
Guss (Gess,)(Gass) George, 402
Guss, William, 70,98,117
Guthrie, James, 13

H

Hackney, Jacob, 403,404,412
Haggard, Henry, 113
Hailey, Claiborne, 405
Hailey, Major David, 9,10,13,40,70
    79,89,94,108,202,214,243,
    244,246,250,254,255,304,337
Hailey, Edward, 151,154,174
Hailey (Haley) John C. 20,31,32,33
    56,68,71,94,113,115,122,155,
    161,220,223,240,241,251,256
    279,280,297,300,331,339,353
    364,371,425
Haines (Hanes) Isabel, 101
Haines, John, 32,43,44,97,100,101
    136,146,163,195
Haines, Peter, 70
Haines, Robert, 176
Haines, William, 165,175,223
Hainey, Spencer, 51
Hall, Adam, 52,55,236,250,265

Hogg, James, 133
Hogg, Obediah, 19
Holley, Mary, 266
Holston, Henry, 102,260,273,278,284
Holston River, 73,82
Holt, Daniel, 121
Holt, David, 19,30,31,-35,41-45,50
   51,55,56,60,83,87,89,93,99,
   104,113,114,116,119,143,158
   187,201,222,243,250,266,288
   295,330,378,393,388,401,421
Holt, Davis, 71
Holt, Edmund, 4,5,-8,17,23,30,40
   47,182,213,223,224,243
Holt, Henry, 201
Holt, James, 100,164,195,348,353,
   354
Holt, John, 28,31,37,69,75,100,
   106,111,136,137,143,158,167
   174,187,301,299,307,345,355
   400,403
Holt, Joseph, 299
Holt, Michael, 164,228,229,299,
   311,318,327,328,330,356
Holt, Sarah, 162
Honeycutt, Robert, 162,176,177,
   179,186,222,224,238,229
Hopper, Archabald, 167,168,169
   175,266,351,427
Hopper, Charles, 20,26,97,100,116
   119,124,129,168,266
Hopping, David, 41,62
Hornback, John, 91,317,354
Horner, George, 32,85,118
Horner, John, 39,45,49,50,51,62
   68,71,80,81,111,112,120
   122,124,134
Horner, Thomas, 314,327,329
Horton, Benjamin James, 380
Horton, Milley, 380
Howard, Abraham, 34,35,47,51
Howard, Absolem, 106
Howard, Henry, 48
Howard, John, 48,64,65
Howard, William, 19,28,30,40,43,44
   47,49,64,72,81,82,90,95
   101,200
Howell, Benjamin, 27,51,102,112,140,
   171,174,194,198,220,247,
   249,259
Howell, Caleb, 61,76,130,146,172,177
   185,198,226,247,251,259,280,
   283,295,296,303,318,320,324,
   325,349,363,371,375,379

Howell's Company, 10,26,91,94,128,185
Howell, Henry, 6,7,12,16,18,22,29,30-
   35,37,47,49,60,65,68,71,73,77
   79,82,83,85,87,88,89,92,93,95
   98,99,101,102,103,105,107,109
   110,121,124,125,128,129,133,
   135,139,141,143,144,146,147
   155,158,167,168,169,171,175
   176,177,178,179,180,184,185
   196,201,204,220,224,228,236
   237,240,244,247,254-259,260-
   267,273,275,277,-284,286,287,
   291,294,295,296,299,300,303,
   307,312,314,315,325,326,328
   330,331,336,337,343,353,357
   363,371,-376,379,381,383,384
   385,388,393,394,400,401,403,
   408,409,416,418,-421,425,426
Howell, John, 48,102,115,229
Howell, Major, 174
Howell, Malacia, 94,97,100,102,105
   107,109,110,176,181,186,
   220,240,241,247,363,371,
   373,374
Howell, Philip, 94,146
Howell, William, 27,48,52,74,82,94
   108,249,418
Huddleston, Benjamin, 266
Huddleston, David, 78,84,89,93,97
   100,122,154,159,168,222,
   227,266,351
Huddleston, Jackson, 266
Huddleston, John, 21,22,55,56,65,
   72,95
Huddleston, Robert, 111,117,374,385
   394
Huddleston, Thomas, 5,111
Hudson, Benjamin, 20,26,98,162,168
   175,182,201,231,233,241
   247,248,259,291,371
Hudson, Culberd, 233,241
Hudson, Hall, 14,233
Hudson, James, 15
Hudson, Joshua, 233
Hudson, Obediah, 15
Humbard, William, 78,84,85,88,90
   122,251
Hume, Alexander, 326,385
Humphreys, George, 83,179
Humphreys, John, 5,7,31,60,73,80,118
   120,130,136,141,145,146,166,176
   198,241,244,247,250,256,277,309
   311,318,325,327,329,330,337,379
   388

Mc Vey, Eli, 30,35
Mc Vey, James, 224
Medlock, Littleberry, 270,343
Medly, James, 32,33,35
Mendinghall, Abaolem, 309
Mendinghall, Joseph, 56,77,102
Michaels Company, 128
Middleton, John, 101,250,254,256
        258,305,308
Middleton, Rebecca, 305,308
Midkiff, Isaac, 33,43,44,45,48,69
        97,100,105,106,107,141
Midkiff, Isaiah, 15,18,22,24,30,32
        46,52,53,60,65,68,70,71,75,
        77,80,81,82,84,85,87,88,89,
        98,101,103,109,111,116,118,
        125,133,135,143,145,154,161
        163,184,185,188,196,197,226,
        227,228,235,237,238,240,241
        242,246,248,253,255,256,258
        259,262,263,266,267,268,270
        272,273,275,277,278,282,283
        288,290,292,297,298,299,300
        302,303,309,311,312,315,320
        321,324,325,327,333,334,336,
        343,349,353,355,360,361,364
        365,370,371,373,381,382,393
        395,396,397,401,406,408,409
        414,416,420,422,423,426,429
Midkiff, Jeremiah, 24,35,41,42,58
        70,83,89,104,114,140,150,
        168,173,211,224,278,259,
        272,278,288,298,299,324,
        350,351,370,409
Midkiff, John, 21,47,288,345
Midkiff, Thomas, 18
Midkiff, William, 58,231,247,259,291
Midly, James, 34
Miller, Batheny, 85
Miller, Betsy, 104
Miller, Frederick, 6,7,343,364
Miller, George, 76,85,104,157,286
        289,292
Miller, John, 85,244,247,271,273,
        282,290
Miller, Martin, 34,85,104
Miller, Nancy, 76,85,157,286,292
Miller, Peter, 5,7
Miller, Pleasant, M. 9,19,21,28,34
        50,52,58,59,76,77,79,80,82
        83,96,110,115,117,135,142
        215,243,255,256,261,382
Miller, Rachel, 171
Miller, Sally, 150

Miller, Sarah, 289
Miller, Stephen, 361
Miller, William, 48,55,74,77
Millican, Elenor, 38
Millican, William, 38,219
Milligan (Millican) Elihu, 123,171
Milligan, (Millican) William, 71,79
        97,111,124,129,153,176,181,
        210,222,227
Millikan (Millican) Solomon, 312
Millikan, (Millican) William, 46,58
        71,89,93,100,104,115
Minet, John, 90,93,223,287,295,318
Minet, Samuel, 383
Minis, Jeremiah, 164
Minor, Henry, 134
Mitchell, Aquilla, 373,374
Mitchell, Isaac, 30,48,56,60,68,69,71
        79,93,95,136,145,154,176,181,
        184,187,251,262,266,274,275,
        278,281,284,288,294,325,327,
        328,329,336,363,371,416,413,
        425,426
Mitchell, James, 137,178,198
Mitchell, John, 125
Mitchell, Richard, 8,88,102,317,334
Mitchell, Ruth, 276
Mitchell, Thomas, 385
Mitchell, William, 10,13,18,21,22,30,
        31,37,43,68,69,75,79,80,89
        97,100,104,115,118,124,129
        135,136,139,143,148,151,166
        167,168,174,177,178,187,201
        213,225,236,237,254,300,325
        333,342,374,401,427
Moffett, Henry, 24
Moffett, John, 62,63,69,75,77,79,80,
        81,88,89,103,105,106,109,110,
        115,124,125,126,129,135,136,137
        139,163,164,182,219,220,252,259
        262,264,280,283,292,294,297,299
        303,309,310,320,321,325,332,337,
        348,350,351,359,360,361,375,388
        401,410,414
Moffett (Moffet) Samuel, 62,70,89,393
Moffett, William, 14,16,18,21,24,62
        105,303,325,332
Monrow's Company, 409
Monrow, Robert, 81
Montgomery, Carrick & Co. 99
Montgomery's Company, 165
Montgomery, Hugh, 225
Montgomery, Michael, 43
Montgomery, Thomas, 257

Moody, George, 140,151,159,167,168
    171,192,198,210,219,221,222
    224,235,241,242,245,247,252
    259,262,263,268,270,274,286
    290,291,292,293,294,297,298
    306,308,314,315,319,320,321,
    329,337,349,352,359,360,361
    372,373,383,385,387,390,392
    395,399,400,401,406,409,412
    417,420,422,423,425,426,428
Moody, James, 372
Moody, John, 359,376,398,400,401,406
Moody, Rachel, 398,399,400
Mooney, William, 117,247
Moore, Benjamin, 30
Moore, Enoch, 371,373
Moore, James, 3,4,10,15,17,25,26,45,
    47,49,50,53,55,57,59,60,65,68
    69,73,88,89,91,93,94,96,97,98,
    105,112,116,119,122,128,132,145,154
    159,162,166,174,176,181,192,194,195
    198,199,201,203,204,211,212,213,216
    219,221,222,225,227,240,241,242,243
    245,247,-250,252,258,262,264,286,288
    292,293,294,297,298,319,320,331,332,
    377-382,388,396,401,402,403,414,429
Moore, John, 203,234,244,254,270,279,316
Moore, Levi, 97,158,196
Moore, Magnus, 50,53
Moore, Martha, 48
Moore, Master, 426
Moore, McNess, 190,205,206,209,287,295,
    349,376,401,417,420,428
Moore's Mill, 117
Moore, Rice, 265,268,349
Moore, Robert, 7,8,30,32,33,42,43,44,79
    97,99,113,124,135,156,162,196
Moore, Sparks, 287
Morgan, Abel, 18,43,57,61,69,76,160,161
    173,205
Morgan, Henry, 56,60,69,75,89,93,97,98
    100,140,142,164,180,203
Morgan, Thomas, 180
Morgan, Valentine, 23,69,70,71,72,107,
    123,157,162,166,167,168,171
    174,175,177,178,180,186,187
    201,202,225,228,229,239,241,247,252,
    263,265,268,270,293,311,312,312
Morgan, ?274,329,330,344,345,351
Morgan, William, 43
Morris Company, 352
Morris, Gideon, 293
Morris, John, 61,94,175,210,219,241

Morris, Martin, 133,154,174,271,334
Morris, Shedrick, 93
Morris, Thomas, 352,363
Morris, William, 120,330,331
Morrison, William, 3
Morrows, Gap, 217
Mossy Creek Iron Works, 363,371
Moulder, Valentine, 45,54,55,57,91
    96,97,128,132,178,186,199
Mountain (Log) 94,112,311,349
    Lane, 11,81,82,328
    Powell, 377
Mourning, Sally, 173,184
Moyers, Adam, 4,8
Moyers, Frederick, 23,30,31,35,48
    50,63,64,67,73,81,82,87,91,
    95,96,109,116,122,143,147,154
    166,169,173,183,185,186,202
    232,234,235,351,404,408,415
Moyers, Henry, 285
Moyers, John, 10,13,41,70,75,77,78
    79,80,81,95,112,210,212,213
    215,218,219,228,229,241,259
Moyers, Michael, 112,122,183,234
Mumpower, John, 50,53
Mumpower, Jonathan, 10,13,167,168
    222,227,287,428
Munrow (Monrow) Robert, 411
Murlock, Sampson, 254
Murphy, Dubart, 62,68,69,190
Murphy, Isaac, 46,172
Murphy, Richard, 46,172
Murphy, Sarah, 46,62,172
Murphy, Thomas, 393
Murphy, William, 9,46,214
Murry, Thomas, 216,408,419
Myers, John, 247

N

Nall, John, 10,13,18,20,28,40,44
    45,48,107,139,217,218,244
    251,252,268,270,271
Nall, Larkin, 15,17,18,40,41,45,49
    73,79,80,97
Nall, Margaret, 52
Nall Meeting House, 195,218,385,
Nall, Rebecca, 273
Nall, Robert, 274,309,349,353,362
    378
Nall, William, 7,15,18,21,22,43,44
    48,50,52,56,57,73,74,77,79

Nall, William, 80,86,88,91,103,104
        112,114,169,174,238,247
        270,273,274,289,309,310
        349,353,362,378,387
Nance, John, 279
Natches Creek, 423
Nation, William, 23,30,31
Neal, Anthony, 245
Neal, Jesse, 282,287
Nenney, Patrick, 123
Nevin, John, 6,49
Newell, Samuel, 8,43,50,59
Newman, John, 243
Newman, Jonathan, 72
Nicely, John, 390,391
Nichol, Isaiah, 99
Nichol, John, 98,99,109
Nichol, Joseph, 156
Nichols, Josiah, 98,109,121,144
Nicholson, Samuel, 377,401,424,
Nisle, John, 95
Niven, John, 49
Noe, George, 3,5,115,178,199,253
        376,383,390,418,419
Noe, Jacob, 125,143,288,388,427
Noe, John, 15,20,25,31,37,50,53,
        129,136,145,175,187,201,217,
        222,224,229,231,252,259,260
        273,278,284,349,361,376
Noe, Joseph, 10,13,41,50,53,54,58,59
        69,71,75,85,99,107,114,124,
        125,129,133,135,143,154,158
        159,162,167,169,173,175,183
        186,-193,194,195,196,201,203,
        229,265,288,290,301,305,307
        325,327,339,352,356,359,363
        368,371,373,377,393,395,396
        400,403,406,423,427
Noe, Joseph Jr. 352
Noe, Peter, 11,13,14,19,24,25,29,30,
        33,34,35,41,42,43,47,51,83
Norman, John, 255,256,259,269,353
Norris, George, 68,69,75,97,100,124
        129,136,145,184,205,210,219
        223,240,261,273,284,407
Norris, Gidion, 126,262
Norris, Janet, 407
Norris, John, 185
Norris, Martin, 121
Norris, Shedrick, 262
Norten, William, 50,132,133,148,154,160
North Carolina, 148,167,189,275
Nott, Edmund, 4
Nugent, Thomas, 251

O

Oaks, Jonathan, 231
Oaks, Joshua, 124,129,168,266
Oansville, 411
Obark, Robert, 311,319,335
Odannell, John, 11,108
Odneil, Sanders, 410
Ogan, John, 143,172,174,175,192,193
Ogle, Harklous, 4,48
Ogle, Hercules, 70,75,79,89,93,96
        104,111,115
Ogle, John, 241
Ogle, Thomas, 180,196,275,370,386
Oldham, Moses, 179
Ore, Colonel, 72
Ore, James, 5,6,14,17,18,19,20,25
        ,28,29,32,35,40,41,43,45
        50,51,52,57,59,60,62,71
        81,82,83,92,98,99,100,
        102,103,104,106,110,124
        131,161,170,184,255
Ore, Joseph, 6,9,10,13,14,17,41,45
        49,87,170,248,261,299
Orr's old Mill, 198
Outlaw, Alexander, 13,31
Overton, John, 85,86
Overton, Moses, 170
Owen, James, 95,183
Owen, Joseph, 38,120,142
Owens, William, 49
Owl Hole Gap, 48,54,56,210,212,223
        248,281,299,338,370,394

P

Pace, Hardy, 33
Paine, William, 48,49
Pangle, Joseph, 122
Pannell, Thomas, 4,267
Panther Springs, 46,56,73,82,87,113
        144,312
Park, Jones, 212
Park, Robert, 44,47,48
Park, William, 212
Parker, James, 370,400,403,406,413
        420,425,427
Parker, Philip, 57,95
Parker, Thomas, 391,393
Parkerson, William, 131,235,237,252
        258,268,270,279,280,284-292
        296,299,305,352
Parsons, Enoch, 85
Patterson Creek, 63,64

Robinson, Daniel, 29,30,31,37,38,58
    69,72,75,87,88,116,120,389
    404,425,426
Robinson, James, 58,78
Robinson, John, 25,
Robinson, William, 42,49,87,297,388
    389,391
Robison, Daniel (Robinson) 25,244,
    262,265,267,268,271
Roddye, James, 61
Rodgers, John, 163,171,181,201,312
    367
Roebeck (Robeck) John, 263,337
Rogers, Joseph, 4
Rogersville, 42
Rooks, Aaron, 97,130,131,228,265,
    268,380
Rose, Elinor, 208
Rose, John, 14,50,51,52,55,58,59,60
    63,68,69,74,83,85,92,98
    99,189,208
Rose, Richard, 285,299
Ross, Edward, 268,280,343
Ross, David, 144
Ross, John, 208
Roulston, George, 184
Rubin, Dixon, 220
Rumney, John, 35,115,137,137,191
Russell, James, 26,27
Rutledge Court House, 13
Rutledge, 8,14,17,23,25,26,29,35,37
    41,42,48,49,50,53,58,60,62
    63,72,75,82,86,87,90,96,100
    106,111,118,119,122,124,128
    140,144,149,150,155,160,161
    164,168,169,172,178,181,183
    186,190,191,199,201,202,206
    211,214,219,221,222,227,230
    231,234,235,239,240,241,247
    250,-259,267,273,276,284,
    295,303,306,310,318,324,326
    333,347,351,354,355,359,360
    362,365,368,373,375,379,380
    381,383,385,392,397,404,405
Ryans, Joseph, 195,249
Ryerson, Thomas, 256

S

Sall (slave) 123
Sally, John, 69,75,81,82,120,123,223,
    239,241,247,249,411
Sand Lick Branch, 64,107,154
Sanders, Alexander H. 331,373

Sanders, Harmon, H.373
Sanders, John, 324,330,353,360
Sanders, Reubin, 74
Sartain, (Sartin) James, 136
Sartain, Lewis, 122
Sartan (Sartain) Margery, 117
Sesseen, William, 39
Satyrfield, John, 421
Saunders, John, 47,48
Saunders, Julius, 399
Saunders, Rubin, 88
Savage, William, 24
Scaggs, James, 53,74
Scott, Burwell, 27
Scott, Charles, 51
Scott, Dennis, 37,204
Scott, Edward, 28,35,80,96,98,155
Scott, Goodin, 203,204,227
Scott, Sarah, 61,101
Scrugge, James, 108
Sourlock, Samuel, 51,59
Seabolt, Andrew, 223,277,288,290
Seamons, Joshua, 317,326,354
Seamons, John, 318
Seawell, Joseph, 34
Selvage (Selvedge) Jeremiah, 17,81,223
    239,240,274,283,330,331,398
Senter's Company, 128
Senter, Milton, 306
Senter, Stephen, W. (of Willis)
    26,29,98,104,132,167,168,179,185
    222,227,232,234,237,238,265,285
    287,295,301,305,326,333,335,337
    339,345,353,354,358,364,365,377
    417,424
Senter, Tandy, 31,32,46,83,86,87,103
    106,109,110,113,121,123,124
    125,126,129,146,148,162,169
    175,178,181,184,192,193,263
    335,377,415
Sertan (Sartain) James, 115
Sertan (Sartain) Lewis, 115
Servis, Nimrod, 384
Sevier, John (Governor) 45,54,66,67
    76,127,150,151,152,242,286,291
Shall, George, 261
Shall, William, 369
Sharkey, Patrick, 38,78,93
Sharp, Aaron, 14
Sharp, Amos, 249
Sharp's Company, 305
Sharp, Dowell, 371
Sharp, Elizabeth, 382
Sharp, George, 21,32,33,34,36,41,42

Sharp, Jacob, 15
Sharp, John, 83,104,113,142,222,227
      304
Sharp, Nicholas, 5,14,35,83,113,
Sharp, Thomas, 126,142,176,181,182,
     252,259,260,265,267,268,
     273,279,283,293,352,262,
     376,384,410,427
Shaw, Benjamin, 23,24,41,45,86,87,88,
     100,103,114,123,263,275,279
Shaw, Joseph, 90
Shaw, William, 5
Shelton Branch, 235,262,281
Shelton, Cutbert (Cutberth) 28,68
Shelton, David, 14,68,83,226,245,312
Shelton, John, 255
Shelton, Palatiah, 55
Shelton, Ralph, 69,275,370
Shelton, Richard, 69,78,84,90,158,
    171,175,176,181,186,195,210
    219,241,247,251,253,256,258
    278,284,290,318,339,341,342
    344,375,422,428
Shelton, Robert, 142
Shelton, Sarah, 238,252,362,378
Shelton, Stephen, 243,268,292,365,366
Shelton, William, 5,6,39,70,75,77,80
    89,93,95,104,111,115,135,
    167-169,176,181,182,222,227
    336,252,362
Sherley, Balsar, 349,355,377,389,401
    404,415,417
Sherley (Shirly) John, 405
Sherman, Edmund, 80,98
Shields, William, 76,104,111,117,123
    136,137,139,163,175,222,227
Shipley, Benjamin, 361
Shipley, Edward, 10,13,39,56,60,146
Shipley, John, 179
Shipley, Samuel, 201,279,344
Shipley, Thomas, 114,136,145,146,175
    187,217
Shire, William, 133
Shockley, Caleb, 214
Shockley, Isaiah, 157
Shockley, Josiah, 141
Shockley, Richard, 23,244,349
Shockley, Thomas, 273
Short, Elizabeth, 397
Short, James, 100
Showman, Jacob, 184,238,276,295,303,
    338,348,355,351,407
Shropshire (Shopshier) John, 103,105
Siddens, James, 27,32,33,43,44

Sigler, M. 56
Sigler, (Siglar) Philip, 15,28,31,37
    41,44,45,55,65,78,79,95,97,
    101,122,138,139,162,163,164
    168,173,178,186,195,197,198
    199,217,228,235,241,242,248
    252,261,262,266,267,268,269
    271,274,275,284,289,297,298
    299,303,309,310,311,319,320
    325,334,335,345,349,353,362
    375,378,383,384,385,386,389
    390,391,396,409,420
Simmons, James, 235
Simmons, John, 240
Simmons, Joshua, 313,326
Simmons, Matthew, 193
Simmons, Zachariah, 267
Simpson, James, 117,180,205,222,226
    268,270,280,294,303,312,343
    349,355,375,376,401
Simpson, Lewis, (or Lewis Sartan) 122
Simpson, Neal, 243
Sims, Elijah, 369
Sims, Elizabeth, 174
Sims, Walter, 254
Sims, William, 62,89,93,106,124,129
    147,200,215,218,220,223
Sirkle (Circle) George, 54
Sirus, Nimrod, 130,139

Slaves—

    Abraham 14
    Aggy, 131
    Alse, 68
    Arthur, 254
    Betsy, 29
    Billy, 386
    Bob, 102
    Bryan, 131
    Clarissa, 254
    Dolly, 380
    Fann, 94,102,219,
    Fill,102
    George, 46,109
    Hampton, 254,
    Hanna, 241
    Harriet, 81
    James, 280
    Jean, 39
    Jeff,380
    Jinny, 82,131
    John, 19,380
    Joshua, 102

Trotman, John, 229
Tucker, John, 147
Turley, Thomas, 105,106,174,176,177
     178,180,222,251,288
Turn Pike Gap, 185
Turner, Abigail, 306,308
Turner, Jonathan, 306,308
Turner, Walter, 77
Tuttle, Peter, 108
Tuttle, William, 108
Tyes, John, 98

U

Umstead, John, 54,95
Underhill, John, 88

V

Vandergriff, Gilbert, 391,393
Vandergriff, Leonard, 166
Vanhooser, Abraham, 8
Varnell, John, 8
Vinyard, John, 20,26,48,56,60,77,79
     121,123,125,126,139,143,144
     151,167,169,210,219,229,231
     251,278,284,288,290,291,293
     337,347,352,359,360,391,393
     427
Virginia, 38,264,390
Vitito, Thomas, 223,248,263,311

W

Waddle, Jonathan, 276,285
Waggoner, Joseph, 163,179
Walker, Alexander, 147
Walker, David, 140
Walker, Edmund, 170
Walker, Joseph, 359
Walker, Richard, 236,237
Wallin, Elisha, 2,29,30,31
Wallin, John, 5
Walters, Obediah, 133,134
Warren, Thomas, 103,114,406,407
Ward, James, 5
Ward, Samuel, 55
Ward, Thomas, 55
Warwick, John, 57
Washington, 264
Waters, (Walters) Obediah, 4,5,18,
     27,28,40,42,44,45,55,76,116
     119,121,167,168,170,305,331
Watson, David, 215,241,247,275,360
     363,368,373,377

Watson, Robert, 341
Watson, William, 267,337
Weaver, Adam, 11,19
Weaver, Jacob, 17,286
Webster, Abigail, 16,18,31,46,79
Webster, Elizabeth, 46
Webster, John, 427
Wells, John, 72,80,107,245
West, Armstead, 169
West, Edward, 8,20,26,69,75,77,80
     91,94,106,136,145,154,218
     276
West, Joel, 280
West, Joseph, 239,251,252,270
West, Samuel, 218,241,247,254,275
     356,368,373,374,375,379,388
Westhirrin, Armstead, 300
West Tennessee, 306
Weyer, Jacob, 380
Weyer, Mary, 380
Whaling, (Whalen) James, 239,252,327
     330,356
White, Allen, 14,20,56
White, Andrew, 26
White, Edward, 26
White, Hugh, L. 16,85,86,95,105,223,
     245,246,266
White, James, 256
White, Joseph, 77
Whitelock, James, 10,13,45,54,55,68
     75,77,78,79,80,84,94
Whitelock, Mary, 84,94
Whitener, Henry, 204,205,210,219
     311,318,327,329,330,373
Whitener, Lewis, 73,197,204,
Whiteside, James, 360
Whiteside, Jenkins, 8,50,59,110,113
     148,149,153,165,233
Whiteside, Thomas, 294,345,347,353
     354,364,377,378,421
Whiteside, William, 121,133,185,251
     253,255,256,259,263,264,289
     307,326,347,348,360,379
Widener, Avery, 223
Widener, Henry, 223,241,250,253,263
     299,303,355,371,376,401,424
Wilhite, Julius, 17
Willet, Francis, 69,99,100,108,113
     118,119,122,124,128,129,136
     143,150,151,152,153,158,170
     190,295
Williams Branch, 78,112
Williams Company, 297
Williams, Daniel, 351

GRAINGER COUNTY

COURT OF PLEAS & QUARTER SESSIONS
1802-1812- Vol.2-
(pages 1 & 2 missing)

(p 3)   Court adjourns till tomorrow 9 o'clock.

Tuesday morning 16th November 1802 -Court met according to adjournment.
         James Moore   )
Present - William Hankins &   ) Esquires
         Peter Harris   )

John Ferry
No. 21 vs   Case
Richard Reynolds ----Whereupon came a Jury towit-

1- David Fields   7- Dennis Condry
2- Benjamin Condry   8- William Morrison
3- Moses Willis   9- John Hamill
4- Alexander Hamilton   10-John Calvin
5- John Gillington   11-George Coe &
6- Edward Davidson   12-Isaac McDonald

     Who being elected tried and sworn the truth to tell on the Issues
joined in this suit retired to consider of their Verdict, afterwards returned to the Box and being asked if they had agreed upon their Verdict
said they had not. Whereupon the Council as well for the Plaintiff as
for the Defendant consent that a mistrial be entered and the Jury discharged; and mistrial is entered accordingly.

(p 4)   Sarah Matlock administratrix & James Moore administrator of
John Matlock -Deceased- With the Will annexed Returns in open Court an
Inventory of said Estate.

Samuel Brown
No. 29 vs -Debt

Spencer Haney &
John Estis   -------Whereupon came a Jury towit-

1- Reubin Riggs   7- Stephen Brundage
2- Benjamin Bell   8- Edmund Nott
3- Adam Moyers   9- Jesse Lay
4- Robert Long   10-Obediah Waters
5- Jonathan Williams   11-David Jackson
6- John Acuff   12-Robert Patterson

     Who being elected tried & sworn well & truly to try & the truth
to speak on the issue joined in this case Do say the writing obligatory
and is the Deed of the Defendants, they further find for the Plaintiff

the sum of one hundred dollars the Debt in the declaration mentioned and assessed his damages ocationed by the detention of that debt to seventeen dollars & seventy five cents & costs.

A bill of sale from Mathew McPhetridge was proven in open Court by Charles Hutcheson & Andrew McPheeters subscribing witnesses thereto ordered to be Recorded.

Ordered by the Court that John Hodges be appointed overseer of the road in the place of Thomas Pannell and that he have the same hands to work under him that worked under said Pannell.
Court adjourned till tomorrow 9 o'clock.

Wednesday morning 17th Novr. 1802-
Court met according to adjournment.

Present
Peter Morris)
Joseph Cobb) Esquires
David McAnally)

A Deed of Conveyance from Joseph Cobb to Haridous Ogle for two hundred and thirty one & one half acres of land was acknowledged in open Court & ordered to be recorded.

Thomas Lea
No. 58 vs Case
Lincoln Anis

Joseph Rodgers being duly summoned a wright to give evidence in this Case on behalf of Defendant Being solemnly called, came not It is therefore considered by the Court that he forfeit one hundred & twenty five dollars according to the Acct. of ——torn

(p 5)
Thomas Lea
No. 58- vs Case
Lincoln Anis   ——Whereupon came a Jury towit-

1- Edmund Holt
2- William Shelton
3- Thomas McBroom
4- Pleasant Dukes
5- Jonathan Williams
6- David Bunch
7- John Hamill
8- Jesse Cheek
9- William Peters
10- Kindrid Dodson
11- John Wallin
12- William Shaw

Who being elected tried & sworn the truth to speak on the Issues joined in this Case Do say they find for the Plaintiff & assesses his damages to one hundred & eighty two Dollars & eight cents and costs.

William Hankins
vs -Cert.
James Ward ——Whereupon came the same Jury as in No. 58. Who being elected tried & sworn the truth to speak on the matter in dispute in this Case Do say they find for the Plaintiff and assess his damages to one cent besides his costs.

Isaac McDonald
No. 87- vs Cert.
Thomas McDonald ----Whereupon came a Jury towit-

1- John Humphreys	7- Robert Long
2- Michael Kearnes	8- Reubin Riggs
3- Peter Miller	9- John Patterson
4- Moses McElheny	10-John Crabb
5- Nicholas Sharp	11-Thomas Ruddleston
6- Obediah Waters	12-John Dorah

Who being elected tried & sworn the truth to speak on the matter in
Dispute in this case Do say they find for the Plaintiff and assess his
damages to eighteen dollars sixty six cents & two thirds of a cent &
costs.

Clisbe Riggs, Assignee of
Martin Ashburn
No. 97- vs Debt
Spencer Griffin and
James Ore   ----Whereupon came a Jury towit, the same Jury as in
No. 87- save only George Noe in the place of Reubin Riggs.
      Who being elected tried & sworn the truth on the Issues joined in
this suit do say that one of the Defendants has paid one hundred & fifteen
dollars, part of the debt on the declaration mentioned,   (p 6)   that
they have not paid neither have they made any accord or satisfaction for
the Ballance of the debt in the declaration mentioned as in pleading they
have alledged; they further find for the Plaintiff seventy seven dollars
sixty cents & two thirds of a cent Debt & assesses his damages accasioned
by reason of the detention of that debt to eleven dollars sixteen cents &
two thirds of a cent to six cents cost- From which Verdict an appeal is
prayed- motion of an appeal withdrawn & execution stayed three months By
order of Plaintiff.

Edward Riggs
No. 98- vs Debt
Spencer Griffin
James Ore and
Ambrose Yancey ----Whereupon came a Jury towit-

1- Edmond Holt	7- Jesse Cheek
2- William Shelton	8- William Peters
3- Walter Evans	9- John Burton
4- Frederick Miller	10-Richard Reynolds
5- Francis Crabb	11-John Nevin and
6- John Howill	12-Elijah Donathan

Who being elected tried & sworn the truth to speak on the Issues
joined in this Case do say the Defendants have not paid the Debt in the
declaration mentioned as in pleading they have alledged, that they have
made no accord or satisfaction for the same as in pleading they have alledged, they further find for the Plaintiff the sum of Four hundred dollars the debt in the declaration mentioned besides his costs- From which
Verdict an appeal is prayed motion for appeal withdrawn & execution directed to stay three months By order of Reubin Riggs.

A Deed of conveyance from Joseph Ore to William Shelton for two hundred acres of land was acknowledged in open Court - Ordered to be Registered.

A Bill of Sale from William Windham to Robert Yancey for a negro man Slave named John was proven in open Court by John Jack a subscribing witness- Ordered to be Recorded.

By order of Court John Conley is released from the payment of Taxes on seventy five acres of land for the year 1802.

Elijah Donathan being charged by Nancy Hayes with being the father of a Bastard child begotten on her body, comes into open Court and enters into Bond with Henry Howell & Robert Yancey his securities in the penal sum of five hundred dollars conditioned that they will indemnify the County of Grainger aginst the maintenence of said child.

(p 7)   William Clay, William Hankins
           Robert Patterson & William Hall -Commissioners.&
           No. 116 vs Debt-
           Joseph Cobb & George M.Combs - Whereupon came a Jury towit-

1- John Humphreys   7- Henry Howell
2- Michael Kearns   8- Reubin Riggs
3- Peter Miller   9- John Crabb
4- Spencer Griffin   10-Merriweather Johnson
5- Edmond Holt   11-John Dorah &
6- John Buller   12-Frederick Miller

Who being elected tried & sworn the truth to speak on the Issue joined in this case Do say the defendants have not paid the debt in the declaration mentioned as in pleading they have alledged; they further find for the Plaintiffs the sum of Fifty Dollars the Debt in the declaration mentioned and assess their damages accationed by reason of the detention of that debt to four dollars thirty three cents & one third of a cent besides their costs; Execution to stay three months by order of Plaintiffs Attorney.

Andrew McPheeters)
No. 135- vs Debt   ) Robert Moore & John Hargraves Special bail of the
John Stewart   ) defendant in this case bring him into Open Court &
surrendered him in discharge of themselves - Defendant is prayed in custody by Plaintiffs Attorney.

Thomas Chinn for the use of) Edmund Holt & William Cooper special
Robert Yancey   ) Bail of the defendant in this case bring
No. 151- vs -Covenant   ) him into open Court & surrender him in
discharge of themselves.

     Court adjourned till tomorrow 9 o'clock.
     Thursday morning Nov. 18th 1802- Court met according to adjournment.
          Joseph Cobb   )
Present- Nimrod Maxwell   ) Esquires
          Daniel Clayton   )

Thomas Chinn for the use of)
Robert Yancey   ) John Stewart the Defendant
No. 151 - vs -Covenant   ) Abraham Elliot, John Hargraves &

Edmond Holt came into open Court and acknowledged themselves in debt to the plaintiffs , they further undertake,agree that if the Defendant be
(p 8)   condemned in this action, he shall pay the condemnation or render himself to pay for the same, and if he fail so to do, that they will do it for him. Afterwards the said John Stewart came into open Court & surrendered himself a prisoner in discharge of his securities in this action & is payed in custody.

By order of Court Martin Ashburn, Philip Combs, Edward West, William Guynn, Michael Massengill, James Alsum, Jacob Arnett, Daniel Clayton,Esqr. thomas McBroom, Miller, Easeley, & Michael Coons are appointed a Jury to view and lay off a road, the nearest & best way from the town of Rutledge to Michael Massengill's Mill and make report to next Court.

Samuel Newell Assignee of   )
Jenkins Whiteside   )   Whereupon came a Jury towit—
No. 119 vs— Debt   )
Spencer Griffin & James Chinn)

1— Reubin Riggs   7— Merriweather Johnson
2— Abraham Vanhooser   8— Adam Moyers
3— Edmond Holt   9— Willis Davis
4— John Hamill   10—George Combs
5— Nicholas Spring   11—William Henderson
6— John Margraves   12—Robert Moor

Who being elected tried and sworn the truth to speak on the Issue joined in this case Do say the defendants have not paid the debt in the declaration mentioned as in pleading they have alledged, they further find for the plaintiff one hundred dollars, the debt in the declaration mentioned and assesses his damages occasioned by reason of the detention of that debt to six dollars and fifty cents besides his costs.

John Varnell   )
No. 129 vs— Debt   )   Whereupon came a Jury towit, Jury as in No. 119—
Richard Mitchel   )   Who being elected tried & sworn the truth to speak on the Issues joined in this case Do say they find the defendant hath paid teo hundred & seventy five dollars part of the debt in the declaration mentioned & no more; they further find the plaintiff the sum of four hundred & seventy five Dollars, the balance of the debt in the declaration mentioned & assess his damage occationed by reason of the detention of that debt to one hundred and two dollars and seventy five cents, besides his cost.

Ordered that William Clay Esqr. have leave to keep an ordinary or house of public entertainment at his dwelling house in Grainger County and
(p 9)   the said William Clay enters into Bond with Noah Jarnagin his security in the sum of two thousand five hundred dollars conditioned according to Law— Whereupon it is ordered that License be granted to the said William Clay.

Andrew McFeters   )
No. 135— vs— Debt   )   Whereupon came a Jury towit, the same Jury as in
John Stewart   )   No. 119.
Who being elected tried & sworn the truth to speak on the Issue joined in this case Do say the defendant hath not paid & satisfied the debt

mentioned as in pleading he hath alledged, they further find for the plaintiff the sum of eight eight dollars & fifty cents the debt in the declaration mentioned and assess his damage occationed by reason of the detention of that debt to one dollar & thirty three cents & six cents cost.

John Rhea)
No. 140- vs- Debt)   Whereupon came a Jury towit, the same Jury as in
David Hailey) No. 119- Who being elected tried and sworn the truth
to speak on the Issue joined in this case Do say they find the defendant
hath paid twenty dollars, part of the debt in the declaration mentioned and
no more; they further find for the plaintiff Forty dollars the balance of
the debt in the declaration mentioned and assess his damage occasioned by
reason of the detention of that Debt to twelve dollars and twenty cents &
six cents costs.

William Murphy)
    vs   )   Wilson Loyd by F.H.Miller his Attorney prefers to
Wilson Loyd)Court a petition praying that a writ of Supersedeas may
issue to stay proceedings in this case, and also a writ of Certiorari directed to William Clay Esqr. commanding him to certify &c. the prayer of
petition is granted.

Thomas Chinn for the use of)
Robert Yancey)   the Defendant
No. 151- vs- Debt)   John Stewart, Abraham Elliot, John
John Stewart) Hargraves, Joseph Ore, Nimrod Maxwell, John
Crabb, John Bird and William Cooper came into open Court and acknowledged
themselves Indebted to the plaintiff in the sum of three hundred dollars,
they also undertake & agree that if the defendant be condemned or render
himself to prison for the same, and if he fail to do so that they will do
it for him.

(p 10)   Andrew McFeters)
          No. 135- vs -Debt)
          John Stewart)   John Stewart the defendant, Abraham
Elliot, John Hargraves, Joseph Ore, Nimrod Maxwell Esqr. John Crabb, John
Bird & William Cooper came into open Court & acknowledge themselves indebted to the plaintiff in the sum of two hundred dollars, they also undertake & agree that if the defendant be condemned in the action he shall pay
the condemnation, or render himself to prison for the same, and if he fail
so to do that they will do it for him.

The following is a list of Jurors appointed by the Court to attend
the next Court of Pleas & Quarter Sessions to be held for Grainger County
on the third Monday of February next.
1- Barclay Marshall   7- John Coulter Senr.
2- Edward Shipley   8- Joseph Noe senr.
3- Henry Beatman   9- Hezekiah Phillips
4- Hugh Larimore   10-Pleasant Duke
5- Henry Ivey   11-Jeremiah Chamberlain
6- Charlie Smith   12-John Benn
                             13-Archelus Gibson
                             14-William Henderson
                             15-Miller Easley

16- Nicholas Countz   26- Henry Bowen
17- James Arwine   27- Robert McElheney
18- Cain Acuff   28- William Peters
19- Peter Beeler   29- Joseph Peters
20- Lemuel Branson   30- Jonathan Harpower
21- Chesley Jarnagin   31- David Bailey
22- John Moyers   32- James Whitlock
23- John Hall   33- Joseph Ore
24- Aaron Smith   34- Edward Churchman
25- John Spencer   35- Joseph Eaton
                            36- William Mitchell

the following is a list of Justices of the Peace appointed by Court
to take in Lists of Polls & taxable property in the respective Captains
Companies in Grainger County & make return thereof to next Court, towit-
1- Robert C. Gordon Esqr. for Captain George Bean's Company.
2- David McAnally Esqr. for Capt. Carmichael's Company.
3- Peter Harris Esqr. for Captain thomas Man's Company.
4- Charles McAnally Esqr. for Captain Smith's Company.
5- Samuel Clark Esqr. for Capt. James Company.
Nimrod Maxwell Esqr. for Capt. Condrey's Company. (6)
7- Charles Hutcheson Esqr. for Captain Dennis Company.
8- Major Lea Esqr. for Capt. Hamilton's Company.
9- Noah Jarnagin Esqr. for Capt. Samuel Punch's Company.
10-William Arnold Esqr. for Capt. Wilson's Company.
11-James Moore Esqr. for Capt. Howell's company.

Willie Blount Esqr. by John F.Jack being duly authorized for that purpose
Returns in open Court the following list of taxable property subject to the
payment of taxes for the year A.D.1802, Towit-   (p 11)   Three hundred acres at the mouth of Caney Creek.
150 acres at the mouth of the cave Spring.
1000 acres on the East side of Williams Creek.
1000 acres Williams Creek.
1000 acres Town house Valley.
320 acres below where Clinch runs thro the lone mountain.

John O'Donnell by John F.Jack, Returns in open Court 5000 acres of land on
Bull Run.

On motion made to Court John Cocke Attorney and it appearing to the
Satisfaction of the Court that the representations of Samuel Low -Deceased
had been charged on the Tax list for the year 1802, with the payment of
the State & County tax on 72150 acres of land more than in truth in fact
they owned in Grainger County. Whereupon it is ordered by the Court that
they be released from the payment of the sum of ninety dollars eighteen
cents & three fourths of a cent being the amount of the Tax due the State
on said Land, and also from the payment of the sum of Ninety dollars
eighteen cents & three fourths of a cent the amount of tax due Grainger
County on said Land.

Ordered by Court that Martin Ashburn Coroner of Grainger County be
allowed the sum of Four dollars for holding an Inquest on the Body of a
certain Adam Weaver Deceased, who was murdered in said County.

Ordered by Court that James Dyer one of the Constables for Grainger

County be allowed the sum of six dollars and fifty cents for summoning a Jury by Virtue of a precept Issued by Martin Ashburn Coroner and to him directed to hold an Inquest on the body of a certain Adam Weaver deceased who was murdered in said County and also for summoning three witnesses to give testimony to said Jury of Inquest.

Court adjourned till tomorrow 9 O'clock.

Friday morning 19th. Nov. 1802 -Court met according to adjournment.

Present —
Noah Jarnagin)
Daniel Clayton) Esquires.
William Clay)

Peter Noe, Constable maketh oath in open Court that he has attended this present term five days as Constable.

(p 12)   By order of Court Grainger County is divided into three Districts, as follows towit-that part of Grainger County which lies South of the richland nobs shall compose one District, that part of Grainger County which lies between said Nobs & Clinch mountain shall compose one other Division, and that part of Grainger County which lies between Clinch Mt. & Clinch River shall compose the third District.

By order of Court Michael Massengill, Henry Howell & Isick Dyer are appointed searchers or Patrollers for the first Division above mentioned.

By order of Court George M.Combs Michael Coons & Jeremiah Jarnagin are appointed Searchers or Patrollers for the second Division above mentioned.

On application to Court by John Cocke Attorney for Robert Yancey Sheriff and collector of the public & County tax in Grainger County and it appearing to the satisfaction of the Court that the representatives of Samuel Lowe -Deceased had been charged on the Tax List for the year 1801 with the pwyment of the State and County tax on 72150 acres of Land more than in truth and in fact they owned in Grainger County. Whereupon it is ordered by the Court that the said Robert Yancey be Released from the payment of the sum of ninety dollars & eighteen cents being the tax due the State on the Land for which the said representatives were overcharged & that he have a credit to that amount in his settlement with the treasurer of the District of Hamilton.

On application to Court John Cocke Attorney for Robert Yancey Sheriff and collector of public & County tax in Grainger County and it appearing to the satisfaction of the Court that the Representatives of Samuel Lowe deceased had been charged on the tax List for year 1801 with the payment of the State and County tax on 72150 acres of Land more then in truth and in fact they owned in Grainger County. Whereupon it is ordered by the Court that the said Robert Yancey be released from the payment of the sum of ninety dollars & eighteen cents being the tax due the County aforesaid on the Land for which the said Representatives were overcharged and that he have a credit to that amount in his settlement with the Treasurer of the aforesaid County.

Court adjourned till Court in Course.

(Signed)   Noah Jarnagin J.P.

(p 13)   At a Court of Pleas & Quarter Sessions begun and held for the
County of Grainger at the Court House in Rutledge on the third Monday of
February A.D. 1803 being the 21st. of the same month.

          Peter Harris   )
Present   William Clay   )   Esquires
          Charles McAnally &)
          Samuel Clark   )

     Robert Yancey Esquire Sheriff of Grainger County returns to Court
that he has executed the following Venire facias on the following Persons
towit- except those marked thus- sd.

1- Barclay Marshall
2- Edward Shipley
3- Henry Boatman -sd.
4- Hugh Larimore
5- Henry Ivey -sd.
6- Charles Smith
7- John Coulter Senr.
8- Joseph Noe Senr.
9- Hezekiah Phillips
10-Pleasant Duke
11-Jeremiah Chamberlain
12-John Bean
13-William Henderson
14-Miller Easeley
15-Nicholas Counts
16-James Arwine
17-Cain Acuff
18-Peter Beeler

19- Lemuel Branson
20- Cheesley Jarnagin
21- John Noyers
22- John Hall
23- Aaron Smith
24- John Spencer
25- Henry Bowen
26- Robert McElhany
27- William Peters
28- Joseph Dennis
29- Jonathan Humpower
30- David Hailey
31- James Whitlock
32- Joseph Ore
33- Edward Churchman
34- Joseph Eaton
35- William Mitchell &
36- Archelus Gidson

     Out of which Venire facias the persons whose names are hereafter
mentioned were appointed a Grand Jury for the present term, towit,
1- Jeremiah Chamberlain- foreman
2- Barclay Chamberlain
3- Henry Boatman
4- Joseph Noe Senr.
5- Pleasant Duke
6- William Henderson
7- Miller Easely
8- Nicholas Counts
9- Cain Acuff
10- Peter Beeler
11- John Noyers
12- Henry Bowen
13- John Spencer
14- William Peters &
15- Jonathan Humpower
Who were sworn and charged by the Solicitor.

     Peter Noe Constable was sworn to attend the Grand Jury during the
present Term.

     A Bill of sale from James Guthrie to Jeremiah Chamberlain for a negro
was proven in open Court by James Carmichael Senr. and ordered to be Recorded.
     A Deed of conveyance from Joseph Evans and Andrew Evans to Thomas
Hodges for one hundred acres of Land was proven in open Court by Peter Lowe
a subscribing witness and ordered to be Recorded.

(p 14)   A Deed of conveyance from Joseph Evans to Peter Lowe for two hundred acres of Land was proven in open Court by Thomas Hodges and ordered to be recorded.

A Deed of conveyance from John Matlock to Allen White for forty seven acres of Land, more or less, was proven in open Court by Joseph Ore a subscribing witness, ordered to be recorded.

Ordered by Court that John Acuff have leave to keep an ordinary or house of Intertainment at his dwelling house in Grainger County, who enters into Bond in the sum of two thousand five hundred dollars with Cain Acuff, his security.

Barcley Marshall comes into open Court & presents a paper purporting to be the last Will and Testament of William Moffit deceased- for probate and the said paper is continued for probate till tomorrow morning.

A Deed of conveyance from Robert Yancey to John Counts for lot No.19 in the town of Rutledge was proven in open Court by Nicholas Sharp a subscribing witness and ordered to be Registered.

Ordered by Court that James Ore have leave to keep an ordinary or house of Entertainment at his dwelling house in Grainger County who enters into bond in the sum of two thousand five hundred dollars with Spencer Griffin, his security.

Ordered by Court that Spencer Griffin have leave to keep an ordinary or house of Entertainment in the town of Rutledge who enters into Bond in the sum of two thousand five hundred Dollars with James Ore, his Securities.

A Deed of conveyance from Thomas Hodges to Aaron Sharp for one hundred acres of Land by estimation was acknowledged in open Court and ordered to be Registered.

Ordered by Court that Robert Yancey have leave to keep an ordinary or house of Entertainment in the town of Rutledge, who entered into Bond in the sum of two thousand five hundred dollars with John Rose & Peter Hoe his securities.

A Bill of sale from David Shelton to Jesse Roggs for a negro fellow named Abraham was proven in open Court by Hall Hudson a subscribing witness & ordered to be Recorded.

A Deed of conveyance from Felps Read to Jacob Wilson for seventy five acres of Land more or less was acknowledged in open Court, ordered to be Registered.

Thomas Chinn for the use of   )
Robert Yancey   )
        vs   )
John Stewart   )   John Hargraves, Nimrod Maxwell,
Joseph Ore, William Cooper, John Crabb and Abraham Elliot bring the body of the said John Stewart the Defendant into Court and surrender him in

discharge of themselves and prayed in custody by the said Robert Yancey.

(p 15)   A Deed of conveyance from Jacob Cox to Jacob Sharp for two hundred acres of Land was proven in open Court by Nimrod Maxwell a subscribing witness- ordered by the Court to be Registered.

Andrew McPheters)
    vs   )
John Stewart   )   John Hargraves Nimrod Maxwell, Abraham Elliot, Joseph Ore, John Crabb and William Cooper being the Body of the said John Stewart into Court & surrendered him in discharge of themselves and ordered to be put into Custody.

A Deed of conveyance from William Hall to Philip Sigler for three hundred acres of Land was acknowledged in open Court and ordered to be Registered.

A Deed of conveyance from William Hall to Larkin Hall for three hundred acres of Land was acknowledged in open Court and ordered to be Registered.

James Hudson Admr. of the estate of Obediah Hudson deceased, returns to Court a supplemental Inventory of said Estate, also an account of the sales of part of said estate.

The following is a List of Jurors appointed by the Court to attend the next Superior Court of Law to be holden for the District of Hamilton at the Court House in Knoxville on the third Monday of March next, towit, Ambrose Yancey, Joseph Cobb, Isaiah Midkiff & Hezekiah Philips.

By order of Court John Noe is appointed overseer of the road that leaves from Marshall's ford to the fork of the road above John Coulter's in place of Hugh Larimore, and that he have the same hands to work under him that worked under the said Larimore.

Ordered by Court that Felps Read be exonerated from the Indenture & discharged from the maintenance of an orphan child supposed bound to him, by the name of Nancy Smith.

The Justices of the Peace who were appointed by the Court at November term 1802 to take in Lists of Polls & Taxable property in the respective Captains Companies in Grainger County for the year A.D. 1803 and make return thereof to the present term- have made Return of their Lists in open Court except Major Lea Esqr. and James Moore Esqr. who have altogether failed to return Lists of Polls and taxable property in their respective Captain's Companies which was assigned to them.
Court adjourns till tomorrow 9 o'clock.

Tuesday morning 22nd. February 1803 - Court met according to adjournment.
          James Blair   )
Present   Peter Harris   ) Esquires
          Nimrod Maxwell)

(p 16)   John Maddison Esquire produced to Court a paper writing signed
by David Campbell and Hugh L. White Judges of the Superior Courts of Law
Equity for the State of Tennessee Licensing him to practice Law as an Attorney in the Courts of said State who took the oath prescribed for Attornies and an oath to support the Constitution of the States (United)
& of the State of Tennessee.

Robert McElhany and James Bowen Executors of the last Will and Testament of William McElhaney —deceased came into open Court & were respectively sworn Executors of the said last Will and Testament, they not having been sworn when the said last Will and testament was proven in Court.

Levi Wilson Executor of William Wilson —Deceased and Lusanna Wilson
Executrix of said Deceased come into open Court & were sworn towit— Levi
Wilson Executor and Lusanna Wilson Executrix of the last Will & Testament
of the said William Wilson they not having been sworn when the said last
Will and Testament was proven in Court.

Barcley Marshall by his Attorney makes a motion to Court that a subscribing witness to a paper purporting to be the last Will and Testament
of William Moffit deceased which was offered to Court for probate yesterday should be sworn to prove the execution thereof and Ansley Clark Admr.
& Peggy Clark his wife administratrix of all and singular the Goods and
chattles rights & credits which were of the said William Moffit deceased
come into open Court by their Attornies and oppose the swearing of the sd.
Witness—and arguments of Council, being heard on the aforesaid motion; it
was ordered by the Court that the witness should be sworn and afterwards
the said Ansley Clark & Peggy his wife by their Council make a motion to
Court that an issue of fact should be made up under the direction of the
Court and a Jury sworn to enquire whether the said paper is the last Will
& Testament of the said William Moffet —deceased, whereupon an Issue of
fact was made up under the direction of the Court in these words, towit—
"Whether the written Instrument purporting to be the last Will and Testament of William Moffet – deceased, and presented to this Court for Probate by Barcley Marshall Executor & Abigail Webster Executrix named therein
is the last Will and Testament of the said William Moffet deceased."

John Spencer   )
       vs   )   Mathew Campbell Special Bail of John Beaty the defendant
John Beaty   )   brings him into open Court and surrenders him in discharge
of himself.   of himself.

John Beaty   )
ad effectum   )
John Spencer   )   John Beaty, the defendant William Hamilton & Henry Howell
come into open Court & acknowledge themselves indebted into the plaintiff
John Spencer in the sum of Two thousand dollars to be Levied of their Goods
& chattles Lands and tenements, to be void upon Condition that if the Defendant be condemned in the above action that he will pay the costs & condemnation or surrender himself to Prison for the same or that they the sd.
William & Henry will do so for him.

(p 17)   James Moore produces the last Will and Testament of Samuel Moore
deceased, to Court for Probate and the due execution thereof is proven by

William Arnold a subscribing witness thereto; and in as much as the said
Samuel Moore deceased, has Omitted appointing any Executor to execute the
same; James Moore has leave to Administer on the Estate of the said dec'd.
with the Will annexed and enters into Bond in the sum of one thousand Dollars with William Arnold and Joseph Eaton his securities.

```
Thomas Colbert    )
13  vs Appeal     )
Francis Crabb     )    Whereupon came a Jury towit—
```

```
1- Aaron Smith              7- Nicholas Spring
2- Robert Mc Elhaney        8- Joseph Ore
3- Edward Churchman         9- John Hamilton
4- Peter Lowe               10-William Harmill
5- Alexander McDonald       11-Alexander Hamilton
6- Jacob Weaver             12-Jeremiah Selvage
```
Who being Elected tried and sworn the truth to speak on the matter in
dispute in this case Do say they find for the Defendant.

Ordered by Court that Michael Coons have leave to keep an ordinary or
house of Entertainment in the town of Tutledge, who enters into Bond in the
sum of two thousand five hundred dollars with James Ore & Pleasant Duke his
securities.

```
Thomas Colbert    )
 14  vs —Appeal   )    Whereupon came a Jury towit— the same Jury as in
Francis Crabb     )    No. 13—
```
Who being elected tried & sworn well and truly to
trye the truth to speak on the matter in Dispute in this case Do say they
find for the plaintiff & assess his damage to six cents & costs.

```
Thomas Colbert    )
15- vs  Appeal    )
Francis Crabb     )    Whereupon came a Jury towit—
```

```
1- Larkin Hall             7- Ezekiel Craft
2- William Christian       8- Thomas Maxwell
3- Joseph Ore              9- Robert Ellis
4- Francis Hunter          10-David Fields
5- Martin Bunch            11-Edmund Holt &
6- Julius Wilhite          12-Benjamin Condry
```
Who being elected tried and sworn the truth to speak on the matter
in dispute in this case Do say they find for the Plaintiff & assess his
damage to Eighteen dollars & sixty six cents besides his costs.

```
John Denn, Lessee of  )    Robert C.Gordon Special Bail of John Griffitts
James Ore             )    the Defendant surrenders him in open Court in dis-
    vs                )    charge of himself.
Richard Fenn &        )
John Griffitts        )
```

(p 18)   Thomas Bunch returns in open Court the following List of Taxable property for the year A.D. 1803 – two hundred acres of Land & 1 white
Poll.

Ordered by Court that Henry Boatman have leave to record the Earmark of his meat, cattle, hogs & sheep as follows, towit- a crop and under keel in the left Ear.

A Deed of Gift from Isaiah Midkiff to Thomas Midkiff his son for 95 acres of Land was acknowledged in open Court & ordered to be Registered.

Ordered by Court that John Hall be appointed overseer of the road Beginning at the creek below William Halls thence to Nicholas Springs and that all the hands within the following Bounds, towit- Beginning at Larkin Halls thence across the Copper Ridge to Combs Ridge a direct course, thence along the Comb Ridges down to William Cooper's thence a direct course across the Copper ridge to Nicholas Spring's so as to include said Spring's, thence along the Road leading by said Spring's to Benj. Elliot's, thence a direct course to the Beginning.

Court adjourns till tomorrow 9 o'clock.

Wednesday morning 23rd. Feby. 1803 —Court met according to adjournment.

Present William Arnold Peter Harris) Nimrod Maxwell) Esquires

Alexander Outlaw Esqr. was admitted to practice Law as an Attorney in this Court & took the necessary oaths.

The following is a Jury sworn to try an Issue of fact made up under the direction of the Court in these words, towit-

"Whether the Written Instrument purporting to be the "last Will and Testament of William Moffet deceased & presented to this Court for probate " by Bardley Marshall Executor & Abigail Webster executrix named therein is the last "Will and Testament of the said William Moffet- deceased, towit

1- Aaron Smith
2- Abel Morgan
3- Obediah Waters
4- Jesse Lay Senr.
5- Henry Howell
6- John Bullard
7- William Hamilton
8- Dennis Condry
9- Samuel Frazier
10-William Mitchell
11-Thomas Henderson
12-James Ore

Who being elected tried & sworn well and truly to try the truth to speak on the above Issue Do say that the Written Instrument purporting to be the last Will and Testament of William Moffet & presented to this Court for Probate by Bardley Marshal Executor & Abigail Webster Executrix named therein is the last Will and Testament of William Moffet deceased.

(p 19) John Bean)
vs) James Blair special Bail of Stephen Bean the
Stephen Bean)Defendant brings into open Court & surrenders him
in discharge of himself.

On motion by Council and Pleasant M.Miller sworn & examined touching a contempt alledged to have been committed by Jeremiah Aulgur in open Court It is considered by the Court that the said Jeremiah Aulgur be fined the sum of five dollars. Rule to remit fine.

State)
vs) William Howard security of Obediah Hog the Defendant,
Obediah Hog)

brings him into Court & surrenders him in discharge of himself to the said Obediah Nog is ordered in custody of the Sheriff.

John Denn, Lessee of James Ore)
vs   ) Trespass Ejectment
Richard Fenn & John Griffitts   )

David Holt comes into open Court & makes oath that he has title to the Land in dispute, that John Griffitts the tenant in possession refuses to defend and the said David Holt David McAnally acknowledge themselves indebted unto James Ore the plaintiff in the sum of five hundred dollars to be Levied of their Goods and Chattles land & tenements, to be void upon condition that if the said David Holt be condemned in the action that he will pay the costs & condemnation or surrender himself to prison for the same, or that they, the said David McAnally & Charles McAnally will do so for him. Whereupon the said David Holt is admitted Defendant.

On motion it is ordered by the Court that the Clerk be allowed thirty Dollars for his ex officio services for the year A.D. 1810 and fifteen Dollars for making out & recording the tax list for said year, which allowance is to be computed from May term A.D. 1801.

Ordered by Court that Robert Yancey Esquire Sheriff of Grainger County be allowed the sum of sixty dollars for his exofficio services for the year 1801, the time to be computed from the May Term 1801 -

Ordered by Court that Peter Noe be allowed the sum of fifteen Dollars for his trouble & expenses in keeping & maintaining Baker Hazard & negro John, Prisoners charged with murdering a certain Adam Weaver.

Ordered that John Countz be allowed the sum of one dollar & fifty cents for aiding and in guarding the above mentioned prisoners.

Ordered by Court that Francis Young an orphan now at the age of thirteen years be bound by Indenture unto John Cocke Esquire, to live with him after the manner of an apprentice & servant until he shall attain the age of twenty one years.

John Lea, Admr. of David Inman deceased returns in open Court an Inventory of the personal Estate of said deceased; and on application to Court It is ordered that the said John Lea have leave to sell the personal Estate of said deceased.

(p 20)   Ordered by Court that the following Tax be laid & collected in the County of Grainger for the year A.D. 1803, towit-
12½ cents on each hundred acres of Land.
25 cents on each Town Lot
25 cents on each Stud Horse
25 cents on each Black Poll
12½ cents on each White Poll &
10 Dollars on each Billiard table.

Ordered by Court that Major Lea Esquire be allowed till May term to return a List of the polls and taxable property in the bounds of Captain

Peter Hamilton's Company he having failed to return a List at the present Term.

The following is a List of persons appointed by the Court to attend as Jurors at May Term A.D. 1803-

1- John Lebo
2- James Ore
3- Joseph Bryant
4- James Blair Junr.
5- John Hoe
6- John Darnel
7- Edward West
8- William Christian
9- David Davis
10-Jacob Arnett
11-Robert Stone
12-James Richardson
13-David Bunch
14-Martin Bunch
15-John Brook
16- Peter Hammock

17- Chelsey Jarnagin
18- John Counts
19- John Coulter
20-George Kisry
21- John Bean
22- Martin Stubblefield
23- John Bunch
24- Henry Hipshur
25- Benjamin Hudson
26- ————————————
27- Richard Chilton
28- Charles Hopper
29- John Bradon
30- John Vinyard
31- Henry Mayo A
32- Benjamin Elliot

Allen White returns in open Court the following List of Taxable property for the year A.D. 1803, towit- forty acres of Land & one white poll.

John Hailey by Allen White returns to Court the following List of Taxable property for the year 1803, towit- one hundred acres of Land & one Stud horse, price of the Season -2 dollars.

an Inventory of the personal estate of said deceased, returns in open Court John Lea Administrator of David Inman deceased, returns in open Court Noah Jarnagin Esquire returns in open Court the following List of taxable property for the year A.D. 1803, 500 acres of Land - 1 white poll and 1 Black poll.

Ambrose Yancey Esq. by Robert Yancey returns to Court the following List of taxable property for the year A.D. 1803 - 1 town lot- 1 white poll.

Robert Yancey returns in open Court the following List of Taxable property for the year A.D. 1803   200 acres of Land 3 town lotts - 1 white poll.

(p 21)   Court adjourns till tomorrow 9 o'clock.

Thursday moring 20th day Feby. A.D. 1803 -Court met according to adjournment.

Nimrod Maxwell   )
Peter Harris A   )   Esquires
David McAnally   )

Ansley Clark administrator & Peggy Clark his wife Administratrix of William Moffet deceased- come into Court and pray an appeal to the Superior Court of Law & equity to be holden in Knox County for the District of Hamilton on the fourth Monday of March next from the Verdict rendered yesterday on an Issue of fact made up under the direction of Court to try the

Validity of a written instrument purporting to be the last Will and Testament of the said William Moffet deceased, and they said Ansley & Peggy by their Attorney filed reasons for their appeal.

William Hall, William Hawkins, Robert Patterson & William Clay, Commissioners. vs

John Crabb & Thomas McBroom

The Plaintiff's in this suit by Pleasant McmIller their Attorney come into Court & make a motion to enter a Judgment against Robert Yancey Sheriff of Grainger County for the sum of one hundred & two dollars sixty three & one half cents Debt, damages & costs being the amount of monies by him collected on an execution issued on a Judgment rendered in this case & which he has failed to pay over, and it being made manifest to the Court by proof that the said Robert Yancey has due notice of this motion, whereupon it is considered by the Court that they said Plaintiff's do recover of the said Robert Yancey the sum of ninety three dollars & fifteen cts. for their debt & damages & also the further sum of nine dollars forty eight & one half cents for their costs & charges by them expended in & about prosecuting this suit.

The Court having given public notice by Proclamation that they were about to elect a Coroner for the County of Grainger, desired that those persons who would be candidates for the said office should come into Court & make it known — Whereupon Robert C. Gordon Esqr. declared himself a candidate; the Court proceeded to Ballot for a Coroner and on counting the votes it appeared that the said Robert C. Gordnon was duly & unanimously Elected Coroner.

State)
vs)
John Huddleston) Whereupon came a Jury towit—
1— Aaron Smith
2— George Sharp   7— William Mitchell
3— Thomas Anderson   8— David Bunch
4— John Clay   9— John Midkiff
5— Moses McElhaney   10—John Countz
6— Jesse Lay   11—Richard Reynolds &
                         12—William Burton

Who being elected, tried & sworn the truth to speak on the Issue joined in this case Do say they find the defendant not Guilty in manner & form as charged in the Bill of Indictment.

(p 22)   State)
              vs)   John Huddleston the Defendant comes into
     John Huddleston) open Court & surrender himself in discharge of
his Bail & is ordered in custody.

John Denn, Lessee of Bartholomew Smith
& Pleasant Duke
        vs   ——Trespass & ejectment.
Richard Fenn & Henry Howell

Henry Howell comes into Court & prays to be admitted Defendant, & is admitted and the said Henry Howell —Willaim Mitchell & Henry Boatman in open Court acknowledge themselves indebted to the Lesors of the Plaintiff in the sum of five hundred dollars to be levied of their respective goods & chattles Lands & tenements to be void upon condition that if the said Henry Howell be condemned in the above action that he will pay the costs & condemnation or surrender himself to prison for the same or that they the said William & Henry Boatman will do it for him.

William Nall, Charles Hutcheson,Esqr. Samuel Clark, Thomas Dennis Andrew McPheters who together with Edmond Clark were appointed by the Court & Jury to view & make a road connecting & altering a road heretofore laid out by order of Court, that is to say, from the meeting house below William Nalls to the foot of the Copper Ridge, towit-to leave sd. Nalls on the left hand & take the ridge by John Nalls & so to the Copper ridge at the same place as before directed make the following report to Court, towit-

We the Jurors appointed by the Court to review & alter a road heretofore laid out by order of Court from a meeting house below William Nalls to the foot of the Copper ridge after being duly sworn have reviewed the same from the said meeting house to the foot of the said Copper ridge by way of a road heretofore cut out by John Nalls. Given under our hand this 10th day of February 1803 which said report is received by the Court.

> (signed)
>
> Wm Nall
> Andrew McPheters   Samuel Clark
> Chas. Hutcheson   Thomas Dennis

Ordered by Court that Edward Field be released from the payment of forty cents being the Tax due the State on 322 acres of Land for the year 1801 & also the payment of the sum of forty cents being the Tax due the County on the aforesaid Land for the year aforesaid, he having made oath that he was charged with the payment of Taxes on three hundred & twenty two acres of Land more or less than he owned in Grainger County.

Court adjourned till tomorrow 8 o'clock.

Friday 25th. February Court met according to adjournment.

	Nimrod Maxwell	)
Present	David McAnnlly &	) Esquires
	Robert C.Gordon	)

(p 23)

A Deed of conveyance from John Counts to Peter Hamilton for one hundred acres of Land was proven in open Court by Stephen McBroom a subscribing witness & ordered to be Registered.

Ordered by Court that Frederick Moyers have leave to build a chimney on the public square in the town of Rutledge adjoining his Lot.

Robert Yancey -Assignee of	)
Martin Ashburn	)
vs	) Whereupon came a Jury towit-
Isaiah Midkiff	)

| 1- Benjamin Shaw | 3- John Dorah |
| 2- James Chinn | 4- John Gillentine |

5- Dennis Condry
6- William Hamilton
7- Valentine Horgan
8- John Hammil

9- Stephen Bean
10-Edmond Holt
11-Alexander McDonald
12-Stephen McBroom

Who being elected tried & sworn well & truly to try the truth to speak on the matter in dispute in this case Do say they find for the Defendant -Rule for a new trial- Rule made absolute.

Thomas Anderson)
vs)
William Nation) John Cantrel a witness in this case being solemnly called, came not- It is therefore considered by the Court that he forfeit one hundred & twenty five dollars according to the Act of Assembly in such case made & provided.

Alexander McDonald)
vs)
Stephen Bean) Whereupon came a Jury towit-

1- James Chinn
2- John Dorah
3- Dennis Condry
4- William Hamilton
5- Valentine Horgan
6- John Gillentine

7- John Hammil
8- Edmond Holt
9- Stephen McBroom
10-David Smuffer
11-Alexander Hamilton A
12-Jesse Lay

Who being elected tried & sworn the truth to speak on the Issue joined in this case retired to consider of their Verdict afterward returned to the bar & being asked whether they had agreed upon their Verdict answered that they had not-Whereupon a mistrial was directed to be retired by consent.

A Deed of conveyance from Joseph Cobb to Richard Shaolday for one hundred acres of Land was acknowledged in open Court & ordered tobe Registered.

A Deed of conveyance from Joseph Cobb to Robert Yancey for a lot No. 11 in the town of Rutledge was acknowledged in open Court & ordered to be Registered.

(p 24) On motion to Court it is ordered that the written Instrument purporting to be the last Will and Testament of William Moffet deceased & which was found by a Jury to be his last Will and Testament be Recovered. Whereupon Barclay Marshal executor & Abigail Webster executrix named therein came into open Court & were sworn to execute the same.

By order of Court Barclay Marshal is appointed Guardian of Henry Moffet Webster a minor orphan who enters into Bond in the penal sum of fifteen hundred dollars with Peter Harris & Benjamin Shaw his securities. William Clay, David McAnally, & Isiah Midkiff -Justices of P.present.

Ordered by Court that Owen Loyd take into his care Jeremiah Midkiff a pauper & support him till next Court.

Alexander McDonald)
    vs   )   Peter Noe special Bail of the Defendant brings
Stephen Bean   ) him into open Court to surrender him in discharge
of himself.

Alexander McDonald)
    vs   )   Stephen Bean the Defendant Benjamin Shaw & Peter
Stephen Bean   ) Noe come into open Court & acknowledge themselves
indebted to Alexander McDonald the plaintiff in the sum of one thousand
dollars to be levied of their respective goods & chattles Land & tenements
but to be void upon condition that if the said Stephen Bean be condemned
in this action that he will pay the costs & condemnation or surrender himself
to prison for the same or that they will do it for him.

By order of Court Peter Noe is appointed overseer of the road from
Bean's Station to where said road intersects the river road at or near
John Coulters in place of John Hodge & that he have the same hands in the
same bounds in the same bounds to work under him that were allotted to
work under the said John Hodge.

By order of Court Robert C. Gordon Esqr. Dennis Condry are appointed
Jurors to attend the next Superior Court to be held at the Court House in
Knoxville on the fourth Monday of March next for the District of Hamilton
in the place of Ambrose Yancey & Isiah Widkiff who had bee appointed.

Ordered by Court that Robert Yancey Sheriff & Collector of the public & County Tax in Grainger County for the year 1801 be released from
the payment of the su, of four Dollars sixty two & one half cents & have
a credit to that amount in his settlement with the Tresurer of the District of Hamilton it being monies due the State aforesaid for taxes in
the year aforesaid William Savage Deputy collector of said Yancey, North
of Clinch river having exhibited to Court a list of Insolvencies to the
above amount to which he was qualified as the Law in that case Requires.

Ordered by Court that Robert Yancey Sheriff & collector of the public & County Tax in Grainger County for the year 1801 be Released from the
payment of the sum of four Dollars sixty two & one half cents & have a
credit to that amount in his settlement with the Tresurer of the County
aforesaid, it being monies due the said County for Taxes in the year
aforesaid — William Savage Deputy collector of said Yancey North of Clinch
river having exhibited to Court a list of Insolvencies to the above amt.
to which he was qualified as the Law in that case requires.

(p 25)   Ordered by Court that Robert Yancey Sheriff & collector of the
public & County tax in Grainger County for the year 1800 be released from
the payment of the sum of seven Dollars eighty seven cents & one half of a
cent & have a credit to that amount in his settlement with the Treasurer of
the District of Hamilton, it being monies due the State aforesaid for taxes
in the year last aforesaid.
     John Word, late Deputy of the said Robert Yancey having exhibited
to Court a list of Insolvencies to that amount to which he was qualified
as the Law in that case requires.

Ordered by Court that Robert Yancey Sheriff & collector of the

public & County Tax in Grainger County for the year 1800 be released from
the payment of the sum of Seven Dollars eighty seven & one half cents &
have a credit to that amount in his settlement with the treasurer of the
County aforesaid, it being monies due the County aforesaid for taxes in
the year last aforesaid for taxes in the year last aforesaid - John Word
late Deputy of the said Robert Yancey having exhibited to Court a list of
Insolvencies to that amount to which he was sworn as the Law in that case
requires.

Usley Campbell returns in open Court the following List of Taxable
property for the year A.D. 1803 -150 Acres of Land.

By order of Court John Counts & Captain George Bean are exempted from
working under Thomas Bunch Overseer of the road from Bean's Station to
Daniel Robinson & that they work under Peter Noe Overseer of the Road
from Bean's Station to the intersection of the River road near John Coulter's.

Peter Noe Constable maketh oath in open Court that he has attended
the Court five days as Constable at the present Term.

Court adjourns till Court in Course.

Joseph Cobb -J.P.

At a Court of Pleas and Quarter Sessions began & holden for the
County of Grainger at the Court House in Rutledge, on the third Monday of
May A.D. 1803 being the 16th of the same month.

James Moore   )
Present Major Lea &   )   Esquires
Noah Jarnagin   )

Robert Yancey esquire Sheriff of Grainger County returns to Court
that he has executed the following Venire facias on the following persons marked thus   sd. towit-

1- John Lebow -sd.
2- James Ore   "
3- Joseph Bryant -sd.
4- James Blair Jr.
5- John Noe
6- John Dannel -sd.
(p 26)
7- Edward West -sd
8- William Christian
9- David Davis - sd.
10-Jacob Arnett-   "
11-Robert Stone   "
12-James Richardson - sd.
13-David Bunch   "
14-Martin Bunch   "
15-John Brock   "
16-Peter Hancock   "

17- Chesley Jarnagin -sd
18- John Counts   "
19- John Coulter   "
20- George Cimry   "
21- John Bean   "
22- Martin Stubblefield
23- John Bunch   "
24- Henry Wipshur   "
25- Benj. Hudson   "
26- Richard Chilton   "
27- Charles Hopper   "
28- John Bradon   "
29- John Vinyard   "
30- Henry Mayo   "
31- Benj. Elliot   "

Out of which Venire Facias the persons whose names are hereafter
written were appointed Grand Jury for the present Term, towit-

1- Chesley Jarnagin foreman	9- John Bean
2- David Davis	10-Henry Kipshur
3- Jacob Arnett	11-Benjamin Hudson
4- Edward White	12-John Bradon
5- Robert Stone	13-John Vinyard
6- David Bunch	14-Benjamin Elliot
7- Peter Hammock	15-John Lebow &
8- John Counts	16-John Darnel

Sworn and charged by the Solicitor William McPhetridge Constable sworn to attend the Grand Jury at the present Term.

James Moore esquire returns in open Court a List of Polls & taxable property in the Bounds of Captain Howell's Company for the year A.D. 1803.

Andrew White esquire produced to Court a License authorizing him to practice Law as an Attorney in the several Courts of this State & took all necessary oaths.

James Moore Admr. of Samuel Moore deceased returns in open Court an Inventory of the estate of Samuel Moore deceased.

A Deed of conveyance from Stephen W. Senter to Merriweather Johnson for Lot No. 15 in the town of Rutledge was proven in open Court by Ambrose Yancey one of the subscribing witnesses & ordered to be Registered.

A Deed of conveyance from Merriweather Johnson to Stephen W. Senter for Lot no. 15 in the town of Rutledge was proven in open Court by John F. Jack one of the subscribing witnesses & ordered to be Registered.

A Deed of conveyance from Richard Conner to John Robinson for twenty five acres of Land was proven in open Court by James Russell one of the subscribing witnesses and ordered to be Registered.

(p 27)   A Deed of conveyance from Robert Dunville to Elijah Clay for one hundred and twenty seven and one half acres of Land was proven in open Court by the oath of William Clay one of the subscribing witnesses & ordered to be Registered.

Ordered by the Court that William Blair be released from paying the tax on fifty six acres of Land for the year A.D. 1802.

A Deed of conveyance from Samuel Carson to William Clay for four hundred and seventy acres of Land was proven in open Court by Noah Jarnagin one of the subscribing witnesses and ordered to be Registered.

A Deed of conveyance from Harwood Jones to Joseph Perrin for four hundred & fifty acres of Land was proven in open Court by Robert Stone one of the subscribing witnesses and ordered to be Registered.

A Deed of conveyance from Harwood Jones to Robert Gaines for fifty acres of Land was proven in open Court by Robert Stone one of the subscribing witnesses & ordered to be Registered.

A Deed of conveyance from James Pendergrass to Benjamin Howell for fifty acres of Land was proven in open Court by William Howell one of the subscribing witnesses & ordered to be Registered.

A Deed of conveyance from Burwell Scott to Dennis Scott for one hundred & fifty acres of Land was proven in open Court by Felps Read the subscribing witness & ordered to be Registered.

A Deed of conveyance from Isaac Barton to Isaac Barton for one hundred & twelve acres of Land (more or less) was proven in open Court by Felps Read one of the subscribing witnesses, and ordered to be Registered.

A Deed of conveyance from Henry Bowen Senr. to Henry Bowen Jr. for two hundred acres of Land was proven in open Court by James Grayson, one of the subscribing witnesses and ordered to be Registered.

Thomas Busby Returns in open Court twenty acres of Land subject to the payment of taxes for the year A.D. 1803-

John Hargraves   )
    vs   )   Obediah Waters & James Siddens special Bail of the
Nicholas Springs   )   Defendant surrender him in open Court in discharge of
themselves.

Absolum Hurst returns in open Court an account of the sale of the personal Estate of Francis Hines deceased, for which he was administrator.

James Russell returns in open Court the following List of taxable property for the year A.D. 1803 -Viz. 300 acres of Land & one white Poll.
Court adjourns till tomorrow 9 o'clock.

(p 28)   Tuesday morning May 17th. Court met according to adjournment.

            Major Lea   )
Present - Charles Hutcheson &   )   Esquires.
            William Hankins   )

John Ferry   )
    vs   )
Richard Reynolds)   Whereupon comes a Jury- towit,

1- Cuthbert Shelton   7- Thomas HoBroom
2- William Hamilton   8- Bartley Marshal
3- James Doson   9- Robert McElhaney
4- Nicholas Counts   10-Elisha Wallin
5- Obediah Waters   11-John Hall &
6- Michael Glinn   12-Philip Sigler

Who being elected tried and sworn the truth to speak on the Issue joined in this case Do say the Defendant did assume in manner & form as the plaintiff in his declaration hath complained against him, and assess plaintiffs damages by reason of his non performance to seventy five dollars besides his costs.

William Howard & Mary Coats widow & relict of Charles Coats deceased-present to Court for probate an written instrument purporting to be the last Will and Testament of the said Charles Coats and Robert Snodgrass a subscribing witness comes into Court makes oath that saw the said Charles Coats. Sign, seal publish and declare the said written Instrument as & for his last Will and Testament and that he saw Thomas Grimes another subscribing witness sign the same as a witness in the presence of the Testator, whereupon the said Will is ordered to be Registered, and the said William Howard was sworn Executer & the said Mary Coats executrix of the said last Will & Testament.

John Terry	)
vs	) Richard Reynolds the defendant surrenders himself
Richard Reynolds	) in open Court in discharge of his Bail.

A Bill of Sail from William Smith to Col. James Ore a negro man slave named Lemon was proven in open Court, Ambrose Yancey one of the subscribing witnesses & ordered to be Recorded.

A Deed of conveyance from James Ore to Elizabeth Center for six hundred & seventeen acres of Land was acknowledged in open Court by the Grantor & ordered to be Registered.

A Deed of conveyance from Alexander Stewart to Major Lea for two hundred acres of Land was proven in open Court by the oaths of William Howard a subscribing witness and ordered to be Registered.

A Deed of conveyance from Elijah Donathan, to John Holt for two hundred acres of Land was proven in open Court by David McAnally one of the subscribing witnesses & ordered to be Registered.

A Deed of conveyance from Joseph Cobb to Joshua Collins for one hundred acres of Land was acknowledged in open Court by Joseph Cobb & ordered to be Registered.

Robert C. Gordon who was elected Coroner for Grainger County at February Sessions A.D. 1803 produces to Court his commission signed by the Governor of the State of Tennessee & the Great Seal of said State thereto affixed & entered into Bond in the sum of Two Thousand five hundred Dollars with Pleasant M.Miller, Edward Scott & James Trimble his securities.

(p 29)

State	)
vs	) Jonathan Barnard surrenders John Bull Jr. in
John Bull & others	) open Court in discharge of himself.

James Ore has leave to administer on the estate of David Allison —dec'd that have not been administered upon & enters into Bond in the sum of thirty thousand dollars with Thomas Henderson — Ambrose Yancey & George Evans esquires, his securities & to take the necessary oaths.

Elizabeth Crabb by Attorney prefers to Court her petition praying the Court to order & adjudge what sum Stephen W.Senter shall pay her for the maintenance of a Bastard child of whom the said Stephen Stanor charged as the reputed father from the birth of the child to the present time; arguments of Council being heard, as well on behalf of the said Elizabeth as the said Stephen; it is considered by the Court that the said Elizabeth take nothing by her petition.

Major Lea esquire returns in open Court a list of Polls & Taxable property in the bounds of Captain Peter Hamilton's Company for the year A.D 1803-

Court adjourns till tomorrow 9 o'clock.

                    Wednesday May the 18th -Court met according to adjournment.
        Joseph Cobb   )
Present Charles McAnally)   Esquires
        Reubin Mason   )

State   )
     vs   )   Whereupon came a Jury towit-
William Kirk   )

1- Elisha Wallin   7- Henry Howell
2- James Arwine   8- Daniel Robinson
3- James Ore   9- Joseph Long
4- Daniel Taylor   10-Stephen W. Senter
5- Bartley Marshall   11-John Patterson &
6- Stephen Brundage   12-Robert Long

Who being Elected tried & sworn the truth to speak on the Issue Joined in this case, Do say they find the Defendant not guilty in manner & form as he stands charged in the Bill of Indictment Rule shew cause why Peter Hoe prosecutor should be taxed with the costs; on argument Rule made absolute.

By order of Court George Rensbarger is appointed overseer of the public road leading from the Town of Rutledge to the top of the Richland nobs in the room of Michael Coons, and that all the hands living between the top of the the Richland nobs and the top of Clinch Mountain from the house of Miller Easely to the house of Joshua Hickey (the aforesaid Easely and Hickey included) be assigned to work on said Road.

By order of Court Asa Street is appointed overseer of the River road from the ford in German Creek to the ford of McCarter's Creek and it is and it is ordered by Court that all the hands living between the mouth of German Creek and between the river & Big ridge be assigned him to work on said road.

A Bill of Sale from William Dyer to Major Lea for a negro girl about thirteen years of age named Betsy was proven in open Court by the oath of James Dyer Jr. a subscribing witness and ordered to be Recorded.

(p 30)
Thomas Lea   )
     vs   )   Peter Hoe special Bail of the Defendant surrenders him
Lincoln Ards   )   in open Court in discharge of himself and the said Defendant is prayed in custody of the Sheriff.

Robert Yancey, Assignee of Martin Ashburn)
   vs   )   Whereupon came a Jury towit-
Isiah Midkiff   )

1- Lincoln Amis   7- Edmund Holt
2- Isaac Mitchell   8- John Crabb
3- Edward Eppes   9- William Mitchell
40 Eli Mc Vey   10-Isaac McDonald
5- Thomas Mann   11-John McAnally
6- Pleasant Duke   12-George Martin

Who being Elected tried and sworn the truth to speak in the matter
in dispute between the parties Do say they find for the plaintiff the sum
of Eleven Dollars & forty cents debt & assess his damages occationed by
the detention of that Debt to two dollars & forty two cents - the Defendant by his Attorney makes a motion in arrest of Judgment & Reasons filed-
and the said Robert Yancey comes into Court in his proper person & releases all the Debt & damages in this case except eleven dollars & forty
cents- Reasons in arrest of Judgment withdrawn by Defendants Council.

Ordered that Frederick Moyers take charge of the Court House untill
November Term next, and keep the same clean and secure, that he make the
necessary repairs for carrying into effect this order for which he is to
receive a reasonable compensation.

Thomas Anderson   )
   vs   )   Whereupon came a Jury towit-
William Nation   )

1- Elisha Wallin   7- Robert Moore
2- Henry Howell   8- Benjamin Moore
3- Daniel Robinson   9- Philip Combs
4- Joseph Long   10-Thomas Bunch
5- David Holt   11-John Hammil
6- Samuel Peery   12-Richard Reynolds

Who being Elected tried & sworn the truth to speak on the Issue
joined in this case -Do say they find for the Defendant -Rule for a new
Trial- Rule discharged.

Ordered by Court that Martin Bunch be released from the payment
of Taxes on 875 acres of Land and one White poll the year A.D. 1802-

William Nation   )
   vs   )
David Lay & Jesse Lay)   Whereupon came a Jury,towit,

1- Lincoln Amis   7- John McAnally
2- Eli McVey   8- William Kirk
3- Thomas Mann   9- Stephen Brundage
4- Pleasant Duke   10-John Lea
5- Edmund Holt   11-Edward Eppes
6- William Mitchell   12-Martin Bunch

Who being elected tried & sworn the truth to speak

on the issue joined in this case Do say they find the Defendant did not
assume in manner & form as the plaintiff in his declaration hath complained aginst him. Rule to shew cause why a new trial should be granted-Court
being equally Divided- Rule Discharged.

William Howard comes into open Court & resigns his appointment of Constable.

(p 31)
William Nation   )
     vs   )   David Lay surrenders themselves in open Court
David Lay & Jesse Lay   )   in discharge of their Bail.

        Ordered that Frederick Moyers repair the Jail of Grainger County in
the following manner, towit- by repairing all the Benches that have been
made in as full & ample a manner as the situation of said Jail shall require, the repairs to be completed by August Term next, for which he shall
be allowed a reasonable compensation.
        The following is a List of Jurors appointed by the Court to attend as
Jurors at August Term A.D. 1803, towit,

1- Jeremiah Jarnagin   7- John Thompson
2- John Spencer   8- Aaron Smith
3- William Mitchell   9- Henry Ivey
4- Richard Acuff   10-Philip Sigler
5- Mathew Campbell   11-Francis Darnel
6- George Martin   12-Daniel Robinson

13- Abraham Elliot   24-Thomas Estes
14- John Lea   25-Danile Taylor
15- Michael Massingill   26-John Holt Senr.
16- James Alsup   27-Harmon Cox
17- Cornelius McCoy   28-John Noe
18- Edward McGinnis   29-Henry Boatman
19- John Humphreys   30-Henry Boatman
20- Joseph Eaton   31- Henry Howell
21- Edward Churchman   32-William Williams
22- Richard Thompson
23- Joseph Stubblefield

        Ordered that David Martin a minor, now of the age of two years &
eight months be bound unto Isaac Martin to live with him after the manner
of an apprentice, until he shall attain to the age of twenty one years.

        A Bill of Sale from Alexander Outlaw to Abigail Webster for a negro
man slave named Paul & a negro woman slave named Moll was proven in open
Court by the oath of Thomas Harm a subscribing witness and ordered to be
Recorded.

        Court adjourns till tomorrow 9 o'clock.

        Thursday May 19th -Court met according to adjournment.
            William Hankins   )
Present Robert C.Gordon &   )
            Charles McAnally   )   Whereupon came a Jury, towit,

Elisha Wallin   )
    vs -Certiorari   )   Whereupon came a Jury, towit,
Willaim Lane   )

1- Pleasanr Duke	7- Philip Combs
2- Henry Howell	8- Barclay Marshall
3- Joseph Long	9- John Hailey
4- Mathew Campbell	10-Miller Easley
5- David Holt	11-John Bird
6- Tandy Senter	12-William Hamilton

(p 32)   Who being elected tried & sworn the truth to speak on the matter in dispute between the parties Do say they find for the plaintiff and assess his damages to forty seven dollars and twenty five cents and costs. From which Verdict the defendant prays an appeal and by his Attorney files his reasons and enters into Bond with security.

A Deed of conveyance from Robert Yancey Sheriff of Grainger County to James Ore for one hundred & fifty acres of Land was proven in open Court by Ambrose Yancey a subscribing witness and ordered to be Recorded.

State   )
  vs   )
Isaiah Midkiff)   Isaiah Midkiff by Thomas Gray Esqr. his Attorney comes into Court & enters a Rule to shew cause why a writ of fieri facias issued on a Judgment rendered in this case & returnable to February Term A.D. 1803 and also a writ of Venditiori Exponas issued in consequence of a Levy made on the said execution and Returnable to the present Term together with the returns thereon should be quashed- Rule Continued.

James Danniel   )
    vs -Debt   )
Joseph Cobb &   )   Whereupon came a Jury, towit,
James Ore   )

1- John Spring	7- James Gidden
2- John Margraves	8- John Hamill
3- John Lea	9- James Nedly
4- Francis Hunter	10-John Hanes
5- Benjamin Allen	11-Robert Moore &
6- Nicholas Spring	12-Andrew Campbell

Who being elected tried & sworn the truth to speak on the Issue joined in this case Do say the Defendants have not paid the debt in the Declaration mentioned as in pleading they have alledged; they find for the plaintiff the sum of five hundred dollars the Debt in the declaration mentioned & assess his damages occasioned by the detention of that debt to sixty two Dollars besides his costs.

George Horner   )
   vs   )
Alexander McDonald)   Whereupon came a Jury, towit,

1- Pleasant Duke	3- Joseph Long
2- Henry Howell	4- Mathew Campbell

5- David Holt   9- John Bird
6- Phillip Combs   10-William Hamilton
7- John Hailey   11- Nathaniel Austin &
8- Miller Easely   12-George Sharp

Who being elected tried & sworn the truth to speak & well & truly to
enquire what damages George Horner hath sustained in a writ of Enquiry by him
brought into this case Do say they find for the Plaintiff and assess his damages to twenty dollars besides his costs- Rule for a new trial- Verdict set
aside by plaintiffs Attorney.

(p 37)

Ferqushard Campbell for the use of)
William Hamilton   ) Whereupon came a Jury, towit,
     Vs   )
Thomas Henderson   )
1- John Spring   7- James Siddens
2- John Hargraves   8- John Howell
3- Francis Hunter   9- James Hedly
4- John Lea   10-John Haines
5- Benjamin Allen   11-Robert Moore
6- Nicholas Spring   12-Mathew Campbell

Who being elected tried & sworn the truth to speak on the Issue joined
in this case Do say they (the Defendants) have not paid the debt in the Declaration mentioned as in pleading they have alledged, but have altogether
failed to pay the same, they find for the Plaintiff the sum of one hundred
dollars the debt in the declaration mentioned, and assess his damages occationed by the Detention of that debt to Ten dollars & fifty cents & costs.
Plaintiff directs execution to stay till next Court- Defendants agree that
interest be calculated till execution Issued.

Thomas Obinn for the use of)
Robert Yancey   )
     Vs   )
John Stewart   ) Whereupon came a Jury, towit,

1- Pleasant Duke   7- John Hailey
2- Henry Howell   8- John Bird
3- Joseph Long   9- George Sharp
4- Mathew Campbell   10-Thomas Ginnings
5- David Holt   11-John Hunch &
6- Philip Combs   12-Peter Hoe

Who being Elected, tried & sworn the truth to speak on the Issue joined
in this case Do say they find the Defendant hath not performed his Covenants
as in pleading he hath alledged, and for the non performance thereof assess
the plaintiffs damages to Eighty four dollars and twenty cents and costs.

A Deed of conveyance from Andrew Evans to George New for one hundred
acres of Land was proven in open Court by the oath of Jacob Cobbs a subscribing witness & ordered to be Registered.

Ordered that the Sheriff take into possession & bring into Court In-
stanter, James John, Thomas & Spencer, children of Elizabeth Ashberry

to be dealt with as the Court may direct.

Stephen Brundage   )
    vs -Certiorari)
George Combs   )   Whereupon came a Jury, towit,

1- Henry Howell   7- Thomas Jinnings
2- Joseph Long   8- John Punch
3- Mathew Campbell   9- Peter Noe
4- David Holt   10-Francis Grabb
5- Nathaniel Austin   11-Joel Harmer &
6- George Sharp   12-Hardy Pace

Who being elected tried & sworn the truth to speak in the matter in dispute in this case Do say they find for the Plaintiff & assess his damages to six dollars & eighty nine cents besides his costs.

(p 34)
Martin Miller   )
    vs   )
Martin Ashburn -Coroner)
        Martin Miller By James Trimble his Attorney comes into Court & makes a motion to inter up a judgment for the sum of one hundred & twenty five Dollars aginst the said Martin Ashburn Coroner for not returning in due time writ of Capias Ad Respondendum caused to be issued by Martin Miller aginst John Hamil, Ambrose Yancey & George Rensbarger from the Clerks Office of Grainger County returnable to May Term A.D. 1803 and it appearing to the satisfaction of the Court that the said Writ came to the said Martin Ashburn more than Twenty days before the return day of May term A.D.1803 -Whereupon It is considered by the Court that the said Martin Miller Do recover aginst the said Martin Ashburn one hundred & twenty five dollars according to the Act of the General Assembly in such cases made & provided; unless he shew sufficient cause at our next Court to be held on the third Monday of August next why the said forfeiture should not be made absolute- Plaintiffs Attorney directs Scire facias to Issue and afterward the said Attorney comes & releases the aforesaid forfeiture.

William Windham   )
    vs   )
Martin Ashburn -Coroner)
        William Windham By Pleasant M.Miller his Attorney comes into Court & makes a motion to enter up a judgment against Martin Ashburn Coroner for one hundred & twenty five dollars for not Returning in due time a Writ of Capias ad Respondendum issued in the name of the said William Windham aginst Robert Yancey out of the Clerks Office for the County of Grainger Returnable to May term A.D. 1803 and it appearing to the satisfaction of the Court that the aforesaid Writ came to the hands of the said Martin Ashburn more than twenty days before the return day thereof; Whereupon it is considered by the Court that the said William Windham Do recover against the sd. Martin Ashburn the sum of one hundred & twenty five dollars according to the Act of Assembly in such cases made & provided unless he shew cause at our next Court of Pleas & Quarter Sessions to be held at the Court House in Rutledge on the third Monday of August next why the said forfeiture should not be made absolute- Scire facias to issue.

Samuel Terry Assignee, &c)
    vs - 156)
Martin Ashburn &)   Whereupon came a Jury -towit,
Philip Combs)

1- John Daniel Junr.   7- Joseph Long
2- Nathaniel Austin   8- Pleasant Duke
3- John Hammil   9- James Medly
4- David Holt   10-William Kirk
5- Thomas Jennings   11-Peter Noe &
6- Abraham Howard   12-George Sharp

Who being Elected tried & sworn the truth to speak on the Issue joined in this case Do say they find the Defendants have not paid the debt in the Declaration mentioned as in pleading they have alledged, they find for the Plaintiff one hundred & two dollars & fifty cents, the Debt in the Declaration mentioned & assess his damages occasioned by the detention of that Debt to seven dollars & seventeen cents besides his costs.

Joseph Stowell)
    vs)   Whereupon came a Jury as in the above case.
John Brown)

Who being Elected tried & sworn the truth to speak on the issue joined in this case Do say they find the Defendant hath not paid the debt in the declaration mentioned as in pleading he hath alledged; they find for the Plaintiff the sum of thirty dollars the debt in the Declaration mentioned & also his damages occationed by the detention of that debt to four dollars & fifty cents Besides his costs.

(p 35)
Dedrick and Conway)
    vs)
Eli McVey)   Whereupon came a Jury, towit,

1- John Daniel   7- William Kirk
2- John Hammil   8- Peter Noe
3- Thomas Jinnings   9- George Sharp
4- Abraham Howard   10-Henry Howell
5- Joseph Long   11-James Ore &
6- James Medly   12-John Acuff

Who being Elected tried and sworn the truth to speak on the Issue joined in this case Do say they find for the the defendant hath not paid the debt in the Declaration mentioned as in pleading he hath alledged they find for the plaintiffs thirty nine dollars & twenty five cents debt and assess their damages occationed by the Detention of that debt to one dollar & fifty nine cents & costs.

A Letter of Attorney from Thomas King to John Counts was proven in open Court by Nicholas Sharp a subscribing witness & ordered to be Recorded.

Ordered by Court that James Ore be appointed overseer of the public road from the fork below Crabb to Bean Station in the room of Thomas Johnson, and all the hands in the same bounds that worked under said Johnson to work under him on said road.

Ordered that John Lebow be appointed overseer of the road from the Line dividing Hawkins County in the same bounds that worked under said Henderson to work under him on said road.

Ordered by the Court that David Holt Senr. take in his charge Jeremiah Middiff one of the poor of this County & provided for him till next Court for which he shall be allowed a reasonable compensation.

Ordered by Court that John Acuff be appointed overseer of the road in the room of John Beaty and that he have the same hands to work under him that worked under said Beaty.

Ordered by Court that Frederick Moyers have leave to keep an Ordinary or house of publick Intertainment in the town of Rutledge, and he enters into Bond with Edward Scott & John Bunch his securities in the sum of twelve hundred & fifty Dollars.

Ordered by Court that David Clayton Esquire have leave to keep an Ordinary or house of entertainment at the dwelling house in Grainger Co. and he enters into Bond in the sum of Twelve hundred & fifty dollars with James Ore and Robert Yancey his security.

By order of Court the following persons, towit, Thomas Henderson, Nimrod Maxwell & Reubin Mason Esquires are appointed Inspectors of an Election to be held on the first thirsday in August next and the succeeding day at the Court House in the town of Rutledge for the purpose of Electing a Governor for the State of Tennessee - Three Representatives to represent said State in the Congress of the United States and one Senator and two Representatives to represent said County in that State Legislature.

John Rumney By George W. Campbell his Attorney & Agent Returns to Court the following taxable property for the year A.D. 1803 towit-Ten thousand acres of Land being the whole of a tract of 12,000 acres originally Granted to Stockley Donalson, that is not taken away by older claims.
Court adjourns till tomorrow 10 o'clock.

(p 36)   Friday Morning 20th May —Court met according to adjournment.
        Joseph Cobb   )
Present David McAnally &) Esquires
        Robert C. Gordon)

Ordered by the Court that the Sheriff exposed to sale 200 acres of Land the property of James Hall or so much thereof as will be sufficient to satisfy the State & County tax due thereon for the year A.D. 1800 & all costs & charges that Has accured thereon, the same having been published in the Knoxville Gazette as the Law directs and the Court directs Execution to issue.

Ordered by Court that the Sheriff expose to sale & sell 200 acres of Land the property of Young Lamar or so much thereof as will be sufficient to satisfy seventy five cents being the tax due the State & County on said Land for the year A.D. 1801 & also further sum of two dollars & thirty five cents, being the Tax due thereon the same having been published in the Knoxville Gazette as the Law directs and the Court direct Execution to issue.

Ordered By Court that the Sheriff take into his custody James, John Thomas and Spencer —children of Elizabeth Asbery and bring them to next Court to be dealt with as the Court May order.

(p 37)   At a Court of Pleas & Quarter Sessions began and holden for the County of Grainger at the Court House in Rutledge on the third Monday of August A.D. 1803 being the 15th day of the same month.

Present
James Blair
William Hankins —Esquires.
Reuben Mason

Robert Yancey Esqr. Sheriff of Grainger County returns to Court that he has executed the following Venire Facias on the following persons, towit on all marked thus (ed).

1- Jeremiah Jarnagin   ed.
2- John Spencer   "
3- William Mitchell   "
4- Richard Acuff   "
5- Mathew Campbell   "
6- George Martin   "
7- John Thompson   0
8- Aaron Smith   "
9- Henry Ivy   0
10-Philip Sigler   "
11-Francis Daniel   0
12-Daniel Robinson   ed.
13-Abraham Elliot   "
14-John Lea   "
15-Mitchel Massengill "
16-James Alsup   "

17-Cornelius McCoy   ed.
18-Edward McGinnis   "
19-John Humphreys   "
20-Joseph Eaton   "
21-Edward Churchman   "
22-Richard Thompson   "
23-Joseph Stubblefield ed.
24-Thomas Estis   "
25-Daniel Taylor   "
26-John Holt Senr.
27-Harmon Cox   ed.
28-John Noe   "
29-Henry Boatman   "
30-Henry Howell   "
31-William Williams   "

Out of which Venire Facias the Persons whose names are hereafter mentioned were appointed a Grand Jury to the present Term, towit-

1- John Lea foreman
2- John Spencer
3- William Mitchell
4- Mathew Campbell
5- Daniel Robinson
6- Abraham Elliot
7- Edward McGinnis
8- John Humphreys

9- Edward Churchman
10-Richard Thompson
11-Harmon Cox
12-Henry Howell
13-Jeremiah Jarnagin
14-Richard Acuff &
15-Mitchell Massengill

Who were sworn & charged William McWhatridge Constable was sworn to attend the Grand Jury.

(p 38) A Mortgage Deed from Thomas Bunch to John Bunch for two hundred acres of Land was proven in open Court by the oath of John F. Jack a subscribing witness & ordered to be Registered.

A Bill of Sale from Thomas Bunch to John Bunch for one Mare & Coult five cows & calves was proven in open Court by the Oath of Daniel Robinson a subscribing witness & ordered to be Registered.

A Deed of conveyance from James Maxey To Thomas Johnston for three hundred acres of Land was proven in open Court by the Oath of Fare Owen one of the subscribing witnesses and ordered to be Registered.

A Deed of conveyance from Mirida Coffy Jr. Abner Lowe for two hundred acres of Land more or less was acknowledged in open Court & ordered to be Registered.

A Deed of conveyance from Chesley Jarnagin to Enoch Winds for one hundred and sixty five acres of Land was proven in open Court by the oath of Noah Jarnagin one of the subscribing witnesses & ordered to be Registered.

Enoch Winds records his mark & brand as follows, towit, his mark a smooth crap in the left ear & a small under bit in the right ear- His brand thus-(#3)

A Deed of conveyance from Patrick Sharkey to Charles Gilbert for a tract of Land supposed to contain six hundred acres was proven in open Court by Joseph Owen a subscribing witness and ordered to be Registered.

A Power of Attorney from James Daniel was proven in open Court by the oath of George H. Combs one of the subscribing witnesses and ordered to be Recorded.

A Deed of conveyance from John Smith -William Milligan & Elenor his wife for about sixty two & one fourth acres of Land to William Smith of Bath County Virginia was acknowledged in open Court.

Nicholas Countz returns in open Court 200 acres of Land the property of John Countz for the Tax of the year A.D. 1803.

John Finley returns in open Court two Lots in the town of Rutledge towit- Nos. 35-38 for the Tax of the year A.D. 1803.

A Deed of conveyance from Thomas Churchman to Edward Churchman for sixty acres & one half of an acre & twenty poles was proven in open Court by the oath of William Hankins one of the subscribing witnesses & ordered to be Registered.

(p 39)   A Deed of conveyance from William Shelton to Samuel Rail for one hundred acres of Land was acknowledged in open Court & ordered to be Registered.

A Bill of Sale from Gideon Johnson to Chesley Jarnagin for a negro girl named Jean was proven in open Court by the Oath of Enoch Winds one of the subscribing witnesses and ordered to be Recorded.

A Deed of conveyance from William Sasseen to Spencer Griffin & Richard Reynolds for one thousand acres Land was proven in open Court by the oath of John McCoy a subscribing witness & ordered to be Registered.

Jacob Elliot Records his mark -Viz.a light smooth crop in each ear.

Abraham Elliot Records his mark a crop off the left ear & a half penny in the right.

Andrew McLusk Esqr. produced to Court a License authorizing him to practice Law as an Attorney in the several Courts of Law & Equity in this State & took the necessary oath & was admitted to practice as an Attorney in this Court.

Simion B.Grigsby Esqr. produced to Court a License authorizing him to practice Law as an Attorney in the several Courts of Law & Equity in this State and took the necessary oaths & was admitted to practice Law as an Attorney in this Court.

Samuel Lowe Esqr. produced to Court a License authorizing him to practice Law as an Attorney in the several Courts of Law & Equity in this State & took the necessary oaths & was admitted to practice Law as an Attorney in this State, or Court.

Court adjourned till tomorrow 9 o'clock.

Tuesday 15th August Court met according to adjournment.

Present
Noah Jarnagin)
William Clay) Esquires
Robert C.Gordon)

Ordered by Court that thomas Harm be appointed overseer of the road from Marshall's Ferry on Holston River to Hawkins Court House, towit, from said ferry to the Hawkins Line in the room of Edward Shipley & that all the hands in the following bounds work under him on said road, towit up Harris' creek to Samuel Coxes & from thence to the County Line.

John Denn, Lessee of Nimrod Dobson)
vs) Whereupon came a Jury, towit-
Fen and Joshua Botts)

1- Clisbe Riggs   7- Richard Reynolds
2- John Horner   8- Jesse Riggs
3- Bartley Marshall   9- John Elsey
4- Benj. Coopwood   10-Isaac Midkiff
5- Nicholas Countz   11-Elijah Donathan &
6- John Harrill   12-William Harmill

Who being Elected, tried & sworn the truth   (p 40)   to speak on the Issue joined in this case Do say the defendant is Guilty of the Trespass & Ejectment in manner & form as alledged in the plaitiff's Declaration as to one eighth of an acre & not guilty as to the residue & assess the Plaintiff's damages to six cents besides his costs.

A Deed of conveyance from Henry Bowen Junr. to James Bowen was acknowledged in open Court containing one hundred and fifteen acres of Land ordered to be Registered.

John Stewart vs Nicholas Spring —Abraham Elliot & Charles Hutcheson Special Bail of Nicholas Spring surrenders him in open Court in discharge

of themselves Defendant prayed in custody by Plaintiffs Attorney and ordered in custody by the Court.

A Deed of conveyance from Henry Rice to Charles Rice for two hundred
acres of Land more or less was acknowledged in open Court by the Grantor
ordered to be Registered.

A Bill of Sale from David Bailey to Charles Hutcheson for a negro girl
named Nance was proven in open Court by the oath of William McPhetridge
& ordered to be Recorded.

Hugh Campbell)
    vs   )   Whereupon came a Jury towit,
James Ore)

1- James Grayson   7- William Howard
2- Stephen Brundage   8- Edmond Holt
3- William Hamilton   9- James Bowen
4- Obediah Waters   10-Robert Smith
5- John Crabb   11-Nicholas Spring
6- John Gillentine   12-Robert McElhaney

Who being elected tried & sworn the truth to speak on the Issue joined
in this case Do say the defendant did assume in manner & form as the plaintiff in his declaration hath complained against him, that he has not paid
the sum in the declaration mentioned as in pleading he has alledged that he
has no set off- that he made no accord & satisfaction and they find for
the plaintiff & assess his damages To forty eight dollars sixteen cents &
one third of a cent besides his costs- rule for a new Trial- rule discharged.

By order of Court the following persons are appointed Jurors to the
next Superior Court of Law & Equity for Hamilton District towit- John Lea
Noah Jarnagin, Robert C/Gordon & Joseph Cobb Esquires.

By order of Court Thomas Dunn is appointed overseer of the road from
the top of said mountain to Peter Beelers old mill in the room of Larkin
Hall & that all the hands in the following Bounds, towit, Beginning at the
aforesaid Gap of the mountain Thence along the mountain till opposite David
Bunch's thence to the top of the Combs ridge till opposite William Roberts
thence to Larkin Halls, so as to leave him in John Halls Bounds, thence
to the Beginning.

(p 41)
John Stewart)
    vs   )   the Defendant was surrendered in open Court in dis-
Nicholas Spring)   charge of his Bail & ordered in custody of the Sheriff
and afterwards the Defendant brings Adam Peck & Francis Hunter into Court
who enter his special Bail in this case- the Court appointed the following
persons Jurors to November Term 1803-towit, Henry Crawley -Josiah Smith,
Benjamin Shaw, John Lebow, Joseph Roe Senr. David Taylor, Joseph Bryant
Hugh Larimore, Robert Long, Miller Easley, Nicholas County, James Blair,Sr.
John Bowen, Henry Bowen, Michael Kearns, Chesley Jarnagin, Aaron Smith,
John Estis, Joseph Stubblefield, Philip Sigler, Larkin Hall, Jacob Arnett
Cornelius McCoy, Bartley Marshall, James Ore, Joseph Ore, William Kirkam,
David Holt,Senr. Edward Churchman, James Carmichael, Duncan Carmichael.

Court adjourns till tomorrow 9 o'clock.

Wednesday August 17th –Court met according to adjournment.

Charles Hutcheson)
Charles McAnally   )   Esquires.
William Hankins   )

A Deed of conveyance from John Crabb to Spencer Griffin for one Lot in the Town of Rutledge No. 25– was acknowledged in open Court & ordered to be registered.

State   )
  vs   )   Whereupon come a Jury, towit,
John Bull   )

1– John Arwine   7– Philip Combs
2– John Boyers   8– Thomas Lea
3– James Arwine   9– John Crabb
4– Jesse Cheek   10–William Jones
5– George Sharp   11–James Grayson
6– Peter Hoe   12–George Combs

Who being Elected tried & sworn the truth to speak on the issue joined in this case Do say they find the defendant not guilty in manner & form as he stands charged in the Bill of Indictment thereupon the Defendant by his Council enters a rule to shew cause why the Prosecutor should be taxed with the costs of the prosecution; on argument the aforesaid rule is made absolute.

A Deed of conveyance from Ambrose Yancey to David Hopping for a Lot in the town of Rutledge No. 1– containing three eights of an acre was acknowledged in open Court by Ambrose Yancey the Grantor & ordered to be Registered.

A Deed of conveyance from Robert Yancey Sheriff of Grainger County to John F.Jack for one third part of four hundred acres of Land was acknowledged in open Court & ordered to be Registered.

Ordered by Court that Owen Loyd be allowed the sum of six Dollars for keeping Jeremiah Midkiff six weeks previous to February Term.

(p 42)   Ordered By the Court that David Holt be allowed the sum of 12 Dollars for keeping Jeremiah Midkiff three months previous to this Term.
A Deed of conveyance from Edward Epps to John S.McFarland for one Lot in the town of Rutledge No. 36– was acknowledged in open Court by Edward Epps & ordered to be Registered.

State   )
  vs   )
Elizabeth Asberry)   Whereupon come a Jury, towit,
William Robinson, Joseph Dennis, Thomas Dennis, William Jones, John Beaty John Hargraves, William Cooper, Thomas Dunn, Nicholas Spring, Robert Moore William Hamilton and Alexander Hamilton, who being Elected tried & sworn the truth to Speak the issue joined in this case, do say they find the Defendant Guilty in manner & form as charged in the Bill of Indictment– Rule for a new trial– Rule made absolute.

Ordered by Court that Robert Yancey Sheriff of Grainger County be allowed the sum of sixty Dollars for his Ex Officio services for the year one thousand eight hundred & two, the time to be computed from May term, one thousand eight hundred & two.

Ordered by Court that Ambrose Yancey Clerk of Grainger County be allowed the sum of thirty Dollars for his Ex officio services for the year one thousand eight hundred & two, and also the further sum of fifteen dollars for making out & recording the Tax Lists for said year, the time to be computed from May term one thousand eight hundred & two.

Ordered by Court that Joseph Cobb Esqr. be allowed the sum of two dollars for his services in laying off the prison Bounds in the town of Rutledge as Surveyor, and also the further sum of one dollar for the Chain-Carriers in laying off said Bounds.

the Grand Jury are discharged from further attendance at this Term.

Ordered by Court that William McFetteredge Constable be allowed the sum of one dollar for each day he has attended on the Grand Jury as Constable at May Term last, and the same for each day he has attended on the grand Jury at the present Term, and the said William McFeteredge comes into Court & proves four days attendance at May Term & three days at the present Term.

State   )
   vs   )
William Grisham)   Whereupon came a Jury, towit,   Jesse Cheek, George Sharp, Peter Hoe, Thomas Lea, John Crabb, James Grayson, George Combs, John Long, James Blair Junr. David Holt, Obediah Waters, & Elisha Williamson, who being Elected tried & sworn the truth to speak on the Issue joined in this case, Do say they find the defendant guilty in manner & form as charged in the Bill of Indictment— Rule for a new trial —Rule discharged by Defendants Attorney & Defendant fined Twenty five Dollars.~

Ordered by Court that Col. Thomas Henderson, Nicholas Countz, Thomas Bunch, Thomas McBroon, Major Lea, Mathew Campbell, be appointed Jurors to view the public road leading from Rogersville in Hawkins County to Knoxville through the Town of Rutledge to begin at the County line above Col. Henderson whare said road crosses the same and to view said road to whare it crosses the town line of Grainger County & make report to next Court.

(p 43)   William Morgan comes into Court & enters into Bond in the sum of five hundred dollars with Able Morgan his security; conditioned that the said William Morgan shall at all times acquit, discharge & save harmless the Inhabitants of the County of Grainger from all costs, charges & troubles whatsoever for & by reason of the birth maintenance of & bringing up a child begotten on the body of a certain Elizabeth Childress with which he stands charged on oath of being the reputed father.

Court adjourns till tomorrow 9 o'clock.

Present— Joseph Cobb— David McAnnlly— Charles McAnnlly —Esquires.

James Guinn   )
    vs   )   Whereupon came a Jury, towit, Dennis Condry, Joseph
John Patterson) Beelor, Nicholas Spring, Benjamin Elliot, John Hamill,
Peter Hoe, Francis Hunter, Robert Moore, James Sidden, John Hains, Benj.
Allen & William Howard, who being Elected tried & sworn the truth to speak
in the matter in controversy in this case Do say they find for the Plain-
tiff & assess his damages to twelve dollars & twenty five cents & costs;
Rule to shew cause why a new trial should be granted- Rule made absolute.

A Deed of conveyance from John F.Jack to James Ore for one hundred &
thirty three & one third acres of Land was acknowledged in open Court &
ordered to be recorded.

George Combs   )
  vs   )
William Hall, William Clay   )
William Hankins & Robert Patterson.)

Whereupon came a Jury, towit, John Countz, Obediah Waters, Isaac
Midkiff, William Jones, James Arwine, John Arwine, John Crabb, John Bird
John Hargraves, John Beaty, John Gillinton, & Pleasant Duke, who being
elected tried & sworn the truth to speak in the Issue joined in this case;
Mistrial by consent.

Samuel Newell   )
    vs   )
Michael Montgomery)   Whereupon came a Jury, towit, Dennis Condry,
Joseph Beelor, Nicholas Spring, Benj. Elliot, John Hamill, William Dyer
Francis Hunter, Robert Moore, James Siddens, John Haines, Benjamin Allen
& William Howard - who being elected tried & sworn well and truly to en-
quire what damages the plaintiff hath sustained on a writ of inquiry by
him brought in this case, Do say they find for the plaintiff & assess his
damages to one hundred & seventeen Dollars besides his costs.

Court adjourns for half an hour.
Court met according to adjournment. Present -William Clay, Charles
McAnally & Joseph Cobb, Esquires.

(p 44)
Charles McClung)
    vs   )
Thomas Mann   )   Whereupon came a Jury, towit, Dennis Condry, Joseph
Beelor, Nicholas Spring, Benjamin Elliot, John Hamill, William Dyer,
Francis Hunter, Robert Moore, James Sidden, John Haines, Benjamin Allen
& William Howard, who being elected tried & sworn the truth to speak in
this case Do say the Defendant hath not paid the Debt in the declaration
mentioned as in pleading he hath alledged, they find for the Plaintiff
the Debt in the Declaration & assess his damages to thirteen dollars and
ninety five cents besides his costs.

A Deed of conveyance from David Holt To Isaac Midkiff for one hundred acres of Land was acknowledged in open Court & ordered to be Registered.
John Denn, Lessee of James Anderson -John Anderson, William Anderson

Andrew Anderson, Thomas Anderson & Samuel Anderson heirs at Law of William Anderson.-Dec'd.

        Whereupon came a Jury -Viz.

vs

James Arwine

        John Countz, Obediah Waters, John Hall, William Jones, Isaac McDonald, Robert Smith, John Crabb, John Bird, John Hargraves, John Beaty Philip Sigler & Pleasant Duke, who being elected tried & sworn the truth to speak on the issue joined in this case do say they find the defendant not Guilty, in manner & form as alledged in the plaintiff's declaration appeal prayed & granted, bond with security given &c.

        By permission of Court William Hall returns in open Court the following List of taxable property for year 1802 towit 520 acres of Land -one town Lot 23 -Black polls.

        Ordered by Court that the Patrolers or searchers for Grainger County be released from the payment of poll Tax for the year 1803.

        James Dyer, one of the Constables of this County returns to Court that he has levied on two hundred acres of Land the property of Charles Bunch bounded & described as follows, towit, bounded by John Bunches Land to satisfy the sum of thirty one dollars & sixty cents debt & seventy five cents costs which sum Robert Parks lately recovered against him before Daniel Clayton, one of the Justices of the Peace for said County, whereupon it is ordered by the Court that the sheriff of said County do sell said Land or so much thereof as will be sufficient to satisfy the aforesaid sum of thirty one dollars & sixty cents Debt & seventy five cents costs besides his costs.

Benjamin McCarty)
     vs   )
Ambrose Yancey   )   Whereupon came a Jury, towit,

Nicholas Countz, Joseph Beelor, Nicholas Spring, Benjamin Elliot, John Hammill, Philip Combs, Francis Hunter, Robert Moore, James Siddens, John Haines, Benj. Allen & William Howard - who being elected tried & sworn the truth to speak on the issue joined in this case, do say they find the defendant hath not paid the debt in the declaration mentioned as in pleading he hath alledged they find for the plaintiff the debt in the declaration & assess his damages to three dollars & fifty cents & costs.

(p 45)

Benjamin McCarty)
  vs   )
Nicholas Coons &)
Ambrose Yancey   )   Whereupon came a Jury, towit, John Countz, Obediah Waters, John Hall, William Jones, Robert Smith, Isaac McDonald, John Crabb John Bird, Francis Crabb, John Carwile, Michael Kearns & John S. McFarland who being elected tried & sworn the truth to speak in the Issue joined in this case Do say the Defendants have not paid the debt in the declaration as in pleading they have alledged & find for the plaintiff the debt in the declaration mentioned & assess his damages to one Dollar & seventy cents & costs.

Motion in Arrest of Judgment reasons filed.

Court adjourns till Court in course.
Signed -Joseph Cobb & Isaac Midliff -Esqrs.

At a Court of Pleas & Quarter Sessions begun and holden for the County of Grainger at the Court House in Rutledge on the third Monday of Nov. A.D. 1803 being the 21st. of the same month.
Present- Major Lea - William Clay- Charles Hutcheson -Esquires.

Robert Yancey Esquire Sheriff of Grainger County returns to Court that he has executed the following Venire Facias on the following Persons Viz. on all marked thus-sd.
Henry Crawley, Josiah Smith sd.- Benj. Shaw sd. John Lebow sd. Joseph Hoe Senr. sd. Daniel Taylor sd. Joseph Bryant sr. Hugh Larimore sd. Robert Long sr. Miller Easely sd. Nicholas Countz sr. James Blair Junr. sd. John Brown sd. Henry Bowen sd. Michael Kearns sd. & Excused Duncan Carmichael Sr. Chesley Jarnagin Sr. Aaron Smith sd. John Estis sd. Joseph Stubblefield sd. Philip Sigler sd. Larkin Hall sd. Jacob Arnett, Cornelius McCoy sd. Bartley Marshall, James Ore sd. William Kirham sd. Joseph Ore sd. David Holt sd. Edward Churchman & James Carmichael sd. out of which Venire facias the persons whose names are underneath was appointed a Grand Jury for the present Term, Viz.

James Ore Foreman, Henry Crawley, Joseph Hoe Sr. Joseph Bryant, Miller Easely, James Blair Jr. Henry Bowen, Aaron Smith, John Estis, Larkin Hall, Joseph Ore, James Carmichael & Hugh Larimore, who were sworn & charged by the Solicitor.

William McFetridge, Constable was sworn to attend the grand jury.

A commission was produced to Court from his Excellency John Sevier Governor in and over the State of Tennessee with the Great Seal of the sd. State thereunto annexed appointing John Bradden, Valentine Houlder, William Christan, Philip Sigler, James Whitlock, James Moore Jr. Henry Boatman Sherod Hayes, Reubin Riggs & John McFarland all of the County of Grainger Justices of the Peace in & for said County Issd. and the said John S. McFarland -William Christian, Philip Sigler & Henry Boatman came into Court & took the necessary oaths & took their seats.

Ordered by Court that John Homer have leave to keep an ordinary or house of public Entertainment in Grainger County & enters into Bond with Samuel Peery & Joseph Long his securities in the penal sum of two thousand five hundred Dollars.

(p 46) A Bill of Sale from Joseph Inman and to Isaac Inman for a negro boy named George was acknowledged in open Court by Joseph Inman and ordered to be Recorded.
A Bill of Sale from Nicholas Spring to John Spring was proven in open Court by William Christian one of the subscribing witnesses and ordered to be recorded.

A Deed of conveyance from Nicholas Spring to John Spring for three hundred acres of Land was proven in open Court by William Christian one of the subscribing witnesses and ordered to be registered.

A Bill of Sale from John Punch to William Christian for a negro girl named Sarah was proven in open Court by Charles Hutcheson one of the subscribing witnesses, ordered by Court that Isaac Barton Jr. be appointed overseer of the road from Moffett's place to where the road runs into Jefferson County at the corner of Isaac Barton's field & that all the hands in the following bounds be assigned to him to work on said road Viz.from Moffett's to Reduss & Kidwell's on Spring Creek thence up said creek including all the hands living on said creek above said Kidwell's.

Ordered by Court that William Smith be appointed overseer of the road from Panther Spring to Jesse Riggs old place, and that all the hands in the following Bounds be assigned him to work on said road, towit-including Welcom Hodge, Henry Ivey, John Howell, William Milliken, Joseph Stephens William Sweaney & all between them and said road.

Ordered by Court that Thomas Reece Jr. be appointed overseer of the road from the bridge at Jesse Riggs old place to where road takes into Jefferson County between said Riggs & Miller Doggetts & that all the hands living on Harmson Coxes Creek below said road down to the mouth of said creek & those living on Reubin Riggs creek from the forks of said Creek up to said road & in the bounds between said creek be assigned on said road under him.

A Deed of conveyance from Stephen Brundage to Tunker Senter for one hundred acres of Land was proven in open Court by the oath of Miller Easeley one of the subscribing witnesses thereto & ordered to be Registered.

A Power of Attorney from Stephen Brundage to Tandy Senter was proven in open Court by Miller Easley one of the subscribing witnesses and ordered to be Recorded.

A Deed of conveyance from Sarah Murphy executrix of William Murphy deceased. Richard Murphy, Isaac Murphy and Jesse Murphy To Isaac Barton for two and fifty eight acres Land was proven in open Court by Felps Beed one of the subscribing witnesses thereto as to all the Grantors except Jesse Murphy and the said Felps Read swears that the said Isaac Murphy and the subscribe the name of Jesse Murphy to said deed but that he does not recollect that he either heard Jesse Murphy authorize the said Isaac Murphy to sign his name to said Deed or heard him acknowledge said Deed, ordered to be Registered, and ordered to be recorded.

A Bill of Sale from Abigail Webster to Elizabeth Webster for her claim to a tract of Land on Holston river & also for horses and cattle &c was proven in open Court by William Bryan one of the subscribing witnesses & ordered to be Recorded.

Thomas Emerson Esqr. produced to Court a License authorizing him to practice Law as an Attorney in the several Courts of Law, and Equity in this State and took all necessary oaths & was admitted an Attorney to practice in this Court.

Thomas Davis Esqr. produced to Court a License authorizing him to practice Law as an Attorney in the several Courts of Law & Equity in this State took the necessary oaths & was admitted, to practice Law as an Attorney in this Court.

Court adjourns till tomorrow 9 o'clock Tuesday morning 22nd. November Court met according to adjournment.
Present - Major Lea, Isaiah Widdiff & John S. McFarland Esquires.

(p 47) William Howard is appointed Constable and enters into Bond with Thomas Hodges his security in the sum of Five hundred Dollars & took the necessary oaths.

Peter Noe)
vs No. 10)
Joseph Cobb) Whereupon came a Jury, towit, William Kirkam, John Widdiff William Alsup, Henry Howell, John Latham, Moses McElhaney -John Gillentine Dennis Condry, James Mayes, William Bryant, thomas Hodges, & Charles Bunch who being elected tried & sworn the truth to speak on the issue joined in this case Do say the Defendant is not guilty in manner & form as the plaintiff in his declaration hath alledged against him.

John Stewart)
vs) Francis Hunter & Adam Peck special bail of Nicholas
Nicholas Spring) Spring surrenders him in open Court in discharge of
themselves.

Peter Noe)
vs) Royal Jinnings being duly summoned a witness in this
Joseph Cobb) suit being solemnly called came not; It is therefore considered by the Court that the said Royal Jinnings Do forfeit according to Act of Assembly Plaintiff's Atty. directs that the fieri facias shall issue on the forfeiture.

John Lea, Admr. for David Inman deceased runs in open Court a supplemental Inventory of said Estate & on application the Court directs an order of sale to Issue.

Isaac McDonald)
vs) Whereupon came a Jury, towit, Nicholas Coumts, Henry
Edmund Holt) McPherson, James Arwine, Robert Parks, George Combs William Henderson, John Crabb, John Spencer, William Streat, John Beeler Abraham Howard, John Saunders, who being Elected tried & sworn the truth to speak in the Issue joined in this case Do say the Defendant is not guilty in manner & form as the plaintiff in his Declaration hath complained against him- Rule for a new trial - Rule discharged.

John Stewart)
vs) Adam Peck and James Moore come into Court and become
Nicholas Spring) special bail for Nicholas Spring. On motion it is considered by the Court that Edmund Holt be fined Five Dollars for a contempt done and committed in open Court.

James Guinn) Whereupon came a Jury, towit, the same Jury as in the
vs) aforegoing suit Peter Noe against Josepg Cobb except
Joan Patterson) Willain Arnold in the place of Dennis Condry, who being Elected tried & sworn the truth to speak on the matter in controversy in this case Do say they find for the Defendant.

(p 47)
Joseph Magoffin & James Magoffin ）
    vs ）
Robert Yancey & thomas Henderson ）

Whereupon came a Jury, towit, the same Jury as in the above suit
Peter Noe against Joseph Cobb, who being elected tried and sworn the truth
to speak in the Issue joined in this case Do say the Defendants have not
paid the debt in the Declaration mentioned and assess their damages by the
detention thereof to Twenty five dollars & sixty six cents besides their
costs.

(p 48)
Peter Harris for the use of Henry Howell）
    vs ）
Ambrose Yancey and Robert Yancey ）

Wherewupon came a Jury, towit,
Nicholas Counts, Henry McPherson, James Arwine, Joseph Eaton, George Combs
Jesse Cheek, William Hamilton, John Spencer, Robert Parks, John Beelor,
Abraham Howard & John Saunders, who being Elected tried and sworn the
truth to speak in the Issue joined in this case; Do say the Defendant have
not paid the debt in the declaration mentioned as in pleading they have
alledged; they find for the plaintiff the debt in the declaration and assess his damages accationed by the Detention thereof to Twenty eight dollars twelve & one half cents besides his costs. Motion in arrest of judgment and Reasons filed.

Ordered by the Court that thomas McBroom, Samuel Perry, John Vinyard
John Spencer, William Mitchell, Eligar Clay & Mathew Campbell, be appointed
a Jury, to view and lay out a road the nearest and best way from the town
of Rutledge to Mathew Campbell & make Report to next Court.

Ordered by Court that Daniel Clayton Esqr. Michael Coons, John Bowen
Thomas Bunch, Thomas Henderson, Thomas Johnson and Frederick Moyers be appointed a Jury to view out and lay off a road from the town of Rutledge
the nearest and best way to the Hawkins County Line where the present
road intersects the same near the house of Col. Thomas Henderson & make
report to next Court.

Ordered by Court that Edward Clark, Cain Acuff, Andrew McPheeters,
Harless Ogles, David Bunch, Martin Bunch and John Brook be appointed a
Jury to view out & lay out a road the nearest and best way from the Ken-
tucky road at Dameron Cheeks to John Halls and make report to next Court.

A Deed of conveynnce from Josiah Smith To Frederick Snider for one hundred & sixty five acres of Land was proven in open Court by David McAnally one of the subscribing witnesses & ordered to be Registered.

Ordered by the Court that Joseph Dennis – John Nall, Samuel Clark,
Esqr. Charles Hutcheson Esqr. Benj. Elliot, John Spring & thomas Dennis
be appointed a Jury, to view out and lay out a road the nearest and best
way from the Powder Spring Gap in Clinch Mountain to William Nalls on flat
Creek and make report to next Court.

A Deed of conveyance from Martin Ashburn To William Miller for two
hundred acres of Land was acknowledged in open Court by Martin Ashburn &

ordered to be registered.

A Deed of conveyance from Isaac Midkiff & William Howell to Elijah Donathan for one hundred acres of Land was proven in Court by William Pain one of the subscribing Witnesses and ordered to be Registered.

Ordered by the Court that Aaron Smith, Jacob Arnett, Michael Massengill, James Callison Jr. William Davis, John Williams, Jeremiah Jarnagin & Elizar Clay be appointed a Jury to view and lay out a road the nearest and best way from Moore's ferry on Holston river to Owl-hole Gap & from thence to the Powder Spring Gap in Clinch mountain & make report to next Court.

A Deed of conveyance from Martha Moore To Alexander Thompson for 80 acres of Land was proven in open Court by William Arnold one of the subscribing witnesses & ordered to be registered.

Ordered by the Court that Robert Yancey Sheriff be allowed the sum of three Dollars & fifty cents for taking care of the Court House & also the further sum of three dollars for reparing the prison.

A Deed of conveyance from Benjamin McCarty to Edward Darnel for three hundred acres of Land was proven in open Court by Isaac Michaell one of the subscribing witnesses; and also an Instrument of writing on the back of sd. Deed explanatory of said Deed was proven in open Court by Henry Mays, one of the subscribing witnesses thereto and ordered to be Registered.

Court adjourns till tomorrow 9 o'clock.

Wednesday 23rd. November 1803 -Court met according to adjournment. Present Major Lea, Peter Harris & Noah Jarnagin, Esquires.

(p 49)
Dennis Condry Overseer)
  Vs   }
Alexander Hamilton   )   Whereupon came a Jury, towit, Nicholas County William Kirkum, William James, Robert McElhiney, John Niven, John Lathom William Howard, William Alsup, Robert Smith, Pleasant Duke, William Paine & John Crabb - who being elected tried and sworn the truth to speak on the matter in controversy in this case do say they find for the plaintiff the sum of sixty two cents & one half of a cent besides his costs. Rule for a new trial- Rule discharged- Appeal prayed Bond with security given, reasons filed and appeal Grantor.

John Elsey   )
  vs   )
Charles Bunch & William Bunch)
    John Horner & Samuel Peery special Bail of Charles Bunch surrender him in open Court in discharge of themselves and the said Charles is prayed in custody of the Sheriff and ordered in custody of the Sheriff by the Court.
John Elsey   )
  vs - qui tam   )
Charles Bunch and William Bunch)   John Horner & Samuel Peery Special Bail of Charles Bunch surrender him in open Court in discharge of themselves

the said Charles is prayed in custody of the Sheriff and ordered in Custody by the Court.

William Owens)
vs)
William Windham) Whereupon came a Jury, towit, Stephen McBroom, Henry Howell, Joel Bean, John Terry, William Kirk, John Finly, John Margraves, James Floyd, William Robinson, John Inman, James Moore & Moses McElhiny who being elected, tried & sworn the truth to speak in issue joined in this case Do say the Defendant hath not paid the debt in the declaration mentioned as in pleading he hath alledged, and find for the plaintiff the debt in the declaration mentioned and assess his damages accationed by the detention of that Debt to Eleven Dollars besides his costs.

John Adair –Admr. of Thomas Cox– dec'd.)
vs)
George H. Combs, Robert Yancey & Joseph Ray) Whereupon came a Jury, towit The same Jury as in the last case, who being Elected, tried and sworn the truth to speak on the Issue joined in this case do say the defendants have not paid the debt in the declaration mentioned as in pleading they have alledged, they find for the plaintiff the debt in the declaration mentioned and assess his damages accationed by the detention of that debt to four dollars and twenty five cents besides his costs.

The Court discharge the Grand Jury from further attendance at the present Term.

William McPhetridge Constable was worn to attend the grand Jury at the present Term, swears in open Court that he has attended on the Grand Jury three days at the present Term.

By order of Court Larkin Hall is appointed Constable who enters into bond in the sum of Five hundred dollars with John Bunch his security & took all necessary Oath.

A Deed of conveyance from Robert Yancey Sheriff to Thomas Graham, for 233 acres of Land was acknowledged in open Court by Robert Yancey and ordered to be Registered, also a release on the back of said Deed was acknowledged in open Court by Ambrose Yancey was ordered to be Registered.

A Deed of conveyance from Martin Ashburn Corinor to Joseph Ore Jr. for a House and lot in the town of Rutledge was acknowledged in open Court & ordered to be Registered.

(p 50) Ordered by the Court that Frederick Noyers be allowed to receive from the County treasure out of the County money the sum of nine dollars & eighty seven cents & one half of a cent for his expenses & trouble in reparing the Jail of Grainger County & taking gear of the Cort House of sd. County from May term 1803 to November term 1803, and that he continues to take gear of the Cort House for which he is to be allowed by the Court.

The Court appointed the following persons Jurors To February term 1804, towit, Joseph Long, Jeremiah Jarnagin, Jessie Jennings, Jr.

Nicholas Massengill, Peter Hamilton, James Moore Senr. Richard Acuff, John Spencer -Capt. Robert Stone, George Martin, Thomas Smith, John Thompson Nimrod Maxwell, Robert Eaton, Daniel Taylor, Archibald McCarver -John Coulter, John Dannel, Joseph Hoe Senr. William Bowman, Harmon Cox, Henry Ivey, John Hoe, Duncan Carmichael, Henry Howell, Joseph Stubblefield, Magnus Moore, John Manpower, Francis Dannel & Cain Acuff.

James Gilbreath)
    vs   )
Robert Yancey) Martin Ashburn, Coroner of Grainger County to whom and Execution issued on a Judgment rendered in this case was directed, having made return thereon that the money demanded by the said Execution was made; and on application failing to pay the same over -whereupon on motion of Pleasant M.Miller -Attorney for the plaintiff It is considered by the Court that the said James Gilbreath, Do recover against the said Martin Ashburn and John Humphreys -James Blair his securities the sum of fifty seven dollars & seven cents and costs.

    Samuel Newell, Assignee of Jenkins Whiteside
        vs
    Spencer Griffin & James Chinn

    Robert Yancey Sheriff of Grainger County to whom an execution issued on a Judgment rendered in this case was directed, having made return thereon that the money demanded by the said Execution was made, and on application failing to pay the same over, whereupon on motion of Pleasant M.Miller Attorney for the plaintiff it is considered by the Court that the said Samuel Newell do recover against the said Robert Yancey & James Ore, Henry Howell, Nicholas Gillentine, William Henderson, Bartley Marshall, Charles McAnally, Robert McElhiney, John Rose, Thomas Bunch, William Bryan, Francis Crabb & Spencer Griffin his securities the sum of one hundred & six Dollars & fifty cents besides his costs.

    Court adjourns till tomorrow 9 o'clock.

              Thursday morning 24th November 1803-
    Court met according to adjournment.
Present -Major Len, Joseph Cobb & John S.McFarland- Esquires.

George Combs
    vs
William Nall, William Clay, William Hankins & Robert Patterson.

    Whereupon came a Jury, towit- John Horner, William Norton, David Holt, William Hamilton, David Abernathy, David Floid, Joshua Hickey, Isaac McDonald, Stephen Smith -John Hammill, Richard Reynolds & John Bean, who being elected tried & sworn the truth to speak on the Issues joined in this case, as to the first plea Do say that within nine months from the making & entering into the Covenant set forth in the plaintiffs Declaration the Defendant did not make to the plaintiff a good & sufficient Title in fee simple to town Lots of Land in the town of Rutledge number 12 & 13 according to the true intent & meaning of the said Covenant as in pleading they have alledged, and as to the third Plea Do say -they the Defendants did not make and Tender to the said Plaintiff a Deed in fee simple for the

Lots number 12 & 13 within nine months from the date of the Covenant set forth in the plaintiffs Declaration according to the tenor & effect of the said Covenant as in pleading they have alledged, and assess the Plaintiff's damages by reason of the performance (p 51) of said Covenant to $489..09 besides his costs- Appeal prayed -Bond and security given.

Ordered by Court that little John Acuff be appointed overseer of the road leading from Robertson's Ferry to the lower end of Clinch mountain towit, from the ford of Richland Creek to the Knox County Line & that all the hands living between the said road & the Knox Line & between the river road & the Clinch Mountain, including William Snodgrass & Isaac Campbell & those that may live on the plantations whereon the said Snodgrass and Campbell now live, except Henry Hawkins the overseer of the richland road & that the hands that did heretofore work on said road not included within the aforesaid Bounds shall work on the richland road under the said Henry Hawkins.

John Spencer)
vs)
John Beatis) Whereupon came a Jury, towit, Nicholas Countz, Martin Ashburn, Pleasant Duke, John Finley, Jeremiah Chamberlain, William Dyer, Wm Windham, Joel Bean, Samuel Sherlock, Thomas Bunch, John Dorah & John Terry who being elected tried & sworn the truth to speak on the issue joined in this case Do say they find for the plaintiff and assess his damages to one thousand Dollars & six cents costs- Rule for a new Trial - Rule discharged- Appeal prayed bond & security given & reasons filed.

By order of Court William Kirk is appointed overseer of the road from Beans Station to where said road intersects the river road at or near John Coulters in the place of Peter Noe, and it is ordered by the Court that all the hands living in the bounds that worked on said road under said Noe be assigned to work under William Kirk on said Road.

William Windham)
vs)
Robert Yancey) Whereupon came a Jury, towit, John Horner, Benjamin Howell, William James, Abraham Pruit, John Hamill, William Hamilton, Isaac McDonald David Abernathy, David Floyd, David Holt and Nicholas Countz, who being elected tried and sworn the truth to speak on the Issues joined in this case do say the Defendant hath well & truly performed the Covenant set forth in the Plaintiffs Declaration and as to the second plea they say the Defendant did offer and tender to deliver to the said Plaintiff before the first day of October next after the date of the Covenant set forth in the plaintiffs Declaration a horse creature as in pleading he hath alledged - Rule for a new trial - Rule made absolute.

Samuel Brown)
vs)
Spencer Hainey & John Estis) Robert Yancey Sheriff of Grainger County to whom an Execution issued on a Judgment rendered in this case was directed having made thereon that he had collected sixty eight Dollars & twenty five cents part of the money demanded by said Execution and on application failing to pay the same over; whereupon on motion of James Trimble Atto. for the plaintiff; It is considered by the Court that the said Samuel Brown

Do recover against the said Robert Yancey, James Ore, Henry Howell, Nicolas Gillentine, William Henderson, Barclay Marshall, Charles McAnally, Robert McElhiney, John Rose, thomas Bunch, William Bryan, Francis Crabb & Spencer Griffin his securities the afresaid sum of sixty eight cents, besides his costs.

A Deed of conveyance from Thomas King by John Counts his Attorney to Abraham Pruit for one hundred and fifty acres of Land was proven in open Court by Samuel Branson one of the subscribing witnesses and ordered to be Registered, and ordered by the Court that the statement & Certificate of William Clay Ranger of Grainger County be entered of Record and that the Clerk furnish the County Trustee with a copy of the same, towit, one Steer valued at Twelve Dollars taken up twentieth Sept. 1802 by Thomas Dodson, taken up 11th Oct. 1802 by Charles Scott – 5 Hoggs valued at three dollars & thirty three cents, taken up 3rd. Nov. 1802 by Joel Bean Abraham Howard two Hoggs valued at 2 dollars & twenty five cents taken up 16th Nov. 1803 by Chesley Jarnagin 2 hoggs valued at 8 dollars.

November Term 1803

(p 52)   I, William Clay Ranger for the County of Grainger Do certify that the above & foregoing specifications of strays entered upon the stray Book, kept by me, twelve months previous to this term & not proven away is just & true.
Signed– W.C.Lay –R.J.C
Nov. 24th 1803–
Court adjourns till tomorrow 9 o'clock.

Friday morning 25th. November 1803 –Cort met according to adjournment

Present– Isiah Middiff– John S.McFarland – Henry Boatman– Esquires.

William Howell –Assignee of William Middiff)
vs)
Spencer Griffin & John Rose) On motion of John Cooke
Attorney for the plaintiff and it appearing to the satisfaction of the Court that the Execution issued on a Judgment rendered in this case, came to the hands of Robert Yancey Sheriff twenty days & upwards, previous to the sitting of the present Term, and the said Robert Yancey neglecting & failing to execute the same & make due return thereon, therefore it is considered by the Court that the said William Howell do recover against the said Robert Yancey the sum of one hundred & twenty five dollars, unless the said Robert Yancey can shew sufficient cause to Cort at next term why said forfeiture should not be made absolute.

William King & John Crozier)
vs)
James Ore) Robert Yancey Sheriff of Grainger County
to whom an execution issued on a Judgment rendered in this case was directed having made return thereon that the money demanded by said Execution was collected and on application failing to pay the same over, whereupon on application of Pleasant M.Miller Attorney for the plaintiff It is considered by the Court that the said William King & John Crozier do recover against the said Robert Yancey and James Ore –Henry Howell Nicholas Gillentine,William Henderson, Bartley Marshall, Charles

McAnally, Robert McElhiney, John Rose, Thomas Bunch, William Bryan, Francis Crabb and Spencer Griffin his securities the sum of fifty dollars twenty cts. & one half of a cent, the balance of the money due on said Execution, besides their costs.

William Clay -William Nall)
William Hankins & Robert Patterson)
  VS)
Martin Ashburn & John Cocke) Robert Yancey Sheriff of Grainger County to whom an Execution Issued on a Judgment rendered in this case was directed having made return thereon that he had sold property by Virtue of said execution for thirty six dollars, and on application failing to pay the same over, whereupon on motion of Pleasant M. Miller Attorney for the Plaintiffs It is considered by the Court that the said Plaintiffs do recover against the said Robert Yancey and James Ore, Henry Howell, Nicholas Gillentine, William Henderson, Bartley Marshall, Charles McAnally Robert McElhiney, John Rose, thomas Bunch, William Bryan, Francis Crabb & Spencer Griffin, his securities the aforesaid sum of thirty six Dollars & costs.

On motion the Court appoint Margaret Nall, widow & relict of James Hall-deceased Guardian of Jinny Hall, Adam Hall, James Hall, Betsy Hall, Illy Hall, John Hall & Archibald Hall, minor heirs of the said James Hall and require her to appear at the next Term of this Court and give bond with sufficient security for her Guardianship.

(p 53) Robert Yancey, Esquire, Collector of Taxes for the County of Grainger report to Court that the taxes remained unpaid on the following Tracts of Land for the year one thousand eight hundred and that he cannot find any goods & chattles of the owners thereof within his County on which he can distress, towit, 5000 acres of Land the property of Robert Anderson - 640 acres of Land the property of David Harbert and that the taxes remained unpaid on the following tracts of Land for the years 1800 1801 and that he cannot find any goods & chattels of the owners thereof within his County on which he can distress- towit, 640 acres of Land the p property of John Jones. It is therefore ordered that the Clerk make a Certificate of the same together with the amount of the taxes & charges hue thereon & cause the same to be twice published in the Knoxville Gazette giving notice that the same will be sold, or so much thereof as will satisfy the said taxes & costs.
Signed- Major Lea-C.P.T.

FEBRUARY SESSIONS A.D. 1804-

At a Cort of Pleas & Quarter Sessions begun and holden for the County of Grainger at the Court House in Rutledge on the third Monday of February A.D. 1804- being the 20th Day of the same month.
      William Clay
Present- Peter Harris
      Noah Jarnagin & Isiah Midcliff -Esquires.

Robert Yancey- Sheriff of Grainger County returns to Court that he has executed the following Venire facias on the following persons Viz.on all marked thus.sd.-

1- Joseph Long	17- John Coulter -sd.
2- Jeremiah Jarnagin	18- John Dannel -sd.
3- Jesse Jennings -sd.	19- Joseph Noe Sr.-sd.
4- Michael Massengill -sd.	20-William Bowman
5- Peter Hamilton	21- Harmon Cox
6- James Moore Sr. -sd.	22- Henry Ivey -sd.
7- Richard Acuff	23- John Noe
8- John Spencer -Capt.	24- Duncan Carmichael
9- Robert Stone	25- Henry Howell
10-George Martin	26- Joseph Stubblefield
11-Thomas Smith -sd.	27- Magnus Moore
12-John Thompson-sd.	28- John Murpower -sd.
13-Nimrod Maxwell	30- Francis Dannel &
14-Robert Eaton	31- Cain Acuff
15-Daniel Taylor-sd.	
16-Archibald McCarver -sd.	

Out of which Venire facias the persons whose names are underwritten were appointed a grand jury to the present term, Viz.

1- Daniel Taylor -foreman	7- Richard Acuff
2- Archibald McCarver	8- John Dannel
3- Robert Stone	9- Joseph Long
4- Joseph Noe sr.	10-Robert Eaton
5- Cain Acuff	sworn and charged
6- Jesse Jennings	

Certificates of attendance Issd.

11- Henry Ivey
12- John Thompson
13- Joseph Stubblefield
14- Francis Dannel &
15- John Spencer

James Dyer Constable to attend the Grand Jury at the present term.

(p 54)   John Umstend)
              vs   )
          John Ripley   )   Samuel Lusk being summoned a Garnaghee
in this case under a late Act of Assembly came into Court & declares under oath that he is not indebted to the Defendant John Ripley & that he
hath no effects of said defendant in his hands nor had at the time of being
summoned as aforesaid, and that he does not know of any person indebted to
the said defendant neither does he know od any effect of the Defendant in
the hands of any person whatever.

Henry Ivey comes into Court and recovers his mark as follows, towit-
an under keel in each Ear and a slit in the right ear.

A Commission was produced to Court from John Sevier Governor in and
over the State of Tennessee appointing amongst others James Whitlock & Valentine Moulder Justices of the Peace in & for the County of Grainger & the
said James Whitlock & Valentine Moulder came into Court & took an oath
to support the Constitution of the State of Tennessee the Constitution of
the United States & also the oath of Office.

Robert C. Gordon Esqr. Coroner of Grainger County resigns his appointment of Coroner in open Court which is received & ordered to be recorded.

Ordered by Court that John Hargraves be appointed a Constable in Grainger County who enters into bond in the sum of Five hundred dollars with John Spring & Nicholas Spring his securities & took all necessary Oaths.

A Deed of conveyance from Henry Bowen to John McElhiney for one hundred acres of Land was proven in open Court by the oaths of James Bowen, one of the subscribing witnesses & ordered to be Registered.

A Deed of conveyance from John Bean to William Bowman for five hundred & twenty acres of Land was acknowledged in open Court by the Grantor & ordered to be Registered.

A Deed of conveyance from Robert McElhiney to James Bowens for one hundred acres of Land was acknowledged in open Court & ordered to be Registered.

A Deed of conveyance from Robert Yancey Sheriff to George Evans Esqr. for 300 acres of Land was acknowledged in open Court & also a release on said deed from Ambrose Yancey to the said George Evans was acknowledged in open Court & ordered to be Registered.

A Bill of Sale from Robert McElhiney to James Bowen was acknowledged in Court & ordered to be Recorded.

A Deed of conveyance from Richard Reynolds & Reubin Riggs to Henry Ivey for two hundred acres of Land was proven in open Court by the oath of Moses Hodges one of the subscribing witnesses and ordered to be Registered.

A Deed of conveyance from Richard Condry to David Davison for two hundred acres of land was proven in open Court by Nimrod Maxwell one of the subscribing witnesses & ordered to be Registered.

A Deed of conveyance from George Sirkle to George Peetarr for 320 acres of Land was proven in open Court by the oath of Daniel Beeloy - one of the subscribing witnesses and ordered to be Registered.

By order of Court Robert Eaton is appointed overseer of the road from the top of Clinch Mountain at the Powder Spring Gap, to the Owl -Hole Gap Aaron Smith on the South side of the Richland Hobbs in the room of Samuel Peery & that he have all the hands in the same Bounds to work under him that said Peery had.

William Clay Ranger returns to Court the following property being strays which were entered on his book and not proven away in twelve months towit- James Dyer Senr. one yearling steer appraised to three Dollars - William Clay one shoat appraised to fifty cents- Cheeley Jarnagin - one steer appraised to twelve dollars- James Piercefield one cow appraised to Eight dollars- Peter Noe two hogs appraised to four dollars-& fifty cts Peter Noe one steer appraised to three dollars & fifty cents.

A Letter of Attorney from William Miller to Ambrose Yancey was proven in open Court by Robert Yancey one of the subscribing witnesses & ordered to be Recorded.

An Article of agreement between Barnabas Butcher to Thomas Ward was proven in open Court by Archibald McCowan & Joseph Stubblefield the subscribing witnesses.

Court adjourns till tomorrow 9 o'clock.

Tuesday February 21st. 1804— Cort met according to adjournment. William Clay, Noah Jarnagin, Peter Harris & Valentine Houlder —Justices of the P. present.

John Crabb)
   vs   )
John Rose)   Whereupon came a Jury, towit— James Moore sr. Peter Hamilton — Nimrod Maxwell, Henry Howell, Nicholas County, Jackson Smith, David McAnally, John County, David Holt, James Harris, Harbert Smith and Andrew McPheeters, who being Elected tried & sworn the truth to speak on the issue joined in this case do say the Defendant is guilty in manner & form as the plaintiff in his declaration hath complained against him & assess his damages to six cents and costs.

Reubin Riggs, who was duly appointed & commissioned a Justice of the peace in & for the County of Grainger in the State of Tennessee came into open Court & took an oath to support the Constitution of the United States the Constitution of Tennessee & also the oath of office.

Palatiah Shelton)
   vs   )   Henry Howell by John Cocke his Attorney enters a
Henry Howell   )   rule to shew cause why an execution issued on a
Judgment in this case returnable to the present Term should not be quashed; continued for argument.

James Cosby)
   vs   )
Robert Yancey)   John Arwine, one of the defendants Bail surrenders
him in open Court in discharge of himself.

The Court having first given due & public notice proceeded to ballot for a Coroner & on counting the ballots it appeared that Abraham Elliot had received fourteen votes, whereupon he was declared to be duly & constitutionally Coroner of Grainger County & the said Abraham Elliot entered into Bond in the sum of five hundred dollars & took an oath to support the Constitution of the United States, the Constitution of Tennessee & also the oath of office.

The Court having first given notice publicly proceeded to Elect a Commissioner of the Revinue for the County of Grainger and on counting the Ballots it appeared that Samuel Bunch was duly Elected who took all necessary oaths.
Margaret Hall, widow & relict of James Hall —deceased comes into

Court & enters into Bond in the sum of two thousand dollars with James Richesoan & John Richards her securities for the Guardianship of Jinny ... Hall, Adam Hall, James Hall, Betsy Hall, Illy Hall, John Hall, & Archibald Hall, minor heirs of the said James Hall -deceased- Justices present Major Lea, Noah Jarnagin, James Blair, David McAnally - Joseph Cobb - Valentine Moulder, James Whitlock, William Clay & Philip Sigler -Vide minutes of last Cort.

By order of Court Uriah York is appointed Constable in Grainger County & enters into Bond in the sum of five hundred dollars with Obediah Waters John Huddleston & Moses Willis his securities & took all necessary oaths.

Ordered by Court that John Cocke & John F.Jack commissioners be allowed the sum of two dollars per day each, for four days each have attended to settle with the Collector & Trustee of Grainger County.

(p 56)   February Sessions A.D. 1804

the Jury who were appointed to view & lay out a road the nearest way from the Powder Spring Gap in Clinch mountain to William Halls on Flat creek makes the following report, Viz. We, the Jurors appointed by the Court to view & lay out a road from the top of Clinch mountain at the Powder Spring Gap to William Halls after being sworn have Viewed & laid out the same Beginning at the top of said mountain running a direct course to Mr. Siglers thence a direct course to William Halls signed by Samuel Clark -Charles Hutcheson, thomas Dennis, Joseph Dennis, John Spring, Benjamin Elliot & John Halls -which report was received & confirmed by Court, and it is ordered by Court that the overseer of the road from said gap to Beelers Mill open said road as viewed & layed out by the above Jury with the hands that were heretofore assigned him.

The Jury appointed at last term to view & lay out a road from the town of Rutledge the nearest & best way to the Hawkins County line where the present road intersects the same made report to Court which was set aside by Court.

The Jury appointed at last Term to view & lay out a road the nearest & best way from the town of Rutledge to Mathew Campbell's made report to Court which was set aside by Court.

The Jury appointed at last Term to View & lay out a road from Dawson Cheeks to John Halls made report to Court, which was set aside by the Court.

The Court appoint Daniel Clayton, John Huddleston, Major Lea & Joseph Cobb, Esquires to attend as Jurors at the next Superior Court to be held for the District of Hamilton at Knoxville on the fourth Monday of March next.

Aaron Smith, Jacob Arnett, Michael Massengill, James Callison,Jr. William Davis, John Willins, Jeremiah Jarnagin & Elizar Clay, who were appointed a Jury at last Term to view & lay out a road the nearest way from Moore's ferry on Holstan river to the Owl Hole gap & from thence to the Powder Spring gap in Clinch mountain are continued Jurors to view & lay out a road as above desired & makes report to next Court.

The Court appoint the following persons Jurors to attend the next term of this term, towit, Thomas Mann, John Estis, Isaac Barton, Edward Shipley, Jeremiah Jarnagin; Michael Massengill, Samuel Peery, Thomas McBroom, David Fields, Richard Condry, Moses Willis, George Kimbro Sr. Duncan Carmichael, Henry Morgan, William Harmon, William Peeters, Joseph Dennis, Benjamin Elliot, William Arnold, James Alsup, Col. James Ore, David Holt, William Henderson, Alexander Blair, David Bunch, John Brock, Daniel Beeler, Edward Clark, Mathew Campbell, John Vinyard, Robert Gaines Jesse Cheek, Royal Jennings, Cornelius McCoy, Allen Christian, David Davis, Isaac Mitchell, Josiah Dawson Cheek.

Ordered by Court that Henry Howell, Henry Ivey, William Smith, Joseph Mendingall, Francis Darnel, & John Cocke be appointed a Jury to view & lay out a road agreeable to Law from the town of Rutledge to the Panther Springs and make report to next Court.

A Deed of conveyance from Allen to John Bailey for 47 acres of Land was proven in open Court by Joseph Ray one of the subscribing witnesses & ordered to be Registered.

A Deed of conveyance from Parnifold Green to Jacob Elliot for three acres of Land was proven in open Court by Abraham Elliot one of the subscribing witnesses & ordered to be Registered.

A Deed of conveyance from James Darnel to James Carmichael for three hundred acres of Land was proven in open Court by John Duke, one of the subscribing witnesses and ordered to be Registered.

(p 57)   February Sessions A.D. 1804

A Deed of conveyance from John Anderson & William Anderson to Joseph Beeler for two hundred acres of Land was proven in open Court by John Beeler one of the subscribing witnesses & ordered to be Recorded.

A Bill of Sale from James Lane to John Warwick was proven in open Court by Philip Parker & Cornelius Archer & ordered to be Registered.

Court adjourns till tomorrow 9 o'clock.

Wednesday 22nd. February 1804- Court met according to adjournment. Justices present- Peter Harris, David McAnally & Valentine Moulder.

Jinny Cox daughter of Thomas Cox deceased, comes into open Court & being of the age of fourteen years & upward chooses John Adair Esqr. of Knox County her Guardian who is approved of by the Court, and the said John Adair enters into bond in the sum of two thousand Dollars with James Moore & William Hamilton his securities.
Justices present- Joseph Cobb, William Christian, Valentine Moulder, Peter Harris, William Clay, Charles McAnally, James Blair & Reubin Riggs.

William Hall - vs John Beeler - Whereupon came a Jury, towit,

James Moore, Nimrod Maxwell, William Hamilton, Nicholas Countz, James Bowen, John McElhiney, Bluford Woodall, Thomas Dyer, John Latham, Able Morgan John Crabb & Asa Street, who being elected tried & sworn the truth to speak on the Issue joined in this case and having retired to deliberate on the Testimony could not agree on a Verdict, whereupon a mistrial is directed to be entered by consent of Attornies William Evans by Henry Boatman Esq. comes into open Court & has leave to record his mark & brand as follows, towit, a swallow fork in the left Ear & smooth crop under keel in the right Ear, and his brand thus- W-

Edward Riggs)
   vs)
Spencer Griffin -James Ore-&)
Ambrose Yancey)

        Robert Yancey Sheriff of Grainger County having made return on an execution Issued on a Judgment rendered in this case that he had sold the property to Thomas Mann, to the amount of $18.80 John Cocke Esquire Attorney for the plaintiff makes a motion to enter upon a Judgment for the aforesaid sum of money against the said Robert Yancey & his securities & it appearing to the satisfaction of the Court that application had been made to the said Robert Yancey for the said money & that he had failed to pay the same over; whereupon it is considered by the Court that the said Edward Riggs do recover the aforesaid sum of money & costs against the said Robert Yancey & James Ore, Henry Howell, Nicholas Gillentine, William Henderson, Barclay Marshall, Charles McAnally, Robert McElhiney, John Ross, Thomas Bunch, William Bryan, Francis Crabb & Spencer Griffin his securities. Execution Issd.

Andrew McPheeters)
   vs)
John Stewart)   John Spring & William Robinson being summoned Garnashees on an execution Issued in this case under an Act of the last general Assembly were examined on oath in open Court and it nor appearing to the satisfaction of the Court that either of the aforesaid Garnashees were indebted to the said John Stewart or had any of his effects in their hands at the time they were respectively summoned garnashees – It is therefore considered by the Court that the said Andrew McPheeters take nothing against the said John & William &c.

(p 58)   February Sessions A.D. 1804

James Cozby)
   vs)
Robert Yancey) In this case Thomas Henderson & John Margraves come into open Court and enter themselves special Bail for the Defendant in this case.

Charles McClung)
   vs)
Thomas Mann) Robert Yancey Sheriff of Grainger County having made return on an execution issued on a Judgment rendered in this case that he had made the money demanded by said execution and it appearing to the satisfaction of the Court that application had been made to the said Robert Yancey for the said money and that he had failed to pay the same over Whereupon on motion of Pleasant N. Miller Attorney for the plaintiff to

enter up a Judgment against the said Robert Yancey & his securities for the sum of $52.50 the sum demanded by said Execution - It is considered by the Court the said Charles McClung do recover the aforesaid sum of money together with his costs against the said Robert Yancey & James Ore, Henry Howell Nicholas Gillentine, Barclay Marshall, William Henderson, Charles McElhiney, John Rose, Thomas Bunch, William Bryan, Francis Crabb & Spencer his securities.

Ordered by Court that Tapley Haygood be allowed the sum of fifteen dollars for keeping & maintaining Jeremiah Midkiff one of the poor of this County from November term 1803-to February term 1804 to be paid out of the poor tax when collected.

A Bill of Sale from James Robinson to Joseph Bealer for a negro girl named Rachael was proven in open Court by John Hunter one of the subscribing witnesses & ordered to be Recorded.

A Deed of conveyance from Thomas Henderson to Joseph Ore for two hundred acres of Land was acknowledged in open Court and ordered to be Registered.

A Deed of conveyance from David Evans to William Evans for one hundred & ninety six acres of Land was proven in open Court by the oath of Joseph Hoe & ordered to be Registered.

A Bill of Sale from John Evans to William Evans for a molato girl named Sall was proven in open Court by William Milliken one of the subscribing witnesses & ordered to be Recorded.

A Deed of conveyance from Robert Yancey Sheriff to Joseph Ore for two hundred acres of Land was acknowledged in open Court & ordered to be Registered.

Ordered by Court that Robert D.Eaton -Noah Jarnagin, William Clay, Jeremiah Jarnagin -Joseph Long, Richard Acuff & Major Lea be appointed a Jury to view & lay out a road from the town of Rutledge to Mathew Campbell agreeable to Law & make report to next Court.

Ordered by Court that Thomas Henderson - Joseph Cobb- Peter Harris William Blair, Daniel Robinson, William Kirkum, David Taylor & Alecander Blair be appointed a Jury to view & lay out a road from where the road crosses the County Line above Col. Henderson's to the town of Rutledge agreeable to Law & make report to next Court.

A Deed of conveyance from Thomas Henderson to John Finley Jack for two lots in the town of Rutledge numbers 27 & 46 containing one quarter of an acre & one half quarter of an acres each was acknowledged in open Court by the Grantor & ordered to be Registered.

Court adjourns till tomorrow 9 o'clock.
        Thursday 23rd. February A.D. 1804- Court met according to adjournment. Justices present- Major Leap Noah Jarnagin- David McAnally and Charles McAnally and Henry Boatman.

(p 59)   February Sessions A.D. 1804.

Ordered by Court that John Cocke & John F. Jack Commissioners make a settlement with Thomas Henderson trustee of Grainger County commencing at the time of his appointment & continuing down to the present time.

The Grand Jury discharged from further attendance at this Term.

James Dyer Constable of the Grand Jury swears that the has attended on the grand Jury four days at this time.

On motion of Pleasant M. Miller Esqr. to remove Robert Yancey Esquire Sheriff of Grainger County from the execution of his office and it appearing to the Court that said Robert had been guilty of permitting a voluntary Escape & other misdemeanors in the execution of said office; It is ordered & adjudged that the said Robert be removed from the execution of said office of Sheriff. From which Judgment said Robert prayed an appeal to the next Superior Court of Law to be holden at Knoxville for the district of Hamilton; and the said Robert by Attorney filed reasons for said appeal, but altogether failed to enter into Bond with security for the persecution of said appeal.

Ordered by Court that Robert C. Gordon Esqr. have leave to keep an Ordinary or house of Public Entertainment and he entered into Bond in the sum of twelve hundred & fifty Dollars with Joseph Hoe his security.

Ordered by Court that William Clay Esqr. have to keep an Ordinary or house of public Entertainment & he enters into Bond in the sum of Twelve hundred & fifty dollars with Noah Jarnagin Esqr. his security.

James Moore Junr. who was duly commissioned one of the Justices of the Peace in & for the County of Grainger comes into Court & took an oath to support the Constitution of the United States — the Constitution of the State of Tennessee & also an oath of office.

On motion of John Cocke Attorney to enter up a Judgment against William McGinnis Constable & his securities for failing to return an execution issued on a Judgment rendered by Joseph Cobb Esqr. in favour of Joseph Hoe against Samuel Sourlock for nine dollars Debt & one dollar costs; It is therefore considered & adjudged by Court that the said Joseph Hoe do recover against the said William McGinnis & Stephen Brundage his securities the aforesaid sum of Ten dollars besides his costs— Execution Issd. to the Coroner.

Cort adjourns till tomorrow 9 o'clock.

Friday 24th. February A.D. 1804 —Court met according to adjournment. Justices present —John S. McFarland— William Clay— David McAnally & Charles McAnally, —

Samuel Newell, Assignee of)
Jenkins Whiteside   )
        vs   )
James Ore   )

Robert Yancey Sheriff having made return on an execution issued on a Judgment rendered in this case that he had sold property of Joseph Ore to the amount of thirteen dollars & seventy five cents, and it appearing to the satisfaction of the Court that the said Robert had failed to pay over said money on application made to him for the same; John Cocke Atto. makes a motion to Court to enter up a Judgment against the said Robert Yancey & his securities for the aforesaid sum of money & costs- It is therefore considered that the said Samuel Newell do recover against the said Robert Yancey & James Ore, Henry Howell, Nicholas Gillentine, William Henderson, Barclay Marshall, Charles McAnally, Robert McElhiney, John Rose, Thomas Bunch, William Bryan, Francis Crabb & Spencer Griffin his securities the sum of thirteen dollars & seventy five cents & costs.

the following List of taxable property is received by Court & ordered to be Recorded, Viz/ Mary Jarnagin by Noah Jarnagin returns 466 acres of Land subject to the payment of Taxes for the year A.D. 1803.

(p 60)   May Sessions A.D. 1804.

Francis Crabb   )
    vs   )
Thomas Colbert   )   Robert Yancey Sheriff having made return on an execution issued on a Judgment rendered in this case that he had made the money Demended by said execution; John Cocke Attorney makes a motion to enter up a Judgment against the said Robert Yancey & his securities for the sum of two dollars & forty cents the sum of which James Armstrong is entitled for his attendance as a witness in the above case and it appearing to the satisfaction of the Court that the said Robert had failed to pay over the said money on application being made to him for the same. It is therefore considered that the said James Armstrong do recover against the said Robert Yancey and James Ore, Henry Howell, Nicholas Gillentine, William Henderson, Barclay Marshall, Charles McAnally, Robert McElhiney, John Rose, William Bryan, thomas Bunch, Francis Crabb & Spencer Griffin his securities the said sum of two dollars & forty cents besides his costs.

        Court adjourns till Court in Course.
             Signed-   Isaiah Midkiff C.P.T.

At a Court of Pleas and Quarter Sessions begun and holden for the County of Grainger at the Court House in Rutledge, on the third Monday of May A.D. 1804 being the 25th day of the same month.

Present Major Lea, Isiah Midkiff, Henry Boatman & James Moore Esqrs.

Abraham Elliot Esqr. Coroner of Grainger County returns to Court that he has executed the following Venire facias on the following persons, except William Henderson, towit,

1- Thomas Mann   5- Jeremiah Jarnagin
2- John Estis   6- Michael Massengill
3- Isaac Barton   7- Samuel Peery
4- Edward Shipley   8- Thomas McBroom

9- David Fields
10-Richard Condry
11-Moses Willis
12-George Kimbro
13-Duncan Carmichael
14-Henry Morgan
15-William Harmon
16-William Peeters
17-Joseph Dennis
18-Benjam Elliot
19-William Arnold
20-James Alsop
21-James Ore
22-David Holt
23-William Henderson
24-Alexander Blair
25-David Bunch

26-John Brook
27-Daniel Beeler
28-Edward Clark
29-Mathew Campbell
30-John Vinyard
31-Robert Gaines
32-Jesse Cheek
33-Royal Jinnings
34-Cornelius McCoy
35-Allen Christian
36-David Davis
37-Isaac Mitchell
38-Josiah Dyer and
39-Dawson Cheek

Out of which Venire facias the persons whose names are underwritten were balloted a Grand Jury for the present Term, Towit,

Thomas Mann, foreman, David Holt, Michael Massengill Joseph Dennis, Samuel Peery, Allen Christian, John Estis, John Vinyard, Edward Clark, Daniel Beeler, William Arnold, James Alsop, David Bunch, thomas McBroom & William Harmon, who were sworn and charged.

(p 61)   May Sessions A.D. 1804

James Dyer Constable sworn to attend the grand jury at the present Term.

On motion John Smith an orphan & minor comes into Court & states that he is upwards of fourteen years of age and chooses Nicholas County his Guardian which is not allowed by the Court, because it is represented to Court that the said John Smith was bound by Indenture by Samuel Smith his father in his lifetime to Colonel James Roddys.

Abraham Wilson & Nancy Wilson widow & relict of Isaac Wilson —deceased come into Court & have leave to administer on all & singular the goods & chattels, rights & credits of the said Isaac Wilson, dec'd.& enter into Bond in the sum of two thousand dollars with Jacob Wilson, John Norris & Isiah Dyer, their securities took the necessary oaths & return an inventory of the personal estate of said deceased, on the application the Court directs an order of sale to issue.

William McCarty administrator of all and singular the goods and chattels rights & credits which were of James McCarty deceased returns to Court an account of the sales of the personal estate of said deceased.

Nathaniel Jackson)
        vs   )
~~~~~~~~~~~~~~~~~~)   Pleasant Duke one of the Bail of James Berry the defendant in this case surrenders him in open Court in discharge of himself; Whereupon John Cocke Esqr. Atty. for Nathaniel Jackson the plaintiff prays him in custody of the Coroner and he is ordered in custody accordingly, the Justices present appoint Major Lea Esqr. Chairman of presiding Justices in & for the Court of Pleas & Quarter Sessions for Grainger County .

By order of Court Caleb Howell is appointed a constable in Grainger County and enters into bond in the sum of five hundred dollars with Duncan Carmichael & Josiah Dyer his securities and took the necessary oaths.

A Deed conveyance from Samuel Carson and Annie his wife to William Clay for four hundred & seventy acres of Land was proven in open Court by the oath of Lewis Harmon one of the subscribing witness thereto & ordered to be Registered.

John Gowing by Caleb Howell record his mark as follows, towit, a crop off the left ear and an under bit off the right ear.

Ordered by Court that Abel Morgan be overseer of the river road from the brance at Henry Mayes to the branch at John Williams in the room of John Jarnagin & that all the hands that worked under said Jarnagin work on said road under said Morgan.

A Deed of conveyance from John Percefield to John Alder for seventy five acres of Land was acknowledged in open Court & ordered to be Registered.

James Reynolds who stands charged according to Law with being the reputed father of two bastard children of which a certain Sarah Scott has been delivered comes into Court & enters into bond in the sum of one thousand dollars with John Cooke and Adleb Howell his securities conditioned.

(p 62)   May Sessions A.D. 1804.

That the said James Reynolds should at all times acquit, discharge & save harmless the inhabitants of the County of Grainger from all costs charges & troubles whatsoever for and by reason of the births, maintenance of & bringing up of said children.

A Deed of conveyance from David Hopping to John Horner for Lot No. 1 in the town of Rutledge was proven in open Court by Ambrose Yancey one of the subscribing witnesses and ordered to be Registered.

A Deed of conveyance from Robert Yancey to John Horner for a Lot in the town of Rutledge being Lot No. 4-in the plan of said town was proven in open Court by Ambrose Yancey one of the subscribing witnesses and ordered to be Registered.

A Deed of conveyance from Ambrose Yancey to John Horner for a Lot in the town of Rutledge being Lot No. 3-in the plan of said town was acknowledged in open Court by the said Ambrose Yancey & ordered to be Registered.

John Moffett comes into Court & has leave to administer on all and singular the goods & chattels rights & credits which were of William Moffit deceased and enter into bond in the sum of five thousand dollars with Samuel Moffit, Isaac L.I.H. Irvine & Daniel Clayton his securities and took the necessary oath.

A Deed of conveyance from Robert Dunville to William Simms for one hundred & twenty seven and one half acres of Land was proven in open Court by Enoch Winds one of the subscribing witnesses and ordered to be Registered.

Jeremiah Jarnagin who was summoned a Juror to February Term 1804 states on oath his reasons for non attendance which are deemed substantial & the fine incurred is remitted by the Court.

William ^Clay Rainger for Grainger County returns to Court the following list of property which has been entered on his book & not proven away in twelve months towit, David McAnally two hogs appraised to two dollars & fifty cents, Joseph Ore one Bull appraised to three dollars & fifty cents -Robert McElhiney one Bull appraised to three dollars thirty three & one third cents.

A Deed of conveyance from Sarah Murphy to Dubart Murphy for two hundred acres of Land was proven in open Court by John Moffit one of the subscribing witnesses and ordered to be Registered.

Ordered by Court that Michael Coons have leave to keep an Ordinary or house of public entertainment in the town of Rutledge & he enters into bond in the sum of twelve hundred & fifty dollars with Abraham Elliot & George Rensbarger his securities.

Ordered that James Byone have leave to keep an Ordinary or house of Public entertainment at Beans Station & he enters into bond in the sum of twelve hundred and fifty dollars with James Ore & John Rose his securities.

(p 63)   May Sessions A.D. 1804.

Duncan Carmichael who was on the Venire as a Juror at february term 1804 states on oath to Court that he was not summoned, therefore the forfiture is remitted.

Ordered by Court that Miller Easley be overseer of the public road leaving from the town of Rutledge to the top of the richland nobbs in the room of George Rensbarger & that all the hands living between the top of the richland nobbs & the top of Clinch mountain from the house of said Easley to the house of Joshua Hickey, the aforesaid Easley & Hickey included work on said road under him.

The Jury appointed at February Sessions A.D. 1804 to view & lay out a road from the town of Rutledge to Mathew Campbell makes the following report to Court, towit, From the town of Rutledge to a small post Oak on the left side of the road in a hollow above thomas McBroom's field, thence to a stake near the corner of said field, thence to a Mulberry tree near sd. McBroom's lower field to three small perciman trees standing in Capt.John Bunch's upper field, thence the same course to the old road, thence along the fence and old road to a red oak marked, thance between the said marked red oak & fence to the old road, thence along the old road to the fordd of Pattersons Creek, thence to a Mulberry tree, marked, between the Creek & Capt. Bunch's field, thence to a small Walnut in the corner of said Bunches field, thence to a dead cherry tree in said field leaving the said dead cherry tree to the right hand of the road, thence to a Mulberry tree marked in said field, thence along said Dunches lane to a Walnut tree near the lower ind of said lane, thence to awhite Oak in a hollow below the old road, thence to a hickory tree, marked near the upper end of John Halls field, thence a direct course to a white oak in said field thence to said Halls Smith shop leaving said Halls shop on the left hand thence to the Meeting house leaving said house on the left also, thence to a large white Oak near the upper end of Mary Chamberlains field thence along the old road to a White oak on the left of the road near the lower end of said field, thence to a white oak near to John Hall Jr. stable, thence to a red oak near the corner of said Halls field thence along the old road to a red oak near Mallacot's fence thence to a pine tree standing in said Mallacot's field leaving the said Oak and pine trees on the right thence along the old road to a hickory tree on the left side -therefore thence to a cherry tree near Isaac Martain's house, thence to a hickory tree near the lower end of said Martain's Lane thence along the old road to the mouth of a small Lane before James Dyers Jr. door, thence to a hickory in said Dyers on the left side of the road thence along the old road to Buffalow hide creek, thence along the road now used to a white oak near the corner of Frederick Moyers lower plantation, thence through the corner of said plantation to a large pine tree, thence along the old road to a white oak on the right of the road, thence along marked trees leaving present road to the left to a white oak on the right of the present road thence along said road to the sand lick branch, thence along the marked trees leaving the road to the right to a red oak near the house of Robert D.Eaton thence to a white oak leaving the said road on the right, to a white oak, thence along the said road to a small post oak, thence a direct course to a large dead pine tree on the right of the said road, thence along said road to a large poplar near the corner of Noah Jarnagin's orchard thence through said orchard to a white oak, thence a direct course to a Bridge across the Powder Spring branch, thence along said road to the lower end of Jeremiah Jarnagin's lane thence leaving the road on the right to a cherry tree near the corner of said Jeremiah Jarnagin's field, thence (p 64) along the road to a blased hickory above the blue spring branch, thence a direct course leaving the road on the left to a red oak on the right thence along the road to a poplar on the left side of said road, thence leaving the road to the right to a small black gum thence along the road, to a blased oak on the left side of the said road, thence to a poplar on the bank of a branch, thence thence to a poplar on the left of the road, thence with the road to a hollow that divides William Clay's & Chesley Jarnagin's Lands to a Gum thence along the blased way to a red oak opposite to said Chesley Jarnagin's field thence along the road to a red oak near the lower corner of said Chesley Jarnagin's lower field, thence to a large white oak leaving the road on the left side thereof, thence to a white oak where the old road crosses a hollow, thence with the old road to a ded pine tree near the corner of William Howard's field, thence a direct course to the shade by said Howard's stable leaving it on the right, thence along said Howard's new Line of fence to the old lane, thence a direct course to a Walnut tree at the lower end of the plantation leaving John Howard's stable on the left thence to a white oak near the road thence along the road now used to Mathew Campbell's (signed) N.Jarnagin - W.Clay- Joseph Long -Robert D. Eaton & Major Lea which said Report is received & confirmed by Court & ordered to be recorded.

Ordered by Court that Frederick Moyers continues to be overseer of

the road laid out as above from Patterson's creek to the Sand-lick branch
and that he opens the same, laid out as aforesaid & keep it in repair &
that he have the hands in the same bounds to work on said road that have
heretofore worked on it.

Ordered by Court that Noah Jarnagin continue overseer of the road
laid out as above from the Sabd-lick branch to the first large spring
above Chesley Jarnagin that he open the same laid out as aforesaid and that
he have the hands in the same bounds to work on said road that worked under him on the former road.

Ordered by Court Daniel Gowing continue overseer of the road laid
out as above from the first big spring above Shealey Jarnagin's to where
John Howard now lives, that he opens the same laid out as aforesaid and
that he have the hands in the same bounds to work on said road that worked
under him on the former road.

The Jury appointed at February Term 1804-to view and lay out a road
from Moore's ferry on Holston river to the Owl Hole Gap & from thence to
Powder Spring Gap in Clinch mountain makes the following report to wit,
we, the Jurors appointed to view and lay out a road from Moore's ferry
on Houlston river to the Powder Spring Gap in Clinch mountain do report
& say the road to continue from said ferry to Aaron Smith, as formerly
did from thence to Samuel Peery's from thence into the richland road
along said road to Noah Jarnagin's field & then the former road by the
Powder Spring to said Gap (signed) Jacob Arnett -Elizar Clay, John Williams - William Davis, Aaron Smith & Jeremiah Jarnagin - which said report
is received & confirmed by Court & ordered to be recorded.

(p 65)   May Sessions A.D. 1804

By order of Court the following persons are appointed overseer of
the road last above mentioned, towit, William Arnold overseer from Moore's
ferry to Crouch's th the Powder Spring Gap in Clinch Mountain & ordered
that the hands in the Bounds formerly laid off to work as usual.

Ordered by Court that Mathew Campbell be overseer of the road from
John Howard's to the Knose Line as lately laid out in the room of Henry
Hawkins and that he have all the hands in the same Bounds that said Haw-
kins had.

Court adjourns till tomorrow 9 o'clock.

Tuesday morning 22nd May A.D. 1804 -Court met according to
adjournment. Justices, Noah Jarnagin, Isiah Midkiff, Reubin Riggs & William Christian.

Ordered by Court that Thomas Dardis Esqr. be Solicitor for the present Term & that he be allowed the same compansation which William Garnett
was allowed.

John Beaty   )
    vs   )   Justices present, Charles McAnally -Philip Sigler
Nathanile Davis   )   David McAnally, William Clay, Isaiah Midkiff,

Noah Jarnagin, Reubin Riggs, William Christian, Henry Boatman, Major Lea
James Moore & Peter Harris. Whereupon came a Jury, towit, David Davis,
Mathew Campbell, Jeremiah Jarnagin, George Kimbro, Robert Gaines, Benj.
Elliot, John McElhiney, Robert McElhiney, Henry Howell, Joseph Long, James
Dyer & Joseph Beeler, who being elected, tried & sworn the truth to speak
on the issue joined in this case do say the defendant did assume in manner & form as the plaintiff in his declaration hath alledged & for the
non performance of said assumption, assess the plaintiffs damages to one
hundred & fifty dollars & six cents costs.

Ordered that the following tax be laid & collected as a County tax
in the County of Grainger for the year A.D. 1804, towit, on each white
poll, twelve & one half cents, on each Black poll, twenty five cents,
on each hundred acres of Land, twelve & one half cents- one each town Lot
twenty five cents on each Stud horse kept for covering mares twenty five
cents, on each merchant five dollars & on each Pedlar five Dollars.

Ordered by Court that the following poor tax be laid & collected
for the year A.D. 1804, towit, on each hundred acres of Land six cents,
on each Black poll six cents & on each White poll three cents.

The Court after giving due & public notice proceeded to ballot for
a Sheriff. John Lea & John Huddleston candidates & on counting the votes
it appears that John Lea is unanimously elected to the office of Sheriff
whereupon proclamation was made accordingly- and the said John Lea took
oath to support the Constitution of the United States, the Constitution
of the State of Tennessee the oath of Office & also the oath prescribed
by Law, for the collection of taxes,

May Sessions A.D. 1804

(p 66)
and the said John Lea enters into Bond with securities which ware approved of by the Court for the faithful discharge of the office of Sheriff
in these words, towit-
State of Tennessee)
Grainger County   )   May Sessions -A.D. 1804

Know all men by these presents that we John Lea, Major Lea, John
Cocke & John Bunch, Esquires all of the County of Grainger are held &
firmly bound unto his Excellency John Sevier Governor in our State of
Tennessee in the sum of twelve thousand five hundred dollars to be paid
unto the said John Sevier or his successors in office, to the which
payment well & truly to be made. We bind ourselves to every of us, our
& every of our heirs, executors & Administrators jointly & severally
firmly by these presents, sealed with our seals and dated the twenty
second day of May in the year of our Lord one thousand eight hundred &
four.

The condition of the above obligation is such, that whereas the
above bounden John Lea hath been duly & constitutionally elected Sheriff
in and for the County of Grainger, if therefore the said John Lea shall
well & truly execute executed & due returns make of process & precepts
to him directed & pay & satisfy all sorts & sums of money by him received or Levied by virtue of any process into the proper office to which

the same by the tenor thereof ought to be paid, or to the person or persons to whom the same shall be due, his, her or their executors Administrators, Attorneys or Agent & in all other things well & truly & faithfully execute the said office of Sheriff during his continuance therein, then the above abligation to be void, otherwise to remain in full force & virtue in Law.

    Signed, Sealed & delivered in open Court.

J.F.Jack -

                Signed - John Lea- seal
                    Major Lea-seal
                    Hooke   seal
                    John Bunch - seal

and the said John Lea Sheriff enters into Bond with securities approved of by the Court for the faithful collection & payment of Public taxes in these words, towit,

State of Tennessee)
Grainger County   )   May Sessions A.D. 1804

    Know all men by these presents that we John Lea, Major Lea, John Cooke and John Bunch Esquires all of Grainger County are held & firmly bound unto his Excellency John Sevier Governor in & over the State of Tennessee in the penal sum of one thousand dollars to be paid unto the said John Sevier or his successors in office to the which payment well & truly to be made, we bind ourselves & every of us, our & every of our heirs -executors & Administrators Jointly & severally firmly by these presents sealed with our seals & dated the twenty second day of May in the year of our Lord, one thousand eight hundred & four, the condition of the above obligation is such that whereas the above bounden John Lea hath been the day of the date hereof duly constitutionally elected Sheriff in & for the County of Grainger - now if the said John Lea shall well and truly & faithfully collect all public taxes that shall or may become due during the time for which he hath been appointed to the office of Sheriff & also well & truly & faithfully pay the same into the hands of the treasury for the districts of Washington & Hamilton for the use of the State aforesaid on or before   (p 67)   the last day of December in each & every year for which he hath been appointed as aforesaid then the above obligation to be void, otherwise to remain in full force & virtue in Law.

Signed, sealed & delivered in open Court.

                      John Lea- seal
                      Major Lea-seal
          Signed-   Hooke   -seal
                      John Bunch -seal

and the said John Lea Sheriff also enters into Bond with securities approved of by Court for the faithful collection & payment of County Taxes in these words towit,

State of Tennessee)
Grainger County   )   May Sessions A.D. 1804

    Know all men these presents that we John Lea, Major Lea, John Cooke & John Bunch Esquires all of the County of Grainger are held & firmly bound unto his Excellency John Sevier Governor in & over the State aforesaid in the penal sum of one thousand dollars to be paid unto the said John Sevier or his successors in office for the use of the County of Grainger to the which payment well & truly to be made - we bind ourselves & every of us, our every of our heirs, executors & administrators jointly

& severally firmly by these presents, sealed with our seals & dated this twenty second day of May in the year of our Lord, one thousand eight hundred & four.

The condition of the above obligation is such that whereas the above bounden John Lea hath been the day of the date hereof duly & constitutionally elected sheriff in and for the County of Grainger now if the said John Lea shall well and truly & faithfully collect all County taxes that shall or may become due in the County of Grainger during the time for which he hath been appointed to the office of sheriff, and also well and truly & faithfully pay the same into the hands of the trustee for the County of Grainger, for the use of the aforesaid County, on or before the last day in Dec. in each and every year for which he hath been appointed as aforesaid then the above obligation to be void -otherwise to remain in full force & virtue in Law.

Signed sealed & Delivered
in open Court
J.F.Jack

Signed- John Lea --seal
Major Lea --seal
Rocks --seal
John Bunch -seal

the Court after giving due & public notice proceeded to ballot for a trustee for Grainger County, Thomas Henderson & Noah Jarnagin Esquires candidates & on counting the votes it appears that Noah Jarnagin is elected Trustee whereupon proclamation was made accordingly and the said Noah Jarnagin enters into Bond with securities in the following words, towit,

State of Tennessee)
Grainger County) May Sessions A.D. 1804

Know all men by these presents that we, Noah Jarnagin -Frederick Moyers & William Clay all of the County of Grainger are held & firmly bound unto the chairman of the County Court of Grainger in the penal sum of two thousand Dollars to be paid unto the said chairman or his successors in office for the use of the County, to the which payment well & truly to be made, we bind ourselves & every of us, our & every of our heirs, executors & Administrators jointly & severally firmly by these presents, sealed with our seals and dated this 23rd. day of May A.D. 1804.

(p 68) May Sessions A.D. 1804

The condition of the above obligation is such that whereas the above bounden Noah Jarnagin hath been duly Elected Trustee in & for the County of Grainger - now if the said Noah Jarnagin shall well & truly pay over all District & County monies which shall be deposited in his hands agreeably to the order of the County Court of Grainger then their obligation to be void otherwise to remain in full force & virtue in Law.

Signed sealed & Delivered
in open Court
J.F.Jack-

Signed- N.Jarnagin -seal
Frederick Moyers -seal
W.Clay -- seal

Cuthbert Shelton)
vs)
David Shelton)

Justices present- Reubin Riggs, David McAnally Philip Sigler, William Christian, & Noah Jarnagin Whereupon came a Jury, towit, Isaac Mitchell

David Fields, Moses Willis, Duncan Carmichael, Josiah Dyer, Dubart Murphy, Joseph Dyer, William Windham, John Rose, William Bryant, Thomas Hodges & John Moffitt who being elected tried & sworn well and truly to enquire what damages the plaintiff has sustained in writ of enquiry by him brought, do say they find for the plaintiff & assess his damages to one hundred & twenty two dollars twenty two & one half cents & costs.

William Peeters has leave to record his mark as follows, towit, a crop and two underbits in the right ear.

George Norris Records his mark as follows, towit, a crop in the right ear and an under bit off the left ear.

Edward Eppes)
vs)
Joshua Moore) Justices present. Charles Hutchinson, James Whitlock, Isiah Midkiff, James Moore & Samuel Clark. Whereupon came a Jury towit, David Davis, Mathew Campbell, Jeremiah Jarnagin, George Kimbro, Robert Gaines -Benjamin Elliot, John McElhiney - Robert McElhiney, Henry Howell, Joseph Long, who being Elected tried & sworn the truth to speak on the issue joined in this case do say they find the defendant guilty in manner & form as the plaintiff in his declaration hath alledged against him & assess the plaintiffs damages to six cents besides his costs, from which the plaintiff prays an appeal to the next Superior Court of Law for the district of Hamilton & enter into bond with J.L. I.M. Irvine & John Horner his securities for the prosecution of said appeal reasons for appeal filed & appeal granted.

Edward Epps)
vs)
Joshua Hickey) Thomas Henderson one of the defendants Bail in this case surrenders the said Joshua Hickey in open Court in discharge of himself & the defendant is prayed in custody by Plaintiffs Council -
   A Bill of Sale from John Hailey to William Mitchhell for a negro girl named Alse was acknowledged in open Court by the said John Hailey & ordered to be Recorded.

John Adair- Administrator, of)
Thomas Cox -Deceased.)
   vs) Justices present, William Clay
Robert Yancey & Ambrose Yancey) James Moore- Peter Harris &c.

(p 69)   May Sessions A.D. 1804
   Whereupon came a Jury, towit, Isaac Mitchell -pd. David Fields, Moses Willis, Duncan Carmichael, Josiah Dyer, Dubart Murphy, Joseph Dyer William Windham, John Rose, William Bryant, Thomas Hodges & John Moffit who being elected tried & sworn the truth to speak on the issue joined in this case do say the Defendant have not paid the debt in the Declaration mentioned as in pleading they have alledged & find for the plaintiff the debt in the Declaration mentioned & assess the plaintiffs damages occasioned by the detention of that debt to four dollars & ninety five cents besides his costs.
   William Hamilton records his mark as follows, towit, a smooth crop

off the right ear and a slit in the left ear, he also records his Brand thus—11 —

Ordered by Court that Samuel Bunch commissioner of the Revenue for Grainger County for the year 1804 be allowed the sum of one hundred dollars for taking in Lists of Polls & taxable property recording the same &.

A Deed of conveyance from Charles Bunch to Valentine Morgan for two hundred acres of Land was proven in open Court by the oath of John Bunch one of the subscribing witnesses & ordered to be Registered.

A Deed of conveyance from James Bowens to Josiah Smith for one hundred & fifteen acres of Land was acknowledged in open Court & ordered to be Registered.

Ordered by Court that Robert Yancey late Sheriff of Grainger County be allowed the sum of sixty dollars for his ex officio services for the year A.D. 1803 ending at the present term and also the further sum of fifteen dollars for making out & recording the tax Lists for said year.

A Deed of conveyance from Robert Yancey Sheriff to Jesse Riggs for one hundred acres of Land was acknowledged in open Court & ordered to be Registered.

A Deed of conveyance from Ralph Shelton to William Street for eighty acres of Land was acknowledged in open Court & ordered to be Registered.

By order of Court Francis Willet is appointed a constable in Grainger County & enters into bond in the sum of five hundred dollars for the due performance of his duty with James Moore & Abel Morgan his securities & took the necessary oaths.

A Deed of conveyance from Isaac Midkiff to Elijah Donathan for one hundred acres of Land was acknowledged in open court & ordered to be Registered.

The Court appoint the following Jurors to August term A.D. 1804 to wit, Jacob Arnett, Chesley Jarnagin, Aaron Smith, Thomas Dennis, Joseph Fields, William Peeters, Evan Harris, Edward Churchman, Edward West, John Moffit, Hugh Larimore, Robert Long, Josiah Kidwell, Jesse Cheek, Neal McCoy, William Snodgrass, Peter Hamilton, William Mitchell, Harmon Cox, John Coulter, Henry Morgan, William Kirkum, John Lebow, George Morris, Daniel Robinson, James Bowen, Joseph Long, John Sally, William Hamilton John Braden, Joseph Noe Sr. John Holt, Hezekiah   (p 70)   Philips Hercules Ogles, David Asher, Martin Bunch, John Moyers, William Shelton, & Henry Bowen.

Ordered by Court that Bluford Woodall be allowed the sum of five dollars for keeping Jeremiah Midkiff one of the poor of the County for the term of one month commencing at February term 1804 and that Tapley Haggard be allowed the sum of ten dollars for keeping said Midkiff from the expiration of said month till May term A.D. 1804.

Court adjourns till tomorrow 9 o'clock.

(p 70)   Wednesday 23rd. May —Court met according to adjournment.
Justices present— Major Lea, Noah Jarnagin, Peter Harris, William Hankins
Charles McAnally, Reubin Riggs & William Clay.

State   )
  vs   )
Aza Street   )   Justices present, Noah Jarnagin, Joseph Cobb, William
Clay, Major Lea, David McAnally, Peter Harris, William Hankins & Reubin
Riggs. Whereupon came a Jury, towit, David Davis, Mathew Campbell, Jeremiah Jarnagin, George Kimbro. Robert Gaines, Josiah Dyer, Thomas Henderson, James Campbell, James Dyer —Sr. David Claxton, Valentine Morgan &
James Blair Jr. who being elected tried & sworn the truth to speak on the
issue joined in this case Do say they find the Defendant not Guilty in
manner & form as charged in the bill of indictment.

     The Court appoint John Bull a constable John Bull a constable in
Grainger County, who enters into Bond in the sum of five hundred dollars
with William Guss & John Bull Sr. his securities & took the necessary
oaths.

     Ordered by Court that William Hankins Esqr. be overseer of the river
road from the Knox County Line to the ford on Richland Creek in the place
of Major David Hailey & that all the hands living between Richland Creek
& the Knox County Line & between the river & said road below work under
him on said road.

     Ordered by Court that Robert Gaines Jr. be overseer of the river
road from the ford on Richland Creek to the Indian Ridge that all the
hands that formerly worked under Harwood Jones work under him.

Edward Epps   )
  vs   )   William Wilson, & David Bunch come into Court &
Joshua Hickey   )   acknowledged themselves indebted to the said Edward
Epps the plaintiff in the sum of one thousand dollars to be Levied of
their respective goods and chattels Lands & Tenements. But to be void
on condition that if the said Joshua Hickey be condemned in this action
that he will pay the costs & condemnation or surrender himself to prison
for the same or that they will do it for him.

State   )
  vs   )   Justices present, William Clay, Noah Jarnagin, Maj-
Samuel, David McAnally, Peter Harris, Charles Hutchison, William Hankins
Reubin Riggs & Isaiah Middiff. whereupon came a Jury, towit, John Brock
Benjamin Elliot, Isaac Mitchell   (p 71)   David Fields —Moses Willis
John Spencer, Jacob Elliot, John Hailey, Aza Street, William Alsup,
Henry Bowen, & Duncan Carmichael —who being elected tried and sworn the
truth to speak on the issue joined in this case do say they find the de-
fendant not guilty in manner & form as he stands charged in the Bill of
Indictment— Rule to shew cause why the prosecutor should not be taxed
with the costs— Rule made absolute.

John Beaty   )
  vs   )   Nathaniel Davis the defendant comes into Court &
Nathaniel Davis)   prays an appeal from the Judgment rendered in this

case to the Superior Court for the District of Hamilton & enters into Bond with John Horner, Samuel Peery & Valentine Morgan his securities reasons filed & appeal granted.

John Denn lessee of James Ore)
    vs)
Fen & David Holt) Justices present, Major Lea, Charles Hutcheson, William Clay, Noah Jarnagin, Peter Harris & William Rankins whereupon came a Jury, towit, John Brock, Benjamin Elliot, Isaac Mitchell, David Fields, Moses Willis, Duncan Carmichael, John Spencer, Jacob Elliot, John Hailey, Aza Street, Daniel Taylor & Henry Bowen, who being elected tried & sworn the truth to speak on the issue joined in this case do say they find the trespass & Ejectment in manner & form as the plaintiff in his declaration hath alledged against him, from which the plaintiff prays an appeal to the Superior Court of Law for the District of Hamilton —reasons for appeal filed & Bond with security given for the prosecution of said appeal— Appeal Granted.

Ordered by Court that Joseph Noe Sr. be overseer of the river road from the ford on Garman Creek to the ford on McCarties Creek in the room of Aza Street & that all the hands in the same bounds, that worked under Aza Street do work under Joseph Noe.

Jonathan Williams for the use of)
George Combs)
    vs)
Michael Massengill, William Milligan,)James Fears, Henry Howell, & John Bristo, James Fears, John Briston non in custody.
Justices present, Isiah Midkiff, William Rankins & Reubin Riggs, whereupon came a Jury, towit, David Davis, Mathew Campbell, Jeremiah Jarnagin, George Kimbro, Robert Gaines, Josiah Dyer, Thomas Bunch, James Campbell, James Dyer, Sr. John Wells, Valentine Morgan, & James Blair Jr. who being elected tried & sworn the truth to speak on the issue joined in this case retired to deliberate on their Verdict, afterwards returned to the bar of the Court & being asked if they had agreed on their Verdict gave for answer that they had not— whereupon a Mistrial was interred by consent &c.

James Dyer constable sworn to attend the Grand Jury at the present term swears that he has attended said Jury three days at the present Term.

The Court appoint Samuel Cox one of the Constables in & for Grainger County, who enters into Bond in the sum of five hundred dollars with Charles Smith & William Millikan his securities & took the necessary oaths.

(p 72)   May Sessions A.D. 1804
Jonathan Newman & Hannah Pope)
    vs)
Jacob Ray & Joseph Ray) Justices present, Major Lea, Noah Jarnagin, William Clay & Reubin Riggs, whereupon came a Jury, towit, David Davis, Mathew Campbell, Jeremiah Jarnagin, George Kimbro, Robert Gaines, Josiah Dyer, Thomas Bunch, James Campbell, James Dyer Jr. John Wells, Valentine Morgan & James Blair Jr. who being elected tried and sworn the truth to speak on the issue joined in this case do say the

defendants have not paid the debt in the declaration mentioned as in pleading they have alledged, they find for the plaintiffs the debt in the declaration mentioned & assess their damages occationed by the detention of that debt to five dollars & fifty cents besides their costs,

Ordered by Court that William Howard constable attend the next term of this Court.

A Bill of sale from Nicholas Opunts for a negro woman named Kate was proven in open Court & ordered to be Recorded.

The Jury appointed at February term 1804 to view & lay out a road from the Line that divided Hawkins & Grainger Counties, makes the following Report, towit, to keep the road as it now is to the place where John Crabb now lives, the overseer straightening some bends where the ground will admit and making a Bridge or causeway across a sinkhole near Crabbs house & moving Crabbs fence from his stacks to the lower end of the field about twelve or fifteen feet in, then taking the left hand fork below Crabbs & keeping it about one hundred & fifty yards, take to the right along a small path leaving William Hendersons house to the right & falling into the old road about one hundred & fifty yards below, then keeping the road across the creek at Col. Ors's & keeping along his meadow fence & up the branch with a former road to a small rising then a direct course so as to go between the old stone house & old stable at Beans old Station then a direct course into the road near the upper end of Russells place, then with the old road a direct course through a field formerly cleared by Joseph Beelor & with said road to the East end of the Race paths, thence along the Race-paths keeping the same course till it falls into the road near Thomas Bunchs plantation, then with the former old road a direct course through the field keeping on a direct course to Daniel Robinson then leaving the road on the right going a direct course so as to strike the old road formerly opened by Jesse Bean near a small drain opposite to Kearns plantation, then with said road that was opened by Jesse Bean to Moses McElhiney & through a small field to the North West side of the house where William McElhiney formerly lived; (here it will be necessary to build a bridge) keeping nearby Beans old road to Miller Easley's passing by his house & into the road near the head of Mr. Claytons Spring, then with the road to the Town of Rutledge -(Signed) -Thos. Henderson, Alexander Blair, William Blair, Daniel Taylor, Peter Harris, whereupon a Petition signed by a number of the citizens of Grainger County was present to Court praying that a part of the foregoing Report might be set aside & the said report is continued over till next Court.

Robert Yancey late Sheriff & collector of Taxes in & for Grainger County by John Huddleston his deputy exhibited to Court a List of insolvents for the year 1801, amounting to twenty five cents and also a list of insolvents for the year 1802, amounting to one dollar & fifty cents & also a List of insolvents for the year 1803 amounting to eighty seven & one half cents amounting in the whole to two dollars sixty two & one half cents and the said John Huddleston also made oaths that the said Lists of insolvents are just & true to the best of his Knowledge   (p 73)   (May Sessions A.D. 1804)   and that he had used all legal ways & means in his power to collect the taxes contained in said Lists from the time he had received the tax lists & that he could not find any property to enable him to collect the said taxes; whereupon the Court order & direct that the said Robert Yancey do receive a credit with the Treasurer of the District of Washington & Hamilton for the afoesaid sum of two dollars sixty two & one half cents and the Court do further order and direct that the said Robert Yancey shall receive a credit with the Trustee of Grainger County for the aforesaid sum of two dollars sixty two & one half cents.

Ordered by Court that Henry Howell, Henry Ivey, William Smith, Francis Dannel, John Cooke, Frederick Moyers, John F. Jack, Edward Dannel, Thomas McBroon & John Bunch be a Jury to view & lay out a road agreeably to Law from the town of Rutledge to the Panther Spring & make report to next Court.

Ordered by Court that all the hands in the following Bounds, towit beginning at the mouth of Harris Creek, thence up said creek to include Samuel Cox, then to include William Riggs & all the hands on his plantation, thence to Porcurile & all his hands, thence to Joshua Brookins & all his hands & from thence to the river Holsten, so as to include all the hands work under Thomas Mann overseer of the road from Marshalls ferry to Hawkins County Line.

Court adjourns till tomorrow 9 o'clock.

Thursday May 24th. —Court met according to adjournment. Justices present, William Clay, Reubin Riggs, Noah Jarnagin, & James Moore.

By order of Court James Dyer Jr. is appointed a constable in Grainger County, who enters into bond in the sum of five hundred dollars with Samuel Peery & John Horner his securities & took the necessary oaths.

Abraham Elliot Coroner of Grainger County, enters his protest against the prison of said County for its insufficiency which is ordered to be Recorded.

Order by the Court that John Kitchen be overseer of the road from the fork of the road at Abraham Elliots field to the Knox County Line below Lewis Whitners field in the room of Abraham Elliot & that he have all the hands that worked under said Elliot.

Nathaniel Jackson)
   vs   )
James Berry   )   John Cooke Atty. for the plaintiff makes a motion to Court to enter up a judgment against Abraham Elliot Coroner & William Hall, Larkin Hall, John Humphreys, Jacob Elliot, & Nicholas Spring his securities for the sum of one hundred & fifty seven dollars & fourteen cents & costs for permitting James Berry to escape & go at large after he had been surrendered by his Bail in open Court prayed in custody of the said Coroner by the ~~said~~ Coroner by the said Attorney & actually in his custody whereupon on arguments it is ordered & adjusted by the Court that the said Plaintiff take nothing by his motion.

(p 74)   May Sessions A.D. 1804

Ordered by Court that Richard Reynolds have leave to keep an Ordinary or house of public entertainment & he enters into Bond in the sum of Twelve hundred & fifty Dollars with Reubin Riggs & Henry Howell his securities.

A Deed of conveyance from William Hall, William Clay, Robert Patterson, William Hawkins Commissioners for the town of Rutledge to Reubin Sanders for Lots Nos. 3 — 34- 39 & ordered to be Registered.

Robert Yancey late Sheriff & collector of the taxes in Grainger County exhibited to Court a List of Insolvents for the year 1804 amounting to one Dollar thirty seven & one half cents & made oath &c. the Law in such cases made & provided requires- It is therefore ordered by the Court that the said Robert Yancey do receive a credit with the Treasurer of the Districts of Washington & Hamilton for the aforesaid sum of one Dollar thirty seven & one half cents, and it is further ordered that the said Robert Yancey do receive a credit for the said sum of one Dollar thirty seven & one hald cents with the Trustee of Grainger County.

Robert Yancey late Sheriff & collector of Taxes in Grainger County by John Rose his Deputy exhibited to Court a list of Insolvents for the year 1801, 1802 & 1803 amounting to six dollars fourteen cents & one half of a cent & made oaths as the Law in such cases made & provided requires- It is therefore ordered by the Court that the said Robert Yancey do receive a credit with the treasurer of the Districts of Washington & Hamilton for the said sum of six dollars fourteen cents & one half of a cent, and it is also ordered that the said Robert Yancey do receive a further credit with the Trustee of Grainger County for the sum of six dollars fourteen cents & one half of a cent.

Robert Yancey Esqr. late collector of the taxes in Grainger County reported to Court that the taxes remained unpaid on the follwong Tracts of Land for the respective years following & that he can not find any goods & chattels of the owners thereof within his County on which he can distress Viz. for the year 1801 James McNair 1500 acres of Land, William Henry 400 acres of Land - William Henry 400 acres of Land -James Scaggs 640 acres of Land - James Spencer 300 acres of Land - John Jones 300 acres - Robert Smith 200 acres - William Howell 100 acres -For the year A.D. 1802- John B.Darnel 5000 acres - David Harts heirs &c. 3,250 acres David Harris Harris 150 acres for the year A.D. 1803- Joseph Jentry 540 acres - John Lebow 200 acres & John O.Darnell 5000 acres - It is therefore ordered by the Court that the Clerk make a Certificate of the same together with the amount of the taxes & charges due thereon cause the same to to be twice published in the Knoxville Gazette giving Notice that the same will be sold or so much thereof as will pay the taxes & charges due thereon.

A Deed of conveyance from Robert Yancey to William Miller for Lot No. 10 in the town of Rutledge was acknowledged in open Court by the said Robert Yancey & ordered to be Registered.

It appears from the tax lists for the year A.D. 1803 that two persons by the name of John Lebow were charged with the tax on one white poll & one black poll for said year amounting for the State & County tax to the sum of seventy five cents & it appearing to the satisfaction of the Court that there is but one person by the name of John Lebow subject to pay taxes in Grainger County & that the above must be an error. It is therefore ordered by the Court that Robert Yancey collector for said County be released from the payment of the aforesaid sum of money & have a credit for the sum of thirty seven cents & one half of a cent with the Treasurer of the Districts of Washington & Hamilton & it is further ordered   (p 75) (May Sessions A.D. 1804)   that he receive a credit for the sum of thirty seven cents & one half of a cent in his settlement with the Trustee for Grainger County.

Ordered by Court that the prison Bounds for Grainger County be altered in the following manner, towit, to run from the N.W. Corner of lot No. 10 S. 76 W. twenty one poles to the corner of Lot No. 11- then on the Line of said Lot N. 14 W. eight poles to a stake thence S. 76 W five poles to a stake of the Line of Lot No. 10 then N.14 on the Line of said Lots seven poles to a stake corner of the original Line thence with the original Line round to the Beginning.

Noah Jarnagin Esqr. Records his mark as follows, towit, a crop & a half crop in the right Ear & a half crop in the right Ear & a half crop off the under part of the left Ear.
                    Noah Jarnagin C.P.T.
Court adjourns till Court in Course.

At a Court of pleas and quarters sessions began holden for the County of Grainger at the Court House in Rutledge on the third Monday of August A.D. 1804 being the twentieth day of the same month.
          Justices present, Isaiah Midkiff, William Christian, Reubin Riggs and James Whitlock.

John Lea Esqr. high Sheriff of Grainger County returns to Court that he has executed the following Venire Facias on the following persons -towit,

1- Jacob Arnett
2- Chesley Jarnagin
3- Aaron Smith
4- Thomas Dennis
5- Joseph Fields
6- William Peeters
7- Evan Harris
8- Edward Churchman
9- Edward West
10-John Moffitt
11-Joseph Moe Sr.
12-Hercules Ogles
13-John Moyers
14-Hugh Larrimore
15-Robert Long
16-Josiah Fidwell
17-Jesse Cheek
18-Neal McCoy
19-William Snodgrass
20-Peter Hamilton
21- William Mitchell
22- Harmon Cox
23- John Coulter
24- John Holt
25- David Asher
26- William Shelton
27- Henry Morgan
28- William Kirkham
29- John Lebow
30- George Morris
31- Daniel Robinson
32- James Bowen
33- Joseph Long
34- John Sally
35- William Hamilton
36- John Bradon
37- Hezekiah Phillips
38- Martin Punch &
39-Henry Bowen

75

Out of which Venire Facias the persons whose names are under written
were drawn a Grand Jury for the present Term towit, Jesse Cheek,foreman
Chesley Jarnagin, John Braden, High Larimore, Henry Morgan, James Bowen
Edward Churchman, Daniel Robinson, John Sally, Thomas Dennis, Joseph Kidwell, Joseph Long, Robert Long, John Holt, & Harmon Cox who took the
oath prescribed for Grand Jurors and were charged by Thomas Davis Esq.
who was appointed by the Court Solicitor for the present Term.

James Dyer Constable is sworn to attend the Grand Jury at the present Term.

(p 76)   August Sessions A.D. 1804

A Commission was produced to Court from John Sevier Governor in &
over the State of Tennessee with the great seal of said State thereunto
annexed appointing Josiah Dyer & Cobb Howell Justices of the place in
and the said Josiah Dyer came into open Court & took an oath to support
the Constitution of the United States & of the State of Tennessee and
also the oath of office prescribed by Law.

William Clay Esqr. Rainger of Grainger County makes a Report to
Court in the following words and figures Viz. "A List of property of
the following specifications not proven away in twelve months remaining
on my Books this date August 20th 1804 - Martin Ashburn - one Steer
five dollars.
        Signed- W.C.Jay -R.G.Co.

The last Will and testament of John Ervine was produced to Court
for probate and Obediah Waters one of the subscribing witnesses thereto
came into Court & proved the due execution thereof and John Carwile one
of the Executors therein, appointed came into Court was qualified &
took upon himself the surrender of the execution thereof and ordered
to be Recorded.

Abraham Wilson & Nancy Wilson Administrators of Isaac Wilson -De-
ceased returns to Court a supplemental Inventory of the estate of said
deceased & also the amount of the sales of the Estate of said deceased.

Ordered by Court that John Acuff have leave to keep an Ordinary or
house of public entertainment and he enters into Bond with James Hamilton his security in the sum of twelve hundred & fifty dollars.

John Condly & Nancy Miller Widow and Relict of George Miller deceased come into Court & have leave to administer on all & singular the
goods and chattels rights & credits of the said George Miller Dec.
enters into Bond in the sum of two thousand Dollars with Pleasant M.
Miller & William Duncan their securities & took the necessary oath -
whereupon the said John Condly and Nancy Miller returned to Court an
Inventory of the goods and chattles &c. of the said Deceased, and an
application the Court directs an order of sale to issue authorizing
them to sell the property therein contained.

Ordered by Court that Noah Jarnagin overseer of the road from the

Sand Lick branch to the first large spring above Chesley Jarnagin have all the hands living between Clinch Mountain & a Direct course from Evan Harris to Jacob Arnett's & below the powder Spring old road as far down as said large Spring thence a direct course to said Harris'.

Ordered by Court that Edward Donnel be overseer of the river road in the place of Abel Morgan and that all the hands that worked under said Morgan do work under him.

Ordered by Court that Michael Massengill be overseer of the River road from Buffalow Creek to the top of the Indian Ridge and that all the hands between said Creek and said Ridge from the river inclosing Evan Harrises plantation thence a direct course including Jacob Arnett's work under him.

William Peeters one of the Jurors to attend the last term of this Court states on oath his reasons for not attending which is deemed sufficient & forfeiture set aside.

A Deed of conveyance from Andrew Evans to William Shields for one hundred and forty acres of Land was proven in open Court by John Braden one of the subscribing witnesses and ordered to be Registered.

A Deed of conveyance from Andrew Evans to Joseph Yeadin for one hundred & forty acres of Land was proven in open Court by John Bradon one of the subscribing witnesses and ordered to be Registered.

(p 77)   August Sessions A.D. 1804

A Deed of conveyance from Abraham Elliot Coroner to Acquilla Jones for the one undivided sixth part of six hundred & forty acres of Land was proven in open Court by the oath of John Lea one of the subscribing witnesses & ordered to be Registered.

A Deed of conveyance from William Miller by Ambrose Yancey his Attorney in fact to George Evans for two hundred acres of Land was proven in open Court by the oath of Abraham Elliot one of the subscribing witnesses & ordered to be Registered.

A Deed of conveyance from Joseph White to Walter Turner for one hundred & ninety five acres of Land was proven in open Court by the oath of Joseph Mendenhall one of the subscribing witnesses and ordered to be Registered.

A Deed of conveyance from Walter Turner to Philip Free for one hundred acres of Land was proven in open Court by William Woodward one of the subscribing witnesses & ordered to be Registered.

A Deed of conveyance from Henry Rice to Michael Massengill for one hundred acres of Land was proven in open Court was proven in open Court by the oath of Lewis Prim one of the subscribing witnesses and ordered to be Registered.

Court adjourns till tomorrow 9 o'clock.

Tuesday 22nd. August A.D. 1804- Court met according to adjournment Justices Present - William Hankins -Reubin Riggs -Charles McAnally - William Reel for the use of)
William Copeland   )
No. 96 -vs - Cont.   )
Henry Howell & John Buller   )

    Justices present William Hankins, Isiah Midtiff, Charles McAnally & Reubin Riggs. Whereupon came a Jury towit, Aaron Smith, John Moffit Peter Hamilton, Evan Harris- pd. John Coulter, Edward West, John Moyers William Peeters, Abraham Hamilton, Nicholas Coontz, Moses McIlhiney,& Himrod Maxwell, who being elected tried and sworn the truth to speak on the issue joined in this case do say, the defendants have not performed their Covenants in pleading they have alledged and assess the plaintiffs damages occationed by reason of the non performance thereof to one hundred and twenty Dollars besides his costs.

William Hall)
No. 17 - vs)
John Beeler)   Justices present Isiah Midtiff, William Hankins, Joseph Cobb, Reubin Riggs, Charles McAnally - Samuel Clark & James Whitlock, whereupon came a Jury, towit, Jacob Arnett, William Mitchell, Henry Bowen, Martin Bunch, William Kirkam, David Asher, William Shelton paid- John Vineyard, William Arnold, David Bunch, John Martin, & Pleasant Duke, who being elected tried & sworn the truth to speak on the issue joined in this case do say the Defendant did not assume & undertake in manner & form as the plaintiff in his declaration hath alledged against him an appeal to the Superior Court of Hamilton District & enter into Bond with security for the prosecution of his appeal & by Pleasant M. Miller files reason for the appeal pursuant to the act of Assembly in such case made & provided.

(p 79)   August Sessions A.D. 1804

John Denn on the Demise of)
James Robertson   )
No. 165 -vs   )
Fenn & Thomas Hodges   )   Justices present, Major Lea, Noah Jarnagin, Philip Sigler, Charles Hutchinson, & James Whitlock, whereupon came a Jury, towit- the same Jury as in No. 96 , who being Elected tried & sworn the truth to speak on the issue joined in this case do say the Defendant is guilty of the trespass & ejectment in manner and form as the plaintiff in his Declaration against him hath complained & assess the plaintiffs damages to six cents besides his costs and afterwards the said James Robertson comes into Court and assumes one half the costs.

William Windham)
No. 212 -vs   )Justices present -Major Lea, Joseph Cobb, Charles Hutcheson, - whereupon came a Jury as in No. 96-except
Robert Yancey   )James Blair in the room of John Coulter & James Robinson in the place of Nicholas Coontz who being elected tried & sworn the truth to speak on the issue joined in this case do say the Defendant hath not performed his Covenant as in pleading he hath alledged and assess the plaintiff he hath alledged and assess the plaintiffs damages to seventy three dollars & ninety three cents & costs.

Benjamin McCarty)
vs)
John Elsey, Spencer Griffin)
Joseph Ray & George Countz)

    Jacob Ray, one of the defendants surrenders him in open Court in discharge of himself —whereupon John Ray and Jacob Ray come into Court & enter themselves special Bail for the said Joseph Ray.

    Ordered by Court that John Moyers be overseer of the road from the Powder Spring Gap in Clinch mountain into Peter Beelors old Mill in the room & stead of Thomas Dennis & that he have the same hands that the said Thomas Dennis had.

    Ordered by Court that William Arnold overseer of the road from Moore Ferry to Crowers have all the hands in the bounds following to work under him, towit, the hands living between said road & the river road, Buffalow Creek & the river.

    The Court appoint the following persons Jurors to November term next, towit, Richard Acuff, James Hamilton, William Rumbard, Jesse McKinney, James Campbell, William Arnold, Robert Alsop, Charles Gilbert, Hezekiah Trogdon, Abner Lowe, William Cook, Joseph Jackson, David Huddleston Duncan Carmichael, William Street, Richard Shelton, Cornelius McCoy, Henry Hipshier, Edward McGinnis, Joseph Bryant, Nicholas Countz, Thomas Henderson, Thomas Johnston, John Estes, Daniel Taylor, Bartley Marshall, Archibald McCarver, Richard Thompson, John Dannel, Francis Dannel, David Davis, Moses Hodges, Archelus Gibson, Jeremiah Jarnagin, Samuel Peery, John Acuff, Joseph Beelor, Peter Hammock & Abraham Pruit.

    A Deed of conveyance from Patrick Sharkey to James Alsop for three acres of Land was proven in open Court by William Arnold one of the subscribing witnesses & ordered to be Registered.

    A Deed of conveyance from Enos Johnston to James Alsop for a tract of Land containing by estimation containing two hundred acres was proven in open Court by William Arnold one of the subscribing witnesses & ordered to be Recorded.

    Ordered by Court that James Alsop be overseer of the river road from Buffalow Creek to William's Branch and that all the hands in the bounds of the road running from Crows to Moores Ferry, thence up the river to Stiffeys Mill Creek thence to said creek to the head, thence a direct,

(p 79)   August Sessions A.D. 1804
course to the Buffalow hollow including Jonathan Massey, William Guinn thence a direct course to the head of Buffalow Creek, work under him.

    Ordered by Court that David Bunch, Martin Bunch, Andrew McPheeters Edward Clark, John Brook, John Bean, William Bowman & Barton McPerson be a Jury to view & lay out a road agreeably to Law leading out of the Kentucky road at Dawson Cheeks, thence down the mountain valley the nearest & best way to the Knox road near William Halls Sr. & make report to next Court.

A Deed of conveyance from Joseph Cobb to Martin Bunch for Fifty acres & one half of an acre of Land was acknowledged in open Court & ordered to be Registered.

Ordered by Court that John Moyers be overseer from the top of Clinch mountain in the Powder Spring Gap to Beelors old mill, in the room of Thomas Dunn and that all the hands in the follow ing bounds work under him, towit, Beginning at the Powder Spring Gap, thence along the mountain till opposite David Bunches, thence to the top of the Comb ridge, thence down the said ridge till opposite William Roberts, thence to Larkin Nulls so as to leave him out of said bounds, thence to the Beginning.

Ordered by Court that Richard Acuff -William Hankins, Peter Hamilton, William Mitchell, James Campbell, Mathew Campbell, John Vinyard be a Jury to view & lay out a road agreeably to Law from the fork of the Roads opposite Major David Haileys on the upper side of Richland Creek to the Knox County Line near the lower end of Clinch Mountain & make report to next Court.

A Bill of sale from Abigil Webster to William Line for a negro woman now in possession of John Moffitt was proven in open Court by James Magee one of the subscribing witnesses & ordered to be Registered.

A Deed of conveyance from Joseph Cobb to David Bunch for fifty acres of Land was acknowledged in open Court & ordered to be Registered.

A Deed of conveyance from Willie Blount to James Robertson for one hundred & fifty acres of Land was proven in open Court by Pleasant M. Miller & ordered to be Registered.

Ordered by Court that Abel Dale be overseer of the road from the Powder Spring Gap in Clinch mountain to the top of the Copper Ridge in the place of Robert Moore & that he have the same hands that said Moore had.
A Deed of conveyance from Hercles Ogle to John Ogle for one hundred & fifteen acres of Land was acknowledged in open Court and ordered to be Registered.

A Deed of conveyance from Charles Smith to Harmon Cox for twenty five acres of Land was acknowledged in open Court and ordered to be Registered.

John Moffitt administrator of all & singular the Goods & Chattels rights, credits of William Moffitt -Deceased, returns to Court an Inventory of the Personal Estate of said deceased.
Court adjourns till tomorrow 9 o'clock,-

Wednesday 22nd. August Court met according to adjournment. Justices present - Major Lea, Joseph Cobb & James Whitlock.

Jonathan Williams for the use of
George Combs   vs   Michael Massingill, William Milligan, James Fears

Henry Howell & John Bristo (James Fears & John Bristo not in custody)
    Justices present, Major lea, Noah Jarnagin, Joseph Cobb, Peter Harris -Philip Sigler, Charles McAnally &c. Whereupon came a Jury, towit,

(p 80)   August Sessions A.D. 1804
Aaron Smith, John Moffitt, Evan Harris, -pd. John Coulter, Edward West
John Moyers- pd. William Peeters- pd. Peter Hamilton, Nicholas County,
John Hammill, Moses McElhiney -pd. & John Horner, who being elected tried
& sworn the truth to speak on the issue joined in this case do say the defendant have not paid the Debt in the declaration mentioned as in pleading
they have alledged and assess the plaintiffs damages by reason thereof to
thirty two dollars & fifty cents & costs.

William King & Edward Sherman
      vs
Robert Yancey
        Edward Scott Attorney for the plaintiff makes a plea in Court to
enter up a Judgment against Martin Ashburn late Coroner of Grainger County & James Blair & John Humphreys his securities for not paying over monies by him collected on a writ of Venditioni exponas issued in this case,
towit, for failing to pay over the sum of Ten dollars & sixty cents which
it appears from his return that he has collected on the aforesaid execution; whereupon it is considered by the Court that the said plaintiffs do
recover against the aforesaid sum of money & costs.

James Graham   )
   vs   )
Thomas McDonald   )   Jane Graham by James Trimble his Attorney makes a
motion in Court to enter up a Judgment against William McGinnis & Stephen Brundage his securities for twenty five dollars & ninety one cents
being the amount of money demanded in an execution issued on a Judgment
rendered in this case by David McAnally Esqr. for this, that the said
William hath failed to pay the aforesaid sum of money or return the execution - whereupon it is considered by the Court that the said plaintiff
do recover the aforesaid sum of money & costs against the said William
McGinnis & Edward McGinnis & Stephen Brundage his securities.

John C.Hamilton)
   vs   )
Felps Reed   )   Justices present - William Clay,James Whitlock,
Josiah Dyer &c. Whereupon came a Jury, towit, Jacob Arnett, William Mitchell,pd- Henry Bowen, David Asher -pd. William Shelton -pd.Martin Bunch
William Kirkum, Pleasant Duke,John Crabb, Daniel Gowing,John Humphreys
& Wilson Loyd, who being elected tried & sworn the truth to speak on the
issue joined in this case do say the Defendant hath not performed his Covenant as in pleading he hath allidged & assess the plaintiffs damages to
one hundred and seven dollars & fifty cents & costs.

John Adair Administrator of   )
Thomas Cox   )
   vs   )
George M.Comb-Robert Yancey   )
and Joseph Ray   )   Pleasant M.Miller Atty. for the plaintiff

makes a motion in Court to enter up a Judgment against Abraham Elliot -Coroner & William Hall, Larkin Hall, John Humphreys, Jacob Elliot & Nicholas Spring his securities for failing to pay over forty dollars, which sum the said Abraham on an execution in this case has returned that he has collected - whereupon it is considered by the Court that the said plaintiff do recover against the said Abraham Elliot & William Hall, Larkin Hall, John Humphreys -Jacob Elliot & Nicholas Spring the aforesaid sum of money & costs.

Francis Crabb)
vs) Justices present, Robert C.Gordon, David McAnally,
Michael Coons) & Isaiah Midkiff, whereupon came a Jury, towit, Jacob Arnett, William Mitchell, Henry Bowen, David Asher -pd. William Shelton, Martin Bunch, William Kirkum, Pleasant Duke, Thomas Henderson, Daniel Gowing, John Humphreys & John Wells, who being elected tried & sworn the truth to speak on the issue joined in this case do say they find the defendant not Guilty in manner & form as the plaintiff in his declaration hath alledged against him.

(p 81)   August Sessions A.D. 1804

The Grand Jury dismissed from further attendance at the present Term/

James Dyer Constable, made oath that he had attended three days on the Grand Jury at the present Term.

Isaac Gibson)
vs) Justices present - Major Lea, Robert C.Gordon & Isaiah
John Crabb).. Midkiff- whereupon came a Jury, towit, Aaron Smith, John Moffitt, Evan nnes -pd. John Coulter, Edward West- pd.-John Moyers, William Peeters-pd. Peter Hamilton, Nicholas Countz, John Hammill, Moses McElhiney -pd. & John Horner, who being elected tried & sworn the truth to speak on the issue joined in this case do say the defendant did assume in manner & form, as the plaintiff in his Declaration hath complained against him and assess the plaintiffs damages to sixty five Dollars & thirty two cents & costs.

James Cosby)
vs) Justices present -William Clay, Joseph Cobb, Isaiah Midkiff &c. whereupon came a Jury, towit, Aaron Smith, John
Robert Yancey) Moffitt,Evan Harris, Edward West, John Moyers, William Peters - Peter Hamilton, Nicholas Countz, John Hamill, Moses McElhiney, John Horner & James Ore, who being elected tried & sworn the truth to speak on the issue joined in this case do say the Defendant hath not paid the debt in the declaration mentioned as in pleading he hath alledged they find he hath paid eighty three dollars -thirty three & one half cents & no more and find for the plaintiff sixty six dollars -sixty two & two third cents & assess his damages occationed by reason of the detention thereof to five dollars & ninety five cents & costs.

Noah Jarnagin Trustee for Grainger County makes a motion in Court to enter up a Judgment against Robert Yancey late Sheriff & Collector of Taxes & his securities for the sum of Five hundred & thirty eight Dollars -four and one fourth cents, being the balance reported by the Commissioners appointed to settle with holders of County money to be due the County aforesaid from the said Robert Yancey & his securities of which motion the Court will advise till tomorrow.

Ordered by Court that Tipley Haygood be allowed the sum of Twenty dollars for keeping & maintaining Jeremiah Midkiff one of the poor of this County from the May term A.D. 1804 till August Term 1804 to be paid out of the Poor tax when collected. Copy Issd.

Ordered by Court that James Dyer constable of the Grand Jury be allowed the sum of one Dollar for each day he has heretofore attended the Grand Jury & also that he be allowed the sum of one dollar for each day he may hereafter attend on the Grand Jury.

Ordered by Court that William Howard Constable be allowed the sum of one dollar for each Day attending the Court at the present Term & that he be appointed the Constable to attend the next Court. Issd.

A Bill of Sale from George Hamill to Aza Street for a negro Girl named Harlot was proven in open Court by John Coulter one of the subscribing witnesses & ordered to be Recorded.

A Deed of conveyance from Abraham Elliot Coroner to Frederick Moyers for Eighteen acres of Land more or less was acknowledged in open Court by the said Abraham Elliot and ordered to be Registered.

Ordered by Court that Dennis Condry overseer of the road lying South of the Lone mountain from William Davidson to William Hamiltons, thence along the road to Thomas Brown in the Copper ridge, thence along the Copper ridge to the Knox Line, thence along the Knox to the Comb ridge, thence along Comb ridge to Robert Monrows to keep in repair the road from the top of the Copper Ridge at a path that leads down said ridge to Jeremiah Selvages & John Salley's. Copy Issd.

Ordered by Court that Seamore York overseer of the road from a new road below Magbees where Dennis Condry's oversight of said road Terminates, to the mouth of the Cave Spring Creek on Clinch River,

(p 82)   August Sessions A.D. 1804
have all the hands below where the road crosses the hickory Valley from John Salley's to Clinch river north of the Lone mountain to the line of Anderson County thence along the Line to the River, thence up the River to where the road crosses, to work under him. Copy Issd.

Ordered by Court that John Sally overseer of the road from the foot of Hindes ridge to the Knox Line have the hands South of the Lone mountain to the Comb Ridge below where the road crosses the Raccoon Valley to the Knox Line to work on said road. Copy Issd.

William Howell   )
     vs   )
Robert Yancey -Ambrose Yancey & William Howard) James Dyer one of the
Constables of Grainger County, to whom an execution issued in this case
by Isiah Midkiff Esqr. was directed whereby he was commanded as he had
before been that of the Goods & chattles Lands & tenements of Robert Yancey -Ambrose Yancey, and William Howard &c he should cause to be made the

sum of forty five dollars and seventy five cents which sum William Howell lately recovered for his debt and the further sum of one Dollar and twenty nine cents for costs, Returned the said Execution to Court with the following Return indorsed thereon, towit, made on said Execution $4.80 Levied on one house & Lot in the town of Rutledge as the property of Ambrose Yancey July 14th. 1804 –James Dyer –Const. whereupon the Court order and direct that the sheriff of Grainger County do expose to sale and sell the house and Lot Levied on as aforesaid to satisfy the said Execution & costs. Ex. Issd.

Samuel Eddins)
   vs)   James Dyer one of the Constables of this County to
Spencer Griffin)   whom an execution issued in this case was directed whereby he was commanded that of the Goods & chattels Lands & tenements of Spencer Griffin he should to be made the sum of Forty six dollars & also the further sum of fifty cents for costs. Returned said execution to Court with the following return endorsed thereon, towit–No personal property found in the hands of the Defendant, James Dyer Const. Levied two tracts or parcels of Land as the property of Spencer Griffin one parcel lying in the Raccoon Valley adjlining William Hamilton's said to be about Eighty acres – the other on Cobb Creek said to be one hundred acres a part of an 800 acre tract on the South side of Holston River– August 14th 1804 James Dyer Const. whereupon the Cort order & direct that the Sheriff of Grainger County do expose to sale and sell the two tracts of Land Levied on as aforesaid or so much thereof as will be sufficient to satisfy the aforesaid sum of forty six dollars & fifty cents & costs. Exc. Issd

Ordered by Court that Henry Howell, Henry Ivey, William Smith, Francis Dannell, John Cooke, John F.Jack, Frederick Moyers, Edward Darnell, Thomas McBroon & John Bunch be continued a Jury to view & lay out a road agreeably to Law from the town of Rutledge to the Panther Springs & make report at the next Court.

Court adjourns till tomorrow 9 o'clock.

Thursday 23rd. August 1804– Court met according to adjournment –Justices present– Major Lea, Joseph Cobb & David McAnally.

A Bill of Sale from Francis Mayberry to James Brown for a negro girl named Jinny was proven in open Court by the oath of William Cook, one of the subscribing witnesses & ordered to be Recorded.

Ordered by Court that Patience Keith otherwise called Patience Crockett personally appeared at the next Court and shew cause if any she can why her children should not be bound out agreeably to Law.

Chaney Bowen)
   vs)   Pleasant W.Miller Atty. for plaintiff makes a motion
James Ore)   to the Court to enter up a Judgment for the sum of Sixty five dollars & fifteen cents against Robert Yancey late Sheriff – James Ore, Henry Howell, Nicholas Gillentine,–

(p 83)   AUGUST SESSIONS   A.D. 1804

     William Henderson, Bartley Marshall - Charles McAnally, Robert McEl-
hiney, John Rose, Thomas Bunch, William Bryant, Francis Crabb, Spencer
Griffin, his securities for failing to pay over the aforesaid sum of sixty five dollars and fifteen cents collected on an Execution in this case
and it appearing to the said Robert Yancey has failed altogether to pay
over the said sum on application made to him; It is therefore considered
by the Court that the said plaintiff do recover against the said Robert
Yancey & his securities the aforesaid sum of money and costs- Exec. Issd

George Humphreys)
          vs   )   Original Judgment obtained before Daniel Clayton
Thomas Harlow   )   Esqr. for 40 dollars on motion of George Humphreys by James Trimble his Attorney to enter up a Judgment against William McGinnis Constable & Edward McGinnis & Stephen Brundage his securities for the sum of forty dollars for failing to return an execution
agreeably to Law & it appearing to the satisfaction of the Court that he
has failed so to do; It is therefore considered by the Court that the
said George Humphreys do recover against the said William McGinnis & his
said securities the aforesaid sum of forty dollars and costs.

     Ordered by Court that John Lebow be continued overseer of the road
from the Line that divides the Counties of Hawkins & Grainger down to the
fork below John Crabb & that the same Bounds be allowed him for hands
that has therefore been to open the road as lately laid out by the Jury.
                         Copy Issd.
     Ordered by Court that Col. James Ore be continued overseer of the
road from the fork below John Crabbs to Beans Station & that the same
Bounds be allowed him for hands that has heretofore been. Copy Issd.

     Ordered by Court that Tandy Senter be overseer of the road from Bean
Station to the first branch below Jesse Beans old place and that Charles
Kidwell -Elijah Donathans hands, Nicholas Sharp, John Sharp, and all the
hands living between the river ridge & the Top of Clinch Mountain & between Beans Station and said Senter except those in William Kirk's bounds
be allowed him to work on said road as lately laid out by the Jury.

     The Report of the Jury heretofore appointed to view and lay out a
road from the Line that divides Hawkins & Grainger Counties to the town
of Rutledge which was returned to last Court records & continued till the
present Term was taken up by the Court and confirmed as follows -towit,
from the Hawkins Line down to the first branch below J.W.Beans old place
where John Sharp now lives and the residue of said Report set aside.

     Ordered by Court that John Bowen, James Ore, David Holt, Thomas John-
ston, Joseph Cobb. Robert C.Gordon and Joel Hammer be a Jury to view &
lay out a road agreeably to Law from the first Branch below Jesse Beans
old place to the town of Rutledge & make report to next Court. Copy Issd.

     The motion of Noah Jarnagin Trustee of Grainger County which was
made to Court yesterday was taken up. It is therefore considered by the
Court that the said Noah Jarnagin do recover the sum of thirty three dollars forty nine & three fourth cents against the said Robert Yancey -

George Bean, Peter Noe, Martin Bunch, David Shelton, & Spencer Griffin
his securities for the use of said County, and it is further considered
by the Court that the said Noah Jarnagin do recover the further sum of
Four hundred and forty nine dollars & forty five cents for the use of said
County & costs against the said Robert Yancey, Richard Reynolds, Thomas
Bunch, Pleasant Duke & William Henderson his securities being the tax due
said County for the years A.D. 1802-1803.

James Cowan Administratrix and Francis A.Ramsey Administrator of Samuel Cowan deceased. vs James Ore – the said Jane & Francis by Thomas Dardis
their Attorney makes a motion to Court to enter up a Judgment against Robert Yancey late Shff. and James Ore, Henry Howell, Nicholas Gillentine,
William Henderson, Bartley Marshall –Charles McAnally, Robert McElhiney
John Rose, Thomas Bunch, William Bryant, Francis Crabb, & Spencer Griffin
his securities for the sum of Ninety two dollars & forty cents which sum
he has collected on an execution in this case as appears from his receipt
produced, to

(p 84)   November Sessions A.D. 1804
Court and on application has altogether failed to pay over; It is therefore considered by the Court that the said Plaintiff do recover against
the said Robert & his securities the aforesaid sum of money besides their
costs &c.
     Court adjourns till Court in Course.
              Signed – Major Lea –Chm.

At a Court of Pleas and Quarter Sessions began and holden at the
Court House in Rutledge for the County of Grainger on the third Monday of
November A.D. 1804, being the 19th of the same month.

Justices present, Isaiah Midkiff, Reubin Riggs, Isaiah Dyer & Henry
Boatman.
     John Lea Esquire high Sheriff of Grainger County returns to Court
that he has executed the following persons except Archibald McCarver,
David Davis, Joseph Beeler,Abraham Fruit, Cornelius McCoy, William Cooke
Joseph Jackson & David Huddleston, towit–
1- Richard Acuff
2- James Hamilton
3- William Humbard
4- Jesse McKinney
5- James Campbell
6- William Arnold
7- Robert Alsop
8- Charles Gilbert
9- Hezekiah Trogdon
10-Abner Lowe
11-William Cooke
12-Joseph Jackson
13-David Huddleston
14-Duncan Carmichael
15-William Street
16-Richard Shelton
17-Cornelius McCoy
18-Henry Hipshir
19-Edward McGinnis
20-Joseph Bryant
21-Nicholas Countz
22-Thomas Henderson
23-Thomas Johnston
24-John Estis
25-Daniel Taylor
26-Bardley Marshall
27-Archibald McCarver
28-Richard Thompson
29-John Daniel
30-Francis Daniel
31-David Davis
32-Moses Hodges
33-Archelus Gibson
34-Jeremiah Jarnagin
35-Samuel Peery
36-John Acuff
37-Joseph Beeler
38-Peter Harnock & Abraham Fruit.

Out of which Venire Facias the persons whose names are underwritten ware drawn a Grand Jury to the present Term -towit,

1- Thomas Henderson
2- Thomas Johnston
3- Hosey Hodges
4- William Street
5- Jeremiah Jarnagin
6- Charles Gilbert
7- Richard Acuff
8- Hezekiah Trogdon
9- Barcley Marshall
10-Peter Haycock
11-James Hamilton
12-Francis Darnel
13-Robert Alsop
14-Nicholas Countz &
15-Samuel Peery

Who were all sworn & charged by Thomas Dardis Esquire.

James Dyer constable sworn to attend the Grand Jury at the present Term.

Mary Whitlock widow & relict of James Whitlock deceased & William Golding come into Court and have leave to administer on the Estate of James Whitlock deceased and enter into Bond in the sum of two Thousand Dollars with Abner Love & Ezekiel Trogdon their securities, whereupon the said Mary & William took the necessary oath & returned an Inventory of said Estate and application the Court direct an order of sale to issue authorizing said Administrators to sell the estate of said Deceased. Order Ised.

Order by the Court that Joseph Beelor be overseer of the road from Beelors old mill to Peeter's ferry & that the same bounds be allowed him for hands that hath heretofore been allowed Joseph Beelor.

(p 85)   November Sessions A.D. 1804

William Carrett who was heretofore appointed Solicitor to prosecute on behalf of the Government in and for the County of Grainger failing to attend to performing the Duties of his said appointment -whereupon the Court after giving due & public notice proceeded to appoint John Cocke Esquire Solicitor in & for the County of Grainger who was immediately qualified.

On application the Court appoint Nancy Miller & John Conley Guardians of John Miller, Martin Miller & Bathiny Miller Minor heirs of Geo. Miller deceased & the said Nancy & John Conley enter into Bond in the sum of two thousand Dollars with James Hamilton & William Humbard their securities- Justices present, Major Lea, Isiah Tidkiff & Henry Boatman.

Joseph Fields who was summoned to attend as a Juror at last Term, states to Court his reasons on oath for his non-attendance which are deemed sufficient & forfeiture set aside.

George Horner
     vs
Robert Yancey late Sheriff and his securities.

James Trimble Esquire makes a motion to Court to enter up a Judgment against Robert Yancey late Sheriff, James Ore, Henry Howell, Nicholas Gillentine, Barcley Marshall, Charles McAnally, Robert McElhiney, John Rose Thomas Bunch, William Brynnt, Francis Crabb & Spencer Griffin his securities for the sum of seventeen dollars for his failing to pay over said sum by the said Robert Yancey Collector on an execution issued on a Judgment recovered By George Horner against a certain Hardin Dunham; and it appearing to the Court that the said Robert Yancey has collected the aforesaid sum of money and failed to pay the same over- It is therefore considered by the Court that the said Plaintiff do recover against the said Robert Yancey & his securities the aforesaid sum of seventeen dollars & costs and afterwards the said James Trimble releases seven Dollars part of the above sum of seventeen dollars.

A Deed of conveyance from Lemuel Hibbard, John Hibbard, Jedediah Hibbard and Samuel Hibbard to Thomas Rice for two hundred & forty acres of Land was proven in open Court by Felps Read one of the subscribing witnesses & ordered to be Registered.

A Deed of conveyance from Hezekiah Phillips to Joseph Noe Sr. seventy acres of Land was proven in open Court by Joseph Rich one of the subscribing witnesses & ordered to be Registered.

A Deed of conveyance from Charles Gilbert to Peter Cotner for one hundred & ninety six acres of Land was acknowledged in open Court by Charles Gilbert & ordered to be Registered.

Ordered by Court that John Alfred an orphan now of the age of eighteen years be bound by Indenture to Thomas Mann to learn the art trade & mistery of a Millwright & Major Lea chairman & the said Thomas Mann interchangeably execute Indenture for that purpose.

Ordered by Court that William Peeters be overseer of the road in the room of Dennis Condry & that the same Bounds be allowed him for the hands that was allowed to said Condry. Order Issd.

A Deed of conveyance from Farnafold Green to William Hamilton for fourteen hundred acres of Land was proven in open Court by the oath of Alexander Hamilton one of the subscribing witnesses & ordered to be Registered.

An Instrument of writing purporting to be the last will & testament of John Gillman deceased was exhibited to Court for probate & Thomas Smith & Peter Gillman the subscribing witnesses came into Court & proved the due execution therefore & ordered to be Recorded.

Nancy Miller & John Condley Administrators of the Estate of George Miller deceased return to Court the amount of the sales of said Estate.

Enoch Parsons Esqr. produced to Court a License signed by David Campbell, Hugh L. White & John Overton Esquires Judges of the Superior Courts of Law & Courts of Equity in & for the State of Tennessee,

(p 86)   November Sessions A.D. 1804
authorizing him to practice Law in the several Courts of Law & Equity in said State & the said Enoch took an oath to support the Constitution of the United States & also an oath to support the Constitution of the State of Tennessee & also the oath of an Attorney of this Court

Luke Lea Junr. Esqr. produced to Court a License signed by David Campbell, Hugh L.White & John Overton Esqrs. Judges of the Superior Courts of Law & Courts of Equity in and for the State of Tennessee authorizing him to practice Law as an Attorney in the several Courts in this State & the said Luke Lea took an oath to support the Constitution of the United States & also an oath to support the Constitution of the State of Tennessee & also the oath of Attorney & is admitted an Attorney of this Court.

William Clay Esqr. Ranger returns to Court a List of Strays in the following words, towit- "A List of strays remaining on my books & not proven away in twelve months of the following specification" -one steer taken up by Isaac Martin appraised to seven dollars & one Heifer taken up William Kirk appraised to six dollars.

(Signed) W.Clay -R.G.C.

Hugh Woolard & Jane Woolard his wife late Jane Cox deceased- prefer a petition to Court, praying to Court to issue a Writ directed to the Sheriff of Grainger County commanding him to summon twelve freeholders unconnected with the parties to allot & lay off the Dower of the said Jane Woolard of a certain tract of Land containing about three hundred & sixty acres lying in Grainger County on Richland Creek of which they alledged the said Thomas Cox died seized & possessed & it appearing to the satisfaction of the Court that John Adair Administrator &c. and Guardian of Jane Cox - Minor heir of said Thomas Cox had notice of filing this petition the Court therefore direct a writ to issue agreeably to the prayer of the said petition.

The Petition of sundry inhabitants of Grainger County was prefered to Court praying a discontinuance of the road that leaves the Kentucky road that leaves on the North side of Clinch mountain, between the mountain & Copper ridge & leads to Claiborne Court House and also two petitions signed by sundry Inhabitants of Grainger County & Claiborne County were prefered to Court praying a continuance of said road; and the said petition were continued over for argument.

The Jury heretofore appointed to view & lay out a road agreeably to Law leaving out of the Kentucky road at Dawson Cheeks, thence down the mountain Valley the nearest and best way to the Knox Line near William Walls, make the following report to Court, towit, We, the Jurors appointed to view & lay lot a road from the Kentucky road at Dawson Cheeks down the mountain Valley make the following Report, From Dawson Cheeks as Jinnings road runs down to Benjamin Shaws, thence to William Browns living him on the right & Joel Bean also on the right from thence to William Bowmans as it is Marked from thence living where Barton McPherson now lives on the left hand, as it is marked, from thence leaving Harris Burks on the right hand as it is marked, from thence as it is marked to the widow Harmons going through the Lane, from thence to Edwards Clarks from thence as the Waggon way now is to the Knox road near William Walls-.

(Signed) David Bunch, Andrew McPheeters, Edward Clark, John Brock,William Bowman, & Barton McPherson which is received & confirmed by Court & the road -ordered to be opened.

Ordered by Court that David Bunch be overseer of the road from Dawson Cheeks to where it intersects the Knox road near William Walls &that all the hands in the following Bounds be assigned to him to open said road & keep the same in repair -Viz. Beginning at Dawson Cheeks, thence down the Copper ridge opposite Edward Clarks thence across to Clinch mountain thence along said mountain till opposite the Beginning & thence a course to the Beginning.

The Jury appointed at last Term to view & lay off a Road agreeably to Law from the first Branch below Jesse Beans old place to the Town of Rutledge make a report to Court ad follows towit, -We the Jurors appointed by Court to view & mark out a road leading from the first branch below Jesse Beans old place to the town of Rutledge do make the following report that is to say Beginning at the first branch below Jesse Beans old place thence along the race paths and along the new cut road by Tandey Senters to where it intersects the old road thence along (Nov. Sessions) (p 87) the old road passing through the corner of Thomas Bunchs field three rod in from the corner, then a straight course into the old road then to a post Oak marked on the right, thence to the right of the old road so as to straighten a bent, thence along the old road to a post oak marked on the right hand on the lower side of a branch, thence on so as to straighten a bent into the old road again, then along the old to the corner of Daniel Robinson Junr's fence so as to move the fence in about a road to the right, thence along the old road to a post oak bush marked on the left in Kearns Lane thence a straight course through the fields so as to pass between hir dwelling house & barn through his clover Lot to a large Pine near the corner of said Lot thence along the ridge to the old road, then on passing through a corner of Clayton's field, to the right about two rod in -then to where the old road intersects the town of Rutledge.
N.B. from the post oak marked at the upper corner of Robert McElhiney's fence on the right a straight course through his field to the lower corner of his fence into the old road again &c. also Kearns's fence on the left across the creek to be moved two rod to the left-
(Signed) J.P.Cobb -James Ore, Thomas Johnson, David Holt & Joel Honner which report is received by Court & continued for argument.

The Jury appointed to view & lay out a road agreeably to Law from the town of Rutledge to the Panther Springs make the following report, Viz. We, the Jury appointed to view the road from the town of Rutledge to the Panther Springs report that we have viewed said road as far as the top of the ridge Beginning at the Court House down the public square to the Creek, thence across the Creek & with the marked trees down the Clift near the upper end of Thomas Mc.Broom's meadow, thence with the marked trees to strike the road near Comb's ferry, thence through the ferry leying the road to the right at flat rock, thence with the road to the top of the ridge -(Signed) - John Cocke -John F.Jack, Francis Dannell, Thomas McBroom, Henry Howell, Frederick Moyers which is received by the Court, confirmed & ordered to be opened.

Ordered by Court that Miller Easley be overseer of the road laid out as above & that he have all the hands in the Bounds heretofore laid off to open said road & keep the same in repair. Issd.

Ordered by Court that Henry Howell, Henry Ivey, William Smith,Francis Dannel, John Cocke, John F.Jack, Frederick Moyers, Edward Dannel,Thomas

McBroom & John Bunch be continued a Jury to view & lay out a road agreeably to Law from the top of the Ridge at the burnt Cabbin to the Panther Spring & make report to next Court.

Cort adjourns till tomorrow 9 o'clock.

Tuesday 20th November -Court met according to adjournment. Justices present, Isaiah Midkiff, Henry Boatman and Rubin Riggs.

Robert Yancey   )
No. 169 -vs   )   Justices present Isaiah Midkiff, David McAnally, Chas.
James Armstrong)   McAnally, Henry Boatman, & Rubin Riggs, whereupon
came a Jury, towit, Daniel Taylor, Abner Lowe, Duncan Carmichael, Edward McGinnis, John Estis, John Dannel, James Campbell, Jeremiah Chamberlain, Royal Jinnings, Benjamin Shaw, Tandry Senter & James Ferguson, who being elected tried and sworn the truth to speak on the issue joined in this case do say the Defendant did assume in manner & form as the plaintiff in his declaration hath complained against him and assess the plaintiffs Damages to six hundred & twenty three dollars thirty three and one third cents & costs from which the Defendant prays an appeal to the next Superior Court of Law to be held at Knoxville on the fourth Monday of March next for the District of Hamilton the defendant enters into Bond with James Blair & C. McCraw his securities for the prosecution of said appeal Reasons for appeal filed & appeal Granted.

(p 88)   November Sessions A.D. 1804

John Dean -Lessee of Bartholomew Smith and Pleasant Duke   )
No. 192- vs In Eject.   )
Henry Howell   )
     Justices present, Isaiah Midkiff, David McAnally, Rubin Riggs, Henry Boatman, Noah Jarnagin, Major Lea & William Clay. Whereupon came a Jury Viz. Joseph Bryant -Abraham Gibson -pd. William Humbard, Richard Thompson, Edward Churchman, Joel Ferrin, William Roberts, George Evans, John Moffitt, Dannel Clayton, John Vinyard, and Hogan Bean; who being elected tried & sworn the truth to speak on the issue joined in this case Do say the Defendant is not Guilty of the trespass & Ejectment in manner & form as the plaintiffs in their declaration have complained against him-Rule for a trial- Rule discharged.

James Armstrong Assignee &c)
         vs   )
Ambrose Yancey   )   John Lea high Sheriff surrenders Ambrose
Yancey the Defendant in open Court in discharge of himself for whom he stood Special Bail by reason of his not holding him to Bail on the arrest or before the return of the Writ, and Benjamin Shaw & Spencer Griffin come into Court and undertake & agree that if the Defendant should be cast in the action that he will pay the costs and condemnation or surrender himself to prison for the same or in case he failed therein that they would do it for him.

Richard Mitchell -Assignee
of Rubin Saunders   - vs   Ambrose Yancey

John Lea Sheriff surrenders Ambrose Yancey the Defendant in open Court in discharge of himself for whom he stood special Bail by reason of his not holding him to Bail on the arrest or before the return of the writ, and Benjamin Shaw & Spencer Griffin come into Court & undertake & agree that if the Defendant should be cast in the action that he will pay the costs & condemnation or surrender himself to prison for the same, or in case he fails therein that they would do it for him.

An Instrument of writing purporting to be the last Will & Testament of William Elliot deceased was presented to Court for probate and Mathew Elliot one of the subscribing witnesses came into Court & proved the due execution thereof and ordered to be Recorded- Thereupon Israel Elliot - Hugh Maxwell & John Underhill executors therein & thereby appointed came into Court were sworn & took upon themselves the Burthen of the execution thereof.

A Deed of conveyance from Thomas King to Archibald McCoy for one hundred & forty acres of Land was proven in open Court by G. McCraw, one of the subscribing witnesses & ordered to be Registered.

William Olay - William Hoskins)
Robert Patterson & William Hall)
vs)
Robert Yancey) Martin Ashburn late Coroner of Grainger County surrenders the said Robert Yancey the Defendant in open Court in discharge of himself for whom he stood special Bail in consequence of his not taking a Bail Bond of the said Defendant on the arrest or before the return of the writ agreeably to the acts of the General Assembly in such case made & provided —whereupon Pleasant M. Miller Attorney for the plaintiff prays the said Robert Yancey in custody of the Sheriff and his taken into Custody accordingly.

James Moore Esqr. Daniel Robinson, Major Lea Esqr. and John Bowen are drawn Jurors to attend the next Term of the Superior Court for Hamilton District.

Ordered by Court that Abraham Elliot Coroner be allowed the sum of Twenty Dollars for Ex officio services heretofore performed by him.
Copy Issd. to J. W. Lea at request of an Elliot.

Ordered by Court that Thomas Davdis Esqr. be allowed the sum of fifteen dollars for his services as Solicitor in Grainger County at August term A.D. 1804.

Ordered by the Court that Topley Haygood be allowed the sum of Twenty five dollars for his attention to Jeremiah Midkiff one of the poor of this County and the said Topley Haygood is to be paid according to Law commencing at August Term 1804 & ending at November Term 1804. Copy Issd.

(p 80)   November Sessions A.D. 1804
Ordered that Isiah Midkiff be allowed to take charge of Jeremiah Midkiff one of the poor of this County and keep & provide for him till next Court for which he is to be allowed the sum of Twenty five dollars or at that rate for what time he shall keep him.   Certificate Issued

The Court appoint the following persons

Jurors for next term, Viz.Seth McKinney, David Spencer, Elijah Clay, Daniel Clayton, William Sims, Josiah Kidwell, Christian Porcupile, Hugh Larimore, Joseph Fields, Thomas Dennis, William Harmon, Henry Bowen, Jr. David Holt, James Carmichael, Henry Morgan, William Williams -Cain Acuff, Hercules Ogle, Joseph Bealer, William Bowman, Rubin Dalton, Cornelius Mc Coy, Thomas Hann, Daniel Gowen, Dennis Gendry, William Hamilton, David Huddleston, Archibald McCarver, John Thompson, James Moore Senr. David Davis, Isaiah Mitchell, Edward Dennell, Henry Ivey, William Millikan, William Shelton, Jesse Cheek, Henry Howell & John Minat.

Ordered by Court that George Evans have leave a public ferry on the South bank of Clinch River where the present Kentucky road crosses the same & he enters into Bond with Joseph Cobb his security.

John Carwile Executor of the last Will & testament of John Irwin deceased returns to Court an account of the sales of the estate of said deceased.

The Jury heretofore appointed to view & lay out a road agreeably to Law from the fork of the roads opposite Major David Hailey's on the upper side of Richland Creek to the Knox County Line near the lower end of Clinch Mountain makes the following Report towit, "We the Jurors after being duly sworn to lay out a road from Major Hailey's to the end of Clinch mountain where the Knox Line intersects to Beginning at the forks of the road opposite Major Hailey's crossing at the upper ford of Richland Creek, Thence along the old road to John Acuffs Senr. thence along said road crossing the creek where the Knox road crosses said creek near John Spencers "thence along said road to William Snodgrass, thence along said road to the Knox line near the end of Clinch mountain.
Given under our hands 11th October 1804- Mathew Campbell, Peter Hamilton Richard Acuff, James Campbell, & William Mitchell, which said report is received & confirmed by the Court.

Ordered by Court that William Snodgrass be overseer of the road leading from Nances ferry to the lower end of Clinch mountain, towit, from the ford of Richland creek to the Knox Line and that the same bounds be allowed him for hands that were allowed little John Acuff.
                                                    Order Issd.

George Rensbarger)
        vs   )
John Hammil   )   John Cooke Esqr. makes a motion to Court to enter
up a Judgment against John Hammil in favor of George Rensbarger for the
sum of Forty dollars & twenty five cents which sum the said George Rensbarger has been obliged to pay as a security of the said John Hammil in part satisfaction of a Judgment recovered by Martin Miller in Grainger County Court against John Hammil principal & George Rensbarger & Ambrose Yancey his securities, and it appearing to the satisfaction of the Court that the said George has paid the aforesaid sum as security aforesaid: It is therefore considered by the Court that the said George do recover the aforesaid sum of Forty Dollars & twenty five cents against the said John Hammill besides his costs.

Court adjourns till tomorrow 9 o'clock.
            Wednesday 21st. November Court met according to adjournment.

Justices present, Major Lea, William Clay, Noah Jarnagin, Joseph Cobb, Rubin Riggs & Henry Boatman.

William Bryant)
vs) Whereupon came a Jury, towit, Daniel Taylor, Abner
John Moffitt) Lowe, Duncan Carmichael, Edward McGinnis, John Estis
Richard Thompson, Pleasant Duke, William Hamilton, Miller Easley, Alexander Hamilton, Henry Howell,& Thomas Bunch, who being elected tried & sworn the truth to speak on the issue joined in this case do say the Defendant did assume in manner & form as the plaintiff in his declaration hath alledged against him & assess the plaintiffs damages to forty five dollars & eighty three cents & costs from which the Defendant prays an appeal to the Superior Court of Hamilton District & he enters into Bond with James Carmichael & Samuel Moffit his securities for the prosecution of said appeal -Reasons for appeal granted.

(p 90)   November Sessions A.D. 1804

William Howard Constable maketh oath in open Court that he attended on the Court four days at August Sessions A.D. 1804. Issd.

Benjamin McCarty
vs
John Elsey, Spencer Griffin
Joseph Ray & George Counts
not in custody the same Justices present as in the above case. Whereupon came a Jury, towit, Henry Hipsher, James Campbell, William Hubbard, Richard Shelton-sd. Archelus Gibson sd- Joseph Bryant, John Daniel, William Windham, John Bean, James Bowen, William Dyer & David Bunch, who being Elected tried & sworn the truth to speak on the Issue joined in this case do say the Defendant have not paid the debt in the declaration mentioned as in pleading they have alledged, they find for the plaintiff the Debt in the declaration mentioned, Twenty five dollars & twenty five cents & assess the plaintiffs damages occasioned by the Detention of that debt, to one dollar & seventy cents & costs.

Royal Jinnings)
vs) the same Justices present as in the above case—whereupon came a Jury, towit- Henry Hipsher, James Campbell,
Hogan Bean)
William Hubbard, Richard Shelton pd. Archelus Gilbert -pd. Joseph Bryant Meredith Coffy, William Windham, Thomas Bunch, James Bowen, William Dyer & David Bunch ; who being Elected tried & sworn the truth to speak in the matter in controversy in this case do say they find for the plaintiff & assess his damages to one dollar & twenty five cents & costs- Rule for a new trial- Rule discharged.

The Grand Jury are discharged from further attendance at the present term- James Dyer Constable comes into open Court and makes oath that he has attended the Grand Jury three days at the present Term.

Ordered by Court that John Hodge be overseer of the Road in the room of William Kirk and that the same bounds be allowed him for hands that hath heretofore been allowed said Kirk -William Hamilton who was summoned to attend a Juror at last Term failed to attend, states to Court on oath the reason of his non-attendance which is deemed sufficient and forfecture set aside.

The reprt of the Jury who was appointed to view & lay out a road from the first branch below Jesse Beans old place to the town of Rutledge which was returned to Court on Monday & Recorded at length is confirmed by Court and ordered to be opened.

Ordered by Court that Thomas Bunch be overseer of the Richland road from the first branch below Jesse Beans old place to the ford of the Creek near Nicholas Carnses plantation and that all the hands living below sd. Branch of said Creek including Elijah Donathan's hands, Charles Kidwell & between Clinch mountain & the River ridge be allowed him to work on said road. Copy Issd.

Ordered by Court that Joel Harmer be overseer of the Richland road from the ford of the creek near Nicholas Kearnses to the public square in the town of Rutledge and that all the hands living between said Creek and Nicholas Countres & between the Richland Hoobs & Clinch mountain be allowed him to work on said Road. Order Issd.

Ordered by Court that James Dyer be allowed to take charge of Benj. Dyer one of the poor of this County for which he is allowed the sum of Two dollars & fifty cents per month for what time he shall keep him. Issd.

A Deed of conveyance from John Brock to Martin Bunch for Twenty five acres of Land was acknowledged in open Court by the said John Brock & ordered to be Registered.

A Deed of conveyance from Christian Rhodes to James Alsop for thirty five acres of Land was proven in open Court by the oath of Philip Combs a subscribing witness & ordered to be Registered.

Ordered by Court that William Windham be Released from the payment of the sum of five dollars and twenty five cents being the State & County tax with which the said William Windham stands chargeable on the tax List for the year A.D. 1804 on a Stud Horse— It appearing to the satisfaction of the Court that the said William Windham did not own said horse on the first day of January in the year A.D. 1804. Copy Issd. as to County and State.

Ordered by Court that the hands heretofore Reported on By the Sheriff that have bin published in the Knoxville Gazette as the Law directs be sold for the payment of Taxes & that the clerk issue Execution.

Ordered by Court that Joseph Shaw an orphan now of the age of nine years be bound to Miller Easley untill he attain to the age of Twenty one years; pursuant of which order Major Lea Chairman and the said Miller Easley have interchangeably signed Indentures &c.

Court adjourns till tomorrow 9 o'clock.

(p 91)   November Sessions A.D. 1804

Thursday 22nd. November Court met according to adjournment -Justices present, William Christian, William Clay, Noah Jarnagin & David McAnally

A Deed of conveyance from Frederick Moyers to John F.Jack for Lot No. 28- in the town of Rutledge was proven in open Court by the oath of John Lea a subscribing witness & ordered to be Registed.

Daniel Clayton States to Court on oath that he served Ten days as a Juror at the March term 1804 of the Superior Court of Hamilton District & that he travelled seventy miles & also that he got a Ticket for said attendance which amount to $12.33 -1/3 which said ticket he alledged was taken or mislaid during his sickness- It is therefore ordered by the Court that the said Daniel Clayton do receive the aforesaid sum of $12.33 -1/3 from the Trustee of Grainger County if the Trustee or collector of said County has not already taken said ticket, on condition that the said Daniel Clayton enter into bond with good & sufficient security for the use of said County in double the aforesaid money in case he may improperly receive said money, and the said Daniel Clayton enters into Bond with John Cocke Esqr. security in pursuance of the above order.

Joseph Cobb)
vs) John Cocke Esqr. makes a motion to Court to enter up
George M.Combs) a Judgment in favor of Joseph Cobb against George M. Combs for the sum of sixty dollars and sixty seven cents which the said Joseph Cobb has been obligated to pay as security of the said George M. Combs on a Judgment recovered in the County Court of Grainger by Nathaniel Davis assignee &c. against George M.Combs principal and the said Joseph Cobb his security and it appearing to the satisfaction of the Court that the said Joseph Cobb has been compelled to pay the aforesaid sum of money as the aforesaid sum of money as security of the said George M. Combs -- It is therefore considered by the Court that the said Joseph Cobb do recover the aforesaid sum of sixty dollars & sixty seven cents against the said George M.Combs besides his costs.

Ordered by Court that William Hall be allowed to take charge of Charles Asher and his wife two of the poor of Grainger County who are likely to become chargeable to the County & provide for them till next Court.

A Deed of conveyance being a deed of gift, from John Bird to John Hanback for one hundred acres of Land was proven in open Court by Ambrose Yancey the subscribing witness & ordered to be Registered.

Ordered by Court that the following Justices take in Lists of Polls & takable property in Grainger County for the year A.D. 1805 and make return to next Court -Viz.

1- William Clay Esqr. for Capt. Bunches Company.
2- James Moore Esqr. for Captain Wilson's Company.
3- Rubin Riggs Esqr. for "   Mann's   "
4- Henry Boatman Esqr. for Captain Carmichael's Company.
5- William Christian Esqr. for "   Hargraves   "
6- David McAnally Esqr. for   " Dodson's   "
7- Valentine Moulder Esqr. for " Alexander Hamilton's Company.

8- Samuel Clark Esqr. for Captain James Company.
9- Joseph Cobb   "   "   "   Bowens   "
10-Major Lea   "   "   "   Peter Hamilton's Company.
11-Josiah Dyer   "   "   "   Howells Company.

Charles McAnally)
    vs   )
Robert Yancey   )   John Cooke Esqr. makes a motion to Court to enter up
a Judgment in favor of Charles McAnally for the sum of Forty five dollars
against Robert Yancey which sum the said Charles McAnally has been obliged to pay on sundry judgments recovered in the Court of Pleas & Quarter
Sessions for Grainger County in the name of sundry persons against the sd.
Robert Yancey late Sheriff and the said Charles McAnally & others securities of the said Robert Yancey and it appearing to the satisfaction of
the Court that the said Charles McAnally has been obliged to pay the above
mentioned sum mentioned sum of Forty five dollars as security of the said
Robert- It is therefore considered by the Court that the said Charles do
recover the aforesaid sum of Forty five dollars against the said Robert
Yancey besides his costs.

(p 92)   November Sessions /A.D. 1804

Henry Howell   )
    vs   )   Henry Howell by John Cooke Esqr. his Attorney makes
Robert Yancey   )   a motion to Court to enter up a Judgment in favor of
Him the said Henry Howell for the sum of thirty nine dollars & fifty cents
against Robert Yancey which sum the said Henry has been obliged to pay
on sundry Judgments recovered by sundry person in the Court of Pleas &
Quarter Sessions for Grainger County against the said Robert Yancey late
Sheriff of said County and the said Henry Howell & others securities of
the said Robert Yancey; and it appearing to the satisfaction of the Court
that the said Henry has been obliged to pay the aforesaid sum of money as
security of the said Robert Yancey- It is therefore considered by the
Court that the said Henry Howell do recover the said sum of thirty nine
dollars & fifty cents against the said Robert Yancey & costs.

Noah Jarnagin Trustee   )
    Vs   )
Robert Yancey late Sheriff)
    John Cooke Esqr. Solicitor makes a motion to Court to enter up a Judg-
ment in favor of Noah Jarnagin Trustee for the use of the County for the
sum of five dollars against Robert Yancey late Sheriff which sum the said
Robert collected on a Bill of costs sogned by the Clerk being a fine imposed by the Court on a Bill of Indictment exhibited on behalf of the Government against a certain Spencer Griffin which sum the said Robert has
failed to pay over; It is therefore considered by the Court that the said
Noah Jarnagin do recover for the use of the County the said sum of five
dollars against the said Robert Yancey besides his costs.

Noah Jarnagin Trustee   )
    vs   )
Robert Yancey late Sheriff)   John Cooke Esqr. Solicitor makes a motion
to Court to enter up a Judgment in favor of Noah Jarnagin Trustee for the

use of the County for the sum of Eleven Dollars to Ten cents against Robert Yancey for so much money by him collected on sundry Executions for fines imposed by the Court & which he has failed to pay over; It is therefore considered by the Court that the said Noah Jarnagin Do recover for the use of the County the said sum of Eleven Dollars & ten cents against the said Robert Yancey besides his costs.

Noah Jarnagin -Trustee }
    vs
Robert Yancey late Sheriff and sis securities.) John Cocke Esqr. Solicitor of Grainger County makes a motion to Court to enter up a Judgment in favor of Noah Jarnagin Trustee for the use of said County for the sum of Four Dollars & seventy cents against Robert Yancey late Sheriff James Ore, Henry Howell, Nicholas Gillington, Bardley Marshall, Charles McAnally, Robert McElhiney, John Rose, Thomas Bunch, William Bryant, Francis Crabb & Spencer Griffin his securities fo so much money by the said Robert Yancey collector for fines in State Prosecutions on sundry Executions & which he has failed to pay over; It is therefore considered by the Court that the said Noah Jarnagin do recover for the use of the County the said sum of Four Dollars & seventy besides his costs against the said Robert Yancey & his said securities.

A Commission was produced to Court from his Excellency John Sevier with the great seal of the State thereto annexed appointing amongst others, John Bradon a Justice of the Peace in and for the County of Grainger and the said John Bradon, in open Court took an oath to support the Constitution of the United States, an oath to support the Constitution of the State of Tennessee and also an oath of Office.
    Court adjourns till Court in Course.
                (Signed) Noah Jarnagin -C.P.T.
(p 93)
             February Sessions A.D. 1805

At a Court of pleas and quarter sessions begun and holden for the County of Grainger at the Court House in Rutledge on the third Monday of February A.D. 1805, being the 18th of the same month. Justices present, William Rankins, William Christian, Henry Boatman and Rubin Riggs.

John Lea Esqr. high Sheriff of Grainger County returns to Court that he has executed the following Venire facias on the following persons except John Thompson & William Williams, towit-

1- Seth McKinney	15- Henry Morgan
2- David Spencer	16- William Williams
3- Elijah Clay	17- Cain Acuff
4- Daniel Clayton	18- Hercules Ogle
5- William Sims	19- Joseph Baelor
6- Josiah Kidwell	20- William Bowman
7- Christian Porcupile	21- Rubin Dalton
8- Hugh Larimore	22- Cornelius McCoy
10-Thomas Dennis	23- Thomas Ham
11-William Harmon	24- Daniel Gowen
12-Henry Bowen Jr.	25- Dennis Condry
13-David Holt	26- William Hamilton
14-James Carmichael	27- David Huddleston

28- Archibald McCarver
29- John Thompson
30- James Moore Sr.
31- David Davis
32- Isaac Mitchell
33- Edward Dannell

34- Henry Ivey
35- William Milliken
36- William Shelton
37- Jesse Cheek
38- Henry Howell A
39- John Minat

Out of which Venire facias the persons whose names are underwritten were drawn a Grand Jury to the present Term.

1- William Hamilton- Foreman.
2- David Holt
3- Thomas Dennis
4- James Carmichael
5- Hercules Ogle
6- Archibald McCarver
7- Josiah Kidwell
8- Henry Howell
9- Seth McKinney

10- Christian Porcupile
11- Elijah Clay
12- Daniel Clayton
13- William Sims
14- Joseph Fields
15- William Harmon

Who were sworn and charged by John Cooke Esqr. Solicitor. The Court appoint John Crow Guardian for Gidion Wilson a monor heir of Isaac Wilson deceased who enters into Bond in the sum of one thousand dollars with John Morris & Shedrick Morris his securities - Justices present Major Lea, Rubin Riggs, Hanry Boatman, William Clay & William Christian.

Nimrod Cyrus By John Bradon Esqr. Records his mark as follows, towit A crop off the right Ear.

A Deed of conveyance from Christian Rhodes to William Arnold for two hundred acres of Land was proven in open Court by the oath of James Alsup one of the subscribing witnesses & ordered to be Registered.

A Deed of conveyance from Patrick Sharkey to William Arnold for 15 acres of Land was proven in open Court by James Alsup one of the subscribing witnesses & ordered to be Registered.

A Deed of conveyance from Christian Rhodes to William Arnold for two hundred acres of Land was proven in open Court by the oath of James Alsup one of the subscribing witnesses & ordered to be Registered.

A Deed of conveyance from James Alsup to William Arnold for ten acres of Land was acknowledged in open Court by James Alsup the Grantor and ordered to be Registered.

A Deed of conveyance from Evan Harris to Robert Harris his son for one hundred & forty acres of Land was acknowledged in open Court by the said Evan Harris the grantor & ordered to be Registered.

A Deed of conveyance from John Winshaw to Robert Harris for fifty two acres of Land was proven in open Court by Evan Harris one of the subscribing witnesses & ordered to be Registered.

A Deed of conveyance from John Estis to John Archer for one hundred acres of Land was proven in open Court by the oath of Christian Porcupile one of the subscribing witnesses & ordered to be Registered.

(p 94)   February Sessions A.D. 1805

A Deed of conveyance from John Morris to Isaac Wilson for two hundred acres of Land was acknowledged in Court by the said John Morris and ordered to be Registered.

A Deed of conveyance from John Morris to Isaac Wilson for forty six acres of Land was acknowledged in Court by the said John Morris & ordered to be Registered.

A Deed of conveyance from John Lea Sheriff of Grainger County to John Cocke for Lot number Ten in the town of Rutledge was acknowledged in open Court & ordered to be Registered.

A Deed of conveyance from Philip Howell To Malachiah Howell for one hundred acres of Land was proven in open Court by the oath of William Hodge one of the subscribing witnesses & ordered to be Registered.

A Deed of conveyance from John Archer to Christian Porcupile for one hundred acres of Land was proven in open Court by the oath of Isiah Kidwell one of the subscribing witnesses & ordered to be Registered.

A Deed of conveyance from Samuel Moore to William Arnold for twenty acres of Land was proven in open Court by the oath of Edward West one of the subscribing witnesses & ordered to be Registered.

A Deed of conveyance from Martin Bunch to William McPheteridge for twenty five acres and one half of an acre of Land was proven in open Court by the oath of Samuel Clark one of the subscribing witnesses & ordered to be Registered.

A Deed of conveyance from John Spring to Nicholas Spring for three hundred acres of Land was proven in open Court by the oath of David Spring one of the subscribing witnesses & ordered to be Registered.

A Deed of conveyance from John Bean to James McFarland for two hundred acres of Land was proven in open Court by the oath of Joseph Cobb one of the subscribing witnesses & ordered to be Registered.

A Deed of conveyance from John Adamson & George Pugh to Jeremiah Brown —James Harmock for one hundred acres of Land was proven in open Court by the oath of Samuel Pruit a subscribing witness and ordered to be Registered.

A Deed of conveyance from Daniel Petree to John Bealor Jr. for one hundred acres of Land was proven in open Court by the oath of Thomas Dunn a subscribing witness & ordered to be Registered.

A Deed of conveyance from John Bealor Sr. to John Bealor Jr. for one hundred acres of Land was proven in open Court by the oath of John Petree a subscribing witness & ordered to be Registered.

A Bill of Sale from John Hailey to Edward West for a negro girl named Sarah was proven in open Court by the oath of James Moore a subscribing witness & ordered to be Registered.

A Bill of Sale from David Hailey to James Richardson for two negroes one named Terra the other named Thomas was acknowledged in open Court by the said David Hailey & ordered to be Recorded.

A Bill of Sale from David Hailey to Thomas Smith for two negroes the one named Poll was acknowledged in open Court by the said David Hailey & ordered to be Recorded.

Mary Whitlock Administratrix & William Golden Admr. of the estate of James Whitlock deceased, return to Court on oath an account of the Statements of said Estate.

Josiah Dyer Esqr. returns to Court a List of Polls & taxable property in the Bounds of Captain Howell's Company for the year A.D. 1805.

Ordered by Court that Daniel Beelor be overseer of the road beginning at William Howells old place thence to the middle of Clinch river & that all the hands in the following Bounds be allowed him to work on said road, towit, Beginning at the grassey shoals thence to William Howells old place including the hands that live at said place, thence to John Beelors Jr. thence to the Cog Mountain.   Copy order issd.

(p 95)   February Sessions A.D. 1805

Ordered by Court that Joseph Hall be overseer of the road from the Powder Spring Gap in Clinch mountain to where it intersects the Flat Creek road near the house of Philip Sigler Esqr. and that all the hands living on the South side of the Copper ridge & formerly in the Bounds of John Moyers be allowed him to work on said road. Copy order issd.

Ordered by Court that Philip Parker be overseer of the road in the room of John Kitchen and that he have the same hands to work under him on said road that ware allowed said Kitchen. Order Issd.

A bill of Sale from John Bolts to John Wisle for an Improvement on the South side of Clinch river above the mouth of Black fox was proven in open Court by the oath of Samuel Ward and ordered to be Registered.

Court adjourns till tomorrow 9 o'clock.

Tuesday 19th February Court met according to adjournment. Justices present -William Christian, Rubin Riggs, John Bradon & Henry Boatman.

Samuel D.Carrick   )
vs- qui Tan   )   Lewis Harmon and Frederick Moyers special Bail
Raphael Jones   )   of the defendant surrenders him in open Court in
discharge of themselves.

John Winstead   )
     vs   )
Mathew Capps & Stephen Austin)   Stephen Austin only in custody.

Justices present -Major Lea, William Clay, William Christian &c.
Whereupon came a jury towit, Hugh Larimore, Henry Bowen Jr. Rubin Dalton
Isaac Mitchell, Henry Ivey, William Shelton, Alexander Hamilton, Nicholas
Countz, William King, John Huddleston, Miller Easley, & Robert D. Eaton
who being elected tried and sworn well & truly to try what damages John
Umstead hath sustained in a writ of Inquiry by him brought in this case
Do say he hath sustained damages to the amount of one cent beside his
costs.

Denn on the Demise of James Ferguson)
    vs --Trespass in Ejectment   )
Fenn and James Hamilton   )   Whereupon came a Jury, towit, the
same Jury as the above case except Robert Harris in the room of John Huddleston and Edward McGinnis in the room of Alexander Hamilton, who being
Elected, tried & sworn well & truly to try the issue joined in this case
do say they find the Defendant not Guilty in manner and form as the plaintiff in his Declaration hath complained against him.

        William Clay Esqr. Ranger for Grainger County returns to Court a
List of Strays as follows, towit, " A List of Strays" remaining on my
Book and not proven away in twelve months of the following specifications
towit- Major Lea Esqr. one yearling Steer $2.50 - one White sweather $1
William Howard - four hoggs towit, first $4.00- second $3.50- third $3
fourth $2.50 -John Spencer - one Sow and nine pigs $3.00 1/3 - 3 others
$1.66 2/3 - James Owen - 1 hog $1.25 - Lewis Collins three Hogs $6.00.
                    (Signed) W.Clay -R.G.C.

Henry Howell   )
     vs   )
Francis Darnel)   Whereupon came a Jury, towit, the same Jury, towit,
as in the last suit except William Dyer in the place of Isaac Mitchell -
who being elected tried & sworn the truth to speak on the issue Joined
in this case do say they find the Defendant not Guilty in manner & form
as the plaintiff in his Declaration hath complained against him- Rule
for a new trial- On argument Rule made absolute.

Hugh L. White   )
     vs   )   John Lea Sheriff surrenders the Defendant in open
Barcley Marshall)   Court in discharge of himself for whom he stands
Special Bail in consequence of not taking a Bail Bond, and the said De-
fendant gives Henry Howell & Thomas Henderson his Special Bail.

(p 96)   February Sessions A.D. 1805

    Ordered by the Court that William Clay, Noah Jarnagin,& Major Lea
Esquires be appointed to settle with Margaret Hall administratrix of the
Estate of James Hall deceased-and make report to the present term.

    Ordered by the Court that Frederick Moyers have leave to keep an
Ordinary or house of public entertainment in the town of Rutledge & he
enters into Bond with Lewis Hammon & Pleasant Duke his securities in the
penal sum of twelve hundred and fifty dollars.

Ordered by the Court that John Cocke and John F. Jack Commissioners be allowed the sum of fourteen dollars each for services heretofore performed by them in settling with the Collector & trustee of Grainger County & Reporting their settlements to Court. Copy issd. in favor of J.F.Jack.

Ordered by the Court that Major Lea Esqr. have leave to keep an Ordinary or house of public entertainment in Grainger County and the said Major Lea enters into Bond with Pleasant M.Miller -Noah Jarnagin & Edward Scott his securities in the penal sum of twelve hundred & fifty dollars.

Robert McElhiney)
 vs   )
Robert Yancey) John Cocke Esqr. Atty. for the said Robert McElhiney makes a motion to Court to enter up a Judgment against the said Robert Yancey for the sum of forty nine dollars & fifteen cents which sum the said Robert Mc.Elhiney has been compelled to pay on sundry executions issued on Judgments recovered against him & others -securities of the said Robert Yancey in the Court of pleas & quarter Sessions for Grainger County and appearing to the satisfaction of the Court that the said Robert McElhiney has been obliged to pay the aforesaid sum of money as security of the said Robert Yancey - It is therefore considered by the Court that the said Robert McElhiney do recover the aforesaid sum of Forty nine dollars & fifteen cents against the said Robert Yancey besides his costs.

A Bill of Sale from Michael Coune to Robert Stone was proven in open Court by the oath of Lewis Harmon and ordered to be Recorded.

A Deed of conveyance from James Moore to Peter Cotner for twenty acres of Land was acknowledged in open Court & ordered to be Registered.

A Deed of conveyance from Abraham Elliot to Charles Hutcheson for Forty acres of Land was acknowledged in open Court and ordered to be Registered.

A Deed of conveyance from Joseph Cobb to Hercules Ogle for Two hundred and thirty seven & one half acres of Land was acknowledged in Court & ordered to be Registered.

Samuel Clark Esqr. returned to Court a List of Polls & taxable property in the Bounds of Captain James Company for the year A.D. 1805.

Valentine Moulder Esqr. Returns to Court a List of Polls & taxable property in the Bounds of Captain Alexander Hamiltons Company for the year A.D. 1805.

William Clay Esqr. returns to Court a List of polls & taxable property in the Bounds of Captain Samuel Bunch's Company, for the year A.D. 1805.
Major Lea Esqr. returns to Court a List of polls & taxable property in the Bounds of Captain Peter Hamiltons Company for the year A.D. 1805.
Rubin Riggs Esqr. returns to Court a List of polls & taxable property in the Bounds of Captain Thomas Hanns Company for the year A.D. 1805.

James Moore Esqr. returns to Court a List of polls & taxable property in the Bounds of Captain Massingill Company for the year A.D. 1805.

Joseph Cobb Esqr. Returns to Court a List of Polls & taxable property in the Bounds of Captain Bowens Company for the year A.D. 1805.

William Christian Esqr. Returns to Court a List of polls & taxable property in the Bounds of Captain Hargraves Company for the year A.D.1805.

(p 97)   February Sessions A.D. 1805.

Ordered by Court that the following Tax be laid and collected in Grainger County for the year A.D. 1805- Towit, On each hundred acres of Land twelve and one half cents.
"   "   White Poll twelve and one half cents.
"   "   Black "   Twenty five cents.
"   "   Stud Horse   "   "   "
"   "   Town Lot   "   "   "
"   "   Merchant - Five Dollars.
"   "   Pedlar or Haker five Dollars.

A Deed of conveyance from Robert Moore to Levi Moore for one hundred acres of Land was proven in open Court by the oath of David Spring one of the subscribing witnesses & ordered to be Registered.

A Deed of conveyance from John Lea Sheriff of Grainger County to James Jackson for three hundred acres of Land was proven in open Court by Alex. Hamilton a subscribing witness & ordered to be Registered.

The Court appoint the following persons Jurors to May Sessions A.D. 1805, to wit, David Huddleston, James Brown, William Cook, Charles Hopper Cornelus McCoy, Henry Hipsher, Dawson Cheek, Isaac Midkiff, Peter Hammond Peter Beeler, Abraham Prue, Thomas Henderson, John Crabb, Joseph Brown, William Blair, James Blair Junr. William Kirkum, Thomas Johnston, William Peeters, John Acuff, George Norris, John Haines, Robert Long, Joseph Stubblefield, Richard Thompson, Barnabas Butcher, Melachia Howell, William Smith, Moses Hodges, William Milligan, Sherod Mays, Henry Morgan, Sr. Duncan Carmichael, George Boatman, Harmon Cox, Enough Winds, William Mitchell, Jesse Jinnings & Samuel Peery.

A Deed of conveyance from Martin Bunch to Bartin McPherson for one hundred & twenty six acres of Land was proven in open Court by Aaron Rooks & ordered to be Registered.

A Bill of Sale from John Spring to Nicholas Spring was proven in open Court by Levi Moore a subscribing witness & ordered to be Recorded.

A Deed of conveyance from Larkin Wall to Philip Sigler for three hundred acres of Land was acknowledged in open Court & ordered to be Registered.
A Deed of conveyance from Joseph Cobb to Aaron Rooks for one hundred & seventy acres of Land was proven in open Court by the oath of James Dyer Jr. and ordered to be Registered.

A Deed of conveyance from Jesse Riggs to Jacob Wilson for one hundred and fifty six acres of Land was acknowledged in open Court & ordered to be Registered.

A Deed of conveyance from John Lea Sheriff, to Jesse Riggs for one hundred & fifty six acres of Land was acknowledged in open Court & ordered to be Registered.

James Moore Esqr. returns to Court a List of his taxable property for the year A.D. 1805 as follows, towit, 600 acres of Land & one White Poll.

James Dyer Deputy Collector of taxes in Grainger County for the year A.D. 1804 exhibited to Court a List of Insolvents to which he was qualified as the Act of the General Assembly in such case made and provided requires amounting in the whole to sixteen Dollars & thirty seven cents-Viz. $7.75 the State tax $7.00 the County tax, and $1.62 the poor tax; It is therefore ordered by the Court that John Lea Collector of Taxes for the aforesaid year be released from the payment of the aforesaid sums of money and have a credit for the sum of $7.75 in his settlement with the Treasurer of the Districts of Washington, and also a credit with the Trustee of Grainger County for the sum of $8.62 in his settlment.

Court adjourns till tomorrow 9 o'clock.

Wednesday 20th February Court met according to adjournment. Justices present, Major Lea, Peter Harris, Noah Jarnagin, Joseph Cobb Rubin Riggs, Charles McAnally & Valentine Moulder.

(p 98)   February Sessions A.D. 1805

Henry Boatman Esqr. returns to Court a List of Polls and taxable property in the Bounds of Captain Stephen W.Senters Company for the year A.D 1805.

Ordered by Court that Josiah & John Nichols Merchants be released from the payment of the sum of Five dollars being the County tax on their Store for the year A.D. 1804; the firm of Harmon & Nichols having paid the tax for said year on the same store, and that the Collector have a credit for the aforesaid Tax in his settlement with the Trustee of Grainger County; and if the collector has paid said tax into the Treasury It is ordered by the Court that the Trustee refund the same to the collector.
                              Copy Issued.
William King & Edmund Sherman   )
        vs   )
John Burton & George Combs   )

Edward Scott Esqr. makes a motion to Court to enter up a Judgment against Robert Yancey late Sheriff and James Ore -Henry Howell, Nicholas Gillentine, Barcley Marshall, Charles McAnally, Robert McElhiney, John Rose, Thomas Bunch, William Bryant, Francis Crabb & Spencer Griffin his securities for the sum of sixty eight dollars and ninety four cents for so much money by him collected on an Execution in this case and which the said Robert Yancey has failed to pay over on application and it appearing to the satisfaction of the Court that on the oath of Edward Scott Esqr. that said Yancey on application made to him by the said Edward Scott Atty. in said suit failed to pay over the aforesaid sum of money; It is therefore considered by the Court that the said plaintiffs do recover the aforesaid sum of sixty eight dollars & ninety four cents & costs against the said Robert Yancey and his securities.

Edward Scott Esqr. makes a motion to Court to discharge William Perrin from his recognizance he standing bound to the present term for begetting a bastard child on the body of a certain Nancy Long and it appearing to the satisfaction of the Court that the said Nancy was a married woman; It is therefore ordered by the Court that the said William Perrin be discharged from his recognizance.

State)
vs)
William Guss & others)

George Bull who was legally summoned a witness in this suit being solemnly called, came not; it is therefore considered by the Court that he do forfeit according to Act of Assembly.

State)
vs) Justices, Major Lea, David McAnally & Josiah Midcliff
William Guss) whereupon came a Jures Moore Senr. William Shelton, pd
Henry Bowne, Thomas Henderson, Nicholas Countz, James Hamilton, Edward McGinnis, James Dyer, Moses McWhiney, Miller Easley & Samuel Bunch, who being elected tried & sworn the truth to speak on the Issue Joined in this case do say they find the defendant Guilty in manner and form as he stands charged in the Bill of Indictment— From which the Defendant prays an appeal to the next Superior Court of Law for Hamilton district & enters into recognizance &c. Reasons for the appeal filed.

Ordered by the Court that William Williams overseer of that part of the road Beginning at the gap of the ridge near the head of Youngs creek to the main road below Read Wilsons have the hands towit, the hands living at John Tyes old place thence to Joseph Stephens thence to Henry Morgans and the hands there, thence to John Crows, thence to Harmon Cox, thence to Thomas Reeces thence to Ambrose Hodges and all the hands in the above Bounds. Copy Issd.

Ordered by Court that Benjamin Hudson be overseer of the road in the room of Simon York, and that the same bounds be allowed him for hands to work on said road that has heretofore bee allowed said York. Copy issd.

Ordered by Court that John Bunch senr. have leave to keep an ordinary or house of public entertainment in Grainger County and he enters into Bond in the penal sum of twelve hundred & fifty dollars with Noah Jarnagin Esqr. his security.

David McAnally Esqr. returns to Court a List of polls & taxable property in the Bounds of Captain Dodsons Company for the year A.D. 1805.

(p 99)   February Sessions A.D. 1805
Ordered by Court that the following persons, towit, David Holt, Pleasant Duke, Joseph Noe, William Kirbon, Alexander Blair, Daniel Tayler,

Robert Long, & Hugh Larrimore be a Jury to View & lay out a road agreeably to Law from Barcley Marshall, ford on Holston river to the Sulphur Springs on the Kentucky road between Beans Station & Clinch mountain and make report to next Court. Order Issd.

Ordered by Court that Jacob Elliot be overseer of the road in the place of John Kitchen, and that he be allowed the same Bounds for hands that said Kitchen had to work on said road.

Henry Hipsher Administrator of)
Mathias Hipsher deceased)
    vs)
Robert Yancey late Sheriff & his securities.)

The plaintiff by John Williams his Attorney makes a motion to Court to enter up a Judgment against Robert Yancey late Sheriff, and James Ore Henry Howell, Nicholas Gillentine, Barcley Marshall Charles McAnally, Robert McIlhiney, John Rose, Thomas Bunch, William Bryant, Francis Crabb & Spencer Griffin his securities for the sum of one hundred & sixty dollars ninety one & one half cents money collected on an execution Issued in favor of the said Henry Hipsher against George Cooper and Isaac Cooper & which he has failed to pay over which said motion is continued over for argument till next Court.

State)
    vs) William Magill the Defendant charged with begetting
William Magill) a bastard child on the Body of Mary Ivey, comes into Court & enters into Bond in the sum of Five Hundred Dollars with Josiah Dyer & Abner Dyer conditioned to indemnity the County of Grainger against raising & maintaining said child.

Court adjourns till tomorrow 9 o'clock.

Thursday 21st. February Court met according to adjournment. Justices Present, Peter Harris, David McAnally & Henry Boatman.

John Crabb returns in open Court a List of polls & taxable property for the year A.D. 1806 as follows, towit, one white poll— two Town Lots & 640 acres of Land.

Carrick Montgomery & Co. By John Cocke returns to Court a retail store subject to the payment of County Tax for the year A.D. 1805.

Josiah and John Nichols By John Cocke returns to Court a retail store subject to the payment of County Tax for the year A.D. 1805.

The Grand Jury dismissed from further attendance at the present Term.

Francis Willet Constable of the Grand Jury maketh oath in Court that he attended four days on the Grand Jury at the present Term— Ordered by Court that Francis Willet be allowed one dollar for each day he has attended as aforesaid.

Willie Blount By John F.Jack returns to Court a List of Lands for which he is subject to pay Taxes for the year A.D. 1805 as follows, towit, 300 acres of Land at mouth of Onny Creek -150 acres at the mouth of Cave Spring 1000 acres East side Williams Creek -1000 acres Williams Creek - 1000 acres Town house Valley.

Ordered by Court that Joseph Fields be overseer of the road from the Powder Spring gap in Clinch mountain to the top of the Copper Ridge in the place of Robert Moore & that he have the same bounds allowed him for hands that hath heretofore bee allowed said Moore. Copy Deliv.to Fields by J.F. Jack.

Court adjourns till Court in Course.

Major Lea Chn.

(p 100)   May Sessions A.D. 1805

At a Court of Pleas & Quarter Sessions begun and holden for the County of Grainger at the Court House in Rutledge on the third Monday of May A.D. 1805 being the 20th of the same month.
Justices present, William Clay, Rubin Riggs and Henry Boatman.

John Lea Esquire high Sheriff of Grainger County returns to Court that he has executed the following Venire Facias on the following persons except Charles Hopper, Joseph Brown, William Smith & Sherod Mays towit-

1- David Huddleston
2- James Brown
3- William Cook
4- Charles Hopper
5- Cornelius McCoy
6- Henry Hipsher
7- Davison Cheek
8- Isaac Midkiff
9- Peter Hammock
10-Peter Beeler
11-Abraham Pruit
12-Thomas Henderson
13-John Crabb
14-Joseph Brown
15-William Blair
16-James Blair Jr.
17-William Kirkm
18-Thomas Johnston
19-William Peeters
20-John Acuff

21- George Norris
22- John Haines
23- Robert Long
24- Joseph Stubblefield
25- Richard Thompson
26- Barnabas Butcher
27- Malachia Howell
28- William Smith
29- Moses Hodges
30- William Milliken
31- Sherod Mays
32- Henry Morgan
33- Duncan Carmichael
34- George Boatman
35- Harmon Cox
36- Enoch Winds
37- William Mitchell
38- Jesse Jennings
39- Samuel Peery

Out of which Venire Facias the persons whose names are underwritten were drawn a Grand Jury for the present Term, towit,

1- Moses Hodges -Foreman
2- William Cooke
3- Joseph Stubblefield
4- Henry Hipsher
5- William Mitchell
6- William Blair
7- David Huddleston

8- Richard Thompson
9- Harmon Cox
10-Thomas Johnston
11-Enoch Winds
12-Cornelius McCoy
13-Peter Beeler
14-John Haines & 15-George Norris.

Who are sworn and charged by the Solicitor.

Francis Willet Constable sworn to attend the Grand Jury during the present Term.

Ordered by Court that Thomas Henderson —Lewis Fammm & William Clay Esqrs. be appointed Commissioners to settle with Col. James Ore Admr. of James Short Deceased and make report to this Court.

John Denn Lessee of Henry Roberts)
vs)
Benjamin Shaw) Joel Bean one of the Special Bail of the Defendant in this case brings him into Court & surrenders him in discharge of himself and the Defendant brings John McElhiney & James Grayson into Court who became his special Bail in this action.

John Williams Esqr. makes a motion to Court that the Sheriff be directed to bring William Royl into Court, who is now confined in the County Jail on a Civil process for the purpose of enabling John Holt & James Holt to surrender said Royl in discharge of themselves for whose appearance at the present Term it has been suggested they stand bound by Recognizance , whereupon the Court direct the Sheriff to bring the Body of the said William Royl into Court and the said Sheriff in pursuance of said order brings him into Court and the said John Holt and James Holt surrenders the said William Royl in discharge of themselves for whose appearance they state they stand bound as above suggested and the Court directs the said William Royl in custody of the Sheriff.

(p 101) May Sessions A.D. 1805

On motion William Howard & Elizabeth Grimes have leave to administer on the estate of David Grimes deceased and they enter into Bond in the sum of Five hundred Dollars with Edward Hankins their security & were qualified as the law in such cases requires.

William Howard & Elizabeth Grimes Administrators of David Grimes deceased returns to Court an Inventory of the estate of the Deceased & upon motion the Court direct an order of sale to issue. Order issd.

On application the Court direct that Jesse Riggs have leave to build a grist mill on a creek that runs into Holston river on the South side of said river nearly opposite the Aple orchard of Peter Harris Esqr. at or near the mouth of said creek.

Justices present, Major Lea, Noah Jarnagin, Philip Sigler, Isaiah Biddiff —Charles Hutchison, Henry Boatman, David McAnnlly,William Hankins & Samuel Clark.

Phebe Coats, a minor heir of Charles Coats deceased — about the age of seventeen years comes into Court & Chooses David Harrison her guardian and the Court appoints the said David Harrison her guardian for

and

also appoint him guardian for Jinny Coats, David Coats, and Amy Coats minor heirs of the said deceased, who are now under age of fourteen years

& the said David Harrison enters into Bond in the sum of six hundred Dollars with Edward Hankins his security.

Kinsey Coats a minor heir of Charles Coats deceased now of the age of fifteen years comes into Court & chooses Edward Hankins his guardian and the Court appoint the said Edward Hankins Guardian for Peggy Coats & Mary Coats minor heirs of the said Charles Coats deceased they being under the age of fourteen years and the said Edward Hankins enters into bond in the sum of five hundred dollars with William Hankins his security.

James Reynolds who is charged with begitting a bastard child on the body of Sarah Scott comes into Court & enters into bond in the sum of five hundred Dollars with Josiah Dyer & Henry Howell his securities conditioned to indemnify the County against the maintenence of said child.

Valentine Spring who is charged with begetting a Bastard child on the body of Isbel Haines comes into Court & enters into bond in the sum of five hundred dollars with Nicholas Spring & John Haines his securities conditioned to indemnify the County against the maintenence of said child.

A Deed of conveyance from Robert Yancey late Sheriff to Ambrose Yancey for ninety five acres of Land was proven in open Court by the oath of John T.Jack one of the subscribing witnesses and ordered to be Registered.

A Deed of conveyance from John Lea Sheriff to Henry Howell for ninety five acres of land was proven in open Court by the oath of Samuel D. Carrick one of the subscribing witnesses and ordered to be Registered.

A Bill of Sale from Thomas Dodson to William Johnston, James Johnson Jesse Dodson -Stephen Johnston, & Samuel Dodson for three negroes & other property was proven in open Court by the oath of Joseph Stubblefield a subscribing witness & ordered to be Recorded.

A Deed of conveyance from Thomas Dodson to Samuel Dodson for one hundred & fifty four acres of Land was proven in open Court by the oath of Joseph Stubblefield one of the subscribing witnesses & ordered to Be Registered.

A Deed of conveyance from John Crabb to Martin Albert for Lot No.48 in the town of Rutledge was proven in open Court by the oath of Luke Lea Junr. a subscribing witness & ordered to be Registered.

Ordered by Court that Martin Albert be overseer of the road from the town of Rutledge to the top of Richland Hobs in the place of Miller Easley & that the bounds for hands that ware allowed said Easley to work on said road be so extended as to include the plantation whereon John Middleton now lives & that the hands in the aforesaid Bounds be allowed said Albert to work on said road. Issd.

(p 102)   May Sessions A.D. 1805

William Clay Esqr. Rainger returns to Court a List of Strays as follows, towit, "A List of strays remaining on my Books not proven away in

twelve months of the following specification, towit, Chesley Jarnagin, one yearling Steer $2.50- John Thomson - one yearling Steer $1.66 2/3 Eliphaz Condry - 1 weather - one ram & one Lamb $2.16 2/3 -
Signed —W.Clay R.O.C.

Thomas Ketland by David Henley his agent returns to Court 20,000 acres of Land for the year A.D. 1805.

A Deed of conveyance from Benjamin Howell To Elijah Donathan for fifty acres of Land was acknowledged in open Court & ordered to Be Registered.

A Deed of conveyance from John Gilmore to George Sparkman for two hundred acres of Land was proven in open Court by the oath of Ambrose Yancey a subscribing witness & ordered to be Registered.

A Deed of conveyance from Henry Ivey to Benjamin Blake for two hundred acres of Land was proven in open Court by Joseph Mendinhall a subscribing witness & ordered to be Registered.

A Deed of conveyance from John Gray to Young Lemar for two hundred acres of Land was acknowledged in open Court & ordered to be Registered.

Richard Mitchell obtained leave & returned the following List of taxable property to Court for the year A.D. 1805 towit, 1500 acres of Land to Jesse Benns place 640 acres mouth of Jerman Creek.

Henry Hawkins obtained & returns the following List Taxable property to Court for the year A.D. 1805 towit, one white poll & two hundred acres of Land.

A Bill of Sale from William James for three negroes towit, one named Fann, one negro man named Fill was acknowledged in open Court and ordered to be Recorded.

Henry Holston obtained leave & returns to Court one hundred & twelve acres of Land for which he is subject to pay tax for the year 1805.

A Bill of Sale from Jessie James to William Hamilton for a negro man named Bob was acknowledged in open Court & ordered to be Recorded.

A Deed of conveyance from Thomas Cunningham to Henry Holston for one hundred & twelve acres of Land was proven in open Court by Nathaniel Austin a subscribing witness & ordered to be Recorded.

A Deed of conveyance from Henry Howell to John Howell for one hundred acres of Land was acknowledged in open Court & ordered to be Registered.

A Bill of Sale from Thomas Galleyon to James Ritcheson for a negro boy named Joshua was acknowledged in open Court & ordered to be Recorded.

A Deed of conveyance from Henry Howell to Malachia Howell for two hundred acres of Land was acknowledged in open Court & ordered to be Registered.

A Deed of conveyance from John Beaty to James Wilson for two hundred acres of Land was proven in open Court by the oath of John Lea a subscribing witness & ordered to be Registered.

A Deed of conveyance to David Spencer for three hundred acres of Land was proven in open Court by John Acuff a subscribing witness & ordered to be Registered.

A Lease from James Ore to Floid Allison & Company for his dwelling house &c on German Creek for the term of four years was proven in open Court by the oath of Thomas Henderson a subscribing witness & ordered to be recorded.

Benjamin Blake who stands charged with begetting a bastard child on the Body of Mary Riggs comes into Court & enters into Bond in the sum of five hundred dollars with Malachia Howell & Henry Ivey his security to indemnify the County against the maintenance of said child.

(p 103)   May Sessions A.D. 1805.

A Bill of Sale from John Burd to Abraham Burd (Bird) for a bay horse & rifle gun was acknowledged in open Court & ordered to be Recorded.

Ordered by Court that George Sparkman be overseer of the road from Crows to the top of Clinch mountain at the Powder Spring Gap in the room of Robert D. Eaton & that the same bounds be allowed him for hands to work on said road that was allowed said Eaton.

An execution was returned to Court by Ashley (Noah) in the following words & figures, towit, "You are hereby "commanded to execute & sell as much of the goods Lands & tenements, the property of John Hunter" as will satisfy a Judgment obtained against him by William Hall with all lawful costs, "the sum of thirty nine dollars & seventy five cents giving under my hand this 21 day of February 1805.
(sign) Philip Sigler.

On which execution an indorsment is found in the work following, towit, "there being no personal property of the defendant found February 2 day 1805 executed by Noah Sahley constable one hundred acres of Deeded Land including one hundred acres of a claim of the property of John Hunter to satisfy a Judgment obtained by William Hall.
(Signed) Noah Ashley.

On motion of John Williams Esqr. the Court direct that an execution issue to the Sheriff of Grainger County commanding him to sell the above tracts of Land Levied on by Noah Ashley or so much thereof as will be sufficient to satisfy the sum of thirty nine Dollars & seventy five cents & costs.

Court adjourns till tomorrow 9 o'clock.

Tuesday 21st. May Court met according to adjournment. Justices present -Major Lea, Noah Jarnagin, David MC Anally & Henry Bowman.

Henry Howell)
    vs)   Justices present, Major Lea, Noah Jarnagin, David
Francis Dannell)   McAnally, Henry Boatman, Charles McAnally, Rubin
Riggs & Josiah Midkiff. Whereupon came a Jury, towit, Thomas Henderson,
William Kirkun, Robert Long, James Brown, George Boatman, Thomas Mann,
John Shropshier, Benjamin Shaw, Samuel Taylor, Tandy Senter, John Moffitt,
& William McPhetridge, who being Elected tried & sworn the truth to speak
on the issue Joined in this case do say they find the Defendant not Guilty in manner & form as the plaintiff in his declaration hath complained
against him; from which the plaintiff prays an appeal to the next Superior Court of Law to be holden for the District of Hamilton at the Court-
House in Knoxville on the fourth Monday of September next, and the said
plaintiff enters into Bond with John Cooke & Josiah Dyer his securities
and the said plaintiff by his Atty. files his reasons for appealing -
appeal granted.

Joshua Roach obtained leave & returned to Court an oth a List of taxable property for the year 1805 towit, sixty acres of Land & one white
poll.

A Deed of conveyance from Henry Ivey to Moses Hodges for fifty acres
of Land was proven in Court by the oath of Francis Darnell a subscribing
witness & ordered to be Registered.

A Deed of conveyance from Thomas Busby to Josiah Dyer for twenty five
acres of Land was proven in open Court by Abner Dyer a subscribing witness
& ordered to be Registered.

Ordered by Court that Jesse Kitchen be overseer of the road from
Coxes old place to the Knox Line in the room of Mathew Campbell & that he
be allowed to call on all the hands on Walter Adays plantation to work
under him on said road in addition to the hands living in the bounds
that were allowed said Campbell.

A Deed of conveyance from Amos Reed to John F. Jack for Lot number
twenty five in the town of Rutledge was proven in open Court by the oath
of Thomas Warren a subscribing witness and ordered to be Registered.

Thomas Henderson -Lewis Harmon & William Clay Commissioners appointed by Court to settle with Col. James Ore Administrator of James Short -
deceased report to Court that the Estate of said deceased is indebted to
the said James Ore fifteen dollars and one half of a cent.

William Kirk obtained leave & returns upon oath to Court one white
poll for taxes for the year A.D. 1805.

(p 104)   May Sessions A.D. 1805

William Kirk for John Sharp obtains leave & returns in open Court
one white poll for which the said John Sharp is subject to pay tax for
the year A.D. 1805.

The Court proceeded to ballot for Jurors to the Superior Court for
Hamilton district to be held at Knoxville September next & on comparing
the Votes it appears that William Mitchell, Pleasant Duke, William Bowman

& Bartley Marshall drawn Jurors.

Ordered by Court that the following Tax be laid & collected as a poor tax in Grainger County for the year A.D. 1805 towit,

On each hundred acres of Land six cents.
" " white poll three cents.
" " Black poll six cents.

James Spradling being sworn saith he is upwards of fifty five years old & on application the Court direct that the said James Spradling be exempt from the payment of a poll tax for time to come.

Ordered by Court that William Hall be allowed the sum of ten dollars for furnishing Charles Asher and Elizabeth Asher his wife with provisions from November term eighteen hundred & four till February Term following agreeably to order of Court at November Term aforesaid. Issd.

The Court appoint John Taylor overseer of the road from Beans Station to the intersection of the river road near John Coulters in the room of John Hodge & that he have the same Bounds for hands allowed him to work on said road that were allowed said Hodge. Issd.

Ordered by Court that David Holt be allowed the sum of twenty five dollars for keeping & maintaining Jeremiah McBriff one of the poor of this County from February Term 1805 till May term following. Issd.

Ordered by Court that John Lea Esqr. high Sheriff be allowed the sum of Eighty Dollars for his Ex Officio services from May term 1804 till May term 1804 till May term 1805. Issd.

Ordered by Court that Ambrose Yancey Esqr. Clerk of Grainger County be allowed the sum of Forty five dollars for his Ex Officio services & making out the tax Lists for the year A.D. 180- commencing at May term 1804 & ending at May term 1805. Issd.

Ordered by Court that John Cocke Solicitor of the County be allowed the sum of fifteen dollars for his services as Solicitor at November Term 1804 and also the sum of fifteen dollars for his services as Solicitor of the County be allowed the sum of fifteen dollars for his services as Solicitor at November Term 1804 and also the sum of Fifteen dollars for his services as Solicitor at the present Term. Issd.

Betsy Miller a minor heir of George Miller deceased aged about sixteen years comes into Court & chooses Martin Miller her Guardian & the said Martin Miller enters into Bond in the sum of one thousand Dollars with John Cocke —John Shropshire & Isaac Thompson his securities.

Ordered by Court that William Hall furnish Charles Asher & Elizabeth Asher his wife with provisions till next Court for which he is to be allowed a reasonable compensation.

James Ore obtained leave & returns upon oath in open Court the following List of taxable property for the year 1805, towit, 2208 acres of

The Court appoint the following persons Jurors to the next Session of this Court, towit, Robert D. Eaton, Chesley Jarnagin, John Thompson, Archibald McCarver, Daniel Taylor, John Estis, William Milligan, Duncan Carmichael -William Bowman, William Shelton, James Macfarland, Mathew Campbell, Richard Acuff, Jesse McKinney, Jesse Jinnings Senr. Benjamin Condry, William Hamilton, Joseph Yeaden, William Shields, William Street Stephen W.Senter, John Holt Senr. Francis Dannell, Sherod Mays, Thomas Dennis, Peter Harmock. Benjamin Elliot, Joseph Bryant, Nicholas Countz, Henry Bowen Jr. Hercules Ogles, James Bowen, George Cirole, Jesse Cheek Hugh Larimore, John Cannon, Dawson Cheek & Pleasant Duke & James Carmichael.

Court adjourns till tomorrow 9 o'clock.

(p 105)   May Sessions A.D. 1805
        Wednesday 22nd. May Court met according to adjournment, Justices present, Henry Boatman, Rubin Riggs, David McAnally & Major Lea.

Nathaniel Davis)
No. 278 vs   )   Justices present, Major Lea, David Lea, David Mc
Joseph Ray   )   Anally, Rubin Riggs, & John Bradon, whereupon came
a Jury, towit, Thomas Henderson, Isaac Midliff, William Kirkum, Robert Long, Henry Howell, Nisbit Allen. Moses McElhiney, John Duke, Jackson Smith, John Shropshire, John Hargraves & John Hammill, who being elected tried and sworn the truth to speak on the issue Joined in this case do say the Defendant did assume in manner and form as the plaintiff in his declaration hath alledged against him & assess the plaitiffs damages to Eighty seven dollars & ninety eight cents besides his costs.

John Gold   )
No. 305 vs   )   Justices present, Charles McAnally Rubin Riggs
Robert C.Gordon)   Major Lea, John Bradon, Henry Boatman, Noah Jarnagin & David McAnally.Whereupon came a Jury, towit, James Bowen, Malachia Howell, James Blair Jr. John Crabb, George Boatman, Abraham Pruit, Thomas Turley, James Conn, William Harris, Stephen Smith, Duncan Philips & James Harris who being elected tried and sworn the truth to speak on the issue Joined in this case having retired to consider of their Verdict & not being able to agree a mistrial is entered by Consent.

Hugh L.White   )
No. 322 vs   )
Bartley Marshall)   Justices present, Rubin Riggs, Peter Harris & James
Moore, whereupon came a Jury, towit, the same Jury as in the suit No.278 who being Elected tried and sworn the truth to speak on the issue Joined in this case do say the Defendant hath not paid the Debt in the Declaration mentioned as in pleading he hath alledged & assess the plaintiffs damages occasioned by the detention of that debt to three dollars forty one cents - Seven mills & costs.

Richard Reynolds)
      vs   )   the plaintiff by John Cocke his Attorney makes a
Robert Yancey   )   motion to Court to enter up a Judgment against
Robert Yancey for the sum of forty two dollars which he alledged he has been compelled to pay as security of the said Robert Yancey on and

execution issued on a Judgment rendered in the Court of Grainger County against the said Robert Yancey & the said Richard Reynolds & others securities of the said Robert Yancey and it appearing to the satisfaction of the Court that the said Richard Reynolds has been compelled to pay the aforesaid sum of money as security of the said Robert Yancey -It is therefore considered by the Court that the said Richard Reynolds do recover the aforesaid sum of Forty two Dollars against the said Robert Yancey besides his costs.

John Moffitt Admr. of
William Moffitt -deceased.
No. 327 vs
William Bryant

   Justices present, Peter Harris, Rubin Riggs & James Moore, whereupon came a Jury, towit, the same Jury as in No. 278- except John McElhiney in the room of Jackson Smith who being Elected tried & sworn the truth to speak on the Matter in dispute in this case do say they find for the plaintiff and assess his damages to Forty four dollars & ninety five cents & costs- Rule for a new trial on Argument Rule discharged.

(p 103)   May Sessions A.D. 1805
State
 vs
Tapley Haygood   Isaac Midkiff surrenders Tapley Haygood in open Court in discharge of himself and the said Tapley is ordered in custody of the Sheriff.

Thomas Bunch
  vs   Thomas Bunch plaintiff by John Cocke his Attorney makes
Robert Yancey a motion to Court to enter up a Judgment against the said Robert Yancey for the sum of one hundred & six Dollars which sum he alledged he has been compelled to pay as security of the said Robert Yancey for the sum of one hundred & six Dollars which sum he alledged he has been compelled to pay as security of the said Robert Yancey on sundry executions issued on Judgment recovered in the Court of Grainger County against the said Robert Yancey & Thomas Bunch & others security of the said Robert Yancey and it being made Manifest to the Court that the said Thomas Bunch has paid the aforesaid sum of money as one of the securities of the said Robert Yancey- It is therefore considered by the Court that the said Thomas do recover the aforesaid sum of one hundred & six dollars against the said Robert Yancey together with his costs. Ex.Isd.26 July 1811

  Ordered by Court that John Lea Sheriff of Grainger County be allowed the sum of four Dollars twelve and one half cents for money he hath heretofore paid for repairing & guarding the Jail of said County. Isd.

  Edward West obtained leave & returns upon oath in Court for Absolem Howard 300 acres of Land the property of the said Howard for the tax of the year A.D. 1805.

  Court adjourns till tomorrow 9 o'clock.

  Thursday 23rd. May Court met according to adjournment.

Justices present, David McAnally, Rubin Biggs. Charles McAnally &
Henry Boatman.

State   )
No. 86- vs   )
John Holt   )   Thomas Henderson, George Boatman, Robert Long, William
Kirkus, James Brown, John Hammill, Moses McElhiney -pd. John Moffitt,
John Bean, Thomas Turley, Tandy Senter & John McElhiney- who being elec-
ted tried & sworn the truth to speak on the issue Jpined in this case
do say they find the Defendant guilty in manner & form as he stands
charged in the Bill of Indictment -Rule for a new trial- on argument rule
discharged whereupon the Court impose a fine of Ten dollars on the said
John Holt.

A Deed of conveyance from Robert King to David McAnally for two Hundred acres of Land was proven in open Court by the oath of Charles Mc
Anally a subscribing witness & ordered to be Registered.

A Deed of conveyance from William Clay To Carrick Montgomery &c for
Lot No. 45- in the town of Rutledge was proven in open Court by the oath
of William Sims a subscribing witness & ordered to be Registered.

Ordered by Court that the firm of Allison, Floid & Conn have leave
to keep a ordinary or house of public Intertainment on German Creek in
the home lately occupied by Col. James Ore & enters into Bond in the
sum of twelve hundred & fifty Dollars with Thomas Mann & Pleasant Duke
his securities.

The Grand Jury is dismissed from further attendance at the present
Term.

Ordered by Court that the Sheriff be directed to summon a Jury of
twelve freeholders to enquire by Inquisition into the situation of Jonathan Pickeral of this County relative to his being in a state of Idiocy
or Lunacy & also what estate he is possessed of real or personal if any
there be & make report to next Court.   Issd.

(p 107)   May Sessions A.D. 1805

Ordered by Court that William Clay Esqr. have leave to keep an ordinary or house of public entertainment at his dwelling house in the richland Valley & he enters into bond in the sum of (penal) twelve hundred &
fifty dollars. with Noah Jarnagin Esqr. his security.

State   )
No. 87- vs   )   Justices present, Charles McAnally, Major Lea, Henry
James Conn   )   Boatman, & William Clay.
Whereupon came a Jury, towit, Isaac Midkiff, Malachia Howell, Abra-
ham Pruit- pd. James Blair-Jr. pd. John Crabb, John Hall, William Windham,
Daniel Clayton, Valentine Morgan, Robert McElhiney, Henry Howell & John
Wells who being Elected tried and sworn the truth to speak on the issue
Jpined in this case do say they find the Defendant guilty in manner & form
as he stands charged in the Bill of Indictment whereupon came the Court
impose a fine of twenty five cents.

Ordered by Court that Francis Willet Constable of the grand Jury be allowed the sum of one dollar each day for four days he has attended the grand Jury at the present Term.

Court adjourns for half an hour.

Court met according to adjournment. Justices present, Major Lea, Noah Jarnagin & Charles McAnally.

State
No. 90- vs
Joseph Noe Senr.
) the Bill of Indictment in this case having been sent to the Grand Jury without the name of the Solicitor signed thereto & being returned to Court with the following Indorsement thereon, towit, "A true Bill —Moses Hodges foreman the grand Jury being dismissed the Solicitor moved for leave to sign his name to the Bill of Indictment —On argument the Court do not grant leave.

State
vs
Joseph Rich
) Justices present, Henry Boatman, Major Lea & Noah Jarnagin, whereupon came a Jury towit, John McElhiney, Malachia Howell, Abraham Fruit, pd- James Blair Jr. pd. John Crabb, John Hall William Windham, Daniel Clayton, Valentine Morgan, Robert McElhiney, Henry Howell & John Wells, who being Elected tried & sworn the truth to speak on issue Joined in this case do say they find the Defendant guilty in manner & form as he stands charged in the Bill of Indictment, whereupon the Court impose a Fine of Twenty five cents.

State
vs
John Green
) John McElhiney who stands bound by Recognizence for the appearance of John Green from day to day surrenders him in Court in discharge of himself.

Ordered by Court that Jeremiah Jarnagin be appointed overseer of the road from the stand Lick branch to the first large spring above Chesley Jarnagins in the room of Noah Jarnagin Esqr. & that the same Bounds be allowed him for hands towork on said road that was allowed said Noah Jarnagin.

Henry Hipsher Admr. of Mathias Hipsher deceased
vs
Robert Yancey late Sheriff and his securities.

The motion made in this case at last term to enter up a Judgment against Robert Yancey & his securities for failing to pay over one hundred & sixty dollars ninety one cents & one half of a cent which the said Robert Yancey had collected on an execution against George Bean & Isaac Cooper in favor of the Plaintiff was taken up for argument & after examination Testimony It is considered by the Court that the said plaintiff take nothing by his motion.

(p 108)   May Sessions A.D. 1805

Ordered by Court that James Dyer Constable be notified to attend the next Sessions of this Court as constable of the Grand Jury.

Ordered by Court that Samuel Cox & Francis Willet Constable attend the next session of this Court.

It is ordered by the Court that the following Tracts of Land which was reported to Court at May Term 1804 and which have been published in the Knoxville Gazette agreeably to Law be sold for the payment of the tax due thereon Viz. For the year 1801 1500 acres of Land the property of James McNair, 400 acres of Land the property of William Henry 640 acres of Land the property of James Scruggs 300 acres of Land the property of James Spencer -300 acres of Land the property of John Jones, 200 acres of Land the property of Robert Smith, 100 acres of land the property of William Howell For the year 1802- 5000 acres of Land the property of John Odonnell, 3250 acres of Land the property of David Harts heirs, 150 acres of Land the property of David Harris- For the year 1803- 640 acres Land the property of Joseph Gentry, 200 acres of Land the property of John Lebow - 5000 acres of Land the property of John Odonnell.

Robert Yancey late Sheriff & collector of taxes in Grainger County reported to Court that the taxes remained unpaid on the following Late in the town of Grantsborough for the year A.D. 1805 and that he can not find any goods & chattles of the owners thereof within his County on which he can distress, towit, 4 lots the property of Charles Lee Burd -3 Lots the property of James V.Ball- 2 Lots the property of Richard Chandler, 2 Lots the property of Patrick Campbell- 1 lot the property of George Wilson- It is therefore ordered by the Court that the clerk make out a Certificate of the same together with the amount of the taxes & charges due thereon and cause the same to be twice published in the Knoxville Gazette giving notice that the same will be sold or so much thereof as will pay the taxes & charges due thereon.

On application the Court release David Hailey from the payment of the sum of three Dollars & twenty five cents the amount of his state & County tax for the year 1802 it appearing to the satisfaction of the Court that the said David Hailey stands charged twice on the tax List for said year- and it is ordered by the Court that Robert Yancey late Sheriff & collector of taxes have a credit in his settlement with the Treasury of the District of Washington & Hamilton for the sum of one dollar sixty two & one half cents; and also a credit in his settlement with the Trustee of Grainger County for the further sum of one dollar sixty two and one half cents.   Issd. Due Treasurer.

On application the Court Release Robert Yancey late Sheriff & collector of Grainger County from the collection & payment of the sum of Twenty five cents being the amount of the State & County tax with which Peter Tuttle stands charged twice on the Tax Lists for the year 1802 and it is ordered by the Court that the said Robert Yancey have a credit for the sum of twelve & one half cents in his settlement with the trustee of Grainger County & also a further credit for the sum of twelve & one half cents in this settlement with the Treasurer of the Districts of Washington & Hamilton.

On application the Court release Robert Yancey late Sheriff & collector of taxes in Grainger County from the collection & payment of the sum of twenty five cents being the amount of the State & County tax with which Peter Tuttle stands charged twice on the Tax Lists for the year 1802 and it is ordered by the Court that the said Robert Yancey have a credit for the sum of twelve and one half cents in his settlement with the trustee of Grainger County; & also a further credit for the sum of twelve & one half cents in this settlement with the Treasurer of the Districts of Washington & Hamilton. Issd. D. Treasurer.

On application the Court release Robert Yancey late Sheriff & collector of taxes in Grainger County from the collection & payment of the sum of twenty five cents, the amount of the State & County tax with which William Tuttle stands charged for the year 1802 and the said Robert Yancey making it appear to the satisfaction of the Court that he could not find any person that he could not find any persons by the name of William Tuttle within this County of whom he could collect the taxes – It is ordered that the said Robert Yancey have a credit for the sum of twelve and one half cents in his settlement with the Treasurer of the districts of Washington & Hamilton & also a credit for the sum of twelve & one half cents in his settlement with the Trustee of Grainger County.
Issd. D. Treasurer.

(p 109)   May Sessions A.D. 1805.

On application the Court release Robert Yancey late Sheriff & collector of Grainger County from the payment of the sum of $2.42 of being the amount of the State & County tax with which it has bee made manifest to Court that David Bunch was overcharged on the Tax Lists & with the collection & payment of which the said Robert Yancey stands bound It is therefore ordered by Court that the said Robert Yancey have a credit in his settlement with the Treasurer of the Districts of Washington & Hamilton for the sum of one dollar twenty one and one fourth cents and also a credit for the sum of one Dollar twenty one & one fourth cents in his settlement with the Trustee of Grainger County. Issd. D. Tres.

Court adjourns till tomorrow 9 o'clock.

Friday 24th May Court met according to adjournment. Justices present, Major Lea, Noah Jarnagin & William Clay.

A Bill of Sale from John Lea Admr. of David Inman deceased to John Keen for a negro boy named George was proven in open Court by Luke Lea a subscribing witness & ordered to be Recorded.

State   )
No. 89- vs   )
Joseph Noe Sr.   )   Whereupon came a Jury, to wit, Thomas Henderson, George Boatman, James Brown, William Kirkum, Malachia Howell, Tendy Senter John Harddll –Abraham Pruit –pd. John Moffitt, James Blair pd. Jr. Robert Long & John Crabb who being elected tried & sworn the truth to speak on the issue Joined in this case do say they find the Defendant Guilty in manner & form as he stands charged in the Bill of Indictment whereupon the Court Impose a Fine of Ten dollars.

A Deed of conveyance from Daniel Clayton to Frederick Moyers for three acres of Land one rod twenty eight & one half polls was acknowledged in open Court & ordered to be Registered.

Denn on the Demise of)
Henry Rowell)
vs) John Lea Sheriff to whom the Defendant in this
Fenn & Isaiah Midkiff) case has been surrendered brings him into Court & surrenders him in discharge of himself —whereupon the Attorney for the plaintiff prays him in custody & he is in custody of the Sheriff.

Josiah & John Nichol)
vs)
John Spring) Luke Lea Attorney for the plaintiffs makes a motion to Court that an order of sale in this may issue to the Sheriff commanding him to sell the property Levied on in this case to satisfy the sum of Twenty one Dollars twenty three and three fourths cents Debt & Costs.

James Cozby
vs- Sci.Fa.
Thomas Henderson and John Margraves securities of Robert Yancey.

In this case after Judgment on the Scire Facias —Thomas Henderson one of the Special of Robert Yancey surrenders him in open Court in discharge of himself & John Margraves from which Judgment the said Thomas and John prays an appeal to the next Superior Court of Law for Hamilton District —Reasons for appeal filed.

(p 110) May Sessions A.D. 1805

James Cozby
vs
Thomas Henderson & John Margraves
securities of Robert Yancey.

Judgment in this case having been entered against Thomas Henderson & John Margraves by Default; and afterwards came the said Thomas by Pleasant M.Miller his Attorney & make a motion to Court to set aside the Judgment by Default; and the said thomas states facts on oath to Court why said Judgment should be set aside; and upon examination & consideration the said Judgment is set aside; whereupon the said Thomas immediately surrenders the said Robert in open Court in discharge of himself & John Margraves the said Robert is prayed in custody of the sheriff by plaintiffs Attorney & is ordered in custody accordingly.

John Lea Sheriff enters his protset against the Jail of Grainger County because he alledges it is insufficient for the safekeeping of prisoners.

William Windham)
vs)
Robert Yancey) the Defendant in this case surrenders himself in open Court in discharge of Spencer Griffin & Philip Combs his securities.

Ordered by Court that John Lebow continue Overseer of the road from the Line of Hawkins County to the house of John Crabb and that the hands

on Thomas Henderson plantation and upwards to the County Line & on the
North side of the road work with him on said road.   Issd.

Ordered by Court that John Crabb be appointed overseer of the road
from his own house to the Line between the Lands of Thomas Johnston &
Col. James Ore and that all the hands below the plantation of Thomas
Henderson down to the upper end of Thomas Johnsons Land & square across
the valley be the hands to work under him on said road.   Issd.

Ordered by Court that John Conn be overseer of the road from the
Line between the Lands of Col. James Ore & Thomas Johnsons to Beans Station and that the hands on Thomas Johnsons plantation, and all below
said Johnsons & above the plantation of Jenkin Whiteside & Joseph Cobb
on both sides of the road from the Hobbs to Clinch mountain be the hands
to work with him on said road & keep the same in good repair, Issd.
according to Law.

John Howmill   )
    vs   )   Justices present, Major Lea, Noah Jarnagin, William
Ambrose Yancey   )   Clay & Henry Boatman, whereupon came a Jury, towit
Thomas Henderson, George Boatman, James Brown, William Kirkum, Malachia
Howell, Tandy Senter, Henry Howell, Abraham Pruit, John Moffitt, James
Blair pd. Jr. Robert Land & John Crabb who being Elected tried & sworn
the truth to speak on the issue joined in this case do say the Defendant hath paid the sum of sixty one Dollars thirty one cents and one half
of a cent & no more, they find the sum of Fifty eight dollars sixty eight
& one half cents the balance of the Debt in the Declaration mentioned &
assess the plaintiffs occationed by the detention of the Debt to nineteen Dollars & eighty four cents, besides his costs.

Court adjourns till Court in Course.

Major Lea -Chn.

(p 111)   August Sessions A.D. 1805

At a Court of Pleas and Quarter Sessions begun and holden for the
County of Grainger at the Court House in Rutledge on the third Monday in
August A.D. 1805 being the nineteenth of the same month.

Justices present, Noah Jarnagin, Henry Boatman, Rubin Riggs, &
Isaiah Midkiff.

John Lea Esquire high Sheriff returns to Court that he has executed
the following Venire Facias on the following persons except William Milligan, John Holt & George Circle. Viz.

1- Robert D. Eaton   7- William Milligan
2- Chesley Jernagin   8- Duncan Carmichael
3- John Thompson   9- Jems Carmichael
4- Archibald McCarver   10-William Bowman
5- Daniel Taylor   11-William Shelton
6- John Estis   12-Jems McFarland
                          13-Mathew Campbell

14- Richard Acuff
15- Jesse McKinney
16- Jesse Jinings
17- Joseph Yeadin
18- William Shiblds
19- William Street
20- Stephen W. Senter
21- John Holt Sr.
22- Benjamin Gondry
23- William Hamilton
24- Francis Daniel
25- Sherod Hays
26- Thomas Dennis

27- Peter Harmock
28- Benjamin Elliot
29- Joseph Bryant
30- Nicholas Countz
31- Henry Bowen Jr.
32- Harcules Ogles
33- James Bowen
34- George Circle
35- Jesse Cheek
36- Hugh Larimore
37- John Cannon
38- Bowman Cheek &
39- Pleasant Duke

Out of which Entire Number the persons whose names are underwritten were drawn a Grand Jury for the present Term Viz.

1- John Estis Foreman
2- Benjamin Elliot
3- Peter Harmock
4- William Hamilton
5- Duncan Carmichael
6- Chesley Jarnagin
7- Henry Bowen Jr.
8- Joseph Bryant

9- Joseph Yeadin
10-John Thompson
11-James Bowen
12-William Shields
13-Jesse Jinings Sr.
14-Stephen W. Senter &
15-Francis Daniel

Who were sworn and charged by John Cooke Esqr. Solicitor.

Samuel Cox Constable sworn to attend the Grand Jury at the present Term.

On motion George Parmpile has leave to administer on the estate of Christian Parmpile deceased it appearing to the satisfaction of the Court that Rachael Parmpile widow and relict of the deceased hath relinquished her right of administration and he enters into Bond in the sum of five Dollars with John Estes & Aaron Dishon his securities and was qualified, Fsd.

Ordered by Court that Robert Huddleston be appointed a constable and he enters into Bond in the sum of five hundred Dollars with Thomas Huddleston & John Peters his securities and takes the oath prescribed by Law.

A Deed of conveyance from Jeremiah Jarnagin to Newberry Jones for forty acres of Land be the same more or less was proven in open Court by John Horner a subscribing witness and ordered to be Registered.

(p 112)   August Sessions A.D. 1805.
The last Will and testament of John Archer was exhibited to Court for probate and the due execution thereof was proven by John Estis and Aaron Dishon two of the subscribing witnesses and ordered to be Recorded.

Ordered by Court that Wilson English be overseer of the River road from Buffalow Creek to Williams branch in the room of James Alsop and that all the hands in the Bounds of the road running from Crows to Moore's ferry, thence up the river to Stiffeys Hill creek thence up said creek to the head, thence a direct course to the Buffalow hollow including Jonathan Theseys & William Guinn, thence a direct course to the head of Buffalow creek work under him on said road.   Order Issd.

A Deed of conveyance from Joel Horner to Noble Keith for seventeen acres of Land & one fourth of an acre was acknowledged in open Court & ordered to be Registered.

A Deed of conveyance from Martin Albert to William Clay, William Hall, William Hankins & Robert Patterson commissioners for a Lot in the town of Rutledge being Lot No. 48 in the plan of said town was proven in open Court by John Cocke a subscribing witness and ordered to be Registered.

A Deed of conveyance from Benjamin Howell to Henry Boatman for three acres of Land was proven in open Court by George Boatman a subscribing witness and ordered to be Registered.

The last Will and testament of Frederick Snyder was exhibited to Court for probate, and the due execution thereof proven in open Court by Edward McGinnis and Joshua two of the subscribing witnesses and ordered to be Recorded thereupon Elizabeth Snyder nominated & appointed executrix therein comes into Court, was qualified & took upon herself the execution thereof.

A Deed of conveyance from John Horner to Michael Moyers for a Lot in the town of Rutledge being Lot No. 4 in the plan of said town was proven in Court by the oath of Samuel Peery a subscribing witness & ordered to be Registered.

A Deed of conveyance from John Cocke to Francis Willet for three hundred acres of Land was acknowledged in Court and ordered to be Registered.

Ordered by Court that Peter Havrock be overseer of the road from the meeting house at William Halls to Beelers old mill in the room of John Moyers and that all the hands in the following bounds work on said road, towit-Beginning at John Havrocks North of the Copper Ridge, thence along said ridge opposite to William Pattons thence to the Log mountain so as to include said Patton, thence along the Log mountain opposite the Beginning.

Israel Elliot one of the Executors of William Elliot deceased returns to Court an account of the property of old by the executers of said deceased.

The last Will and Testament of Archelic Gibson deceased was exhibited to Court for probate and the due execution thereof was proven in Court by James Moore and William Gibson subscribing witnesses and ordered to be Recorded.

Ordered by Court that James Kinneys be overseer of the road from Begms Station to the intersection of the river road near John Coulters in the room of John Taylor and that he have the same bounds allowed him for hands to work on said road that was allowed said Taylor. Order Issd.

A Deed of conveyance from Bartholomew Smith to John Howell for a

Lot in the town of Rutledge being Lot No. 42 was proven in open Court by William Stone a subscribing witness & ordered to be Registered.

(p 113)   August Sessions A.D.1805

A Deed of conveyance from William Hall, Robert Patterson, William Clay & William Haskins Commissioners &c. to Bartholomew Smith for a Lot in the town of Rutledge being Lot No. 49 was proven in open Court by William Stone a subscribing witness & ordered to be Registered.

Ordered by Court that John Hailey be overseer of the road in the place of William Arnold and that he have the same bounds allowed him for hands to work on said Road that was allowed said Arnold. Order Issd.

It appearing to the satisfaction of the Court by an Inquisition duly taken & returned pursuant to the Statute in such cases made and provided that Jonathan Pickeral is insane and incapable of taking care of himself wherefore the Court appoint James Reddin Guardian to take charge of the person & Estate of the said Jonathan Pickeral and he enters into Bond in the sum of five hundred Dollars with Edwin Riggs & Felps Reed securities &c. Justices present, Hugh Jernigin, William Clay, Henry Bratton.&c

By order of Court James Kennedy has leave to keep an ordinary or house of public entertainment at Beans Station and he enters into bond in the sum of twelve hundred and fifty Dollars with Jenkins Whiteside his security.

Ordered by Court that David Holt be overseer of the road in the room of Tandy Senter from Beans Station to the first branch below Jesse Beans old place and that Charles Kidwell, Elijah Donathans hands, Nicholas Sharp John Sharp and all the hands living between the river ridge & the top of Clinch Mountain and between Beans Station and Tandy Senters (except those in William Kirks bounds be allowed him to work on said road as lately laid out by the Jury.

A Bill of Sale from William Windham to Jacob Lebow for a negro fellow named Wittim was proven in Court by John Lebow a subscribing witness & ordered to be Recorded.

A Release from Henry Hoggard to William Williams for one hundred & forty acres of Land was proven in open Court by John Morris, a subscribing witness & ordered to be Registered.

Samuel Adkins   )
     vs   )   On an execution issued in this case by William Clay
Spencer Griffin   )   Esqr. for forty six dollars principal & two dollars
& seventy six cents interest and one dollar for costs –

James Dyer Constable makes the following return, towit,   Levied the within execution on different Lands as follows Viz. one hundred and fifty acres at the Panther springs a part of 500 acres., also 300 acres on the North side of Clinch mountain adjoining Samuel Clarks the place John Spencer formerly occupied also Levied on three lots in the town of

Rutledge Levied on all as the property of Spencer Griffin as could find no personal property- James Dyer- Const.

It is ordered by the Court that an execution do issue to the Sheriff of Grainger County commanding him to sell the Lands Levied on as aforesaid by James Dyer constable or so much as will be sufficient to satisfy the aforesaid sum of forty eight dollars & seventy six cents Debt and damages & one Dollar for costs- Exr. Issd.

Major Lea)
   vs)
John Spring & Robert Moore)

Ordered by Court that John Lea Sheriff be allowed twenty five cents per day for each day he has kept a Stud horse Levied on by attachment in this case.

Ordered by Court that Robert Long be released from the payment of fifty cents, he having been so much overcharged on the tax Lists for the Season of a Stud horse for the year A.D. 1805. Copy Issd.

(p 114)   August Sessions A.D. 1805.

Court adjourns till tomorrow 9 o'clock.

Tuesday 20th August Court met according to adjournment.
Justices present, Peter Harris, Robin Riggs and John Breaden.

John Crabb)
No. 335- vs)   Whereupon came a Jury, towit-William Bowman, Hugh Lari-
John Bull)   more, Thomas Dennis, James McFarland, Archibald McCarver
John Corman, William Arnold, Joseph Noe Sr. Joseph Rich, William Mc Phetridge, Thomas Warren & Thomas Bunch who being elected, tried & sworn the truth to speak on the Issue Joined in this case do say they find the Defendant not guilty in manner & form as the plaintiff in his Declaration hath alledged against him- Rule for a new Trial.

Stewart Harris who stands bound by Recognizance to the present Term charged with begetting a bastard child on the body of Aley Troglon comes into Court and enters into bond in the penal sum of five hundred dollars with Robert Harris -Meredith Coffy his securities, conditioned to indemnify the County against the maintnence of said child.

John Denn lessee of Henry Roberts)
   vs)
Venn and Benjamin Shaw)

John McElhiney one of the special Bail of Benjamin Shaw surrenders him in open Court in discharge of himself whereupon Charles McAnally & John Dodson comes into Court and become special bail for the said Defendant.

Ordered by Court that William Hall be allowed the sum of Eleven Dollars and fifty cents for furnishing Charles Asher and Elizabeth Asher his wife with provisions from May term A.D. 1805 till Aug. term following.

Issd.

127

On motion of John Cooke Solicitor to fine Stephen Bean for a contempt committed in open Court and testimony being given touching said contempt It is considered by the Court that the said Stephen Bean be fined Ten dollars for said contempt, and for a continuance of his contemptuous behavior in open Court that the said Stephen Bean be fined another sum of ten dollars and for a repetition of his contempt to the Court and a further continuance of the contemptuous conduct in the presence of the Court; It is considered by the Court that the said Stephen Bean be fined in the sum of Thirty dollars and that he be & remain in the custody of the Sheriff till fine and costs are paid; and it is ordered by the Court that the Sheriff do summon a sufficient guard, to guard the County Jail till tomorrow morning.

On application to Court by Major Lea Esqr. It is ordered by the Court that the said Major Lea have leave to erect a Grist-mill on his own Land on Richland Creek.

Ordered by Court that Thomas Shipley be overseer of the road from Marshalls ford on the South bank of Holston river to the County Line in the direction of Cheeks Cross roads in the room of Thomas Mann and that he have the same bounds allowed him for hands to work on said road that was allowed said Mann. Issd.

Ordered by the Court that David Holt be allowed the sum of Twenty five dollars for keeping and maintaining Jeremiah Midkiff one of the poor of this County from May Sessions A.D. 1805 till Aug. Term following. Ord.

(p 115)   August Sessions A.D. 1805

A Deed of conveyance from Duncan Carmichael to James Carmichael for 250 acres of Land more or less was acknowledged in open Court & ordered to be Registered.

A Deed of conveyance from James Carmichael to Duncan Carmichael for 50 acres of Land more or less was acknowledged in open Court & ordered to be Registered.

Johnbury by John F.Jack has leave and returns in open Court Ten thousand acres of Land for which he is bound to pay taxes for the year A.D. 1805.

William Clay esqr. returns to Court a list of strays as follows, towit, A List of strays remaining on my books & not proven away in twelve months, of the following specifications, towit, John Howell one mare, ten dollars -Spencer Griffin one yearling heifer three Dollars thirty three and one third - John Amuff Sr. one mare thirty seven dollars.

John Taylor
   vs
Samuel Cox Constable -Charles Smith & William Milliken his securities.

John Taylor by Pleasant M.Miller his Attorney makes a motion to Court to enter up a Judgment for the sum of ten dollars & of fifty cents, with interest to be calculated on ten dollars from the first day of November AD. 1804 against Samuel Cox Constable, Charles Smith and William Milliken his securities for this that the said Samuel Cox has failed to pay over the aforesaid sum of money or return an execution issued on a Judgment rendered in favor of John Taylor against John Estis within thirty days &c It is therefore considered by the Court that the said John Taylor do recover the sum of Eleven dollars & eighty cents against the said Samuel Cox and his securities besides his costs.

Court adjourns till tomorrow 9 o'clock.

Wednesday 21st. August Court met according to adjournment. Justices present, Major Lea, Peter Harris, David McAnally & Charles McAnally.

State   )
  vs   )
Benjamin Yates)   Benjamin Yates Sr. surrenders the Defendant in open Court in discharge of himself.

State   )
  vs   )
Royal Jinnings)   Justices present, Major Lea, Charles McAnally, John Breeden, William Clay & Noah Jarnagin. Whereupon came a Jury towit, William Bowman, Hugh Larimore, Hugh Larimore, Thomas Dennis, William Street, Richard Acuff, Archibald McCarver, Nicholas Countz, Hercules Ogles, William Shelton, George Noe, John Moffitt & Joseph Rich, who being elected tried and sworn the truth to speak on the issue joined in this case do say they find the defendant not guilty in manner & form as he stands charged in the Bill of Indictment.

Ordered by Court that James Brown be directed to bring to this Court at this Term, Lewis Sertan, & James Setman, two orphans whom he has in his possession, the grand Jury having presented him for maltreating & abusing said orphans, the Grand Jury is discharged from further attendance at the present Term.

(p 116)   August Sessions A.D. 1805

State   )
  vs   )
Stephen Bean)   John Williams Esqr. makes a motion to Court— Cause why the three fines imposed yeasterday amounting to fifty dollars should be mitigated; —Rule discharged by Atty.

Ordered by the Court that Major Lea, Noah Jarnagin Esquires and Chesley Jarnagin be Commissioners to settle with John Adair Admr. of Thomas Cox deceased & make report to next Sessions of this Court.

Ordered by the Court that the Sheriff do summon a sufficient guard to guard the Jail till tomorrow morning for the purpose of safekeeping the prisoners now confined therein.

The Court appoint the following persons Jurors to the next Sessions of this Court, towit— David Spencer —Peter Hamilton, Mathew Campbell,

---

William Mitchell, Jesse Cheek, Dodson Cheek, Edward McGinnis, Joshua
Collins, Isaac Barton, Barnabas Butcher, Thomas Mann, John Hodge, William
Reddie, Semore York, William Blair, William Kirkum, James Blair Jr.
David Robinson, Charles Hooper, Benjamin Condrey, Peter Beelor, Thomas
Dunn, Cain Acuff, Cornelius McCoy, Martin Stubblefield, David Holt, Stephen
Johnston, William Williams, Robert D. Eaton, Samuel Peery, Joseph Long,
Abner Lowe, Joseph Dennis, Jacob Elliot, Obediah Waters, Daniel Smith
Edward Churchman, Thomas Henderson & Edward Dannell. Venire Facias issd.

Ordered by the Court that John Bunch Sr. John Conley, John Hailey
Michael Massengill, Rubin Dixon, James Moore & Frederick Moyers be a
Jury to lay out & make a road according to Law from the Town of Rutledge to Smith's ferry on Holston river, and report to next Court. Ord. Issd.

Ordered by Court that Jacob Arnett be overseer of the river road
from Buffalow Creek to the top of the Indian ridge in the room of Michael Massengill and that all the hands between the said creek & said
ridge from the river including Evan Harris's plantation & Isaac Thompson
thence a direct course including Jacob Arnett's work under him on said
road. Order Issd.

George Porcupile Admr. of Christian Porcupile deceased returns to
Court an inventory of the Estate of said deceased.

Court adjourns till tomorrow 9 o'clock.

Thursday 22nd. August Court met according to adjournment.
Justices present, Peter Harris, William Clay and John Breeden.

State)
vs) Indictment for Petit Larceny, General demurrer and Join-
Isaiah Midduff) der – Demurrer standing for argument– Justices present, William Clay,
John Breeden, Charles McAnally and Noah Jarnagin –the said Demurrer coming on for argument and on hearing arguments of Council as well on behalf
of the Defendant –It is considered by the Court that the demurrer be sustained &c whereupon the said Isaiah Midduff is discharged on proclamation.

(p 117) August Sessions A.D. 1805.

A Deed of conveyance from David Davis to John Kidwell for seventy
acres of Land was proven in open Court by Moses Hodges a subscribing witness & ordered to be Registered.

A Deed of conveyance from Henry Ivey to John Kidwell for fifty acres
of Land was proven in open Court by Moss Hodges a subscribing witness &
ordered to be Registered.

A Deed of conveyance from Henry Bowen Jr. to Nicholas Kearns for
fourteen acres of Land was acknowledged in open Court and ordered to be
Registered.

John Cocke Solicitor, makes a motion to Court to take two orphan boys
apprentices bound by Indenture to James Brown out of his possession towit,

Lewis Simpson & James Simpson & for this that the said James Brown maltreats & abuses said boys-the said orphan boys being brought into Court & witnesses being examined touching the treatment of the said James Brown to the said orphans -the said James proposes delivering up said orphans to the Court on conditions that he be exonerated from the Indentures heretofore entered into between him & the chairman of the Court for said orphans -whereupon the said James does deliver up said orphans to the Court and it is ordered and adjudged by the Court that the said James be freed and exonerated from the force and obligations of the said Indentures.

Ordered by the Court that Lewis Simpson otherwise called Lewis Sertan and James Simpson otherwise called James Sertan remain with Margery their Mother, and the said Margery Sertan enters into Bond in the sum of five hundred dollars with William Shields -George Martin, & Joseph Yeadin her securities conditioned that she provide for said Boys till the next Sessions of this Court & have them forthcoming at next Court.

Abraham Elliot)
    vs   )   The attachment issued in this case is returned to
John Hargraves)   Court with the following endorsed thereon, towit.
the within attachment Levied on the Land and Buildings thereon John Hargraves levied lying on the head of a branch that empties into Flat Creek at Moore's mill at the property of said Hargraves-August 19th 1805-by me (Signed) -Robert Huddleston -Constable - On motion it is ordered and directed by the Court that an order of Sale do issue to the Sheriff commanding him to sell the Land Levied on as above or so much thereof as will satisfy the sum of Forty four Dollars and all costs.
Court adjourns till tomorrow 9 o'clock. Exec. Issd.

Friday 23rd. August Court met according to adjournment. Justices present -Peter Harris, David McAnally.

Royal Jinnings   )
    vs   John Bull Constable, William Gass &   )
John Bull Senr. his securities.   )   Pleasant M.Miller
makes a motion to Court to enter up a Judgment against John Bull constable and William Gass and John Bull Senr. his securities for one dollar & twenty five cents for this that the said John Bull Constable hath failed to make return of an execution within the time limited by Law, issued on a Judgment obtained by the said Royal Jinnings against William Mooney - It is considered by the Court that the said Royal Jinnings do recover the aforesaid sum of money against the said John Bull & his securities. Exec. Issd.

(p 118)   August Sessions A.D. 1805

Richard Reynolds)
    vs   )   Richard Reynolds by John Cooke Esqr. his Atty. makes
George Horner)   a motion to Court to enter up a Judgment against Geo.
Horner for thirteen Dollars eighty eight cents & one half of a cent for so much money he has paid over as security of the said George Horner- It is considered by the Court that the said Richard do recover the aforesaid sum of money against the said George, together with his costs.

William Clay and others -Commissioners. vs- Martin Ashburn late Coroner

James Blair Junr. and John Humphreys his securities.

Pleasant M.Miller Atty. makes a motion to Court to enter up a Judgment against the said Martin Ashburn and James Blair & John Humphreys his securities for the sum of $24.90 for money by the said Martin collected on an execution in the suit, William Clay & others Commissioners against Robert Yancey which he has failed to pay over; It is considered by the Court that the said plaitiffs do recover the aforesaid sum of money and costs aginst the said Defendants. Exec. Issd.

The same)   Pleasant M.Miller Atty. makes a motion to Court to enter up
   vs   )   a Judgment against Martin Ashburn late Coroner and James
The same.and   Blair Jr. and John Humphreys his securities for the sum of
thirty two dollars and thirty cents for monies by him collected on an
execution issued in favor of William Clay & others Commissioners against
Robert Yancey late Sheriff and his securities which he has failed to pay
over- It is considered by the Court that the said plaintiffs do recover
the aforesaid sum of money together with costs against the said Defendants.

A Deed of conveyance from Luke Lea to John Lea for two Lots in the
town of Rutledge, being the Lots No. 23 & 24 was acknowledged in open Court
& ordered to be Registered.

A Deed of conveyance from John Lea Sheriff to Luke Lea for two Lots
in the town of Rutledge being Lots No. 23 & 24 was acknowledged in open
Court & ordered to be Registered.

A Deed of conveyance from John Bunch to Martin Albert for two Lots
in the Town of Rutledge being Lots No. 42, 43 was acknowledged in open Court
& ordered to be Registered.

Ordered by Court that Francis Willet Constable be allowed the sum of
one dollar per day for each day he has attended on the Court at the present Term.

Ordered by Court that Samuel Cox Constable be allowed the sum of one
dollar per day for each day he has attended on the grand Jury and Court
at the present Term and the said Samuel Cox maketh oath that he has attended on the Grand Jury and Court five days.

Ordered by Court that Francis Willet & Samuel Cox Constable be sum-
oned to attend the next Session of this Court.

David McAnally   )
   vs   )
Robert Yancey late Sheriff and his securities.)
       David McAnally by Luke Lea his Atty. makes a motion to Court to enter
up a Judgment against Robert Yancey late Sheriff & his securities for the
sum of five Dollars & fifty cents which sum he is entitled to for his attendance as a witness in the suit the State against Isiah Midkiff which
sum the said David McAnally alledges the said Robert has collected and failed to pay over- on examination of witnesses &c and arguments of Council
being heard thereon It is considered by Court that the said plaintiff take
nothing by his motion.

(p 119)   November Sessions A.D. 1805

Ordered by Court that John Cocke, John Bunch & Thomas Bunch be Patrollers in the Richland Valley, beginning at Beans Station and as low down as Buffalow Hide Creek, and the said John Cocke & Thomas Bunch took the oath prescribed by Law.

Court adjourns till Court in course.
                    (Signed) Noah Jarnagin C.P.T.

At a Court of Pleas & Quarter Sessions began & holden in and for the County of Grainger at the Court House in Rutledge on the third Monday of November A.D. 1805 being the 18th of the same month-
Justices Present - Major Lea, William Hankins - James Moore and Joseph Cobb Esquires.

John Lea Esquire Returns to Court that he has executed the following Venire Facias on the following persons except Peter Hamilton -William Mitchell, John Hodges, Martin Stubblefield & Stephen Johnston (towit)

David Spencer   Martin Stubblefield
Peter Hamilton   David Holt
Mathew Campbell   Stephen Johnston
William Mitchell   William Williams
Jesse Cheek   Robert D. Eaton
Dawson Cheek   Samuel Peery
Edward McGinnis   Joseph Long
Joshua Collins   Abner Lowe
Isaac Barten   Joseph Dennis
Barnabis Butcher   Jacob Elliot
Thomas Harn   Obediah Waters
John Hodges   Daniel Smith
William Redis   Edward Churchman
Simon York   Thomas Henderson &
William Blair   39-Edward Daniel
William Kirkhan
James Blair Jr.   Out of which Venire Facias the persons
Daniel Robertson   whose names are underwritten were drawn
Charles Hopper   as Grand Jurors for the present Term-Viz.
Benjamin Condrey
Peter Beeler
Thomas Dunn   Thomas Henderson -Forman
Cain Acuff   Mathew Campbell -
Cornelius McCoy   Abner Lowe   Benj. Condrey
                                Obediah Waters   Joseph Long
                                Cornelius McCoy   Jesse Cheek
                                Samuel Peery   Robert D. Eaton
                                Joshua Collins   William Kirkhan
                                Edward Churchman   Thomas Dunn &
                                                    Peter Beeler

All of whom were sworn and charged by John Cocke Solicitor & Francis Willit Constable sworn to attend the Grand Jury at the present Term.

State
vs   -Thomas Bowling one of the securities of the Defendants Surrenders
William McGill   ders him in open Court in discharge

of himself & James Carmichael the other security.

Ordered by Court that John Doyd have leave to keep an ordinary or house of Publick Entertainment & he enters into Bond in the sum of Twelve hundred & fifty Dollars with James Kennedy his security -

On application Dawson Cheek have leave to keep an ordinary or house of publick Entertainment & he Enters into Bond in the sum of Twelve hundred & Eighty Dollars with George Evans his Security.

(p 120)   November Sessions A.D. 1805.

The last Will and testament of William James Jr. was exhibited to Court for probate and the due execution thereof proven by John Bolton & William Morris two of the subscribing witnesses thereto and ordered to be Recorded. Whereupon Jesse James one of the Executors therein named was qualified.

A Deed of conveyance from Joseph Green to John Sally for four hundred acres of Land was proven in open Court by the oath of Benjamin Condrey one of the subscribing witnesses and ordered to be Registered.

A Deed of conveyance from John Sally to Benjamin Condify for two hundred and seventy five acres of Land was acknowledged in open Court and ordered to be Registered.   .

The Court appoint Henry Hawkins a Constable and he enters into Bond in the penal sum of five hundred dollars with William Hawkins his securities and took the necessary Oaths.

Ordered by Court that Daniel Robinson be overseer of the road from the first branch below Jesse Bewns old place to the ford of the creek near Nicholas Fearns plantation in the room of Thomas Bunch and that all the hands living between said branch and said creek including Elijah Donathan's hands -Charles Kidwells hands and between Clinch mountain and the river ridge be allowed him to work on said road. Order Issd.

Ordered by Court that Robert McElhiney be appointed overseer of the road in the room of Joel Hammer from the ford of the creek near Nicholas Kearns plantation to the public Square in the town of Rutledge and that all the hands living between said creek and Nicholas Countz's and between the Richland Hobbs and Clinch mountain be allowed him to work on said road. Order Issd.

Ordered by Court that Joseph Bryant be appointed overseer of the road in the room of John Lebow from the Line of Hawkins County to the house of John Crabb and that the hands on the plantation of Thomas Henderson and upwards to the County Line and on the North side of the road be allowed him to work on said road. Order Issd.

A Deed of conveyance from Martin Ashburn to Jesse Christian for one hundred acres of Land was proven in open Court by the oath of John Humphreys a subscribing witness and ordered to be Registered.

A Deed of conveyance from Allen Christian for fifty acres of Land was proven ip open Court by John Humphreys one of the subscribing witnesses and ordered to be Registered.

A Bill of Sale from William Rayl To Washington Rayl for a sorrel horse was proven in open Court by John Green one of the subscribing witnesses & ordered to be Registered.

A Deed of conveyance from James Hickman To John Sullins for ninety four acres of Land was proven in open Court by John Horner a subscribing witness & ordered to be Registered.

A Deed of conveyance from Charles Gilbert To Joseph Owen for two hundred acres of Land was acknowledged in open Court & ordered to be Registered.

William Clay Rainger for Grainger County returns a list of Strays in the words & figures following –Viz."A List of strays remaining on my book & not proven away in twelve months of the following specifications towit, James Dyer Junr. one red and black spotted Hogg —$1.25.

(p 121)   November Sessions A.D. 1805

James Dyer Senr. one Barrow –$1.00– John Horner one Barrow –$1.50– William Hall one Steer –$6.00.
                    (Signed) W.C.Lay –R.G.C.
Court adjourns till tomorrow morning nine o'clock.

Tuesday 19th November Court met according to adjournment. Justices present Major Lea, Noah Jarnagin & Henry Boatman.

John Bean   )
    vs   ) Justices present, Major Lea, Noah Jarnagin & Henry
Robert Yancey   ) Boatman.
    Whereupon came a Jury, (towit)

1- Daniel Robertson   8- Thomas Bunch
2- William Blair   9- Nicholas Counts
3- Stephen Smith   10-Tandy Senter
4- John Green   11-Robert McElhiney &
5- Martin Morris   12-David Holt
6- James Bryant
7- Henry Howell
    Who being Elected Tryed and sworn well & truly to enquire what damages the Plaintiff hath sustained in a writ of enquiry by him brought in this case, do say they find for the plaintiff & assess his damages to two hundred & nine dollars & twenth one cents besides his costs.

Josiah Nichol Assinee of)
Lewis Harmon   )
    vs   ) John Vinyard one of the Defendants Bail
Nicholas Spring   ) surrenders him in open Court in discharge
of himself & defendant prayed in custody of the Sheriff by the plaintiffs Atty.
John Gold   Vs   Robert C.Gordon – Justices present as above.

Whereupon came a Jury (towit) the same Jury, as in the above case except John McElhiney in the room of Stephen Smith -who being elected tried and sworn the truth to speak on the issue Joined in this case, do say they find the Defendant hath paid all the Debt in the declaration mentioned, except Sixteen and two thirds of a cent & find for the plaintiff sixteen & two thirds of a cent besides his costs- rule to shew cause why the Verdict should be set aside & a non suit entered -rule discharged.

Josiah Nichâl -Assignee)
    vs   )
Nicholas Spring   )   Nicholas Spring comes into open Court -Obediah Waters & Joseph Dennis became the Special Bail of the Defendant.

Andrew Campbell - Admr. & Ex. of)
Hugh Campbell -Dec.   )
    vs   )
John Cocke   )   Justices present, Major Lea, William Hankins - A Jury sworn -Thomas Dardis Atty. for the plaintiff enters a non suit- Rule to set aside non suit-Rule discharged.

William Dyer Sr.)
    vs   )
Edward Cormok &)   Justices present, Major Lea, William Hankins & Jo
Francis Mayberry)   Cobb. Whereupon came a Jury, towit-

1- Joseph Dennis   4- John Dodson
2- William Whitesides   5- Joseph Taylor
3- William Harris   6- Stephen Smith

(p 122)   November Sessions A.D. 1805

7- Frederick Pangle   10- William Horner
8- Joseph Yeaden   11- William Arnold &
9- John Hailey   12- Valentine Morgan

Who being elected tryed & sworn the truth to speak on the issue Joined in this case do say they find for the plaintiff & assess his damages to two hundred & two dollars & eighty cents & costs, the plaintiff comes into Court & directs Execution to stay three months.

Robert Alsup comes into open Court & proves to the satisfaction of the Court that a certain John Robinson did sometime in the month of September 1805 bite a large piece out of the upper part of his Right Ear. Whereupon the Court direct an Entery thereof to be made of Record.

Ordered by the Court that Noah Ashley be appointed Constable in this County and he enters into Bond in the sum of five hundred Dollars with Philip Sigler & James Brown his securities and takes the necessary oaths.

A Deed of conveyance from John Horner to Michael Moyers for a Lot in the Town of Rutledge it being Lot No. 3- was proven in open Court by Luke Lea a subscribing witness and ordered to be Registered.

A Deed of conveyance from John Robertson to Enos Horner for twenty

five acres of Land was proven in open Court by Francis Willitt a subscribing witness thereto ordered to be Registered.

A Deed of partition Between Uri Campbell & Bill Ganaway Campbell of
a Tract of Land containing four hundred acres, was proven in open Court
by William Campbell a subscribing witness and ordered to be Recorded.

Ordered by the Court that William Rimbard be overseer of the Road
from the ford of Richland Creek to the top of the Indian Ridge in the room
of Robert Gaines and the same bound be allowed him for hands, that was
allowed said Gaines.   Order S -Ised.

Ordered by the Court that John Hall have leave to keep an ordinary
or house of Public Entertainment and he enters into Bond in the sum of
Twelve hundred & fifty Dollars with William Hall & Valentine Morgan his
securities.

Ardeoadshyouhenfoprededthes Johfcourt from his Excellency John Sevier
Governor with the Great Seal of the State thereunto annexed appointing
William Peeters & others Justices of the piece for Grainger County and
the said William Peeters comes into open Court and took the necessary
oaths.

Ordered by the Court that Lewis Sartin an orphan Boy now of the age
of thirteen years be bound by Indenture to David Huddleston until he shall
attain to the age of twenty one years. Therefore Major Lea, Chairman of
the Court & David Huddleston execute Indenture in pursuance of said Order.

The Report of the Jury heretofore (towit) at last Term appointed to
lay out & make road according to Law from the town of Rutledge to Smith's
Ferry on Holston River & make Report to this Term being Returned to Court
and the same being so Vague and uncertain it is considered by the Court
that the said Report be not confirmed - It is therefore ordered by the
Court that the said Jurors (towit) John Bunch Sr. John Conley, John Hailey
Michael Massengill, Rubin Dixon James Moore & Frederick Moyers be con-
tinued a Jury, towit to lay out & mark a road according to Law from the
Town of Rutledge to Smith's Ferry on Holston River & make report to next
Court- Court adjourns till 9 o'clock.

(p 123)   November Sessions A.D. 1805

Wednesday 20th November Court met according to adjournment. Present
William Henning Charles McAnally & Henry Boatman. Esquire.

Roberts Ledsee   )
        vs   )
Benjamin Shaw   )   John Dodson Special Bail of Defendant surrendered
him in open Court in discharge of himself & Charles McAnally the other
Security.

Ordered by the Court that Francis Willitt Constable shall be allowed
the sum of one dollar per day for each day he has heretofore attended on
the Grand Jury.

Ordered by the Court that John Lea Sheriff be allowed the sum of two
Dollars & seventy five cents being monies he expended in hiring a Guard

to guard the Jail on the nights of the 20th & of August 1805.

State   )
  vs   )
Elihu Milligan) John Hodge surrenders the Defendant in open Court in
discharge of himself as Bail.

John Jodson   )
vs   appeal   )
Patrick Nenney &)
William Grayham   ) Warrant Executed only on William Grayham Justices
present, William Clay -William Hankins & Henry Boatman -thereupon came a
Jury (towit)
1- Danile Robertson   7- John Crabb
2- John McElhiney   8- Thomas Bunch
3- John Green   9- John Vinyard
4- William Blair   10-John Hodge
5- John Patterson   11-Stephen Smith
6- Robert McElhiney   12-David McAnally

     Who being Elected tryed and sworn the truth to speak on the matter in
dispute in this case do say they find for the plaintiff & assess his damages to five Dollars and costs. Appeal prayed by William Grayham -Rule
discharged - A rule for a new trial -Rule discharged.

     Deed of conveyance from Jeremiah Brown & James Harmock to Peter Ham-
mock for one hundred acres of Land was proven in open Court by William
Shields a Subscribing witness thereto and ordered to be Registered.

     George Porcupile Admr. of Porcupile Returns to Court the amount of
the sales of the personal Estate of Christian Pocupile -Deceased.

     A Deed of conveyance from Elijah Donathan to Landy Senter for fifty
acres of Land was proven in open Court by Thomas Johnston - a witness &
ordered to be Registered.

     A Deed of conveyance from Samuel Davidson to John Archer for one hun-
dred acres of Land was proven in open Court by Ralph Ford a witness & ordered to be Registered.

     Ordered by the Court that William Hamilton be appointed overseer of
the road from the top of the Copper Ridge to John Sallies in the Raccoon
Valley in the Room of William Peeters & that he be allowed the same bounds
for hands to work on said Road that was allowed said Peeters.

(p 134)   November Sessions A.D. 1805

William Cooper   )
     vs   )
Robert Moore -John Spring &)
John Margrave   ) John Cooke Atty. for plaintiff makes a
motion to Court to Enter up a Judgment against Robert Moore -John Spring
& John Margrave for the sum of one hundred & five dollars & five cents
for money he has been compelled to pay as security for said Defendants
and it appearing to the Satisfaction of the Court that the said William

Cooper has been compelled to pay the aforesaid sum of money as Security of the said Defendants— It is therefore considered by the Court that the said plaintiff do Recover the aforesaid sum of one hundred & five Dollars and five cents against the said Defendants.

William McGill enters into Bond in the sum of five hundred Dollars with Josiah Dyer his security conditioned that he will indemnify the County from all costs & charges whatsoever for & by Reason of the birth, maintenance & bringing up of a bastard child of which he stands charged according to Law of being the Reputed father of which a certain Nancey Davis has been lately delivered of and also that he will perform such order as the County Court may make in the premises.

A Deed of conveyance from John Harner to John Bactor Grannett for Lot No. 2— in the town of Rutledge was proven in open Court by James Dyer & Ambrose Yancey the subscribing witness thereto and was ordered to be Registered.

A Bill of Sale from James Ore to James Johnston in the nature of a Mortgage for three Stills was acknowledged in open Court by the said James Ore &ordered to be Registed.

The Court appoint Noah Ashley Constable to attend on the Court at each Term for one year & that he shall Receive one Dollar per day for each day he shall attend he proving his attendance.

The Court appoint Francis Willit Constable to attend on the Grand Jury at each Term for the Term of one year and that he shall be allowed the sum of one dollar per day for each day that he shall attend on the Grand Jury on proving his attendance.

Ordered by the Court tat Richard Acuff David Spencer, Peter Hamilton William Snodgrass. James Campbell & William Hankins be appointed a Jury to view & lay out a Road agreeably to Law from William Hankins ford on Holston River to the fork of the Road near Major James Campbells field and make Report to next Court.

The Court appoint the following persons Jurors to February Term 1806 (towit) David Spencer —Peter Hamilton-Seth McKinney— Enoch Winds, William Mitchell —William Sims, Elijah Clay, Jesse Jinnings,Senore York, Charles Hooper, Joshua Oaks, William Milligan, James Carmichael, Harmon Cox, Joseph Beelor, George Norris, William McPhetridge, David Bunch,Robert Long Rubin Riggs, Hugh Cain, John Moffitt, Benjamin Elliot, Tandy Senter, Moses Hodges, Henry Howell, Francis Darnell, Joseph Hoe Senr. —John Lebow & James Blair Jr.

Court adjourns till Tomorrow 9 o'clock.

(p 125)   November Sessions A.D. 1805

Thursday 21st. November Court met according to adjournment. Justices present, Joseph Cobb, David McEnally —Henry Boatman & Major Lea Esqr.

William Rail vs   trover Joseph Hoe Senr. — Whereupon came a Jury towit-

1— Daniel Robertson
2— William Dyer
3— Tandy Senter
4— Joseph Dennis
5— John Vinyard
6— Thomas Bunch

7— Moses McElhiney
8— John Crabb
9— James Hamilton
10—William Whitesides
11—Henry Howell
12—John Patterson

Who being Elected Tried & sworn the truth to speak on the Issue Joined in this case do say they find the Defendant not Guilty in manner & form as the plaintiff in his Declaration hath complained against him.

A Deed of conveyance from George Kimbro to Joseph Hoe Sr. for one hundred acres of Land was proven in open Court by the oath of Joseph Rich a witness & ordered to be Registered.

Jacob Hoe by Joseph Hoe Sr.)
his next friend &c   )
    vs   )
William Rail   )   Justices present, David McElhiney, Major Lea
Charles McElhiney — Henry Boatman & Joseph Cobb. Whereupon came a Jury, towit—

1— William Blair
2— John Bean
3— Thomas Bunch
4— Henry Smith
5— Thomas Henderson
6— John Mitchell

7— Daniel Clayton
8— Robert McElhiney
9— William Windham
10—John Dodson
11—David McEnelley
12—John Moffett

Who being Elected tried and sworn the truth to speak on the Issue Joined in this case, do say they find the Defendant Guilty in manner & form as the Plaintiff in his declaration hath complained against him that he hath no Justification and assess the plaintiffs Damages to five hundred Dollars & costs.

Court adjourns till tomorrow 9 o'clock.

Friday the 22nd. November Court met according to adjournment —Present Major Lea, David McEnelly & Charles McEnelly, Esquires.

Denn on Demise of)
Henry Howell   )
    vs   )
Isaiah Midkiff   ) Thereupon came a Jury, towit—

William Blair
Thomas Henderson
Thomas Bunch
William Dyer
Joseph Dennis
John Vinyard

Daniel Taylor
Hugh Craig
Tandy Senter
Henry Smith
James Harris
James Hamilton

(p 126)   November Sessions A.D. 1805

Who being Elected tryed & sworn the Truth to speak on the Issue Joined

in this case do say they find the ^Defendant Guilty of Trespass & Ejectment in manner & form as the plaintiff in his declaration hath complained
against him & assess the plaintiffs damage by Reason thereof to six cents
and costs - Therefore it is considered it is considered by the Court that
the said Henry Howell do recover against the said Pleasant Duke - Term
yet to come of & in the said Tennements with the appurtenances & the said
damages aforesaid by the said Jury in form aforesaid besides his costs.

Tandy Senter	)
vs	)
Thomas Bunch	)

Pleasant Duke, Major Lea. David McEnally & ^Charles Mc-
Enalley Esquires. Whereupon came a Jury (towit)

1- William Blair	7- John Taylor
2-John Vinyard	8- Dennis Condry
3- James Harris	9- John Patterson
4- Joseph Dennis	10-Thomas Henderson
5- John Moffett	11-Daniel Taylor
6- William Dyer	12-James Hamilton

Who being Elected tryed & sworn the truth to speak on the Issue Joined in this case do say they find the Defendant not guilty in manner & form
as the plaintiff in his declaration hath complained against him. Therefore
it is considered by the Court that the Defendant do recover his costs aforesaid.

A Deed of conveyance from James Robertson to James Hodges for one hundred & fifty acres of Land was proven in open Court by the oath of Edward
Churchman & ^Thomas Sharp & ordered to be Registered.

Tandy Senter	)
vs	)
Thomas Bunch	)

Daniel Robertson being summoned a witness in behalf of
the plaintiff the case being called for trial & the said Daniel Robertson
being solemnly called came not it is therefore considered by the Court
that the said Daniel Robertson do forfeit one hundred Dollars & twenty
five Dollars according to Act of Assembly.

John Crabb	)
vs	)
John Brown	)

On application to ^Court by John Cooke Atty. for plaintiff
that writs of Certiorari Supercedeas may issue in this case- It is ordered
by the Court that writs do issue according to the prayers of the petition
filed in this case.

Hugh Craig Assignee of	)	
Gidion Morris	)	
vs	)	Justices present, David McAnally, Major Lea
James Byrns	)	Charles McAnally -Henry Boatman.

1- William Blair	7- Dennis Condry
2- Joseph Dennis	8- Daniel Taylor
3- Nicholas Countz	9- James Harris
4- Thomas Henderson	10-William Dyer
5- John Vinyard	11-John Patterson
6- John Moffitt	12-James Hamilton

(p 127)   November Sessions A.D. 1805

Who being Elected tryed and sworn the truth to speak on the issue Joined in this case do say they find for the plaintiff the sum of of twenty
three Dollars Debt and asses the plaintiffs damages occationed by the detention of that debt to one Dollars & three fourths of a mill.

John Lea Sheriff Exhibits to Court a list of Insolvents for the year
1805 amounting in the whole for the State tax to two Dollars eighty seven
and one cent for the County tax to three Dollars fifty six & one half cent
(towit) $2.87½ cents for the poor tax to which the said John Lea was qual-
ified as the Law directs — it is ordered by the Court that the said Sheriff be released from the payment of the aforesaid sum of money & have a
credit in his settlement with the Treasurer of the District of Washington
& Hamilton for the sum of $2.87½ and that he have a credit in his settle-
ment with the Trustee for the sum of $3.56½ — Issued.

John Lea Esquire Sheriff Returns to Court that he cannot find any goods
& chattles on which he can distrain to make the taxes on the following
tracts of Land for the year 1804 (towit) —George M.Combs — 870 acres —John
Cathcart 50 acres — William Bowling 200 acres — Jesse Coats 100 for the
year 1805— Lewis Clapier by Thomas Dardis 30,000 acres the heirs of Thomas
Cox Deceased — 340 John Hargraves 200 — Geo. M.Combs 120 — Geo. M.Combs 150
acres — Michael Cook 100 acres — John Bull Junr. 25 acres — It is therefore considered by the Court that the clerk make out a Certificate of the
amount of tax due on the same together with the amount of costs & charges
due thereon & cause the same to be twice published in Knoxville Gazette
giving notice that the same will be sold. Order to the Printer Issued.

Ordered by the Court that John Lea Sheriff be released from the collection & payment of the sum of $0.46½ being the State and County Tax due
on 150 acres of Land the property of David Bunch, it appearing to the sa-t
isfaction of the Court that the said David Bunch is twice charged for the
same Land in the present year & it is further ordered that he have a credit
for the old sum of money in the settlement of his accounts. Issd.

Ordered by the Court John Lea Sheriff be released from the collection
& payment of the sum of $1.21 being the State and County Tax due on 300
acres of Land the property of James Blair- It appearing to the appearing
to the satisfaction of the Court that te said James is charged twice for
the same tract of Land in the present term —it is further ordered that he
have a credit for the aforesaid sum of —— in the settlement of his accts.

(p 128)   November Sessions A.D. 1805

Francis Willitt constable makes oath in open Court that he has attended five Days on the Court at last Term (towit) August Term 1805 & five Days
at the present Term Certificate Issed.to F.Willit.

Samual Bunch having been appointed Deputy Sheriff by John Lea Esquire
high Sheriff of Grainger County and comes in open Court & took an oath to
support the Constitution of the United States also the Constitution of the
State of Tennessee & also the oaths prescribed by Law.

Court adjourns till tomorrow morning.

Saturday 21st. November Court met according to adjournment.

Justices present -David McAnally, Charles McAnally & Henry Boatman -The
Court appoint the following Justices of the peace to take in Lists of Polls
and Taxable property in Grainger County for the year A.D. 1806 & make Return to next Court (towit)

Josiah Dyer Esquire for Captain Howells Company.
Henry Boatman Esquire for Captain Senters Company.
Peter Harris Esqr. for Captain Manns Company.
Joseph Cobb Esqr. for Captain Bowens Company.
Charles McAnally Esqr. for Captain Dodsons Company.
Samuel Clark Esqr. for Captain James Company.
Charles Hutcheson Esqr. for Captain Hargraves Company.
Valentine Holder Esqr. for Captain A.Hamilton's Company.
William Clays Esqr. for Captain Bunches Company.
Major Lea Esqr. for Captain Micheals Company.
James Moore Esqr. for Captain Massengill's Company.

Court adjourns Till Court in Course.

David McAnally C.C.T.
February Sessions A.D. 1806.
At a Court of Pleas and quarter Sessions began & holden for the County
of Grainger at the Court House in Rutledge on the third Monday of February
A.D. 1806 being the 17th of the same month.

(p 129)　　　February Sessions A.D. 1806.

Justices present, John Breaden, William Peters, Charles Hutcheson Esqr.
John Lea high Sheriff of Grainger County by Samuel Bunch his Deputy returns
to Court that he has Executed the following Venire facias on the following
persons Except David Spencer & Benjamin Elliot.(towit)

1- David Spencer
2- Peter Hamilton
3- Seth McKinney
4- Enoch Wynds
5- William Mitchell
6- William Sims
7- Elijah Clay
8- Jesse McKinney
9- Semore Yorke
10-Charles Hopper
11-Joshua Oaks
12-William Milligan
13-James Carmichael
14-Harmon Cox
15-Joseph Beelor
16-George Norris
17-William McPhetridge

18- David Bunch
19- Robert Long
20- Rubin Riggs
21- Hugh Kain
22- John Moffit
23- Benjamin Elliot
24- Tandy Senter
25- Moses Hodges
26- Henry Howell
27- Francis Daniel
28- Joseph Noe Sr.
29- John Lebow A
30- James Blair Jr.

Out of which Venire facias the persons whose names are underwritten
are appointed a grand jury for the present Term (towit)

1- William Milligan
2- Peter Hamilton

3- Seth McKinney
4- Enoch Winds

5- William Sims
6- Elijah Clay
7- Jesse McAnally
8- Semore York
9- Charles Hopper
10-Joshua Oaken

11- James Carmichael
12- Harmon Cox
13- William Mofetredge
14- Robert Long &
15- Rubin Riggs

And were qualified and charged by the Solicitor accordingly Francis Willet Constable to attend on said Jury at this Term.

The last Will & testament of Drury Solomons was proven in open Court by the oaths of Edward Daniel & Henry Hays and ordered to be Recorded and filed.

The last Will and testament of Benjamin Elliot was proven in open Court by the oath of Nicholas Spring & Littier Fields Two of the subscribing witnesses & was ordered to be Recorded & filled in the Clerks office and Executor qualified accordingly.

Ordered by the Court that Hugh Larrimore be appointed overseer of the road in the Room of John Moe. Issd.

(p 130)   February Sessions A.D. 1806

State   T.A.B.)
   vs   )
Sarah Going   )   In this case the Defendants Securities comes into Court and surrenders hir in discharge of themselves as Bail.

State - Pettilarceny)
     vs   )
Sarah Going   )   the defendants Securities comes into Court and surrenders her in discharge of themselves as Bail.

State T.   )
   vs   )
Sarah Going   )   Clayborn Going acknowledged himself indebted to the State of Tennessee in the sum of one Hundred Dollars for the appearance of Sarah Going his wife Caleb Howell & James Bryant in the sum of fifty dollars currency for the appearance of sd. Sarah Going.

State   )
   vs   )
Sarah Going)   forfeiture against the Bail —Cachor Bound as above & Caleb Howell & James Bryant Bound as above. Sci- fa. Issd.

Ordered by the Court that Aaron Book be appointed a constable in Captain Thomas Jameses Company and he enters into Bond in the sum of five hundred Dollars with Barton Moferson and David Bunch his securities and he was qualified according to Law.

Nimrod Sirus comes into open Court & gives in his taxable property for the year 1806 (towit) fifty acres of Land and one free Poll.

Hardy Clifton comes into open Court and on oath Gives in his List of taxable property for the year 1806 (towit) one white Poll.

Ordered by the Court that John Arwine be appointed overseer of the road in room of Daniel Beeler and that he be allowed the same Bounds for hands that the said Daniel Beeler was authorized to have. Issd.

A Bill of Sale from William Arnold to Robert Dunville proven in Court by the oath of John Humphries and ordered to be recorded.

Ordered by the Court that Aaron Rooks be appointed constable in the County of Grainger who gave security (towit)
Barton McPherson & David Bunch as securities in the sum of   (p 131)
(February Sessions A.D.1805)   five Hundred Dollars and te said Aaron Rook took the necessary oaths &c.

Ordered by the Court that William Parkerson gives in his Taxable property for the year 1805 (towit) two hundred acres of Land & one white poll in Capt. Alex. Hamiltons Company.

A Bill of Sale from John Smith to Nicholas Countz for two negroes Slaves one named Aggy about twelve years of age the other named Bryan about ten years of age was proven in open Court by John F.Jack a subscribing witness and ordered to be Recorded.

A Deed of Trust from John Smith to Nicholas Countz for negroes was proven in open Court by John F.Jack a subscribing witness & ordered to be Recorded.

A Bill of Sale from John Smith to John Cocke for a negro man slave named Lot was proven in open Court by the oath of John F.Jack the sub-scribing and ordered to be Recorded.

A Bill of sale from Henry Bowen Jr. for a negro Girl named Jimmy to Michael Kearns was proven in open Court by the oath of John Cocke a sub-scribing witness and ordered to be Recorded.

William Clay Esquire Returns the following amount of Strays to him up in the County of Grainger and posted with him as Ranger of Grainger County (towit)

James Ore one cow ----$6.50 -Edward Clark - eight head Hogs $15.50
Labourn Jones one steer -- 10.00 -John Acuff - 1 heifer & 1 steer- 9.00
Aquilla Jones - one cow -- 8.00 Thomas Bunch -1 bull ------ 4.00
Daniel Going 1 heifer --- 7.25- Isaac Martin one shoat ---   75
Jacob Gallion one steer -- 8.00- Joseph Eaton two hogs --   4.50
Jeremiah Brown one cow - 6.00-
    My fee not paid by said Brown.

(p 132)   February Sessions A.D. 1806

William Clay Esquire who was appointed at last term to take in list of Taxable property in the Bounds of Captain's John Bunches Company for the year A.D. 1805.

Josiah Dyer Esquire who was appointed to take in Lists of Taxable prop-erty for the year A.D. 1806.Made his returns in open Court.

Valentine Moulder who was appointed to take in Lists of taxable property in the bounds of Alexander Hamilton's Company made his return for the year 1806 in open Court.

Charles Hutchison Esquire who was appointed to take in Lists of taxable property for the year 1806 made his Return in open Court.

Samuel Clark who was appointed to take in Lists of taxable property for the year A.D. 1806 made his Return in open Court.

James Moore was appointed to take in Lists of taxable property in the Bounds of Captain Robert Massengill's Company for the year 1806 was Returned in open Court.

Charles McAnally Esquire who was appointed to take in Lists of Taxable property in the Bounds of Captain Doddons Company for the year 1806 was returned in open Court.

Henry Boatman Esquire who was appointed to take in Lists of Taxable property for the year 1806 in the Bounds of Capt.S.W.Senters Company was Returned in open Court.

Tuesday the 18th of Febr. the Court met according to adjournment - Justices present John Breeden, William Peters & William Norten Esquires. A motion by Thomas Dardis Esquire against John Hargraves constable his securities in favour of William T.Lewis for failing to pay over monies he collected from a Judgment before a Justice of the peace in the County of Grainger to the satisfaction of the Court that John Hargraves one of the constables of this County hath collected Twenty Dollars and sixty five cents being principal and Interest of a Judgment Recorded by the said William T.Lewis against Spencer Griffin before a Justice of the peace which he has failed to pay over it is therefore considered   (p 133) (February Sessions A.D. 1806)   By the Court that the said William T. Lewis Do recover the aforesaid sum of money & costs against the said John Hargraves —Nicholas Spring & John Spring his securities — Execution has Isd.

A Bill of Sale from John Cooke to Michael Kearns for one negro slave named Lott was acknowledged in open Court & ordered to be Recorded.

James Hogg Received in the name of Waller Alvis & Galven Alvis Executors of the last Will & Testament of the said James Hogg Dec'd— vs No. 103 T.V.A. Writ of Inquiry Willoughby Lewis	Justices present John Breeden— Mah Midcliff & William Norten. Whereupon came a Jury (to wit)

1- Henry Ewell
2- James Blair Jr.
3- Joseph Rich
4- Robert Alsup
5- John Crabb
6- Joseph Noe Jr.

7- John Hodges
8- James Brown
9- William Street
10- Benjamin Condrey
11- Nicholas Countz &
12- Robert McElhiney

Who being Elected tryed and sworn the truth to speak and well and truly to Inquire what Damages the plaintiffs have sustained in a writ of Inquiry by them Brought in this case do say they assess the plaintiffs Damages to Twenty six Dollars & costs- Bill costs Issued to Major Grant.

Ordered by the Court that Jonathan Williams be appointed overseer of the Road in the Room of Edward Daniel & that he be allowed the same hands that the said Edward Daniel was allowed. Issd.

Samuel Carick & Co.)	
vs)	Justices present William Clay, William Rankins
David Hunt &c.)	William Peters Esquires.

1- Joseph Hoe Sr.	7- William Arnold
2- William Wilson	8- John Cannon
3- Thomas Johnston	9- Obediah Waters
4- Thomas James	10-William Shire
5- Martin Morris	11-William Mitchel
6- William Whiteside	12-John Moffett

(p 134)   February Sessions 1806

Who being Impaneled in his writ of Inquiry do say they find for the plaintiff and assess his damages to seventy two dollars and thirty three cents, it is therefore considered by the Court that the plaintiff have Judgment against the Defendant David Hunt for the aforesaid sum of Seventy two Dollars and Thirty three cents besides costs.

The Chairman of the Court having give due & public Notice according to Law for the Election of a Coroner in & for the County of Grainger for the Ensuring two years Obediah Waters offered himself as a candidate upon counting the Votes Ordered it appears that the said Obediah Waters was duly & constitutionally Elected as Coroner of said County who failed to give Bond with security as the Law Directs.

Thomas James one of the Executors of the Last Will and Testament of William James Deceased which was proven in open Court & was qualified as an Execution of the Estate of the Dec'd agreeable to the Tennor of the Will.

Ordered by the Court that the Jurors who was appointed at the last of this Court to view and lay off Roads and Report to this Court be continued Jurors to view and lay off said Roads that they were then appointed to view & make report to next Court.

Henry Minor Esquire produced to Court a License authorizing him to practice law as an Atty. in the several Courts in this State who takes an oth to support the Constitution of the United States & the State of Tennessee and also the oath of an Attorney and admitted as an Attorney to practice in this Court.

Thomas Jinnings	)
vs	)
James Dyer Constable	)
and Samuel Perry & John Horner his securities.	)

Thomas Jinnings by John F.Jack his Attorney makes a motion to Court to enter up a Judgment against the said James Dyar constable & Samuel Perry his Securities for the sum of forty two Dollars eleven & one half cents being the amount of monies.

(p 135)   February Sessions A.D. 1806

Demanded in an Execution issued by William Clay Esquire in favour of the said Thomas Jinnings against Spencer Griffen for failing to Return said Execution on which motion the Court will advise therefore it is considered by the Court that Thomas Jinnings the plaintiff in this case do Recover nothing by his motion - Thomas Dardis & Pleasant H.Miller entitled to a tax fee - Execution Issued.

William Cooper)
     vs   )
Abraham Elliot)   The plaintiff by John Cocke makes motion to Court to enter up a Judgment against Abraham Elliot who was summoned a garnashee on an Execution Issued in favour of the said William Cooper against Robert Moore -John Spring & John Hargraves, the said Abraham Elliot appearing in open Court and being sworn and it appearing to the Court that he owes Robert Moore sixty five Bushels of Indian Corn which is considered in his hands and it is ordered that Execution Do issue to the Sheriff to sell the same & the monies arising therefrom be applied in Satisfaction of the plaintiff demanded in the aforesaid Execution - Order sale Isd.

Andrew Campbell   )
Administrator of the   )
Estate of Hugh Campbell)   Justices present Noah Jarnagin -Philip
     vs   )   Sigler, Isaiah McDiff Esquires- therefore
Robert C.Gordon   )   came a Jury towit-

1- Henry Howell   7- James Brewer
2- Jas. Rich   8- William Street
3- Robert Alsup   9- Benj. Coulrey
4- John Crabb   10-Nicholas Counts
5- Joseph Hoe Jr.   11-William Shelton
6- John Hodge   12-William Hamilton

Who being elected tryed and sworn the truth to speak on the issue joined in htis case do say they find that the Defendant hath not paid the Debt in the Declaration and assess the plaintiffs damages by Reason thereof to Two Hundred and seven Dollars & fifty cents besides his costs.

State T.A.B.)
     vs   )   In this case the Defendants Security surrenders him
Ronalds Brogan)   in discharge of themselves as Bail.

Ordered by the Court that the following persons be appointed Jurors to the Superior Court of Hamilton District- Robin Riggs, Joseph Cobb Esqr. William Peters & William Hamilton-
Ordered by Court that the following persons be appointed Jurors to May Term. A.D. 1806.   Isd.

(p 136)   February Sessions A.D. 1806

1- William Mitchell   2- Mathew Campbell

3— Richard Acuff
4— James Alsup
5— Miller Easley
6— Evan Harris
7— Samuel Perry
8— Robert D. Eaton
9— Thos. Smith
10—William Golden
11—William Street
12—Abraham Wilson
13—John Eatis
14—James Arwine
15—Peter Beelor
16—John Thomson
17—John Humphreys
18—William Arnold
19—William Cook

20— Thomas Branson
21— John Hains
22— George Norris
23— John Hoe
24— Edward West
25— Josiah Kidwell
26— Thomas Shipley
27— Daniel Beelor
28— John Dennis Jr.
29— Isaac Mitchel &
30— Pleasant Duke

Court adjourns till tomorrow 9 o'clock.

At a Court continued and held in and for the County of Grainger A.D 1806 being the 19th of Feby.

Justices present —Major Lea, Isaiah Midcliff and William Clay.

Ordered by the Court James Sartin an orphan Boy now of the age of Eleven years & Eleven months be bound an apprentice to William Keith till he shall attain to the age of twenty one years to Learn the art trade & ministry of a Hatter and Major Lea Chairman of the Court & the same William Keith in pursuance of an order of Court interchangeably inter into Indenture for the purposes aforesaid.

State   )
   vs   )
Joseph Fields)   Justices present, Major Lea, William Clay & David Mc-
Anally Esquires. Thereupon came a Jury towit,

1— John Moffett
2— James Blair
3— Stephen Smith
4— James Reddis
5— James Conn
6— John Green

7— Nicholas Countz
8— John Crabb
9— Edward Breeden
10—William Shields
11—John Hodges
12—John Holt

Who being Elected tried & sworn the truth to speak on the Issue at Traverse do say they find the Defendant not guilty in manner & form as charged in the Bill of Indictment and the Defendant Discharged from the payment of all costs.

The Grand Jury Dismissed for the present Term.

Francis Willet proved his attendance as constable of the Grand Jury at the present three Days.

(p 137)   February Sessions A.D. 1806

State   )
   vs   )   Present— Major Lea, David McAnally & Charles McAnally
Sairah Going)   Esquires. Thereupon came a Jury (towit)

1- Francis Daniel
2- William Kirkham
3- William Street
4- Thomas Lea
5- John Wells
6- Benj. Condrey

7- Joseph Fields
8- Thomas Ball
9- John Hunter
10-Thomas Dunn
11-Joseph Rich &
12-William Dyer

Who being elected tried and sworn the truth to speak on the Issue Traverse in this do say they find the Defendant not guilty in manner & form as charged in the Bill of Indictment -rule to tax the prosecution with the costs - rule discharged.

Benjamin Atkinson by John F.Jack his agent has leave to Return 314 acres of Land subject to the payment of Taxes for the year 1806.

John Rumney by John F.Jack his Agent has leave to Return 10,000 acres of Land subject to the payment of Tax for the year 1806.

State   )
   vs   )   the Defendant
Tapley Haygood)

State   )
   vs   )   A.B.
Sarah Going)   Whereupon came the following Jury (towit)

1- John Moffet
2- James Blair
3- Valentine Morgan
4- James Reddis
5- James Conn
6- John Green

7- Nicholas Counts
8- John Bean
9- Edward Breeden
10-William Shields
11-John Hodges
12-John Holt

Who being Elected tryed and sworn the truth to speak on this Issue of Traverse in this do say they find the Defendant -Indictment - Mistrial by consent of Counsel.

Major Lea Esquire who was appointed at last Term to take in the list of Taxable property in the Bounds of Captain James Mitchel's company for the year 1806 was returned in open Court.

Ordered by the Court that Luke Lea Esquire be allowed to receive from the trustee of Grainger County the sum of Eight Dollars in order to enable him to purchase a Book or Books for the purpose of Transcribing the Records belonging to the Registers office of Grainger. Issd.

Ordered by the Court.that David McAnally & Charles McAnally

(p 138)   February Sessions A.D. 1806 -
Esquires be appointed Commissioners to Settle with John Adair Admr. of all and singular the goods and chattles Rights and credits of Thomas Cox -Deceased and make Report to this Court or next May Term.

Felps Reed Register of Grainger County in obedience to an Act present at the Last Session of the General Assembly Intitled an Act for the Better Regulation of Registers office &c Brought into Court all the Records of

Office and Exhibited to the worshipfull Justices for their Inspection &
examination and the Court having proceeded to inspect and Examine the same
are unanimously of opinion that the said records have not bin kept as
Contemplated by the above Recited Act and are further of opinion that it
is highly expedient that all the Records of the Registers office for the
County of Grainger should without delay be Transcribed pursuant to the
Act aforesaid whereupon the Court appointed Luke Lea Esquire To transcribe
the same in well Bound Books, and in a fair and Legible hand writing and
the said Luke Lea Immediately takes the oath prescribed by the above Recited Act before David McAnally Esquire in open Court.

Ordered by the Court that the following Tax Be laid and collected for
the year 1806 (towit) for each Hundred acres of Land twelve and one half
of a cent on each Free Poll twelve and one half cents - on each Town Lot
twenty five cents - on each Merchant or pedlar Five Dollars.

Ordered by the Court that the following Tax be laid & collected for
the purpose of Defraying the expengis of copying the Books Belonging to
the Registers office in the County of Grainger agreeably to an act of the
General Assembly passed at Knoxville on the thirtieth day of October 1805
for each hundred acres of Land six and one fourth cents - on each Free poll
6¼ cents on each negro slave 12½ cents on each Town Lott 12½ cents - on
each Merchant or Pedlar $2.50.

Thirsday the 20th of Feby. A.D. 1806 - present Court meet according
to adjournment -Major Lea, Philip Sigler, Henry Boatman.

Ordered by the Court that the Land Reported on by John Lea Esquire
Sheriff at Last Term of this Court which have been published in the
Knoxville Gazette as the Law   (p 139)   February Sessions A.D.1806.
Directs be sold by the Sheriff to satisfy the taxes due thereon (towit)
for the year 1806 -George M.Combs 870 acres - John Cathcart 50 acres -
William Bowling 200 -Jesse Coats 100 For the year 1805 -Lewis Clipper
30,000 acres the Heirs of Thomas Cox -Dec'd -260 acres -John Hargraves -
200 acres Geo. M.Combs 120 acres -Geo.M.Combs 150 acres Michael Cook 100
acres -John Bull Jr. 25 acres -Geo.M.Combs 600 acres. Order Issd.

John Denn - Lessee of
Henry Howell
      vs
Fenn & Pleasant Duke
towit-
1- Thomas Dunn
2- Nimrod Sisns
3- John Hunter
4- John Crabb
5- Joseph Long
6- John Hodges

Justices present -David McAnally -Peter Harris & Joseph Cobb. Whereupon came a Jury

7- William Mitchell
8- James Hamilton
9- William Shields
10-John Patterson
11-John Vineyard
12-John Moffet

Who being Elected tryed & sworn the truth to speak on the Issue Joined
do say they find the Defendant guilty of the Trespass Complained of in
Ejectment.

John Adair Admr. on the Estate of Thomas Cox -Dec'd Returns in open
Court 260 acres of Land as Taxable property for the year 1806.

Ordered by the Court that Samuel Clark, Charles Hutchison —Joseph Beeler - John Hall, Joseph Fields, William McPhetridge and Philip Sigler be Jury to view —lay out and mark a Road agreeable to Law from the Powder Spring Gap in Clinch Mountain to Circle Ferry on Clinch River and make Report to next Court.

Ordered by the Court that Francis A. Ramsey Esquire Be allowed the sum of Ten Dollars for Services rendered the County of Grainger for making out a statement of Jurors from Grainger County to the Superior Court of Hamilton District.

Ordered by the Court that John Cooke & John F. Jack Esquire be allowed the sum of Twenty Dollars for their services as Commissioners in settling with Thomas Henderson the former trustee of Grainger County.

(p 140)   February Sessions A.D. 1806

Ordered by the Court that John Cooke & John F. Jack Esquires be allowed the sum of Twelve Dollars for their services as Commissioners in settling with the present Sheriff and trustee of Grainger County.

Ordered by the Court that Tapley Haygood be allowed the sum of $25 for keeping Jeremiah Midkiff one of the poor of this County from August Term 1805 to November Term 1805 and also the further sum of $25 be allowed for keeping Jeremiah Midkiff from November Term 1805 To February Term 1806.   Issd. to D. McAnally.

Willie Blount by his agent Joseph Robertson Returns in open Court 650 acres of Land subject to taxation for the year A.D. 1806 also 600 acres on the waters of Bull Run known by the name Crain Town also 300 acres at the mouth of Williams Creek also 250 acres of Land on Flint Creek also 2000 acres of Land on Williams Creek.

The Commissioners David McAnally & Charles McAnally Esquires who was appointed at the present term to settle with John Adair Admr. on the Estate of Thomas Cox Deceased Report to Court that they have settled with the said Admr. and a settlement thereof filed in the Clerks Office which was examined by the Court.

Joseph Cobb Esquire who was appointed to take lists of Taxable property in the Bounds of Capt. Bowen's made his return &c.

A Deed of conveyance from Thomas Chin to Mary Hickey for a lot in the Town of Rutledge it being Lott No six in the plan of said was proven in open Court by oath of John F. Jack subscribing witness thereto & ordered to be Registered.

A Deed of conveyance from John Bunch to Walker John Horner, Nancy Harmon & Samuel B. Harmon heirs of James Harmon Deceased for two hundred acres of land acknowledged in open Court by the subscribing - John Bunch & ordered to be Registered.

A Deed of conveyance from Ambrose Hodge to Henry Pulnall and Henry Morgan for one Hundred and sixty acres of Land proven in open Court by

the oath of Benjamin Howell one of the subscribing witnesses & ordered to
be Registered.

A Deed of conveyance from John Jarnagin to George Moody for two hundred acres of Land acknowledged in open Court & ordered to be Registered.

A Deed of conveyance from John Hargraves to Thomas Dennis for ninety acres of Land proven in open Court by the oath Abraham Elliot.

(p 141)   February Sessions A.D. 1806
subscribing witness and ordered to Be Registered.

A Deed of conveyance from John Countz to Nicholas Countz for Lott No.
18 in the town of Rutledge was proven in open Court by the oaths of Henry
Bowen Jr. a subscribing witness thereto & ordered to be Registered.

A Deed of conveyance from James Blair -John Bristo-Isaac Midkiff to
John Griffin for one hundred acres of Land was proven in open Court by the
oath of Griffetts as to the signature of John Bristo & Isaac Midkiff and
James Blair Jr. came into open Court and acknowledged his signature thereto
for it was ordered to be Registered.

A Deed of conveyance from Loyd Aby to Edward Churchman for forty nine
acres of Land was proven in open Court by the oath of John Sutton one of
the subscribing witnesses and ordered to be Registered.

A Deed of conveyance from Thomas Dennis to Benjamin Elliot for sixty
acres of land was acknowledged in open Court and ordered to be Registered.

A Deed of conveyance from John Lea Sheriff of Grainger County to Benjamin Cropwood was acknowledged in open Court containing fifty acres & is
ordered to be Registered.

A Deed of conveyance from Henry Crowley to Josiah Shoadley for ninty
three acres of Land acknowledged in open Court and ordered to be Registered.
A Deed of conveyance from Elijah Donathan to Henry Howel for one Hundred and seventy acres of land was proven in open Court by the oath of
Peter Hamilton one of the subscribing witnesses and ordered to be Registered.
A Deed of conveyance from Young Lamar to Thomas Dennis for two hundred and seventy six acres was proven in open Court by the oath of William
Harmon one of the subscribing witnesses and ordered to Be Registered.

A Deed of conveyance from Robert Alsup to Solomon Massengill for 99
acres was proven in open Court by the oaths of John Humphreys & James
Carmichael two of the subscribing witnesses thereto and ordered to be
Registered.
A Deed of conveyance from Joshua Collins to Joel Barkwell for 100
acres of Land acknowledged in open Court and ordered to be Registered.

A Deed of conveyance from Josiah Dyer to David Tate for 25 acres of
Land and one Grist Mill acknowledged in open Court and ordered to be
Registered.

A Deed of conveyance from Josiah Dyer to David Tate for one hundred & fifty acres of Land and was acknowledged in open Court & ordered to be Registered.

(p 142)   February Sessions A.D. 1806

A Deed of conveyance from Robert Shelton to Andrew Cofman for two hundred acres of Land and was acknowledged in open Court and ordered to be Registered.

A Deed of conveyance from Henry Boatman to Joseph Owens for thirty seven & one half acres of Land acknowledged in open Court & ordered to be Registered.

A Deed of conveyance from John Robertson to Royal Jinnings for 200 acres of Land was proven in open Court by the oaths of George Jinnings & Pleasant Duke two of the Subscribing witnesses & ordered to Be Registered.

A Deed of conveyance from Wiat Stubblefield for forty three acres of Land was proven in open Court by the oaths of Joseph McelIy two of the subscribing witnesses & ordered to be Registered.

A Deed of conveyance from Thomas Dennis to Joseph Dennis for eighty acres of Land was acknowledged in open Court and ordered to be Registered.

A Bill of Sale from James Johnston -Stephen Johnston-Thomas Dodson & Samuel Dodson was proven in open Court by the oath of Joseph Stubblefield one of the subscribing witnesses thereto & ordered to be Recorded.

A Bond or Instrument of writing purporting to be a Deed of conveyance from John Sharp to Thomas Sharp for 88 acres of Land was proven in open Court by the oath of Thomas Churchman & Elizabeth Churchman two of the subscribing witnesses & ordered to be Registered.

Friday the 21st. of Feby. A.D. 1806
Court met according to adjournment -present Peter Harris -Charles Mc Anally & John Breeden Esquires.

John Baxter   )
     vs   )
Thomas Henderson   )
William Windham   )
John Wilson &
Rachel Wilson his wife formerly Rachel Windham.

Executor of Rubin Windham Dec'd- on motion of John Baxter by his Atty. Pleasant M.Miller filed his petition after the same being Read in open Court Ordered by the Court that the petition be filed & Summons Issue accordingly with the copy of the petition.

James Reddis   )
Guardian to Jonathan Pulnull   )   Petition for a Legacy of the
     vs   )   said James Reddis by his Atty.
Henry Morgan Executor of the   )   Thomas Dardis Exhibited his
Last Will and Testament of   )   petition in open Court against
Henry Pulnull -Deceased.   )   the said Henry Morgan Executer

as aforesaid whereupon it is ordered by the Court that the same be filed
and that a summons & copy of Petition be issued according to Law.

(p 143)   February Sessions A.D. 1806
     John Holt Sr. Samuel Rayl & John Hodges appearance Bail for William
Rayle in the suit Jacob Noe by Joseph Noe his father and next friend against
William Rayle Brought into Court the Body of William Rayle and surrendered
him in discharge of themselves as Bail.

     Ordered by Court that Frederick Moyers have Leave to move the publick
Gail of Grainger County from the place where it now stands on the public
square till opposite the Court House on said square about ten feet back
from the alley towards the Court House on condition that he leaves the
same in as good repair as it now is in.

     Ordered By the Court that Jesse Cheek have leave to Keep a house of
public intertainment where he now lives upon his given bond and Security
as the Law Direct who Gives Bond with David Mcenelly his security in the
sum of 1250 Dollars.

     Peter Harris Esquire who was appointed to take in Lists & Polls and
taxable property in the Bounds of Capt. William Bryants Company for the
year 1806 was returned in open Court agreeable to Law.

     Saturday Feby. 22nd. 1806 the Court meet according to adjournment.
Present Major Lea, Isaiah Midkiff- Charles McAnally Esquires.

John Vinyard   ) Justices present, William Clay, David McEnelly
   vs -appeal   ) & Charles McAnally Esquires.
No. 366 -James Hamilton   ) Thereupon came a Jury (towit)

1- John Crabb   7- Miller Easley
2- Henry Howell   8- Samuel D.Carrick
3- John Ogan   9- William Mitchel
4- Nicholas Bull   10-David Holt
5- James Bryant   11-David Clayton
6- Jesse McAnally   12-William Harris
     Who being Elected tryed & sworn the truth to speak on the matter in
dispute in this case do say they find for the plaintiff and assess his damages to seven Dollars & fofty cents besides his costs.

Thomas Jinnings)
     vs   ) Noe Ashley one of the constables of this County to
Spencer Griffin) whom an Execution issued Signed by Major Lea one of
the Justices of Grainger County was directed wherein & whereby he was commanded that of the Goods & chattles of Spencer Griffin in said County &
if no Goods & chattles in said County then of the Lands and Tenements of
said Spencer Griffin he should to be made the sum of Forty two Dollars
Eleven & one half cents to satisfy a Judgment -Thomas Jinnings Recovered
against Spencer Griffin Before Major Lea one of the Justices of this County and also the further sum of Seventy five cents for costs and charges &
that he should make due Return hereof the said Execution to Court with a
Return endowed thereon in the words and figures following (towit) Levied

the written Execution,   (p 144)   on the following Tracts of Land
towit- Levied on one hundred & fifty acres of Land being a part of a 500
acres Survey known by the name of the Panther Springs also on 300 acres
of Land Lying on the North side of Clinch mountain adjoining the lands of
Samuel Clark being the tract of Land whereupon John Spencer formerly
Lived and also on a Lot in the Town of Rutledge being the same Lot said
Griffin bought of Thomas Jinnings lying opposite William Keiths Lot Levied
on the above described Land on the property of Spencer Griffin on 22nd.
Feby. 1806 not being able to find any personal property whereupon Thomas
Jinnings By John F.Jack his Atty. makes a motion to Court to enter up a
Judgment against the said Spencer Griffin for the aforesaid sum of money
& that the Lands Levied on as above may be sold -It is considered by the
Court that the said plaintiff do recover the said sum of $42.11½ & costs
against the said Defendant & that an Execution do issue to the Sheriff
commanding him to sell the above Land Levied on as aforesaid -Order of
Sale issued.

Josiah Nichol -Assignee)
of Lewis Harmon   )
       vs   )   Whereupon came a Jury (towit) the same Jury
Nicholas Spring   )   as in the suit John Vinyard against James
Hamilton Except James Dyer in the place of Samuel D.Carrick who being
Elected tryed & sworn the truth to speak in the issue joined in this case
do say the Defendant hath not paid the Debt in the Declaration mentioned
as in pleading he hath alledged and find the Debt in the Declaration mentioned and assess the plaintiffs damages occationed by Reason of the Detention thereof to $15.75 Besides his costs.

Ordered by the Court that Jesse McAnnily be appointed constable in
the Bounds of John Dodson's Company of Militia who gave Bond in the sum of
$500 with Thomas Henderson & Henry Howell his securities and take the
necessary oaths.

Ordered by the Court that Thomas Henderson former Trustee be allowed
a credit for $9.39 and three fourths of a cent on a former settlement with
the Commissioners of Grainger County -also that he Returned from the Trustee of Grainger County the sum of $39.60 and one fourth of a cent it being
a sum which appears to be Due him from said County of Grainger as trustee
aforesaid.   Order Issd.

John Coake comes into open Court and gives in his Lists of taxable
property for the year A.D. 1806 -1780 acres of Land -Four town lots -1
white poll - 9 black polls also 600acres of Land the property of David
Ross.
(p 145)   February Sessions A.D. 1806

David Hanley Agent for Thomas Kitt and Lewis Clipahier Esquires Returns 20,000 acres of Land subject to Taxation for the same year A.D.1806.

Ordered By the Court that Joseph Cobb & Peter Harris Esquires be appointed Commissioners to settle with John Crabb admr. of Joseph Crabb
deceased & make Report to May Term.

Noe Ashley proves his attendance as constable six Days.

Court adjourns Till Court in Course.

D.Mcenally

May Sessions A.D. 1806
At a Court of Pleas and Quarter Sessions began and held at the Court
House in Rutledge on Monday the 19th day of May in the year of our Lord
one thousand eight hundred and six. Justices present, Noe Jarnagin, James
Moore, John Breeden and Isaiah Midkiff, Esquires.

John Lea high Sheriff of Grainger County by his Deputy Samuel Punch
Returns to Court that he Executed the following Venire facias on the following persons Except William Cock & Thomas Branson (towit)

1- William Mitchel
2- Mathew Campbell
3- Richard Acuff
4- James Alsup
5- Miller Easley
6- Evan Harris
7- Samuel Perry
8- Robert D.Eaton
9- Thomas Smith
10-William Golders
11-Thomas Branson
12-William Street
13-Abraham Wilson
14-John Estis
15-James Arwine
16- Peter Beeler
17- John Thompson
18- John Humphreys
19- William Arnold
20- William Cook
21- John Haynes
22- George Norris
23- John Noe
24- Edward West
25- Josiah Kidwell
26- Thomas Shipley
27- Daniel Beeler
28- John Dennis Jr.
29- Isaac Mitchel
30- Pleasant Duke

(p 146)   May Sessions A.D. 1806
Out of which Venire facias the persons whose names are underwritten
are appointed a Grand Jury for the present Term(towit)

1- William Street foreman
2- William Michel
3- Mathew Campbell
4- Richard Acuff
5- James Alsup
6- Evan Harris
7- Samuel Perry
8- Robert D.Eaton
9- Thomas Smith
10-Abraham Wilson
11-Peter Beeler
12-John Thomson
13-John Humphreys
14-William Arnold
15-John Haines

Sworn and charged

Francis Willet appointed Constable of the Grand Jury.
20th. May 1806 Grand Jury Discharged.

Ordered by the Court that Cobb Howel be appointed constable in the
County of Grainger who entered into Bond in the sum of $500 with Henry
Howell & Josiah Dyer his securities.

Ordered by the Court that David Porcupile an orphant of Eleven years
of age be bound to William Bryant as an apprentice untill he attain the
age of twenty one years & the said Bryant enters into Bond with the Chairman of the Court accordingly.

A Deed of conveyance from Edward Shipley to Thomas Shipley for one hundred & fifty acres of Land in open Court by oath of John Estis and ordered bo be Registered.

A Deed of conveyance from Edward Shipley to Thomas Shipley for 70 acres of Land was proven in open Court by the oath of John Estiis and ordered to Be Registered.

Jesse Callison Returns list of polls and taxable property for the year 1806 in open Court one white poll and 150 acres of land.

James Callison Jr. Returns in open Court his Lists of Taxable property for the year 1806 350 acres of land all Returned by Jesse Callison.

James Callison Returns his Lists of Taxable property for the year 1806 in open Court 700 acres of Land.

A Deed of conveyance from Henry Howell for 200 acres of Land proven in open Court by the oath of William Hodges & ordered to be Registered.

A Deed of conveyance from Elijah Donathan to Tandy Senter proven in open Court by the oath of William Kirk a witness thereto & ordered to be Registered.

(p 147)   May Sessions A.D. 1806

A Deed of conveyance from James Hodges to John Hodges for 150 acres of Land proven in open Court by the oath of Alexander Walker & John Tucker & ordered to be Registered.

A Bill of Sale from Francis Mayberry to Mathew Campbell for a negroe Girl proven in open Court by the oath of Robert Blair and ordered to be Recorded.

A Bill of Sale from Henry Bowen Sr. to John Bowen for a negro Girl proven in open Court by the oath of Robert Massengill & ordered to be Recorded.

A Bill of Sale from Robert Dunville to Elijah Clay for a negro proven in open Court by the oath of William Sims a witness thereto & ordered to be Recorded.

A Bill of Sale from Robert Dunville to William Sims for a negro proven in open Court by the oath of Elijah Clay & ordered to be Recorded.

A Deed of Gift from Henry Bowen Sr. to James Bowen a negroe Boy was proven in open Court by the oath of Frederick Moyers a witness thereto & ordered to be Recorded.

A Power of Attorney from Joseph Boon to William Hamilton was proven in open Court and ordered to be Registered.

A Bill of Sale from Francis Mayberry to James Wilson for a negro & other property was proven in open Court by the oath of Thomas Grimes & ordered to be Recorded.

A Deed of conveyance after the nature of a Deed of Gift from James Wilson to Elsey Wilson his sister was acknowledged in open Court & ordered to be Recorded.

Ordered by the Court that John Cocke & John F. Jack have leave to keep a house of public entertainment in the County of Grainger who together with themselves enters into Bond with Henry Howell their security in the sum of $1250.

Ordered by the Court that John Estis be Excused from serving as a Juror at the present Term for Reasons Stated in his petition to Court.

Falps Reed Register of the County of Grainger transmitted his Resignation to Court as Register for the said County and Received By the Court.

Noble Keith returns in open Court his Lists of Taxable property for the year 1806 fifty acres of Land and Town Lott.

(p 148)   May Sessions A.D. 1806

Tandy Senter Returns his lists of Taxable property in open Court for the year 1806 300 acres of Land – one white poll & one black poll.

Joel Harmers Returns in open Court his Lists of Taxable property for the year 1806 33 acres of Land & one white poll.

William Clay Rainger of Grainger County made the following Return (towit) – A list of Strays Remaining on my books and not proven away 12 mos. of the following specifications,(towit)

John Bunch Sr. 5 Hoggs — $5.00
Henry Hawkins Sr. one heiffer ——$3.00
John Bean – one Steer ———— 7.00
Signed   N. Clay – R.G.C.

Court adjourns Till 9 o'clock.
Court met according to adjournment –Present Henry Boatman – William Hortin & William Peters, Esquires.

Jinkins Whitesides By Attorney presents a petition to Court for a partition of a certain Tract of Land in the words and figures following (towit) Grainger County (towit) May Term 1806–
To the Worshipful Court of Pleas and Quarter Sessions in & for the said County of Grainger – Your petitioner Jenkins Whiteside of Davison Co. and State of Tennessee respectively represents to your Worships that the State of North Carolina by pattent bearing date the 12th Day of July 1796 & No. 623 Granted unto Robert King & John Blair a tract of Land containing 200 acres situated lying & being in what was Hawkins County & Grainger County on German Creek Between the Lands of John Coulter and the tract on which Joseph Cobb now lives in said State of Tennessee and bound as follows (towit) Beginning on a Black Oak and two white oaks Running thence South 240 poles to two white oaks on the Top of a Ridge on the South side of the creek thence West 170 poles to a stake thence North 240 poles to a Stake near the line of the tract on which said Joseph Cobb now lives and thence to the Beginning that the said John Blair previous to the first day of January in the year of our Lord 1796 –Died intestate leaving a wife Sarah who has since Intermarried with said Joseph Cobb a Daughter named Catharine Blair and a son John Blair both them(towit) at the Death of said John, yet an infant under the age of 21 years that said John Blair was the only son and heir at Law of said John –Dec'd and the legal Title to one equal undivided moiety of said Tract of 200 acres of Land as intended and is now

Vested in him as heir to the said John Blair Deceased- your petition further (p 149)   May Sessions A.D. 1805

Represents to your Worships that said Robert King soon after the date of said patent sold and afterwards conveyed his equal and undivided moiety of said Tract of 200 acres of Land to James Blair for a valuable consideration (towit) for the sum of $100 to him paid by which said James Blair became seized and possessed of said undivided moiety of said tract of land and the said Blair so being seized and possessed of said equal and undivided moiety of Land 200 acres of Land afterwards on the 17th Day of April 1805 sold and conveyed the same to your petitioner by said Indenture bearing date the said day and year lasts aforesaid for the consideration of $200 to him paid that your petitioner and the said infant John Blair are now seized and possessed of said tract of 200 acres of Land as

Tenants in common and your petitioner is desirous to have the same divided between them that each may hold his part in severalty distinguished by proper meets and bounds - your petitioner therefore requests that your Worships may appoint five suitable free holders as Commissioners to enter upon examination and make partition of said tract of land between your petitioner and said John Blair son and heir of said John Blair- Dec'd and Due returns to make of this proceedings under their hands and seals at next Term of your Worships Court in conformity with the Directions prescribed by the Act of the Assembly (General) in such case made and provided and your petitioner &c.

J. Whitesides

Which petition being heard by the Court & it further appearing to the satisfaction of the Court by the acknowledgment of Joseph Cobb Guardian to the said John Blair being a Minor being made in Court that he Joseph Cobb Guardian as aforesaid had been duly served with a written Notice of the time & intention Exhibiting the above petition more than ten days previous to the Exhibiting the same, whereupon it is ordered by the Court that said petition be filed & that the prayers thereof be Granted & it is further ordered by said Court that William Clay, Robert Stubblefield, Thomas Henderson, David Hoenelly & John Cooke Esquires be Commissioners to partition & set apart to the said Jenkins Whitesides & John Blair in severalty each his own half part of said tract of Land by the said Jenkins Whitesides & John Blair as tenants in common containing two hundred acres of Land lying & being in what was called Hawkins But now Grainger County on German Creek between the Lands of John Coulter and the Lands where Joseph Cobb now lives bounded as follows (towit) Beginning at a Black Oak & two white oaks running thence South 240 poles to a stake &c & that the said Commissioners do make & designate by proper meets and boundaries the several portions of said Claiments in said tract of Land & make due return of their proceedings to the Justices of our next Court of Pleas & Quarter Sessions to be held for aforesaid County of Grainger at the Court House in Rutledge on the third Monday in August next in form according to the Act of the General Assembly in such made & provided.

(p 150)   May Sessions A.D. 1805

At an Election opened and held at the present Term for a Trustee of the County of Grainger and upon counting and examining the Votes it appears that Charles Hoenelly Esquire was duly & constitutionally Elected Trustee in and for said County who entered into Bond in the sum of two thousand Dollars with John Cooke & John F. Jack his securities as trustee.

John Cocke & Thomas Henderson produced a commission from his Excellency John Sevier Governor appoited them Justices of the peace in and for
the County of Grainger who took the oath to support the Constitution of
the State of Tennessee & also the oath of office.

Ordered by the Court that Tapley Haygood be allowed the sum of $25
for keeping and supporting Jeremiah Ridcliff one of the poor of this County
from Feby. 1803 till the present Term. Issd.

Richard Reynolds)
    vs   )   John F.Jack Atty. for Richard Reynolds makes motion
Robert Yancey)   in open Court against Robert Yancey late Sheriff for
the sum of $18.50 it Being monies he was compelled to pay over as Security
for the said Robert Yancey — it is, therefore ordered by the said Richard
Reynolds to Recover from the said Robert Yancey the aforesaid sum of $18.50
besides his costs.
    Ordered by the Court that James Dyer be appointed Constable in the
County of Grainger who entered into Bond in the sum of $500 with Robert D.
Eaton & Samuel Perry his securities.

Sally Miller now of the age of fifteen years comes into Court and
makes choice of Thomas Carney as her Guardian of the minor heirs in the
sum of $500 with Meredith Coffee, Isaac Thomson his securities.

Ordered by Court that Joseph Peters be appointed Constable in the Co.
of Grainger who enters into Bond in the sum of $500 with William Peters
& Charles Hutchison his securities.

At an Election open & held at the Court House in Rutledge on the
20th day of May A.D. 1806 for high Sheriff in and for the County of Grainger whereupon counting the votes it appears that James Conn was duly &
constitutionally Elected High Sheriff in and for said County who entered
into Bond in the sum of $2500 with Thomas Henderson —Pleasant Duke, John
Allison & Francis Willet his securities.

(p 151)   May Sessions A.D. 1806

John Cocke Esquire Solicitor for the County of Grainger Resigns his
appointment as Solicitor & appoint Thomas Dardis Esquire in his place for
Term.
    At an Election open & held for the County of Grainger at the Court
House in Rutledge for Register in and for said County upon counting the
Vote it appears that Samuel Perry was duly & Constitutionally Elected
Register in and for said County who enters into Bond in the sum of $2500
with John Thomson —William Mitchel & John Vineyard his securities.

State   )
    vs   )   Bastardy
James Kemp)   the Defendant security of Jacob Gibson surrenders the De-
fendant in discharge of himself as Bail and prayed in custody of the Sher-
iff.
State   )
    vs   )   By order of Court the Defendant Chargeable of the mainten-
James Kemp)   ance & support of a Bastard child for which he stands

chargeable after begot on the body of Elizabeth Hawkins and afterwards on the 21st. Day of the present Term the said James Kemp comes into Court and Enters into Bond in the sum of $500 with Edward Haley & Jacob Gibson his securities for the Indemnification of the County.

Know all men by these presents that We James Conn -Thomas Henderson Pleasant Duke -John Allison & Francis Willet all of the County of Grainger and State Tennessee are held & firmly bound unto John Sevier Governor of the State of Tennessee in the sum of Thousand five hundred dollars Lawful Currency of the United States to be paid unto the said John Sevier or his successors in office to the which payment well and truly to be made -We bind ourselves and each other of us our every of our heirs Executors & Administrators jointly & severally firmly by these presents sealed with our seals and dated the 25th day of May in the year of our Lord 1796.

The condition of the above obligation is such that whereas the above bounded James Conn hath the day and date hereof hath been duly and constitutionally Elected Sheriff of Grainger County - If therefore the said Jas. Conn shall well and truly Execute and due return make & make of process to him Directed and pay and satisfy all fees and sums of money by him Received or Levied by Virtue of any process into the proper Office by which the same by the Tennor thereof ought to be paid or to the person or persons to whom the same shall be due his hir or their Executors Administrators Attorneys or Agents and in all other things well Truly and faithfully Execute the said Office of Sheriff during his Term.

(p 152)   May Sessions A.D. 1806

Continuance therein the above obligation to be Void otherwise to Remain in full force and effect.

                                    James Conn   -seal
                                    Thomas Henderson -seal
Test-   Pleasant Duke -seal
Saml. C.Yancey   John Allison -seal
                                    Francis Willet -seal

Know all men by these presents that We, James Conn- Pleasant Duke- Thomas Henderson-John Allison & Francis Willet all of the County of Grainger Co. and State of Tennessee are held and firmly Bound unto John Sevier Governor of the State of Tennessee in the sum of $2000 lawful current money of the United States to be paid unto John Sevier or his successors in Office to the which well and truly to be made, we bind ourselves our heirs Executors and Administrators Jointly and severally firmly by these presents sealed with our seals and dated this 20th day of May A.D. 1806.

The condition of the above obligation is such that whereas the above bounded James Conn hath the day of the date hereof hath been duly and constitutionally Elected Sheriff of Grainger County - If therefore the said James Conn shall well and truly faithfully and honestly pay the same unto the Trustee or Treasurer for Grainger County -then the above obligation to be void otherwise to remain in full force or effect.

Signed sealed and Delivered in open Court -   Jas. Conn- Thos. Henderson
Saml. C.Yancey   Pleasant Duke-John Allison
                                              Francis Willet   -Seal.

Know all men by these present that we James Conn- Thomas Henderson-
Pleasnt Duke- John Allison & Francis Willet all of the County of Grainger
& State of Tennessee are held and firmly Bound unto John Sevier Governor
of the State of Tennessee in the sum of $2000 lawful current money of the
United States to be paid unto the said John Sevier or his successors in
office to the which payment well and truly to be made —we being ourselves
and every of us our and Every of our heirs —Executors and Administrators
Jointly and severally firmly by these presents sealed with our seals and
Dated the 20th Day of May A.D. 1806.

(p 153)   May Sessions 1806
The condition of the obligation is such that whereas the above bounded Jas.
Conn hath the Day of the Date herwof hath been Duly & constitutionally
elected Sheriff of Grainger County - If therefore the said James Conn shall
well and truly Collect all Taxes that shall become due to said State in
said office and also well and truly faithfully & honestly pay the same to
the treasurer for the District of Washington & Hamilton then the above obligation to be void -otherwise to Remain in full force and Effect.

Signed Sealed and
Delivered in open Court

Seal. C.Yancey -James Conn -seal
               Thomas Henderson -seal
               Pleasnt Duke -seal
               John Allison -seal
               Francis Willet -seal

     Ordered by the Court Thomas Edington be appointed overseer of the Road
from Thomas Johnston's Line to Bean Station in the place of James Conn and
that he have same hands within the Bounds heretofore allowed to James Conn
to keep the same in Repair according to Law. Issued.

     A releasment or acquitance from Richard Reynolds to William Miligan
for 350 acres of Land was proven in open Court by the oath of William Crump
a witness & ordered to be Recorded.

     A Deed of conveyance from Richard Reynolds to William Miligan for 170
acres of Land proven in open Court by the oath of William Crump a witness
thereto and ordered to be Registered.

     A Deed of conveyance from Joseph Green to Abraham Elliott for four-
teen acres of Land proven in open Court by the oath of Jacob Elliott a witness and ordered to be Registered.

     A Deed of conveyance from Joseph Cobb to Jinkin Whitesides for 17 acres
of Land was acknowledged in open Court by Joseph Cobb the subscribing thereto and ordered to be Registered.

     A Deed of conveyance from Nicholas Spring to John Dennis for one hun-
dred acres of Land was proven in open Court by the oath of Joseph Fields
a witness thereto & ordered to be Registered.

     A Deed of conveyance from Jesse Jinnings Sr. to Christopher Conway
for100 acres of Land proven in open Court by the oath of Ambrose Yancey

a witness thereto & ordered to be Registered.

(p 164)   Ordered by the Court that following persons be summoned to attend at August Term 1806 as Jurors (towit)

1- John Beeler
2- Peter Hamilton
3- Joseph Fields
4- Jesse Cheek
5- Joseph Cobb
6- Peter Harris Sr.
7- Joseph Moe Jr.
8- David Tate
9- Jacob Arnet
10-David Huddleston
11-Chesley Jarnagin
12-Miller Easley
13-William Golden
14-John Estes
15-Peter Beeler

16- William Cook
17- Josiah Kidwell
18- Abraham Pruit
19- William Kirkham
20- Major Lea
21- Moses Hodges
22- Thomas Johnston
23- Dennis Condrey
24- Cornelius McCoy
25- Joseph Eaton
26- Joseph Stubblefield
27- David Fields
28- Robert Stone
29- John Bunch
30- George Moody

Ordered by the Court that Philip Frae be appointed overseer of the road in the Room of Frederick Moyers from Pattersons Creek to the Sand Lick Branch on the Richland Road and that he have all the hands that said Moyers had to the same in repair according to Law. Issd.

Wednesday 21st. May A.D. 1806 —Court met according to adjournment . Justices Present —Josiah Midkiff- Henry Boatman & William Martin, Esqrs. James Kemp who charged with Bastardy on the Body of Elizabeth Hankins comes into Court and enters into Bond in the sum of $500 to endemnify the County from the charge and maintenance of the above named Bastard child Edward Haley & Jacob Gibson his securities.

State   )
  vs   )
Caleb Going &)   Pettilarceny –
James Going   )   Thomas Henderson- James Moore & Charles Mc Anally
                   Esquires. Thereupon came a Jury (towit)

1- Edward West
2- Isaac Mitchell
3- John Hodges
4- Nicholas Countz
5- James Redis
6- Joseph Yeadin

7- Jacob Arnett
8- Martin Morris
9- William Kirkham
10-Thomas Nance
11-John Moffit &
12-Johnston

Who being elected tried & sworn in this case do say they find for the defendant not Guilty in manner   (p 165)   and form as charged in the Bill of Indictment —Rule Tax the Prosecutors with costs —Rule Discharged.

State   )
  vs   )   John Williams motion by Edward Scott Atty. for the De-
James Brown   )   fendant for to discharge the Indictment in this case.

State – vs James Brown –   Edward Scott & John Williams Esqr.maketh motion in open court to have the Bill of Indictment in this case discharged.

State)
vs)
James Brown)   John Williams & Edward Scott Esquires maketh motion in open Court to discharge the Bill of Indictment in this case.

    Ordered by the Court that $20 be appropriated for the use of Stephen Collins one of the poor of this County to be placed in the hands of Chas. McAnally Esquire for the use of said Stephen Collins.

State)
vs)
James McGinnis)   Mary Bawldwin a witness in this case being solemnly called came not - it is therefore considered by the Court that forefeit according to an Act of Assembly-

State)
vs)
James McGinnis)   Present Thomas Henderson -David McAnally & John Breeden, Esquires.

    Thereupon came a Jury towit-

1.- Pleasent Duke   7- John Hailey
2- Thomas Dunn   8- Zachariah Keith
3- Samuel Perry   9- Thomas McBroom
4- Robert McElhany   10-Rubin Dixon
5- Henry Howell   11-Ezecal Craft &
6- Thomas Edington   12-Nicholas Countz

    Who being Elected tryed & sworn the truth to speak on the Issue in traverse in this case do say mistrial by consent.

    Ordered by the Court that Joshua Hickey be appointed overseer of the road from the town of Rutledge to the top of the Richland   (p 156) (May Sessions) A.D. 1806 -   Knobs in the place of Martin Albert Resignee & that he have the same bounds for hands that the Albert had.Isd.

Nicholas Spring)
vs)
Robert Moore &)
John Spring)   On motion of Nicholas Spring by James Trimble his Attorney to enter up Judgment against the said Robert Moore and John Spring for $354.24 for so much monies recovered of him and by him paid to Joseph Nichol Assignee of Lewis Harmon as their security and it appearing to the satisfaction of the Court that said sum of $354.24 was paid by said Nicholas by Virtue of a Judgment obtained in the Court of Grainger County at the suit of Josiah Nichol assignee against him as security of the said Robert & John on a note-- It is therefore considered by the Court that the said Nicholas Spring do Recover of the said Robert Moore & John Spring said sum of $354.24 besides his costs & that execution Issue and Execution Issd.

Nicholas Spring)
vs)
John Margraves)   On motion of Nicholas Spring by James Trimble his Atty. and it appearing to the satisfaction of the Court that said Nicholas Spring has been compelled to pay the sum of $26.33 by a Judgment obtained in Grainger County against him as security of the said John Margraves Constable - it is therefore considered by the Court that the said Nicholas Spring do Recover of the said John Margraves Constable

the aforesaid sum of $26.30 with costs of motion & that execution Issue accordingly.

Ordered by the Court that the ones of the Ferry on Clinch River where the Kentucky road crosses the same be allowed the following Rates (towit) For Man & Horse 12½¢ for each four wheel Carriage one Dollar – for each two wheel Carriage fifty cents – for each footman single horse or head of Cattle six and one fourth of a cent.

Ordered by the Court that David McAnally & Josiah Dyer Esquires be appointed Commissioners to settle with Thomas Henderson –William Windham and Rachel Windham now Rachel Wilson Executors & Executrix of the estate of Rubin Windham Deceased. and make report to next Court.

Ordered by the Court that the following Tax be Laid & Collected in the County of Grainger for the year A.D. 1806 on each white poll 3 cents on each black poll six cents and on each Hundred acres of Land six cents.

(p 157)   May Sessions A.D. 1806
Ordered by the Court that John Lea late Sheriff of Grainger County be allowed the sum of $80 for his Ex Officio Servis as Sheriff from May term 1805 To May Term 1806.

Ordered by the Court that John Cocke Esquire be allowed the sum of $20 for his services as Solicitor in the County of Grainger from May Term 1806. Issd.
Ordered by the Court that Ambrose Yancey Clerk of Grainger County be allowed the sum of $40 for his Ex Officio Servises from May Term 1805 to May Term 1806. Issd.

Thomas McBroom comes into open Court and Returns his Lists of Taxable property for the year 1806 One white poll.

Allen Christian comes into Court and Returns his Lists of Taxable property for the year 1806– one white poll.

Henry Crowley comes into open Court and Returns his Lists of Taxable for the year 1806. One white poll & 200 acres of Land.

Isaiah Shockley comes into Court & Returns his lists of Taxable property for the year 1806 – one white poll.

Riland Birks comes into Court & Returns his lists of Taxable property for the year 1806 – one white poll & 40 acres of Land.

Richard Birks comes into open Court & Returns his lists of Taxable property for the year 1806 – one white poll.
Joseph Brown comes into Court & Returns his lists of Taxable property for the year 1806 – one white poll & 50 acres of Land.

Ordered by the Court that William Clay, Noe Jarnagin and Major Lea Esquires be appointed Commissioners to settle with the Administrators of the Estate of George Miller Deceased & make report to next Court –whereupon the said Commissioners so appointed made their report to this Court in the words and figures following (towit)

We, William Clay, Noe Jarnagin and Major Lea being appointed by the Court Grainger County to settle with John Conley Admr. and Nancy Miller Admr. of George Miller -Deceased and report to this Term and it appears on settlement that the said John Conley and Nancy Miller stands indebted to the heirs of George Miller Dec'd. the sum of eight hundred ninety eight dollars and seventy nine & one half cent.

                     Contri   Cr.
To amount of Sales   - $541.59½ By cash pd-
George Tinly —— $11.50
Cash ——————————   157.20 -Contingent
Expences -$29.27
T. Harmon Note —— $10.00 - J.Harmon's.
Note $10.00
T.Roach's Note ——180.00 - J.R. Roach
Note $180.00 —— $898.79½

John Brys Note   7.00
  "   "   "   9.75

(p 158)   May Sessions A.D. 1806
D.Day ————$14.00
L.Moore — 345.43
           385.26
We the undersigned Do certify that the foregoing Statement to be Just & true agreeable to the statement and Vouchers to us produced May 21st. 1806.
                    W.Clay   )
                    N.Jarnagin) Com.
                    Major Lea   )
     Thursday 22nd. May A.D. 1806 -Court met according to adjournment by Jas. Dyer Const. -Present Thomas Henderson, John Cocke, John Breeden & Henry Boatman Esquires.

     The Court having proceeded to ballot for a Chairman whereupon counting the Ballots it appears that Thomas Henderson Esquires is duly Elected Chairman of the Court of Grainger County.

     Joseph Noe Jr. resigns his appointment as overseer of the road & Recommends Richard Shelton & George Boatman.

     Ordered by the Court that the order of Court at last Term for viewing a road from the Powder Spring Gap in Clinch Mountain to Sircles Ferry on Clinch River be continued till next Court for Consideration.

     Francis Willet appointed Deputy Sheriff in the County of Grainger & took the necessary oath of Office as such.

Reynolds Brogan)
    vs   )
Benjamin Yates   )   Present, Thomas Henderson, William Clay & John Breeden Esquires. Thereupon came a Jury (towit)

1- Henry Howell - 2- Thomas Edington- 3- Jesse Cheek- 4- Samuel Williams

5— Washington Aryl
6— John Holt
7— David Holt
8— Pleasant Duke

9— John Green
10—Joseph Noe Sr.
11—Nicholas County
12—Joseph Rich

Who being Elected tryed and sworn the truth to speak on the matter in dispute in this case do say they find for the Debt, therefore it is considered by the Court that the Defendant Benjamin Yates do recover his costs accrewing as assessed by the Jury aforesaid & that the plaintiff Reynolds Brogan take nothing by his fals Clamor

Noe Ashley Constable who was appointed at last Court to attend the Court at the present Term proves four days such.

Francis Willet Constable who was appointed to attend on Grand Jury proved his attendance as such Two days. Isd,—

(p 159)   May Sessions A.D. 1806
Ordered by the Court that Noe Ashley be appointed a Constable to attend on the Grand Jury at August Term & that Joseph Peters be appointed a Constable at August Term to attend on the Court.
The Court then adjourned untill Court in Course.
                                        Thomas Henderson.
          August Sessions A.D. 1806
At a Court of Pleas & Quarter Sessions began and held in and for the County of Grainger at the Court House in Rutledge on the third Monday in August A.D. 1806, it being the Eighteenth of the same month— Present Thomas Henderson, James Moore, John Breeden and Henry Boatman, Esquires.

James Conn, high Sheriff of Grainger County made his Returns to Court that he had executed the following Venire facias on the following persons (towit) Except John Bunch, David Fields, Major Lea, Jesse Cheek & Joseph Stubblefield.

1— John Beelor
2— Peter Hamilton
3— Joseph Fields
4— Jesse Cheek
5— Joseph Cobb
6— Peter Harris
7— Joseph Noe Jr.
8— David Tate
9— Jacob Arnett
10—David Huddleston
11—Chesley Jarnagin
12— Miller Easley
13—William Goldin
14—John Estis
15—Peter Beelor

16— William Cook
17— Josiah Kidwell
18— Abraham Pruit
19—William Kirkham
20—Major Lea
21— Moses Hodges
22— Thomas Johnston
23— Dennis Condray
24— Cornelias McCoy
25— Joseph Eaton
26— Joseph Stubblefield
27— David Fields
28— Robert Stone
29— John Bunch Sr.
30— George Moody

Out of which Venire facias the following persons were appointed a Grand Jury at the present Term as follows (towit)
1— John Estes —foreman — 2— Joseph Eaton— 3— David Huddleston—

4- John Dellor
5- Abraham Pruit
6- Moses Hodges
7- Charley Jarnegin
8- William Pirkham

9- George Brady
10- Josiah Kidwell
11- William Cook
12- Joseph Hoa Jr.
13- Miller Ensley

Joe Ashley sworn to attend the Grand Jury.

(p 130)   August Sessions A.D. 1806
Ordered by the Court that Henry Boatman pJosiah Dyer & William Mortin Esquires be appointed Commissioners to settle with Abraham Wilson—Admr. of the Estate of Isaac Wilson —Deceased & make Report to our next Court.Isd.

John Gold   )
     vs   ) Abraham Wilson being Summoned as a Garnishee in this
Robert C.Gordon) Court and in the present case deposeth on oath that he
oweth unto the Defendant Robert C.Gordon 130 gallons of good Merchantable Whisky which he says he is redy to render as the property of Robert C. Gordon's - it is therefore considered by the Court that the said whisky be condemned and made pymble to the plaintiffs Demand & that an Order of Sale do issue accordingly.

Ordered by the Court that Joseph Eaton be released from the payment of the poll Tax in the County of Grainger for the year A.D. 1806. It appearing to the satisfaction of the Court that he is over age.

Ordered by the Court that William Hall be appointed Constable in and for the County of Grainger who gave Bond in the sum of $500 with security for his faithful performance (towit) Abraham Pruit -Able Morgan &c -who took the necessary oaths and also the oath of Office.

Ordered by the Court that infuture all causes in the Court will be put to trial as they come in order at the next Term of this Court when no Legal cause can be shewn to the satisfaction of the Court - a continuance.
Ordered by the Court the several of Ferry's on Holston River within the Bounds of Grainger County shall be entitled to Receive the following Rates- For each wagon & Near Load & Driver $1- For each mand and horse 12½ For each Lead horse 6¼ for each footman 6¼ - For each Cart 50¢ For each four wheel pleasure Carriage $1.25 - For each Two wheel pleasure Carriage 75¢ For each cow 6¼.

To the Worshipful Court of Grainger County -Jesse McAnelly who was heretofore appointed one of the Constables for said County finding extremely inconvenient to Serve any Longer in that capacity begs leave to tender his resignation to your Worships which he hopes you will receive and prays to be exonerated from all further Services as Constable.
                    Jesse McAnelly
Rutledge August 18th 1806 - Rec'd by the Court.

(p 161)   August Sessions A.D. 1806
To the Court of Grainger County please to Except of my Resignation as Ranger in the County of Grainger.
                    William Clay 18th of August 1806

Ordered By the Court that Richard Acuff be appointed overseer of

Grainger County in the room of William Snodgrass with the same Bounds & hands that were allowed to Mr. Snodgrass.

Jones Bowen Records his mark — one smooth crop off each ear and two slits in the Right ear and one slit in the left.

Ordered by the Court that Richard Duvall be appointed overseer in the Room of George Sparkman with the Bounds & hands that were allowed to Mr. Sparkman— Issued.

Ordered by the Court that James Arnold be appointed overseer of the road in the rim of John Haley with the Bounds & hands that were allowed to Mr. Haley. Issued.

Ordered by the Court that Acquilla Jones be appointed overseer of the road from the house of John Crabb to the lines between the Lands of Thomas Johnson & James Ore's & have the same Bounds for hands as were allowed John Crabb. Issued.

Ordered by the Court that Abel Morgan be appointed overseer of the road from the Branch at John Williams to the ford of Buffalow Creek and have the same Bounds for hands as William English had. Issued.

Ordered by the Court that Joseph Fields – David Tate & Joseph Cobb be excused from serving as Jurors at the present Term as per affidavits shewn to the Court.

A Bill of Sale from James Ferguson to William Ferguson was acknowledged in open Court and ordered to be Recorded.

A Deed of conveyance John Sutton to William Hall for 544 acres of Land was proven in open Court by the oaths of William Clay & John Hall Sr. and ordered to be Registered.

A Deed of conveyance from John Cocke to William Keith for Lott No. 24 in the Town of Rutledge, was acknowledged in open Court and ordered to be Registered.

A Power of Attorney from Isaac Inman to Isaiah Midkiff was acknowledged in open Court and ordered to be Registered.

A Power of Attorney from Isaac Inman to Isaiah Midkiff was acknowledged in open Court and ordered to be Recorded.

A petition filed at the present Term for opening of a Road from John Bunches to William Arnolds &c.

Court adjourns till 9 o'clock tomorrow morning.

(p. 162)   August Sessions A.D. 1806

Court met according to adjournment — Tuesday 19th of August A.D. 1806 Present – Thomas Henderson–John Cocke and John Breeden Esquires.

State	)	
vs	)	Sarah Holt who at Last Term of this Court was bound
John McGinnis	)	in Recognizing to Give Evidence and prossecute in the

above suit after being solemnly called came not - therefore it was considered by the Court that she forfeit her Mei-

Ordered by the Court that Benjamin Hudson be released from the payment of the Tax- one Stud Horse- called Hector for the year A.D. 1806.

William Cooper)
vs)
Robert Moore -John Spring) William Robertson being summoned a Guarni-
John Margraves) shee on an execution Issued in this case
to appear and Declare on oath what sum he is indebted to John Margraves,
appears personally in Court & being sworn as the Act of Assembly in that
case directs Declares that he gave John Margraves a Note for ninety Dollars to be Discharged in a Horse creature to be valued at trade rates &
that he has no Notice the said John Margraves has transferred his interest
in said Note, on Motion the Court order & adjudged that the above mentioned property be condemned in the hands of the said William Robertson for
the use of said William Cooper & it is further ordered that an order of
Sale do issue to the Sheriff commanding him to sell the above mentioned
property.

State)
vs) Justices present, Thomas Henderson -William Clay,
James McGlants) John Breeden, James Moore & Philip Sigler Esquires.
   Whereupon came a Jury towit,

1- Peter Harris   7- Joseph Hoe Sr.
2- Martin Ashburn   8- James Richardson
3- Abraham Elliott   9- James Reddis
4- Valentine Horgan   10-James Arnold
5- John Green   11-William Williams
6- Robert Honeycutt   12-Wm Smith
   Who being Elected tryed and sworn the truth to speak on the Issue at
traverse do say they misstrial -submits to the Court & that Court proceeds to assess his fine to the amount of Twelve cents & one half cents
with costs.

State)
vs)
Elisha Williamson) In this case the Defendant is surrendered by his Bail
in discharge of themselves as such who gives Daniel Clayton & Cobb Reese
his securities for the the Defendants appearance at next Court to answer
the charge of Bastardy against him himself 200 Dollars & each of his securities in one hundred dollars each.

(p 163)   August Sessions A.D. 1806

State)
vs)
John Rogers)   The security in this case William Wirdham surrenders him
the Defendant in open Court in discharge of himself as Bail.

State vs Squire Harlow ------Philip Sigler, Charles McAnally & William
Hankins Esquires. Thereupon came a Jury (towit)

1- Peter Harris
2- John Crabb
3- John Arwine
4- Jeremiah Jarnagin
5- John Haines
6- Henry McPherson

7- William Street
8- William Jones
9- William Shields
10-Joseph Waggoner
11-William Bowman
12-Thomas Dunn

Who being Elected tryed and sworn the truth to speak on the Issue at Traverse do say they find the Defendant not Guilty in manner and form as charged in the Bill of Indictment —Rule to Tax prosecutor with costs.

A list of Strays remaining on my Books and not proven away in twelve months of the following specification &c.
William Hamilton — one Blue Boar —$1.00.

A Bill of sale from James Richardson to William McNeal for a negro Girl was acknowledged in open Court by the subscriber thereto & ordered to be Recorded.

A Deed of conveyance from John McElheney to Nicholas Kearns for one hundred acres of Land was proven in open Court by the oaths of Joseph Cobb & Henry Bowen witnesses thereto and ordered to be Registered.

A Bill of sale from Francis Mayberry to James Richardson for two negroes was acknowledged in open Court by the subscriber thereto.

A Deed fo conveyance from James Bowen to Robert McElheney for 200 acres of Land was proven in open Court by the oaths of John Finley— Jack & John Mc elheney and ordered to be Registered.

The Grand Jury Discharged and Hoe Ashley Constable of the Grand Jury proved his attendance as such Two days. Issued.

Ordered by the Court that the following persons be appointed Jurors to the Superior Court of Hamilton District at Sept. Term A.D. 1806 —David Tate Sr. John Moffitt —Joseph Cobb and Michael Massengill.

Court adjourned till 9 o'clock tomorrow morning.

(p 164)   August Sessions A.D. 1806

At a Court Continued and held in and for the County of Grainger at the Court House in Rutledge on the 20th Day of August A.D. 1806— Present —Thomas Henderson —John Cocke & John Breeden Esquires.

State   )
  vs   )
Owen Brummett)   Present —Thomas Henderson —Philip Siglar, John Breeden
William Clay Esquires. Thereupon came a Jury (towit)

1- Major Lea
2- John Moffitt
3- William Haiths
4- John Breeden
5- Jeremiah Hinis
6- William Jones

7- Michel Holt
8- Dawson Cheek
9- James Reddis
10-William Williams
11-Henry Morgan
12-James Holt

Who being Elected tryed and sworn the truth to speak on the Issue at traverse in this case do say they find the defendant not Guilty in manner and form as charged in the Bill of Indictment.

A motion made by Thomas Dardis Esquire Solicitor for the County of Grainger that a Scire facias Do Issue Directing John Crow Guardian by appointment of this Court to Gidion Wilson a Minor to appear & shew cause if anything be can say, why he should not be removed from his said Guardianship and it appearing to the satisfaction of the Court that there is danger to be apprehended from suffering said Minor longer to remain in custody of said John Crow it is therefore ordered that Abraham Wilson have the custody of said Minor until next Term of this Court and ordered that Scire facias do issue accordingly.

William Keith who intermarried with the widow Coons comes into Court & relinquishes his Right of administration on the Estate of the Deceased Michael Coons ordered by the Court that John Cocke Esquire be admitted Administrator on the Estate of the said Michael Coons Deceased who enters into Bond in the sum of five hundred Dollars with security for his the sd. John Cocke's faith ful performance as such and gives David Tate & William Keith his securities and qualified accordingly.

Ordered by the Court that John Cocke the administrator on the Estate of Michael Coons Deceased do expose to sale the property in his possession as per Inventory returned according to Law in such cases made and provided.

Ordered by the Court that the Order of Last Court Directing & appointing Commissioners to settle with Thomas Henderson.

(p 165)　　　　August Sessions A.D. 1806

William Windham – Rachel Wilson the wife of John Wilson on the Estate of Rubin Windham's Deceased be continued for Report till next Court.

Ordered by the Court that Copy of a Petition of Jinkin Whitesides for a partition of Land Granted to Robert King & John Blair the 12th day of July 1794 – No. 623 for a tract of Land containing 200 acres be Recorded at Length with the Report of the Commissioners annexed thereto and the Court order that each Commissioner be allowed the sum of three dollars each for their services in full.

Ordered by the Court that John Lea late high sheriff and Collecter of the county of Grainger have a credit with the trustee of said County & also with the treasurer of the District of Washington & Hamilton for the taxes not collected & report on for the year 1804–& 1805 (towit) on 1220 acres of Land for the year 1804 also 31,645 acres of Land for the year 1805 which was reported on at November Sessions A.D. 1805.

Joseph Peters who was appointed constable to attend on the Court at the present Term in Discharge and was qualified to two Days attendance which he is to be allowed one Dollar per day for his attendance.

On motion of James Gaines by John Cocke his Attorney to enter up Judgment against Benjamin Bradford high Sheriff of the County of Jefferson for the sum of Two hundred and twenty three Dollars & Eighty four cents besides costs.

Samuel D.Carrick &)
Montgomery Co.)
    vs)   On motion of the plaintiff in this case for an
Moses Ballenger)   order of sale to Issue to sell 200 acres of Land
of William Quirn's attached as the property of said Ballengers - it is therefore ordered by the Court that order of Sale do Issue to the Sheriff to
sell said Land to satisfy the Debt of the plaintiff agreeable to their
Legal Demand.

Ordered by the Court that Luke Lea Jr. be Released from his undertaking to Transcribe the Registers the Registers Books of this County it appearing to the satisfaction of the Court that said Luke Lea can not perform the Duties of said appointment in a short time and it is further ordered by the Court that Thomas Henderson Esquires be appointed in his sted
who was qualified according to Law before Charles McEnelly Esquire one of
the acting Justices for said County.

(p 166)   August Sessions A.D. 1806

A Deed of conveyance from Daniel Clayton to Martin Albert for one acre
and a half of Land was proven in open Court by the oaths of Joseph Cobb &
Frederick Moyers and ordered to be Registered.

Ordered by Court that John Dennis be appointed overseer of the Road
leading from the Powder Spring Gap in Clinch mountain to the top of the
Copper Ridge in the room of Joseph Fields and that he have the same bounds
for hands that said Fields had. Issued.

Ordered by Court that Valentine Morgan be within the Bounds & a work-
er on the Richland Road under Thomas McBroom overseer.

Ordered by the Court that Jesse McKinney -Samuel Dunlay, Robert Harris Richard Acuff, William Mitchell, Peter Hamilton,James Wilson & William
Hankins be appointed as Jurors To view and lay off a road according to Law.
Leading from the Ford of Holston River at William Hankins ford to the fork
of the Road near Major Campbell's and make report to next Court. Issd.

Inventory of the Estate of Drury Solomon's Deceased was exhibited &
sworn to in open Court by Francis Solomon & John Cocke Admr. on the said
Estate.
Ordered by the Court that John McPheeters be allowed the sum of ninety
cents for taxes paid to John Lea, late Sheriff of Grainger County, by him
the said John McPheeters for the year 1805, he not being liable to pay taxes
that year. Order Issued.

Ordered by the Court that Lewis Kirby be appointed overseer of the
road from the Powder Spring Gap to where it intersects with State Creek
Road below Philip Spangler's in sight of Joseph Halls giving him the same
hands that belonged to the said Hall with the addition of John Birdwell-
Jesse Birdwell, William Patton, John Hunter -Lenard Vendergriff & William
Roberts & the hands at Nicholas Springs. Issued.

Ordered by the Court that Tapley Haygood be allowed the sum of $25 for the keeping and supporting Jeremiah Midriff one of the poor of the County from May Term 1806 until August Term 1806. Issued.

Ordered by the Court that James Moore Jr. Esquire, John Humphreys Rubin Doxon, William Arnold, James Slaup, John Martin Sr. & Philip Free be appointed to view and Lay out a road from John Bunches to the end of William Arnolds Lain and make report to next Court. Issued.

Ordered by the Court that the following persons whose names

(p 167)   are herto annexed be appointed Jurors at November Sessions A.D. 1806.

1- Jonathan Barnard	21- William Mitchell
2- William Shelton	22- Seth McKinney
3- Henry Hipsher	23- Richard Acuff
4- William Davidson	24- Joseph Noe Sr.
5- Obediah Waters	25- Robert Long
6- Thomas Brown	26- Tandy Senter
7- Daniel Beelor	27- Moses Hodges
8- Thomas Dunn	28- Jesse Cheek
9- Stephen W.Senter	29- Jos. Stubblefield
10-David Fields	30- Martin Stubblefield
11-Archabald Hopper	31- Alexander Blair
12-Harmon Cox	32- Daniel Taylor
13-William Shields	33- Henry Ivy
14-John Hodges	34- —————
15-Thomas James	35- Abraham Wilson
16-John Bunch Sr.	36- George Moody
17-Joseph Long	37- Henry Howell
18-Valentine Morgan	38- Major Lea
19-Jonathan Marpower	39- John Vinyard
20-Thomas Johnston	

Issued to the Sheriff &c.

Court met according to adjournment August 21st. 1806 -Present Thomas Henderson, William Clay, David Mcenelly & William Rankins,Esquires.

Samuel Carrick & Co.   )
        vs   )
Spencer Griffen & David Hunt)
                    Joshua Mickay comes into Court & surrenders David Hunt in Release of himself and John F.Jack who was special Bail and the plaintiff Samuel D.Carrick prays the Defendant in custody of the Sheriff in Execution.

Ordered by the Court that Joseph Noe Sr. be released from three days attendance of John Green a witness on behalf of the State against Joseph Noe Sr. and that he also be released from three days attendance of John Holt, a witness in the above stated case, and it is further ordered by the Court that the monies due said John Holt be paid over to Joseph Noe against John Holt, which Execution was Issued by Thomas Henderson Esquire.

Ordered by the Court that the petition of Thomas Henderson which was filled at Last Term, be granted for the alteration or amendment of a patent Grant, and ordered by said Court, that the Clerk of said County -do Settify to the secretary of the State of North Carloina for the alteration according to the prayers of the petitioners.

Ordered by the Court that James Reddis as formerly appointed Guardian for Jonathan Purchul an Idiot of this County be released from his Guardianship and that William Williams be appointed to take charge of said Jonathan Purchul an Idiot who enters into Bond with security as the Law in such cases Directs in the sum of five   (p 168)   Aug. Sessions A.D. 1806 --   Hundred Dollars for his faithful performance as Guardian to the said Idiot and Gave James Reddis & Henry Howell as his securities in the sum of Two hundred and fifty dollars Each.

David Mcenelly Jr. is appointed Constable in this County and wit h Henry Howell his security enters into Bond in the sum of Five hundred Dollars for his true and faithful performance in that office and took the Oath prescribed by Law.

An Inventory of the Estate of Michael Coons Deceased was Returned in open Court by John Cocke Esquire the Admr. on the Estate of the Deceased and ordered to be Recorded.

Ordered by the Court that David Huddleston, Charles Hopper, David Fields, Seimore York, Benj. Hudson, Archabald Hopper & Joshua Oaks, be a Jury to view and lay out & make a road agreeably to Law from the forks of the Road in the Hickory Valley near the cave Spring to the County Line where it Intersects the said Valley and make report to next Court.Issd.

A Deed of conveyance from Josiah Smith to James Bowen for one Hundred & fifty acres of Land was proven in open Court by the oath of John Bowen & David Robertson the subscribing witness thereto and ordered to be Registered.
Court adjourns till Court in Course.

Thomas Henderson

November Sessions A.D. 1806
At a Court of Pleas & Quarter Sessions began and held in and for the County of Grainger at the Court House in Rutledge on the third Monday of November A.D. 1806 it being the 17th of the same month. Prestn, Isaiah Midkiff, Hoe Jarnagin, Philip Siglar & Henry Boatman., Esquires.

1- Jonathan Barnard
2- William Shelton
3- Henry Upsher
4- William Davidson
5- Obediah Waters
6- Thomas Brown
7- Daniel Beelor
8- Thomas Dunn
9- Stephen W.Senter
10-David Fields
11-John Hodges
12-Thomas James
13-John Bunch Sr.

14- Joseph Long
15- Valentine Morgan
16- Jonathan Hampower
17- James Johnson
18- William Mitchell
19- Seth McKinney
20- Richard Acuff
21- Moses Hodges
22- Jesse Cheek
23- Joseph Stubblefield
24- Martin Stubblefield
25- Alex. Blair
26- Daniel Taylor

27- Henry Ivy
28- Samuel Machel

29- Abraham Wilson
30- George Moody

(p 169)   November Sessions A.D. 1806

31- Archabald Hopper
32- Harmon Cox
33- William Shields
34- Joseph Noe Sr.
35- Robert Long

36- Tandy Senter
37- Henry Howell
38- Major Lea
39- John Vinyard

James Conn high Sheriff of the County of Grainger returned the above Venire facias Executed on all but William Shelton -William Davidson -Obediah Waters, Thomas Brunson, David Fields, Samuel McBee & Seth McKinney.

Out of which Venire facias the following persons whose names are hereunto annexed were drawn as Grand Jurors at the present Term, towit-

1- Major Lea foreman
2- Joseph Noe Jr.
3- Obediah Waters
4- Martin Stubblefield
5- William Shields
6- Thomas Johnston
7- John Vinyard
8- Jesse Chisick

9- Joseph Long
10-Thomas Dunn
11-Joseph Stubblefield
12-Archibald Hopper
13-Daniel Taylor
14-Stephen W. Senter
15-Tandy Senter

Who as sworn & charged.

Ordered by the Court, that Amsted West Herein be released from the payment of a Tax for the year 1806 on five Black Polls he being entitled to pay a Tax on but one Black poll for the same year- It is therefore consudered by the Court that he be released accordingly. Copy issued.

Ordered by the Court that Chesley Jarnagin have Leave to keep a House of public Entertainment in the County of Grainger for the Term of one year who gave Bond in the sum of one thousand dollars with Frederick Moyers, his securities &c.

Ordered by the Court that Frederick Moyers have leave to keep a House of public entertainment in the County of Grainger for the Term of one year who gave Bond in the sum of one Thousand Dollars and Gave Chesley Jarnagin his securities.

Ordered by the Court that Gidion Wilson a minor orphan now about the age of five years & six months be bound by Indenture to Jacob Wilson to serve him untill he shall attain the year of twenty one &c.

David Tate Esquire produced a Commission from the Excellency the Governor appointing him a Justice of the peace in and for the County of Grainger -Took the oath of office & the oath to support the Constitution.

A Deed of conveyance from William Hall, Robert Patterson, William Clay & William Hawkins to John Dorah a Lott No. 47 in the Town of Rutledge was proven in open Court by the oaths of Ambrose Yancey & Luke Lea witnesses thereto and ordered to be Registered.

A Deed of conveyance from William Hall -Robert Paterson - William Clay
& William Hawkins to John Dornh for Lott No. 20 in the town of Rutledge was
proven in open Court by the oath of Ambrose Yancey.

(p 170)   November Sessions A.D. 1806

Luke Lea the witness thereto and ordered to be registered.

A Bill of sale from Moses Overton to Obediah Waters was proven in open
Court & ordered to be Recorded.

A Deed of conveyance from Abraham Elliot Coroner to Nicholas Count
for 212 or 213 acres of Land was proven in open Court by the oaths of Ambrose Yancey & John Cooke Esquire witnesses thereto & ordered to be Registered.
A Deed of conveyance from Francis Willet to Enos Hammers for one hundred acres of Land was acknowledged in open Court by the subscriber thereto
and ordered to be Registered.
A Power of Attorney from James Paul to Samuel McBee was proven in op-
en Court by the oath of William Hamilton and ordered to be Recorded.

James Conn high Sheriff & collector of Grainger County made report to
Court that the following Tracts of Land have been Given in as Taxable prop-
erty of the Reputed owners, whereof he can make the taxes due thereon (towit)
James Ore, 1000 acres on Germantown Creek - James Ore 400 acres poor Valley
Joseph Ore 375 acres not said where, Joseph Stephen 200 acres not said where
Robert King 440 acres Given in by David Mcenelly - Thomas King 122 acres
given in by David Mcenelly -Edmund Walker 125 acres Given in by David Mc
enelly -Jesse Callison 150 acres - Willie Blount 640 acres Given in by I.
Robertson- Willie Blount 400 acres B.R. -Willie Blount 300 acres W.C. -
Willie Blount 250 acres -F.C. Willie Blount 2,000 acres W.E. -Solomon Massengill 100 acres waters of Buffelow.
Therefore it is considered by the Court that the Clerk do certify to
the Public printer of this State and cause the same to be twigt published
as the Law Directs.

James Conn, high Sheriff and Collector of the public & County Taxes
for the year A.D. 1806 report to Court, that the following Tracts of Land
were not Given in by the owner thereof as Lands Taxable for the year A.D
1806 therefore it is ordered by the Court that the Clerk of the said County
do cause them to be published-as the Law Directs, James Cooper 400 acres
of Land in Jamesses Company -John Adler 600 acres of Land in said Company.

(p 170)   Godfrey Cariger -500 acres of Land Richland Creek -Wilson Hunt
200 acres Panther Creek.

November A.D. 1806
Court met according to adjournment. Present Henry Boatman, David Tate
& Josiah Dyer, Esquires.

Ordered by the Court that Henry Boatman -Josiah Dyer & Joseph Cobb
Esquires be appointed Commissioners to settle with Abraham Wilson Admr. on
the Estate of Isaac Wilson Deceased and make report to next Court.

(p 171)   November Sessions A.D. 1807

Andrew Campbell
Admr. of Hugh Campbell Dec'd
    vs
Robert C. Gorden   Abraham Wilson, being summoned as a
Guarnishee in this case, Deposeth on oath that He oweth unto the Defendant
Robert C. Gorden, one hundred & thirty Gallons of Good Merchantable Whisky
which he is ready to render as the property of Robert C. Gorden, it is there-
fore considered by the Court, that the said whisky be condemned and made
liable to the plaintiffs Demand and that an order of sale Issue accordingly.

    Elihu Miligan came into open Court and Entered into Bond in the sum
of one hundred Dollars for the purpose of Indemnifying the County from the
charge and maintainance of a Bastard child be gotten on the Body of Rachel
Mills and he the said Miligan being the Reputed father thereof, and Gave
Benj. Howell & Abraham Wilson as his securities.

    At an Election opened & held in and for the County of Grainger a ran-
ger for said County, upon counting the Votes it appears William Keith was
legally and constitutionally Elected to that appointment who gave Bond to
the Chairman of the Court, in the sum of one Thousand Dollars with his securities John Cocke & David McAnally and was qualified.

State
    vs
Elisha Williamson)   Elisha Williamson came into open Court and entered
into Bond in the sum of five hundred Dollars for the support & mathtenance
of a Bastard child of which he is the Reputed father, begotten on the Body
of Nancy Mc.Master and gives Caleb Reese & Daniel Clayton his securities.

State
    vs
John Rodgers)   Ordered by the Court that Judgment be Entered up against
the Defendant in this cause for the sum of one Dollar as a fine and also
for all costs —therefore it is considered by the Court that he pay the
sum aforesaid &c.
    Fine paid Clerk. Fi.Fa. Issd.
State)
    vs
John Bull)   Present, Charles McAnally, Josiah Dyer & David Tate Esquires.
    Whereupon came a Jury (towit)

1- David Bllor   7- John Jimison
2- Valentine Morgan   8- Daniel Clayton
3- Henry Howell   9- William Treat
4- Abraham Wilson   10-John Hodge
5- Jesse McAnally   11-William Windham
6- Benjamin Howell   12-Richard Shelton

(p 172)   November Sessions A.D. 1806
    Who being Elected tryed and sworn the truth to speak on the Issue of
traverse in this case do say they find the Defendant is Guilty in manner
and form as charged in the Bill of Indictment and the Court proceeded to
assess the fine & do assess the fine to Ten Dollars.

State vs Claiborne Going —Sarah his wife & others.

Caleb Howell who was security for the appearance of Nancy Davis a witness in this case surrenders her in open Court in Discharge of himself.

State)
  vs)
Claiborne Going &) The Defendants in this case are Discharged on
Sarah Going his wife) proclamation.

State)
  vs) Ordered by the Court that Judgment be entered up against
John Bull) the Defendant for the sum of Ten Dollars fine and also
the further sum of all costs that have or may accrue in said action and Gave John Ogun & Patrick Donohoe his securities for fine and costs by the consent of the principle & his securities.

Ordered by the Court that a pounder Pen be Erected in the Town of Rutledge for the purpose of confining Strays as the Law Directs (towit) a strong Pound or pen thirty feet square six feet high of Locust Posts and white Oaks Rails four Rails in each Pannel - no pannel to be more than Ten feet long the the Posts set into the Ground Two feet with a good Gate Hung on strong Iron hinges a good & sufficient strong lock. Isd. to Moyers.

Whereas Richard Murphy together with Sariah Murphy -Isaac Murphy and Jesse Murphy on the 18th day of November in the year 1802 Executed a Deed of conveyance to Isaac Barton for two hundred and fifty Eight acres of Land situate lying and being on the County Line which Divides Grainger & Jefferson County and the said Richard Murphy being then a monor under the age of Twenty one years, now I, the said Richard Murphy at the date of this being above the age of Twenty one years Do hereby confirm the said Deed of conveyance unto the Isaac Barton his heirs & assigns forever confirmed in open Court this 18th Day of November 1806.

Charles F. Keith & Isaac S. McNeans Esquires produced a License authorizing them to practice as Attornies, in the respective County's in this State who being duly qualified as the Law Directs,were admitted to the practice as such in the County of Grainger.

Court adjourns till 9 o'clock tomorrow morning.

Court met according to adjournment Wednesday 19th of November A.D. 1806 -present Thomas Henderson-David McAnally, William Hankins & John Breeden, Esquires.

(p 173)   November Sessions A.D. 1806

Ordered by the Court that Elizabeth Harmons -Sally Mourning & Elizabeth Densoh be Cited to appear at our next Term of this Court to shew cause if any they can why their children Reputively should not be Bound out for their Better support and maintenance. Issued.

Ordered by the Court that Frederick Moyers be allowed the sum of $20 for his taking charge care & cleaning Court House up to the present Term of this Court and that he be paid accordingly.

Ordered by the Court that Luke Lea Esqr. Be allowed to Receive out of the County Treasury the sum of four Dollars & fifty cents monies by him expended for Books to Copy the Records of the Registers Office.

Ordered by Court that Taply Haygood be allowed the sum of $25 for taking and supporting Jeremiah Midliff one of the poor of this County till the present Term. Issued.

Ordered by the Court that the register of this County be allowed the sum of Ten Dollars for to purchase a Book for the Registering Deeds in this County out of any County monies not otherwise applied.

Ordered by the Court that Abel Morgan be appointed overseer of the road be allowed the same bounds for hands that Wilson English formerly had.

Peter Harris Esquire produced a commission from his Excellency the Governor appointing him a Justice of the peace & for said County who took the oath of office & all the necessary.

Ordered by the Court that Frederick Hoyers be allowed the sum of $3.25 for repairing the goal of this County agreeable to an account Exhibited & that he be paid accordingly. Issued.

Ordered by the Court that James Conn high Sheriff be allowed the sum of Two dollars for monies he has Expended in purchasing Locks for the goal of said County as per account Rendered. Issued.

Ordered by the Court that Edward Clark —Joseph Beeler, Daniel Beeler William McPhetridge —John Haynes, Thomas Dunn, Philip Sigler—Joseph Dennis Peter Beeler. Abraham Pruit & Charles Hutcheson be a Jury to view & lay out a Road the nearest and best way from the Powder Spring Gap to Circles ford on Clinch River according to Law and make report to next Court. Issued.
Ordered by the Court that Charles Hutcheson, Joseph Fields, Thomas Dennis, William Peters, Abraham Elliot, Jacob Elliot be appointed. Issed. to view and Lay out a Road the nearest and best way from the Powder Spring Gap of Clinch mountain to Hodges ford on Clinch River according to Law and make report to next Court.
Ordered by the Court that William Blair, Alex. Blair, William Kirbham, John Cannon, Joseph Hoe Sr. Pleasant Duke &   (p 174) November Sessions A.D. 1806 —————James Carmichael be a Jury to view and lay off a Road from the County line above William Blairs to the Branch at Major Howell's and make report to next Court. Issued.
Ordered by the Court that Henry Henry, Henry Hays —Edward Daniel, George Moody, John ?. Ivins —James Moore Sr. William Arnold be a Jury to View and lay out a Road from Howell's Branch to Buffalow Creek & make Report to next Court.
Ordered by the Court that Jacob Arnet, James Richardson, Robert Stone Joseph Ferrin, Rubin Groves, Evan Harris & Robert Gaines be a Jury to view and Lay out a Road fro, Buffalow Creek to the Line Dividing Grainger and Knox Counties and make Report to next Court. Issued.

Ordered by the Court that William Mitchell, Peter Hamilton, Richard Acuff, William Hankins, & Edward Haley be a Jury to view & lay out a Road from the ford of Holston River near William Hankins Esqr. across the River Road & the Richland Road unto the Road that passes by Major Jas. Campbell plantation & report to next Court.

William Nall vs Martin Morris — Present, William Clay, James Moore & Joseph Cobb Esquires. Thereupon came a Jury, towit—

1- William Mitchel
2- Valentine Morgan
3- Wm Paterson
4- Thomas Bunch
5- John Holt
6- John Hodges
7- Thomas Turley
8- Daniel Clayton
9- Pleasant Duke
10-Abraham Wilson
11-Daniel Robertson
12-Robert Honeycut

Who being Elected tryed and sworn the truth to speak on the Issue Joined, do say they find the Defendant did speak words in the Declaration mentioned, of the plaintiff and that he was not justified as in pleadings he hath alledged, and assess the plaintiffs Damage occationed by reason of the speaking and publishing said word, to five dollars besides his costs- rule to shew cause why the plaintiff, in this case should not be taxed with the costs of William Hains a witness in this case, rule made absolute- It is therefore considered by the Court, that the said William Hall do recover off the Defendant Martin Morris the sum of Five Dollars in form aforesaid and assess by the Jury aforesaid and the Defendant in Mercy &c.

William Hall)
     vs)
Martin Morris) Elizabeth Sims, who was summoned as a witness in this case being solemnly called came not - it is therefore considered by the Court that she forfeit according to an Act of Assembly and Sci.Fa.t8 Issue.

John Ogan Assignee)
John Bull)
     vs) Present, Thomas Henderson, John Breeden & Joseph Cobb
John Crabb) Esquires.
                    Whereupon came a Jury,(towit)

(p 175)   November Sessions A.D. 1807

1- Henry Howell
2- John Morris
3- Martin Ashburn
4- Robert Long
5- William Keith
6- Nicholas Countz
7- Christopher Conway
8- John Bean
9- John Green
10-Henry Bowen
11-Martin Albert &
12-Hardimon Taylor

Who being Elected tryed and sworn the truth to speak on matter in Dispute do say they find for the plaintiff thirty dollars to be Discharged by the payment of seventeen Dollars & forty four cents & costs it is therefore considered by the Court that the said John Ogan assignee of John Bull do recover of the Defendant John Crabb, thirty dollars, to be Discharged by the payment of seventeen Dollars & forty four cents & costs as in form aforesaid and assess by the Jury aforesaid and the Defendant in mercy &c

Ordered by the Court Thomas Bunch be appointed overseer of the road in the room of Daniel Robertson, and to work from the six mile Tree or post at the fork of the road below Tandy Senters to the three mile post near John McElhaneys and that all the hands in the following Bounds shall work under said Bunch Beginning at a Post on the Top of Clinch mountain opposite the said six mile post thence a Direct Course to said post thence a Direct course to said post to the top of the Bigg Ridg so as to include Charles Kidwell thence along the Top of said Ridge to a point opposite the three mile post thence a straight line to the said three mile post thence on the same course to the Top of Clinch Mountain thence along the top of said Mountain to the Beginning and all the hands in said Bounds liable to work on Roads are assigned to the said Thomas Bunch to keep the aforesaid road in repair according to Law. Copy issued.

Ordered by the Court that John Estes, Thomas Mann, Robert Long, John Noe, Thomas Shipley, Bartly Marshal & Henry Boatman be appointed a Jury to view and lay off the Road leading from Beans Station to Cheeks Roads beginning at the fork that leads to Sheltons ford thence along the road crossing at Marshals Ferry to the Line of Hawkins and make report to next Court. Issued.

Ordered by the Court that William Shields, Joseph Yeaden, Edward Brown, Benj. Hudson, John Hodges & William Cook be a Jury to view and lay out a road from the Island Ford on Clinch River to the forks of the road, near Joseph Yeadens and make report to next Court. Or. Copy Issued.

Ordered by the Court Archabald Hopper be appointed overseer of the road in the place of Benj. Hudson and have the same Bounds for hands. Isd.

Ordered by the Court that Henry Boatman, Charles Smith, David Tate Josiah Dyer, Joseph Noe Jr. Thomas Reese Sr. Peter Harris, Duncan Carmicoal and Richard Shelton, be a Jury to view a Road leading from Abraham Wilsons and crossing at Sheltons ford on Holston River to Beans Station & make report to next Court. Copy issued.

(p 176)   November Sessions A.D. 1806

A Deed of conveyance from William Street to Andrew Coffman for Eighty acres of Land acknowledged in open Court and ordered to be Registered.

Grainger County November the 9th 1806- We the Jury appointed & sworn to lay out a Road from John Bunches to William Arnolds Do say that the nearest and best way is to follow the old Road Going through Philip Frees lane from thence following the old Road to Martin Ashburns Bigg field leaving said field on the Right hand then taking the left fork to the mouth of William Arnolds Lane aforesaid, William Arnold -John Humphreys, Philip Free, John Martin- Rubin Dixon & James Moore which report being heard and was confirmed by the Court.

Ordered by the Court that the following persons be Summoned as Jurors to February Term A.D. 1807 (towit)

1- William Milligan
2- Malachiah Howell
3- John Daniel
4- James Carmichael
5- Duncan Carmical
6- Richard Shelton
7- Robert Long
8- Febbs Reed
9- Thomas Munn
10-Hugh Larimore
11-Jas. Bryant
12-John Lebow
13-Richard Thomson
14- William Kirkham
15- John Cannon
16- James Brown
17- Henry Hipshier
18- Th Bowman
19- Wm Shelton
20- Edward McGinnis
21- Samuel McBee
22- Dennis Cundry
23- James Campbell
24- Thomas Sharp
25- John Bunch & Jacob Elliot

27- Joseph Yeaden
28- John Hodges
29- Robert Hains
30- Miller Easley
31- Isaac Mitchell
32- John Beeler
33- Joseph Fields

34- Alex. Hamilton
35- Hugh Woolard
36- Martin Albert
37- Thomas Brown
38- Andrew McPheeters

Court adjourns till tomorrow morning 9 o'clock.

Thursday November 20th -Court met according to adjournment -Present Thomas Henderson- David McAnally -Charles McAnally Esquires.

William Windham)
vs)
William Harris) Elizabeth Smith being summoned as a witness in this case & being solemnly called came not - it is therefore considered by the Court that she forfeit according to an Act of Assembly.

James Brown)
vs)
John Breeden) Present, David McAnally- Charles McAnally & Noe Jarnagin Esquires. Whereupon came a Jury, towit-
1- Valentine Morgan
2- Thomas Turley
3- Henry Howell
4- Nicholas Counts
5- John Hodges
6- Robert Honeycutt
7- Thomas Bunch
8- Martin Ashburn
9- William Harris
10-Samuel Perry
11-William Wilson
12-William Paterson

(p 177) November Sessions A.D. 1806

Who being Elected tryed and sworn well and truly to try and the truth to speak one the Issue Joined, in the above case do say they find the Defendant is not Guilty in manner and form as the plaintiff against him in his Declaration hath complained - It is therefore considered by the Court that the said James Brown plaintiff take nothing by his writ that he be punished for his false clamor and that the Defendant John Breeden do the Defendant John Breeden do Recover said Defendant his costs by him in and about Defending his said suit in that behalf Expended &c. and the Defendant prays an appeal to the next Superior Court of Hamilton District who gives Bond with security and is Granted.

David Brown Gives in five Hundred acres of Land as the property of Allen Christians subject to Taxation for the A.D. 1806.

Mary Ashburn by her)
father & next friend)
vs)   Whereupon came a Jury (towit)
James Kennedy)

1- Valentine Morgan
2- James Turly
3- Henry Howell
4- Nicholas Counts
5-John Hodge
6-Robert Honeycutt
7-Thomas Bunch
9- William Harris
9- Samuel Perry
10-William Wilson
11-Caleb Howell

12-William Mitchell

Who being Elected tryed and sworn the truth to speak on the Issue
Joined in the above case do say they find the Defendant Guilty of the Tra-
verse Conversion set fourth in the plaintiffs Declaration and assess her
damages by reason thereof to one hundred dollars besides his costs, the
Defendant in this case prays an appeal to the Superior Court of Hamilton
District appeal withdrawn by Consent.

James Brown by John Williams his Attorney maketh a motion to Court
to have an Instrument of writing purporting to be an Indictment made
Between James Blair Chairman of the Court and James Brown -Bearing Date
the 18th day of August one thousand eight hundred and one to be Recorded
at Length but upon hearing the Argument of the Council on both sides are
of the opinion that the said Instrument of writing purporting to be an
Indenture be not committed to Record.

At a Court continued & held for the County of Grainger at the Court
House on Friday 21st. November 1806. Present, Thomas Henderson- David
McAnally & Charles McAnally Esquires, and

James Kain   )   the said John Crabb in his proper person comes into open
vs   )   Court and saith that he cannot Deny but that he the said
John Crabb is)indebted to the said James Kain in the sum of Forty seven
Dollars & seventy nine cents on account of the money Demanded in the plaintiffs Declaration and thereupon the said James prays that the Debt so acknowledged together with his costs & charges laid out by him about his
suit in this behalf, may be awarded to him, therefore it is ordered and
adjudged by the Court that the said James Do Recover against the said
John his said Debt above acknowledged to Forty seven Dollars & seventy
nine cents and also the further sum of seven Dollars 37½ cents for his
costs & charges by him in & above prosecuting his said Writ in that behalf
Expended and the said John in mercy &c -Whereupon Execution on the above
Judgment is ordered to stay one month by plaintiffs Attorney.

Ordered by the Court that the following Justices be appointed to take
in the Lists of Taxable property in the several Companys in Grainger County
for the year 1807 and make report to next Court.

1- For Captain John Bunches Company -William Clay Esqr.
2- For Captain Bowens -Thomas Henderson Esquire.
3- "   " James Mitchell - William Hawkins -Esqr.
4- "   " William Bryant --Peter Harris Esqr.
5- "   " John Smiths -   James Moore Sr. Esqr.
6- "   " George Noe's - Henry Boatman -Esqr.
7- "   " John Dodson's - David McAnally Esqr.
8- "   " Howells - David Tate Esqr.
9- "   " Alex. Hamilton - Valentine Moulder Esqr.
10-"   " John Margraves - William Peters Esqr.
11-"   " James's - Philip Siglar Esqr.
Notifications have Issued to the Justices agreeable order.

Ordered by the Court that Henry Bowen Be appointed overseer of the
road from the town of Rutledge to the three mile post near John McElheney
in the room of Robert McElheney and that he have the same Bounds for hands.
                                                    Errow.

185

Ordered by the Court that Tandy Senter be released from the payment
of a Tax on 300 acres of Land and one white poll for the year 1805 he
twict charged for the same for the year 1806.

William Windham)
      vs   )   Ordered by the Court that Di Do. do issue to take the
William Harris   )   Depositions of Elizabeth Smith for the Defendant and
Elizabeth Biggs for plaintiff with three days notice and notice acknow-
ledged by plaintiff & Defendant.

Jesse Jinnings   )
      vs   )   Covenant
Christopher Conway)

1- Henry Howell   7- John Coulter
2- Valentine Morgan   8- Miller Easley
3- Thomas Turly   9- William Mitchell
4- William Patterson   10-William Harris
5- John Hodges   11-Thomas Bunch
6- Pleasant Duke   12-George Combs

(p 179)   November Sessions A.D. 1805
      Who being Elected tryed and sworn the truth to speak on the issue
Joined in this case Do say they find that the Defendant hath not well and
truly kept and performed his said Covenant as in pleadings he hath alledged and assess the plaintiffs Damage by reason of the non performance to
Two hundred & thirty five Dollars and thirty four cents besides his costs.

John Coulter   )
      vs   )
Robert Honeycutt)   Asa Street who was summoned as a witness in this case
being solemnly called came not - It was therefore considered by the Court
that he forfeit according to an Act of Assembly and Sci.Fa. to issue.

George Humphreys)
      vs   )
Nathaniel Davis)   William Hall one of the Constables of this County made
Return to this Court that he had Levied an attachment in favour of plaintiff on two Lotts of Land in the Town of Rutledge being Lott No. 34 & 39
in the plan of said Town as the property of Nathaniel Davises -therefore
it is considered by the Court that the Lotts & Land so Levied on by the
said Constable be condemned and that an order of sale do issue accordingly for the sum of Eleven Dollars and twenty five cents on motion of
John Cocke Esquire.

Moses Clifton)
      vs   )   Debt
Henry Howell)   Therefore came a Jury (towit)

1- David McInally   7- Jacob Amet
2- John Shipley   8- Thomas Conway
3- Daniel Clayton   9-Joseph Wagoner
4- John Crabb   10-Peter Edwards
5- Thomas Province   11-James Kennedy
6- William Keith   12-William Mitchell

Who being Elected tryed and sworn well and truly to try and the truth
to tell to speak on the issue Joined in the above case do say they find
the Defendant hath not paid the Debt in the Declartion mentioned as in
pleadings he hath alledged and assess the plaintiffs Damage by reason of
the Detention of that Debt to six dollars and ninety cents besides his
costs.

John Williams   )
   vs   )   Debt
Stephen W.Senter)   Whereupon came a Jury (towit)

(p 180)   November Sessions A.D. 1808

1- Henry Howell   7- John Coulter
2- Valentine Morgan   8- Miller H.Easley
3- Thomas Tarly   9- Wm McPheeters
4- William Patterson   10-William Harris
5- John Hodges   11-Thomas Bunch &
6- Pleasant Duke   12-George Combs

Who being Elected tryed and sworn upon oath they say they find the
Defendant hath not paid the Debt in the Declaration mentioned as he in
his plea hath alledged and assess the plaintiffs Damage by reason of the
Detention of that Debt to nine Dollars sixty six & one third of a cent &
cents costs.

A Deed of conveyance from Archabald McCarver to Richard Grantham
for one hundred and fifty acres of Land acknowledged in open Court and ordered to be Registered.

A Deed of conveyance from Henry Morgan to William Williams for one
hundred and sixty acres of Land was proven in open Court by the oaths of
Thomas Dardis & Ambrose Yancey witnesses thereto & ordered to be Registered.

A Deed of conveyance from Samuel Dodson -Thomas Dodson & William
Dodson to Stephen Johnston for one hundred & fifty acres of Land was proven in open Court by Joseph Stubblefield & Thomas Johnston and ordered to
be Registered.

A Deed of conveyance -William Dodson to Stephen Johnston for four
acres of Land proven in open Court by the oaths of Joseph Stubblefield &
James Johnston witnesses thereto and ordered to be Registered.

A Deed of conveyance from William Davis to James Simpson for 25 acres
of Land was proven in open Court by the oaths of Thomas Willet & Thomas
Morgan witness thereto & ordered to be Recorded.

A Deed of conveyance from William McPhetridge to Thomas Ogle for 25
acres of Land was acknlwledged in open Court and ordered to be Registered.

A deed of conveyance -Dubart Murphy to John Eates for one hundred acres
of Land was proven in open Court by the oaths of Thomas Doghart & George
Carley witnesses therto and ordered to be Registered.

(p 181)   November Sessions A.D. 1806

Ordered by the Court that John Bull be appointed overseer of the road from the six mile Post below Tandy Senters to Bean Station in the room of Tandy Senter and that he have the same Bounds for hands that was allowed (seven hands) by an order entered this present Term.   Issued.

Ordered that Henry Bowen Jr. be appointed overseer of the road in the room of Robert McElheney Dec'd and to have the same Bounds and hands that formerly was allowed said McElheney. Issued.

Ordered by the Court that Rubin Dixon be appointed overseer of the road from John Bunches to the end of William Arnolds Lane as viewed and Laid out by the Late Jury that he have all the hands from the top of the Ridge below the road leading from John Bunches to William Arnolds down the Richland Knobs to include Christopher Conways thence to the head of Buffalow Creek thence down the Creek to the mouth of Alsups Branch up said Branch to William Arnolds thence along the road to the Beginning. Issued Copy order.

Joseph Peters who was appointed Constable to attend on the Court and Jury proved his attendance to five days. Issd.
Court adjourns till Court in Course.
                                Thomas Henderson

                              February Sessions 1807
At a Court of Pleas & Quarter Sessions began and held for the County of Grainger at the Court House in Rutledge on the third Monday of Febr. A.D. 1807 it being the sixteenth of the same month.
Present, John Breeden- James Moore & David Tate Esquires.

1- William Milligan
2- Malachiah Truwall
3- James Carnical
4- John Daniel
5- Duncan Carnical
6- Richard Shelton
7- Robert Long
8- Felps Reed
9- Thomas Mann
10-Hugh Larimore
11-William Kirkham
12-John Carnon
13-James Bowen
14-Henry Hipshir
15-William Bowman
16- William Shelton
17- Edward McGinnis
18- Samuel McGinnis
19- Dennis Condry
20- Thomas Sharp
21- Joseph Bryant
22- John Lebow
23- Richard Thomson
24- John Bunch
25- Jacob Elliot
26- Joseph Yeaden
27- John Rodgers
28- Robert Harris
29- Miller Easly
30-Isaac Mitchell

(p 182)   February Sessions A.D. 1807

31- John Beelor
32- Joseph Fields
33- Alex. Hamilton
34- Hugh Woolard
35- Martin Albert
36- Thomas Brown
37- Andrew McPheeters
38- James Campbell

Out of which Venire facias the persons whose names are underwritten were Drawn a Grand Jury for the present Term.

1- Thomas Mann foreman - 2- James Carnical - 3- Robert Harris

4- Richard Thomson   10-John Daniel
5- Jacob Elliot   11-Martin Albert
6- William Kirkham   12-Thomas Sharp
7- William Shelton   13-Henry Hipsher
8- Edward McGinnis   14-Andrew McPheeters
9- Hugh Larimore   15-Miller Easley

      Who being Duly sworn and charged by Charles F.Keith.

      Micagah Defoe Records his mark —one straight slit in each Ear.

      John Moffit & Mathew Campbell produced commissions from his Excellency the Governor appointing them Justices of the peace in and for said County of Grainger and were quallified as the Law Directs in that case.
      By order of Court Charles F.Keith was appointed Solicitor for the County of Grainger pro Tem and entitled to the Emoluments thereto belonging. Issued.

      Ordered by the Court that Sairah Hammons —Baxter Hammons & Martha Hammons be bound apprentices to Welcome Hodge that is to say Sarah Hammons Martha Hammons be bound unto Welcome Hodge until they attain the age of Eighteen years and that Baxter Hammons be bound also unto Welcome Hodge till he shall attain the age of Twenty one years and oblige himself to teach or cause to be taught the two to read and write and the Boy to read write and subtract.

Rial Jinnings   )
    vs -gui Tm)   George Evans and Benjamin in Hudson came unto Court
Edmund Holt   )   & acknowledged themselves indebted to the plaintiff in the sum of $300 but to be void on condition that if the Defendant Edmund Holt be cast in this action that he will pay the costs & condemnation or surrender himself to prison in Execution for the same or that they will do it for him.

(p 183)   Ordered by the Court that William Dyer be appointed Constable in the County of Grainger who gave Bond with security in the sum of $500 with Peter Hammock —Absolem Garret & Joseph Dyer his Securities.

      A Bill of Sale from Noe Jarnagin to Chealey Jarnagin was acknowledged in open Court and ordered to be Recorded.
      A Deed of conveyance from Joseph Crabb to John F.Jack proven in open Court by the oaths of John Cocke & Isaac S.McMenns for one hundred six & two thirds of an acre and ordered to be registered.

      A Deed of conveyance from Henry Boatman to James Owen for thirty acres of Land was acknowledged in open Court & ordered to be registered.

      William Magill enters into Bond with William Hodges & John Cocke his securities in the sum of $500 taken in open Court and ordered to be Recorded.
      Ordered by the Court that John Boyd has leave to keep a House of publick intertainment in the County of Grainger and Gave James Kennedy as security.
      Ordered by the Court that James Kennedy have leave to keep a house of public entertainment in the County of Grainger and Gives John Boyd as security.

A Deed of conveyance from Jonathan Williams to John Cocke & John F. Jack for an undivided part of six hundred & forty acres proven in open Court by the oaths of Henry Baker & James Conn and ordered to be registered.

A Deed of conveyance from Michael Moyers to William Lively for Lott No. 4— in the plan of the Town of Rutledge proven in open Court by the oaths of Frederick Moyers & John Cocke and ordered to be registered.

A Deed of conveyance from Jacob Elliot to James Dyer Jr. for two acres of Land acknowledged in open Court and ordered to be registered.

A Deed of conveyance from Joseph Noe to Joseph Rich for seventy acres of Land acknowledged in open Court and ordered to be registered.

A Deed of conveyance from Robert Harris to Rubin Groves for one hundred & forty acres of Land acknowledged in open Court and ordered to be registered.

A Deed of conveyance from Robert Harris to Rubin Groves for fifty two acres of Land acknowledged in open Court and ordered to be Registered.

(p 184)   A Deed of conveyance from James Conn Sheriff of Grainger County to Jonathan Williams for two undivided sixth parts of six hundred and forty acres of Land was acknowledged in open Court by the said James Conn & ordered to be registered also proven in open Court.

A Mortgage Deed from Samuel Cox for one half of an undivided Tract of 250 acres of Land —horses &c was acknowledged in open Court and ordered to be Recorded.

At a Court continued and held in and for the County of Grainger on the 17th Day of February A.D. 1807 —Present, Isiah Midkiff— John Breeden Henry Boatman and Mathew Campbell, Esquires.

```
Derieux Gillem                              )
Hugh Dunlap —John Lavender                  )
acting Executors of Geo.Roulston —Dec'd.)      Case
        vs                                  )
James Ore                                   )
```
        Thereupon came a Jury (towit)

1— Isaac Mitchell	7— Henry Howell
2— John Beelor	8— John Coulter
3— Duncan Carmical	9— Meredith Coffee
4— John Cannon	10—Thomas Ray
5— Nicholas Counts	11—George Jinnings
6— Tandy Senter	12—Jacob Showman

    Who being Elected tryed and sworn the truth to speak on the Issue Joined in this case Do say they find a mistrial.

    Ordered by the Court that Sally Mourning & Elizabeth Denson be Discharged from the citation Issued Last Term of this Court.
    Ordered by the Court that Jacob Arnett be appointed Constable in the County of Grainger who gave Bond with George Sparkman & Absolem Garrett as his securities in the sum of $500.

Ordered by the Court that Isaiah Midkiff -Joseph Cobb & Henry Boatman Esquires be appointed Commissioners to settle with Abraham Wilson Admr. for the Estate of Isaac Wilson Deceased and make Report to the present Term.

Ordered by the Court that William Hamilton -George Norris- Obediah Waters- James Harnock & Joseph Yeaden be a Jury to view and Lay off a road from the Knox County Line near the Widow   (p 185)   McMasters to Bullers Ford on Clinch River and make Report to next Court. Issued.

Ordered by the Court that Rial Jinnings- John Daniel-Francis Daniel Henry Howell-Henry Moys -Samuel Clark-David Bunch -Edward Clark- & Andrew McPheeters be a Jury to view and lay out a Road from the turn pike Gap to Edward Clarks & make report to next Court. Issued.

Ordered by the Court that the order heretofore made appropriating a sum of $3 a month for the support of Elisha Dyer son of William Dyer be Resinded.

Ordered by the Court that the sum of $100 be appropriated to Thomas Henderson in part of Discharge of his Services as Transcribed of the Registers Books of Grainger County. Issued.

Ordered by the Court that James Kennedy- Joseph Cobb- Peter Harris High Larimore- Stephen W.Senter -William Whitesides- William Kirkham- be appointed a Jury to view the Road Leading from Beams Station to Cheek's Cross Roads beginning at the fork that Leads to Sheltons Ford. Issd.

Ordered by the Court that Isaiah Midkiff be Released from paying a Tax in Capt. Bowens Company.

Ordered by the Court that William Driver be Released from paying Tax in Capt. Howells Company.

Ordered by the Court that in future John Coulter have Leave to return his taxable property in the Bounds of Capt. McAnally Company.

A Deed of conveyance from Henry Howell & Caleb Howell to John Jamison for 50 acres of Land was acknowledged in open Court and ordered to be registered.

A Deed of conveyance from Daniel Clayton to Frederick Hoyers for 21 acres of Land was proven in open Court by the oaths of Robert Massengill and James Richardson & ordered to be registered.

A Deed of conveyance from David Spencer to Robert Harris for one hundred and seventeen acres of Land was proven in Court by the subscribing witnesses and ordered to be registered.

A Deed of conveyance from William Williams to John Norris for one hundred acres of Land proven in open Court by the oaths of Elisha Williamson & Caleb Reese & ordered to be registered.

A Bill of sale from James Conn Sheriff to Robert Massengill for a negro Girl named Lett was acknowledged in open Court by James Conn the subscriber thereto & ordered to be Recorded.

(p 186) A Deed of conveyance from Abraham Elliott to James Dyer Jr.for 234 acres of Land was acknowledged in open Court and ordered to be registered.

Ordered by the Court that Alexander Blair be appointed overseer of the road from the Hawkins Line to the ford of German Creek on the River Road and that he be allowed the same Bounds for hands that he has been heretofore for working on said Road. Issued.

Ordered by the Court that Frederick Moyers be allowed the sum of $16 for prosecuting Stone steps to be putt at the Court House in Rutledge.

At a Court continued and held in and for the County of Grainger on the 18th day of February A.D. 1807—Present— John Cocke— David McAnally —Henry Boatman & William Peters Esquires.

Valentine Moulder Esquire who was commissioned as a Justice of the peace in & for said County of Grainger resigns his appointment as such.

Thomas Ray)
   vs)
John Ray)   John Cocke the Defendants security in this case surrenders him in discharge of himself as Bail who gives in place thereof James Alsup & Absolem Garrett.

Ordered by the Court that John Hutcheson be appointed and is hereby appointed a constable be entered into Bond in the sum of $500 with Philip Sigler his security and is quallified as the Law Directs.

Ordered by the Court that all the Overseers heretofore appointed on the Roads which have been Reviewed & Reports made & confirmed at the present be continued overseers on the Roads as Lately reviewed & Reported within the Bounds for which they have bee appointed Respectively and that they shall have the same Bounds for hands as heretofore.

Jesse Rayl by his
Father and next friend)
   vs)
Joseph Noe & Joseph Rich)   Thereupon came a Jury (towit)

1- James Bowen
2- Malachia Howell
3- Richard Shelton
4- Joseph Yeaden
5- Henry Howell
6- William James
7- Charles Matlock
8- Robert Honeycutt
9- George Jinnings
10- Valentine Morgan
11- James Alsup
12- Meredith Coffee

(p 187)   Who being Elected tryed & sworn the truth to speak on the Issue Joined in this case Do say they find the Defendant guilty of the assault & battery and assess the plaintiffs Damages occationed thereby to $1.25 besides costs —Rule for a new trial.

Ordered by the Court that William Clay be allowed to keep a House of publick entertainment in the County of Grainger for the Term of one year from the Date thereof and Give Noe Jarnagin his security in the sum of $500.

Ordered by the Court that William Hamilton —Felps Reed —Joseph Cobb and Rubun Riggs be appointed Jurors to the next Superior Court of Hamilton. Issued.

John F. Jack Returns the following list of Taxable property in open Court for the year 1807 - 100 acres of Land North of Clinch Mountain -100 acres of Land Southside of Richland Creek - 4 Town Lotts - 1 White- 320 acres of Land on German Creek being one moiety or undivided half -640 acres of Land adjoining Col. Hendersons & others.

Benjamin Addinson by John F. Jack his agent returns the following List of Taxable property in open Court for the year 1807 towit-314 acres of Land.

Ordered by the Court that the following persons be summoned to attend as Jurors at the May Term of this Court.-1807.

1- Daniel Beelor
2- Joseph Beelor
3- Peter Harnock
4- Henry Howell
5- Henry Mays
6- Sherod Mays
7- William Hamilton
8- William Mitchell
9- Robert Gains
10-Robert Stone
11-John Dodson
12-Cornelius McCoy
13-Joseph Noe Sr.
14-Nicholas Countz
15-Daniel Robertson
16- William Arnold
17-Cain Acuff
18-John Noe
19-Martin Stubblefield
20-Abner Low
21-Thomas Shipley
22-Benjamin Hudson
23-John Kidwell
24-William Williams
25-William Cook
26-David Holt
27-John Holt
28-Jos.Fields
29-William Davidson
30-Thos. Brown
31-Harmon Cox
32-Thos.Johnson
33-James Alsup
34-Valentine Morgan
35-Jas.Richardson
36-Enoch Winds
37-Chesley Jarnagin
38-Jas.Blair &
39-Andrew Cofman

A list of Strays Remaining on my Books & not proven away in Twelve months of the following Specifications (towit)
Daniel Robertson - one Black Barrow $1.75- one saw $1.16 2/3.

(p 188)

Daniel Robertson one saw $1.16 2/3 - 1 sheat 75¢
George Brock one cow ——————————— $8.00
John Thomason - one cow ——————— 9.00
David Smith   "   " ~~A yearling~~ — — 10.00
Hugh Woolard - 1 saw ——————— 2.66 2/3
Noe Jarnagin Esq. 4 head sheep ——— 5.50
Henry Hawkins Sr. 1 yearling ——————— 1.00
John Estes Esqr. 1 cow ——————— 7.00
"   "   "   "   ——————— 5.00
"   "   "   "   ——————— 6.00
"   "   "   "   ——————— 4.00
James Ferguson 1 Heiffer ——————— 4.00
Major Len Esqr. 1 Boar ——————— 1.66 2/3

William Keith -S.M. Gr. C.
Court met according to adjournment -Present -John Cooke -James Moore William Clay- Noe Jarnagin & Josiah Midriff Esquires.

Ordered by the Court that William Hall appointed as Constable to attend on the Grand Jury at next Term.

William Windham)
    vs   ) Case
William Harris)   Thereupon come a Jury (towit)

1- Isaac Mitchell	7- Thomas James
2- John Beeler	8- John Duke
3- Dunkin Carmichl	9- Joseph Noe Jr.
4- John Cannon	10-Nicholas Countz
5- William Lively	11-Pleasant Duke &
6- John Hodges	12-John McElheny

Who being Elected tryed & sworn the truth to speak on the Issue Joined in this case do say the Defendant is guilty in manner & form as the
plaintiff in his Declaration hath complained against him & assess the
plaintiffs Damages by reason thereof to one hundred Dollars besides his
costs William Stubblefield one of the securities in this case surrenders
the Defendant in Discharge of himself alone.

Ordered by the Court that John F.Jack -John Humphreys and Samuel Bunch
be appointed Commissioners to settle with the Collector & Trustee of the
County of Grainger.

(p 189)   William Keith returns the lists of Taxable property in open Court
for the year 1807 -towit-Two town Lotts - one white poll.
A Deed of conveyance from Elijah Donathan to Tendy Senter for one hundred acres of Land was proven in open Court by the oaths of William Kirk
and ordered to be registered.

John Cocke & John F.Jack by John Williams Esqr. their Attorney present-
ed a petition to Court for partition of a certain tract of Land on German
Creek in said County containing six hundred and forty acres of Land in the
words & Figures following towit-
                    Grainger County (towit)
February Term A.D. 1807 to the Worshipful Court of Pleas & quarter
Sessions in and for the said County of Grainger your petitioners John Cocke
& John F.Jack of the County of Grainger & State of Tennessee Respectively
represents to your Worships that Joseph Crabb of the County in the A.D.
1798 Died intestate leaving six children (towit) four sons -one named
John Crabb- one named Francis Crabb - one named Joseph Crabb & one named
Stephen Crabb and two Daughters - one named Elinow Crabb who intermarried
with John Rose - one other named Elizabeth Crabb who afterwards married
with Hilsman King that the State of North Carolina by patent bearing Date
the 15th day of Dec. A.D. 1802 and number 316 Granted unto the said Joseph
Crabb Dec'd - a tract of Land containing 640 acres situated lying & being
in Grainger County on German Creek Beginning at a Gum and white oak a corner to William Hendersons land & runs with his line South 14 East 190 poles
to a Double white oak & a Dogwood then East 325 poles to a white Oak & post
Oak in Thomas Hendersons line then with his line North 188 poles to two
Black Oaks then East 110 poles to a post Oak then North 128 poles to a
white oak & Hickory sapling then West 300 poles to a stake then South 44
West 220 poles to the Beginning that the said tract of 640 acres of Land
Desended to & rested in the sons and Daughters of the said Joseph Crabb
to be equally Divided amongst them share & share alike your petitioners
further Represents to your Worships that said Stephen Crabb after the
Death of the said Joseph Crabb sold & transferred all the Estate right title Interest & claim of in & to the said tract of 640 acres of Land to John
Crabb one of the sons & heirs of the said Joseph Crabb-Dec'd for a valuable
consideration (towit) for the sum of three hundred & thirty three Dollars
& one third of a Dollar to him paid whereby said John Crabb became seized

194

and possessed of one undivided sixth part of said tract of land (six)
(p 190)   Hundred & forty acres and the said John Crabb being seized &
possessed of Two undivided sixth parts of six hundred and forty acres of
Land, afterwards on the fifth day of February 1807 - James Conn, then
high Sheriff of Grainger County by virtue of two writs of Fieri facias
issued from the worshipful Court of pleas & quarter sessions for Grainger County and to him directed sold and conveyed said two undivided sixth
parts of said six hundred and forty acres of Land & all the Estate right
title interest & claim of the said John Crabb of in and to the same unto
Jonathan Williams of said County for a valuable consideration (towit)
for the sum of fifty cents and the said Jonathan Williams so being seized
and possessed of said two undivided sixth parts of said 640 acres of Land
afterwards on the sixth day of February in the year one thousand eight
hundred and seven sold and conveyed the same to your petitioners by indenture bearing date the same day and year last aforesaid for a valuable consideration towit, for the sum of one hundred and fifty dollars to him pd.
that your petitioners & a certain Aquilla Jones are now seized & possessed of said tract of six hundred & forty acres of Land as tennants in
common and your petitioners all desirous to have the same Divided between
them the said Aquilla Jones & those claiming under the heirs & representations of the said Joseph Cobb Dec'd-that each may hold his part in severally Distinguished by proper meets & bounds - your petitioners therefore
request that your worships may appoint five suitable freeholders as commissioners to enter upon Examined & make partition of said tract of six
hundred and forty acres of Land between your petitioners the said Aquilla
Jones & those claiming under the heirs of said Joseph Crabb Dec'd & due
return to make of their hands and seals at next Term of your Worshipful
Court in conformity with the direction prescribed by the Act of the General Assembly in such case made & provided and your petitioner as in
Duty bound will ever pray.
            Rutledge February 19th 1807.
                  John Cocke
                  John F.Jack
Which petition being heard by the Court & it further appearing to the
satisfaction of the Court by the acknowledgment of the said Aquilla Jones
had been duly & legally notified of the time & intention of exhibiting
the above petition ten days previous to the Exhibiting the same whereupon it is ordered by the Court that said petition be filed and that the
prayer thereof be Granted and it is further ordered by the Court that
Thomas Henderson -Peter Harris, Joseph Cobb, David McAnally and Mac-
ness Moore be Commissioners to make partition and set apart
(p 191)   to the said John Cocke -John F.Jack- Aquilla Jones and those
claiming under the heirs and representatives of Joseph Crabb-Dec'd in
severally each his own share of said tract of six hundred & forty acres
of land held by the said John Cocke -John F.Jack -Aquilla Jones &c.as
tennants in common suitable lying and being on German Creek bound & described as stated in the following petition and that the said commissioners do make and designate by proper meets & boundaries the several petitioners of said Claimants in said tract of Land & make due Return of
their proceedings to the Justices of our next Court of Pleas & Quarter
Sessions to be held for the County of Grainger aforesaid at the Court House
in Rutledge on the third Monday of May next in conformity with and according to the Directions prescribed by the Acts of the General Assembly
in such case made & provided.

Ordered by the Court that John Cooke have leave to enter his Lists
of taxable property and polls in the County of Grainger for the year 1807
(towit) 1780 acres of Land - 9 black polls - 1 white poll -4 town lots.

John Cooke & John F.Jack Returns 200 acres of Land - 1 black poll
300 acres of Land at the foot of Clinch Mountain 100 acres of Land Mot-
cha Creek improvements 50 acres of Land on Clinch mountain on the Kentucky Road.
Ordered by the Court that Thomas Beelor -Cain Acuff- Nicholas Countz
Thomas Dunn, Peter Hammoch -John Bunch Sr. & ordered McPheeters be a jury
to view and lay out a road from Thomas McBroom crossing Clinch Mountain
at Bunch's Trace to Edward Clark's & from thence to Joseph Bealor's &
make Report to next Court. Issued.

Ordered by the Court that Daniel Clayton have leave to return his list
of Taxable and polls in the County of Grainger for the year 1807 (towit)
125 acres of Land - 1 white poll.

Ordered by the Court that John Rumney by John F.Jack his agent have
leave to return his Lists of Taxable property and polls in the County of
Grainger for the year 1807 (towit) - 10,000 acres of Land on the South
side of Holston River.

Ordered by the Court that Pleasant Duke have leave to return his
Lists of taxable property and polls in the County of Grainger for the yr.
1807 (towit) - 280 acres of Land on the North side of Holston River.

Ordered by the Court that David McAnally Sr. have leave to return
his lists of polls and taxable property in the County of Grainger for the
year 1807 (towit) 500 acres of Land.

William Hall constable of the Grand Jury proved his attendance 3
days as such at the present Term for which he is to be allowed the sum of
Dollar per day for which he is to be paid accordingly agreeable to Law.Is.

(p 192)   FEBRUARY SESSION A.D. 1807.

Ordered by the Court that James Moore, John Williams, William Arnold
William James & George Moody be a Jury to view and lay off a Road from
Moore's Ferry to Blackwells Branch at John Cooke's still house & make re-
port to next Court. Issued.

Ordered by the Court that Lidy Wood have leave to return her lists
of taxable property in the County of Grainger for the year 1807 - 80
acres of Land.
Amount of clothing found for Stelehn Collins from May Term 1806
to August Term 1807 - 1 cotton shirt $2.00- 1 sheet $3- 2 handkerchiefs
$1.75 one pr. of stockings $1.50- amounting in all to $8.25 - Charles
McAnelly ordered by the Court that the above amount be admitted.Issd.
          Court adjourns till tomorrow 9 O'clock.
Court met according to adjournment 20th Feby. 1807. Present -Thomas
Henderson -Peter Harris & David McAnally Esqrs.

John Backford for the use of
David Hunter Vs James Kennedy - Thereupon come a Jury (towit)

1- John Beeler   7- William Lively
2- John Cannon   8- John Crabb
3- John Hodges   9- Harliman Taylor
4- Tandy Senter   10-Gabriel Fry
5- Joseph Ray   11-John Ogan &
6- John Coulter   12-Pleasant Duke

Who being elected tried and sworn the truth to speak on the issue joined in this case do say the Defendant hath not paid the Debt in the declaration mentioned as in pleadings he hath alledged and asses the plaintiffs Damages occasioned by reason of the Detention thereof to Twenty Eight Dollars & Eighty cents & costs &c. and the Court having inspected & Examined the Record set forth in the plaintiffs Declaration have considered that there is such Record for considered by the Court that the plaintiffs do recover his debt in the Declaration mentioned together with the Damages in form aforesaid assessed together with his costs in and about prosecuting his said suit in that behalf expended & the Defendant in Mercy &c from which Judgment the Defendant prays an appeal to the next Superior Court for Hamilton District & enters into Bond in the sum of $500 with John Coulter & John Williams his securities.

William Cook comes into open Court & returns his Lists of Taxable property for the year 1807 - one white poll & 200 acres of Land.

Ordered by the Court that James Dyer Constable be appointed to attend on the Court at the present Term- James Dyer proves his attendance at the present Term Five Days.

(p 193)   FEBRUARY SESSIONS A.D. 1807.

John Blackford for the use of
David Hunter   )
        vs   )   Whereupon came a Jury (towit)
James Kennedy   )   the same Jury in the preceding case who being elected tried and sworn the truth to speak on the Issue Joined in this case do say they find the Defendant hath not paid the Debt in the Declaration mentioned as in pleadings he hath alledged and assess the plaintiffs Damages occasioned by reason of the Detention thereof to twenty four Dollars sixty nine cents besides his costs &c. and the Court having inspected the Record set forth in the plaintiffs Delaration have considered that there is such Record &c it is therefore considered by the Court that the plaintiff do recover his Debt in the Declaration mentioned together with his Damages in form aforesaid assessed together with his costs by him in & about prosecuting his suit in that behalf expended & the Defendant in Mercy &c -From which Judgment the Defendant prays an appeal to the next Superior Court for Hamilton District & enters into Bond in the sum of $500 with John Coulter & John Williams his securities.

Jesse Riggs   )
    vs   )
Pleasant Duke)   Thereupon came a Jury (towit)

1- John Beeler   4- Joseph Ray
2- John Cannon   5- John Crabb
3- Tandy Senter   6- William Lively

7- John Crabb
8- Hardiman Taylor
9- Gabriel Fry

10- John Ogan
11- Nicholas County
12- William Kirk

Who being elected tryed and sworn the truth to speak on the Issue joined in this case do say they find the Defendant hath not paid the Debt in the Declaration mentioned as in pleading he hath alledged and assess the plaintiffs Damage by reason of the detention thereof to twenty two Dollars & fifty cents besides his costs from which Judgment the Dedendant prays an appeal to the Superior Court of Hamilton District -reasons filed.

Tandy Senter)
vs) Appeal
Mathew Simmons) thereupon came the same Jury as above Except Joseph Moe in the place of Tandy Senter who being Elected tryed and sworn the truth to speak on the matter in Dispute do say they find for the plaintiff & assess his damages to three Dollars besides his costs.

(p 194)   FEBRUARY SESSIONS A.D. 1807

No. 1- General John Cocke Returned a List of Taxable property for the year 1807.
No. 2- John F.Jack Esqr. Returns a List of Taxable property for the year 1807.
No. 3- Charles McInally is allowed $10.25 as per acct.
No. 4- James Corn Sheriff $2 as per acct.
No. 5- Report of the revenues of a road &c.
No. 6- David McInally Returned a List of Taxable property for the year 1807.
No. 7- James Kennedy appointed overseer of the Road.
No. 8- Jury appointed to view and lay out a Road.
No. 9- Report of the viewers of a Road &c.
No. 10- Report of the viewers of a Road &c.
No. 11- Return of the viewers of a Road or crossing at Selton's Ford.
No. 12- Order to view a Road.
No. 13- Report of the viewers of a Road &c.

We, the Jurors on the Road from the County line above William Blair's to Howell's Branch Report the Road as it now stands from the Hawkins to the third Branch Down the Road and from thence a Direct way to Alexander Blairs fence and from thence a Direct course to the mouth of his line & from thence as the road now runs to the meeting house Branch thence a Direct road to the fork of the Ferry Road and from thence the old Road to German Creek from thence a Direct course to the Big Hill between German Creek & Joseph Moe's and from thence to the old road to Howell's Branch -Alex. Blair- Joseph Moe- John Cannon- James Carmical- William Middlem the above Report received by the Court and ordered to be Recorded.

February the 16th 1807- Ordered by the Court that Alexander Blair be appointed overseer of the Road from the Hawkins line to the ford of German Creek on the River Road & that he be allowed the same hands that he had heretofore allowed him to work on said Road.

Ordered by the Court that Rubin Dixon -John Williams- Philip Free John Bird- James Moore Sr. John Martin- Thomas May be a Jury to view & lay out a Road from Blackwells Branch to James Richardsons on the river Road agreeable to Law and make report to next Court.
                              Order Issued.

State of Tennessee)
Grainger County) Agreeable to an order to us directed - we being summoned and sworn according to Law to view a road from Abraham Wilson's to Beans Station on the Knox Road near Abraham Wilsons running the direct way near Bishop's meeting house by Harmon Coxes through William Williams Lane by Charles Smith by (p 195) Squire Boatman's thence by the house where James Holt now lives that is to say to the left through the field from thence by Joseph Noe's from thence crossing at Shelton's ford from thence through Square Cobbs lane unto Beans Station us as Jurors Given under our hands & seals this fifteenth Day of January 1807-

Henry Boatman (seal)
Charles Smith (seal) Thomas Reese (seal)
David Tate (seal) Duncan Carmical (seal)
Joseph Noe (seal) Richard Shelton (seal)

We, the within named Jurors appointed at November Term to review and lay off a Road from Holston River near William Hankins Esq. have Reviewed & laid out the same as follows- Beginning at William Hankins Ford thence by Richard Acuffs thence by Joseph Ryans from thence to the forks of the road near James Campbell's and we recommend Joseph Ryans overseer of said road -Peter Hamilton- Richard Acuff- Wm Snodgrass -Robert Harris William Hankins, therefore it was considered by the Court that the above Report be confirmed.

State of Tennessee)
Grainger County) this is to certify that the Jurors appointed at November Term to review the Road from the Powder Spring Gap to Circles ford on Clinch river as use to be following the old Road with some small alterations which are marked by the Jury & all agree Edward Clark- Daniel Beelor- Joseph Beelor- Peter Beelor- John Hains- Joseph Dennis- Philip Siglar, therefore it was considered by the Court that the above Report be confirmed.

Abraham Pruit is appointed overseer of the public Road from Peter Beelor's old mill to the ford of Flat Creek near Nell's meeting house in the room of Peter Hammock allowing him all the hands in the same bounds to work under him that worked under said Hammock ordered by the Court February Sessions 1807. Copy Issued.

Court met according to adjournment 21st. Feby. 1807. Present James Moore- Charles McAnnlly -David McAnnlly Esqrs.

A Bill of Sale from James Conn Sheriff to John Cooke for a negro Girl named Lucn was proven in open Court by the oath of William Baker one of the subscribing witnesses & ordered to be recorded.
Thomas Henderson.

(p 196) FEBRUARY SESSIONS A.D. 1807.

February 14th 1807- We who was appointed to view the road from Big Buffalow to Knox Line have this Day met & has found no cause to alter the Road in any part in said District -Jacob Arnet, Evin Harris- Rubin Groves James Richardson & Robert Gains -ordered by the Court that the above Report be confirmed.

A Deed of conveyance from John Bean to Thomas Ogle for 100 acres of for 100 acres of Land be the same more or less was acknowledged in open Court & ordered to be registered.

A Deed of conveyance from Levi Moore to Joseph Fields for 82 acres of Land proven in open Court by the oath of Robert Moore & Joseph Fields & ordered to be Registered.

A Deed of conveyance from Nicholas Spring to Robert Fields for 200 and ten acres of Land proven in open Court by the subscribing witnesses thereto and ordered to be Registered.

A Deed of conveyance from Wm Hall to Rubin Dixon for one hundred acres of Land acknowledged in open Court and ordered to be Registered.

A Deed of conveyance from Joseph Hoe for 70 acres of Land was acknowledged in open Court and ordered to be Registered.

A Deed of conveyance from Henry Howell & Caleb Howell to John Jamison for fifty acres of Land was acknowledged in open Court & ordered to be Registered.

A Deed of conveyance from David Spencer to Robert Harris for one hundred and seventeen acres of Land was proven in open Court by the oath of Evan Harris & Rubin Groves witnesses thereto & ordered to be registered.

A Deed of conveyance from Robert Harris to Rubin Groves for one hundred & forty acres of Land was acknowledged in open Court and ordered to be registered.

A Deed of conveyance from Robert Harris to Rubin Groves for one hundred acres of Land was acknowledged in open Court and ordered to be registered.

State of Tennessee)
Grainger County) February Sessions 1807 -We, Joseph Cobb, Henry Boatman & Josiah Midkiff appointed by Court to settle with Abraham Wilson Administrator of the Estate of Isaac Wilson Dec'd have made the following settlement & Report to Court as follows (towit) it appears to us that the personal Estate of Isaac Wilson Dec'd amounts to 1766.86 and it also
(p 197)   appears to us on settlement that the said Abraham Wilson Admr. as aforesaid has paid 2080.86 settling the Debts due by said Estate and it also appears to us that the said Abraham Wilson & Isaac Wilson was in partnership in trading the Lifetime of the said Abraham has paid $314 over & above the amount of said Estate is indebted to the said Abraham & the further sum of 55.31 Exclusive of the partnership which amounts to $212.31 in the whole that is due from said Estate Abraham Wilson as before stated The amount of the Estate of Isaac Wilson Dec'd $1766.86 paid by Abraham Wilson Admr. $2080.86 said Abraham Wilson's acct. Exclusive $55.31 of the partnership we also allowed the Abraham Wilson $25 as a full compensation for his services as Administrator -25 -Given under our hands and seals this 17th Day of February 1807.

                    Joseph Cobb (seal)
                    Henry Boatman (seal)
                    Isaiah Midkiff (seal)

State of Tennessee)
Grainger County) We, Joseph Cobb & Peter Harris appointed by Court to

settle with John Crabb & Joseph Crabb Admrs. of the Estate of Joseph Crabb
Dec'd that is the personal property amounts to $1007.72 and it appears to
us on the settlement that the said John Crabb & Joseph Crabb has paid up
a settled the full amount of said Estate as stated $1007.72 —Given under
our hands & seals this 16th February 1807 —We have also allowed the said
Joseph Crabb, John Crabb Admr. the sum of $100 as a full compensation for
their services to be paid to them by said Estate to that amount.

       Joseph Cobb (seal)
       Peter Harris (seal)

State of Tennessee)
Grainger County) Feby. Sessions 1807 —Ordered by the Court that Lewis
Whitner— Thomas Brewer, Jacob Elliot— James Dyer Jr. Charles Hutcheson —
Robert Fields— Joseph Dennis —Philip Siglar & William McPhetridge be appointed Jurors to review and lay off and mark the same Road Leading
(p 198) Down Flat Creek Flat Creek from where it intersects with
the Powder Spring Gap road at Philip Siglar's the nearest and best way to
the Knox Line and make Report to next Court.

State of Tennessee)
Grainger County) Agreeable to an order of Court we, the undersigned
Jury Did on the 17th of Jan. 1807 —Did view and lay out a road from Howel
Branch to Buffelow Creek (towit) Beginning at Howell's Branch then along
the old road by Moody's Cabbins then along said road near Henry Mayes then
to keep the old road to Edward Daniels then by George Moody's then to
Blackwells Branch then to John Williams then to Martin Sahburn's then by
William Addinson's then to the ford of the Branch at Michael Massengill's
Henry Mays, Edward Daniels, George Moody, John Williams & James Moore the
above report was received by the Court & confirmed and ordered to be recorded.

  The Court appoint James Kennedy overseer of the Road confirmed by
the Court from Beans Station to Shelton's Ford on Holston River and to
have all the hands in the following bounds to work under him on said road
that is to say Beginning at the Sulphur Springs on the Kentucky Road then
a Direct course to the Cabins on the Knox Road where Coopwood formerly
lived on Groves Land thence a Direct Course to said Shelton's ford, then
a Direct course to the old Meeting house between Coulter & Kirkham's,
thence a Direct course to Orr's old mill on German Creek thence a straight
Line to the Beginning. Issued.

  William Clay Esqr. who was appointed to take in Lists of Taxable
property in the Bounds of Capt. John Bunches Company for the year 1807
made return at the Present Term.

  William Peters Esqr. who was appointed to take in Lists of Taxable
property in the Bounds of Capt. Hargroves Company for the year 1807 made
his return at the present Term.

  David Tate Esqr. who was appointed to take in lists of Taxable property in the Bounds of Captain Mayes Company for the year 1807 made his
return at the present Term.

  William Hankins Esqr. who was appointed to take in Lists of Taxable
property in the bounds of Capt. James Mitchell's Company for the year 1807
made his return at the present Term.

Henry Bratten Esqr. who was appointed to take in Lists of Taxable property in the bounds of Capt. George Hoe's Company for the year 1807 and made return at the present Term.

David McAnally Esqr. who was appointed to take in Lists of taxable property in the bounds of Capt. John Dodson's Company for the year 1807 made return at the present Term.

Peter Harris Esqr. who was appointed to take in Lists of Taxable property in the bounds of Captain Bryan's Company for the year 1807 made return at the present Term.

Thomas Henderson Esqr. who was appointed to take in Lists of Taxable property in the Bounds of Capt. McAnally's Company for the year 1807 made return at the present Term.

Philip Sigler Esqr. who was appointed to take in lists of Taxable property in the Bounds of Capt. James Company for the year 1807 made return at the present Term.

Valentine Mouhder Esqr. who was appointed to take in lists of property in the Bounds of Captain Alex. Hamilton's for the year 1807 made Return at the present Term.

James Moore Esqr. who was appointed to take in lists of Taxable property in the Bounds of Capt. John Smith Company for the year 1807 made return at the present Term.

Ordered by the Court that the same Taxes be laid & collected for the year 1807 that was laid and collected for the year 1806.
     Thomas Henderson Chrm.

Ordered by the Court that James Conn high Sheriff of Grainger County which he purchased from William McNeal and allowed of by the Court. Issd.

To the Worshipfuls the Justices of the Court of pleas & quarter Sessions of Grainger County we your petitioners humbly Represents that public road Leading from Rutledge to Knoxville runs on a part of our Lands in such a direction that it renders a very Great inconveniency to us, therefore pray your Worships that you would appoint a Jury to review from where said road crosses the first hollow above Hoe Jarnagin to the first Bridge below, also from the first branch above Chesley   (p200) Jarnagin to where the road that now goes by said Chesley Jarnagin's house intersects with said publick road below and we believe that a near or better way may be had than where the road now Runs Hoe Jarnagin, Chehley Jarnagin, William Clay ordered by the Court that the prayer of the within petition be Granted Abner Low, William Sims, James Brown, Hugh Woolard, Jacob Arnet, Geo. Sparkman, John Richard, Newberry James are appointed by the Court Jurors to view the road agreeable to the prayers of the within petition and make Return to next Court.

Ordered by the Court that David McAnally have leave to return his lists of Taxable property & polls in the County of Grainger for the year 1807 (towit) 500 acres of Land.

We the Jurors appointed by the Court to view and lay out the road from the Powder Spring Gap to Clinch Mountain to Hodges Ford at Clinch River have complied with the appointment and gave it our Judgment that it be continued as it now is with some small alterations, believing it the best way. Given under our hands and seals this 22nd. Jany. 1807.

Charles Hutcheson	(seal).
Wm McPhetridge	(seal)
Joseph Philips	(seal)
Thomas Dennis	(seal)
Wm Peters	(seal)
Abraham Elliot	(seal)
Jacob Elliot	(seal)

Luke Lea)
vs) Attachment
William Howard) William Hall one of the Constables of Grainger County made his return to Court that he had levied an attachment on the 16th day of January 1807 on one hundred and fifty acres of Land situated lying and being in the County of Grainger on the waters of Richland Creek as the property of the said William Howard's – no personal property to be found therefore it is considered as adjudged by the Court that order of sale Do issue to the Sheriff of said County commanding him to expose to sale the above Described tract of Land or so much thereof as will be sufficient to satisfy the plaintiffs Damages besides his costs.

Court adjourned till Court in course.

(p 201)   May Sessions A.D. 1807

At a Court continued and holden for the County of Grainger at the Court House in Rutledge on the third Monday of May A.D. 1807 it being the 18th of the same month. Present —James Moore Sr. David Tate & James Moore Jr. Esqrs.

James Conn high Sheriff of said County made his Return that he had Executed the following Venire Facias on all.

1– Daniel Beeler	21– Cornelius McCoy
2– Joseph Beeler	22– Thomas Shipley
3– Peter Hammoch	23– Benjamin Watson
4– Henry Howel	24– John Kidwell
5– Henry Hays	25– Wm Williams
6– Sherod Hays	26– William Cook
7– Wm Hamilton	27– David Holt
8– Robert Gains	28– John Holt
9– Robert Stone	29– Wm Davidson
10–Joseph Hoe Sr.	30– Thomas Brown
11–Nicholas Counts	31– Harmon Cox
12–Daniel Robertson	32– Thomas Johnston
13–Wm Arnold	33– James Alsup
14–Cain Acuff	34– Valentine Morgan
15–John Hoe	35– Jas. Richardson
16–Abner Low	36– Enoch Winds
17–Martin Stubblefield	37– Chesley Jarnagin
18–Wm Mitchell	38– James Blair Jr.
19–John Dodson	39– Andrew Cofman

Out of which Venire Facias the persons names who are under written were chosen a Grand Jury at the present Term.

1- Daniel Beeler foreman	9- Joseph Hoe Sr.
2- Peter Hammock	10-Nicholas Countz
3- Henry Howel	11-Daniel Robertson
4- Henry Hays	12-Joseph Fields
5- Abner Low	13-John Hoe
6- Sherod Mays	14-Benj. Hutson
7- Robert Gains	15-John Holt
8- Valentine Morgan	

John Rogers Esqr. produced a commission from two of the Judges of the Superior Court of Law and Equity for the State of Tennessee to practice as an Attorney in the said State and was qualified accordingly.

Henry Holt)
vs) In this case the petition of the Defendant having been
John Allison) read and heard praying that a writ of Certiorari Do issue Directed to Charles McAnally commanding him to transmit inclosed under his hand & seal the Judgment &c. in this case to the next Term of this Court.

(p 202)   May Sessions A.D. 1807
and also a writ of Supercedeas Directed to David McAnally Constable commanding him &c. to direct &c. whereupon ordered that writs Do issue agreeable to the prayer of this Petition.

Ordered by the Court that Shedrick Brown have leave to return his lists of Taxable property and polls for the year A.D. 1807 (towit) 1 white poll- 3 black polls.
Ordered by the Court that David Brown have leave to return his lists of Taxable property and polls for the year A.D. 1807 (towit) 500 acres of Land.
Ordered by the Court that David Haley have leave to return his Lists of Polls & taxable property by Robert Stone for the year 1807 (towit) 450 acres of Land.
Ordered by the Court that Robert Massengill have leave to return his Lists of Taxable property & polls for the year 1807 (towit) 1 white poll.
Ordered by the Court that John Dorough have leave to return his Lists of Taxable property for the year A.D. 1807 (towit) 1 Town Lott No. 3- 1 Town Lott No. 47.

Ordered by the Court that Harmon Cox be Released from the payment of one Dollar and eighty nine cents & a half which he was taken more than his Taxable property amounted to for the year 1806.

The Court appoints John Cocke & Henry Bentman Esqr. Commissioners to settle with Thomas James Executor of the Last Will and Testament of the Estate of William James -Deceased and make report to Court.

A Deed of conveyance from Hilsman King & Elizabeth his wife late Elizabeth Crabb to John F.Jack for one undivided sixth part of six hundred & forty acres of Land on German Creek formerly the property of Joseph Crabb Dec'd- was acknowledged in open Court by the said Hilsman King & Elizabeth King & Elizabeth King his wife she having been first privately examined by David Tate Esqr. a member of the County Court of Grainger appointed

by said Court to Examine her whether she Doth voluntarily assent thereto
and the said David Tate after the examination aforesaid reports to Court
that she Did assent thereto voluntarily.

A ^Deed of conveyance from Frederick Foyers to ^Edward D.Hobbs for a
Lott in the town of Rutledge being Lott No. 44- was proven in open ^Court
by the oaths of John F.Jack & Wm Baker subscribing witnesses thereto and
ordered to be Registered.

A Deed of conveyance from James Paul & John Paul to Joseph Beeler for
163 acres of Land was acknowledged in open Court by the subscribers thereto and ordered to be recorded.

A Deed of conveyance from David Haley to Robert Stone for one Thousand acres of Land was proven in open Court by the oaths of Robert Blair
& Thomas Grimes subscribing witnesses & ordered to be registered.

(p 203)   May Sessions A.D. 1807

A Deed of conveyance from William Cooke to the heirs and representatives of Robert McElhiney Dec'd- for 159 acres of Land was acknowledged
in open Court by the subscribers thereto and ordered to be registered.

The Last Will and Testament of James Thomason Dec'd was proven in op-
en Court by the oaths of James Moore & John Moore subscribing witnesses
thereto and ordered to be Recorded.

Ordered by the Court that Joseph Noe Jr. be appointed overseer of the
Road leading from Shelton's Ford to the top of the Ridge where Henry Boatman formerly lived and all the hands that Lives in the following bounds
to work under said overseer that is to say beginning at a Stake on the bank
of Holston River on the Southside corner to Abraham Wilson's bounds thence
Down the meanders of said river to the lower corner of James Camical's
Land thence to the top of Boatman's Ridge so as to include all the Lands
from Ambrose Hodges up thence a straight line to the Beginning. Issued.

Ordered by the Court that Abraham Wilson be appointed overseer of the
Road leading from his house from the top of the Ridge where Henry Boatman
formerly lived as it was laid off by a Jury appointed Nov. Term 1806 and
said Wilson to have all the Hands in the following Bounds Described as
works under said Wilson's beginning at Redis Mill thence Down the meanders of said Creek to the mouth or confluence with Holston River thence
Down said river opposite to where Henry Boatman Lived thence to where
Henry Morgan formerly Lived thence to Abraham Wilson's and from thence to
the beginning. Issued a copy.

A bond or relinquishment from Alexander Thomason to Samuel West &c.
was acknowledged in open Court by the subscriber thereto and ordered to
be registered.

Nancy McElhaney comes into Court and was admitted as administratrix
on the Estate of Robert McElhaney -Dec'd who enters into Bond in the sum
of six hundred dollars with her securities- Ambrose Yancey -John Paul &
John McElhaney who took the necessary oaths &c.

Goodin Scott came into open Court and entered into Bond in the sum
of five hundred dollars for the purpose of indemnifying the Court from

(p 204)   May Sessions A.D. 1807
charge and maintenance of a Bastard child begotten on the Body of (   )
and he the said Scott being the reputed father thereof and Gives Henry
Rowell & Dennis Scott as his securities.

Court adjourns till tomorrow morning 9 o'clock.
Court met according to adjournment 19th May 1807- Present James El-
lison- Henry Boatman, Noe Jarnagin -David Tate Esquires.

Ordered by the Court that Robert Harris be released from the payment
of a Tax on one hundred and Seventeen acres of Land for the year 1807,
also for one free poll Tax for the same year.

State   )
   vs   )   For feloniously stealing a smooth bored Gun this Day
Thomas Pounders)   William Hankins Esqr. one of those who was bound in Recognizance for the appearance of the above named Defendant at this Court
to answer the above charge appeared in Court and surrendered in open Court
the said Thomas Pounders in Discharge of his undertaking and thereupon it
was ordered by the Court that the said will and be considered Discharged
from his undertaking and Recognizance aforesaid and it is further ordered
that the said Thomas Pounders be in custody of the Sheriff of this County
to answer the aforesaid charge.

N. the last Will and Testament of Lewis Whitner Dec'd was proven in
open Court by the oaths of Isaac Taylor & Lewis Whitner Jr. two of the subscribing witnesses thereto and ordered to be recorded and Henry Whitner
one of the Executors mentioned in the said Will was qualified & took the
upon himself the due Execution thereof.

Ordered by the Court that Sariah Glosset a minor Orphant be bound
unto David Tate Esqr. until she attains to the age of Eighteen years as
by Indenture will appear.

State   )
   vs   )   Who was bound in Recognizance to appear at the present
Thomas Pounders)   Term to answer to the charge the State against the Defendant and he being solemnly called came not therefore

(p 205)   May Sessions A.D. 1807
it is considered by the Court that he forfeit his Ni 51.

James Simpson was appointed Constable for Grainger County and enters
into bond in the sum of $500 with Martin Ashburn and Abel Morgan his se-
curities was qualified according to Law.
Ordered by the Court that William Hamilton, George Norris, Henry
Whitner - Wm Peters, Samuel McBee, Obediah Waters and Joseph Yeaden be appointed as Jurors to view and lay out a road from the Knox County Line
near the widow Minets to Beelors ford on Clinch River and make report to
next Court. Issued,- a copy.

State   )
   vs   )   Robert Harris comes into Court and surrenders the Defend-
Hugh Woolard   )   ant in Discharge of himself as bail and prayed in custody

of the Sheriff who gives George Martin his security in place thereof.

State)
vs)   John Richards who was summoned as a witness in this case
~~Thos. Woodlarxy~~) called came not - therefore it was considered by the Court
that he forfeit according to the Act of Assembly.

State)
vs)
Meredith Coffee)
Thos. Ray, commonly)
called Big Thomas Ray)
Benj. Ray & John Aytes)   Thereupon came a Jury (towit)
1- Harmon Cox   7- Gabriel Fry
2- Thomas Johnston   8- George Sparkman
3- Evan Harris   9- Thomas Jones
4- Wm Lively   10- John Duke
5- Zachariah Kieth   11- James Grayson
6- Thomas James   12- David Countz

Who being elected tryed and sworn the truth to speak on the Issue at
traverse do say they find the Defendants not Guilty as charged in the Bill
of Indictment.

In pursuance of an order of Last Court a commission Issued in the
words and figures following (towit)
State of Tennessee)
Grainger County   ) To Thomas Henderson, Peter Harris, Joseph Cobb. David
McAnally Esquires & Moness Moore -
By order of Court you and each of you are hereby appointed Commis-
sioners, to make petition and set apart

(p 206)   May Sessions A.D. 1807
John Coake - John F. Jack -Acquilla Jones & those claiming under the heirs
and Representatives of Joseph Crabb Deceased in severalty each there own
share of a tract of Land of 640 acres held by John & John F. Jack -Aquilla
Jones &c as tenants in common situate lying & being on German Creek bounded and Described as follows (towit) beginning at a Gum and white oak a corner to Wm Henderson's Land and runs with his line South 90 poles to a double white oak & a Dogwood then East 326 poles to a white oak & post Oak
in Thomas Henderson's Line then with his Line North 188 poles to two black
oaks then East 110 poles to a post oak then North 126 poles to a white oak
& Hichory saplin then West 300 poles to a stake then South 44 West 220 poles
to the Beginning.   You are therefore hereby Required to make & disignate
by proper meets & boundaries the several portions of said claimants in sd.
tract of Land & make due return of your proceedings under your hands and
seals to the Justices of our next Court of pleas and quarter Sessions to
be held for the County of Grainger aforesaid at the Court House in Rutledge
on the third Monday of May next in conformity with and according to the
Directions prescribed by the Act of the Assembly in such case made and provided - Witness Ambrose Yancey Clerk of our said Court at Office the third
Monday in Febr. A.D. 1807 and in the XXXI st. year of American Independ-
ence.   Saml. Yancey C.G.C

In obedience to and by Virtue of the foregoing Commission the Commissioners to whom it was Directed made their report to Court in the words &

figures following (towit)

In obedience to a commission Issued from the Worshipful Court of
pleas & Quarter Sessions for the County of Grainger in the tate of Tennessee & Directed to us whose names are underwritten (towit) Thomas Hen-
derson- Peter Harris, Joseph Crabb, David McAnally Esquires & Mackness
Moore Commissioners appointed by said Court to make pertition & set apart
to John Cooke -John F.Jack -Acquilla Jones & thos clciming under the heirs
and Representatives of Joseph Crabb Dec'd in severally each their own share
of a certain tract of Land containing 640 acres held by John Cooke -John
F.Jack- Acquilla Jones as tenants in   (p 207)   common situated
lying and being on German Creek bounded and Described as follows(towit)
Beginning at a Gum and white oake a corner to Wm Henderson's Land and runs
with his line 14 East 190 poles to a double white oak and a dogwood then
East 325 poles to a white oak and post oak in Thomas Henderson's Line then
with his line North 188 poles to two black Oaks then East 110 poles to a
post oak then North 128 poles to a white oak & hickory saplin then West
300 poles to a stake then South 44 West 225 poles to the Beginning which
said Commission bars test Monday of Febr. A.D. 1807 in pursuance to and
by Virtue of said Commission we the undersigned Commissioners being first
Duly sworn as the Act of the General Assembly in such cases made and provided requires have entered upon and examined the above mentioned tract
of Land (640) acres & have made partition thereof amongst the Respective
Claimants as follows towit-We Do hereby allot & set apart to John F.Jack
claiming under Joseph Crabb one of the heirs of Joseph Crabb Dec'd -Lot
No. 1- bounded and described as follows (towit) Beginning at a stake in
the middle of German Creek on Thomas Henderson's Line of a tract of Land
whereupon Wm Henderson Dec'd formerly lived thence up the middle of said
creek as it mianders to the mouth of the spring branch thence up the middle of said branch as it mianders to a marked white oak Dividing the
spring then South 8 degrees East to a stake on the East Line of the original tract thence West on said Line to a Double white oak corner of the
original survey thence North 14 West to the Beginning to have and to hold
said Lot to the sd. John F.Jack his heirs and assigns forever - We Do
hereby further allot and set apart Lot number 2 to John F.Jack claiming
under Elizabeth Crabb one of the heirs of Joseph Crabb Dec'd who intermarried with Hileman King bounded and Described as follows(towit) beginning at a Gum & white oak beginning at a Gum and white oak beginning corner of the original tract Running thence South 14 East to a stake in the
middle of German Creek corner of Lott No. 1- thence up the middle of said
creek to the mouth of Campbell's fork thence up the middle of said fork
as it mianders to a stake on the closing line of the original tract &
from thence to the beginning to have and to hold said Lott number 2 to
the said John F.Jack.

(p 208)   May Sessions A.D. 1807
his heirs and assigns forever- We do hereby further allot and set apart
Lott number 3 to John F.John claiming under Elinor Rose & John Rose the
said Elinor late Elinor Crabb one of the heirs of the said Joseph Crabb
Deceased having intermarried with the said John Rose bounded and Described as follows (towit)   Beginning on a stake in the middle of Campbell's
fork on the closing Line of the original Tract corner to Lott No. 2-
Running thence Down the middle of said fork as it mianders to the middle
of German Creek as it mianders to the moth of Cany fork to a white oak
& sugar tree at the mouth of as small branch thence North 49 West to a

stake in the closing line of the original tract and from thence with said
Line to the Beginning to have and to hold said Lot number 3 to the said
John F.Jack his heirs and assigns forever and we do adjudge that Lot No.
3 is thereby three dollars and one third of a Dollar more valuable than
Lot No. 4- herein after mentioned that said Lot No. 3- is sixteen and two
thirds of a Dollar more valuable than Lott No. 1- that said Lot number three
is sixteen Dollars & two thirds of a Dollar more valuable than Lot No. 2-
that said Lot No. 3- is sixteen Dollars & two thirds of a Dollar more valuable than Lot no. 6- herein after mentioned - We do hereby further allot
& set apart Lot No. 4- to John F.Jack claiming under Atephen Crabb one of
the heirs of said Joseph Crabb Deceased bound and described as follows
(towit) Beginning at a stake in the middle of the spring branch corner to
Lot number 1- Running thence up the middle of said branch to a marked white
oak at the head of the spring thence South 8 East with the line of Lot
No. 1- to a stake on the East Line of the original tract to a Post oak -
Dogwood and Hickory running thence North crossing German Creek till it intersects the Caney fork thence down the middle of said Caney fork as it
mianders to its junction with German Creek & from thence down the middle
of German creek as it mianders to the Beginning. To have and to hold sd.
Lot no. 4- to said John F.Jack his heirs and assigns forever we do hereby
further allot and set apart Lot. No. 5- to John Cooke claiming under John
Crabb one of the heirs of said Joseph Crabb Deceased bounded and described
as follows(towit) Beginning at a white oak & post oak corner of the original tract thence North 128 poles to two black oaks thence South 79 West
92 poles to a white oak   (p 209)   and sugar tree at the mouth
                 May Sessions A.D. 1807
of a small branch running into the Cany fork corner to lots No. 3- & 6
thence down the middle of Cany fork to a stake corner to Lot No. 4-
thence South with the line of Lot No. 4 crossing German Creek to a post
oak Dogwood and Hickory corner to Lot No. 4- thence East to the Beginning
to have and to hold said Lot No. 5- to the said John Cooke his heirs and
assigns forever and we do hereby adjudge said Lot No. 5- to be worth 188.
dollars and one third of a dollar more than Lot No. 4- We do hereby further allot and set apart Lot. No. 6- to Acquilla Jones claiming under
Francis Crabb one of the heirs of said Joseph Crabb Dec'd bounded and Described as follows (towit) Beginning at a white oak & sugar tree at the
mouth of a small branch running into the Cany fork corner to Lot No. 3-
thence North 49 West with the Line of Lot No. 3- to a stake in these closing Line of the original tract thence North 54 East to a white oak corner
of the original tract thence East 300 poles to a white oak & hickory Saplin
corner of the original tract thence South and 128 poles to a post oak thence
West 110 poles to two black oaks thence South 79 West to the Beginning to
have and to hold said Lot No. 6- to the Acquilla Jones his heirs and assigns forever in witness thereof We have hereunto set our hands and seals
this 16th Day of May A.D. 1807 -

                    Thomas Henderson (seal)
                    Peter Harris   (seal)
                    Joseph Cobb   (seal)
                    David McAnally   (seal)
                    Mackness Moore   (seal)

     The above and foregoing Report of the proceedings of the aforesaid
Commissioners being presented to Court whereupon motion it is confirmed
and ordered to be Registered.
     Ordered by the Court that John Bunch Sr. Thomas McBroom -Miller

Easly -Nicholas Counts -Martin Albert- John Bowen, Daniel Robertson-&
Thomas Bunch be a Jury to view and lay out a road from Blackwell's branch
to James Richardson's on the river road and make report to next Court.

(p 210)   May Sessions A.D. 1807

    Ordered by the Court that the following persons under named be ap-
pointed as Jurors to August Term A.D. 1807.

1- Henry Whitner
2- George Norris
3- Robert Fields
4- Rubin Dixon
5- James Richardson
6- John Williams
7- Evan Harris
8- David Bunch
9- John Myers
10-Cain Acuff
11-Wm Milligan
12-Francis Daniel
13-George Moody
14-Moses Hodge
15-Wm Blair
16-Rubin Riggs
17-John Estes
18-Daniel Taylor
19-Martin Stubblefield
20-Samuel McBee

21- Dennis Condry
22- Richard Shelton
23- Lewis Edwards
24- Jeremiah Jarnagin
25- Newberry James
26- Robert Harris
27- Major Lea
28- John Vinyard
29- Thomas Mann
30- Miller Easly
31- Hugh Larimore
32- John Norris
33- Jeremiah Chamberlain
34- Edward Daniel
35- Peter Hamilton
36- Henry Bowen
37- John Bowen
38- William Windham

    Ordered by the Court that Richard Dunville be appointed overseer of
the road From the top of Clinch mountain to Crosses plantation and to have
the following bounds for hands to work on said road(towit) beginning at
the lower end of William Clay's Lane thence to the top of said Mountain
thence along the mountain to the Gap where the road crosses the same thence
along said road to the owl hole Gap in the Richland Knobs thence adross
so as to include Thomas Ray Jr. and all the hands on John Birds plantation
across the valley to the Beginning and the hands are to work on the Valley
road so far as said road intersects with the same. Issued.

    Ordered by the Court that Samuel Reed have leave to return his Lists
of Taxable property for the year A.D. 1807 (towit) 1 white poll.

    Ordered by the Court that John Spencer by John Bunch Jr. have leave
to return his Lists of Taxable property for the year A.D. 1807 (towit)
two town lotts No. 40 & 41.

    Ordered by the Court that the Solicitor Thomas Dardis Esqr. be allowed
the sum of Thirty Dollars for his Services from May Term 1807 inclusive.Is.

(p 211)   May Sessions A.D. 1807
    Ordered by the Court that James Conn high Sheriff be allowed the sum
of $80 for his Exofficio Services from May term 1807 inclusive. Issued.

    Ordered by the Court that Ambrose Yancey Clerk of Grainger County be
allowed the sum of fifty dollars for the ExOfficio services from May Term

1806 until May term 1807 inclusive.

A Deed of conveyance from Aaron Smith to Abraham Garret for two hundred acres of Land was proven in open Court by the oaths of Abner Low & Meredith Coffee subscribing witnesses thereto and ordered to be registered.

A Deed of conveyance from James Robertson to Major Lea for one hundred and forty six acres and the quarter of Land was proven in open Court by the oaths of John Howll & Rubin Cotrel subscribing witnesses thereto and ordered to be registered.

A Deed of conveyance from Nicholas Countz to John F.Jack for two undivided parts of 640 acres of Land say 213 acres & one third of an acre was proven in open Court by James Conn & John Cocke subscribing witnesses thereto and ordered to be registered.

Court adjourns till tomorrow morning 9 o'clock.

At a Court continued and held in and for the County of Grainger in the town of Rutledge on the 20th Day of May A.D. 1807. Present James Moore- Henry Boatman David Tate Esqrs.

Ordered by the Court that Tapley Haygood be allowed the sum of $25 for each three months that he hath not been allowed for the keeping supporting Jeremiah Midkiff one of the poor of this County. A copy Issd.

Ordered by the Court that Francis Daniel be appointed overseer of the road from the fork of the road near Henry Mayes to the top of the Ridge above widow T—— & that he have the following bounds for hands to work under him all the hands on German Creek & including the hands at Sherod Mays & Francis Daniels -

(p 212)   May Sessions A.D. 1807

Ordered by the Court that Isaac Jones be appointed overseer of the road from James Moore's Ferry on Holston River to Crosses old place in the Owl Hole Gap and that he have the same Bounds for hands that James Arnold had to work under him-. Issued.

State   )
  vs   )
Meredith Coffee)   In this case John Cooke Atty. for the Defendant maketh motion to the Court to have rule entered for the Mitigation of the fine of five dollars imposed on the Defendant by the Court at the present Term which motion was granted by the Court.

John Brown)
   vs   )
John Crabb) Whereupon came a Jury towit-

1- Enoch Winds   5- Thomas Bunch
2- Chesley Jarnagin   7- Gabriel Fry
3- Andrew Coffman   8- Nathan Lawson   11-Thomas Jones
4- Thomas Dunn   9- John Tabber   12-John Woolard
5- Edward McGinnis   10-Thomas Kerney

Who being elected tryed and sworn the truth to speak on the Matter in Dispute Do say they find for the Defendant rule for a new trial, the Grand Jury for the present Term Dismissed.

James & Wm Park)
    vs   )   Whereupon came a Jury (towit)
Francis Mayberry)

1- Harmon Cox	7- John Moyers
2- Thomas Cox	8- Benjamin Ray
3- James Alsup	9- William Jones
4- Meredith Coffee	10-Thomas Ray
5- Robert Long	11-Joseph Ray
6- George Sparkman	12-John Griffits

Who being elected tryed and sworn the truth to speak on the Issue Joined do say that the Defendant hath not paid the Debt in the Declaration mentioned nor any part thereof as in pleadings he hath alledged and assess the plaintiffs Damage by reason of the Detention thereof to seven Dollars fifty seven cents besides his costs, therefore it is considered by the Court that the plaintiffs Do recover the Debt in the Declaration mentioned also the damages assessed as aforesaid in manner and form aforesaid besides his costs.

(p 213)   May Sessions A.D. 1807

Edmund Holt)
    vs   )
Gabriel Fry)   Thereupon came a Jury towit, the same Jury as above - Non-suit entered by order of Council - Rule to set non-suit aside -Rule made absolute.

Thomas Ray   )
    vs   )
John Ray & Jesse Baxly)   James Alsup comes into Court and surrenders John Ray the Defendant in this case in Discharge of himself as Bail who gives James Alsup & Joseph Ray as his securities in lieu thereof.

James Grayson)
    vs   )
William Keith)   Thereupon came a Jury (towit)

1- Thomas Johnston	7- Benjamin Ray
2- James Alsup	8- William Jones
3- Meredith Coffee	9- Thomas Ray
4- Robert Long	10-Joseph Ray
5- George Sparkman	11-John Griffits
6- John Myers	12-William Mitchell

Who being elected tryed and sworn the truth to speak on the Matter in Dispute do say they find for the plaintiff and assess his damage to seventy five cents and costs- rule for a new trial- rule made absolute.

Ordered by the Court that John F.Jack -Samuel Bunch and Chesley Jarnagin be appointed Commissioners to settle with the Sheriff and trustee of the County of Grainger who enters into bond with their securities in the sum of $100 each agreeable to an act of the General Assembly in such case made and provided.

A Deed of conveyance from Christian Roads to James Moore for seventy five acres of Land was proven in open Court by the oath of James Alsup a subscribing witness thereto and ordered to be registered.

A Deed of conveyance from William Cocke to Nicholas County for one hundred acres of Land was proven in open Court by the oaths of Josiah Cobb & Wm Hamilton subscribing witnesses thereto and ordered to be registered.

A Deed of conveyance from Christian Roads to James Moore for 300 acres of Land was proven in open Court by the oath of James Alsup a subscribing witness thereto and ordered to be Registered.

(p 214)   May Sessions A.D. 1807

A Deed of conveyance from James Wilson to Henry Hawkins for 3 acres and three eights of an acre was acknowledged in open Court by the subscribing members thereof and ordered to be Registered.

A Bill of Sale from William Fulcher to Noe Jarnagin for a negro woman named Pegga was proven in open Court by the oaths of Enoch Winds a subscribing witness thereto and ordered to be recorded.

Lewis Clippier by his Agent David Haly returns his Lists of Taxable property for the year 1807(towit) 1000 acres of Land. E-

Thomas Keeland by David Haly his agent returns his Lists of Taxable property for the year 1807(towit) 14000 acres of Land. E-
Ordered by the Court that the Lands reported on by the Sheriff of Grainger County subject to Taxation for the year A.D. 1806 and published as the Law Directs be condemned and sold for the taxes Due thereon and that the Clerk Do issue orders of sale accordingly.

Court adjourns till tomorrow morning 9 o'clock.

At a Court continued and held for the County of Grainger at the Court-House in Rutledge on the 21st. Day of May 1807.

Present ——— Henry Boatman- William Clay-Thomas Henderson —David Tate Peter Harris Esquires.

John Cooke Esqr. Admr. returns into all the Book Accounts as a suppliments Inventory of the Estate of Michael Coons —Dec'd.

Caleb Shockley)
      vs   )
Noe Ashly   )   Thereupon came a Jury (towit)

1- Enoch Winds   7- Jesse Cheek
2- Chesley Jarnagin   8- Samuel Perry
3- Andrew Cofman   9- Joseph Long
4- James Sullens   10-Wm Murphy
5- Thomas Bunch   11-Samuel Reed
6- James Hickey   12-Joseph McElheney

Who being elected tryed and sworn the truth to speak on the matter

in Dispute in this case do say they find for the plaintiff and assess his
Damage to four dollars besides his costs therefore it is considered by the
Court that the plaintiff do recover of the Defendant the aforesaid as as-
sessed by the Jury aforesaid besides his costs.

(p 215)   May Sessions A.D. 1807

William Hall constable of the Grand Jury at the present Term proved
his attendance three Days as such which he is to be allowed the sum of
one dollar per day for each day he attends.   Issued.

A Deed of conveyance from James Conn sheriff to John Cooke for 500
acres of Land was proven in open Court by the oaths of Pleasant M.Miller
& John F.Jack subscribing witness thereto and ordered to be registered.

A Deed of conveyance from James Conn Sheriff to David Stewart for 150
acres of Land was proven in open Court by the oaths of John Cooke & John
F.Jack subscribing witnesses thereto and ordered to be registered.

We, the Jurors appointed by Court to view and lay out a road from
Thomas McBroom to Edward Clark's from thence to Joseph Bealor report and
say the road we viewed will be profitable from Bealors up the road to the
upper end of the Gap near Thomas Dunn's fence causing Dunn's to the right
hand from thence a marked way leaving John Moyers on the right hand from
thence a marked crossing the Creek below Peter Harnocks fence from thence
up the creek a marked way to Clarks Mill from thence along a marked way
to Edward Clarks from thence along the Valley road to the far end of
David Watson's land from thence a marked way crossing the mountain at
Bunches tract a marked way over said mountain from the foot of the mountain a marked way crossing Bunches Meadow to the right hand a marked way
to Thomas McBrooms concluded this 2nd.day of May 1807 -Cain Acuff,Nicholas
Conntz. Peter Harnock, John Bunch, Andrew McPheters present to an order
of the Court of Pleas and Quarter Sessions of Grainger County -We Abner
Low- Wm Sims- James Brown, Hugh Woolard- Jacob Arnet -Geo.Sparkman, John
Richards & Newberry James have this day provided to view the road as in
said order Directed and agree for the road to turn off at the first hollow
above Moe Jarnagin's by a small Poplar marked then a Direct course to the
upper end of said Jarnagin's then along said Land to the first Bridge below said Jarnagin's also to turn off at the first Branch above Chesley
Jarnagin's by some marked trees then a direct course to the end of said
Jarnagins land then along the road that goes by said Jarnagins House to
where it intersects with the old road below said Jarnagins -given under
our hands and seals this 9th day of May 1807 -Abner Low, Wm Sims, James
Brown, Hugh Woolard, Jacob Arnet, Geo.Sparkman, John Richards, Newberry
James.------

(p 216)   May Sessions A.D. 1807
Which report was received by the Court and confirmed and ordered to be
recorded.
We, the undersigned appointed to view and Lay out a road from Moore's
Ferry on Holston River have agreed as follows -Beginning at the bank of
the River at the said James Moore's ferry Landing keeping the old Mill
Road to where it intersects with the River road from thence along the
said road up the river to Blackwells branch as per order -Given under our
hands the 13th day of April A.D. 1807.

John Williams, William Arnold, William James, James Moore, which Report was received and confirmed by the Court and ordered to be Recorded.

We, the Jurors appointed by the Court to view the road leading from Beans Station to Cheeks cross roads do make the following Report to Court (towit) —Beginning at the fork of the road near John Coulters that leads to Shelton's ford then towards Cheeks cross roads then along said old road to the going down into the first Hollow then turn to the Left a cross the Hollow marked by the Jury into the old road on the side of the hill thence along said old road past Stephen Smith along the Dug Hill with a small alteration to the right marked by the Jury near John Coulters from thence on said road turning to the right so as to run through a corner of said Coulters field and into the old road near Thomas Murrys house as marked by the Jury thence along said old road by Samuel Rayls shop and on the Dug Hill turn to the left going down to the branch past the Diging cross the branch into the old road as marked by the Jury thence on said road to Squire Harrises thence along the Hollow a little to the right opposite his house thence on turning to the left leaving two of said Harris cabins to the right intersecting the old road in the Hollow thence on to the fork that turns off the ferry leading along said ferry Landing near the River thence down the side of the River to the ford in the old road thence across the River along said old road by Bartley Marshall to a black oak marked to the right hand has a large swell on it about one half mile from Jackson Smiths field thence on the right of said Smiths field to two marked white oaks thence on a Line marked by the Jury to a stake on the County Line in Moffitts fields nearly opposite to Moffits old cabins — Given under our hands this 9th Day of May 1807 —Joseph Cobb- Peter Harris- James Kennedy- William Whitesides -Hugh Larimore, which report was received by and confirmed and ordered to be Recorded.

(p 217)   May Sessions A.D. 1807

Ordered by the Court that Hugh Taylor be appointed overseer of the road from the fork in the Hollow above John Coulters to Bartley Marshals ford on Holston River and all the hands in the following bounds (towit) to work under said overseer that is to say —Beginning 50 poles above Daniel Taylor's house at a stake on the river bank thence down the meanders of said river opposite to the mouth of Clark'ston Creek thence across said River to include the tract of Land whereon John Noe & James Harris lives called the Brack Bottom thence down the river including John Coulters Island thence to the Beginning so as to include John Cannon's -Jas. Taylor, Stephen Smiths and John Coulters hands. Copy issued of the order.

Ordered by the Court that Thomas Shipley be continued overseer in his former bounds with the same bounds for hands that was formerly allowed him and that he cut and open the same according to the report of the Jury within mentioned and keep the same in repair according to Law. Is.

Ordered by the Court that John Hall Jr. be appointed overseer of the road from the ford of Pattersons creek to where the Powder Spring road turns off to Moore's ferry and that he have all the hands in the following bounds to work on said road (towit) Beginning at John Bunchs Sr. so as to include said Bunches hands thence to the top of the Richland Knobs thence along the top of said Knobs to Morrows Gap thence across the Valley so as to include Wm Clays hands thence to the top of Clinch Mt.

thence along the top of said mountain so as to include Justice Mulls & John Mathews hands thence around to the Beginning.

State of Tennessee)
Grainger County) We, the Jurors appointed by Court to view & lay off and mark the road leading from Philip Siglars at the fork of the road down Flat Creek to the Knox line – We met and was qualified – We agree to keep the old down to the plantation formerly occupied , then we made an alteration & crossed the creek and marked the way down to Joseph Dennis thence intersects with the Powder Spring Gap road to sycamore tree near a spring branch that breaks out of a plantation where Abel Dale now lives thence round the head of said Spring near 100 yards unto the old road again thence along the old road to the Knox line near Aron L——— Given under our hands and seals this 16th Day of May 1807 –Thomas Brown –Chas. Hutcheson, Robert Fields, Joseph Dennis & Wm McPhetridge which report was confirmed by the Court and ordered to be recorded.

(p 218)   May Sessions A.D. 1807

Ordered by the Court that James Dyer Jr. be appointed overseer of the road from his house down to the County line & that he have the hands in the same bounds that was formerly to Jacob Elliott. Issued.

Ordered by the Court that Joseph Dennis be appointed overseer of the road from the ford of the creek at Halls meeting house to Robert Fields and that he have the hands in the same bounds formerly allowed to John Hall to cut and open said road as laid out by the Jury agreeable to the within report and keep the same in repair according to Law. Issued.

A Deed of conveyance from James Robertsons to Major Lea for one hundred & fifty six & three quarters of an acre of Land was proven in open Court by the oaths of John Hamil & Rubin Cotrel subscribing witnesses thereto and ordered to be registered.

Ordered by the Court that Williams Sims be appointed overseer of the road in room of Jeremiah Jarnagin from the first hollow above Chesley Jarnagin and open out said road agreeable to the report of a Jury to this Term and have the same bounds for hands that was allowed said Jeremiah Jarnagin. Issued.

A Bill of Sale from John Conly to Edward West was proven in open Court by the oath of Rubin Dixon a witness thereto and ordered to be Recorded.

An Instrument of writing from Alex. Thompson to Samuel West to purporting to be a Relinquishment of my right or proportion of the Estate of James Thompson –Dec'd was acknowledged in open Court by the subscriber thereto and ordered to be recorded.

An Instrument of writing purporting to be marriage contract between Lewis Edwards & Mary Chamberlain was proven in open Court by the oaths of John Hall Sr. & Wm Hall subscribing witnesses thereto and ordered to be Recorded.

Ordered by the Court that Real Jinnings –Samuel Clark, Edward Clark David Punch, Andrew McPheters, Abraham Pruit, John Moyers, & John Acuff be & are appointed Jurors to view a road from the turn pike on the Kentucky road to where it may intersect the road passing by Halls Meeting

house and marked and Designate the same so viewed and report to next Court.
Signed - Peter Harris-   Issued

(p 219)   August Sessions A.D. 1807

At a Court of pleas and quarter sessions began and holden for the
County of Grainger at the Court house in Rutledge on the third Monday of
August A.D. 1807 it being the 18th of the same month. Present -James Moore
John Moffitt & Peter Harris, Esquires.

James Conn Sheriff of Grainger County made his return to Court that
he had executed the following persons (towit) Henry Whitner -Geo.Norris
Robert Fields, Rubin Dixon, James Richardson, John Williams, Evan Harris,
David Bunch, John Moyers, Cain Acuff, Wm Millican, Francis Daniel, George
Moody, Moses Hodges , Wm Blair, Rubin Riggs, John Estis, Daniel Taylor
Martin Stubblefield, Samuel McBee, Dennis Condry, Richard Shelton, Lewis
Edwards, Jeremiah Jarnagin, Newberry James, Robert Harris, Major Lea,
John Vineyard, Thomas Mann, Miller Easley, Hugh Larimore, John Morris,
Jeremiah Chamberlain, Edward Daniel, Peter Hamilton, Henry Bowen, John
Bowen, John Bowen & William Windham out of which Venire facias the per-
sons whose names are underwritten are chosen as Grand Jurors for the pre-
sent term (towit) Major Lea, foreman -Hugh Larimore Robert Fields,Jer-
emiah Jarnagin, Thomas Mann, Peter Hamilton, Daniel Taylor, David Bunch
Evan Harris, Lewis Edwards, John Moyers, Henry Whitner, Newberry James,
Dennis Condry & John Vineyard.

Peggy Bradberry comes into open Court & returns an inventory of the
Estate of Hezekiah Bradberry deceased-therefore it was ordered by the
Court that an order of sale do issue accordingly. Order accordingly.

Ordered by the Court that John Williams be released from the payment
of one poll tax for the year 1807.

William Keith Rainger for the County of Grainger returns to Court
that the following is a list of strays remaining in his office not proven away in twelve months.

    Ruebin Dolton two heiffers --$5.50
    One other to four dollars   4.00
                    W.M.Keith -R.G.C.
A Bill of Sale from Jesse James to William James Sr. for one negro
woman named Fen and 4 head of horses - six head of cattle which was proven in open Court by James Dyer Jr. a subscribing witness thereto and ordered to be Recorded.

Isaac Campbell was appointed constable for Grainger County who enters
into Bond in the sum of $500 with Mathew Campbell & Major Lea his secur-
ities & was qualified according to Law.

A Deed of conveyance from John Percifield to Jacob Wolf for 20 acres
of Land was acknowledged in open Court by the Grantor and ordered to be
Registered.

John Den Lessee &c.
    vs   Thomas Johnston the Defendants security comes into
John Crabb

Court & surrenders him in discharge of himself as Bail who gives in place thereof James Brown and Thomas Dyer as his Bail.

A Deed of conveyance from George Ransbarger to William Keith for a lott in the town of Rutledge it being Lot. No. 16,was proven in open Court by the oath of William Baker and John F.Jack subscribing witnesses thereto and ordered to be Registered.

Daniel Gowing overseer reports to Court that the part of the road from the first branch above Chesley Jarnagin through said Jarnagins lane as laid out by the 1st Jury is opened and in repair.

(p 220)   August Sessions A.D. 1807

William Sims overseer reports to Court that the part of the road from the first hollow above Noah Jarnagin through said Jarnagins Lane as laid out by the late Jury in open and in repair.

Ordered by the Court that Malachiah Howell be appointed overseer of the road from the fork near to Henry Mays's and to cross Holston River at Mays ford and by Tate's Mill and to the top of the Ridge near to Claiborn Gowing's and that the following hands be appointed to work on said road (towit) Sherod Hays hands the hands from Francis Daniels –John Daniels Moses Hodges and including all the hands on the waters of Young Creek & Samuel and Willis Jones and all the hands at Benjamin Howell's.

A Deed of conveyance from Aron Smith to Abner Low for 200 acres of Land was proven in open Court by the oaths of Absolem Garrett and Meredith Coffee subscribing witnesses thereto and ordered to be Registered.

John Hunter   )
    vs   )
James Robertson   )   On motion of John Hunter by John Williams his Atty

Ordered by the Court that the said John Hunter do recover of the said Jas. Robertson the sum of $237.93 money he has been compelled to pay over as security for the said James Robertson –Execution issued and satisfied by Defendant.

State   )
    vs   )
William Roberts   )   the Defendant in this case being solemnly called came not, it was considered by the Court that he forfeit his Recognizance.

At a Court continued and held in and for said County of Grainger on the 18th day of August A.D. 1807– Present Peter Harris. David Tate & John Moffit Esquires.

State   )
    vs   )
Hugh Woolard   )   Whereupon came a Jury (towit) Rubin Riggs, Rubin Dixon John Bowen, Robert Harris, Henry Bowen, Henry Howell, James Sullins, George Jinnings, Edward Tate, Seth Cullen, John Haley, & John Taylor who being elected tried and sworn the truth to speak on the issues of traverse in this case do say they find the Defendant guilty in manner and

form as he stands charged in the Bill of Indictment the Defendant in this
case by his Council enters a rule to shew cause why a new trial should be
granted.

A Deed of conveyance from George Spartman to Thomas Ray for 200 acres
of Land was proven in open Court by the oath of Meredith Coffee & Absolem
Garrett subscribing witnesses thereto and ordered to be Registered.

State	
vs	William Roberts who was bound in Recognizances
Oloe Cowings and	to appear at the present Term and give Evidence
Nancy Davis	

on behalf of the State being solemnly called came not. It is therefore
considered by the Court that the said Roberts do forfeit,

(p 221)   August Sessions A.D. 1807
his recognizance and also that James Bryant securities of the said Roberts
do forfeit agreeably to the tenor of his Recognizance.

A Bill of Sale from John Smith to John Lebow for negroes named Judith
Mary Washington one not yet named which was proven in open Court by the
oath of Thomas Henderson & Daniel Lebow subscribing witnesses thereto &
ordered to be Recorded.

Nancy McElhiney Admrix. of Robert McElhiney Dec'd returns in open
Court an inventory of the Estate of the deceased.

A Bill of Sale from William Fields to Jeremiah Jarnagin for a negro
girl named Violet was proven in open Court by the oaths of Enoch Winds &
William Dunn subscribing witnesses thereto and ordered to be Recorded.

Ordered by the Court that James Hickey have leave to return his List
of Taxable property for the year 1807 (towit) sixty acres of Land & one
white poll.
Ordered by the Court that Edward Tate be appointed Deputy Sheriff
under James Conn high Sheriff of Grainger County & was qualified as the
Law Directs.

State	
vs	The Defendants security in this case surrenders him in
Hugh Woodlard	

discharge of themselves as Bail who gives James Grayson & John Bird in
place thereof.

State	
vs	Whereupon came a Jury towit, George Moody, Moses Hodge,
Nancy Davis	

John Williams -James Richardson, Miller Easley, Nathan Lamson, Meredith
Coffee, Henry Matlock, Enoch Winds, Samuel Perry, James Long, & Richard
Dunville who being elected tried and sworn the truth to speak on the
issue of traverse in this case Do say they find the Defendant not guilty
in manner & form as she stands charged in the Bill of Indictment.

Ordered by the Court that Joseph Cobb, Henry Howell, Dennis Condry
& Nicholas Counts be appointed Jurors to attend the next Superior Court

of law for Hamilton District.

A Deed of conveyance from John Pickens to John Jarnagin for 338 acres of Land was proven in open Court by the oaths of John Clark & James Clark prescribing witnesses thereto & ordered to be Registered.

A Deed of conveyance from Noah Jarnagin —Major Lea, Levina Lea, Daniel Gowing, Percella Gowing, Jeremiah Jarnagin, Major Lea, Rodah Lea, Samuel Carson, Anna Carson & Benj. Jarnagin to John Jarnagin for 338 acres of Land was proven in open Court by the oaths of John Clark and James Clark subscribing witnesses thereto & ordered to be Registered.

Court adjourns till tomorrow morning 9 o'clock.

At a Court continued & holden for the County of Grainger at the Court House in Rutledge on the 19th day of August A.D. 1807. Justices present Thomas Henderson, David Mc Anally & James Moore.

(p 222)   August Sessions A.D. 1807

State
vs
Cloe Gowing   } Justices present, Thomas Henderson, David McAnally & James
Moore, whereupon came a Jury, towit, Robin Dixon, Robert
Harris, Joseph Ray, Richard Melone, Aza Street, John Richards, Gabriel Fry
Samuel Ramsey, Nathan Lawson, Valentine Morgan, David Holt, Jr. & Thomas
Dunn who being elected tried and sworn the truth to speak on the issue of
traverse in this case do say they find the Defendant not guilty in ——
ner and form as she stands charged in the Bill of Indictment.

A Deed of conveyance from John Counts to Miller Easley for 200 acres of land was proven in open Court by the oaths of Robert Hasengill and Ambrose Yancey subscribing witnesses thereto and ordered to be Registered.

Ordered by the Court Richard McPherson have leave to return his Lists of Taxable property for the year 1807 towit—one negor fellow.

Ordered by the Court that the Grand Jury be discharged from further attendance at the present Term.

State
vs
John Bird   }
John Williams, James Richardson, Miller Easley, Thomas Turley, Robert
Honeycutt, David Counts, Henry Howell, Joseph Long, Wm Windham, & Nicholas Counts, who being elected tried & sworn the truth to speak on the
issue of traverse in this case Do say they find the Defendant guilty in

per day for 3 days attendance on the Grand Jury as Constable at the present Term & was quailified accordingly.

State)
vs)
Abraham Bird) Abraham Bird & John Bird the Defendants security comes into open Court & confesses Judgment for the sum of one dollar fine with the additional sum of $6.50 costs.

Ordered by the Court that the following persons be summoned to attend as Jurors at the Court House in Rutledge on the third Monday of Nov. 1807 Viz. Wm Milligan, Francis Daniel, John Kidwell, John Estis, Robert Long, John Roe, Richard Grantham, Harmon Cox, Andrew Coffman, James Carmichael Thomas Churchman, Joseph Perrin, John Sharp, Wm Hamilton, Wm Shields, David Huddleston, Jacob Elliot, John Dennis, Wm Davidson, Josiah Kidwell Felps Reed, Duncan Carmichael, Wm Shelton, Neal McCoy, Henry Hipsher, Rubin Dolton, Jonathan Mumpower, Stepehn W.Senter, Wm Blair, Max.Blair Wm Kirkham, Martin Stubblefield, James Alsup, Wm James, Wm Arnold, John Bunch Sr. Wm Bowman, Geo.Sparkman & Eliza Clay.

(p 223)   August Sessions A.D. 1807

John Dennis resigns his appointment as overseer of the road from the powder Spring Gap in Clinch Mt. to the five mile post on Cypper Ridge and that the said hands with said road to be divided and overseer appointed as follows, ordered by the Court that Wm McPhetridge be appointed overseer from the fork of the road near the Gap in Clinch Mt. down the road till opposite Able Dales house and that Joseph Fields -Wm Harmon, Thomas Dennis Thomas Vetito, Wm Haines, John Dennis, Andrew Seabolt, Philip Sword be the hands belonging to Wm McPhetridge.

Ordered by Court that Wm Dodson be appointed overseer of the road from Abel Dales house to the five mile Post on Copper Ridge & that David Elkins, Wm Hutcheson, Benj/Coats, Lewis Hutcheson, Able Dale, Jonathan Dale Wm Jack, Wm James be the hands to work under Wm Dodson on said road.

Ordered by the Court that James Brown be appointed overseer of the road in the room of Richard Dunville from the top of Clinch Mt. to Cross's place in the owl hole Gap and that he have the same bounds for hands that said Dunville had, and it is to be understood that said hands are to work on the Richland Land road as far as the Powder Spring Gap road intersects with the same except that part is between the first hollow below Robert D. Eatons.
Ordered by the Court that Wm Sims be appointed overseer from the 1st. large spring above Chesley Jarnagin's to the first hollow above Noah Jarnagins and shall have his bounds intended from the said first hollow below Robert D.Eatons and have the same bounds for hands as heretofore.

Ordered by the Court that Jeremiah Selvage be appointed overseer of the road leading from the Powder Spring Gap in Clinch Mt.to Hodges Ferry on Clinch River and said Selvage to work on the road from the five Mile post on the Copper Ridge to the top of Gap Creek in the Copper Ridge and that all the hands living about said road on Bull run & who formerly did work under said road be the District or bounds of hands to work under said Selvage on said road.

Ordered by the Court that Wm Hamilton be appointed overseer of the road from John Sallys to the fork of Gap Creek then up the said creek and so on to the foot of Hinds ridge at George Smiths and that he have the same hands that formerly worked on said road.

Ordered by the Court that George Norris be appointed overseer of the road from the fork of the road at Gap creek to the cross roads that came down Flat Creek by Henry Wideners field and that all the hands on the North side of Bull Run and ablove Knox County Line up to the Quaker Gap path then with said path to the top of Copper ridge, to where the road that Jeremaih Selvage works on, goes down said ridge, thence with said road to the fork and that all the hands living on Bull run within said Bounds work under said Norris.

Ordered by the Court that John Minet Jr. be appointed overseer of the road from the cross roads at Henry Wideners field to the Knox County Line near the Widow Minet's and that all the hands living on Bull run below the Quaker Gap path to Knox County line, thence with said Line to Clinch Mt. then up said Mt. so as to include all the hands that lives below the Mt. fork of Flat Creek & below said road in Grainger County work on said road under said John Minet.

At a Court continued & holden in and for the County of Grainger at the Court House in Rutledge on the 20th day of August A.D. 1807 — Justices present, Thomas Henderson —David McAnally & Charles McAnally.

Rial Jinnings who sues Dec'd)
  vs   qui Tam   )
Edmund Holt   )   Whereupon came a Jury, towit— Rubin Dixon Robert Harris —John Haley, John Hodges, Aza Street, John Duke, Nicholas Counts, John Arnold, James Sullins, William   (p 234)   Arnold

(p 234)

August Sessions A.D. 1807

James Richardson, & James McCoy who being elected tried and sworn the truth to speak on the issue joined in this case Do say they find the Defendant oweth the plaintiff nothing as in pleading he hath alledged, therefore it is considered by the Court that the plaintiff take nothing by his writs, that the Defendant do recover of said plaintiff his costs and charges by him in and about defendant his said suit in that behalf expended and the plaintiff in Mercy for his fals clamor.

Charles Matlock)
   vs   )
Joseph Dyer   )   Whereupon came a Jury, towit, Henry Bowen, John Bowen George Moody, Moses Hodge, Miller Easley, Henry Howell, Robert Honeycut, John Duncan, John Griffits, Seth Coulter, Jesse McAnally, & Thomas Bunch who being elected tried & sworn the truth to speak on the issue joined in this case do say the Defendant did assume & undertake in manner & form as the plaintiffs in his Declaration hath complained against him and assess the plaintiffs Damages occationed by reason of the non performance thereof to $20 besides his costs, and the Defendant by his Attorney with

the abscents of Court enters a Rule to shew cause why a new trial should be granted and on argument it is considered by the Court that said rule be discharged, therefore it is considered by the Court that said plaintiff Do recover of the Defendant the Damages aforesaid in form aforesaid assessed together with his costs by him in & about prosecuting his said suit in that behalf expended &c.

Edmond Holt)
   vs   )
Gabriel Fry   )   Whereupon came a Jury, towit- Robert Harris -Nicholas Counts, John Hodge - John Arnold, James Sullins, James Richardson, James McVey, Thomas Smith -Joseph Ray - Wm Hall, Levi Miller & Barton McPherson who being elected tried and sworn the truth to speak on the matter in controversy in this case and after having retired from the Bar to deliberate of their Verdict could not agree, whereupon with the assent of Court & the agreement of Council a mistrial is entered.

Ordered by the Court that Sion Bruce be appointed overseer of the road from Beans Station to Thomas Johnston's Line above Ousville in the place of Thomas Edington and to have the same Bounds for hands that the said Edington had.

Ordered by the Court that Joseph Bryant have leave to return a stud horse subject to taxation for the year 1807.

Ordered by the Court that Tupley Haygood be allowed the sum of $25 for keeping and maintaining Jeremiah Midkiff one of the poor of this County from May Term A.D. 1807 to August Term 1807.

A Deed of conveyance from James Fears to John Roe for 140 acres of Land was proven in open Court by the oaths of Wm Harris & John Estis subscribing witnesses thereto and ordered to be Registered.

A Deed of conveyance from James Fears to Peter Harris for one hundred and ten acres of Land was proven in open Court by the oaths of Wm Harris & John Estis subscribing witnesses and ordered to be Registered.

A Deed of conveyance from Absolam Garrett to George Sparkman for 150 acres of Land was acknowledged in open Court and ordered to be Registered.

Ordered by the Court that Elisha Williamson be released from the payment of Tax on a cotton Gin containing 40 saws which he was not in his possession the first day of January 1807 therefore ordered by the Court that he be released from the payment of the tax on the said saw Gin.

(p 225)   August Sessions A.D. 1807.

Ordered by the Court that the following persons be appointed to view, mark & lay out a road from the branch which crosses the Richland road above said Mayberry's, towit, Henry Hawkins, Peter Hamilton, Joseph Perrin, Robert Stone, Robert Harris, Richard Acuff & Wm Mitchell & make report to next Court. Issued.

Ordered by the Court that James Conn high Sheriff of Grainger County be allowed the sum of $30.25 for his services performed in conveying John Davis

to the District Jail of Hamilton at Knoxville & also for supporting &
maintaining a Guard for the safe keeping as per account Rendered & sworn
to in the open Court. Issued.

David McAnally one of the Constables proved his attendance on the Court
at the present time three days.   Issued.

At a Court continued & holden in and for said County of Grainger on the
21st. day of August A.D. 1807 —Justices present, Thomas Henderson, James
Moore & Wm Clay.

Hugh Montgomery Assignee &c.)
vs)
Nicholas Kearns)   Whereupon came a Jury, towit, Ruebin Dixon
Henry Bowen, John Williams, Miller Easley, Nicholas Countz, John Hodge, Jas.
Sullins, Valentine Morgan, Thomas Bunch, George Jinnings, James Grayson
and Thomas James, who being elected tried and sworn the truth to speak on
the issue joined in this case Do say they find the Defendant hath not paid
the debt in the Declaration mentioned, or any part thereof as in pleading
he hath alledged and assess the plaintiffs Damages occationed by reason
of the detention thereof to three dollars thereby three cents & one third
of a cent besides his costs, therefore it is considered by the Court that
the plaintiff recover of the Defendant that Debt in the Declaration mentioned and also his damages in form aforesaid assessed together with his costs
by him in and about prosecuting his said suit in that behalf expended & the
defendant in mercy &c.

John Denn Lessee of)
Youngs)
vs)
Ann Gillmore)   Thereupon came a Jury, towit, the same as above
who being elected tryed and sworn the truth to speak on the issue joined
do say they find the Defendant guilty of the trespass set forth in the plaintiffs declaration in Ejectment & assess their damages to six cents & costs
It is therefore considered by the Court that the plaintiff recover against
the Defendant his Term yet to come of in and to the tract of Land with the
appurtenances in his declaration mentioned together with his damages aforesaid in form aforesaid assessed & also his costs in that behalf expended
& the defendant in Mercy &c.

Dedrick & Comway)
vs)
George Jinnings)   Thereupon came the same Jury as before except John
Bowens in the place of George Jinnings who being elected tryed and sworn
the truth to speak on the matter in dispute in this case do say they find
for the plaintiffs and assess their damages to seventeen Dollars thirty
eight cents & costs, It is therefore considered by the Court that the plaintiffs do recover of the defendant their damages aforesaid in form aforesaid
assessed together with the costs by them in and about prosecuting their sd.
suit in this behalf expended & the Defendant in mercy &c.

(p 226)   August Sessions A.D. 1807
Jesse Riggs
vs   David Shelton —   Attachment—

Caleb Howell, one of the Constables of this County made return to Court that he had levied an attachment on 200 acres of Land the property of David Shelton to satisfy Jesse Riggs in the sum of $47.98 Debt and costs, therefore it is ordered by the Court that order of sale do issue commanding the sheriff to sell the Lands so levied on for the satisfaction of the said Debt & costs accordingly.

Edmund Tate)
   vs   )
Isiah Midkiff)   David McAnally one of the Constables of this County made return to Court that he had levied an execution on 100 acres of Land as the property of said Midkiff to satisfy thereof $26.34 & costs to satisfy the Demand of the Plaintiff; It is therefore considered by the Court that order of sale do issue accordingly to the sheriff commanding him to sell the before recited Land to satisfy the demand of the plaintiff.

Ordered by the Court that John Finly Jack Esqr. be appointed to the Transcripts of the register's Books in this County agreeably to Law.

Ordered by the Court that Wm Hall be appointed Constable to attend on the Grand Jury at next term of this Court.

Ordered by the Court that James Simpson be appointed Constable to attend on the Court at next Term of this Court.

Thomas Henderson

(p 227)   November Sessions A.D. 1807

At a Court of Pleas & Quarter Sessions began and holden for the County of Grainger at the Court House in Rutledge on the third Monday of Nov. A.D. 1807 it being the 16th of the same month.   Present, William Clay, David Tate & Isiah Midkiff Esquires.

James Conn, Esquire high sheriff of said County makes his return to Court that he has Executed the following Venire facias on all except Martin Stubblefield & Felps Reed. Viz.

1- William Milligan	20- Josiah Kidwell
2- Francis Daniel	21- Felps Reed
3- John Kidwell	22- Duncan Carmichael
4- John Estis	23- Wm Shelton
5- Robert Long	24- Neal McCoy
6- John Noe	25- Henry Hipshir
7- Richard Grantham	26- Rubin Dolton
8- Harmon Cox	27- Jonathan Mumpower
9- Andrew Coffman	28- Stephen W. Senter
10- James Carmichael	29- William Blair
11- Thomas Churchman	30- Alexander Blair
12- Joseph Perrin	31- William Kirkum
13- John Sharp	32- Martin Stubblefield
14- William Hamilton	33- James Alsup
15- William Shields	34- William James
16- David Huddleston	35- William Arnold
17- Jacob Elliot	36- John Bunch Jr.
18- John Dennis	37- William Bowman
19- Wm Davidson	38- George Sparkman 39- Elizar Clay

Out of which Venire Facias the following persons were appointed as Grand Jurors for the present Term -towit,

1- John Estis foreman
2- William Milligan
3- Francis Daniel
4- Andrew Coffman
5- James Carmichael
6- Jacob Elliot
7- John Dennis

8- Duncan Carmichael
9- Elizar Clay
10-William James
11-William Arnold
12-John Bunch Sr.
13-George Spaxman

State)
vs)
Goodin Scott)   For begitting a bastard child on the Body of Susannah Car-
rol alias or in other words Smith- It appearing to the
satisfaction of the Court that he said Goodin Scott has since the last Term
of this Court intermarried with the said Susannah it is therefore ordered
by the Court that the said Goodin be discharged from his recognizance
all fees paid in this case.

Court adjourns till tomorrow morning 9 o'clock.

Court met according to adjournment -Justices present, James Moore,
Noah Jarnagin and Isaiah Midkiff Esquires.

(p 238)   November Sessions A.D. 1807
State)
vs)
Meredith Coffee)   John Burd the security of the Defendant comes into
Court and surrenders him in discharge of himself as Bail who gives Jacob
Arnet in place of &c.

State)
vs)   Justices present, Isaiah Midkiff, David McAnally, Noah
Hugh Woolard)   Jarnagin & David Tate- Thereupon came a Jury, towit-

1- Thomas Bunch
2- John Woodall
3- Aron Rook
4- Miller Easley
5- Nicholas Counts
6- Meredith Coffee

7- John Martin
8- John Arnold
9- Jacob Arnet
10-James Boatright
11-Philip Free &
12-John Kidwell

Who being elected tried and sworn the truth to speak on the issue
of Traverse do say they find the Defendant not guilty in manner & form as
charged in the Bill of Indictment.

The Grand Jury at the present Term discharged.

State)
vs)
Samuel Ray)   In this case Jacob Arnett comes into open Court & confesses Judgment for fine and costs with the Defendant Samuel
Ray.

Court adjourns till tomorrow morning 9 o'clock.

Court met according to adjournment - November 18th 1807. Justices
present, Philip Siglar, John Braden and David Tate, Esquires.

State)
  vs) Thereupon came a Jury, towit—
John Ray Sr.)
1— Robert Hunnicut   7— John Moyers
2— Henry Howell   8— Michael Holt
3— Hugh Carrick   9— John Arnold
4— James Alsup   10—William Windham
5— John Kidwell   11—Thomas Bunch
6— Samuel Williams   12—Valentine Morgan

Who being elected tried and sworn the truth to speak on the issue Joined of Traverse in this case do say they find the Defendant Guilty in manner and form as charged in the Bill of Indictment and the Court fined him 25 cents & costs, comes into open Court and gives John Burd and Martin Ashburn as securities for all costs in the above case.

(p 229)   November Sessions A.D. 1807.

State)
  vs)
Meredith Coffee) Thereupon came a Jury, towit,
1— Lewis Gallyon   7— Thomas Harris
2— Thomas Dunn   8— Joseph Noe
3— Lewis Edwards   9— Gabriel Fry
4— Philip Free   10—James Dyer
5— David Bunch   11—John Noe &
6— Lewis Combs   12—Martin Ashburn

Who being elected tryed and sworn the truth to speak on the Issue of Traverse do say they find the Defendant not guilty in manner and form as charged in the Bill of Indictment.

John Howell comes into open Court and has leave to record his mark as follows a crop & slit in the Left Ear.

Denn on the Demise of)
Willie Blount)
  vs) Thereupon came a Jury towit,
Thomas Dunn)

1— Robert Hunnicutt   7— Michael Holt
2— Henry Howell   8— John Arnold
3— Hugh Carrick   9— William Windham
4— James Alsup   10—Thomas Bunch
5— John Kidwell   11—Valentine Morgan
6— Samuel Williams   12—Joseph Fields

Who being elected tried and sworn the truth to speak on this issue Joined in the above case do say they find the Defendant guilty in manner and form as the plaintiff hath complained against him & assess the plaintiffs damages by reason thereof to six cents.

Ordered by the Court that Solomon Massengill be appointed Inspector of Cotton at his Cotton Machine in this County who gave his bond with security as the Law directs and was qualified as the Law Directs.

Ordered by the Court that John Trotman have the right of administration on the Estate of Curtis Trotman Dec'd who gave John Vinyard as his security in the sum of $200 and was qualified accordingly.

Denn on the Demise)
of Willie Blount)
   vs)   Whereupon came the same Jury as in the above cause
John Moyers)   who being elected tried and sworn the truth to speak
on the Issue joined in this case do say they find the Defendant guilty in manner as the plaintiff in his Declaration hath complained against him & assess the plaintiffs damage by reason thereof to six cents and costs, it is therefore considered by the Court that the plaintiff recover of the Defendant his Damages aforesaid together with his costs in & about prosecuting his said suit that behalf expended & the Defendant in mercy &c.

(p 230)
Peter Edwards)
   vs)   Whereupon came the same Jury as before Except Mil-
William Windham)   ler Easley in the place of William Windham who being
elected tryed and sworn the truth to speak in the Matter in dispute do say they find for a mistryal.

Ordered by the Court that James Boatright be appointed overseer of the road from John McElhaney to the town of Rutledge in the place of Henry Bowing & that he be allowed the same for hands to work under him as the said Bowing had. Issued.

Ordered by the Court that Armstead Kirk be appointed overseer of the road from the five mile post to Beans Station in place of John Bell and that he be allowed the same hands to work under him that the said Bell had. Issued.

Ordered by the Court that James Grayson be appointed overseer of the road in place of Rubin Dixon and to have the same bounds for hands that the said Dixon had. Issued.

A Deed of conveyance from Hugh Woolard to Mathew Campbell for Dower assigned of the tract of Land whereon Thomas Cox formerly lived on, containing 120 acres of Land was acknowledged in open Court & ordered to be registered.

A Deed of conveyance from Elizar Clay to Richard Coats for 127 acres and one half of an acre of Land was acknowledged in open Court & ordered to be registered.

(p 231)   August Sessions 1808

At a Court of pleas and quarter sessions began and held for the County of Grainger at the Court House in Rutledge on the third Monday of August A.D. 1808 it being the 15th of said month - Justices present, Thomas Henderson David Tate, Noah Jarnagin & William Clay Esquires.

James Conn Esquire high sheriff of said County of Grainger made return to Court that he had executed the following Venire facias, towit-
1- Thomas Smith - 2- James Richardson - Cer. isd, 3- Edward Strong -Cer.isd.

4- John Williams Cer.Isd.
5- Sherod Mays cer.Isd.
6- Benj.Hudson
7- Jesse Cheek
8- John Vinyard
9- John Crow Cer.isd.
10-Richard Grantham
11-Edward Daniel cer.isd.
12-Francis Daniel
13-Isaac Mitchell
14-Richard Coats
15-John Bunch isd. to
James Con on Jones order
16-Aquilla Jones
17-John Bowen
18-James Bowen
19-Nicholas Karnes
20-Joseph Beelor

21- Peter Hamilton Isd.
22- Rubin Dalton
23- Rubin Riggs
24- Hugh Kain
25- Jonathan Oaks
26- John Arwine
27- Peter Hammock
28- William Peeters
29- Able Dale A
30- Robert Fields

Out of which Venire Facias the following
persons were as grand Jurors, towit-

1- William Peeters
2- James Bowen
3- Nicholas Karnes
4- Richard Coats
5- Able Dale
6- Isaach Mitchell
7- Edward Daniel
8- Rubin Dalton

9- Benjamin Hudson
10-Peter Hammock
11-Joshua Oaks
12-Thomas Smith
13-Jesse Cheek
14-John Bowen
15- John Vinyard

Sworn and charged.

King Q.Baker)
       vs   )   James McDaniel who was summoned as guarnishee in this
Lewis Edwards)   case on his oath in open Court that he gave a bond for
four hundred dollars to the heirs of Ninian Chamberlain Dec'd to be discharged in horses not exceeding seven years old to be valued at the rate
of a second rate cow and calf at Ten dollars by the beginning of March
next $100 of said $400 Note was to be paid to the said Lewis Edwards as
his division of said Note as this Deponant verily believes therefore it
is ordered by the Court that Judgment be entered up against the said Thomas McDonald for the sum of $100 as aforesaid forty three dollars & thirty
cents and one half of a cent to be applyed to the Discharge of the aforesaid Judgment - King and Baker against the said Lewis Edwards besides
costs of this Judgment -Execution isd.

      Ordered by the Court that Robert Long be released from the payment of
the sum of four dollars it being a Tax Due on a Stud Horse for the year
A.D. 1808 he being Twice charged.

William Midkiff   )
Assignee &c for the use of   )
John Coake & Henry Howell   )
       vs   )   In this case the Defendants securities
Benjamin Hudson   )   comes into Court and surrenders him in
Discharge of his Bail & prayed in   (p 232)   custody of the sheriff
and ordered by the Court in custody and the Defendant comes into Court

and gives George Evans and Joseph Fields in room of.

Cornelius Hickey by James Hickey comes into Court and returns his Lists of Taxable property for the year 1808 -one town lott.

Ordered by the Court that William Piatt have leave to return his taxable property for the year 1808 - 200 acres of Land on Bull run Grainger County.

Ordered by the Court that Thomas Henderson -Peter Harris and David Tate Esquires be appointed to settle with Joseph Cobb Admr. of John Blair Dec'd and also to settle with said Joseph Cobb guardian to the heirs of John Blair-Dec'd

Ordered by the Court that William Clay have leave to keep a house of publick Entertainment where he now lives and gives Noah Jarnagin as his security in the sum of $500.

Ordered by the Court that James Kennedy have leave to keep a public house of Entertainment where he now lives at Bens Station in the County of Grainger who enters into Bond with Stephen W.Senter his security in the sum of $1000.

Ordered by the Court that John Jarnagin be appointed overseer of the road from the first big spring above Chesley Jarnaging down to Coxes old place in the room of Daniel Goings and have the same hands for hands that the said Goings had to work under him.

The last Will and testament of Henry Bowen Sr. Dec'd was proven in open Court by the oaths of Ambrose Yancey -Robert Massengill and Frederick Moyers subscribing witnesses thereto and ordered to be recorded.

Ordered by the Court that David Bowling have leave to give in his taxable property for the year 1808 - one free poll.

Ordered by the Court that Henry Hawkins Guardian to the heirs of Chas. Coats Dec'd have leave to return his lists of taxable property for the year 1808 - 640 acres of Land on the waters of Richland Creek.

Andrew Donelson)
   vs)
Thomas Reece Sr. &)   Ralph Ford one of the Constables of this County
Yarnel Reece)   made return to Court an execution whereby he was
commanded that of the Goods and chattels Lands and Tenements of Thomas Reece & Yarnel Reece in this County he should cause to be made the sum of $32.83 to satisfy a Judgment and Execution -Andrew Donelson obtained against them before Henry Boatman Esqr. and the said Constable made return to Courts that he had Levied on 150 acres of Land whereon the said Thomas Reece now lives.
           Execution Issued.
           Signed Ralph Ford.

(p 233)

August Sessions A.D. 1808

Therefore it is ordered by the Court at the motion of Thomas Dardis Esqr. that order of sale do issue to the Sheriff commanding him to Expose to sale and sell the Lands so levied on to satisfy the sum of $32.83 - so recovered as aforesaid and costs.

Andrew Donelson)
    vs)
Thomas Reece Sr.)   Ralph Ford one of the Constables of this County
& Yarnel Reece)   made return to Court an Execution whereby he was
commanded that of the Goods and chattels Lands and Tenements of Thomas Reece
& Yarnel Reece in his County he should cause to be made the sum of $40 which
sum of Andrew Donelson recovered against them for debt before Henry Boatman Esqr. and the said Constable made return to Court that he had levied
on 160 acres of Land being the same Lands whereon the said Thomas Reece
now lives.
        Signed   Ralph Ford.
therefore it was ordered by the Court that order of sale do issue to the
Sheriff commanding him to Expose to sale and sell the Lands so levied on ,
to satisfy the sum of $40 the sum so recovered and costs by the Motion of
Thomas Hardie Esqr. Exec.Issd.

A Deed of conveyance from Benjamin Hudson to Cuthberd Hudson, Hall
Hudson & Joshua Hudson for 200 acres of Land was acknowledged in open Court
by the said Benjamin Hudson & ordered to be registered.

A Deed of conveyance from John Adair Jr. for forty acres of Land was
acknowledged in open Court by the said John Adair and ordered to be Registered.
A Deed of conveyance from Reubin Grove to Robert Harris for 52 acres
of Land was proven in open Court by the oath of Thomas Smith & George Martin subscribing witnesses thereto & ordered to be registered.

A Deed of conveyance from Rubin Groves to Robert Harris for 140 acres
of Land was proven in open Court by the oath of Thomas Smith & George Martin
& ordered to be Registered.

A Deed of conveyance from John Coulter to Jinkin Whiteside for 400
acres of Land was acknowledged in open Court by the said John Coulter &
ordered to be Registered.

A Deed of Release from John Bunch -Thomas Bunch for 300 acres of Land
was proven in open Court by the oath of John Williams & Hugh L.White subscribing witnesses thereto & ordered to be Registered.

A Deed of conveyance from William Arnold to Solomon Humphries for 49
acres of Land and three quarters acres was acknowledged in open Court &
ordered to be registered.

(p 334)   August Sessions A.D. 1808

A Deed of conveyance from George Martin to Robert Harris for three &
one fourth acres of Land was acknowledged in open Court and ordered to be
Registered.
A Deed of conveyance from Stephen W.Santer to William Keith for Lot
No. 15 in the town of Rutledge was proven in open Court by the oath of Wm
Baker & John Moore subscribing witnesses thereto & ordered to be Registered.

A Deed of conveyance from John Cooke to William Keith for Lot No.14
in the town of Rutledge was acknowledged in open Court by said John Cooke
& ordered to be Registered.

A Deed of conveyance from Mary Hickey to Cornelius Hickey for Lot No. 6— in the town of Rutledge was proven in open Court by oaths of Frederick Moyers & Wm Kalth two of the subscribing witnesses thereto & ordered to be registered.

A Deed of conveyance from Wm Arnold to David Tate for 473 acres & 7 poles of Land was proven in open Court by the oaths of Edward Tate and John Noe, two of the subscribing witnesses thereto & ordered to be Registered.

A Deed of conveyance from Michael Moyers to John Cocke for Lot No. 3 in the town of Rutledge was proven in open Court by the oaths of John P. Jack & Isaac T.Williams subscribing witnesses thereto and ordered to be registered.

A Deed of conveyance from James Cooper to John Arwine for one hundred & ninety acres of Land was acknowledged in open Court by the Grantor & ordered to be Registered.

A Deed of conveyance from Wyatt Smith to Alexander Thomason for 200 acres of Land was proven in open Court by the oaths of John Donaldson 2 of the subscribing witnesses thereto & ordered to be registered.

A Deed of conveyance from Nicholas Spring to William Harmon for 19 acres of Land was proven in open Court by the oaths of Joseph Fields & Joseph Dennis subscribing witnesses thereto & ordered to be Registered.

A Deed of conveyance from Joseph Cobb to Elisha Bowman for forty acres of Land was acknowledged in open Court by the Grantor & ordered to be Registered.

(p 235)   August Sessions A.D. 1808

At a Court continued and held in and for the County of Grainger at the Court House in Rutledge on the 15th. day of August A.D. 1808, present, Thomas Henderson — Wm Clay — John Brasden— & Noah Jarnagin Esqrs. Jacob Peck Esqr. produced a License to practice as an Attorney in this State, from the Judges of the Superior Court and was quailified accordingly.

Ordered by the Court that Samuel Perry Esqr. be allowed the sum of $12.50 it being the amount of the purchase money for a Book for the use of his office as register of Grainger County-. Copy order issd.

Ordered by the Court that the order of Court and the report of the Jury who ware appointed to view and lay out a road at the last term of this Court, from the Kentucky road at or near the mouth of Sheltons Branch to Clinch river at Bristows Bent be quashed.

The Petition of sundry of the inhabitants North of Clinch Mt. for the purpose of viewing and laying out a publick road from the Kentucky road or near the mouth of Sheltons branch to Bristows Bent on Clinch river was presented to Court for consideration —Justices present Thomas Henderson, Chas. McAnally, Mathew Campbells — Joseph Cobb, David McAnally, David Tate, Philip Sigler, Wm Parkerson, Isaiah Midkiff, Wm Clay, Henry Boatman, Noah Jarnagin, Chas. Hutcheson, George Moody Esquires and upon argument before the Court that the prayer of the petitioners is unreasonable & ought not to be Granted.

William Parkerson presents to Court a petition praying for a writ of Certiorari and superadeas to Supersead the proceedings in the suit

William Dyer against Wm Patterson, which was sworn to in open Court by the prayer thereof and ordered to be granted.

The last Will and Testament of Joseph Eaton Dec'd was proven in open Court by the oaths of Jeremiah Chamberlain and Hiram Chamberlain subscribing witnesses thereto and ordered to be recorded and Robert D. Eaton, William Eaton Executors and Mary Eaton Executrix of the Last Will and Testament of Joseph Eaton Dec'd were qualified as the Law Directs. Copy W-ised.

Ordered by the Court that Frederick Moyers be allowed the sum of six Dollars up to the present Term for taking charge of the Court House and cleaning it out— a majority of the Justices present. Copy order issd.

Ordered by the Court a majority of the acting Justices being present (to wit) Charles McAnally, Thomas Henderson, Charles Hutcheson, David McAnally, David Tate, Philip Sigler, Wm Patterson, John Cooke, Isiah Witcher, Joseph Cobb, Noah Jarnagin, George Moody that Robert Stone, Evan Harris, Thomas Smith, Joseph Dyer, Meredith Coffee, Peter Gilmore and John Hinshaw be appointed a Jury to view and lay out a road from Blackwells branch where the River road crosses the Land to James Richardson and Report to next Court according to Law. Copy order issued.

(p 236)   August Sessions A.D. 1808

Ordered by the Court that John Dodson Sr. be allowed the sum of $2.50 for making a Coffin for Stephen Collins who was one of the poor of this County. Issued.

Ordered by the Court that Sarah Shelton —widow and relict of William Shelton Dec'd have leave to administer on all and singular the goods and chattels rights & credits of said William Shelton Enters into Bond in the sum of $1000 for the faithful administration on the estate of the Deceased and gives David McAnally & George Evans as his securities and was qualified accordingly.

A Deed of conveyance from James Campbell to Mathew Campbell for 130 acres of Land was proven in open Court by the oaths of John Adair & John Acuff, subscribing witnesses thereto & ordered to be registered.

Ordered by the Court that James Arwine be released from the payment of his poll tax for the year 1808 and also that the Sheriff be released from the collection thereof & have a credit to the amount thereof in the settlement of his accounts.

an order or orders to the trustee for the Ballance due said Henderson.

        (Signed) John F.Jack
                     Jos.Cobb
                     C.McAnally
                     Luke Lea Jr.

State
  vs
Adam Hall   Richard Walker comes into Court and maketh oath that he is afraid of the said Defendant doing him some Boddy hurt or harm & the Defendant comes into Court and enters into recognizance in the sum of $500 and John Patterson, Henry Hawkins & Levi Ady, Wm Mitchell, Henry Howell, Meredith Coffee in the sum of $250 each the said Adam Hall keeping the peace towards the Good people of this State and particularly towards Richard Walker for the Term of one year from the date hereof.

(p 237)   August Sessions A.D. 1808

State
  vs
Margret Hall   Richard Walker comes into Court and maketh oath that he is afraid of his life or some bodily harm being done him by the said Margret therefore it was considered by the Court that the said Margaret Hall be bound in the sum of $500 who gives John Patterson, Henry Hawkins & Levi Ady, Wm Mitchell, Henry Howell, & Meredith Coffee in the penal sum of $250 each for her faithful keeping the peace towards the Good people of this State and more especially towards Richard Walker for the term of one year from the date hereof.

State
  vs
Mary Hall   Richard Walker comes into Court and maketh oath that he is afraid of his life or some bodily hurt from the said Mary Hall and the Defendant comes into Court and enters into recognizance in the sum of $500 and gives John Patterson -Henry Hawkins and Levi Ady - Wm Mitchell - Henry Howell, & Meredith Coffee as her securities in the sum of $250 for her faithful performance in keeping the peace towards the Good people of this State and more especially towards Richard Walker for the Term of one year from the date hereof.

State
  vs
Jean Hall   Richard Walker comes into Court and maketh oath that he is afraid of his life or some bodily hurt from the said Jean Hall and the Defendant -Jean Hall came into Court and enters into recognizance in the sum of $500 and gives John Patterson -Henry Hawkins-& Levi Ady - Wm Mitchell, Henry Howell & Meredith Coffee as securities in the sum of $250 each for her strict observance of the piece towards the Good people of this State and especially towards Richard Walker, for the term of one year from the date hereof- Be it remembered that the interlineations in the foregoing recognizance were Interlined before acknowledgment and afterwards acknowledged by the persons in open Court.

      Ordered by the Court that David Tate -William Pardison, Isaiah Midkiff & Henry Howell be appointed as Jurors to the Superior Court of Hamilton District for the year 1808. Copy order Issued.

Ordered by the Court that Charles McAnally act in conjunction with David Tate and Thomas Henderson Esqrs. in place of Peter Hunt Esqr. to settle with Joseph Cobb Esqr. admr. and Guardian in right of his wife of the Estate of Col. John Blair Dec'd and make Return to next Court.

Ordered by the Court that the bounds of the road formerly allotted to Joseph Briant from the County line down to John Crabb be continued down to a white oak with three forks from one root near the forks of Austins old road the same hands to be continued to him as at present and that Capt. Stephen W. Senter work here after from that place to Beans Station with all the hands allotted to him by his former order.

Ordered by the Court that James Boatright overseer be authorised to draw the sum of $7.00 from the Trustee in order to procure a hammer and crow bar to be used on publick roads. Copy order issued.

(p 238)   August Sessions A.D. 1808

Ordered by the Court that Samuel Peery overseer be authorised to draw the sum of $7.00 in order to procure a hammer and crow bar to be used on publick roads. Copy order issued.

August Sessions 1808- Ordered by the Court that Stephen Coard be appointed overseer of the road leading from Peter Beelers old mill to the ford of Flat Creek at Wm Nalls meeting house in the room of & stead of Abraham Pruitt giving him the same Bounds for hands that formerly belonged to Pruitt.   Copy order issd.

Ordered by the Court that Jacob Capps be appointed overseer on the road from the fork of the road leading from the County line of Knox and Grainger where it crosses the Raccoon Valley to the Island ford on Clinch river and that he have all the hands from the mouth of Dodsons Creek to the top of Lindses Ridge thence on said Ridge to the path leading from James Dickinsons to William Cappses to the mouth of Black Creek. Copy or. Is.

Ordered by the Court that Samuel Bunch be overseer of the road from Pattersons Creek Down to opposite the house of John Hall Sr. and that he have all the hands on the plantation of John Bunch Sr. to work under him.
Copy order issued.

Ordered by the Court that Jacob Showman be overseer of the road from opposite the house of John Hall Sr. down to where the road turns off to go to Moses Ferry and that he have the same bounds of Hands to work under him that John Hall had, the hands on the plantation of John Bunch excepted.

Ordered by the Court that Isaiah Midkiff be allowed the sum of $35 for maintaining Jeremiah Midkiff one of the poor of this County from May Term untill August Term 1808- issued.

Ordered by the Court that Jeremiah Midkiff one of the poor of this County be left to the lowest bidder that will undertake to maintain him for three months & Isiah Midkiff undertook the same for nineteen Dollars, he being the lowest bidder and last bidder.   Copy issued.

Ordered by the Court that the bounds formerly allotted to Joseph Bryant from the County line down to John Crabbs be continued down to a white oak with three forks from one root near the fork of Austins old road and that Stephen W.Senter work from the said white oak to Bean Station each to retain the same hands to work as present and that the said Joseph Bryant and Stephen W.Senter or either of them be authorized to draw on the Trustee for the sum of $7.00 to procure a banner and crowbar to be used by them on said road as the law directs.

(p 239)   August Sessions A.D. 1808

Samuel Riggs

Caleb Reece & Thomas Reece Sr. }   Ralph Ford one of the Constables of this
vs   County made return to Court an Execution signed by Henry Boatman Esqr. where-
Caleb Reece A Thomas Reece Sr. by he was commanded that of the goods and chattels Lands and Tenements of
Caleb Reece & Thomas Reece Sr. of his County he should cause to be made the
sum of $46.71½ Debt which Samuel Riggs recovered against him, and the said
Constables made his return to Court that he had levied on one hundred and
sixty acres of Land being the Land whereon said Thomas Reece now lives.

Signed— Ralph Ford

Therefore it is ordered by the Court that order of sale do issue to the Sheriff commanding him to Expose to sale the before recited Land & levied on
or so much thereof as will be of value sufficient to satisfy and pay the
sum of $6.75½ besides his costs.

Ordered by the Court that William McPhetridge be appointed overseer
of the road of the Powder Spring Gap to the top of the Copper ridge in the
room and stead of John Dennis former overseer and that he be allowed the
same bounds for hands that John Dennis has when he was overseer by making
such alterations as by the Jury laid off. Copy order issued.

Ordered by the Court that Joseph West appointed overseer of the road
from the town of Rutledge to the top of the Richland Knobs on the road
leading from the Town of Rutledge to Hayses ford on Holsten River and which
he have the following bounds and hands as labourers under him towit, Wm
Guynn, Richard Lutrill, Samuel Williams, Valentine Morgan, Hardiman Taylor
Miller Eadley, James Whaling, and every other person aw persons living
with them or on their premises as workers under him. Copy order let.

20th Aug. 1808

Ordered by the Court that Nicholas Karnes be appointed overseer of the
road in the place of Thomas Bunch resigned and to have the same bounds for
hands that said Bunches had.

Ordered by the Court that Wm Hamilton be appointed overseer of the road

(p 240)   August Sessions A.D. 1808

Ordered by the Court that George Norris be appointed overseer of the road from the fork of the road at a Gap Creek to the Gap Creek to the cross roads at Henry Wideners field on Flat Creek and that all the hands that lives on the North side of Bull run in said Valley up the Quaker Gap path and thence with said path to the extreme height of the Copper ridge to the road Jeremiah Salvage works on thence with the same to the fork of said road & that all the hands that lives in said Bounds work under him said Norris that is all the hands on both sides of the Creek.

Ordered that the Court by Henry Widener be appointed overseer of the road from the cross roads at his field to the County Line near the widow Minets that all the hands between Knox County Line and Clinch Mt. & Copper Ridge up as high as the fork of Flat Creek at said Wideners field thence across to John Simenes in Copper ridge thence with the hight of the ridge to the Quaker Gap path thence with said path to Bull run, thence down the run to Knox County Line work under said Widener.

At a Court continued and held in and for the County of Grainger at the Court House in Rutledge on the 17th day of August A.D. 1808. Present- Wm Clay, Daniel McAnally, James Moore, Noah Jarnagin and Isaiah Midkiff, Esquires.

State)
 vs) Thereupon came a Jury towit-
Isabel Hall)

1- Francis Daniel   7- Wm Stubblefield
2- John Williams   8- Malakiah Howell
3- Thomas Ray   9- John Jimmison
4- Henry Matlock   10-Joseph Long
5- John C.Haley   11-Samuel Peery &
6- Joseph Daniel   12-Thomas Dunn

Who being elected tryed and sworn the truth to speak on the issue at Traverse do say they find the Defendant not guilty in manner and form as charged in the Bill of Indictment.

State)
 vs)
Betsy Hall) Thereupon came a Jury, towit-

1- James Richardson   7- Henry Howell
2- Edmond Strange   8- George Martin
3- Richard Granthan   9- Samuel Williams
4- Aquilla Lane   10-Alex.Thomason
5- Sherod Hays   11-D.Abernathy
6- Peter Hamilton   12-Samuel Richardson

Thereupon came a Jury, towit- .
Who being elected tryed and sworn the truth to speak on the Issue at Traverse do say they find for the Defendant Guilty in manner and form as charged in the Bill of Indictment- Rule for new trial -Rule made absolute.

(p 241)   August Sessions A.D. 1808

Ordered by the Court that the following persons be appointed Jurors to attend the next Term of this Court Viz. Newberry James, Geo. Sparkman, Valentine Morgan, Rubin Dixon, Robert Massengill, Samuel West, John Humphreys -John Griffits, Richard Thomason, Joseph Stubblefield, Stephen Johnson, Joseph Rich, Richard Shelton, David County, Thomas Bunch, Henry Howell, John Estis, Daniel Taylor, Malichiah Howell, Moses Hodges, George Taylor, Robert Gaines, Wm Snodgrass, Peter Beeler, John Moyers, John Sally Wm Lane, Robert Fields, George Isom & Nicholas County. Ordered issued.

Ordered by the Court a majority of the acting Justices being present that Jesse Clark -Edward McGinnis, Henry Hipshir Rubin Dalton, Andrew Elder, Edward Franklin, & Neal McCoy or any five of them be a Jury to view & lay off a road from the Kentucky road up Copper Valley to the Hawkins line & make report to next Court.

A Deed of conveyance from Rubin Riggs to John Morris for 200 acres of Land was acknowledged in open Court by the Grantor & ordered to be Registered.

A Deed of conveyance from James Moore to Joseph Blackburn for 75 acres of Land was acknowledged in open Court by the oaths of Miller Easley and Jesse Hammer two of the subscribing witnesses thereto and ordered to be registered.

A Deed of conveyance from John Ogle to David Watson for one hundred & fifteen acres of Land was proven in open Court by the oath of David Watson Sr. & Robert Watson two of the subscribing witnesses thereto & ordered to be registered.

A Bill of sale from Benjamin Hudson to Cuthbert Hudson for sundry horse creatures, meat cattle, feather beads, & furniture & two stills was acknowledged in open Court by the said Benj. Hudson & ordered to be Recorded.

A Bill of sale from Robert Massengill to Samuel West for one negro girl named Hanna was acknowledged in open Court & ordered by the Recorded.

A Bill of sale from John C. Haley to Robert Massengill for a negro girl named Hannah was acknowledged in open Court by the said John C. Haley and ordered to be Recorded.

At a Court continued and held in and for the County of Grainger at the Court House in Rutledge on the 18th day of August A.D. 1808. present, John Cooke, Peter Harris, Philip Sigler, David McAnally -James Moore -Joseph Cobb, Isaiah Midkiff, George Moody & David Tate, Esquires.

Wyett Smith a monor comes into Court and prays the liberty of choosing his guardian whereupon the said Wyett Smith in open Court maketh choice of Thomas Dardis Esquire as his guardian who enters into Bond for the plaintiffs performance of his duty as such.

Ordered by the Court that Samuel Peery -Noah Jarnagin, Abraham Pruit Joseph Fields, John Moyers, Philip Sigler, Robert Fields, Charles Hutcheson & Peter Beeler be appointed to view and lay off a road the nearest and best way from the foot of Clinch Mountain, to the top thereof at the Powder Spring Gap and make report thereof to next Court there being a majority of the acting Justices present.

(p 242)   August Sessions A.D. 1808

    Ambrose Yancey resigns his appointment as Clerk of said County which
was received by the Court.
    The Grand Jury dismissed at this Term.

    Elisha Norman Constable who attended on the Grand Jury at this Term
proves his attendance as such four days. Issd.
    Court adjourns 2 hours Court met according to adjournment. Present,
Thomas Henderson, John Cooke, Joseph Cobb, David McAnally - Peter Harris,
Charles McAnally -George Moody, James Moore, Philip Sigler, David Tate,
Isaiah Midkiff, & Wm Clay Esquires who are a majority of the acting Jus-
tices for this County.

    The said Court composed of the said Justices caused proclamation to
be made that the office of Clerk of this Court was vacantly the resignation of Ambrose Yancey Esquire and that said Court would immediately proceed to the Election of a Clerk to supply said vacancy - the Court proceeded accordingly to the Election of a Clerk and upon counting the votes
it appears that John F.Jack Esquire had eleven votes and Charles McAnally
had one vote for said office the Court then Directed the Sheriff to make
proclamation that the said John F.Jack Esquire was duly and constitutionally elected Clerk of the County Court of Pleas And Quarter Sessions in and
for the County of Grainger which was done accordingly.

    Court adjourns till tomorrow morning nine o'clock.
Friday morning - August 18th -Court met according to adjournment.
          Thomas Henderson)
Present- David McAnally   )   Esquires
          Isaiah Midkiff   )

    John F.Jack comes into Court & enters into Bond in the sum of $5000
with John Cooke & Henry Howell his securities for the keeping of the Records & for the faithful discharging of the duties of his office of Clerk
which is in the following words and figures Viz.
    Know all men by these presents that we, Joh F.Jack, John Cooke, &
Henry Howell, all of the County of Grainger in the State of Tennessee are
held & firmly bound unto John Sevier Governor of the State of Tennessee
in the sum of $5000 to be paid to the said John Sevier or his successors
in office to the which payment well and truly to be made we bind ourselves
and every of us & every of our heirs -executors and Admrs. Jointly and severally firmly by these presents sealed with our seals and Dated this 19th
Day of August A.D. 1808.
    The condition of the above obligation is such that whereas the above
bounded John F.Jack hath been duly & constitutionally elected Clerk of the
County Court of Pleas & Quarter Sessions in and for the County of Grainger.

(p 243)   August Sessions A.D. 1808

    Now if the said John F.Jack shall safely keep the Records & faithfully
discharge the Duties of his office. Then this obligation to be void, otherwise to remain in full force and virtue.
    Signed sealed & Delivered in open Court -Thomas Henderson -

Presiding Justices of the Court of Pleas & Quarter Sessions of Grainger Co.
John F. Jack (seal)
Henry H. Howell (seal) x his mark
John Cooke (seal)

Which said Bond with the securities were approved of & accepted by the Court and the said John F. Jack took an oath to support the Constitution of the United States & on oath to support the Constitution of the State of Tennessee and also took the oath of Office as prescribed by Law.

Edmond Holt)
vs)   This cause being regularly called for trial and Stephen
Gabriel Fry)   Shelton who was summoned a witness in said cause came not it is therefore considered by the Court that the said Stephen Shelton shall forfeit $125 according to the Act of Assembly. Sci.Fa.Issued.

Edmond Holt)
vs)
Gabriel Fry)   This cause being regularly called for trial and David Holt Jr. commonly called Razor David, who was summoned a witness in said cause being solemnly called, came not - It is therefore considered by the Court that the said David Holt do forfeit $125 according to Act of Assembly.
Sci.Fa.Issd.

Neal & Simpson *
vs   *   In this case an Execution signed by James Moore Esqr.
John Newman *   is produced to Court whereby was commanded that of the Goods & Chattels Lands and Tenements of John Newman there should be made three fourth cents for costs and charges which sum Neal and Simpson recovered for debt & costs on the fourth of February 1808, on which Execution James Conn Sheriff makes a return in the words and figures Viz. Levied the within Execution on 100 acres of Land as the property of John Newman lying in the County of Grainger - no goods chattels to be found in my County - August 12th 1808 whereupon Neal and Simpson by John Williams Esq. makes a motion to Court to award an order of Sale directed to the Shff. commanding him to sell the Land levied on as above or so much thereof as will be sufficient to satisfy the sum of $23.60 whereupon it is considered that an order of sale do issue to the Sheriff commanding him to sell the tract of Land above levied or so much thereof as will be sufficient to satisfy the said sum of $22.60 and costs.

Joseph Breeden by Susannah Breeden his Mother & next friend.
No. 158 vs
David Haley -
Present, Thomas Henderson, David McAnally, Mathew Campbell & Joseph Cobb Esqrs.
Whereupon came a Jury, towit-
1- Edmond Strange
2- John Williams
3- Sherod Mays
4- Thomas Jones
(p 214)
5- Martin Albert   9- Nicholas Counts
6- David Abernathy   10-Henry Howell
7- John Humphreys   11-John Estis
8- Richard Harris   12-Daniel Robison

Who being elected tryed and sworn the truth to speak on the Issue joined in this case Do say the Defendant did assume in manner and form as the plaintiff in his Declaration hath complained against him assess the plaintiffs Damages occationed by reason of the non performance thereof to ten Dollars besides his costs, therefore it is considered by the Court that the said Plaintiff Joseph Breeden do recover against the said Defendant David Haley his Damages aforesaid by the Jurors aforesaid in form aforesaid assessed together with his costs by him in and about prosecuting his said suit in that he held expended &c.

Thomas Breeden)
No. 454   vs   )   Present, Thomas Henderson, David McAnally & Joseph
David Haley   )   Cobb, Esquires.
     Pleas - Non assump- set and payment.
     Whereupon came a Jury, towit-
1- Francis Daniel   7- John Moore
2- James Richardson   8- James Campbell
3- Peter Hamilton   9- Henry Hawkins
4- Richard Shockley   10-Walter Addys
5- George Martin   11-Justice Hall &
6- Meredith Coffee   12-Solomon Massengill
Who being elected tried and sworn the truth to speak on the Issue joined in this case and having retired to consideration of their Verdict afterwards returned to the bar & being interrogated whether they had agreed in the negative & that they could not agree -whereupon a misstrial was directed by the Council of the parties.

     Thomas Henderson, Charles McAnally & David Tate Esquires who had heretofore be appointed by the Court to settle with Joseph Cobb Esqr. Admr. and Guardian in Right of his wife of the Estate of Cobb. John Blair Dec'd submit their Reports to Court which is as follows, towit-
     The Estate of Col. John Blair Dec'd-
               To Joseph Cobb Dr. To services rendered by going to Cumberland & security of the rights of Land belonging to said Estate including Services and expences in attending to Law suits wherin the Estate was a party up to this Day-$100.00
     We, the undersigned being appointed by the Worshipful Court of Grainger County to settle with Joseph Cobb Esqr. Admr. & Guardian of the Estate and minor heirs of the Estate of Col. John Blair Dec'd after hearing the allegations of the said Joseph Cobb & maturely considering the premises do mutually agree that the aforesaid Estate is justly indebted to the said Joseph Cobb the sum of $100 for his Services rendered agreeable to the above statement exclusive of the settlement & report made by us bearing equal date with this-Given under our hands and seals this 17th day of August A.D. 1808-
               Thomas Henderson (seal)
               C. McAnally   (seal)
               David Tate   (seal)

Joseph Cobb - Dr. to -
     The amount of the Estate of Col. John Blair Dec'd sold at Public Vandue on the 24th of July 1797-
Total ————————————$1598.11
To collect since sale from
John Miller ————————   49.00   —— $1640.11

(p 245)   August Sessions A.D. 1808

Joseph Cobb -Credit-

By an obligation on John Blair Dec'd- to David Shelton for 300 acres of
Land ———————————————————————————— $600.00
To paid Lawyer Campbell for conducting a Law suit -
George Gordon against said Estate ——————————   65.75
To paid half of the Judgment & costs James Daniel against the Admr. and A
Amrx. of said estate & Thomas King including the Bill of in Equity
                                               961.21½
Paid Martin Ashburn Shff. his commission on the sale of said property
of said Estate ————————————————————————   77.75
To paid Anthony Neals proven account ——————————   4.00
To paid the costs of the suit the Admrs. of said Estate against
James Daniel ————————————————————————   2.00
Amount Brot. forward —————————————————— $1710.71½

To paid the Direct Tax on the land in Cumberland
belonging to the heirs of said Estate —————————— $7.90
To paid the state & county tax on said Cumberland
Land by H.L.White————————————————————   5.00
To paid Mr.Williams Ewing for his attention to
Catharine Blairs Land -1000 acres ——————————   3.00
To paid the costs of the suit the Admrs. of the
Estate of John Blair Dec'd against James Blair Jr. -   7.77½
The amount of credit —————————————————— $1734.39
The amount of the sales ——————————————————   1640.11
Balance due J.Cobb ——————————————————   94.28

We, the undersigned Commissioners appointed by Court to settle with
Joseph Cobb Admr. and guardian in right of his wife of the Estate of Col.
John Blair Dec'd having examined the accounts & vouchers produced to us
by the said Joseph Cobb have made and do report the following settlement
to Court as it stands stated (toait) that the said Joseph Cobb has paid
for the said Estate $1734.39 and that there is Balance of ninety four dol-
lars & twenty eight cents due from said Estate to the said Cobb as appears in the foregoing statement -Given under our hands and seals this 17th
of August 1808 -

            Thos. Henderson (seal)
            C.McAnally   (seal)
            David Tate   (seal)
and the two foregoing Reports were received & confirmed by the Court.

James Callison who was appointed sole Executor of the Last Will and
Testament of James Callison Dec'd which was heretofore proven in open Court
comes into open Court and taken an oath to execute the last Will & testament of the said Deceased so far as the Laws of the State will permit,
and the said James Callison returns an inventory of the personal property of James Callison Deceased.

James Harris &   )
William Stubblefield   )
          vs   )
Caleb Reece   )   The plaintiff in this case by John Cooke
                                 Esqr. makes a motion to Court to enter

up a Judgment against Caleb Reece for $22.87½ which sum they alledged they have been compelled to pay John S.Wells as security of the said Caleb Reece and it appearing to the satisfaction of the Court that the said James Harris & William Stubblefield have paid the aforesaid sum of $22.87½ as aforesaid for Charles Reece- It is therefore considered by the Court that the said James Harris & Wm Stubblefield do recover the aforesaid sum of twenty two dollars and eighty seven and one half cents against the said Caleb Reece and costs. Exec. Issd.

(p 246)   August Sessions A.D. 1808

Thomas Breeden)
    vs   )   Miller Easley one of the Defendants Bail comes into
David Haley   )   open Court and surrenders David Haley in discharge of
himself & the said David Haley, John Cocke & Henry Hewell comes into open
Court & acknowledged themselves indebted to the plaintiff Thomas Breeden
in the sum of $200 and undertook that the Defendant David Haley will pay
the condemnation & costs in this suit or surrenders himself into prison
for the same or that they will do it for him.

        Thomas Dardis Esqr. who was yesterday chosen Guardian by Wyett Smith
& who was approved of by the Court comes into open Court and enters into a
bond in the sum of $5000 with Hugh L.White & Pleasant M/Miller conditioned for the faithful discharge of his Guardianship.

        Richard Boatman Constable proves that he has attended on the Court
five days at the present term. Issd.

William Cocke)
    vs   )   Pleas Replication Issue Demurrer and Joinder on Reading
Ezekiel King   )   the papers & arguments of Council being heard on the Demurrer & Joinder - it is considered by the Court the Demurrer be overruled- Contd.

        Ordered by the Court that Thomas Henderson, George Moody, James Moore
Joseph Cobb, David Tate, David McAnally Esqrs. or any three of them be
commissioners to settle with John Cocke Esqr. Admr. of the Estate of
Michael Coons Dec'd & make report to next Court.

Edward Tate   )
    vs   )   Whereas heretofore David McAnally Esqr. Issued and
Isaiah Midkiff)   Execution whereby it was commanded that of the Goods
and chattels Lands and Tenements of Isaiah Midkiff there should be made
the sum of Twenty four Dollars Debt, two Dollars thirty four cents Int.
with all Lawful costs, it being the amount of a Judgment obtained against
said Midkiff by Edward Tate which Execution was Directed to David McAnally to Execute and return and he returned said Execution to the August
Term 1807-of this Court with his Return indorsed thereon that he had Levied
on 100 acres of Land the property of said Isiah Midkiff whereon the Court
ordered and adjudged that an order of sale should issue directed to the
Sheriff of this County commanding him to sell said Land to satisfy said
Judgment, which order of sale issued in conformity with the Judgment &
Decree of said Court and it appearing to the satisfaction of the Court that
said Land did not sell for a sum large enough to satisfy the Court costs

It is therefore ordered by the Court that a notification of these proceedings be issued to David McAnally Esquire and that he be directed to issue a new Execution.

Court adjourns till Court in course.

(p 247)   November Sessions A.D. 1808

At a Court of Pleas & Quarter Sessions began and holden for the County of Grainger at the Court House in Rutledge on the third Monday of November A.D. 1808 and 21st. of said month. Present, James Moore, David Tate, and George Moody, Esquires.

James Conn Esquire high Sheriff of said County makes his Return to Court that he has Executed the Venire Facias on the following persons, towit

1- Newberry James
2- George Sparkman
3- Valentine Morgan
4- Reubin Dixon
5- Robert Massengill
6- Samuel West
7- John Griffitts
8- Richard Thompson
9- John Humphreys Cert.is.
10-Joseph Stubblefield
11-Stephen Johnson
12-Joseph Rich
13-Richard Shelton cert. isd.
14-David Counts
15-Thomas Bunch
16-Henry Howell
17-John Estis
18-Daniel Taylor
19-Malachia Howell
20-Moses Hodges Issd.

21- George Taylor -Cert.Isd.
22- Robert Gaines Excused
23-Wm Snodgrass
24-Peter Beeler
25-John Moyers
26-John Salley
27-Wm Lane Excd.
28-Robert Fields
29-George Isom &
30-Nicholas Counts

Out of which Venire Facias the following persons were Ballotted a Grand Jury for the present Term.

1- John Griffitts -Foreman
2- Henry Howell Issd.
3- Geo.Sparkman Isd
4- Newberry James Isd.
5- Thomas Bunch issd.
6- Wm Snodgrass Issd.
7- Richard Thompson Issd.
8- Samuel West Issd.
9- Valentine Morgan Issd.

10- Malachia Howell Isd.
11-Stephen Johnson Isd.
12-Nicholas Counts Isd.
13-Reubin Dixon Isd.
14-Peter Beeler Isd.
15-David Counts

Who were sworn as the Law directs and charged by Thomas Dardis Esquire Solicitor. Issd.

Caleb Howell is appointed to attend the Court at the present Term.

Ordered by the Court Gibbons Cross be appointed a Constable in Capt. James District and he enters into bond in the sum of $500 with William Hall and Edward Clark his securities & is qualified as the Law Directs.

William Midkiff Assignees &c. for the use of Henry Howell & John Cocke vs Benjamin Hudson -

Joseph Fields one of the Bail of the Defendant surrenders him in open Court in discharge of himself whereupon Benjamin Howell & Isaac Stanley comes into open Court & acknowledged themselves indebted to the plaintiff in this case in the sum of Twelve hundred dollars but to be void upon condition they do it for him.

Pearson Barney)
    vs   )
John Miller   )   John Miller the Defendant comes into open Court and surrenders himself in discharge of his Bail whereupon Dedmore Mallicoat & Wm Mooney came into open Court and acknowledged themselves indebted to the plaintiff in the sum of $400 but to be void upon condition that said John Miller pay the costs and condemnation in case this suit should be determined against him or surrender himself to prison for the same or in case they do it for him.

Ordered by the Court that David Watson be appointed overseer of the road in the room of David Bunch and that he be allowed the same bounds for hands that were allowed to said David Bunch. Copy order issued.

(p 248)   November Sessions A.D. 1808

Ordered by the Court that Joseph Ore be apppinted overseer of the road from the Owl Hole Gap in the Richland Knobbs to Moore's Ferry on Holston River in the room of Isaac James and that he have the same bounds for hands that said James had to work under him. Order Issued.
Justices present, Philip Sigler, William Clay, Isaiah Midkiff & James Moore

Ordered by the Court that John Kidwell be appointed Guardian of Nancy Bradberry & Hezekiah Bradberry minor heirs of Hezekiah Bradberry deceased and he enters into Bond with David Tate and Jesse Cheek his securities in the sum of $557.75 for the faithful discharge of his Guardianship.

Ordered by the Court Thomas Vitteto be appointed overseer of the road from the top of Clinch mountain at the Powder Spring Gap to where said road intersects the Flat Creek road at Philip Sigler in the room of Joseph Fisherm giving him the same bounds for hands to work under him on said road that said Fisher last had. Order Issd.

A Deed of conveyance from John Hodges to Golder Davidson for 150 acres of Land was duly proven in open Court by the oaths of Benjamin Hudson subscribing witnesses thereto and admitted to record - Let it be registered.

A Deed of conveyance from Nicholas Karnes to William Kirk for a tract of Land containing 111 acres and three fourths of an acre was acknowledged in open Court by the Grantor and admitted to Record -Let it be Registered.

A Deed of conveyance from Richard Harris to Shedrick Williams for 90 acres of Land was acknowledged in open Court by Richard Harris the Grantor and admitted to record - Let it be Registered.

Present, Noah Jarnagin, Philip Sigler, William Clay & John Breeden Esqr. the under signed who were appointed at August Term 1808, to view and lay off a road the nearest and best way from the foot of Clinch Mt. to the top thereof at the Powder Spring Gap and make report have made their report in writing to the Court in the words and figures following towit, We, the undersogned being appointed by the Worshipful Court of Grainger County to view and lay off a road the nearest and best way from the foot of Clinch mountain to the top thereof at the powder spring Gap have met this 12th day of November A.D. 1808 and after being duly sworn have proceeded to view and lay off the road as follows turning off the old road to the right hand at the foot of the mountain at two white oaks marked, then directly up the spur of the mountain, then turn off said spur by some marked trees to the old road, then along said road to the top of the mountain. Signed, Samuel Peery, N.Jarnagin, Joseph Fields, Philip Sigler, Charles Hutcheson & Peter Beeler, which Report was received confirmed by the Court the road ordered to be opened as laid out.

(p 249)   November Sessions A.D. 1808

Ordered by the Court that Robert Harris be appointed overseer of the road from the ford of Richland Creek to the end of Clinch mountain of the Knox Line in the room of Joseph Ryan and that he have the same bounds for hands to work under him on said road that said Ryan had. Order Issd.

Present William Clay, David Tate, Isaiah Midkiff & John Breeden Esqr

Rachael Carmichel a monor under the age of Twenty one years comes into open Court & chooses James Alsup he guardian which choice is confirmed & allowed by the Court and the said James Alsup enters into Bond with David Tate and Robert Massengill his securities in the sum of 260 dollars for the faithful discharge of his Guardianship.

A Bill of Sale from Thomas James to Job Sally for a negro woman named Violet was acknowledged in open Court by the said Thomas James and admitted to record- Let it be recorded.

A Deed of conveyance from Henry Ivey to Benjamin Howell for a certain tract of Land containing for one hundred acres was proven in open Court by the oaths of Wm Howell and Moses Hodges subscribing witnesses thereto & admitted to Record- Let it be Registered.

John Cocke   )
    vs   )   In this case an Execution signed by James Moore Esqr.
Pearson Barney)   and directed to any Lawful officer to Execute and re-
turn is produced to Court whereby it is commanded that of the Goods and chattles Lands and Tenements of Pearson Barney if to be found there should be made the sum of thirty one dollars & fifty cents which sum John Cocke recovered before said James Moore for debt & further sum of forty three and three fourths cents for costs & charges in said suit Expended, whereof the said Pearson Barney is Liable as to me appears &c. on which execution James Conn Sheriff makes the following return towit, No goods and chattles to be found I have levied this Execution on 150 acres of Land whereon Pearson Barney now lives on Puncheon Camp Creek 12th October 1808 whereupon John Cocke by John Williams Esquire makes a motion to Court to award and order of sale directed to the Sheriff commanding him to sell the Land Levied on as above or so much thereof as will be sufficient to satisfy the

sum of thirty one dollars ninety three & three fourths cents whereupon it is considered by the Court that an order of sale do issue to the Sheriff commanding him to sell the tract of Land above leviedon or so much thereof as will be sufficient to satisfy the said sum of thirty one dollars ninety three cents & three fourths of a cent & costs -Exec. Issd.

A Deed of conveyance from Nathaniel Taylor to John Bean for a tract of Land containing 329 acres and three quarters of an acre was proven in open Court by James Conn & Jesse Cheek subscribing witnesses thereto admitted to Record. Let it be Registered.

A Bill of sale from James Wilson to Robert Blair for a negro girl named Mariah was proven in open Court by the oaths of Wm Hutcheson & Amos Sharp subscribing witnesses thereto & admitted to Record. Let it be Recorded.

(p 250)   November Sessions A.D. 1808

A Bill of Sale from Francis Mayberry to Robert Blair and James Armstrong for a negro woman named Sarah was proven in open Court by the oath of Wm Hutcheson and Amos Sharp subscribing witnesses thereto and admitted to Record. Let it be Recorded.

A Bill of Sale from Wm Windham to James Chinn for a negro woman named Syna was acknowledged in open Court by the said Wm Windham and admitted to Record. Let it be Recorded.

The Last Will and testament of Joseph Perrin was Exhibited to Court for probate and the due Execution thereof was proven in open Court by the oaths of William Mills & Edward Churchman subscribing witnesses thereto & admitted to Record. Let it be Recorded, whereupon Joel Perrin and Wm Perrin executors wherein named comes into open Court & took upon themselves the burthen of the Execution of said Will and were qualified Executors.

Court adjourns till tomorrow morning 9 o'clock.
At a Court continued and held for the County of Grainger at the Court House in Rutledge on the 22nd. day of November A.D. 1808.

Court met according to adjournment. Present, Isaiah Midkiff, John Breeden, & Charles Hutchison Esquires.

State   )
No. 448 vs   )
Betsey Hall   )   Present- Isaiah Midkiff, John Breeden, Charles Hutchison & James Moore. Whereupon came a Jury, towit-

1- John Humphreys	7- David Haley
2- Mose Hodges	8- John Middleton
3- Henry Widener	9- Thomas Breeden
4- Abner Low	10-Joseph Breeden
5- Charles Smith	11-Jesse Cheek &
6- David Holt	12-James Campbell

Who being elected tried and sworn well and truly to try and the truth to speak on the issue of Traverse in this case do say they find the Defendant not Guilty in manner and form as charged in the Bill of Indictment - Rule to shew cause why the prosecutor should be taxed with costs and also a Rule to shew cause why the defendant should be taxed with the costs-first Rule made absolute & the Second discharged.

```
State        )
No.452  vs   )
Adam Hall    )   Present -Isaiah Midkiff, John Breeden, Charles Hutcheson
```
James Moore, Mathew Campbell & Wm Hankins Esquires, whereupon came a Jury towit, the same Jury as in the last case No. 448- who being elected tried and sworn well and truly to try & the truth to speak on the issue of traverse in this case do say   (p 251)   they find the Defendant
(November Sessions A.D. 1808)
and the Jury having retired to considered of their verdict returned to the Bar & being as said if they had agreed on their verdict said they had not whereupon a mistrial is concented by the Council & Directed to be entered by the Court- mistrial.

Ordered by the Court that Caleb Howell be allowed the sum of one Dollar and twenty five cents for two small Pitchers & one glass Tumbler furnished for the use of the Court. Order Issd.

Ordered by the Court that John McElheney be appointed overseer of the road from the house where the said John McElheney lives to the Town of Rutledge in the room of James Batright & that he have the hands in the same bounds to work under him on said road that was allowed said Boatright.

A Bill of sale from John Chaney to Samuel McBee for a negro boy named Miles was acknowledged in open Court by the said John Haley and admitted to record. Let it be Recorded.

The Last Will and testament of Henry Hawkins was exhibited to Court for probate and the due execution thereof was proven in open Court by the oaths of David Abernathy and Wm Hankins subscribing witnesses thereto & admitted to Record. Let it be Recorded.

```
State        )
vs           )   Present-
Joseph West  )   Isaiah Midkiff, John Breeden, & William Hankins, Esquires

1- Richard Shelton       7- Thomas Turley
2- John McBroom          8- James Bowen
3- John Vinyard          9- Thomas James
4- Samuel Williams      10-James Richardson
5- George Martin        11-Justice Hall &
6- Joel Martin          12-Robert Massengill
```

Who being elected, tried and sworn well and truly to try, and the truth to speak on the issue of traverse in this case Do say they find the defendant Guilty in manner and form as charged in the Bill of Indictment.

Ordered by the Court that James Conn Sheriff be allowed the sum of $24 for his trouble & expenses in arresting Guarding and conveying Thomas Conway to the District Jail at Knoxville.Copy order issued.

Ordered by the Court that Thomas Nugent be appointed overseer of the road from the ford of Richland Creek to the top of the Indian Ridge in the room of Wm Bumbard and that the same bounds be allowed him for hands that was allowed said William Bumbard. Order issued.

Joseph West who was appointed overseer of the road from the town of Rutledge to the top of the Richland Knobs at the last term of this Court comes into Court & resigns said appointment which is expected by the Court on account of his infirmity & inability to attend to the Duties of said appointment.

(p 252)   November Sessions A.D. 1808

Ordered by the Court that Valentine Morgan be appointed overseer of the road from the town of Rutledge to the top of the Richland Knobs on the road leading from said town to Mayes ford on Holston River in the room of Joseph West and that he have the following Bounds and hands as laborers under him (towit) William Guinn, Richard Luttrell, Samuel Williams, Valentine Morgan, Hardiman Taylor, Miller Easley, James Whaling, and every other persons living with them or on their premises as workers under him, and that his bounds be extended to induce Josiah Gallion, Justice Hall & James Whaling & that they be exuused from working on any other road. Order Issd.

Ordered by the Court that following Justices be appointed to take the Lists of Taxable property for the year A.D. 1809 and make report to next Court (towit)
1st. Noah Jarnagin Esqr. for Capt. Richard Coats Company.
2nd. Retd. William Hankins Esqr. for Capt. Thos. Sharps Company.
3rd. Retd. Charles Hutcheson Esqr. for Capt. Wm McPhetridge Company.
4th. Retd. Philip Sigler Esqr. for Capt. Thomas James Company.
5th. Retd. Charles McAnally Esqr. for Capt. Geo. Griffords Company.
6th. Retd. Isaiah Midiff Esqr. for Capt. Abraham Wilsons Company.
7th. Retd. John Breeden Esqr. for Capt. Williams Parkersons Company.
8th. George Moody Esqr. for Capt. William Mayes Company.
9th. Thomas Henderson Esqr. for Capt. Aquilla Jones Company.
10th.Retd. James Moore Esqr. for Capt. John Smith Company.
11th.Retd. John Moffit Esqr. for Capt. William Bryants Company.

Ordered by the Court that the following persons be appointed Jurors & that they be summoned to attend the next term of this Court, towit-
Robert D.Eaton, John Thompson, Miller Easley, Evan Harris, William Cook, James Brown, Golden Davidson, Seth McKinney, Major Lea, Henry Hawkins, Robert Firlds, Thomas Dennis, Abraham Pruit, John Moyers, John Beeler,Jr. James Carmichael, Duncan Carmichael, Joseph Rich, Thomas Johnston, John Noe, Wm Whitesides, Thomas Bunch, Daniel Robison, Rubin Dalton, Joshua Collins, Andrew McRheeters, Wm Bowman, Daniel Taylor, Hugh Larimore & Thomas Mann.

A Deed of conveyance from John Bull to Joshua Collins for a tract of Land containing two hundred acres was proven in open Court by the oaths of Edward McGinnis & Charles McAnally the subscribing witnesses thereto & admitted to Record- Let it be registered.

Sarah Shelton Administratrix of William Shelton Dec'd returns the amt. of the sales of said estate to Court.

Court adjourns till tomorrow morning 9 o'clock.

(p 253)   November Sessions A.D. 1808
At a Court of Pleas and Quarter Sessions continued and held for the County of Grainger at the Court House in Rutledge on the 23rd. day of Nov A.D. 1808 -
Court met according to adjournment -Present- Charles McAnally, Isaiah Midkiff & Joseph Cobb Esquires.

William Cooke   )
     vs   )   Whereupon came a Jury, towit-
Ezekiel King   )

1- George Taylor   7- Henry Widener
2- Peter A.Campbell   8- Thomas James
3- Edward McGinnis   9- Henry Matlock
4- George Noe   10-Andrew Longmore
5- Stephen Smith   11-William Keith
6- Thomas Dorset   12-James Campbell

Who being elected tryed and sworn well and truly to try & the truth to speak on the Issue joined in this case do say they find the defendant guilty of the traverse & conversion in manner and form as the plaintiff in his declaration hath complained against him and assess the plaintiffs damage occationed by reason thereof to four hundred dollars besides his costs.

Whereas the Court of Grainger County have laid Sundry taxes to be collected in said County for the year 1808 (towit) a County tax - a tax to defray the expenses of transcribing the Registers Books, a tax for the support of the poor and a tax to pay the Jurors - now if it shall so happen that there shall remain a surplus after satisfying the purposes for which any of said Taxes were laid - It is hereby ordered by the Court that such surplus shall be allyed to any County purposes.

Nathan Humphreys records his mark & Brand as follows Viz. the mark & Brand of Nathan Humphreys, the mark a smooth crop of the right Ear and under bit in the Left, Brand thus- NH

Thomas N.Clark)
No. 401 vs   )   Present, Isaiah Midkiff, William Parkison, & Joseph
William Reese   )   Cobb Esquires. Whereupon came a Jury, towit-

1- Michael Massengill   7- Miller Easley
2- Moses Hodges   8- Wm Whiteside
3- Richard Shelton   9- Ambrose Yancey
4- Thomas James   10-Martin Albert
5- Abner Low   11-Nimrod Cyrus
6- Wm Tulley   12-Ira Patterson

Who being elected, tried and sworn well & truly to try and the truth to speak on the Issue joined in this case, do say they find the defendant hath not kept & performed his covenant as in pleading he hath alledged and assess the plaintiffs damages occationed by reason of the non performance thereof to ninety one Dollars eight cents & two thirds of a cent besides his costs.

(p 254)　　　　　November Sessions A.D. 1808

Isaac Campbell comes into open Court & proves that he has attended on the Grand Jury three days at the present Term. Issued.

A Bill of sale from John Coffman to Samuel West for a negro boy named Hampton was acknowledged in open Court by the said John Coffman & admitted to record. Let it be registered.

A Deed of conveyance from John Baker to Michael Massengill for 27 acres of Land was acknowledged in open Court by the Grantor and admitted to record Let it be Registered.

A Deed of conveyance from John Baker to Robert.Solomon Massengill for 25 acres of Land was acknowledged in open Court by the Grantor and admitted to record. Let it be registered.

A Deed of conveyance from John Baker to Solomon Massengill for 225 acres of Land was acknowledged by the Grantor and admitted to record -Let it be registered.

A Deed of conveyance from David Haley to William Mitchell for 245 acres of Land more or less was acknowledged in open Court by the Grantor and admitted to record. Let it be registered.

A Deed of conveyance from John Middleton to Henry Howell for one fifth part of an undivided tract of Land containing 640 acres was proven in open Court by the oath of Peter Campbell & John Moore subscribing witnesses to and admitted to record -Let it be Registered.

A Bill of sale from Sampson Murdock to Stephen Johnson for two negroes named Arthur & Clarissa was proven in open Court by the oaths of James Johnson & William Johnson subscribing witnesses thereto & admitted to Record. Let it be registered.

A Power of Attorney from Walter Sims to John A. McKinney was proven in open Court by the oaths of James Conn & John Moore subscribing witnesses thereto and admitted to Record. Let it be registered.

It appearing to the satisfaction of the Court that the stray horse taken up by James Brown died within twelve months after the appraisement thereof - It is therefore ordered by the Court that the said James Brown be released from any liability of paying any part of the appraised value of said James Brown be released from paying any part of the appraised value of said horse in the County Treasury.

Court adjourns till tomorrow morning　9 o'clock.

(p 255)　　　　　November Sessions A.D. 1808

At a Court of Pleas & Quarter Sessions continued and holden 1808.

Court met according to adjournment. Present, David McAnally, Isaiah Midkiff & Charles McAnally, Esqrs.

Thomas Breeden)
No. 454   vs   )   Justices present, David McAnelly, Charles McAnally &
David Haley)   Henry Boatman. Whereupon came a Jury, towit-

1- George Taylor   7- Joseph Luttrell
2- William Whiteside   8- Samuel Ramsey
3- Abner Low   9- John Harris
4- Stepehn Smith   10-Nicholas Counts
5- John Arwine   11-John Shelton &
6- John Norman   12-John Allison

Who being elected tried and sworn well and truly to try & the truth to speak on this issue joined in this case do say they find the defendant did assume in manner and form as the plaintiff in his Declaration against him hath complained that the Defendant hath not paid the Debt in the Declaration mentioned as in pleading he hath alledged, and assess the plaintiffs Damages occationed by reason of the non performance thereof to fifty Dollars seventy three and one half cents & costs. It is therefore considered by the Court that the said Thomas do recover of the said David the damages aforesaid in form aforesaid assessed together with his costs by him in and about prosecuting his said suit in that behalf expended &c. from which Judgment the said David prays an appeal to the next Superior Court of Law for Hamilton District & the said David enters into Bond with John Cocke & Henry Howell his securities- reasons filed and appeal granted by the Court.

Campbell Martin &c)
No. 527   vs   )
Caleb Reece & Thomas Reece)   Charles Smith one of the Special Bail of Caleb Reece one of the Defendants in this case brings the said Caleb Reece into open Court and surrenders him in discharge of himself & the other Bail- ordered in custody of the Sheriff by the Court.

Thomas A.Claiborne)
  vs   )
Ambrose Yancey)   Pleasant M.Miller Esqr. makes a motion to Court to enter up a Judgment against Ambrose Yancey late Clerk & Thomas Henderson & John Estis his securities for ten dollars and eighty six cents money pd. into office by George Snuffer Sheriff of Claiborne County on an execution Thomas A.Claiborne against James Ore & which on application he has failed to pay over to Pleasant M.Miller Attorney the truth of the foregoing facts appearing to the satisfaction of the Court. It is therefore considered by the Court that said Thomas A.Claiborne recover of said Ambrose, Thomas & John said sum of Ten dollars & eighty six cents & costs. Exon. Issd.

William Woodward
Guardian &c.
  vs   )
Caleb Reece -Tho Williams)   Henry Howell special Bail of Caleb
& Thomas Reece Sr.)   Reece one of the defendants in this case brings the said Caleb in open Court and surrenders him in discharge of himself & Robert Long the other Bail whereupon John Cocke Esqr. Council for the Sheriff & he is ordered in custody by the Court.

(p 256)   November Sessions A.D. 1808

Ordered by the Court that Pleasant M.Miller Esquire & John Haley be
fined two dollars each for a contempt of the Court -Fine paid into office.

Ordered by the Court that Wm Whiteside be released from the payment
of a tax on a stud horse of $4.00 for the year A.D. 1806, which said White-
side once paid to Ambrose Yancey late Clerk of Grainger County as appears
to the satisfaction of the Court.

Court adjourns till tomorrow morning 9 o'clock.

At a Court of Pleas and Quarter Sessions continued and holden for the
County of Grainger at the Court House in Rutledge on the 25th day of November A.D. 1808.

Court met according to adjournment. Present, Isaiah Midkiff, Henry
Boatman & John Cocke.

William McNeill   )
No. 500 vs   )
John Purd   )   Whereupon came a Jury, towit-

1- Richard Shelton   7- David Holt Jr.
2- John Humphrey   8- Henry Howell
3- Ambrose Yancey   9- Samuel Ramsey
4- John Calvin   10-John Middleton
5- Thomas Reece   11-Elisha Bowman &
6- Caleb Reece   12-John Norman

Who being elected tryed and sworn well and truly to try and the truth
to speak on the Issue joined in this case do say they find the Defendant
hath not paid the Debt in the declaration mentioned as in pleading he hath
alledged but hath only paid $8.14 and assess the plaintiffs damages to $2.82
& costs.

James White)
  498 vs   )   Justices present, David McAnally -Charles McAnally & Isaiah
Neal McCoy   )   Midkiff, whereupon came a Jury,(towit) the same Jury as
in the other case who being elected tried and sworn well and truly to enquire what damages the plaintiff hath sustained in a writ of inquiry by
him brought in this case- Do say the plaintiff hath sustained by reason of
the non performance of said Covenant be sides his costs.

Ordered by the Court that Richard Boatman Constable be allowed the sum
of one dollar per day for each day he attended on the Court at August Term
1808. Order Issued.

(p 257)   November Sessions A.D.1808

Moses Free   )
No. 511 vs   )
John Henderson & Uraley his wife)   Present, David McAnally, & Henry Boatman Esqrs. Whereupon came a Jury, towit the same Jury as in No. 500 who being elected tryed and sworn well and truly to try & the truth to speak in
the matter in Dispute in this case do say they find for the Defendants.

William Woodward Guardian &c.　　　　　)
No. 526　vs　　　　　　　　　　　　　　)
Caleb Reece -Wm Williams &Thos. Reece Sr.)
　　　　Whereupon came a Jury (towit) the same Jury as in the Last case except
Abner Low in the room of Thomas Reece Sr. & Richard Dunville in the room of
Caleb Reece who being elected tried and sworn well and truly to say & the
truth to speak in the Issue joined in this case do say they find the Defend-
ants have not paid the Debt in the Declaration mentioned as in pleading they
have alledged & assess the plaintiffs damages occasioned by reason thereof
to $2.95 & costs.

Trunstill Qunls　)
No. 534　vs　　　)
Richard Grantham)　　　Whereupon came a Jury(towit) the same Jury as in the
last case -Who being elected tried and sworn well and truly to try & the
truth to speak on the Issue joined in this case do say the Defendant hath
not paid the debt in the Declaration mentioned as in pleading he hath alledged & assess the plaintiffs damages occasioned by reason of the Declaration thereof four Dollars eighty five cents besides his costs.

Thomas Montgomery)
No. 535　vs　　　　)
Richard Grantham)　　Whereupon came the same Jury as in the last case, who
being elected tried and sworn well & truly and the truth to speak on the
Issue joined in this case do say the Defendant hath not paid the Debt in the
Declaration mentioned as in pleading he hath alledged & assess the plain-
tiffs Damages occasioned by Reason thereof to $4.85 besides his costs.

(p 258)　　　　　November Sessions A.D. 1808

James Conn　　　)
No. 537　vs　　)
Caleb Reece　　)　　　Whereupon came a Jury (towit) the same Jury as in the
last case, who being elected tried and sworn well and truly to try and the
truth to speak on the matter of controversy in this case- Do say they find
for the plaintiff & assess his Damages to five Dollars & costs.

　　　Ordered by the Court that Isaiah Midkiff take the charge of Jeremiah
Midkiff one of the poor of this County from the present term till the next
of this Court.

Thomas Ryerson　　　　　　　　　　　　　)
No. 558　vs -Sci.Fa.to reive Judgment.)
Samuel Acklin　　　　　　　　　　　　　　) Whereupon came a Jury(towit) the
same Jury as in the last case, who being elected tried and sworn well and
truly to try and the truth to speak on the sum joined in this case Do say
they find the Defendant hath not well and truly paid & satisfied the Judgment & costs which the said Scire Facias is intended to review as in his
plea he hath alledged.

Philip Sword)
　　vs　　　　)
Wm Parkinson)　　Whereupon came a Jury (towit)

1- Richard Shelton　　　　　　　4- John Calvin
2- John Humphreys　　　　　　　5- Abner Low
3- Ambrose Yancey　　　　　　　6- Richard Dunville
4- John Calvin

7- David Holt
8- Henry Howell
9- Samuel Rumsey
10- John Middleton
11- Elisha Bowman
12-John Norman

Who being elected tried and sworn - appeal Dismissed by Isaac S.McMeans plaintiffs Atty. the Jury Discharged from further attendance at the present Term- ordered by the Court that Caleb Howell attend the next term of this Court.

A Deed of conveyance from James Conn Sheriff of Grainger County to Samuel Riggs for one hundred and sixty acres of Land was acknowledged in open Court by the said James Conn & admitted to record. Let it be Registered.

A Deed of conveyance from John Dorah to William Baker for Lot. No. 20 in the town of Rutledge was proven in open Court by the oaths of Sterling Cocke and John Hoare subscribing witnesses thereto & admitted to record Let it be registered.

A Deed of conveyance from John Lea late Sheriff of Grainger County to Henry Howell for Lot No.11-in the town of Rutledge was proven in open Court by the oaths of John F.Jack & William Baker subscribing witnesses thereto & admitted to record -Let it be Registered.

Court adjourns till Court in Course.

(p 259)   February Sessions A.^{D}. 1809
At a Court of Pleas & Quarter Sessions A.^{D}. 1809 begun and holden for the County of Grainger at the Court House in Rutledge on the third Monday of February A.D. 1809 & 20th of said month. Justices present, John Moffit Wm Clay, David Tate, Isaiah Midciff & George Moody.

James Conn Esqr. high Sheriff of said County makes his return to Court that he has executed the Venire facias on the following persons except John Beeler Jr.

1- Robert D.Eaton
2- John Thompson
3- Miller Easley
4- Evan Harris
5- Wm Cook Cert.Issd.to Jas.Conn per order W.Cook.
6- James Brown
7- Golder Davidson Cer.Isd.
8- Seth McKinney (Excused)
9- Major Lea (Excused)
10-Henry Hawkins (Excused)
11-Robert Fields
12-Thomas Dennis
13-Abraham Prewit (Excused)
14-John Byers
15-John Beeler Jr.
16-Jas.Carmichael
17-Duncan Carmichael Cer.Issd.
18-Joseph Rich Cer.issd.
19-Thos.Johnston
20-John Hoe
21-Wm Whiteside
22-Thomas Bunch
23- Daniel Robertson Cert.issd.
24- Reubin Dalton
25- Joshua Collins Cert. Issd.
26- Andrew McWheeters
27- William Bowman Cert.issd.
28- Daniel Taylor
29-Ruth Larimore &
30- Thomas Mann

Out of which Venire facias the following persons were Ballotted.

a Grand Jury to the present Term(towit)
1- Issd. James Carmichael -Four
2- Evan Harris -Issd.
3- Robert D.Eaton Or.Issd.
4- Thomas Mann -Issd.
5- Andrew McPhetridge -Issd.
6- Reubin Dalton -Issd.
7- Robert Fields
8- Miller Easley
9- Thomas Johnston Issd.
10-John Moyers -Issd.
11-Hugh Larrimore -Issd.
12-Thomas Bunch -Issd.
13-Thomas Dennis -Issd.
14-Daniel Taylor Issd. &
15-James Brown

Who being qualified as the Law Directs & charged &c.

William Midkiff -Assignee)
for the use of John Cocke)
& Henry Howell)
     vs)
Benjamin Hudson) Who were qualified as the Law Directs & charged.
Isaac Stanley & Benjamin Howell Special Bail of Defendant surrendered him
in open Court in discharge of themselves whereupon the Defendant is prayed
in custody by plaintiffs Atty. and ordered to be in custody of the Sheriff.

     William Rankins Esqr. who was appointed to take in a List of Polls &
taxable property in the bounds of Capt. Thomas Sharps Company Returns his
List to Court.
     Charles Hucheson Esqr. who was appointed to take in a List of polls &
taxable property in the bounds of Capt. Wm McPhetridge Company- Returns his
Lists to Court.
     Noah Jarnagin Esqr. who was appointed to take in a List of Polls & tax-
able property in the Bounds of Capt. Richard Coats Company Returns his List
to Court.
     By order of Court the following persons are appointed to attend the
next Term of this Superior Court to be holden for the District of Hamilton
at the Court House to be holden at the Court House in Knoxville on the 4th
Monday of March next as Jurors, towit, John Moffitt, Wm Clay, Jos.Cobb
Esqrs. & Henry Howell. Ven.Fa.Issd.

(p 260) By order of Court the following persons are appointed to attend
the next Term of this Court as Jurors(towit) Abner Low,Richard Coats,New-
berry James, John Kitchen, Abraham Prewit, John Dennis, Major Lea, Thomas
Sharp, Edward Churchman, Seamor York, Samuel McBee, Isaac Stanley, Royal
Jinnings, Henry Hipshir,Henry Howell, John Daniel, John Kidwell, James Bow-
en, Henry Bowen, Wm Blair, Wm Kirkham,John Noe, John Williams, Meredith
Coffee, Moses Hodges, John Crow, Harmon Cox, Andrew Coffman, Henry Holston
& Josiah Kidwell.

     On motion it is ordered by the Court that Nancey Lively -Widow and re-
lict of Wm Lively -Dec'd. have leave to administer on all and singular the
goods and chattels rights and credits of the said Wm Lively Dec'd -where-
upon she enters into bond in the sum of $1000 with George Evans her secur-
ity for the faithful administration & she is qualified as the Law directs,
whereupon it is ordered by the Court that Letters of administration do
issue to the said Nancy Lively.
     The said Nancy Lively returns to Court an inventory of the goods and
&c of Wm Lively Dec'd and on motion it is ordered that an order of sale
Do issue to the said Nancy Lively Administratrix.

Ordered by the Court that John Boyd have leave to keep an ordinary or house of publick intertainment where he now lives & he enters into Bond in the sum of $1250 with James Kennedy his security.

Ordered by the Court that William Dyer be appointed be appointed a constable and he enters into Bond in the sum of five hundred dollars with Samuel McBee, Samuel Peery & Alex. Hamilton his securities and the said William Dyer takes an oath to support the Constitution of the United States the Constitution of the State of Tennessee and also the oath of Office as prescribed by Law.

On motion of John Cocke Esqr. and after arguments of Council be overruled by the Court. It is ordered by the Court and adjudged that the foregoing order appointing William Dyer a constable Me overruled cancelled & of none effect and afterwards Wm Dyer by Isaac S.McMeans, his Atty. makes a motion to Court to reconsider the above motion made by John Cocke Esqr.

The Last Will and Testament of Joseph Douglas deceased was Exhibited to Court for probate and the due execution thereof was proven in open Court by the oaths of Major Lea & James Perkins, subscribing witnesses thereto & admitted to record -Let it be recorded, and Mathew Campbell Esqr. who is therein and thereby appointed executor comes into Court & takes upon himself the burthem of the Execution of said Will & is qualified as executor.

(p 261)   February Sessions A.D. 1809

The Last Will and testament of Peter Cotner deceased was exhibited to Court for probate & the due execution thereof was proven by Solomon Massengill & John Sanders subscribing witnesses thereto & admitted to record - Let it be recorded, and Joseph Ore and Robert Massengill, Executors therein named comes into Court & are quallified as the Law directs.

George Shall)
    vs   )   In this case an aexcution signed by Philip Sigler Esqr.
William Peeters)   and directed to any lawful officer to execute & Return
is produced to Court, whereby it was commanded that of the goods & chattels Lands & Tenements of William Peeters if to be found there should be made the sum of nine dollars eighty cents principal on a Judgment, George Shall obtained against said defendant with the further sum of Eighty one & one fourth cents in this suit expended with the further sum of twelve and one fourth cents in this suit expended with the further sum of twelve and one half cents for this execution &c. on which execution John Hall constable makes the following return, towit-Levied within execution on a certain tract or parcel of Land as the property of William Peeters lying and being in the County of Grainger North of Copper Ridge & on the waters of Bull run adjoining the Land of George & others - no goods & chattles found by me John Hall Const. whereupon said plaintiff by Pleasant M.Miller makes a motion to Court to award an order of sale directed to the Sheriff Commanding him to sell the Lands levied on as aforesaid or so much thereof as will be of value sufficient to satisfy the sum of Ten dollars seventy three and three fourths cents, whereupon it is ordered by the Court that an order of sale do issue to the Sheriff commanding him to sell the tract of Land levied on as aforesaid or so much thereof as will be sufficient

to satisfy the aforesaid sum of money & costs.

Pritchet & Shall)
    vs   )   The plaintiffs in this case by Pleasant M.Miller Esqr.
William Peters   )   their Atty. makes a motion to Court to award an order
of sale directed to the Sheriff commanding to sell a certain tract or Parcel
of Land as the property of William Peters lying and being in the County of
Grainger North of Copper ridge & on the waters of Bull run adjoining the
Land of George Norris & others (which had been Levied on by John Holt Constable by Virtue of an execution Issued by Philip Sigler Esqr. or so much
thereof as will be sufficient to satisfy the sum of twenty nine dollars
seventy seven & three fourth cents. Whereupon it is considered by the Court
that an order do issue to the Sheriff commanding him to sell the tract of
Land levied on as aforesaid to satisfy the said sum of money & costs.

Pritchet & Shall)
    vs   )   The plaintiff in this case by Pleasant M.Miller Esqr.
William Peters   )   their Atto. makes a motion to Court to award an order
of sale directed to the Sheriff commanding him to sell a certain tract or
parcel of Land the property of William Peters lying and being in the County
of Grainger North of Copper ridge & on the waters of Bull run adjoining the
Land of George Norris & others,

(p 282)   February Sessions A.D. 1809
which had been levied on by John Hall constable by Virtue of an execution
Issued by Philip Sigler Esqr. or so much thereof as will be sufficient to
satisfy the sum of twenty six dollars seventy two and three fourth cents.
Whereupon it is considered by the Court that an order of sale do Issue to
the Sheriff commanding him to sell the tract of Land levied on as afd.to
satisfy the aforesaid sum of twenty six dollars seventy two and three fourth
cents & costs.

    Ordered by the Court that Henry Mays have all the hands in the fol-
lowing named persons to work under him on the road of which he is overseer
towit-John Mays, David Brown, Abraham Southerland, William Lacey,and all
the hands that now lives or that may hereafter live on the plantation on
which the above named persons now lives including the plantation said
Henry Mays.

    Court adjourns till tomorrow mourning 9 o'clock.

    Tuesday 21st.February A.D. 1809
    Court met according to adjournment. Justices present, David Tate,
John Breeden & Henry Boatman.

Campbell & Martin, surviving partners &c)
        vs   )
Gideon Morris and John Crow   )

    Henry Howell and Shedrick Norris comes into Court and acknowledged them-
selves indebted to the plaintiffs in the sum of $400 but to be void on con-
dition that if the defendant shall be cast in this action they, that is sd.
Defendants will pay the costs & condemnations, surrenders themselves to
prison for the same or that is to say Henry & Shadrach will do it for them.
    The petition of Jesse Cheek signed by Inhabitants of the Counties of

Greiffger and Claiborne praying the Court to appoint a Jury to view, make and lay out a road from the mouth if Shelton's Branch on Indian Creek on the Kentucky Road to Bristow's Bend on Clinch River was presented to Court a majority of the acting Justices being present, towit, James Moore, Noah Jarnagin, Isaiah Midkiff, Joseph Cobb, Philip Sigler, David Tate, Wm Clay George Moody, John Breeden, David McAnally, John Moffitt & Charles Mc Anolly- the Court after examining witnesses touching the premises order that the following persons Viz. Thomas Johnston, John Estis, Henry Howell, Nicholas Counts, Thos.Henderson, Jas.Carmichael, Chealey Jarnagin, Moses Hodges Robert Long, Joseph Rich, Henry Mays, & Isaac Mitchell be a jury to view the road leaving the Kentucky road at the mouth of Sheltons branch to the County Line at Bristows Bend and also that the view the present Kentucky road from the same point to the County Line at George Evans Ferry and report to the next Term of this Court the advantages and disadvantages attending each road and whether a road from the mouth of Sheltons branch to the County line at said Bend will be greater publick utility than the present road.

(p 263)   February Sessions A.D. 1809

Ordered by the Court a Majority of the acting Justices being present that John Daniel, Henry Howell, Henry Kipsher, Edward McGinnis, Reubin Dalton, Samuel Dodson & Royal Jinnings be a Jury to view & lay off a road the nearest & best way from the present road leading down the Valley North of Clinch Mountain from a point at or near where Benj.Shaw formerly lived to the ford on Clinch River where Elijah Evans now lives and make report to next Court. Copy order issued.

Ordered by the Court that William McIlhetridge be allowed the sum of seven dollars for the purpose of procuring a sledge hammer and crow bar to be used on the Road on which he is overseer also on the road on which Wm Arwine, Thomas Viteto and Stephen Goard are overseers to be paid out of any County money not otherwise appropriated. Copy order issd.

Ordered by the Court that Valentine Morgan be allowed the seven dollars in order purchased a sledge hammer and crow bar to be used on the road on which he is overseer to be paid out of any County money not otherwise appropriated. Copy order issued.

Ordered by the Court that Isaiah Midkiff, Wm Clay and Noah Jarnagin settle with Nancy McElhany Administratrix of the Estate of Robert McElhany Dec'd-& make report to next Court.

John Robeck returns the following List of Taxable property for the year 1809 (towit) 100 acres of Land.

Noah Jarnagin Esqr. has leave to return his list of Taxable property for the year 1809 Viz. 500 acres of Land - 1 white poll and 2 black.

Jacob Duratt by Henry Widener has leave to return his List of Taxable property for the year 1809 towit- 200 acres of Land.

Ordered by the Court that George Boatman be appointed overseer of the road from the top of the Ridge at Henry Boatmans old place to Jesse Riggs old place & that said Boatman be allowed the following Bounds for hands towit, Beginning at John Crows runing down Turkey Creek to the mouth, thence down the river to the upper end of Boatman ridge thence on said ridge to

Ambrose Hodges old place thence to the Beginning. Copy order issued.

By order of Court William Copeland is appointed overseer of the road leading to Knoxville From Beans Station to the Six mile post, Kearns Bounds and all the hands in the following bounds are assigned to work under him on said Road, that is to say Beginning on William Whitesides bounds on said road running with the line of said Bounds to the top of the Big Ridge & to the top of Clinch Mountain down to Kearnes Bounds so as to include Tandy Senters plantation on said ridge where Jones lives & all the hands thereon. Copy order issued.

(p 264)   February Sessions A.D. 1809

A Certificate of the probate of the Last Will and testament of William King duly autnenicated from the County Court of Washington in the commonwealth of Virginia was exhibited to the Court for the purpose of having the same recorded and admitted to record. Let it be recorded.

James Moore Esqr. who was appointed to take in a List of Polls and taxable property in the bounds of Capt. John Smiths Company returns his Lists to Court.
John Moffitt Esqr. who was appointed to take in Lists of Polls and taxable property in the Bounds Capt. Wm Harris makes his return to Court.

Ordered by the Court that the following tax be laid & collected as a County tax for the year A.D. 1809 Viz. on each hundred acres of Land 12½¢ on each free poll 12½¢ on each black poll 25¢ on each town lott 25¢ and on each storehouse $5.00.

Ordered by the Court that the following tax be laid and collected as a County Tax to pay the attendance of the Jurors to the County Court for the year A.D. 1809 - on each hundred acres of Land 12½¢ and each town lot 25¢ on each free poll 12½¢ on each black poll 25¢ and on each retail store $5.00

Ordered by the Court that Wm Whitesides be appointed overseer of the road from Beans Station to Sheltons ford on Holston River in the room of Henry Smith & that he have all the hands in the same bounds to work under him that ware assigned to said Smith.

Ordered by the Court that the Bounds of John Arwine overseer of the road from John Petres to Josiah Maples be extended in the following manner towit- to extend along the Northside of the Copper Ridge to Griffy Griffits & from thence to Clinch River at Casey's old place then down the river to the Grassy point, then across to John Peters & that all the hands in the aforesaid Bounds in future do work under the asid John Arwine overseer and also the following hands towit-John Beelor, John Petres, Thomas Kee, Griffit Griffits & Josiah Maples. Copy order issd.

Courts adjourns till tomorrow morning 9 O'clock.

Wednesday 22nd. February A.D. 1809.

Court met according to adjournment-Justices present-Henry Boatman & John Breeden.
(p 265)
February Sessions A.D. 1809

State
vs (No.452)
Adam Hall   Justices present, David Tate, Henry Boatman & John Breeden, whereupon came a Jury, towit,

1- Duncan Carmichael   7- Thomas Key
2- Nimrod Cyrus   8- Edmund Strange
3- Daniel Robinson   9- Richard Harris
4- Joseph Rich   10-Valentine Morgan
5- William Cook   11-Aaron Rooks &
6- Henry Howell   12-Nicholas Counts

Who being elected tried and sworn well and truly to try and the truth to speak on the Issue of Traverse in this case do say they find the Defendant Guilty in manner & form as he stands charged in the Bill of indictment.

On motion of David Tate by John Cocke Esqr. his Atto. to release him from the tax of a Saw Gin or cotton machine in as much as it was not worked or used or in situation to be used. It is therefore ordered by the Court that the said David Tate for the cause aforesaid be Released from the payment of the tax.

Francis Daniel
   vs No. 523
Pleasant Duke – Whose Death was suggested at Nov. Term 1809– Joseph Noe & Stephen W.Senter – Justices present– David Tate, Henry Boatman, Charles Mc-Anally –Thomas Henderson & David McAnally.

1- Henry Hawkins   7- Samuel Peery
2- John Thompson   8- John Richards
3- Joshua Collins   9- Aquilla Jones
4- William Bowman   10-Rice Moore
5- Golder Davidson   11-Seth Coulter &
6- Thomas Sharp   12-John Stiffy

Who being elected tried and sworn well and truly to try and the truth to speak on the Issue joined in this case do say the Defendants have not pd. the Debt on the Declaration mentioned as in pleading they have alledged and assess the plaintiffs Damages occationed by reason of the detention thereof to sixteen dollars & eighty cents & costs.

On motion the Grand Jury are dismissed from further attendance at the present term.
Isaac Campbell proves in open Court that he has attended three days on the Grand Jury at the present Term. Order Isd.

Ordered by the Court that all constables or other Officers who have heretofore or shall hereafter attend on the Grand Jury or the Court in obedience to the order of Court shall be allowed one Dollar out of the County Treasury for each & every day they have attended or shall attend.

(p 266)   February Sessions A.D. 1809

John Renfro by Hugh L.White Esqr. his Agent has leave to return his Lists of Taxable property for the year 1809, towit, 360 acres of Land.

Isaiah Midkiff Esqr. who was appointed to take in a List of Polls & taxable property in the Bounds of Capt. Abraham Wilsons Company.

Returns his Lists to Court.

Philip Sigler Esqr. who was appointed to take in a List of polls & taxable property for the year 1809 makes his Return to Court.

Ordered by the Court that Mary Holley an orphan girl now between seven & eight years old be bound as an apprentice to Rice Moore untill she shall arrive at the age of eighteen and Thomas Henderson Chairman of said Court and the said Rice Moore enters into indentures for that pur ese pursuant to act of Assembly.

The petition of sundry Inhabitants praying an order of Court for opening a road Beginning at the County Line & running up the Hickory Valley to the Road that leads from Bullers ferry was read, whereupon a majority of the acting Justices being present- It is ordered by the Court that Isaac Stanley, Seamore York, David Huddleston, Charles Hopper, Archibald Hopper, Joshua Oaks, James Jackson & Benjamin Huddleston be a Jury to view and lay out a road Beginning at the County Line and running up the hickory Valley the nearest and best way to intersect the road that leads from Bullers ferry and maketh report to next Court.

John Jones and Ruth Jones exhibit their petition to Court praying that Commissioners may be appointed to lay off the Dower of one third part of a tract of land containing 600 acres on the Southside of Holston River which Land is particularly Discribed in the copy of a Graint accompanying said petition to the widow of James Callison Deceased and afterwards that said Commissioners shall make pertition of the residue among the claimants thereto & named in said petition according to Law and said petition being read and it appearing to the satisfaction of the Court that notice had been given to the several Claimants od the time of filing said petition, whereupon the Court appoint Jeremiah Chamberlain -George Moody, Henry Mays, Sherod Mayes & Isaac Withhall Commiss ioners to lay off the dower & make partition agreeable to the prayer of said petition.

James Conn Esqr. collector of taxes for the County of Grainger reported to Court that the taxes Remained unpaid on the following tracts of Land for the year 1809 and that the overseer thereof have not Goods or chattels within his County on which he can distress(towit)

(p 267)   February Sessions A.D. 1809
Lewis Edwards, 250 acres - Richland Cu. taxes $1.24½ -
Clerk & Printers $2.35 - Total   ——— $3.59½
Bartholomew Smith 320 acres, Richland Knobs taxes $159
Clerk and Printers $2.35   total   ———$3.94
Geo. Combs - 120 acres taxes $0.58½ Clerk & printers -$2.35
Total $2.94½- William Watson 150 acres taxes $0.74½ - Clerk & Printers
$2.35 total $3.97½- John Burd 350 acres takes $1.74 - Clerk & printers
$2.35 total $4.9 - Zachariah Simmons 150 acres poor Valley taxes $0.74½
Clerk & printers $2.35 total $3.97½- Wm Smith 100 acres taxes $0.49½
Clerk & printers $2.35 total $2.84,7½ -Thomas Pannell - 1 lot in the town
of Rutledge taxes $0.75 - Clerk & printer $2.35 total $3.10 -Mathew Mc
Clane 130 acres taxes $0.65,7½- Clerk & printers $2.35 total $3.00,7½
Wm Barnet 188 acres taxes $0393,2½ - Clerk & printers $2.35 total $3.20,2½
John Crawford 500 acres taxes $2.40,7½ -Clerk & printers $2.35 total $4.83½

Therefore it is considered by the Court that Judgment be entered up against said tracts of Land for the taxes severally due thereon together with the costs and charges thereon respectively annexed and that the sd. tracts of Land be sold or so much of them Respectively as will be sufficient for the payment of the said taxes, costs and charges on the first Monday of July next and on the succeeding day unless said taxes costs and charges be previously satisfied and it is ordered by the Court that the Sheriff of Grainger County carry this Judgment into Execution according to Law.

Court adjourns till tomorrow morning 9 o'clock.

Thursday 23rd. February Court met according to adjournment. Justices present— Thomas Henderson, Isaiah Midkiff & Wm Parkinson.

Henry Hays comes into Court and has leave to record his mark as follows, towit— a smooth crop off each Ear and a slit in the right ear.

State   )
  vs   )
Elisha Bowman)   Justices present, Noah Jarnagin Philip Sigler —Isaiah Midkiff & Wm Parkison.
    Whereupon came a Jury, towit—

1— Duncan Carmichael   7— Nimrod Cyrus
2— Daniel Robison   8— Peter Lowe
3— Golder Davidson   9— Henry Howell
4— Joseph Rich   10—Wm Robison
5— William Cook   11—Thomas Jones
6— Thomas Sharp   12—William Hall

Who being elected tried and sworn well and truly to try and the truth to speak on the Issue of Traverse in this case do say they find the Defendant not Guilty in manner and form as he stands charged in the Bill of Indictment.
(p 268)   February Sessions A.D. 1800

Campbell Martin &c.   )
No. 527 vs   )
Caleb Reece & Thomas Reese)   Justices present, Philip Sigler, Isaiah Midkiff —Wm Clay —John Breeden & George Moody. Whereupon came a Jury, towit

1— Henry Hawkins   7— Stephen Shelton
2— John Thompson   8— Samuel Peery
3— Joshua Collins   9— James Peery
4— Wm Bowman   10— William Kirby
5— Nicholas Counts   11— William Dyer
6— Aaron Rooks   12— Pearson Barney

Who being elected tried and sworn well and truly to try and the truth to speak on the issue joined in this case do say the Defendants have not paid the Debt not paid in the Declaration mentioned as in pleading they have alledged and assess the plaintiffs Damages accationed by reason of the Detention thereof to nineteen dollars eighty five cents and one half of a cent besides their costs.

Edward Ross)
   vs)   Justices present, John Breeden, George Moody,& William
James Simpson)   Parkison - Whereupon came a Jury, towit- The same Jury
as in the last case No. 527- who being elected tried and sworn well and truly to try and the truth to speak on the issue joined in this case, do say
the Defendant hath not paid the debt in the Declaration mentioned as in
pleading he hath alledged but hath only paid fifty dollars and assess the
plaintiffs Damages occasioned by reason of the residue of said Debt to 3
Dollars & ninety cents besides his costs.

William Dyer)
   vs)
Wm Parkison)   Justices Present, Thos.Henderson, David McAnally's -Isaiah
Midkiff & Philip Sigler.

1- Duncan Carmichael   7- Nicholas Counts
2- Daniel Robison   8- Wm Solomon
3- Golder Davidson   9- Valentine Morgan
4- Joseph Rich   10-Wm Robison
5- Justice Hall   11-Thomas James
6- Thomas Sharp   12-William Hall

Who being elected tried and sworn well and truly to try and the truth
to speak on the issue the matter in controversy in this case do say they
find for the Defendant,

(p 269)   February Sessions A.D. 1809

John Bunch Sr. has leave to return a list of his taxable property for
the year A.D. 1809 as follows, towit- six negroes 570 acres of land & four
town Lots.
Court adjourns till tomorrow morning 9 o'clock.

Friday 24th February -Court met according to adjournment -Justice present - Thos.Henderson, Philip Sigler & John Breeden. The motion of Isaac
S.McMeans made on Monday to reconsider the motion of John Cocke relative
to the appointment of Wm Dyer Const. was taken up and after arguments heard
on both sides - It is ordered by the Court that the order resinding the appointment of Wm Dyer Const. be resinded & that he order appointing said Wm
Dyer a Constable be in full force and Virtue.

Denn on Demise of)
Campbell Martin &c)
  vs In Ejectment)   John Vinyard Special Bail of the Defendant brings
Samuel Clark)   him into open Court and surrenders him in open Court
in discharge of himself -Whereupon John Williams Atto. for plaintiff prays
him in custody of the Sheriff and said Defendant is ordered in custody of
the Sheriff. James Conn Sheriff reports to Court that he has put Samuel
Clark the defendant in prison.

Benjamin Yates)
No. 542 vs continued)   Justices present, Thos.Henderson, Chas.McAnally
John Norman)   John Breeden & George Moody, whereupon came a

Jury, towit,

1- Henry Hawkins
2- Daniel Robertson
3- Joseph Rich
4- William Cooke
5- John Thompson
6- Nicholas Counts

7- James Brown
8- Thomas James
9- Peter Haymond
10-John Vinyard
11-James Campbell
13-Francis Young

Who being elected tried and sworn well and truly to try and the truth to speak on the matter in dispute in this case do say they find for the defendants.

(p 270)　　　　February Sessions A.D. 1809

Little Berry Hedlock　　）
No. 546　vs Certiorari　） Justices present, Thos. Henderson, John Breeden
William Robertson　　　）　and Wm Parkerson. Whereupon came a Jury, towit
the same Jury as in the last case except Justice Hall in the room of James
Campbell & Samuel Clark in the room of Francis Young who being elected
tried and sworn well and truly to try & the truth to speak on the matter
in dispute in this case do say they find for the plaintiff and assess his
damages to two Dollars & costs.

By order of Court John Moore is appointed a Commissioner to settle
with the collector of Taxes of Grainger County & with the trustee of said
County and the said John Moore enters into bond in the sum of one hundred
Dollars and fines -John Cooke his security.

William Kirk　）
No. 552　vs ）　Justices present, Thos. Henderson, William Parkerson
Jesse Cheek ）　Isaiah Midkiff and George Moody. Whereupon came a jury
towit-

1- Duncan Carmichael
2- Golder Davidson
3- Joshua Collins
4- Wm Bowman
5- Joseph West
6- Valentine Morgan

7- Philip Long
8- Ambrose Yancey
9- Wm Robertson
10-John Hunter
11-John Boyd
12- James Simpson

Who being elected tried and sworn well and truly to try and the truth
to speak on the issue joined in this case do say the fine the defendant
hath not paid the debt in the declaration mentioned as in pleading he hath
alledged and assess the plaintiffs damages occasioned by reason of the detention thereof to eight dollars and seventy one cents besides his costs.

Robert McAry ）
No. 553　vs ）
William Hall (　Justices present Thomas Henderson, Isaiah Midkiff & Geo.
Moody- Whereupon came a Jury, towit- the same Jury as in the last case,
who being elected tried and sworn well and truly　(p 271)　　to try
& the truth to speak on the issue joined in this case do say the Defendant hath not paid the debt in the plaintiffs declaration mentioned as in
pleading he hath alledged and find for the plaintiff the debt in the declaration mentioned to be discharged by the payment of two hundred & four

dollars eight cents & one mill & costs.

Benjamin Yates)
No. 564   vs   )   Justices present, Thos.Henderson, whereupon came a Jury
John Norman   )   towit-

1- Henry Hawkins   7- James Brown
2- Daniel Robertson   8- Thomas James
3- Joseph Rich   9- Peter Harmock
4- William Cook   10-Martin Albert
5- John Thompson   11-Justice Hall
6- Nicholas Counts   12-Samuel Clark

Who being elected tried and sworn well and truly to try & the truth to
speak on the matter in dispute in this case do say they find for the plaintiff & assess his Damages to two Dollars thirty three and one third cents
and costs.

Benjamin Yates)
       vs   )   In this case Elisha Bowman who was summoned a witness
John Norman   )   on behalf of the plaintiff being solemnly called to
come into Court and give Evidence on behalf of said Plaintiff fails to appear it is therefore considered by the Court that the said Elisha Bowman
Do forfeit one hundred and twenty five dollars.

Peter Harmock)
    vs appeal)   Justices present, Thos.Henderson, Philip Sigler & John
Martin Morris)   Breeden, whereupon came a Jury, towit-

1- Henry Hawkins   7- James Brown
2- Daniel Robertson   8- Thomas Key
3- Joseph Rich   9- John Miller
4- Wm Cocke   10-Martin Albert
5- John Thomson   11-Justice Hall
6- Nicholas Counts   12-James Kennedy

Who being elected tried and sworn well and truly to try & the truth to
speak on the matter in dispute in this case do say they find for the plaintiff and assess his damages to nine dollars & costs.

(p 272)   February Sessions   A.D. 1809

By order of Court James Conn Sheriff was directed to let Jeremiah Midkiff one of the poor of this County to the person who would keep him for
the lowest sum, till the Term of this Court Reports to Court that Isaiah
Midkiff offered to keep the said Jeremiah till the next term of this Court
for fifty Dollars which is the lowest sum bidden.

James Conn Esqr. collector of Taxes for the year 1808 reported to Court
the following tracts of Land, as not having been given in as taxable property for the year 1808 and that the owners thereof hath no goods or chattels that he knows of within his County on which he can distress, towit-
Esa Johnston 550 acres Double tax $5.45 - Clerk and printers $2.35 total
$7.80 -James Cooper 150 acres Double tax $1.49,5 -Clerk & printers $2.35
total $3.84,5 -Heirs of James Callison Dec'd - 1175 acres Double tax

$11.68,7½ -Clerk & printers $2.35 total $14.3,7½, therefore it is consid-
ered by the Court that Judgment be entered up against said tracts of Land
for the taxes severally due thereon, together with the costs and charges
thereto respectively annexed and that the said tracts of Land be sold or
so much of them respectively as will be sufficient for the payment of the
said taxes costs and charges on the first Monday of July next & on the succeeding day unless said taxes, costs and charges be previously satisfied;
and it is ordered by the Court that the Sheriff of Grainger County carry
this Judgment into Execution according to Law.

A Bill of sale from Wm Peeters -Brullen Peeters was proven in open Court
by William Prat one of the subscribing witnesses thereto.

Court adjourns till Court in Course.
Thomas Henderson

(p 273)   May Sessions A.D. 1809
At a Court of Pleas & Quarter Sessions begun and holden for the County of Grainger at the Court House in Rutledge on the third Monday of May
A.D. 1809 and 15th of said month. Justices present, John Coake, Henry Boatman & Isaiah Midkiff.

James Conn Esqr. high Sheriff of said County make his return to Court
that he has executed the Venire Facias on the following persons Viz.

1- Abner Lowe cer.issd.
2- Richard Coats
3- Newberry James
4- John Kitchen
5- Abraham Pruit
6- John Dennis cer. Isd.
7- Major Lea cer.Isd.
8- Thomas Sharp cer.Isd.
9- Edward Churchman Isd.
10-Samuel McBee
11-Seamore York
12-Isaac Stanley (Exl. No.Sci.fa.)
13-Royal Jinnings
14-Henry Hipsher cer. Isd.
15-Henry Howell cer.Isd.
16-John Daniel
17- John Kidwell cer. Isd.
18- James Bowen
19- Henry Bowen
20- William Blair cer. Isd.
21- William Kirkham cer. Isd.
22- John Hoe
23- John Williams
24- Meredith Coffee
25- Moses Hodges
26- John Crow
27- Harmon Cox

29- Andrew Coffman
29- Henry Holston &
30- Isaiah Kidwell cer.Isd.

Out of which Venire facias the following persons were balloted a Grand
Jury to the present Term, towit-

1- Moses Hodges Foreman
2- James Bowen
3- Meredith Coffee
4- Henry Hipsher
5- Andrew Coffman
6- Richard Coats
7- Newberry James
8- Abraham Pruit
9- John Williams
10-John Kitchen
11-Henry Bowen
12-John Daniel
13-Samuel McBee
14-Seamore York &
15-Rial Jinnings

Who was sworn & charged by Thomas Dardis Esqr. Solicitor - Isaac Campbell sworn to attend the Grand Jury at the present Term.

Rebeccah Hall widow and relict of William Hall deceased comes into open
Court and relinquishes her right of Administration on the Estate of WmHall.
Order Issued for $3.00

Pearson Darney)
vs)
John Miller &) John Miller the Defendant in this case surrenders
Thomas Shooley) himself in open Court in discharge of his bail,
whereupon William Bowman undertake that the defendant John Miller will pay
the costs and condemnation in this case if the suit shall be determined
against him or surrender himself to prison for the same or that they will
do it for him.

(p 274)   May Sessions A.D. 1809

Ordered by the Court that the following tax be laid & collected for
the year 1809 (towit) 6 cents on each hundred acres of Land three cents
on each white poll for the support of the poor of this County.

Ordered by the Court that John Hodges be allowed the sum of six dollars for attending on & dressing the wounds of Benj. Davis one of the poor
of this County.

On motion of Robert Hall said Robert Hall & Philip Sigler Esqr. have
leave to administer on all and singular the Goods & chattels rights & credits of Wm Hall died intestate and said Robert Hall & Philip Sigler enter
into Bond in the sum of $12,000 with John Cocke, Wm McPhetridge, John Den-
nis & James Brown their securities for their faithful Administration &c.
Whereupon the said Robert Hall & Philip Sigler were qualified as Admrs.
and returned an inventory of said Estate and on motion it is ordered by
the Court that said Administrators have leave to sell said Estate.

Whereas the petition of John Jones and Ruth Jones was presented to
the last Term of this Court praying the Commissioners might be appointed
to lay off the Dower or one third part of a tract of Land containing six
hundred acres on the Southside of Holston River which land is particularly described in the copy of a Grant accompanying said petition to the
Widow of James Callison Dec'd and afterwards that said Commissioners
should make pertition of the residue among the Claimants thereto & named
in said petition according to Law and said petition being read and it appearing to the satisfaction of the Court that Notice had been given to
the several Claimants of the time of filing said petition -Whereupon the
Court appointed Jeremiah Chamberlain, George Moody, Henry Mays, Sherod
Mays & Isaac Mitchell Commissioners to lay off the Dower and make partition agreeably to the prayer of said petition and said Commissioners having
failed to make report to this Term, the Court reappoint said Commissioners
& direct a new Commission to Issue to them to lay off the dower or one third
part of said land to the Widow of said James Callison & afterwards to make
pertition of the residue among the several Claimants named in said petition
and make report of their proceeding to the next term of this Court according to Law.

(p 275)   May Sessions A.D. 1809
On motion the Court appoint Wm McPhetridge a Constable in Capt. William

McPhetridge's Company and the said William enters into Bond in the sum of five hundred dollars and Philip Sigler and Jeremiah Selvedge his securities and was qualified according to Law.

Ordered by the Court that Thomas Ogle be overseer of the road from opposite David Bunch to the Kentucky road and that he have the hands in the following bounds to mark under him Viz. from Clinch Mt. to Clinch River & below the Kentucky road, down to opposite Ralph Shelton's then across so as to include said Bunches and it is further ordered by the Court that David Watson overseer be released from working on that part of the road from David Bunches to the Kentuck road.

Ordered by the Court that Samuel West be overseer of the road in the room and place of James Grayson and that he have the same bounds for hands to work under him that said Grayson had. Copy order Issd.

Ordered by the Court a majority of the acting Justices being present, that Isaiah Midkiff Esqr. Geo.Taylor, Sherod Mays, Mose Hodges, Isaac Mitchell Edward Churchman Sr. Joseph Rich, Joseph Noe Sr. Henry Mays - Jos. Noe Jr. be a Jury to view lay out and mark a road agreeably to law from Blackwell's Branch where the river road crosses the same to James Richardsons on said road & make report to next Court. Copy order Issd.

The Jury appointed at last Court to view and lay out a road the nearest and best way from the present road leading down the valley of Clinch Mt. from a point at or near where Benj. Shaw formerly lived to the ford on Clinch river where Elijah Evans now lives made the following report to Court Viz. We the undersigned Jurors appointed to view and lay off a road the nearest and best way from where Benj. formerly lived to Clinch River report that they have viewed the road beginning at the present fork of the road near the clearing of Cooke & Jack thence with a road now cleared to Milcons field leaving the field on the left hand thence to where Elijah Evans now lives thence to the river bank, thence between the fence & river to Royal Jinnings horse pen on the Bank of the River Samuel X Dodson -Royal x Jinnings -Rubin Dalton, Edward McGinnis & Henry x Howell a majority of the acting Justices being present - it is ordered by the Court that the said Robert be confirmed & the said road be opened.

The petition of Alexander Blair was presented to Court stating that Thomas King the surveyor had committed error & mistake in making out a plot of a tract of Land Granted to him by the State of North Carolina by Grant No. 101 and dated 16th day of Nov. 1790 for 150 acres and praying that said error and mistake may be corrected and it appearing to the satisfaction of the Court that the persons having Lands as adjoining to said tract were duly notified of the time of filing said petition, it is ordered by the Court that said petition be received & filed.

(p 276)   May Sessions A.D. 1809

On motion of John Cocke Esqr. Jesse Riggs has leave to administer on all and singular the goods and chattles rights & credits of Fuller Grissum deceased- whereupon the said Jesse Riggs enters into Bond in the sum of $2000 with John Cocke & David Brown his securities and the said Jesse Riggs enters into Bond in the sum of $2000 with John Cocke & Daniel Brown his securities and the said Jesse Riggs is qualified as administrator.

On application Ruth Mitchell an orphan aged six years the 27th of Mar. 1809 is ordered to be bound by Indenture till she shall attain to the age of eighteen years to James Dyer Sr. whereupon William Hankins Chairman of the Court for the time being & the said James Dyer interchangeably sign Indentures in pursuance to said order.

James Dyer Esqr. one of Constables of this County presents his resignation of his office of Constables in writing to Court and it is Excepted by the Court.

Benjamin Nall for the use of)
Adam Lyttle   )
                vs   )   Robert Blair being summoned a Garnashee
Francis Mayberry   )   in this case declares on oath that he is
not now nor was not at the time he was summoned, indebted to Francis Mayberry in any sum whatever that he has not now nor had not at the time he was summoned any of the effects of said Francis Mayberry in this hands & that he does not know any person who is indebted to said Francis or has any of his effects in their hands.

Nancy Lively administratrix of William Lively Deceased to Court an account of the sales of said Estate.

Shedrick Williams has leave to return his list of taxable property for the year 1809 Viz. 179 acres of Land and one white poll.

George Brock has leave to return one white poll subject to taxation for the year 1809.

John Spencer by Samuel Bunch has leave to return his List of Taxable property for the year 1809 Viz. two lots in the town of Rutledge -No's not recollected.

Ordered by the Court that the Bounds of Jacob Showman overseer of the Valley road be so extended as to include Jacob Long, Geo.Bridget & James Brown to work under him on said road.   Issd.

Mathew Cyrus one of the Constables of this County presents his resignation of said office of Constable in writing to the Court and it is accepted by the Court.

Jonathan Woddle by Edward West has leave to return his taxable property for the year 1809, Viz. 200 acres of Land.

(p 277)   May Sessions A.D. 1809

Noble Keith has leave to return his taxable property for the year 1809 (towit) 100 acres of Land.

William Keith Ratnger of Grainger County makes his return to Court as follows Viz. A List of strays remaining on my books now proven away according to Law, John Crabb one saw and six pigs $1.60 David Ray one mare $10 —John McElhiney one heifer $5.00

Court adjourns till tomorrow morning 9 o'clock.
Tuesday 16th May 1809- Court met according to adjournment. Justices present, Henry Boatman, Joseph Cobb & Isaiah Midkiff.

State)
5F9 No. vs)
Andrew Seaholt) Justices present, Noah Jarnagin, Wm Clay & Wm Hankins
whereupon came a Jury, towit-

1- John Kidwell   7- John Humphreys
2- Henry Howell   8- John Harris
3- Joshua Kidwell   9- Thomas James
4- John Dennis   10-Alexander Hamilton
5- Abner Lowe   11-Francis Hunter &
6- Thomas Ray   12-James Lane

Who being elected tried and sworn well and truly to try and the truth to speak on the Issue of Traverse in this case the Jury having retired to consider of their Verdict returned to the Bar & not being able to agree on their Verdict – a mistrial is entered by consent.

Samuel Williams has leave to return the following taxable property for the year 1809 Viz. one white poll.

Willie Blount by John Williams Esqr. has leave to return his List of taxable property for the year 1809 Viz. 2300 acres of Land.

Mathew Campbell Executor of the Last will and testament of Joseph Douglass deceased returns to Court an account of the sales of the personal Estate of his testator.

State)
vs)
Samuel Bishop) John Churchman one of the Defendants security brings the Body of Samuel Bishop into Court & surrenders him in discharge of himself.

Benjamin David)
vs) Felps Reed appeared in open Court having been summoned
Wyatt Smith and)being duly sworn declares on oath that he is guilty, and justly indebted to Wyatt Smith on the 25th day of Decr. next the sum of two hundred dollars, deducting therefrom for three attachments that he has been garnisheed upon previous to the present – first James Conn against Wyatt Smith –Second Jesse Evans against West Smith –third Dudley Cox against Wyatt Smith and $12 to Thomas Dardis the precise amount of said several attachments he cannot at present state – but he is of opinion that the sum claimed by said Benj/ David towit, $83.33 1/3 yet remains due from him to said Wyatt Smith.

(p 278)   May Sessions A.D. 1809

A majority of the acting Justices being present it is ordered by the Court that Isaiah Midkiff be allowed the sum of fifty dollars in full compensation for keeping and maintaining Jeremiah Midkiff one of the poor of this County up to the present Term. Order Issd.

A majority of the acting Justices being present – it is ordered by the Court that Thomas Dardis Esqr. be allowed the sum of $25 for his Services as Solicitor from May term 1808 till the present Term. Order Issd.

A majority of the acting Justices being present – It is ordered by the Court that James Conn Sheriff be allowed the sum of $80 for his Ex Officio services from the May term 1808 till the present Term. Order Issued.

A majority of the acting Justices being present – It is ordered by the Court that John F.Jack Clerk be allowed the sum of fifty dollars for his Ex Officio services up to the present Term. Order Issd.

John Gaw)
  vs)
Thos.Henderson) The plaintiff John Gaw by Jacob Peck Esqr. his Atto.makes a motion to enter up a Judgment against James Conn Sheriff for failing to return an Execution agreeably to Law, which issued in favor of said John Gaw against Thomas Henderson for the sum of $33.60 and five mills and costs and after arguments of Counsel in support of said motion & in opposition to it was heard. It is considered by the Court that the plaintiff John Gaw take nothing by his motion.

A majority of the acting Justices being present, it is ordered by the Court that the Clerks –Solicitors & Sheriffs fees on State prosecutions where nolle prosequi's have been entered shall be paid out of any money in the County Treasury.

Court adjourns till tomorrow morning 9 o'clock.
             Wednesday 17th May Court met according to adjournment.
Justices present, Mathew Campbell, Henry Boatman & William Hankins.

Ordered by the Court that the following persons be appointed Jurors to attend the next Term of this Court Viz. Joseph Fields, George Morris, John Arwine,Jr. Peter Hunnock, Richard Shelton, David Counts, Elijah Clark Francis Daniel, Edward Daniel, Isaac Mitchell, Richard Thomson, Joseph Stubblefield, Stephen Johnston, Henry Holston, Peter Hamilton, John Vinyard Daniel Gowin, John Estis, Harmon Cox, John Hoe, John Crow, Joseph Yeaden, William Haynes,Daniel Taylor, Nicholas Counts, Henry Howell, Thomas Bunch Jeremiah Jarnagin and George Sparkman. Venire Issd.

(p 279)   May Sessions A.D. 1809

Ordered by the Court that Rial Jinnings be overseer of the Road from the place where Benj. Shaw formerly lived to Clinch river near said Jinnings Flat Landing and that he have the following Bounds for hands to work under him on said Road (towit) Between the Valley road and Clinch river from the line Dividing the Counties of Grainger & Puncheon Camp Creek and down the creek to the river and up the river to the County Line. Copy isd.

Ordered by the Court a majority of the acting Justices being present that John Moore , Chesley Jarnagin, & Samuel Bunch each be allowed the sum of two dollars per Day for each day they have attended as Commissioners to settle with the Sheriff & trustee of this County –towit, two days each for the year A.D. 1808. Issd. as to ad.Bunch & order Isd. in full.

Jesse Cheek by John Cocke his Atto. makes a motion to Court that he
have leave to keep a publick Ferry on his own Land on Clinch river in
Bristow's Bend.

George Evans by John Williams his Atto. makes a motion to Court that
he have leave to keep a public Ferry on his own Land on Clinch river in
Bristows Bend.

```
John Haley       )
558   vs         )
Thomas Breeden   )   Justices present, Wm Hankins, John Breeden, Mathew Camp-
bell -Noah Jarnagin & James Brown - Whereupon came a Jury, towit,
```

```
1- Thomas Sharp          7- Thomas Jones
2- Edward Churchman       8- Nicholas Kearnes
3- William Blair          9- Samuel Peery
4- William Kirkham        10-Peter Hammock
5- John Dennis            11-Lemuel Branson &
6- John Fuller            12-John Hance
```

Who being elected tried and sworn well and truly to try and the truth
to speak on the Issue joined in this case do say the Defendant did assume
in manner and form as the plaintiff in his declaration hath complained
against him and assess the Plaintiffs Damages occasioned by reason of the
non performance three dollars and fifty cents & costs -Rule for a new trial
after arguments heard -Rule discharged.

On motion the Grand Jury are discharged from further attendance at the
present Term.

```
Samuel Shipley    )
511   vs          )
William Robertson )   Justices present, Viz. Wm Hankins, Wm Parkison, Ma-
thew Campbell, Wm Clay & Noah Jarnagin- Whereupon came a Jury, towit-
```

(p 330)   May Sessions A.D. 1800

```
1- John Bidwell          7- John Haley
2- Henry Howell          8- John Green
3- Josiah Bidwell        9- Jesse Cheek
4- Major Lea             10-Edmund Strange
5- Joseph Long           11-Joel West
6- David Bunch           12-William Kirk
```

Who being elected tried and sworn well and truly to try & the truth
to speak in the Matter in dispute in this case do say they find for the
Defendant.

```
Edward Ross      )
529   vs         )
James Simpson    )   Justices present, John Breeden, David Tate & William
Parkison, whereupon came a Jury, towit- the same Jury as in the last Case
of No. 511 except Aaron Peeks, in the room of Joseph Long who being elect-
ed tried and sworn well and truly to try and the truth to speak in the
```

matter in dispute in this case do say they find the defendant hath not
paid the debt in the diclaration mentioned as he hath in pleading alledged
but hath only paid $25 - they further find for the plaintiff sixty dollars
Debt & assess the plaintiffs damages occasioned by reason of the detention
thereof to six dollars seventy seven & one fourth cents besides his costs.

Luke Lea   )
   vs.   )
Jesse Riggs   )   John Buller & Caleb Howell came into Court and undertake
that if the defendant shall be cast in the suit that he will pay the costs
& condemnation or that they will do it for him.

     William Kirkham by John Moffit Esqr. has leave to return his list of
Taxable property for the year 1809 Viz. 200 acres of Land and one white
poll.

(p 281)   May Sessions A.D. 1809
     The Jury appointed at the Last term of this Court to view the road
leaving the Kentucky road at the mouth of Shelton's Branch to the County
Line at Bristow's Bend &c -Have made a report to the Court as follows-
towit,   State of Tennessee)
     Grainger County   ) We the Jurors appointed by Court have
viewed the road leaving the Kentucky road at the mouth of Shelton's
Branch to the County Line at Bristow's Bend & also we have viewed the present Kentucky road from the same point at the mouth of Shelson's branch
to the County Line at Evans Ferry and went on to comply with the request
of the Worshipful Court, and we the aforesaid Jurors were duly sworn and
do report to the next Worshipful Court as follows, towit, that the road
leaving the Kentucky road at the mouth of Shelton's road branch to the
County Line at Bristows Bend is the levelest easiest and best way for Car-
riages and passengers to pass along & it is our judgment will be of the
most publick utility altho, some the farthest the advantages attending the
aforesaid Kentucky road by our judgment is that it is some the nearest and
the water at the flat landing is some the the Eddies; the disadvantages
attending said Kentucky road is the river hill and Raven hill on the North
side of the river Clinch - the advantages attending the other road leading from the mouth of Sheltons branch crossing at Bristows Bend is that
the aforesaid river hill is not near as bad and misses the said Raven hill
Given under our hands this 6th of May 1809 -N.B. We could not examine the
fords at the crossing of the aforesaid roads the river being high and mud-
dy - James Carmichael - Thomas Johnston- Isaac Mitchell, Chesley Jarnagin
Henry Hays, John Betis, Henry Howell, and Nicholas Counts, a majority of
the acting Justices present - It is ordered by the Court that the aforesaid
report be confirmed.

     Ordered by the Court that Jesse Cheek Sr. be overseer of the new road
from the mouth of Sheltons Branch at the present Kentucky road to the County
Line at Bristows Bend as viewed and laid out by the Jury, and that he open
and clear the same according to Law and the said Jesse Cheek's own hands
are assigned him, to work under him on said road.

     Ordered by the Court that Robert D.Eaton be overseer of the road from
the top of Clinch Mt. at the Fowler Spring Gap to Crows old place in the
Richland Knobs at the Owl Hole Gap in place of Samuel Peery and that he have
the same Bounds for hands that said Peery had to work under him except

Jacob Long, George Bridget, and James Brown and it is further ordered by the Court that the said Robert D. Eaton be authorized to draw the sum of seven dollars from the County Treasury for the purpose of purchasing a sledge hammer and crow bar to be used on public roads, which sums had been appropriated to said Samuel Peery at August Sessions 1808-for the aforesaid purpose and never drawn from the Treasury.

(p 282)   May Sessions A.D. 1809

Pearson Barney)
    vs   )
John Miller) Gabriel Fry who was subpoened to give Evidence on behalf of Pearson Barney in this case being solemnly called, failed to appear; It is therefore considered by the Court that he do forfeit $125 according to Act of Assembly.

        Ordered by the Court that Allen McElhaney an orphan child now of the age of eight years and thirty five days be bound by Indenture to James Bowen untill he shall attain the age of twenty one years, whereupon Thomas Henderson Esqr. Chairman of the Court & the said James Bowen interchangeably enter into Indentures according to Law.

        Court adjourns till tomorrow morning 9 o'clock.

        Thursday May 18th --Court met according to adjournment- Justices present, Isaiah Sidwell, Mathew Campbell and Joseph Cobb.

John Smith   )
    vs   )
William Smith)   Justices present, Joseph Cobb, Wm Clay & Mathew Campbell.
        Whereupon came a Jury, towit--

1- John Fidwell   7- John Miller
2- Henry Howell   8- Nicholas Counts
3- Josiah Fidwell   9- Jesse Neal
4- Abner Lowe   10-Aquilla James
5- John Dennis   11-Jesse Riggs
6- Samuel Clark   12-Richard Drwville

        Who being elected tried and sworn well and truly to Enquire what Damages John Smith hath sustained &c. Do say the plaintiff hath sustained Damages to the amount of Twenty Dollars besides his costs.

George Payne for the use of)
Wm B. King   )
No. 544   vs   )
James Kennedy   )   In this case James Kennedy the Defendant by John Williams Esqr. his Atto. at November Term 1808 filed a plea of abatement to the writ of the plaintiff in this case and afterwards, towit-at May term 1809 the plaintiff by John Cocke Esqr. his Atto. files his Demurer to the aforesaid plea of said Defendant & afterwards -towit- at the same term the said Defendant James by John Williams Esqr. his Atto. files his Joinder to said Demurer and afterwards, now here at the same term after Solemon argument being heard as well on the part of the said plaintiff as on

behalf of said Defendant.

(p 283)   It is therefore considered by the Court that said Demurrer be sustained and that the Defendant James answer over to the Declaration of the said plaintiff.

Campbell Martin &c.   )
        vs   )
Caleb Reece & Thomas Reece)   In this case Henry Boatman Esqr. one of the securities of Thomas Reece Sr. one of the Defendants in this case brings the body of said Thomas Reece into Court & surrenders him in discharge of himself and the other security, whereupon Charles F.Keith Atto. for the plaintiffs prays the said Thomas Reece in Custody of the Sheriff and the said Thomas is ordered by the Court to be in custody of the Sheriff, and afterwards James Conn Sheriff Reports to Court that he has deposited the body of said Thomas Reece in the County Jail.

John Hembeck Burd by Mary Burd has leave to return his list of taxable property for the year A.D. 1809 towit- 100 acres of Land.

On application the Petit Jury are discharged from further attendance at the present term.

Jeremiah Selvage   )
        vs   )
Philip Oxford   )   The defendant Philip Oxford presents his petition to Court praying that writs of Certiorari & Super cedeas may issue &c said petition being read after arguments of Council heard as well in favor of the prayer of the petition as against it, it is ordered by the Court that writs of Certiorari & Supercedeas do issue agreeably to the prayer of said petition he complying with the Law.

Mathew Reddin   )
        vs   )
Isaiah McTaff   )
Wm Payl & Caleb Howell   )   The petition of Isaiah McTaff one of the defendants in this case is presented to the Court praying that a writ of Certiorari may issue directed to John Moffitt Esqr. requiring him to transmit inclosed under his hand and seal the papers and proceeding in this case to the next term of this Court and also a writ of Supercedeas directing the Sheriff -Coroner and all other officers, directing them to desist from all other and further proceedings in this case untill a decision can be had thereon in this Court, whereupon after arguments heard thereon it is ordered that writs of Certiorari & Supercedeas issue agreeably to the prayer of said petition agreeably to Law.

James Conn Sheriff, reports to Court that the County Jail is totally insufficient for the safe keeping of prisoners deposited therein by him; he therefore enters his protest against said Jail & prays that the same may be entered of record; and the Court direct the same to be entered of Record.

Court adjourns till Court in Course.

                                    Isaiah McTaff -Chairman

(p 284)   August Sessions A.D. 1809

At a Court of Pleas & Quarter Sessions begun and holden for the County of Grainger at the Court house in Rutledge on the third Monday of August A.D. 1809 and 21st. of said month- Present, Thomas Henderson, David Tate & William Davidson Esquires.

James Conn Esqr. high Sheriff of said County makes his return to Court that he has executed the Venire Facias on the following persons, towit-

1- Joseph Fields	17- Daniel Gowen
2- George Morris	18- John Eatis
3- John Arwine Jr.	19- Harmon Cox
4- Peter Harrock	20- John Noe
5- Richard Shelton	21- John Crow
6- David Counts	22- Jos. Yeaden
7- Elijah Clark	23- Wm Haynes
8- Francis Daniel	24- Daniel Taylor
9- Isaac Mitchell	25- Nicholas Counts
10-Edward Daniel	26- Henry Howell
11-Richard Thomson	27- Thomas Bunch
12-Jos. Stubblefield	28- Jeremiah Jarnagin
13-Stephen Johnston	29- George Sparkman
14- Henry Holston	
15- Peter Hamilton	
16-John Vinyard	

Out of which Venire Facias the following persons were balloted a grand jury, to the present term, towit-

1- Peter Hamilton	9- John Noe
2- Richard Thompson	10-Wm Haynes
3- George Sparkman	11-Francis Daniel
4- Jeremiah Jarnagin	12-Richard Shelton
5- David Counts	13-Joseph Fields
6- Edward Daniel	14-Daniel Gowen &
7- Elijah Clark	15-Henry Holston
8- Henry Howell	

and the said grand jury are sworn according to law. It appearing to the satisfaction of the Court that Thomas Dardis Esqr. Sl. is rendered unable to attend the present term in consequence of indisposition - it is ordered by the Court that Wm Kelly be appointed Sol. for the present term, where-upon the said Wm Kelly charges the grand jury.

Isaac Campbell- Deputy Sheriff attends on the Grand Jury at the present Term.

On motion the Court appoints Charles Hutcheson, Philip Sigler and James Brown Esqires to settle with Jane Clark Administratrix & Edward Clark Admr. of Samuel Clark Dec'd and make return to next Court.

James)
vs)   Thomas Henderson being summoned a Garnashee on an Execution
John Gaw)   in this case appeared in open   (p 285)   Court and being sworn deposeth & said that he is indebted to the defendant John Gaw in the sum of thirty three dollars - It is therefore considered by the Court that the plaintiff Do recover of the Defendant the amount of the costs demanded in the Execution aforesaid -towit- sum of $3.90 together with the costs of this case.

James Simmons being charged on the tax Lists for the year 1809 with the tax due on fofty acres of Land; and it appearing to the satisfaction of the Court that said Simmons does not own any Land in this County. It is therefore ordered by the Court that he be released from the payment of six and one fourth cents being the Tax due the State on 50 acres of Land and also from the payment of $6¼ the County tax from 6¼¢ the Jury tax and the sum of three cents the poor tax & it is further ordered by the Court that James Conn Sheriff & collector of Taxes be released from the collecting & payment of the aforesaid sum & that he have a credit for the same on the settlement of his accounts with the Treasury of Washington & Hamilton District & the County trustee respectively for the sum due them respectively.

Ordered by the Court that the bounds of the road formerly allotted to Joseph Bryant from the County Line down to John Crabbs be continued down to John Crabbs be continued down to a white oak with three forks from one root near the forks of Austons old road the same hands to be continued to him as at present and that Richard Rose work hereafter from that place to Beans Station in the room of state of Capt. Stephen Senter & that he have the same hands and the same bounds allotted him for hands to work on said road that said Senter had. Order Issued.

Ordered by the Court that Henry Boyers be appointed overseer of the road leading from Peter Beelors old mill to the ford of flat creek at Williams Malls meeting house in the room & place of Stephen Goard and that he be allowed the same bounds for hands that Stephen Goard was allowed. Order Issued.

William Parkison has leave to return his lists of taxable property for the year 1809, towit- one free poll.

Francis Willett being charged on the tax lists for the year 1809 with the tax lists for 200 acres of land and it appearing to the satisfaction of the Court that Jonathan Waddle is charged on the tax Lists for the year 1809 for the same tract of Land; it is therefore ordered by the Court that the said Francis Willett be released from the payment of 25 cents being the tax due the State on the said tract of land & also for the payment of 63 cents being the tax due the County- it is further ordered that James Conn Sheriff & collector of taxes be released from the collecting & payment of the aforesaid sums and that he have a credit for the sum of 25 cents being the tax due the state on said tract of Land in this settlement with the Treasurer of the district of Washington and Hamilton & that he have a credit for the sum of 63 cents being the tax due the County on said tract of land in his settlement with the County Trustee.

(p 286)   August Sessions A.D. 1809

Ordered by the Court that James Brown & George Bridget be added to the list of hands to work under Robert D. Eaton overseer of the road from the top of Clinch Mountain at the Powder Spring Gap to Crows old place in the Richland Knobs and it is ordered that the said James Brown & George Bridget do work under said Robert D. Eaton on said road.

Ordered by the Court that Wm Parkinson & David Tate –Henry Howell & George Moody Esquires attend the next term of the Superior Court for Hamilton District as Jurors. Order Issued.

On motion the Court appoint Wm Clay -Noah Jarnagin and James Moore Esquires Commissioners to settle with John Conley Admr. and Nancy Miller Administratrix of George Miller deceased & make report to the present Term.

A commission was produced to Court signed by the Excellency John Sevier with the great seal of the State annexed appointing Thomas Brown and other Justices of the peace for this County - whereupon the Thomas Brown appeared in open Court and took an oath to support the Constitution of the United States & also to support the Constitution of the State of Tennessee and also the oath of office as prescribed by Law.

Ordered by the Court that John Beelor be appointed overseer of the road from John Petrees to Josiah Maples in the room of John Arwine and the said John Beelor be allowed the same bounds for hands and the same hands that the said John Arwine had. Order Issd.

Ordered by the Court that Josiah Dunlap be overseer of the river road from Buffalow Creek to the top of Indian Ridge in the room of Jacob Arnett and that all the hands between the said creek & ridge from the River including Evan Harris plantation and Isaac Thompson thence a direct course including Jacob Arnetts work under said Joseph Dunlap on said road.
                                        Order Issued.
Ordered by the Court that James Elkins be overseer of the road as confirmed by the Court from Coxes old place to the Knox County line in the room of Robert Blair and that he have the same bounds for hands that said Blair had to work under him on said Road.   Order Issd.

Ordered by the Court that Robert Fields be appointed overseer of the road from the forks of the road at the Powder Spring Gap to the top of Copper ridge in the room of Wm McPhetridge former overseer & that the sd.Fields be allowed the same bounds for hands that McPhetridge had & that such alterations be made as the Jury laid off.

(p 287)   August Sessions A.D. 1809

Ordered by the Court that Talley. be overseer of the road from Jacob Weaver to the Island Ford on Clinch river in the room of Edward Breeden and that he have the same hands & the same bounds for hands to work under him on said road that said Breeden had. Order Issd.

A Bill of sale from David Abernathy to Sethe McKinney for a negro wench was proven in open Court by the oath of Sparks Moore a subscribing witness.

Ordered by the Court that the following persons be appointed Jurors to attend the next Term of this Court & that a Venire facias do issue to the Sheriff to summon them Viz. James Carmichael, Duncan Carmichael, Jos. Rich, Isaac Stanley, Thomas Lay, Edward Churchman, Solomon Massengill, James Richison, John Arwine,Jr. Peter Harrock, Daniel Chanler, Edward Breeden -Miller Easley, Thomas Bunch, Jonathan Hunpower, Hackness Moore, Henry Hays, Sherod Mays, Henry Howell, John Minet, Joel Perrin, Wm Snodgrass, Joseph Long, Abner Lowe, Aquilla Jones, Stephen Senter, Wm Blair, Wm Kirkham, Alex. Thompson & David Holt. Venire facias.

Jesse Cheek by John Cocke Esqr. his Atto. reviews his motion of Last

Term that he may have leave to keep a Publick Ferry on his own Land, on Clinch river in Bristows Bend.

William Kelly Esqr. produced to Court a License signed by two of the Judges of the Superior Court of Law and Equity authirizing him to practice Law as an Attorney in the several Courts of Law and Equity in this State and the said Wm Kelly took an oath to support the Constitution of the United States, an oath to support the Constitution of this State and also the oaths of an Attorney and is admitted as an Attorney in this Court.

Court adjourns till tomorrow morning 9 o'clock.

Tuesday morning 22nd. August 1809 -Court met according to adjournment. Present, Thomas Henderson, David Tate, John Breeden, Joseph Brown and Chas. Hutchison Esquires.

State)
558 vs) John Churchman Special Bail of the Defendant surrenders
Samuel Bishop) him in open Court in discharge of himself whereupon
Wm Kelly Solicitor for the County prays him in custody of the Sheriff and the County order him in custody of the Sheriff.

State)
 vs)
Samuel Bishop) Justice present, Wm Clay, Noah Jarnagin, Philip Sigler
Charles Hutchison, Thomas Brown, John Breeden, Wm Parkinson, David Tate
Mathew Campbell & Joseph Cobb.

(p 208) August Sessions A.D. 1809
Whereupon came a Jury, towit-

1- Thomas Bunch   7- David Tate Jr.
2- John Vinyard   8- William Hall
3- Nicholas Counts   9- Wm Hammer
4- Joseph Noe Jr.   10-Thomas Ray
5- John Allison   11-Thomas Ray
6- John McBroom   12-Edward Tate

Who being elected tried and sworn well and truly to try and the truth to speak on the Issue of Traverse joined in this case and the Jury having retired from the bar to consider of their Verdict and afterwards the Jury returned to the bar and being asked if they had agreed on their verdict answered they had not, nor could not agree in their verdict, whereupon a mistrial is ordered to be entered by consent of Council.

State)
559 vs)
Andrew Seabolt) Justices present, James Moore, Mathew Campbell, Charles
Hutchison, William Parkinson, John Breeden, Philip Sigler, Moses Hodges,
Noah Jarnagin & Wm Clay, whereupon came a Jury, towit-

1- Joseph Yeaden - 2- Isaac Mitchell- 3- Wm Copeland- 4- Thomas Sharp
5- Gibbons Cross - 6- Wm Bowman- 7- Samuel Williams- 8- Thomas Turley
9- James Harris - 10-Jacob Noe- 11-Wm Bryant -Welcome Hodges - who being
elected tried and sworn well and truly to try and the truth to speak

on the issue of traverse in this case do say they find the defendant not guilty in manner and form as he stands charged in the Bill of Indictment on motion -Rule to shew cause why the prosecutor should be taxed with the costs on motion -Rule to shew cause why the defendant should be taxed with the costs.

Ordered by the Court a majority of the acting Justices being present that Isaiah Midkiff be allowed the sum of $25 for keeping and maintaining Jeremiah Midkiff one of the poor of this County from the May term 1809 till the present Term.

John Green   )
    vs   )
John Midkiff)   Wm Bowman being summoned a garnashee in the case appeared in open Court and being sworn deposeth and saith that heretofore he gave his note to John Midkiff for $300 to be discharged in horses on the first day of November next, the horses to be vallued equal to second rate cows & colves at ten dollars apiece before he was summoned as garnashee.

(p 289)   August Sessions A.$^{D.}$ 1809
He heard that said Note was assigned that since he was summoned as aforesaid he saw the said Note with an assignment indorsed thereon - It is therefore considered by the Court that so much of the aforesaid debt be condemned in the hands of the aforesaid Wm Bowman as will be sufficient to satisfy the Demand of said John Green.

Ordered by the Court that Wm Whiteside overseer of the road from Beans Station to Sheltons ford be allowed the sum of seven dollars for the purpose of purchasing a sledge hammer and crow bar for the use of the County to be used on that part of the road over which he is overseer to be paid out of any money in the County treasury not otherwise appropriated. Copy Isd.

Philip Sigler one of the Administrators of the Estate of Wm Nall Dec'd returns to Court an account of the sales of said Estate.

Gibbons Cross one of the Constables of this County presents to Court his resignation of the Office of constables which is received by the Court.

John Gaw   )
    vs   )
James Conn Sheriff)   The plaintiff in this case by Jacob Peck Esqr. his Atto. makes a motion to Court to enter up a judgment against James Conn for failing to return an execution issued by Thomas Henderson Esqr. in favor of said John Gaw against Thomas Henderson for the sum of $33.60,5 and costs, whereupon after hearing arguments - It is considered by the Court that said Plaintiff take nothing by his said motion, and that sd. Defendant recover of said Plaintiff his costs in and about defending said motion in that behalf expended &c.

On application the Court appoint Meredith Coffee Guardian of Sarah Miller one of the monor heirs of George Miller Dec'd in the room and stead of Thomas Carney and the said Meredith Coffee enters into Bond in the sum of two hundred and fifty dollars with James Conn his security whereupon the said Thomas Harvey is released by the Court from his guardianship.

Ordered by the Court that Isaac Campbell be appointed one of the Constables of this County and he enters into bond in the sum of $500 with Mathew Campbell and John Sharp his securities whereupon the said Isaac Campbell took an oath to support the Constitution of the United States and an oath to support the Constitution of the State of Tennessee and also the oath of office.

(p 290)   August Sessions A.D. 1809

Ordered by the Court that Wm Hutchison be appointed one of the Constables of this County and he enters into Bond in the sum of $500 with Obediah Waters and Daniel Gowing his securities whereupon the said Wm Hutchison took an oath to support the Constitution of the United States and an oath to support the Constitution of the State of Tennessee and also the oath of office.

Ordered by the Court that Richard Coats be overseer of Benj. Jarnagin from the first Big Spring above Chesley Jarnagins to the first hollow below Robert D. Eatons and that he have the same bounds for hands that said Jarnagin had.   Order Issd.

Ordered by the Court that Richard Sheltons be overseer of the road leading from Sheltons ford to the top of the ridge where Henry Boatman formerly lived and all the hands that lives in the following bounds do work under him on said road, that is to say, Beginning at a stake on the bank of Holston river, on the Southside corner to Abraham Wilsons bounds thence down the meanders of said river, to the lower end of James Carmichaels Land thence to the top of Boatmans ridge so as to include all the hands from Ambrose Hodges up thence a straight line to the Beginning in the room of Joseph Noe Jr.

State   )
  vs   )
Andrew Seabolt)   Edward Davidson who was summoned a witness in this case to give evidence on behalf of the State the cause being under examination being solemnly called to come into Court and give Evidence agreeable to the tenor of his Subpoena altogether failed to appear. It is therefore considered by the Court that the said Edward Davidson to forfeit $250 according to Act of Assembly.

Court adjourns till tomorrow morning 9 o'clock.

Wednesday morning 23rd. August Court met according to adjournment. Present, Thomas Henderson, Moses Hodges, Henry Boatman & George Moody.

Pearson Barney)
530 vs   )
John Miller   )   Present, Thomas Henderson, Moses Hodges, Peter Harris Wm Parkinson, Isaiah Midkiff & George Moody, Esquires. Whereupon came a Jury, towit-
1- Thomas Bunch   5- Wm Hamilton   9- Robert Chandler
2- John Vinyard   6- Wm Harris   10-Samuel McBee
3- Nicholas Counts   7- Charles Matlock 11-Joseph Buller
4- Alex.Hamilton   8- Ambrose Yancey   12-Richard Durville

(p 291

Who being elected tried and sworn well and truly to try and the truth to speak on the issue joined in this case do say the Defendant did and after examining witnesses as well on behalf of plaintiff as Defendant.

John Cooke Esqr. Atto. for plaintiff directs a non suit to be entered.

William Widdiff Assignee &c for the use of John Cocke and Henry Howell Revived in the name of Abel Pursell Adnr. of Wm Widdiff Dec'd
vs
Benjamin Hudson
Present, Thomas Henderson, Charles McAnelly & Wm Parkerson Esquires.

1- Thomas Bunch	7- Wm Hamilton
2- John Vinyard	8- Ambrose Yancey
3- Nicholas Counts	9- Robert Chandler
4- Alex. Hamilton	10-Samuel McBee
5- Thomas James	11-Joseph Beeler
6- Charles Matlock	12-Richard Durville

Who being elected tried and sworn well and truly to try and the truth to speak on the issue joined in this case to say the Defendant hath not performed his Covenant as in pleading he hath alledged and assess the plaintiffs Damages occasioned by reason of the non performance thereof to four hundred and ninety one dollars thirty three cents & one third of a cent, and costs.

A Commission was produced to Court signed by his Excellency John Sevier with the great seal of the State annexed appointing Moses Hodge a Justice of the piece for the County, whereupon the said Moses Hodge appeared in Court and took an oath to support the Constitution of the United States an oath to support the Constitution of the State of Tennessee and also the oath of office as prescribed by Law.

William Keith ranger returns to Court a list of strays remaining on his Books & not proven away according to Law, towit- George Moody Esqr. one horse $60- George Moody Esqr. $40.

Ordered by the Court that Samuel Dunlap be released from the payment of a poll tax for the year 1809, he having paid a poll tax in Knox County for the present term, and it is ordered by the Court that James Conn Sheriff & collector of taxes for this County be allowed a credit for the amt. of the same in his settlement with the Trustees of the District of Washington & Hamilton & also with the County Trustee for the sum due then respectively for said poll. Order Issued.

(p 292)   August Sessions A.D. 1809

William Clay -Noah Jarnagin & James Moore Esquires Commissioners who were appointed to settle with John Conley Adnr. of George Miller Dec'd make their report to Court, shewing a balance of $485.99½ due from said Adnr.& and Administratrix to the heirs of said Dec'd which report is received confirmed by the Court and ordered to be recorded.

Ordered by the Court that Elisha Bowman Constable be allowed the sum of four dollars for attending on the Grand Jury four days at August term 1808 agreeably to the order of Court.

Jesse Riggs Administratrix of the Estate of Fuller Grisham deceased returns to Court Admr. of the Estate of said deceased.

The petition of Alex. Blair which was filed last Term & set for hearing at the present Term setting for that Thomas King the Surveyor made a mistake in making out the plat courses & distance of a tract of Land granted to the said Alex.Blair for one hundred & fifty acres of Land by the State of North Carolina by Grant No. 101 and dated the 16th day of Nov. 1790 was taken up heard and examined and it appearing to the satisfaction to the Court, that the Surveyor hath committed error and mistake asset forth in said petition &c. It is therefore ordered and adjudged by the Court that the Clerk Do certify to the security of the State the said Error and mistake that the same may be corrected, agreeably to Law.

Jesse Cheek by John Cocke his Atto. present, Thomas Henderson, Moses Hodge, Wm Clay, David McAnally -Charles McAnally -David Tate, Peter Harris Isaiah Midkiff, John Moffitt, George Moody, Henry Boatman & Wm Parkerson Esqrs. that he have leave to keep a public ferry on his own Land on Clinch River in the Bristows Bend.

George Evans by John Williams his Atto. present, Thomas Henderson, Moses Hodge, Wm Clay, David McAnally, David Tate, Peter Harris, Isaiah Midkiff, John Moffett, George Moody, Henry Boatman, & Wm Parkerson, Esqrs. that he have leave to keep a public ferry on his own Land on Clinch river in Bristows Bend. Present, the above named Justices and arguments heard on the above motions- It is ordered by the Court that George Evans have leave to keep a public Ferry on his own Land on the Southside of Clinch river in the place called and known by the name of Bristows Bend at the place where the new road crosses said River,

(p 293)   August Sessions A.D. 1809
which Judgment the said Jesse Cheek prays an appeal to the next term of the Superior Court to be held in the Court House in Knoxville on the fourth Monday of September next for the District of Hamilton and the said Jesse Cheek enters into Bond with John Cocke & Stephen Shelton his securities for the prosecution of said appeal granted- reasons filed and appeal granted.
        Court adjourns till tomorrow morning 9 o'clock.

Thursday 24th August 1809- Court met according to adjournment. Present, David McAnally, Peter Harris & Henry Boatman, Esquires.

Campbell Martin &c.   )
556   vs   )   Present, Peter Harris, George Moody,
Gidion Morris & John Chowly)   David McAnally, Henry Boatman, John
James Moore   )   Moffitt, Charles McAnally,

Whereupon came a Jury, towit-

1- Thomas Bunch   6- Robert Winslow
2- John Vinyard   7- Edward Churchman
3- Nicholas Counts   8- Thomas James   11-Wm Davidson
4- Thomas Sharp   9- Samuel McBee   12-George Evans
5- Joel Perrin   10-Jesse Cheek

Who being elected tried & sworn well & truly to try and the truth to speak on the issue joined in this case do say the defendant have not paid the debt in the Declaration mentioned as in pleading they have alledged & assess the plaintiffs Damages occationed by reason of the detention thereof to seven & seventy two cents & costs. It is therefore considered by the Court that the said plaintiff.

Campbell & Martin surviving partners &c &c7 vs Edward Churchman and Joel Perrin	Present, James Moore, Peter Harris, Henry Bowman & James Brown Esquires.

1- Thomas Bunch
2- Joel Hammer
3- Nicholas Counts
4- James Campbell
5- Valentine Morgan
6- Robert Winslow

7- David McAnnlly Jr.
8- Thomas James
9- Samuel McBee
10- Jesse Cheek
11- Th Davidson
12- George Evans

Who being elected tried and sworn well and truly to try and the truth to speak on the issue joined in this case do say the Defendants are not guilty in manner & form as the plaintiffs in their declaration have complained against them.

Ordered by the Court that George Brock be overseer of the road in the room of John Arwine and that the bounds of said George Brock be so altered as to allow Joseph Mellor and John Petree on his part of the road and that said Brock shall have all the other hands in the bounds that were allowed said John Arwine.

(p 284) August Sessions A.D. 1809

On application the Grand Jury are discharged from further attendance at the present term.

Isaac Campbell Deputy Sheriff made oath in open Court that he has attended the Grand Jury four days at the present term for which he is authorized to receive four dollars agreeably to a former order.

On application James Kennedy has leave to keep an ordinary or house of public intertainment at Booms Station and the said James Kennedy enters into Bond in the sum of one thousand dollars with John Boyd his security.

On argument- It is ordered by the Court that the appeal prayed for yesterday by Jesse Cheek from the order of Court. Granting George Evans a ferry on the Southside of Bristows Bend and granted -Shall be disallowed.

Benjamin Davis vs Wyatt Smith	Present, James Moore, George Moody, James Brown, & Henry Bentman, Esquires. Whereupon came a Jury, towit-

1- Joseph Yeaden - 2- Isaac Mitchell- 3- Jas.Simpson- 4-Richard Dunville

Ambrose Yancey   7- Dudley Cox   10-Thos.Whiteside
David Counts   8- Wm Copeland   11-Edward Churchman
                   9- Nicholas Counts12-Henry Howell

Who being elected tried and sworn well and truly to inquire what Damages the plaintiff has sustained in this case do say the plaintiffs hath sustained damages to the amount of fifty dollars & costs.

George Evans who had leave to keep a public ferry on the Southside of Clinch river in Bristows Bend where the new road crosses the said river comes into Court and enters into Bond with John Moffitt & Felps Reed his securities according to Law, whereupon it is ordered by the Court that Geo. Evans shall receive the following toll at his new ferry in Bristows Bend, towit, for each wagon & team seventy five cents - for each cart and horse 37½¢ for each gig & horse 50¢ for each four wheeled pleasure Carriage $1.00 for each footman 6¼¢ for each man & horse 12½¢ for each loose horse 6¼¢ for each head of cattle two cents - for each head of hoggs or sheep 2 cents.

(p 295)   August Term A.D. 1809

Ordered by the Court that James Bowen and George Bridgett be taken from the lists of Robert D.Eatons hands and annexed to Jacob Shummans hands & ordered to work under him on the road over which he is overseer.

Caleb Howell Deputy Sheriff proves in Open Court that he has attended on the Court four days at the present term for which he is authorized to receive four dollars agreeably to a former order of Court.
Court adjourns till Court in Course.

At a Court of Pleas & Quarter Sessions began and holden for the County of Grainger at the Court House in Rutledge on the third Monday of Nov. A.D. 1809 being the 20th of said month. Present, David Tate, Henry Boatman Mathew Campbell & James Brown, Esqrs.

James Conn Esqr. high Sheriff of said County makes his return to Court that he has Executed the Venire Facias on the following persons except Wm Kirkham, Joseph Rich & William Blair, towit-

1- James Carmichael   17- Henry Mays
2- Duncan Carmichael   18- Sherod Hays
3- Joseph Rich   19- Henry Howell
4- Isaac Stanley   20- John Minet
5- Thomas Lay   21- Joel Perrin
6- Edward Churchman   22- Wm Snodgrass
7- Solomon Passengill   23- Joseph Long
8- James Richeson   24- Abner Lowe
9- John Arwine Jr.   25- Acquilla Jones
10-Peter Harmock   26- Stephen Senter
11-David Chandler   27- William Blair
12-Edward Breeden   28- William Kirkham
13-Miller Ensley   29- Alex.Thompson
14-Thomas Bunch   30- David Holt
15-Jonathan Hurpower
16-Hackness Moore   The Court appoint Charles F.Keith Esqr. Solicitor

The Court appoint Charles F.Keith Esqr. Solicitor for Grainger County
Out of which Venire Facias the following persons were Ballotted a Grand
Jury to the present term, towit—

1— Stephen Senter Foreman
2— Isaac Stanley x
3— Thomas Lay x
4— Solomon Massengill
5— James Richeson x
6— John Arwine Jr. x
7— Peter Murdock x
8— Edward Breeden x

9— Thomas Bunch x
10—Maclness Moore x
11—Henry Howell x
12—John Minet x
13—Joel Perrin x
14—Joseph Long x
15—Abner Lowe x

Were sworn and charged by the Solicitor.

The Court appoint Isaac Campbell to attend on the grand Jury, at the
present term.

The Court appoint Caleb Howell Deputy Sheriff to attend on the Court
at the present Term. Issued.

By order of Court Edward Tate is appointed a constable in the bounds
of   (p 296)   Capt. Richardsons   (Nov.Sessions A.D. 1809)
Company in Grainger County took an oath to support the Constitution of the
United States — an oath to support the Constitution of the State of Tennessee and also the oath of Office and entered into Bond in the sum of
$500 with David Tate, Henry Howell & Caleb Howell his securities.

Chesley Jarnagin one of the Commissioners appointed to settle with the
holders of County money comes into Court and resigns his appointment of Commissioners which is received by the Court.

Ordered by the Court that Edward Tate be appointed a commissioner to
settle with the holders of County monies in the room & stead of Chesley Jarnagin resigned, and he enters into Bond in the sum of $100 with James
Conn, Henry Howell, David Tate & Caleb Howell his securities.

William Mix   )
    vs   )
David Abernathy)   Seth McKinney, one of the Defendants securities in this
case being the said David Abernathy into open Court and surrenders him in
discharge of himself, whereupon John Williams Esqr. Council for plaintiff
prays him in custody of the Sheriff;and the said David is ordered in custody of the Sheriff by the Court.

An Instrument of writing purporting to be the Last Will and Testament
of Narson Cox deceased was exhibited to Court for probate and the due execution thereof was proven by the oaths of William Cox and Joseph Cox, two
of the subscribing witnesses thereto and admitted to record. Let it be Recorded; whereupon Solomon Cox one of the Executors therein named came into
open Court and was qualified &c.

Ordered by the Court that Abel Dale be appointed overseer of the road
in the room of and stead of William Lane and that he have the same bounds
for hands to work on said road that said Lane had. Ised.

Ordered by the Court that the following Justices be appointed to take
the List of Taxable property in the bounds of the several Captains Company

in Grainger County for the year A.D. 1810 and make return thereof to next
Court, towit-
1- Mathew Campbell Esqr. for Capt. Sharps Company-
2- David Tate Esqr. for Capt.Richeson's Company-
3- William Clay Esqr. for Capt. Coats Company.
4- William Parkerson Esqr. for Capt. Hundrsa Company.
5- Thomas Brown Esqr. for Capt. Peters Company.
James Brown Esqr. for Capt. Hall's Company. (6)
7- Charles McAnally Esqr. for Capt. Giffords Company.
8- Joseph Cobb Esqr. for Capt. Copelands Company.

(p 297)   November Sessions A.D. 1809
9- John Moffitt Esqr. for Capt. Bulls Company.
10-Henry Boatman Esqr. for Capt. Williams Company.
11-Moses Hodges Esqr. for Capt. Moyses Company.

An application to the Court by John Hood and Samuel Clifton who are
stated to be charged on the tax Lists for the year 1809 with a poll tax
each and it appearing to the satisfaction of the Court on oath that each
of of them were on the first day of January A.D. 1809 under the age of
21 years, whereupon it is ordered by the Court that they and each of them
be released from the payment of a poll tax for the year 1809 and that the
Sheriff have a credit in his settlement with the trustee of Grainger County
and with the Treasurer of the District of Washington & Hamilton for the
sums respectively due them on the two of the above mentioned Polls.

Court adjourns till tomorrow morning eight o'clock.

Tuesday the 21st. November 1809- Court met according to adjournment.
Present, Mathew Campbell, Henry Boatman and George Moody, Esquires.

State   )
    vs   )
Samuel Bishop -   John Churchman securities of the Defendant brings him
into open Court and surrenders him in discharge of himself, whereupon the
said Samuel is prayed in custody of the Sheriff & is ordered in custody by
the Court.

State   )
353 vs   )
Samuel Bishop)   Justices Present, Mathew Campbell, Henry Boatman &
George Moody, whereupon came a Jury- towit-

1- Miller Easley   7- Edward Benn
2- George Evans   8- Peter Lowe
3- John Haley   9- Barham Easley
4- Ambrose Yancey   10-Mc Robertson
5- Andrew McPheeters   11-Josiah Eidwell
6- Edward Clark   12-Jesse Cheek

Who being elected tried and sworn well and truly to try & the truth
to speak on the issue of Traverse in this case do say, they find the Defendant Guilty in manner and form as he stands charged in the Bill of
Indictment.

State   )
No. 553 vs   )   Present, Isaiah Midkiff, David Tate, Moses Hodges, Ma-
Richard Atkins)   thew Campbell, Joseph Cobb, Philip Sigler, Henry Boatman
Wm Clay and Noah Jarnagin Esquires.

(p 298)   November Sessions A.D. 1809

        Whereupon came a Jury, towit, the same Jury as in the last case- No.558
who being elected tried and sworn well and truly to try and the truth to
speak on the issue of Traverse in this case do say they find the Defendant
not guilty in manner and form as he stands charged in the Bill of Indictment.

William Fix   )
     vs   )
David Abernathy)   Seth McKinney special Bail of the Defendant surrenders
him in open Court in discharge of himself, whereupon the said David Abernathy is prayed in custody of the Sheriff and ordered in custody of the Sheriff by the Court.   Justices present, James Moore, Isaiah Midkiff, Mathew
Campbell, Henry Boatman, George Moody, Wm Clay, whereupon the Court appoint
Edward Clark & Jinny Clark Guardians of William Clark, Joseph Clark, John
Clark & Mary Clark minor heirs of Samuel Clark deceased- and the said Edward Clark and Jinny Clark enter into Bond in the sum of twenty four Dollars with Philip Sigler and Andrew McPheeters their securities for the faithful discharge of their guardianship.

Den on demise of   )
Jeremiah Chamberlain & others)
     vs   )
Richard Durville   )   Samuel Peary & Thomas Janes special Bail
of the Defendant surrenders him in open Court in discharge of himself, whereupon the said Richard Durville is ordered in custody of the Sheriff.

William Fix   )
     vs   )
David Abernathy)   John Williams & Chas.F.Keith Esquires, come into Court
and undertake that the Defendant David will pay the costs and condemnation
in case he shall be cast in the action or surrenders himself into prison
in execution for the same or that they will do it for him.

        Ordered by the Court, a majority of the acting Justices being present
that Isaiah Midkiff be allowed the sum of $25 for keeping and maintaining
Jeremiah Midkiff one of the poor of this County from August term 1809 till
the present Term. $10 transferred to Wm Forsyth- Issd.

(p 299)   November Sessions A.D. 1809
        Ordered by the Court that Isaiah Midkiff be allowed the sum of $24.19
for keeping & maintaining Jeremiah Midkiff one of the poor of this County
from November Term 1809 till the next Term of this Court. Order Issd.

        Charles Hutcheson, Philip Sigler and James Brown Esqrs. who were ap-
pointed at Last Court to settle with Edward Clark and Jinny Clark Administrators of Samuel Clark deceased report their settlement to Court dated

November 18th 1809 whereby it appears that Twelve hundred and twenty two Dollars and eleven cents remain in the hands of said administrators, which said Report is received and confirmed by the Court and ordered to be recorded.

Ordered by the Court that Abner Lowe be appointed overseer of the road from the owl hole gap in the richland Knobs to Moore's Ferry on Holston river in the room and stead of Joseph Ore and that he have the same bounds for hands to work on said road that said Ore had. Issd.

William Leith Rainger returns a List of Strays to Court as follows, towit- a list of strays remaining on my Book not proven away according to Law- Elisha Bowman - one horse $20 - Jeremiah Chamberlain - one horse $10 Nov. 21st. 1809.   William Keith
                                Ranger for Grainger County.

Ordered by the Court, that the following persons be appointed Jurors to attend the next Term of this Court, towit- Benjamin Jarnagin, George Sparkman, Evan Harris, Wm Snodgrass, Henry Hawkins, James Carmichael, Jos. Rich, David Counts, James Alsup, Edward Churchman, Michael Massengill, Nicholas Counts, Nicholas Kearns, Thomas Bunch, Henry Howell, Sherod Mays George Taylor, Josiah Kidwell, John Estis, Alex. Thompson, Winrod Cyrus John Hodges, Robert Winslow, Peter Beeler, John Beeler,Jr. John McPheeters Henry Widener, Robert Fields, Edward McGinnis, and Jesse Cheek. Venire Fa. Issued.

Ordered by the Court that Wm Stephenson be appointed overseer of the road in the room and stead of Richard Rose and that the same bounds be allowed him for hands to work on said road that ware allowed said Rose.Isd.

State   )
   vs   )
John Holt & Joseph Holt)   Justices present, David Tate, Mathew Campbell, Noah Jarnagin, Wm Parkerson, Moses Hodges, Henry Boatman and John Moffitt, whereupon the above named John Holt, together with Michael Holt Ambrose Hodges & John Hodges entered into recognizance in the penal sum of $500 to Willie Blount Governor and his successors in office, conditioned that the said John Holt & Joseph Holt do well and truly keep the peace towards all the good people of this State and in particular towards James G.Harris- John Williams Esqr Council of the said John Holt and Joseph Holt makes a motion to Court that the said   (p 300)   Recognizance may be quashed because the said Recognizance is taken to his Excellency Willie Blount Governor and his successors in Office where it should have been to the States and after arguments being heard by the Court as well in support of said motion as in opposition to it-It is therefore considered by the Court that the said Recognizance be quashed from which Judgment Chas. F.Keith Esqr. Sol. for the County prays an appeal to the next Superior Court of Law to be holden for District of Hamilton, at the Court House in Knoxville on the fourth Monday of March next; and the fourth Monday of March next and the said appeal is granted by the Court.

Court adjourns till tomorrow morning 9 o'clock.
Wednesday 22nd. November 1809 -Court met according to adjournment.Present Isaiah Midkiff, Mathew Campbell and Henry Boatman Esquires.

Peter Lowe)
549 vs)
James Brown)   Vincent Coe, Armstead, Westherrin & James Fowler who had
been summoned to appear and give evidence in this suit on behalf of the plaintiff Peter Lowe being solemnly called came not and altogether made default
although solemnly called- It is therefore considered by the Court that the
said witnesses -towit- Vincent Coe, Armstead -Westherrin and James Fowler
do each of them forfeit one hundred and twenty five dollars according to
Act of Assembly in such cases made provided.

Robert Blair)
   vs)
Alex.Campbell) William Mitchell, one of the special Bail of the Defendant
brings him into open Court in discharge of himself, whereupon Henry Howell
Wm Mitchell, Jeremiah Chamberlain, Seth McKinney & John Haley comes into
Court and undertake that if the Defendant Alex. Campbell will pay the costs
& condemnation in case he shall be cast in the action or surrenders himself
into prison for the same or that they the said Henry, Jeremiah -Seth & John
will do it for him.

(p 301)   November Sessions A.D. 1809

Stephen W.Senter and)
Joseph Noe)
   vs)
John Duke Admr. of)
Pleasant Duke)   In this case the plaintiffs Stephen W.Senter &
Joseph Noe by their Council make a motion to the Court to enter up a Judgment against John Duke Admr. of Pleasant Duke Deceased. for one hundred &
thirteen dollars which they have been compelled to pay to Francis Daniel
as security of the said Pleasant Duke with the Interest thereon from the
time of payment and it appearing to the satisfaction of the Court that the
said Stephen W.Senter & Joseph Noe have been compelled to pay the aforesaid
sum to the said Francis Daniel as securities of the said Pleasant - It is
therefore considered by the Court that the said Stephen & Joseph do recover the afresaid sum of one hundred and thirteen dollars Debt which they
have paid as aforesaid and also the sum of four dollars & fourteen cents
interest on said sum since paid till this time & all costs.Exec.Issd.

George Evans)
   vs)
Jesse Cheek)   In this case the Defendant Jesse Cheek presents his petition to Court praying that a writ of Supercedeas may issue to stay the
proceedings in this case and also that a writ of Certiorari may issue to
David McAnally Esqr. to certify the proceedings to Court in this case,
after argument had on the petition it is considered by the Court that the
petitioner Jesse Cheek take nothing by his petition.

George Evans)
   vs)
Jesse Cheek)   In this case the Defendant Jesse Cheek presents his petition
to Court praying that a writ of Supercedeas may issue to stay the proceedings in this case and also that a writ of Certiorari may issue to David Mc-
Anally Esqr. to certify the proceedings in this case to Court, after argu-

ments heard by the Court it is considered by the Court that the petitioner to be nothing by his petition.

The Same)
vs)
The Same) In this case the Defendant Jesse Cheek presents his petition to Court praying that a writ of Supersedeas may issue to stay the proceedings in this case and also that a writ of Certiorari may issue directed to David McAnally Esqr. directing him to Certify the proceedings in this case to the next Court after arguments heard by the Court- it is considered by the Court that the petitioner takes nothing by his petition.

(p 392)   November Sessions A.D. 1809

The Same)
vs)
The Same) In this case Jesse Cheek presents his petition to Court praying that a writ of Supersedeas may issue to stay proceedings in this case, and also that a writ of Certiorari may issue directed to David McAnally Esqr. directing him to certify the proceedings in this case to the next Court, after arguments being heard by the Court – It is considered by the Court that the petitioner Jesse Cheek takes nothing by his petition &c

Den on Demise of)
Jeremiah Chamberlain & others)
vs)
Richard Durville) In this case Charles Keith & Joel Witt came into Court & undertook that the Defendant Richard Durville will pay the costs & condemnation in case he should be cast in the action or surrenders himself into prison in execution for the same or that they the said Charles & Joel will do it for him.

William Hix)
vs)
David Abernathy) In this case John Williams and Charles F.Keith special Bail of the Defendant brings him into open Court & surrenders him in discharge of themselves, whereupon the said David is prayed in custody of the sheriff and ordered in custody.

On application the grand Jury are discharged from further attendance at the present term.

Isaac Campbell proves that he has attended three days on the grand Jury at the present term. Order Issd.

Ordered by the Court that Samuel Dunlap be overseer of the river road from buffalow creek to the top of the Indian Ridge in the room of Jacob Arnett and that all the hands between the said creek & ridge from the river including Evan Harris plantation & Isaac Simpson's thence a direct course including Jacob Arnetts work under said Samuel Dunlap on said road.Issd.

James Conn High Sheriff makes his protest in open Court against the County Jail as being insufficient &c.

Court adjourns till Court in Course.
Isaiah Midkiff -Chairman Pro tem

(p 303)   February Sessions A.D. 1810
     At a Court of pleas and quarter sessions began and holden for the
County of Grainger at the Court House in Rutledge on the third Monday of
Feb. A.D. 1810- Present, David Tate, Philip Sigler, Isaiah Midkiff and
Moses Hodges, Esquires.

     James Conn Esqr. high Sheriff of said County makes his return to Court
that he has executed the Venire facias on the following persons-Viz.

1- Benjamin Jarnagin   17- George Taylor
2- George Sparkman   18- Josiah Kidwell
3- Evan Harris   19- John Estis
4- Wm Snodgrass   20- Alex. Thompson
5- Henry Hawkins   21- Nimrod Cyrus
6- James Carmichael   22- John Hodges
7- Joseph Rich   23- Robert Winslow
8- David Counts   24- Peter Beelor
9- James Alsup O-issd.   25- John Beelor Jr.
10-Edward Churchman   26- John McPheaters
11-Michael Massengill   27- Henry Widener
12-Nicholas Counts   28- Robert Fields
13-Nicholas Kearns   29- Edward McGinnis
14-Thomas Bunch   30- Jesse Cheek
15-Henry Howell
16-Sherod Mays

     On argument being had to the Court, it is considered by the Court that
no Grand Jury shall be impannelled at the present Term. Justices present,
Wm Hankins, Philip Sigler, Noah Jarnagin & Wm Clay -Jane King minor heir
of John King Dec'd came into open Court & by her Attorney Jacob Peck Esqr.
prays that a Guardianship may be appointed her, whereupon the Court appoint
Abel Morgan he Guardian -whereupon the said Abel Morgan enters into bond
in the sum of one Thousand Dollars with John Stiffey & James Simpson his
securitys for the faithful discharge of his Guardianship.

     The Court proceeds to ballot for a Constable in Captain Coats Compa-
ny to fill the vacancy occasioned by the removal of John Hall, Jacob Showman & Joel Witt, candidates-on counting the ballots it appears that Jacob
Showman has nine votes & Joel Witt two only. It is therefore ordered by the
Court that Jacob Showman is appointed Constable in said Company to fill sd.
vacancy, whereupon the said Jacob Showman came into open Court & entered
into Bond in the sum of $500 with Wm Keith & James Brown his securities
and the said Jacob Showman took the necessary oath.

     Ordered by the Court that Caleb Howell be appointed to attend the
Court at the present Term. Issued.

     On motion of John Moffitt Admr. of all & singular the goods & chat-
tels rights and credits of Wm Moffit Dec'd the Court appoint John Cooke,
Thomas Henderson & Isaiah Midkiff Esqrs. to settle with said Admr. and
make report to the present Term.

293

(p 504)   February Sessions A.D. 1810

     Clement C.Clay Esquire produced to Court a license signed by Samuel
Powell & David Campbell, late two of the Judges of the Superior Courts of
Law & Equity authorizing him to practice Law with the several Courts of Law
& Equity in this State —whereupon the said Clements C.Clay took an oath to
support the Constitution of the United States & the Constitution of the
State of Tennessee and also the oath prescribed for Attornies at Law and
was admitted an Attorney of this Court.

     Samuel Anderson Esqr. produced to Court a License signed by the Honor-
able James Trimble Judge of the 2nd. Circuit & the Hon. Wm Cocke Judge of
the first Circuit, authorizing him to practice Law in the Different Courts
in this State, whereupon on motion the said Samuel Anderson took an oath
to support the Constitution of the United States & the Constitution of the
State of Tennessee and also the oaths prescribed for attornies at Law &
was admitted an Attorney of this Court.

     Ordered by the Court that Joel Perrin be overseer of the road from Rob-
ertsons Ferry on Holston river to the ford of Richland creek at or near Maj.
Haleys old plantation in the place of John Sharp & that he have the same
bounds for hands that said Sharp had to work on said road. Order Issd.

     Ordered by the Court that John Griffits be appointed a Constable for
this County, whereupon on motion the said John Griffits entered into Bond
in the penal sum of $500 with Rial Jinnings & David Bunch his securities
and the said John Griffits took the necessary oaths.

     Ordered by the Court that John Boyd be appointed a Constable for this
County whereupon the said John Boyd came into open Court & entered into
Bond in the sum of $500 with James Kennedy & Wm Stephenson his securites
and the said John Boyd took all necessary oaths.

     Ordered by the Court that Meredith Coffee be appointed overseer of the
river road from Buffalow Creek to the top of the Indian ridge in room of
Samuel Dunlap and that all the hands between the said creek and ridge from
the River including Evan Harrises plantation and Isaac Thompsons, thence
a direct course including Jacob Arnetts work under said Meredith Coffee
on said   (p 505)   February Sessions A.D. 1810

Stephen W.Senter &   )
Joseph Noe   )
     vs   )
John Duke Admr. &c.of)
Pleasant Duke -Dec'd.)   A Writ of Fieri facias having issued in this case
and George Taylor being summoned Garnashee- The said George Taylor appears
in open Court and being sworn saith that he purchased a tract of Land from
said Pleasant Duke for the sum of Eighteen hundred dollars; that he has paid
all the purchase money but nine hundred & ninety dollars or thereabout that
he executed three Bonds to said Pleasant Duke for the remainder of said purchase money for the sum & payable at the time herein after mentioned towit-
one for $500 payable the first of February A.D. 1810 one other for $200 or
thereabouts payable the first of February A.D. 1812 and one other for $300

or thereabouts payable the first of February A.D. 1814 -that he is indebted
to the said Estate of said Pleasant Duke the aforesaid Bonds unless they
have bee assigned and that he has no notice of the assignee of either of
said Bonds whereupon the said plaintiffs come into Court by their Attorney
John Cocke Esqr. and move to condemn one hundred & seventeen dollars and
fourteen cents, together with the interest due thereon from the 22nd. Nov.
1809 together with four dollars & thirty five cents for costs being the
sum demanded by said Execution -It is therefore considered by the Court that
the aforesaid sum of one hundred and seventeen Dollars and fourteen cents
and one Dollar seventy five cents & two mills the Interest due thereon
together with the costs attending this motion be condemned in the hands of
the said George Taylor & that an execution do issue for the same. Exec.Isd.

The following Justices of the piece who, at Last Term, were appointed
to take lists and polls of Taxable property for the present year makes return thereof to Court, towit- Wm Parkerson, Esqr. for Capt. Morris Company.

Mathew Campbell Esqr. for Capt. Sharps Company.
William Clay Esqr. for Capt. Coats Company.
Moses Hodges Esqr. for Capt. Hays Company.
William Keith Ranger makes the following report to Court, towit,
"A list of strays remaining on my Books" proven away according to Law,
John Bunch -one heifer ——$3.50 -John Campbell six hoggs -$7.00-
Total $10.00

(p 306)   February Sessions   A.D. 1810
John Finley by John Cocke Esqr. his Atto. makes a motion to Court to be re-
lieved from the payment from the State and County taxes due on one Lott in
the town of Rutledge he being charged with the taxes on three lots in said
town for the year 1809 and it appearing to the satisfaction of the Court
that said John Finley owns but two lots in said Town - It is therefore ordered by the Court that the said John Finley be released from the payment
of the State & County tax due on one Lot in said town due on one Lot for sd.
year & that the Sheriff have a credit in his settlement with the Treasurer
of the Districts of Washington & Hamilton and also on his settlement with
the County Trustee for the sums due them respectively.

Robert Long by his Attorney makes a motion to the Court to be released
from the payment of the tax wherewith he stands charged on the tax lists
for the year 1809 on a Stud Horse insinuating that the tax for the said year
had been paid on said Horse in Franklin County West Tennessee, and it appearing to the satisfaction of the Court that said said Tax had been paid
as aforesaid- It is ordered by the Court that the said Robert Long be released from said tax and that the sheriff have a credit for the same in the
settlement of his accounts &c.

A Deed of conveyance from John Middleton & Rebekah Middleton his wife
Jonathan Turner & Abigail Turner his wife John Kelly & Mary Kelly his wife
& John Mathews & Ann Mathews his wife to John Cocke & John F. Jack for all
their Estate, right, title interest, property claim & demand both at Law
and in Equity of in and to six hundred acres of Land on the Southside of
Holston river being the same which James Callison Dec'd bequeathed to his
Daughters above named and others was presented to the Court for probate &
registration, on motion the Court appoint George Moody Esqr. one of their

own body to examine said Rebeccah Middleton, Abigal Turner, Mary Kelly
& Ann Mathews privately and apart from their said Husbands whether they
executed the same Dec'd voluntarily of their own free will & accord and
without any threats, compulsion or restraint of their said Husbands or of
any other persons whatsoever.

(p 307)   February Sessions   A.D. 1810
      Court adjourns till tomorrow morning 9 o'clock.
Tuesday 20th February 1810 - Court met according to adjournment. Present,
Wm Hankins, Esquire, Martin Albert has leave to return his List of Taxable
property for the year A.D. 1810 as follows, towit- one white poll, four
town lots & one acre of Land.

John Holt   )
     vs   )
Elisha Williamson)   John Ivey, one of the securities of William Reece
brings the said William Reece into open Court & surrenders him in discharge
of himself whereupon Henry Howell & Alex. Thompson come into Court & undertake for the Defendant, William Reece that if he shall be cast in the above
suit he will pay the costs & condemnation or surrender himself in execution
for the same or that they will do it for him.

      Ordered by the Court a majority of the acting Justices being present,
that the County tax & poor tax for the present year be the same as for the
year 1809.

Wyett Smith   )
     vs   )
Noah Jarnagin   )   John Williams & Wm Clay Esqrs. come into open Court &
undertake for the Defendant that if he be cast in this action that he will
pay the costs & condemnation or surrender himself in Execution for the
same or that they will do it for him.

State   )
     vs   )
David Tate   )   In this case a writ of procedendo from the Superior Court
of Law for Hamilton District is read to the Court by Charles F.Leith Solicitor for the County and wished to be filed, whereupon came the said Defendant by John Williams and John Cocke their Attornies and object to the
filing said writ alledging that this Court has no Jurisdiction of the case
and can not proceed thereon and and after arguments being heard thereon
it is considered by the Court tha they have no Jurisdiction of this case.

State   )
     vs   )
Wm Whiteside)   In this case a writ of procendo from the Superior Court
of Law for Hamilton District is read to the Court by the Solicitor for the
County & wished to be filed, whereupon came the said Defendant by John Cocke
his Atto. and objects to the filing said writ insisting that this Court
has no Jusrisdiction of this cause and can not proceed thereon and after
arguments being heard thereon it is considered by the Court that they have
no Jurisdiction of this case.

(p 308)   February Sessions A.D. 1810

Jesse Cheek comes into Court by Jacob Peck & John Cooke his attornies and applys to the Court to be released from the payment of Tax fee in four cases on motion made at last Term of this Court by said Jesse Cheek founded on a petition for writs of Certiorari & Supercedeas to remove four suits wherein George Evans is plaintiff & Jesse Cheek is Defendant in this Court & in the meantime to stay proceedings, whereupon after arguments being heard by the Court as well in support of said motion as against it, it is considered by the Court that the said Jesse Cheek be released from the payment of the four Tax fees in the above cases, from which Judgment the said George Evans prays an appeal to the Circuit Court to be held for Grainger County on the second Monday of April next.

David Tate Esqr. who was appointed to take in a List of Polls and Taxable property in the Bounds of Capt. Richardsons Company Returns his List to Court.

Thomas Brown who was appointed to take a List of Polls and taxable property in the Bounds of Capt. Peters Company makes his return to Court.

George Moody Esqr. who was appointed at the present Term by the Court to examine Rebecca Middleton -Abigail Turner, wife of Jonathan Turner - Mary Kelly wife of John Kelly & Ann Mathews wife of John Mathews privately & apart from their said Husbands, whether they execute a Deed signed by them selves & Husbands except Jonathan Turner to John Cooke and John F.Jack for a certain tract of Land on the Southside of Holston river containing six hundred acres called the Bent Tract and being the same bequeathed by James Callison Dec'd to his daughters, begs leave to report to Court that he has in obedience to the appointment of Court examined the above named Rebecca Abigail, Mary & Ann, privately & apart from their said Husbands & that they and each of them did execute said Dec'd voluntarily of their own free will and accord and without any threats, compulsion or restraint of their said Husbands or of any other person whatsoever.

(p 309)   February Sessions A.D. 1810

Absolem Mendinghall have leave to return his taxable property for the present year, towit- one free poll.

Samuel Peery has leave to rerurn his Lists of Taxable property for the present year as follows, towit-238 acres of Land & one free poll.

Court adjourns till tomorrow morning 9 o'clock.
Wednesday 21st. February 1810 -Court met according to adjournment. Justices Present, Thomas Henderson, David McAnally & John Breeden, Chas. McAnally Esqr. Trustee of this County by John Cocke and Charles F.Keith his attornies makes a motion to the Court to enter up a Judgment against Wm Clay, Wm Hankins, Robert Patterson, & Robert Hall & Philp Sigler Admrs. of all & singular the Goods &c of Wm Hall Dec'd acting Commissioners for the town of Rutledge for two hundred & fifty three dollars eleven & three fourths cents the sum reported by John Cocke & Ambrose Yancey being a majority of the Commissioners appointed by Law to settle with said Commissioners to be due this County and after arguments had to the Court as well in support of said motion as against it- It is therefore considered by the Court that the said Charles McAnally trustee recover the aforesaid sum of $253.11 and three fourths of a cent of the said Wm Clay, Wm Hankins, Robert

Patterson, & Robert Nall & Philip Sigler Admrs. of Wm Nall Dec'd for the
use of this County together with the costs attending this motion from which
Judgment the said Defendants pray an appeal to the Circuit Court to be held
for Grainger County on the second Monday of April next and enters into Bond
in the sum of $506.23½ with John Williams & Wm McNeill securities & the sd.
defendants by John Williams file their reasons in writing for said appeal
is granted by the Court.

James Thompson)
   vs T.A.B.&c)   John Williams & Noah Jarnagin Esquires, came into
William Clay)   Court and undertake for the defendant William that
he will pay the costs & condemnation if he shall be cast in this action or
surrender himself in Execution for the same or that they will do it for him.

John Anderson)
   vs   )   Justices present, John Moffitt, Noah Jarnagin, John Bree-
John Humphreys)   den, Thomas Henderson, Isaiah Midkiff & Henry Boatman.

     Whereupon came a Juty, towit-
1- Benj. Jarnagin- 2- Evan Harris - 3- Wm Snodgrass

(p 310)   February Sessions   A.D. 1810
4- Henry Hawkins   9- Nicholas Kearns
5- Joseph Rich   10-Thomas Bunch -11- Sherod Mays
6- David Counts   12-George Taylor
7- Edward Churchman
8- Nicholas Counts
    Who being elected tried and sworn well and truly to enquire and the
truth to speak on the issue joined in this case do say the Defendant did
assume within three years in manner and form as the Plaintiff in his Declaration hath complained against him and assess the plaintiffs Damages by reason of the non performance thereof to $71 and costs and the said Plaintiff
by his attornies has a Rule entered to shew cause why a new trial should be
granted- Rule made absolute.

    The following Justices of the peace who were appointed to take Lists
of taxable property for the year 1810 returns their Lists to Court, towit
John Moffitt Esqr. for Capt. John Bulls Company.
Henry Boatman Esqr. for Capt. Williams Company.
Charles McAnally Esqr. for Capt. Criffords Company.

    On motion David Tate has leave to administer on all and singular the
Goods and chattels rights and credits of Samuel Wilson, Dec'd.and the said
David Tate enters into Bond in the sum of $500 with John Cocke his secu-
rities, whereupon the said David Tate took the necessary oaths and afterwards on application it is ordered by the Court that the said Admrs. do
sell the personal estate of the Dec'd.

    Philip Sigler, one of the Admrs. of the estate of William Nall Dec'd
returns to Court a supplimental account of the sales of the estate of said
Dec'd.
    Ordered by the Court a majority of the acting Justices being present
that Ambrose Yancey be allowed the sum of one dollar and fifty cents per day
for five days spent in making a settlement with Wm Clay and others acting
Commissioners of the Town of Rutledge. Order Issued.

Ordered by the Court a majority of the acting Justices being present that Lewis Harmon be allowed the sum of one dollar & fifty cents per Day for two days spent in making settlement with Wm Clay & other acting Commissioners for the town of Rutledge.

(p 311)   February Sessions   A.D. 1810

Ordered by the Court, a majority of the acting Justices being present that Charles McAnally Trustee be allowed the amount of costs which he was compelled to pay in a suit brought by him as trustee against James Ferguson.

Ordered by the Court a majority of the acting Justices being present that the representatives of Thomas Dardis Esqr. Dec'd late Solicitor of this County be allowed the sum of $25 in full satisfaction for services performed by him as Solicitor.

Ordered by the Court a majority of the acting Justices being present that Charles F. Keith Esqr. Sol. be allowed the sum of $25 in full compensation for all services performed by him as Solicitor. Issued.

The Court appoint the following persons Jurors to attend the next Term of this Court towit- Samuel Bunch, Thomas McBroom, Valentine Morgan, Reuben Dixon, Wm Burton, Stephen Johnston, Richard Hitson, Wm Stephenson, Wm Lane Michael Holt, John Humphreys, Henry Whitner & James Dyer Jr. and that a writ of Venire facias do issue to the Sheriff to summon them. Issued.

Ordered by the Court that William Harmon be appointed overseer of the road from the Powder Spring Gap in Clinch Mountain to where it intersects with the Flat Creek road at Philip Sigler Esqrs. and that he have the same bounds for hands that formerly belonged to Thomas Viteto with an addition of all the hands from Stephen Adkins, so as to include all the hands between the Copper ridge and the Log Mt. so as to include Robert Obars.
                              Order Issued.
Court adjourns till tomorrow morning 9 o'clock.
Thursday wend. February 1810- Court met according to adjournment. Justices present, Josiah Midkiff & Henry Boatman.

Peter Lowe   )
549 vs   )
James Brown   )   Justices present, Thomas Henderson, Peter Harris & Isaiah
                   Midkiff.
          Whereupon came a Jury, towit-

1- Josiah Kidwell   7- Edward McGinnis
2- John Estis   8- Michael Massengill
3- Henry Hawkins   9- Joseph Rich
4- John Hodges   10- Benj. Jarnagin
5- John Beeler Jr.   11- Evan Harris
6- John Mc Pheeters   12- Wm Snodgrass

Who being elected tried and sworn well and truly to try & the truth to speak on the Issue joined in this case do say they find the Defendant guilty of speaking the words in manner & form as the plaintiff in his Declaration hath complained against him and that the said Defendant was Justified in speaking them.

(p 312)   February Sessions A.D. 1810

David Shelton   )
554   vs   )
John Thompson   )   Justices present, Thomas Henderson, Henry Boatman -Peter
Harris, James Brown.

     Whereupon came a Jury, towit-

1- David Counts   7- Nimrod Cyrus
2- Edward Churchman   8- Henry Howell
3- Nicholas Counts   9- Thomas Bunch
4- Sherod Mays   10-James Carmichael
5- George Taylor   11-Valentine Morgan
6- Alex.Thompson   12-James Simpson

     Who being elected tried and sworn well and truly to try and the truth
to speak on the issue joined in this case do say they find the Defendant
did not assume in manner & form as the plaintiff in his Declaration hath
complained against him.

     James Brown Esqr. who was appointed to take a List of Polls & Taxable
property in the Bounds of Capt. Halls Company makes return to Court.

     John Bullard has leave to return a List of his taxable property for
the year 1810 towit- four hundred acres of Land.

     Robert D.Eaton has leave to return a List of taxable property for the
heirs of Andrew Chamberlain Dec'd towit- 250 acres of Land Southside of Richland Creek.

     Ordered by the Court that Solomon Millikan be overseer of the road from
Panther Springs to John Rogers in room of William Smith and that he have the
same bounds for hands that said Smith had. Issued.

     Court adjourned till tomorrow morning 9 o'clock.

Friday 23rd. Feby. 1810- Court met according to adjournment. Justices,pre-
sent, Thomas Henderson, Peter Harris and Isaiah Midkiff.

Luke Lea Jr.)
582 vs   )
Jesse Riggs)   Justices present, Thomas Henderson, Wm Keith & Peter
Harris.
     Whereupon came a Jury, towit-
1- Evan Harris - 2- Wm Snodgrass- 3- Henry Hawkins - 4- Jos.Rich-
-
(p 313)   February Sessions A.D. 1810
5- Nicholas Counts- 6- Josiah Kidwell - 7- John Estis- 8- Alex.Thompson
9- Nimrod Cyrus - 10- John Hodges -11-John Beeler- 12-Edward McGinnis
     Who being elected tried and sworn well and truly to try & the truth
to speak on the issue joined in this case do say they find the Defendant

hath not paid the Debt in the Declaration mentioned as in pleading he hath alledged and assess the plaintiffs damages occasioned by reason thereof to $7.50 & costs.

Den on Demise of Joshua Simmons)
    vs   )
John Gallion Tenant in possession.)   Justices present, Thomas Henderson, Peter Harris & Wm Keith, whereupon came a Jury, towit-the same Jury as in the last case, who being elected tried and sworn well and truly to try & the truth to speak in this case do say they find the Defendant not guilty of the trespass & Ejectment in manner and form as the plaintiff in his declaration hath complained against him.

    A Commission from Wille Blount Governor, with the Great seal of the State annexed appointing Wm Keith a Justice of the peace for the County, was produced to the Court - whereupon the said Wm Keith named in said Commission appeared in Court, took an oath to ~~support~~ the Constitution of the United States and oath to support the Constitution of the State of Tennessee and also the oath prescribed by Law for Justices of the peace & took his seat on the Bench.

Den on demise of Jeremiah Chamberlain, Elizabeth Chamberlain & others &c
593   vs
Richard Dumville --------Justices present, Thomas Henderson, Peter Harris & William Keith. Whereupon came a Jury, towit- the same Jury as in the last case except Thomas Bunch in the place of Alex. Thompson, who being elected tried and sworn well and truly to try & the truth to speak on the issue joined in this case do say they   (p 314)   find the Defendant Guilty of the Trespass & Ejectment in manner and form as the plaintiff in his Declaration hath complained against him & assess his Damages to six cents & costs.

Thomas Horner   )
No. 555 vs   )
Thomas James & Jesse James   )
Executors of Wm James Dec'd   )
Thomas James only in custody &c.)   Justices present, Thomas Henderson
Wm Keith, Peter Harris & Henry Boatman.
    Whereupon came a Jury, towit- the same Jury as in the last case, who being elected tried and sworn well and truly to try & the truth to speak on the issues joined in this case and the Jury having retired to consider of their Verdict returned to the bar and being asked if they had agreed on their verdict answered that they could not agree, whereupon a mistrial is entered by consent of Council.

Den on demise of   )
Campbell & Martin   )
No. 589 vs Ejectment   )
Samuel Clark.   )   Justices present, Thomas Henderson, Wm
Keith, & George Moody.

    Whereupon came a Jury, towit-
1- Benj. Jarnagin- 2- Edward Churchman - 3- David Counts -4- Nicholas Counts
5- Sherod Mays- 6- George Taylor- 7- Alex. Thompson- 8- James Carmichael

9- James Carmichael- 10- John McPheeters -11-Nicholas Massengill-
12- Robert D.Eaton

Who being elected tried and sworn well and truly to try and the truth
to speak on issue joined in this case do find the Defendant guilty of the
trespass & Ejectment in manner and form as the plaintiff in this Declaration
have complained against him and assess the plaintiffs Damages to six cents
& costs.

(p 315)   February Sessions   A.D. 1810
Elizabeth Bean)
623   vs   )
Wyett Smith   )   Justices present, Thomas Henderson, Peter Harris, Wm Keith
Isaiah Midkiff, George Moody & Henry Boatman- Whereupon came a Jury, towit-

1- Evan Harris   7- John Estis
2- Wm Snodgrass   8- Thomas Bunch
3- Henry Hawkins   9- Nimrod Cyrus
4- Joseph Rich   10-John Hodges
5- Nicholas Counts   11-John Beelor Jr.
6- Josiah Kidwell   12-Edward McGinnis

Who being elected tried and sworn well and truly to try and the truth
to speak on the issue joined in this case do say the Defendant did assume
in manner and form as the plaintiff in her Declaration hath complained
against him and that he had not paid as in pleading he hath alledged & assess the plaintiffs damages to fifty nine dollars & one cent besides her
costs.

Joseph Cobb and Sarah Cobb his wife late Sarah Blair present their
petition to the Court praying that Dower of the said Sarah be laid of according to Law of the Lands whereof the said John Blair died seized and
possessed; On motion the Court appoint Henry Howell, Nicholas Counts, Thos.
Mann, Wm Copeland, Thomas Gill, John Harell & Thomas Bunch Commissioners
to lay off said Dower according to Law & report to next Court.

Ordered by the Court that the overseer of the road from near John Coulters to Marshalls Ferry have an equal pridiledge & benefit of the Hammer &
crow bar with the overseer from Beans Station to Sheltons ford to be made
use of for the benefit of both the aforesaid roads. Order Issued.

John F.Jack having presented to the Court his resignation of Clerk
of this Court which was accepted by the Court, present Thomas Henderson
Henry Boatman, Isaiah Midkiff, George Moody, John Cocke, Wm Keith & Peter
Harris the said Court composed of the said Justices caused proclamation to
be made that the office of Clerk of this County was vacant by the resignation of John F.Jack Esqr. and that this Court would immediately proceed to
the election of Clerk to supply said vacancy the Court proceeds according ly
to the election of a clerk and upon counting the votes it appeared that Sterling Cocke was unanimously elected Clerk of said County, the Court then directed the Sheriff to make proclamation that the said Sterling Cocke was
duly & Constitutionally elected Clerk of the County Court of Pleas & Quarter sessions in & for the County of Grainger which was done accordingly.

(p 316)   February Sessions A.D. 1810
Know all men by these present that we Sterling Cocke, John Cocke,and

John F.Jack all of the County of Grainger in the State of Tennessee are
held to firmly Bound unto Willie Blount, Governor of the State of Tennessee
in the sum of five thousand Dollars to be paid to the said Willie or his
successors in office to the which payment well and truly to be made and
done we bind ourselves and every of us our & every of us, heirs, executors
and administrators jointly & severally firmly by these presents stated
with our seals and dated this 23rd. day of February 1810.

The condition of the above obligation is such that whereas the above
bounden Sterling Cocke hath bee duly and constitutionally elected Clerk
of the County Court of Pleas & Quarter sessions in and for the County of
Grainger - Now if the said Sterling Cocke shall safely keep the records
of said Court & faithfully Discharge the Duties of his office, then this
obligation to be void otherwise to remain in full force & virtue.
Signed Sealed & Delivered in open Court.
Thomas Henderson
Presiding Justice   Steling Cocke -seal
                                   J.Cocke -   seal
                                   John F.Jack -- seal

James Conn Sheriff of Grainger County Exhibits to Court a Last of Insolvents for the year Eighteen hundred & eight amounting to three dollars
thirty seven & one half cents. It is therefore ordered by the Court that
James Conn Sheriff and collector of the State and County Taxes for said
year be released from the payment of three Dollars thirty seven & one half
cents, it being the amount Due the State from said insolvents and that he
have a credit to that amount in his settlement with the Treasurer of District of Washington and Hamilton.

James Conn Sheriff of Grainger County Exhibits to Court a List of insolvents for the year 1809 amounting to six Dollars seventy five cents. It
is therefore ordered by the Court that James Conn Sheriff and collector of
State and County Taxes for said year be released from the payment of six
Dollars seventy five cents, it being the amount due the State from said
Insolvents and that he have a credit to that amount on his settlement with
the Treasurer of the District of Washington and Hamilton.

John Moore & Samuel Bunch who had bee appointed Commissioners to settle with the Holders of County Monies came into open Court & resign said
appointment, whereupon the Court appointed Wm Copeland & Robert Massengill
Commissioners to fill said vacancies & the said Wm Copeland & Robert Massengill enters into Bond in the sum of two hundred dollars with John Cocke
their securities.

(p 517)   February Sessions A.D. 1810

James Conn Esqr. collector of Taxes for the County of Grainger reported to Court that the taxes remained unpaid on the following tracts of Land
for the year 1808 and 1809 and the owners thereof have no goods or chattels
within her county on which he can distress for said taxes towit, for the
year 1809 -Benjamin Barney 114 acres of Land taxes and costs $2.98½
John Hornback Burd by Mary Burd - 100 acres of land taxes and costs $2.84½
Joshua Seamons 10 acres of Land taxes and costs $2.79 for the year 1808.
Richard Mitchell 200 acres of Land on German Creek taxes and costs $3.34½

Joseph Burnett 50 acres of Land Puncheon Camp Creek taxes and costs

$3.31- George Combs 120 acres of Land taxes and costs $2.94½- Luke Matheny
33 acres of Land taxes and costs $2.51 -Pearson Barney 183 acres of Land
taxes and costs $3.23. Therefore it is considered by the Court that Judgment
be entered up against said tracts of Land for the taxes severally due thereon together with the costs and charges thereto respectively annexed and that
the said tracts of land be sold or so much thereof respectively as will be
sufficient for the payment of said taxes costs and charges on the first Monday of April next and on the succeeding day unless said taxes costs and charges be previously satisfied and it is further ordered by the Court the Sheriff of Grainger County carry this Judgment into Execution according to Law.

James Conn Esqr. collector of taxes for Grainger County reported to
Court the following tracts of Land as not having been given in as taxable
property, towit- Samuel Blyth 10,000 acres of Land as not having been given
in as taxable property for the year 1809 and that the owners thereof have no
goods or chattels that he knows of within her county on which he can distress towit- Samuel Blyth, 10,000 acres of land double tax for the year 1806
D. 74.50 Clerk and printer $2.35 -Samuel Blyth ,10,000 acres of Land
double tax for the year 1807 $74.50 -Clerk and printer $2.35 - Samuel Blyth
10,000 acres of Land double tax for the year 1808- $99.50 -Clerk and print-
er $2.35- Samuel Blyth , 10,000 acres of land, double tax for the year 1809
$87 -Clerk & printer $2.35 - Joseph Gentry 200 acres of Land double tax for
the year 1809 $1.74- Clerk and printer $2.35. therefore it is considered by
the Court that Judgment be entered up against the owner of the said tracts
of land for the taxes severally due thereon together with the costs and
charges thereto respectively annexed and that the said tracts of land be
sold or so much thereof respectively as will be sufficient for the payment
of said taxes costs and charges on the first Monday of July next and on the
succeeding day unless the said taxes and charges be previously satisfied &
it is ordered by the Court that the Sheriff of Grainger County carry this
Judgment into execution according to Law.
                              Thomas Henderson

(p 318)   Monday 21st. May Sessions A.D. 1810

At a Court of pleas and quarter sessions began and holden for the County of Grainger at the Court House in the town of Rutledge on the third Monday of May A.D. 1810 and on the 21st. of said month.
Present David Tate, Moses Hodges and Henry Boatman, Esquires.

James Conn high Sheriff of said County makes return to Court that he
has executed the Venire Facias on the following persons towit-

1- Samuel Bunch -Excused   7- Richard Hitson x
2- Thomas McBroom- Excused   8- Wm Stephenson -Exc.
3- Valentine Morgan   9- William Lane
4- Rubin Dixon   10-Michael Holt
5- Wm Burton   11-John Humphreys
6- Stephen Johnston Excused   12-James Dyer Jr. & Henry Whitener

The following persons are sworn to attend as Jurors at the present term
towit-
1- Rubin Dixon   3- Michael Holt   5- James Dyer Jr.
2- William Lane   4- Henry Whitener 6- John Humphreys

7- Valentine Morgan

8- William Burton

Ordered by the Court that Richard Shelton be appointed a constable in the Bounds of Captain Joseph Riches Company and the said Richard Shelton enters into Bond in the sum of $500 together with John Cocke and Caleb Howell his securities and the said Richard Shelton took an oath to support the Constitution of State of Tennessee and also the oath prescribed by Law for Constables to tak &c.

Ordered by the Court that John Minet be appointed overseer of the road in the room of and stead of Henry Whitener and that he have the same bounds for hands to work under him that said Whitener had towit, from the cross road at Henry Whitener field to the County line near the widow Minets and that all the hands between Knox County line Clinch Mt. and Copper ridge up as high as the ford of Flat Creek as said Whitener's field then crossing to John Seamons in Copper Ridge then with the height of said Ridge to the ᵗnaker Gap path thence with said path to Bull run thence down the run to Knox County, Line. Issued.

George Sparkman who was summoned to attend the Court as a Juror of Feb. Term of said Court A.D. 1810 makes known his Excuse for his non attendance at said term which is deemed sufficient by said Court.

Martin Bunch)
    vs   )
Robert Young) On motion of Martin Bunch by John Cocke Esquire, his atty. to enter up a Judgment against Robert Yancey for forty six dollars and fifty cents which he alledged he has bee compelled   (p 319)   to pay as one of the securities of Robert Yancey and it appearing to the satisfaction of the Court that the said Martin Bunch has paid the aforesaid sum of forty six dollars and fifty cents as aforesaid - It is therefore considered by the Court that the said Martin Bunch do recover of the said Robert Yancey the sum of Forty six dollars and fifty cents togeather with the costs attending this motion and the Defendant in mercy &c.

Thomas James)
    vs   )
Robert Obar) In this case an Execution signed by Philip Sigler Esquire and Directed to any lawful officer to Execute and return, is produced to Court whereof it was commanded that of the goods and chattles Lands and tenements of Robert Obar if to be found there should be made the sum of seven dollars ninety nine cents principal on a Judgment -Thomas James against sd. Defendant on which Execution Wm Hutcheson one of the Constables of this County makes the following return towit, Levied the within Execution on one hundred acres of Land the property of Robert Obar no goods nor chattels to be found in my County May 10th 1810.

William Hutchison Const.

Whereupon the said plaintiff Thomas by John Cocke Esquire makes a motion to Court to award an order of sale directed to the Sheriff of this County commanding him to sell the tract of Land levied on as aforesd. or so much thereof as will be of value sufficient to satisfy the sum of seven dollars & ninety nine cents, whereupon it is ordered by the Court that an order of sale do issue to the Sheriff aforesaid commanding him to sell the tract of Land levied on as aforesaid or so much thereof as will be of value sufficient to satisfy the aforesaid sum of money together with all costs and the Defendant in mercy &c.

Court adjourns till tomorrow morning 9 o'clock.
Court met according to adjournment, Justices present, Peter Harris, James Moore, George Moody, David Tate, Moses Hodges, John Breeden, Wm Keith, Noah Jarnagin and Mathew Campbell, Esquires.

Ordered by the Court that hereafter all drafts on this County for money on the succor of the poor Tax shall be presented to the trustee of this County for payment whose duty it shall be to mark on the back of each Draft aforesaid the day and date he rec'd it and it shall be the duty of the trustee to pay all drafts as they are presented having regard to the first presented as it shall   (p 320)   be first satisfied the next presented shall be paid and so on until all are paid.

Ordered by the Court a majority of the acting Justices being present that Wm Copeland and Edward Tate be allowed the sum of Four dollars each for two days spent in services as Commissioners in settling with the Sheriff of this County. Issd.

The Court having caused proclamation to be made that they would proceed to the Election of a Sheriff of Grainger County for the two ensuing years present, Henry Boatman, Philip Sigler, Charles Hutcheson, James Moore, Peter Harris, Joseph Cobb, Mathew Campbell, Wm Keith, Noah Jarnagin. Thomas Brown David McAnally, Chas. McAnally, John Moffit, Isaiah Midkiff, Mose Hodges, John Cocke, David Tate, Wm Clay, Geo. Moody, James Brown and John Breeden Esqrs. produced to ballot accordingly and on counting the votes it appeared that James Conn had thirteen votes and Caleb Howell had eight votes the Court then directed proclamation to be made that James Conn was duly and Constitutionally elected Sheriff of Grainger County for the two ensuing years which was done accordingly.

The Court having caused proclamation to be made that they would proceed to elect a trustee for Grainger County for the two years ensuing. Present, Henry Boatman, Philip Sigler, Charles Hutcheson, James Moore, Peter Harris Joseph Cobb, Mathew Campbell, Wm Keith, Noah Jarnagin, Thomas Brown, John Moffit, Isaiah Midkiff, John Cocke, David Tate, George Moody, James Brown and John Breeden Esquires, the above named Justices then proceeded to Ballot for a trustee accordingly, and on counting the votes whereupon the Court directed proclamation to be made that Chas. McAnally was duly and constitutionally elected Trustee of Grainger County for two years next ensuing which was done accordingly.

The Court having caused proclamation to be made that they would proceed to the election of Coroner for Grainger County for ensuing years- present Philip Sigler, Charles Hitcheson, James Moore,   (p 321)   Peter Harris Joseph Cobb, Mathew Campbell, Noah Jarnagin, John Moffit, Isaiah Midkiff, John Cocke, David Tate, George Moody, James Brown, & John Breeden Esquires the above named Justices then proceeded to Ballot for a Coroner pursuant to said proclamation & on counting the votes it appeared that Brown Edward had fourteen votes for said Office - the Court then Directed proclamation to be made that said Brown Edward was duly & constitutionally Elected Coroner of Grainger County for two years next ensuing which was done accordingly, and the said Brown Edward not giving security was not sworn as Coroner.

Know all men by these present that we James Conn, James Campbell,Geo. Evans, Wm Copeland, John Harrell and Bradley Marshall all of the County of Granger in the State of Tennessee are hald and firmly bound unto Willie Blount Governor of the State of Tennessee in the sum of $500 to be paid unto the said Willie Blount Governor as aforesaid or his successors in office to the which payment well and truly to be made and done. We and each of us do bind ourselves and each and every of our heirs Executors -Admrs. and assigns jointly and severally firmly by these presents sealed with our seals and dated this twenty second day of May A.D. 1810 -The condition of the above obligation is such that whereas the above bounden James Conn hath the date hereof been duly and constitutionally elected Sheriff of Grainger County - if therefore the said James Conn shall well and truly Execute and due return make of all precepts and process to him Directed and pay and satisfy all sums of money by him received or levied by virtue of any process into the proper office by which the same by the tonor thereof ought to be paid or to the persons to whom the same shall be due his or her or their Executors Admrs. Attorney or Agents and in all other things well and truly and faithfully execute the said office of Sheriff his continuance therein then the above obligation to be void and of non effect otherwise to remain in full force and virtue.
Signed sealed and Delivered
ip open Court
Sttest
Sterling Cocke Clk.

        James Conn (seal)
        James Campbell (seal)
        George Evans (seal)
        Will Copeland (seal)
        John Harrell (seal)
        Bartley Marshall(seal)

Know all men by these presents that we, James Conn, Nicholas Kearns, Wm Copeland, George Evans and Bartley Marshall all of the County of Grainger and State of Tennessee are hald and firmly bound unto Willie Blount Gov. of the State of Tennessee in the sum of one thousand dollars to be paid unto him the said Willie Blount or his successors in Office to the which payment well and truly to be made, we bind ourselves and every of our and every of our heirs Executors and Admrs. jointly and severally firmly by these presents sealed with our seals and dated   (p 322)   this 22nd day of May A.D. 1810 the condition of the above obligation is such that whereas the above bounden James Conn hath the day of the date hereof been duly and constitutionally elected Sheriff of Grainger County if therefore the said James Conn shall well and truly collect all taxes that shall become due the State in the said County of Grainger during his continuance in said Office and shall also well & truly and faithfully and honestly pay the same to the Treasurer of the District of Washington and Hamilton then the above obligation to be void and of none effect, otherwise to remain in full force and virtue in Law.
Signed Sealed and Delivered
ip open Court   James Conn (seal
Attest   Bartley Marshall (seal
Sterling Cocke Clk.   Wm Copeland (seal) Geo.Evans (seal)
                              Nicholas Karnes (seal)

Know all men by these presents that we, James Conn, James Campbell, John Harrell, and Bartley Marshall all of the County of Grainger and State of Tennessee are held and Firmly bound unto Willie Blount Governor of the State of Tennessee, in the sum of one thousand dollars to be paid unto the said Willie Blount or his successors in office to the which payment well & truly to be made, we bind ourselves and every of us our and every of our heirs Executors, Admrs. jointly and severally, firmly by these presents sealed with our seals and dated this twenty second day of May A.D. 1810. The condition of the above obligation is such that whereas the above condition of the above obligation is such that whereas the above bounden James Conn hath the day of the date hereof duly and constitutionally elected Sheriff of Grainger County. If therefore the said James Conn shall well and truly collect all taxes that shall become due the County of Grainger during his continuance in said office and also well and truly faithfully and honestly pay the same to the Trustee of said County of Grainger then the above obligation to be void otherwise to remain in full force and virtue.
Signed sealed and Delivered   (p 323)   May Sessions A.D. 1810
in open Court
Attest
Sterling Cooke Clk.   James Conn (seal)

        James Campbell(seal)   George Evans (seal)
        Will Copeland (seal)   John Harrell(seal)

  Know all men by these presents that we, Chas. McAnally, John Cooke and John F.Jack all of the County of Grainger in the State of Tennessee are held and firmly bound unto Thomas Henderson Chairman of the Court for sd. County, and his successors in office in the penal sum of two thousand Dollars to be paid unto the said Thomas Henderson Esquire Chairman as aforesaid or his successors in office to the which payment well and truly to be made and done. We bind ourselves every of us every and every of our heirs, Executors & Admrs. jointly and severally firmly by these presents sealed with our seals and dated this 22nd. day of May A.D. 1810- the condition of the above obligation is such that whereas the above bounden Charles McAnally hath the day of the date hereof been duly and constitutionally elected Trustee of Grainger County. If therefore the said Charles McAnally shall satisfy keep faithfully and honestly pay all County money which shall be Deposited in his hands agreeably to the orders of the Court of said County & the Laws of the State and in all other things well and truly and faithfully demean himself as Trustee during his continuance in office according to the Laws & Constitution of this State then the above obligation to be void otherwise to remain in full force and virtue.
Signed and sealed & Delivered.
in open Court
Attest
Sterling Cooke Clk.   C.McA nally (seal)
        John F.Jack (seal)
        John Cooke (seal)

  Ordered by the Court that Wm Brock as hereafter bereleased from the payment of a Poll Tax, he being a cripple as appears to the satisfaction of the Court.

  Ordered by the Court, a majority of the acting Justices being present, that John Sanders be allowed the sum of Four dollars for his Services as Coroner in holding an inquest over a negro man supposed to be murdered near Bean Station.

(p 324)   May Sessions A.D. 1810

Ordered by the Court, a majority of the acting Justices being present that Edward Tate be allowed the sum of six dollars for Services by him performed as Constable at an inquest held over a negro man near Bean Station.

Ordered by the Court, a majority of the acting Justices being present, that Abel Dale overseer of the road be allowed the sum of seven dollars, to purchase a sledge hammer & crow bar for the use of the rod on which he is overseer.

Ordered by the Court, that Andrew McPheeters have leave to record his ear mark, towit- a swallow fork in the left ear & a hole in the right Ear.

Ordered by the Court, a majority of the acting Justices being present, that Isaiah Midkiff be allowed the sum of Thirty dollars as full compensation for keeping & maintaining Jeremiah Midkiff one of the poor of this County from February Term A.D. 1810 till the present Term. Issued.

Ordered by the Court, that the Clerk of Grainger County be authorized to issue orders to Caleb Howell for attending on the Court from the time Richard Boatman was appointed to attend on the Court till the present term in all cases where is marked to attend at the next Term of this Court and there appearing no record of any person having attended.

Ordered by the Court, a majority of the acting Justices being present that John F.Jack late Clerk be allowed the same for his exofficio Services as for the last year, towit-fifty dollars as full compensation for his exofficio Services up to the present Term. Order Issued.

A majority of the acting Justices being present. It is ordered by the Court, that James Conn Sheriff be allowed the sum of Eighty Dollars for his Exofficio services up to the present Term. Issd.

Ordered by the Court, that Caleb Howell be allowed the sum of two dollars for attending on the Court two days at the present Term.

Ordered by the Court that the following persons be appointed Jurors to the next Circuit Court to be holden for Grainger County at the Court House in Rutledge on the second Monday of Oct. next, towit-

(p 325).   May Sessions A.D. 1810

1- Ralph Reed
2- Hugh Larimore
3- Richard Thompson
4- David McCoy
5- Samuel Dodson
6- Andrew McPheeters
7- Royal Jinnings
8- Nicholas Counts
9- John McElhiney
10-Samuel Peery
11-Abner Lowe
12-Wm Hodges
13-Henry Howell
14-Isaac Mitchell
15-Peter Harris
16- John Moffitt
17- David McAnally
18- David Tate
19- Isaiah Midkiff
20- Robert Fields
21- John Breeden
22- Robert Blair
23- Joel Perrin
24- Henry Hawkins
25- John Humphreys
26- Philip Sidler
27- Joseph Beeler
28- Joseph Rich
29- Jas. Carmichael
30-James Brown & 31-Nicholas Karnes

32- Wm Copeland
33- Thomas Henderson
34- David Proffitt
35- Solomon Massengill

36- Henry Ivey
37- Major Lea
38- Wm McFhatridge
39- Edward Tate

Ordered by the Court that the following persons be appointed as Jurors
at August Term 1810, towit-

1- John Daniel Sr.
2- David Counts
3- John Bowen
4- John Bunch
5- William Mitchell
6- Wm Bryant

7- John Dennis
8- Robert McGinnis
9- Thomas Johnston
10-Stephen W.Senter
11-George Taylor
12-James C.Harris   Issued.

Joseph Noe Sr.)
    vs   )
Elijah Clark   )   In this case an Execution signed by Moses Hodges, directed
to any lawful officer to Execute & return is produced to Court whereupon it
was commanded to Execute the goods and chattels lands and Tenements of Elijah Clark, if to be found there should be made the sum of fifty dollars
Debt & interest one month fifty cents costs on which Execution the following indorsements are made, towit- April 15th 1810 then Levied the within Execution on one hundred acres of Land, the property of Elijah Clark the Land
lying on the North side of Holston river below Joseph Noe Sr. Caleb Howell
D.Sher. whereupon said plaintiff by John Cocke his Atto. makes a motion to
Court toward an order of sale Directed to the Sheriff commanding him to proceed to sell the Lands levyed on aforesaid or so much thereof as well be of
value sufficient to satisfy the aforesaid sum of fifty dollars Debt & entered
as aforesaid - whereupon it is considered by the Court that an order of sale
do issue to the Sheriff commanding him to sell the Tract of Land levyed on
as aforesaid or so much thereof as will be of value sufficient to satisfy
the aforesaid sum of money and costs.

John Cocke -Thomas Henderson and Isaiah Midkiff, who was appointed by
the Court to settle with John Moffitt Admr. of the Estate of Wm Moffitt
Dec'd Exhibited their report to Court which was confirmed by the Court &
ordered to be filed.

(p 326)   May Sessions   A.D. 1810

David Tate Admr. of Samuel Wilson Dec'd returns to open Court an Inventory of said Deceased on oath which is received by the Court and ordered
to be recorded.

Wm Keith Ranger of Grainger County returns his List of Strays remaining on his books not proven away according to Law, towit-

Elijah Williams to be paid by Edward Churchman ------ $30.00
Edward Churchman   ---------------------   30.00
Thomas Bunch 1 mare   ------------------------   30.00
Noah Jarnagin   one mare   ------------------   5.00
John Renfroe 1 mare yearling Steer----------   2.25
Alex. Hime   one horse ------------------------   45.00 $112.25

John Gallion)
   vs)
James Conn Sheriff of Grainger County)   This day came the said John Gallion by his Attorney, John Williams, came into Court and moved for a Judgment against said James Conn and John Cocke, Wm Whiteside, Henry Howell, John F Jack, Wm Baker, Wm Cocke & Jesse Cheek his securities for failing to return an execution John Gallion against Joshua Seasons on the second day of this Term which Execution was returnable to May Term 1810 of Grainger County Court and it appearing to the satisfaction of the Court that said Execution came to the hands of said James Conn Sheriff of Grainger County and that he failed to return on or before the second day of the Term.. It is therefore ordered by the Court that said John Gallion recover of the said James Conn Sheriff of Grainger County as aforesaid & his said securities the sum of twelve Dol- & sixty four cents the amount of the Execution in said suit John Gallion against Joshua Simmons, from which Judgment the said James Conn prays an appeal to the next Circuit Court, to be holden at the Court House in the town of Rutledge for Grainger County on the second Monday of Oct. next; and the said James Conn plaintiff comes into Court &enters into Bond together with George Evans & Samuel Williams his securities in the sum of Thirty Dollars conditional for the prosecution of said appeal and the said James Conn by Chas.F.Keith Esqr. his Attorney files his reasons, in   (p 327)   writing for said appeal; whereupon the said appeal is granted by the Court.

On motion of the Court appoint Charles Hutchison & James Brown Esquires to settle with Nancy Lively Administratrix of William Lively Deceased & make report to the next Court.

George Payne for the use of)
William B.King)
546 vs Debt)
James Kennedy)   Justices present, Thomas Brown, Wm Keith
Mathew Campbell, Noah Jarnagin, whereupon came a Jury, towit-

1- Robin Dixon	7- Richard Conts
2- Wm Lane	8- Peter Hermond
3- Michael Holt	9- Nicholas Counts
4- Henry Whitener	10-Henry Howell
5- Joseph Hoe	11-Samuel Williams
6- James Whaling	12-Samuel McBee

Who being elected tried and sworn well & truly to try and the truth to speak on the Issue joined in this case, do say the Defendant hath paid the Debt in the Declaration mentioned Except twenty two dollars fifty cents principal and assess the plaintiffs Damages occasioned by reason of the Detention thereof to one hundred & thirty eight Dollars nineteen and three fourth cents - Rule for a new trial.

James Conn Esqr. high Sheriff of Grainger County comes into open Court and appoints Isaac Campbell his Deputy and the said Isaac Campbell came into open Court & took an oath to support the Constitution of the United States an oath to support the constitution of the State of Tennessee and also the oath prescribed by Law for Sheriff, so verefied as to suit the case of Deputy Sheriff.

Ordered by the Court that John Hamill have leave to return his Lists of Taxable property for the year 1810, towit- one town Lott.

Thomas Horner
    vs   )
Thomas James & Jesse James)
Executors of Wm James Dec'd)   Justices present, Isaiah Midkiff, Wm Keith,
Noah Jarnagin, Thomas Brown, whereupon came a Jury, towit-

1- Reuben Dixon	7- Valentine Morgan
2- William Lane	8- William Burton
3- Michael Holt	9- Isaac Mitchell
4- Henry Whitener	10-John Kelley
5- James Dyer	11-Robert D.Eaton
6- John Humphreys	12-John Cotner

(p 328)   May Sessions A.D. 1810

Who being elected tryed and sworn well and truly to try & the truth to speak on the Issue joined in this case Do say Isaac Campbell Deputy Sheriff makes returns to Court copies of orders to overseers of roads being Served, towit- Joel Perrin Received his orders as overseer of the road April the 16th day 1810 - Isaac Campbell Deputy Sheriff, William Harman received his orders as an overseer of the April the 17th day 1810.

                        Isaac Campbell Deputy Sheriff.

John Breeden comes into Court and resigns his appointment as a Justice of the peace which is accepted by the Court.

The Former Jury who ware appointed to lay off Sarah Cobbs Dower not agreeing as to the portion of said Dower, the Court appoint the following persons, towit- Col. Thomas Henderson, Henry Howell, Nicholas Counts, David Counts, Isaiah Midkiff, Henry Moys, Isaac Mitchell, Wm Keith,Esqr. Henry Bowen, John McElhaney, Chas.McAnally, John Bowen, George Taylor, or any five of them to lay off the Dower of the said Sarah Cobb, late Sarah Blair and make report to next Court.

Ordered by the Court that John Haynes be appointed overseer of that part of the road that lies between the Valley road and Hinds ridge where John Smith now and have all the hands between said ridge & the Lane Mt. up to the Black Fox Creek and also as far as to include Isaac Long.

Court adjourns till tomorrow morning eight o'clock

Thursday May the 24th -Court met according to adjournment. Justices present, Wm Keith, Isaiah Midkiff & Noah Jarnagin.

(p 329)   May Sessions A.D. 1810

Thomas Horner
    vs   )
Thomas James & Jesse James)
Executors of Wm James -Dec'd.-)   Whereupon come the following Jury, towit-

1- Reuben Dixon	4- James Dyer	7- Henry Whitener
2- Wm Lane	5- John Humphreys	8- William Burton
3- Michael Holt	6- Valentine Morgan	9- Isaac Mitchell

10- John Kelley -11- Robert D.Eaton - 12- John Cotner

Who being elected tried and sworn well and truly to try and the truth
to speak on this Issue joined in this case do say they find the Defendant
did not assume & take upon himself in manner & form as the plaintiff in pleading hath alledged.

John Cocke)
   vs)
John Jarnagin) This day George Moody comes into open Court, having been
summoned a Garnishee in this case and being sworn on his garnishment declares that he Executed and delivered a Bond to John Jarnagin for four hundred & sixteen Dollars & two thirds of a Dollar - payable the Eleventh day
of Nov. in the year one thousand eight hundred & eight, that a few days after
said Bond became due, he made a payment of seventy five Dollar on account of
said Bond, that the Ballance of said Bond after deducting said sum of seventy five dollars is yet due said John Jarnagin, so far as he knows; that he
does not know of any other person indebted to said Jarnagin, or of any of
his property in the hands or possession of any other person. This Day came
the said plaintiff by John Williams Esqr. his Atto. & moves the Court to condemn the residue of said Bond, in the hands of said George Moody. It is
therefore considered by the Court that the residue of said Bond, towit-the
sum of $341.65 & two thirds cents, together with the Interest due thereon be
condemned in the hands of said George Moody, to satisfy the Judgment to be
recovered in the suit John Cocke against John Jarnagin & also the costs in
that Behalf Expended.

(p 350)   May Sessions A.D. 1810

William Baker surviving partner of)
King & Baker   )
622   vs   )
Thomas James   ) Justices present, Joseph Cobb,Peter
Harris & William Keith; whereupon came a Jury, towit-

1- Nicholas Counts   7- John McElhaney
2- Peter Hancock   8- David Proffitt
3- William Dodson   9- John Sanders
4- Jeremiah Selvedge   10-Edmond Bean
5- William Morris   11-Alex.Thompson
6- Henry Howell   12- Jeremiah Dixon

Who being elected, tried and sworn well and truly to try & the truth
to speak on the issue in this case Do say the Defendant hath not paid the
Debt in the Declaration mentioned as in pleading he hath alledged and assess
the plaintiffs Damages occasioned by reason of the Detention thereof to six
Dollars & nine cents besides his costs.

William Baker surviving partner of)
King & Baker   )
625   vs   )
Peter Hancock   ) Justices present, Peter Harris, William Keith & James Brown- Whereupon came a Jury, towit-

1- Reuben Dixon
2- William Lane
3- Michael Holt
4- Henry Whitener
5- James Dyer Jr.
6- John Humphreys
7- Valentine Horgan
8- Wm Burton
9- James Whaling
10- David Holt
11- Warham Easley
12- Felps Reed

Who being elected tried and sworn well & truly to try and the truth to speak on the Issue joined in this case do say they find the Defendant hath paid the debt in the Declaration mentioned as in pleading he hath alledged; except $240.82 and assess the plaintiffs Damages occasioned by reason of the Detention thereof, to fifteen Dollars seventy one & three fourth cents besides his costs.

(p 331)   May Sessions A.D. 1810

Alex. H. Sanders)
vs   )
John C. Haley   ) Justices present, James Brown, Chas. Hutcheson & Wm Keith whereupon came a Jury, towit-

1- Nicholas Counts
2- Peter Hammock
3- Wm Dodson
4- Jeremiah Selvedge
5- Wm Morris
6- Henry Howell
7- John McElhaney
8- David Proffitt
9- Thomas James
10- Edmund Bean
11- Alex. Thompson
12- Jeremiah Dixon

Who being elected, tried & sworn well & truly to try & the truth to speak on the Issue joined in this case - The Jury in this case having returned from the Bar to consider of their Verdict; having returned to the Bar of the Court & being asked if they had agreed on their Verdict answered in the negative, whereupon a mistrial is Directed to be entered by the consent of Council, and the Jury are discharged from the further consideration of this case.

James Conn Esquire high Sheriff comes into open Court and appoints Warham Easley Dep. Sheriff of Grainger County and desired that said appintment shuld be entered of Record, whereupon the said Warham Easley comes into open Court & took an oath to support the Constitution of the United States, also on oath to support the Constitution of the State of Tennessee and also the oath prescribed by Law for Sheriff so modified as to suit the case of Deputy Sheriff.

Isaac Campbell Deputy Sheriff attended on the Court, two days at the present Term for which he is allowed one dollar per day. Issued.

Ordered by the Court, that Obediah Waters, be overseer of the road in the room of Jeremiah Selvage and that he have the same bounds for hands, to work under him that said Selvage had. Issd.

Ordered by the Court that John Henderson, an orphan child now of the age of fourteen years & four months be bound by indenture to John McPheeters until he shall attain the age of Twenty one years, whereupon James Moore Esqr. Chairman pro tem, of the Court and the said John McPheeters interchangeably enter into Indenture according to Law.

Ordered by the Court that Harmon Henderson an orphan child now of the age of six years Eight months & nineteen Days be bound by Indenture to Andrew McPheeters until he shall attain the age   (p 332)   of twenty one years, whereupon James Moore Esqr. Chairman of the Court pro tem; and the said Andrew McPheeters have interchangeably entered into Indentures according to Law.

Ordered by the Court, a majority of the acting Justices being present, that John Moffat Admr. of the Estate of Wm Moffit Deceased be allowed the sum of $280 for services by him performed as Admr. of said Estate.

Court adjourns till Court in Course.

John Cocke -Chairman pro tem

(p 333)   August Sessions A.D. 1810
At a Court of pleas & quarter sessions began and holden at the Court House in Rutledge on the third Monday of August A.D. 1810 and 20th of said month.

James Conn Esqr. High Sheriff of Grainger County makes return to Court that he has executed the Venire Facias on the following persons, Viz.

1- James Daniel Sr Exod.
2- David Counts   8- Robert McGinnis
3- John Bowen   9- Thomas Johnston
4- John Bunch Sr. Exod.   10-Stephen W.Senter
5- Wm Mitchell   11-George Taylor
6- Wm Bryant Exod.   12-James G.Harris
7- John Dennis Exod.

Out of which Venire Facias the following persons are appointed to attend as Jurors at the present Term, towit- Justices present, Henry Boatman,David Tate, Peter Harris, Warham Easley is appointed to attend on the Jury for the present Term and Isaac Campbell attends on the Court three days at the present Term. W/Easley order issd. Issd. in chief.

1-   Chosen,David Counts   5- Stephen W.Senter
2-Robert McGinnis   6- George Taylor
3- Thomas Johnston   7- James G.Harris
4- John Bowen   8- Wm Mitchell

Ordered by the Court that James Richardson Jr. be released from the payment of a poll Tax for the year 1810, it appearing to the satisfaction of the Court that said James Richardson stands charged on the Tax List for one poll and it further appearing to the Court that said James is under the age of 21 years- It if therefore considered by the Court, that the said James be released as aforesaid and that James Conn Sheriff & collector of the State and County Tax for said year be allowed a credit on his settlement with the treasurer of the District of Washington & Hamilton for that amount and also with his settlement with the Trustee of this County.

Ordered by the Court, that James Elkins Sr. be released from the payment of the Tax on one hundred acres of Land, he being charged on the Tax lists for that amount and it appearing to the satisfaction of the Court, that said James Elkins did not return said one hundred acres. It is therefore considered by the Court that the said James Elkins be released from the payment of the tax on said 100 acres and that James Conn Sheriff and Collector for the County for said year have a credit on his settlement with the treasurer of the Districts of Washington and Hamilton for that amount and also on his settlement with the Treasurer of this County.

(p 334)   August Sessions A.D. 1810
On motion the Court releases Polly Witcher from her recognizance, an article of agreement in the following words and figures, towit-Articles of agreements made between Robert Bean of the one part and John Blair of the other part, witnesseth that the said Robert Bean agrees to make a right to the conditional line that was made between Patterson and English if he obtains the Land by the warrant he bought of Landon Carter and the said John Blair agrees to pay one half of the purchase money whether the said Beans keeps the land or not in consideration of the said Land which is the lower end of the said tract- I witness our hands and seals this 19th of Nov. 1790 -   his
Richard Mitchell   Robert x Bean
Wm McClin   mark
                                              John Blair

The Execution of the within and foregoing instrument of writing was proven in open Court by Richard Mitchell one of the subscribing witnesses thereto and admitted and recorded at Length on the Minutes of said Court.

Ordered by the Court that the Bounds of the road from Peter Beelors old mill be altered so as to include Morris and the road be Extended to the ford of Flat Creek at Philip Sigler's, the hands in the above Bound to work under Henry Clevenger overseer. Issd.

Jacob Peck Esqr. makes a motion to Court to set aside the report of the Jury, who were appointed at last Term by the Court to lay off the dower of Sarah Dobb late Sarah Blair & after argument has as well in support of said motion as against it- It is considered & ordered by the Court that said report be received confirmed & recorded.

William Trigg   )
Executor of   )
William King Dec'd   )
    vs   )   Justices present, Isaiah Midkiff, Mathew Campbell
Abraham Prewit   )   & Peter Harris Esqrs. John Kitchen Special Bail
                               for   (p 335)   Abraham Prewit the De-
fendant in this case, brings the said Abraham in open Court & surrenders him in discharge of himself -whereupon the said Defendant is prayed in custody of the Sheriff &c. whereupon Charles Hatlock and Andrew McPheeters comes into open Court and acknowledged themselves indebted to the plaintiff in the sum of $216.00 void on condition that if the said Abraham Pruit be cast in said suit that he will pay the costs & condemnation money or surrenders himself in prison for the sum, or that they will do it for him.

James Charles by Charles F.Keith Esqr. his Atto. presents to Court an affidavit describing that sometime in the year 1799 Stephen Senter Died possessed of a considerable Estate and that he made & Executed his Last Will & Testament & appointed his sons Stephen W.Senter & Tandy Senter his Executors and that said Will did come to the hands and possession of said Stephen W.

Senter & Tandy Senter &c Whereupon the said Chas.F.Keith makes a motion to
the Court that a subpoena may Issue calling on the said Stephen W.Senter &
Tandy Senter to appear at the next Term of this Court & give up said Will
or shew cause to the contrary and after arguments of Council being heard as
well in support of said motion as against it, and the Court being equable
divided, the motion is lost.

State of Tennessee)
Grainger County   )   August Term A.D. 1810

Ordered by the Court that Alexander Cabbage be appointed overseer of
the road in the room of George Brock & the said Cabbage be allowed the same
bounds for hands that the said Brock was allowed.   Issd.

Ordered by the Court that William Kirby be overseer of the road North
of Clinch Mt. from his house to the entucky road and that he have all the
hands in the following Bounds -Beginhing at the head of Shockleys between
Clinch Mt. & said road up to the Kentucky road thence up McGinnises path &
between the mountain up to the County Line.

Ordered by the Court that the Bounds of the Powder Spring road to where
it intersects the flat Creek road be altered so as to include Philip Sigler
Benj.Hickman and thence to include Robert Obar and Richard Adkins the above
hands to work under Wm Harman.   Issd.

(p 336)   August Sessions A.D. 1810

The Jury who ware appointed at the Last Term of this Court to lay off
the Dower of Sarah Cobb late Sarah Blair makes their report to Court in the
following words & Figures (towit) State of Tennessee)
                          Grainger County   ) In obedience to an
order of the Worshipful Court of Grainger County &c We, the undersigned
Jurors have laid off the dower of Sarah Cobb late Sarah Blair relict of Col.
John Blair -Dec'd of the Lands and Tenements whereof the said John Blair
her late husband died seized and possessed of the said County of Grainger
as follows (towit) Beginning at a white oak a conditional Corner between
Robert Patterson and Wm Inglish running North five degrees East 34 poles
to a post oak & hickory then South 20 degrees East, 105 poles to a Spanish
oak & Ash on the line of the Patterson tract, then South forty three poles
to two white oaks on the top of the ridge, then South 55 Degrees West 60
poles to the middle of the Creek then on the same course 70 poles on the
other line of said Patterson tract, then North 40 West, with said line 130
poles to a black oak, thence a straight line to the Beginning containing
130 acres be the same more or less -Given under our hands this 3rd. day of
August A.D. 1810

Nicholas Counts   Isaiah Midkiff
C.McAnally   George Taylor
Henry Mays   Henry Bowen
Isaac Mitchell   Henry Howell
David Counts   John Bowen
John McElhaney   Wm Keith

Court adjourns till tomorrow morning 9 o'clock.

Court met according to adjournment. Justices Present, Thomas Henderson Mathew Campbell & David Tate Esqrs. Issued in full.

Ordered by the Court that Alexander Hamilton be released from the payment of the Taxes due on two hundred & twenty nine acres of Land he being charged on the tax list for that amount more than what he has in the County of Grainger- It is therefore considered by the Court that the said Alex. Hamilton be released from the payment of the taxes due on said two hundred & twenty nine acres and that James Conn Sheriff and collector of the State and County tax have a credit to   (p 337)   that amount on his settlement with the treasurer of the Districts of Washington and Hamilton also on his settlement with the County Trustee.

Ordered by the Court that Levy Ady by John Vinyard be released from the payment of the Taxes due on 200 acres of Land he being charged for that amt. on the tax lists for the year 1810 and it appearing to the Court that said Ady held a Bond on David Haley for a title to said Land; and that said David Haley has caused a larger tract of Land including said 200 acres to be returned as his taxable property for said year and it is further ordered by the Court that James Conn Sheriff & collector of the public & County taxes have a credit for the tax due the State on said tract of Land in his settlement with the treasurer of the district of Washington & Hamilton and also a credit for the taxes due County on said Land in his settlement with the County Trustee. Issued in full.

On motion it is ordered by the Court that John Vinyard Jr. be released from the payment of a poll tax with which he stands charged on the tax lists for the year A.D. 1810 it appearing to the satisfaction of the Court that John Vinyard was under 21 years of age on the first day of January last, & it is ordered by the Court that James Conn Sheriff and collector of public & County taxes have a credit for said taxes in his settlement with the Treasurer of the District of Washington & Hamilton & also a credit in his settlement with the County Trustee. Issd. in full.

On motion it is ordered by the Court that John Vinyard Jr. be released from the payment of a poll tax with which he stands charged on the tax Lists for the year A.D. 1810 it appearing to the satisfaction of the Court that John Vinyard was under 21 years of age on the first day of January last, & it is ordered by the Court that James Conn Sheriff and collector of public & County taxes have a credit for said taxes in his settlement with the Treasurer of the Districts of Washington & Hamilton & also a credit in his settlement with the County Trustee. Issd. in full.

John Anderson   )
517 vs   )
John Humphreys   )   Justices present, George Moody, John Moffett, Moses Hodges, Mathew Campbell, David Tate, Thomas Brown, Chas.McAnally, Peter Harris & Thomas Henderson.
            Whereupon came a Jury, towit-

1- Robert McGinnis   5- Jas. G.Harris   9- John McElhaney
2- Thomas Johnston   6- Levi McGee   10-John Williams
3- John Bowen   7- John Robeck   11-Henry Bowen
4- Stephen W.Senter   8- Henry Howell   12-David Proffit

Who being elected tried and sworn well and truly to try & the truth to speak on the issue joined in this case do say they find the Defendant did assume in manner & form as the plaintiff in his Declaration hath complained against him and assess the Plaintiffs damage occasioned by reason thereof to sixty six dollars besides costs. Whereupon the said John Humphreys by his Atto. moved the Court for a writ of Error and enters into Bond with David Tate & Wm Watson his securities in the sum of $200 & tendered his Bill of exceptions to the Court, which is allowed of and signed by the Court.

(p 338)   August Sessions   A.D. 1810
    William Keith produces to Court a list of Strays which remains on the Rangers Books of this County in the following words & Figures (towit)
James Richardson   -one heifer -$4.00
    August 22nd. 1810 -Wm Keith -Ranger for Grainger County-

Charles Hutchison Esquire, one of the Justices of the peace for Grainger County comes into Court and resigns his commission as a Justice of the peace for said County which is accepted by the Court accordingly.

Ordered by the Court that James Peery be overseer of the road from the Powder Spring Gap to Crows old place in the Richland Knobbs at the owl hole Gap in the place of Robert D.Eaton and that he have the same bounds for hands that said Eaton had to work under him Except Thornton Chersher & Byram Gibson and it is further ordered by the Court, that the said Peery be authorized to draw the sum of seven Dollars from the County Treasury for the purpose of purchasing a sledge hamer & crow bar to be used on public roads w which sum had been appropriated to Samuel Peery at August Sessions 1809 for the aforesaid purpose and never was drawn from the Treasury. Issd.

Ordered by the Court that Jacob Showman overseer of the road have the same bounds for hands that he formerly had and it is further ordered by the Court, that Bryan Gibson & Thornton Chersher be annexed to his List of hands in line of James Brown & George Bridget who have been taken from said Showman & Given to James Peery. Issd.

Ordered by the Court that Wm Dodson be appointed overseer of the road in the room of Robert Fields and that the said Dodson have the same Bounds & hands that was allowed the said Fields. Issd.

Court adjourns till tomorrow morning 9 O'clock.

Court met according to adjournment. Justices present, Thomas Henderson Charles McAnally & David McAnally Esqrs.

(p 339)   August Sessions A.D. 1810

John Cooke   )
    vs   )
John Jarnagin Sr.)   Justices present, Thomas Henderson, Charles McAnally and David McAnally Esqrs. Whereupon came a Jury, towit-

1- David Counts   5- George Evans   9- John Arwine
2- James G.Harris   6- Philip Combs   10-Nicholas Counts
3- Thomas Johnston   7- Richard Shelton   11-Joseph Noe Jr.
4- Stephen W.Senter   8- Felps Reed   12-John O.Waley

Who being elected tried and sworn well and truly to enquire what damage John Cocke the plaintiff hath sustained on a writ of enquiry wherein he is plaintiff & John Jarnagin is Defendant- Do say they assess the plaintiffs Damages by reason of non performance of the Covenant set forth in the plaintiffs Declaration to Thirteen hundred & fifty Dollars besides his costs. It is therefore considered by the Court that the said John Cocke do recover of the said John Jarnagin Sr. his Damages aforesaid in form aforesaid assessed and the Defendant in mercy &c\
John Cocke in his proper person comes into Court & returns the above Judgment.

George Evans)
    vs   )
Jesse Cheek)   Justices present, Charles McAnally, Thomas Henderson & Wm Keith Esqrs. Whereupon came the same Jury as in the last case except Robert McGinnis in the room of George Evans & David Proffit in the room of Richard Shelton who being elected tried and sworn well and truly to try and the truth to speak on the issue joined in this case having returned from the Bar to consider of their Verdict; having returned to the Bar of the Court, & being asked if they had agreed on their Verdict, answered in the negative. Whereupon a mistrial is Directed to be enetered by consent and the Jury are discharged from the further consideration of this case/

George Evans)
    vs   )
Jesse Cheek) Justices present, Charles McAnally, Thomas Henderson & Wm Keith Esqrs. Abel Langham who was summoned as a witness on behalf of Jesse Cheek in the case and at August term 1810 the cause being regularly called for trial and the said Abel Langham being solemnly called to appear and give Evidence on behalf of said Jesse and after being solemnly called out and failing   (p 340)   to attend as a witness in said suit. It is therefore considered by the Court that the said Abel Langham do forfeit 125 Dollars according to Act of Assembly in such case made & provided.

Joseph Cobb)
    vs   )
James Daniel)   James Carmichael who was summoned as garnashee in this case & being sworn saith that he Executed and obligation to James Daniel for the sum of $1.75 Dated the second Day of Decr. 1803 payable Sept. 15th 1805 that on or about the 11th of Nov. 1805 he paid Fifty dollars part of the above mentioned Note to said James Daniel, that the balance of said Note is yet due but he does not know where said Note now is or whether it is transferred by said James Daniel or not and further that he does not know of any person who either is indebted to said James Daniel or who has any of his property in their possession — Whereupon the said Joseph Cobb by John Cocke Esqr. his Atto. makes a motion to Court to enter up a Judgment against James Carmichael who was summoned as garnashee in this case and after argument had the Court of the opinion that no Judgment be enetered against James Carmichael on his garnashee.

John Chaney)
    vs   )
James McDonald)   Justices present, David McAnally, Chas. McAnally & WmKeith Esqrs. In this case an execution having Issued signed by Henry Boatman, one

of the Justices of the peace for Grainger County for the sum of Five Dollars
and seventy five cents against the said James McDaniel together with the sum
of fifty cents for costs &c and it appearing to the satisfaction of the Court
that said execution came to the hands of Ralph Ford, one of the Constables
of this County commanding him to make the sum of five dollars and seventy
five cents,

(p 341)   August Sessions A.D. 1810
Principle and fifty cents costs before mentioned and it further appearing to
the satisfaction of the Court, that said Execution was not returned by said
Ralph Ford, according to Law but he having failed and neglected so to do-
Therefore on motion of John Chaney by John Cocke Esqr. his Atto. to enter
up a Judgment against Ralph Ford Constable for Failing to rerurn said Execution John Estis and Isaiah Kidwell his securities for five dollars seventy five cents Debt together with the costs in that behalf Expended &c. It
is therefore considered by the Court that the said John Chaney do recover of
the said Ralph Ford Constable as aforesaid and John Estis and Josiah Kidwell
his securities the sum of five dollars and seventy five cents Debt and 50¢
costs in that behalf expended together with the costs attending this motion
and the Defendant in mercy &c.   Exec,Issd.

Ordered by the Court that Andrew Coffman be appoited overseer of the
road from Sheltons ford to the top of the ridge where Henry Boatman formerly
lived in the room of Richard Shelton and that he be allowed the same Bounds
for hands that said Shelton formerly had. Issd.

Ordered by the Court that Wm B.Hinds be overseer of the road from the
First Big Spring above Chesley Jarnagin to the first Hollow below Robert D
Eaton's in the place of Richard Coats had.

A Deed of conveyance from Wm Stewart & Rebecca Stewart his wife to Henry B.Jackson was acknowledged in open Court by the said Wm Stewart to be
his act and Deed for the uses and purposes therein named and on motion the
Court appoint Mathew Campbell Esqr. one of the members of this Court to examine the said Rebecca Stewart, Separate and apart from her Husnabd touching the premises whether she had executed said Deed of conveyance Voluntary and of her own free will and accord & without any threats., compulsion
or restraint of her Husband and afterwards said Mathew Campbell Esqr. reports
to said County of Grainger that he had examined said Rebecca Stewart touching the premises before mentioned and that she acknowledged she had executed
the same voluntarily and of own free will & accord and without any threats
compulsion   (p 342)   or restraint of her said husband -whereupon
said Deed of conveyance was admitted to record -let it be recorded.

Court adjourns till tomorrow morning 9 o'clock.

Court met according to adjourmant. Justices present, David McAnally
Isaiah Midkiff and Joseph Cobb, Esqrs.

Frederick Miller   )
      vs   )
Christopher Bradshaw   ) Justices present, Wm Keith, David McAnally & Isaiah
Midkiff, Esqrs.   Whereupon came the following Jury (towit)

according to law, doth on his oath make the following declaration in order
to obtain the provisions made by the act of Congress of the 18th of March
1818, and and the 1st of May 1820, that he the said James Philips, en-
listed for the term of fifteen months, on the . . . . . day of in the year
. . . . . . the date not recalled, in the State of Virginia in the Company
commanding by Captain John Powell in the Regiment commanded by Colonel
John Flood Edwards in the line of the State of Virginia on the continental
Establishments, that he continued to serve in the sd. Corps untill the Expiration - of his said term of service, when he was discharged from the
said service in the State of Virginia - That he was in no battle except
a Battle at the aforesaid place when he was discharged - That he was discharged by Genrl. John Crawford, & has had said discharge accidently con-
sumed by fire and that he has no other evidence now in his power of his
said Services - and in pursuance of an Act of the 1st of May 1820, I do
Solemnly swear, that I was a resident citizen of the United States on the
18th day of March 1818, and that I have not since that time by gift sale
or in any manner disposed of my property, or any part thereof with intent
thereby so to diminish it as to bring myself within the provision of an
Act of Congress, entitled an act to provide for certain persons engaged
in the land and naval services of the United States - in the Revolutionary
War - passed on the 18th of March 1818, & that I have not, nor has any
person in trust for me, any property or security, contracts or debt, due
to me, nor have I any interest other than   (p-423)   what is contained in
the schedule hereto annexed & by me subscribed - Schedule of the property
of the above declarant, I am by profession,(or rather when I was able)
a cultivator of the earth - I am now altogether unable to pursue my profession, My wife who is near eighty years of age is the only member of my
family, she is unable to contribute any thing to my support, as to my
property except one bed, & one axe I have nothing.

              his
          James X Philips
              Mark

Sworn to and declared on the 24th May 1825, in open court.

              Gorman Lester Clerk

William Banks Plt.   )   In Covenant
  Against   )
Wm. P. A. McCabe Deft.) From the Judgment of the court in this case
) rendered the Defendant prayed an appeal to
the honorable the Circuit Court to be held for the County of Giles, and
having executed bond and Security as the law directs, the same was granted
him.

John Abernathy Plt.   )   In Debt
  Against   )
Robert Oliver Deft.   ) This day came the parties aforesaid by their
) attornies and thereupon the plaintiff de-
murres to the Defendants rejoinder being argued by the court now here fully
understood. It is ordered by the court that sd. Demurres be sustained,
and that said plaintiff recover against said Defendant five thousand dollars,
the debt in the writing obligatory in the declaration mentioned, together
with his costs by him about this suit in this behalf expended -
But the same is to be discharged by the payment of the damages by the Jury

in this cause in this court at this term assessed, and his costs by him
about his suit in this behalf Expended.

Elizabeth Philips Plt.   )   In Debt
       Against   )
Thomas B. Jones &) Defts   )   From the Judgment of the court in this
Thomas Harwood   )   )   case rendered the Defendants prayed
)   an appeal to the honourable the Cir-
cuit court to be held for the County of Giles – and having executed bond
and security as the law directs, the same was granted him.

P-424   Tuesday 24th May 1825

William Worsham Plt!   )   In Case
       Against   )
Ira C. Goff . . . Deft.   )   This day came the parties by their
)   attornies and thereupon came a Jury
of good and lawful men, towit, Thomas Wilkinson, Henry J. Cooper, Beverly
B. Watson, Nathan Davis, William Bodenhamer, John Abernathy, Nathaniel
Hammet, Thomas Bratton, Charles C. Abernathy, Henry McAnnick, George Barnes
& William Roberts, who being elected tried and sworn well and truly to try
the issue joined between the parties in this case upon their oaths do say
that they find said issue in favour of the plaintiff, and assess his damages by occasion of the non performance of the assumpsit in the declaration
mentioned to one hundred & two dollars, besides costs.

It is therefore considered by the court that the plaintiff recover of
said Defendant the damages aforesaid, in form aforesaid by the Jurors
aforesd. assessed, and his costs about his suit in this behalf expended.

A Deed of conveyance from Nathaniel Young to Robert Oliver for fifty
acres of land was produced in court and the Execution thereof acknowledged
by the said Nathaniel Young and ordered to be certified for registration.

The Grand Jury returned into court the following Presentments, towit,
The State against Henry Kimbrough, for obstructing Richland Creek – Same
against Daniel Puryear, for neglect of duty as overseer of the road –
Same against Matthew Johnston for neglect of duty as overseer of the road
& withdrew to consider of further presentments.

John McAnnually Plt.   )   Sci – Fa –
       Against   )
Edward D. Jones & Henry M. Newlin Deft)   This day came the plaintiff by
)   his attorney and the defendant
being solemnly called came not but made default, and it appearing to the
satisfaction of the court that the Scire facias in this cause has been
served upon them, and that they were the bail of James Read in the case
of John McAnnally against said James Read in this court in which case said
McAnnally recovered against said Read, the sum of two hundred & twenty
dollars and twenty five cents, together with the sum of forty five dollars
damages, and also nine dollars   (p-425)   thirty six and a half cents costs

John Green   )
    vs   )   Justices present, James Moore, Wm Keith & David McAnally Esqr.
John Midkiff)

1- David Counts	7- Wm W. Easley
2- Robert McGinnis	8- Thomas Breeden
3- James O. Harris	9- David McAnally
4- Henry Howell	10-Joel Martin
5- Samuel Peery	11-Valentine Morgan
6- Robert Winslow	12-Joseph Breeden

Who being elected tried and sworn the truth to Enquire what Damages the plaintiff hath sustained in his writ of Enquiry brought and by you to be tried do say they assess the plaintiffs Damages to $60 besides his costs.

A list of Jurors to November Term A.D. 1810

1- Thomas Bunch	8- James Richeson
2- Thomas Gill	9- David Bunch
3- Tead McGee	10-John Vinyard
4- John McCarty	11-John Arwine
5- John Harrold	12-Alex. Hamilton
6- Martin Albert	13-John Kitchen
7- John Bunch	

Charles Hutcheson, Philip Sigler & James Brown, who were appointed at the Last Term of this Court to settle with Nancy Lively, Administratrix of William Lively Dec'd produced said settlement to Court, which is ordered to be recorded. Issued.

Court adjourns till Court in course.

John Cooke Chairman —pro tem.

(p 346)   Blank page

(p 347)   November Term A.D. 1810

At a Court of Pleas & Qr. Sessions began and holden at the Court House in Rutledge on the third Monday November A.D. 1810 and on the nineteenth day of said month James Conn high Sheriff of Grainger County makes return to Court that he has Executed the Venire facias on the following persons towit—

1- Thomas Bunch
2- Thomas Gill
3- Zern McGee x
4- John McCarty
5- John Harrell x
6- Martin Albert x
7- John Bunch
8- James Richeson
9- David Bunch Excused
10-John Vinyard Excused
11-John Arwine Jr. x   Justices present, William Clay, John Cooke
12-Alex. Hamilton   Esquires.

A paper was Exhibited to Court purporting to be the Last Will and testament of Wm Copeland Dec'd by Thomas Gill which was proven by the oath of the said
Thomas Gill to have been found amongst the valuable papers of the

said William by the said Thomas and the hand writing of the said Wm Copeland Dec'd was proven in open Court by the oath of John F. Jack -James Conn and Joseph Cobb, who swore they Believed the Will as presented was all in the handwriting of the said William Deceased whom it appeared appointed Ethel A Williem and Thomas Gill his sole Executors who came into Court and took upon themselves the execution of said Will and ware qualified as executors of the last will and testament of William Copeland Deceased - Whereupon it is ordered by the Court that said Will be Recorded.

Ordered by the Court that Thomas Whiteside be appointed overseer of the road in the room of Wm Whiteside and that he have the same bounds for hands to work under him that said Wm Whiteside had. Issued.

Ordered by the Court that Wm Stephenson be appointed overseer of the road in the room of and stead of Wm Copeland and that he have the same hands that said Copeland had. Ised.

Ordered by the Court that Richard Acuff be released from the payment
(p 349) November Sessions A.D. 1810
of the taxes due on two hundred acres of Land returned for the year 1810, it appearing to the satisfaction of the Court that said 200 acres has been twice given in as taxable property for the same year- It is therfore considered by the Court that the Sheriff and collector of the State and County taxes for the year 1810 be released from the payment of the State and County taxes due on said land for year and that he have a credit for the amount due the State on his settlement with the treasurer of the District of Washington and Hamilton and also a credit for the amount due the County on his settlement with the County Trustee. Issued in full.

Ordered by the Court that James Brown be overseer of the road in the room of Jacob Showman and that he have the same bounds for hands that said Showman had and that his bounds be so as to include the place whereon Geo. Bridget lives and also including Byrem Gibson and Thornton Chersher.

Court adjourned till tomorrow morning 9 o'clock.

Tuesday Nov. 20th 1811- Court met according to adjournment -Justices present, Wm Keith, Wm Clay, Noah Jarnagin, John Moffit, and Joseph Cobb,Esqrs.

William Keith ranger returned to Court a list of Strays in these words towit- a list of strays remaining on my books not proven away according to Law.
Lewis Collins one bay Horse ------ $60.00
John Tanner - one Sorrel horse --- 20.00
Jesse Hall one Sorrel horse ------ 6.00
John Anderson - one 2 year old heif.5.00
                                  $91.00
William Keith ranger for Grainger County.

George Payne) for the use of Wm B.King
   vs   )
James Kennedy)   Justices present, Charles McAnally, Thomas Brown and James
Brown Esquires - Whereupon come the following Jury, towit-

1- Thomas Bunch -2- Thomas Gill- 3- John McCarty- 4- Andrew Stone-

5- Thomas Whiteside - 6- David Proffitt- 7- Jeremiah Haney -8-Wm Jones
9- James Holt - 10-John Bull- 11- Wm Whitesides -12-John Patterson
Who being elected tryed and sworn well & truly to try and the

(p 349)   November Sessions 1810
thuth in this case do say the defendant hath paid the Debt in the declaration mentioned except $150.90 and assess the plaintiffs damages occasioned by reason of the detention of that sum to six cents besides costs. It is therefore considered by the Court that the plaintiff do recover of the Defendant the sum of $150 together with the damages and costs aforesaid in form aforesaid assessed and the Defendant in mercy &c. Exec.Issd.

Ordered by the Court that David Chandler be appointed overseer of the road from Peter Beelors old Mill to the ford of Flat Creek at Philip Sigler and that the said Chandler be allowed all the hands between the Copper Ridge and the Log Mountain so as to include Martin Morris down the Valley and include old John Hawmock up the Valley.

A List of Jurors appointed by the Court to the next Circuit Court to-wit,

1- James Campbell
2- Mathew Campbell
3- Caleb Howell
4- Zeniah Midkiff
5- John Harrold
6- John Estis
7- Henry Boatman
8- Thomas Johnston
9- McHess Moore
10-Rice Moore
11-Wm Windham
12-Henry Bowen
13-Thomas Bunch
14-Rial Jinnings
15-Charles McAnally
16-Richard Shockley
17-Valentine Morgan
18-Thomas Brown
19-Meredith Coffee
20-George Moody

21- Henry Mays
22- Jonathan Williams
23- Joseph Bealor
24- John Bealor
25- James Moore
26- Daniel Taylor
27- James Simpson
28- Joseph Stubblefield
29- Michael Massengill
30- Edward Churchman
31- Malcom Hodges
32- Shedrick Williams
33- John Noe
34- Henry Whitener
35- Wm Snodgrass
36- Noah Jarnagin
37- Zern McGee
38- Wm Keith &
39- Balsar Sherley

Ordered by the Court that Philip Sigler and Robert Hall Admr. of Wm Hall Deceased be released from the payment of the taxes due on six hundred acres of Land for the year 1810 it appearing to the satisfaction of the Court that said Land has been twice returned for said year. It is therefore considered by the Court that said Admrs. be released as assd. and that the Sheriff and collector of the State and County taxes for said year be released from the payment of the taxes due on said land and that he have a credit for the amount due the State on said land for said year in his
(p 350)   settlement with the treasurer of the Districts of Washington & Hamilton and also in his settlement with the County Trustee.

Ordered by the Court that Thomas Gill be appointed Commissioner to settle with the Sheriff and trustee of this County in the room of Wm Copeland

Deceased the said Gill having given bond & security as directed by the Court.

On motion it is ordered by the Court that James Blair have leave to administer on all and singular the goods and chattels rights and credits of James Blair the elder deceased and the said James Blair enters into bond in the sum of $5000 together with Joseph Cobb -Robert Blair and Samuel Blair his securities, whereupon the said James Blair took the necassary oath as administrator of the Estate of James Blair Deceased.

The following is the relinquishment of Catharine Blairs rights of Administrator of her late Husbands Estate which is ordered to be recorded - towit, To the Worshipful Court of Grainger County -I, Catharine Blair, widow of the late James Blair Dec'd respectfully maketh known to your Worships that old age and infirmity renders me entirely incapable of taking the Administration of my late Husbands Estate upon me and I do hereby relinquishes and give over all my rights and claim in that case to my son James Blair Witness my hand and seal this 20th day of November 1810
Thomas Henderson   her
Hugh Bragg   Catharine x Blair   -seal
                                   mark
Ordered by the Court a majority of the acting Justices being present that Sterling Cocke Clerk of Grainger County be allowed the sum of $3.60 he having produced the treasurers receipt for the amount of the taxes for the year 1809 and 1810.

Ordered by the Court, a majority of the acting Justices being present that Isaiah Midkiff be allowed the sum of thirty dollars for each three months since his last allowance towit-thirty Dollars from May term 1810 at August term 1810 and from August term 1810 up to the present term for keeping and maintaining Jeremiah Midkiff one of the poor of this County.

Ordered by the Court that Joseph Cobb and John Moffet Esquires be appointed to take the examination of Elizabeth Albert and Jenny Eaton to ascertain whether they signed a Deed of conveyance from Jaermiah Chamberlain & others to John Bunch of their own free will and choice or whether they did it by the compulsion of their husbands or any other person.

(p 351)   November Sessions 1810

Ordered by the Court that James Conn Sheriff be directed and required to bring Daniel,Williams, and Joseph Chambers into Court at the present term.

Ordered by the Court that Ann Roane be hereafter considered as one of the poor of this County and it is further ordered by the Court a majority of the acting Justices being present that Daniel Chandler be allowed the sum of twelve Dollars for keeping and maintaining Ann Roane one of the poor of this County until the next term of this Court. Issued.

Joseph Cobb who ware appointed at the present term to Examine Elizabeth Albert and Henry Eaton separate and apart from their Husbands whether they had Executed a Deed of conveyance from Jeremiah Chamberlain and others to John Bunch for fifty acres more or less make their report to Court as follos, towit-
State of Tennessee -Grainger County - We, Joseph Cobb and John Moffitt

being appointed by the Court to examine Jenney Eaton and Elizabeth Albert separate from their Husbands whether they had executed a Deed from them & others to John Bunch for fifty acres of said freely and voluntarily without any compulsion, threats or restraint of their said Husbands. We beg leave to report that we have made the above examination according to Law and that the said Jenney Eaton and Elizabeth Albert did sign and Execute said Deed voluntarily without any compulsion, threats or restraint of their said Husbands. Given under our seals & hands this 20th day of Nov. 1810—

John Moffitt)

Jos.Cobb   ) Justices of the peace

A majority of the acting Justices being present it is ordered by the Court that Frederick Moyers be allowed the sum of twenty Dollars for keeping and taking care of the Court House up to May term 1810 of this Court.Isd.

Ordered by the Court, a majority of the acting Justices being present that Isaiah Midkiff be allowed the sum of twenty five Dollars which has not heretofore been allowed for keeping and maintaining Jeremiah Midkiff, one of the poor of this County. Issd.

Ordered by the Court that David Huddleston be appointed overseer of the road in the room and stead of Archabald Hopper and that he have the same bounds for hands to work under him on said road that said Hopper had. Issd.

Ordered by the Court that William Guinn be appointed overseer of the road from the town of Rutledge to the top of Richland Knobbs in the room of Valentine Morgan and that he have the same bounds for hands that said Morgan had. Issued.

Ordered by the Court that Stephen Smith be appointed overseer of the road in the room of Wm Stephanson and that he have the same bounds for hands that said Stephens had. Issued.

(p 352)   November Term A.D. 1810

Ordered by the Court that James Moore Esquire be appointed to take in lists of polls and taxable for the year 1810 in the bounds of Captain Samuel Richardson's Company and return the same to next Court.Issued.

Ordered by the Court that Wm Hankins Esquire be appointed to take in lists of polls and taxable property in the bounds of Capt. Thomas Sharp's Company for the year 1811 and return the same to next Court.

Ordered by the Court that Wm Keith Esqr. be appointed to take in lists of polls and taxable property in the bounds of Captain Wm McBrooms Company for the year 1810 and return the same next Court.

Ordered by the Court that George Moody Esquire be appointed to take in lists of polls and taxable property in the bounds of Captain Wm Mayeses Co. for the year 1811 and return to next Court.

Ordered by the Court that Isaiah Midkiff Esquire be appointed to take in lists of polls and Taxable property in the bounds of Capt. Joseph Riches Company for the year 1811 and return the same to next Court.

Ordered by the Court that Peter Harris Esqr. be appointed to take in lists of polls and taxable property in the bounds of Capt. Thomas Mann's Company for the year 1811 and return the same to next Court.

Ordered by the Court that Thomas Henderson Esquire be appointed to take in lists of polls and taxable property in the bounds of Capt. Wm Copeland's Company for the year 1811 and return the same to next Court.

Ordered by the Court that Charles McAnally be appointed to take in lists of polls and taxable property in the bounds of Capt. David McAnally's Company for the year 1811 and return the same to next Court.

Ordered by the Court that James Brown Esqr. be appointed to take in lists of polls and taxable property in the Bounds of Capt. James Brown's Company for the year 1811 and return the same to next Court.

Ordered by the Court that Thomas Brown Esqr. be appointed to take in lists of polls and taxable property in the bounds of Capt. Thomas Morrises Company for the year 1811 and return the same to next Court.

Ordered by the Court that Wm Parkerson Esqr. be appointed to take in lists of polls and taxable property in the bounds of Capt. Morrises Company for the year 1811 and return the same to next Court.

A list of Jurors appointed to attend at February term 1811 of this Court.

1- John Vinyard		7- John Arwine Jr.	
2- Wm Perrin		8- Samuel Lucas	
3- Samuel McBee		9- Daniel Robertson	
4- James Dyer		10-Thomas Mann	
5- Joseph Long		11-Joseph Noe Jr.	
6- Richard Coats		12-Francis Daniel &	
		13-William Bryant	

(p 353)

November Term 1810

Court adjourns till tomorrow morning 9 o'clock.

Wednesday November 21st. 1810 - Court met according to adjournment- Justices Present, Wm Keith, Wm Clay, Mathew Campbell, Joseph Cobb and Thomas Brown, Esquires.

William McNeill)
    vs   )
James Conn Shff.) William McNeill by Clement C.Clay Atto. makes a motion to Court to enter up a Judgment against James Conn Sheriff for the sum of $12.99 being the amount of a Judgment which was obtainable by Wm McNeill against John Norman and on which an order of sale has issued for said Judgment and costs by said Isaiah Midkiff Esqr. and property sold to different persons to the amount of ninety three Dollars and fifty cents by Virtue of said order of sale by said James Conn cotd. for argument.

Ordered by the Court that Wm Clay -Noah Jarnagin and James Brown Esqrs. be appointed commissioners to settle with Philip Sigler and Robert Nall Administrators of Wm Nall Dec'd and make report to next Court.

John C.Haley)
   vs   )
John Sanders) Justices present, David Tate, Mathew Campbell and Wm Keith
Esqrs.)

      Whereupon came the following Jury, towit-

1- John Bunch   7- William Jones
2- James Richardson   8- John Hardl
3- John Kitchen   9- Henry Widener
4- Alex. Hamilton   10-Andrew Stone
5- Stephen W.Senter   11-Thomas Whiteside
6- William Stone   12-James Holt

     Who being elected tryed and sworn well and truly to try and the truth
to speak in this issue joined in this case, they find the defendant hath not
paid the debt in the Declaration mentioned and assess the plaintiffs damage
occasioned by reason of the detention of that sum to $17.49 besides costs.
It is therefore considered by the Court that the plaintiff do recover of the
Defendant the sum of ——— the Debt in the declaration mentioned together
with the damages and costs aforesaid in form aforesaid assessed in and about
prosecuting said suit in that behalf expended and the Defendant in mercy &c.

Denn on demise of)
Henry Howell   )
   vs   ) Justices Present, David Tate, Mathew Campbell and Wm
Alex.Thompson) Clay, Esquires. Whereupon came the parties by their
Attornies and a Jury, towit-

(p 354)   November Term 1810

1- James Richardson   7- William Jones
2- David Proffitt   8- John Hardl
3- John Kitchen   9- Henry Widener
4- Alex. Hamilton   10-Andrew Stone
5- Stephen W.Senter   11-Thomas Whiteside &
6- Wm Stone   12-James Holt

     Who being elected tried and sworn well and truly to try and the truth
to speak on the issue joined in this case do say they find the Defendant not
guilty of the trespass & Ejectment in manner and form as complained of in
the plaintiffs Declaration. It is therefore considered by the Court that the
Defendant Alexander do recover of the plaintiff Henry his costs by him in
and about Defending his said suit in that behalf expended and that the said
plaintiff go hence without day from which Judgment the said plaintiff hath
prayed an appeal to the next Term of the Circuit Court to be holden for the
County of Grainger at the Court House in Rutledge on the second Monday of
April next & files his reason for his said appeal in writing, enters into
Bond with John Cooke and John F.Jack his securities in the sum of $500.00
for the prosecution of his said appeal, whereupon said appeal granted by the
Court.

     James Conn, Sheriff and collector of the State and County taxes for the
year 1807 by Edward Tate his Deputy returns to Court a list of Insolvents
for said year amounting to three Dollars thirty seven cents. It is considered by the Court that said collector be released from the payment of the taxes
due on said Insolvents for said year that he have a credit in his settlement

with the treasurer of the Districts of Washington and Hamilton for the amount
due the State and also a credit for the amount due the County on his settlement with the County Trustee.

James Conn, Sheriff submitted the following Lands to Court which had been
reported and which could not be sold according to Law, in the following words,
towit- I, James Conn, Sheriff of Grainger County in pursuance of a Judgment
and order of Court on the first Monday 1810 exposed in the following tracts
of Land for the taxes for the year 1808 and 1809.

Benjamin Barney - 144 acres of Land taxes and costs ----------- $278½
John Hornback Bird by Mary Bird- 100 acres of Land taxes -costs 284½
Joshua Seamon's - 10 acres of Land -taxes and costs --------- 279
Joseph Burnet - 50 acres of Land -Puncheon Creek taxes &c.   346 3/4
Joshua Wimble - 100 acres of Land, taxes and costs ---------- 351
George Combs - 120 acres &c ------------------------------- 296
Luke Matheny - 33 acres &c. ------------------------------- 257

(p 355)   Pearson Barney - 188 acres of Land ------------- $328
On the sale no person would bid for the above lands. I, therefore pray
to be released from the above taxes and costs and charges for the years above
specified- It is therefore considered by the Court that James Conn Sheriff&
collector of the State and County taxes for said year be released from the
payment of the taxes due on said lands for said year and that he have a credit for the amount due the State on his settlement with the treasurer of the
Districts of Washington and Hamilton and also a credit on his settlement with
the County trustee for the amount due the County for said years.

Court adjourns till tomorrow morning 9 o'clock.

            Thursday November 22nd. 1810- Court met according to ad-
journment - Present, Wm Keith, Joseph Cobb and Mathew Campbell, Esqrs.

John Brown   )
    vs   )
William Peters) On motion of John Brown by John Cocke Esquire, his Atto.
to award a fieri facias and direct the same to Issue against the goods and
chattels lands and tenements of William Peters on a Judgment which has heretofore bee obtained in this Court in favour of John Brown against said Wm
Peters for $100 with interest and costs or thereabouts. It appearing to be
satisfaction of the Court that the lands attached in this suit had been sold
to satisfy three several Judgments recovered in this case. It is therefore
ordered by the Court that a writ of fieri facias issue accordingly.Ex.Issd.

Ordered by the Court that Wm Chambers of the age of fifteen years be
bound by Indenture to Joseph Long until he arrives to the age of twenty years.

Ordered by the Court that Joseph Chambers of the age of eleven years be
bound by Indenture to Balsar Sherley until he shall arrive to the age of 21
years.

John Holt   )   Justices present, Wm Keith, Mathew
    vs   )   Campbell, and William Clay, Esqrs.
Wm Reece -Elisha Williamson)
and William McGill   )

Thereupon came the parties by their attornies and a Jury, towit-

1- Thomas Bunch
2- Thomas Gill
3- John McCarty
4- David Proffitt
5- Jacob Showman
6- Jesse Cheek
7- Reubin Dixon
8- John Bull
9- William Jones
10-Andrew Stone
11-Henry Widener
12-James Simpson

Who being elected tried and sworn well and truly to try and the truth to speak on the issue joined in this case do say they find the Defendant Guilty of the traverse & conversion as charged in the plaintiffs Declaration and assess the plaintiffs Damages occasioned by reason thereof to Eight dollars besides costs. It is therefore considered by the Court that the plaintiff do recover of the Defendant the sum of Eighty Dollars,

(p 356)   November Term 1810
the damages aforesaid in form aforesaid assessed together with the costs in and about prosecution of said suit in that behalf expended and the Defendants in mercy &c. Ex.Issd.

Ordered by the Court that George Bridges be fined the sum of twenty five cents for neglecting to serve as a Juror after being summoned by the Sheriff.
                                        Ex. Issd.
Ordered by the Court that Absolem Roach be appointed overseer of the road in the room and stead of Samuel West and that he have the same bounds for hands to work under him that said West had.

Benjamin Dixon)
      vs   )   Justices present, Mathew Campbell, Isaiah Midkiff and
Thomas Breeden)   Joseph Cobb, Esqrs. Thereupon came the parties by their
attornies and a Jury, towit-

1- James Richardson
2- John Kitchen
3- Alex. Hamilton
4- John Dorner
5- Joseph Hoe Jr.
6- Charles Matlock
7- James Whaling
8- William Reece
9- Wm Stone
10-Th: Crump
11-Caleb Reece
12-Michael Holt

Court adjorns till tomorrow morning 8 o'clock.
            Friday November 23rd. 1810- Court met according to adjournment.
Justices Present, Wm Keith, Mathew Campbell, Wm Clay and Charles McAnally,
Esquires.

Benjamin Dixon)
      vs   )   This day came the parties by their Attornies and the Ju-
Thomas Breeden)   rors aforesaid, who being elected tryed and sworn well &
truly to try and the truth to speak in this issue joined in this case do say
they find the Defendant not guilty of the traverse and conversion as complained of in the plaintiffs Declaration - It is therefore considered by the
Court that the Defendant do recover of the plaintiff the costs in and about
prosecuting said suit in that behalf expended and the plaintiff in mercy &c.
from which Judgment in said Benj.Dixon hath prayed for and obtained an appeal
to the Circuit Court of Grainger County to be holden for said County at the

Court House in Rutledge, on the second Monday in April next files her reasons in writing for said appeal enters into Bond together with John Cooke and Sterling Cocke his securities in the sum of $500 for the prosecution of his said appeal, whereupon said appeal granted by the Court.

James Conn bought of Wm McNeill for the use of the County -
One Stock Lock of the price of ---------------- $2.50
To one testament for use of County for Election- .41 2/3
$2.91 2/3

It is considered by the Court that the said James Conn be allowed the sum of two dollars ninety one and two third cents the amount of the money by him expended for the use of the County as above stated.

Joseph Cobb)
vs)
James Daniel) Justices present, Wm Clay, Wm Keith

(p 357)   November term 1810
and Charles McAnally, Esquires. Whereupon came the same Jury as above cause. Dixon vs Breeding, who being elected tryed and sworn well and truly to enquire what damages the plaintiff hath sustained do say they do assess the plaintiffs damages to $24.65 besides his costs. It is therefore considered by the Court that the plaintiff Joseph do recover of the Defendant James the sum of $24.65 his Damages aforesaid in form aforesaid assessed together with the costs in and about prosecuting said suit in that behalf expended and the Debt in mercy &c. Ex.Issd.

John Den lessee of Henry Howell vs Richard Fen -trespass in Ejectment with notices to William Peters. Justices present, Wm Keith, Wm Clay & Chas. McAnally, Esqrs.
In this cause it appearing to the satisfaction of the Court that a notice & copy of the declaration of Ejectment in this case had been served by the Sheriff of Grainger County on the said William Peters tennant in possession and the said Richard Fen being solemnly called to come into Court and defend this suit & the said William Peters being also solemnly called to come into Court and by a rule of this Court cause himself to be made Defendant in this suit in the room and stead of the said Richard Fen the Caveat Ejector came not, therefore it is considered by the Court that the sd. John Den recover against the said Richard Fen the residue of his term yet to come and correspond as laid in his declaration and on motion of John Williams attorney for the plaintiff a writ of possession, an order to him to turn the said Wm Peters out of possession and it is also considered by the Court that the said Plaintiff recover against the said Wm Peters his costs about his suit in this behalf expended and the said Richard be in mercy &c

John Den, Lessee of John Cocke   )
vs)
Richard Fen with notice to Wm Kirk   )   Justices present, Wm Clay, William
Amount in possession)   Keith and Charles McAnally, Esqrs.

In this case it appearing to the satisfaction of the Court that a notice and copy of the declaration of Ejectment in this cause had been served by the Sheriff of Grainger County on the said Wm Kirk tennant on the premises and the said Richard Fen being solemnly called to come into Court and

defend this suit and the said Wm Kirk being also solemnly called to come into
Court, and by rule of this Court to cause himself to be made Defendant in
this suit in the room of and stead of Richard Fen the ousted Ejector, came
not. Therefore it is considered by the Court that the said John Den to recover of the said Richard Fen the residue of his term yet to come and unexposed
as laid in his Declaration and on motion of John Williams Attorney for the
plaintiff a writ of possession be awarded to him to turn the said William
Kirk out of possession and it is further considered by the Court that the sd.
plaintiff recover against the said Wm Kirk his costs in and about prosecuting said suit in that behalf expended and the said Richard in mercy &c.

(p 358)   November Term 1810

James Charles   )
    vs   ) Motion cont'd.
Stephen W. Banter)

Isaac Campbell, Deputy Sheriff proves that he has attended on the Court
five days at the present Term for which he is allowed agreeably to a former
order- one dollar per day.

Court adjourns till Court in Course.
                                        Jos.Conn -Chairman pro tem.
(p 359)   February Term 1811

At a Court of Pleas & Quarter sessions began and held for the County of
Grainger at the Court House in Rutledge on the third Monday of February A.D.
1811 being the 18th day of said month.

James Conn, Esquire High Sheriff of said County makes return to Court
that he has Executed the Venire facias on the following persons, towit-

1- John Vinyard
2- Wm Perrin
3- Samuel McBee
4- James Dyer
5- Joseph Long
6- Richard Coats
7- John Arwine
8- Samuel Lucas
9- Daniel Robertson
10-Thomas Mann
11-Joseph Hoe Jr.
12-Francis Daniel &
13-Wm Bryant

Justices present, John Cocke, David Tate and George Moody Esquires.

Ordered by the Court that John Moody be appointed a constable in the
bounds of Capt. Wm Mays Company and the said John Moody enters into Bond together with John Cocke and George Moody his securities in the sum of $500
for his faithful execution of his said office of Constable.

Ordered by the Court that Zera McGee be released from any fine that may
have been taken against him for failing to attend as a Juror at November
Term 1810.
Ordered by the Court that James Dyer be excused from attending as a
Juror at the present term of this Court.

James Blair Admr. of the Estate of James Blair Deceased, returns to

Court an Inventory of the Estate of said Deceased,which is received by the Court and ordered to be recorded.

Mary Copeland, widow and relict of William Copeland Deceased- by John F.Jack Esquire, her Attorney makes a motion to Court to enter and file a protest dissenting from the will of her said Husband which is received by the Court and ordered to be recorded, which is in the following words and figures towit- To the worshipful Court of Grainger County this is to signify to your Worships that I have thought proper to wave and I do hereby wave the provisions made for me, in the Will of my late Husband William Copeland late of said County of Grainger and State of Tennessee deceased-and claim my dower of his Estate - I therefore pray that your Worships would order the same to be assigned and set off to me as the law in such case directs.

Mary Copeland

John Moffett

The prayer of the above petition being granted by the Court, it is ordered by the Court that the said Mary Copeland have her dower laid according to Law.

Ordered by the Court that Thomas Bunch have leave to return his list of polls and taxable property for the year A.D. 1811, towit- 270 acres of Land, one white poll.

Edward Tate and Thomas Gill commissioners appointed by the Court to settle with the collector of publick money and with the Trustee of this County exhibits an account of said settlement to Court which is received by the Court and confirmed by the same.

Ordered by the Court that Joseph Walker be appointed overseer of the road from the first big spring above Chesley Jarnagins down to Coxes old place in the room and stead of John Jarnagin and that he have the same bounds for hands to work under him as overseer on said road that said John Jarnagin had.

Issued.

(p 360)   February Term 1811

James Conn, Esqr. high Sheriff of Grainger County comes into Court and appoints Isaac Campbell Deputy Sheriff to attend on the Court at the present Term.

Ordered by the Court that Charles Matlock be appointed overseer of the road in the room and stead of David Watson and that he have the same bounds for hands to work under that said Watson had.

Court adjourns till tomorrow morning 9 o'clock.

Tuesday February 19th 1811- Court met according to adjournment- Justices present, John Moffett -David Tate, James Brown,Geo.Moody & I.Midkiff.

Isaiah Midkiff Esquire, who was appointed to take in lists of polls & taxable property for the year 1811 returns his list to Court.

Justices present, Isaiah Midkiff, George Moody, David Tate and John Moffett, Daniel Stone a minor of the age of seventeen years, comes into Court and chooses John Cocke Esquire, his guardian -whereupon the Court appoints the said John Cocke Guardian of the said Daniel Stone.

George Evans)
    vs)
Jesse Cheek and)
Wm Maliney) Justices present, Isaiah Widkiff, James Brown and John
Moffett, Esquires.

1- John Vinyard	7- David Counts
2- Wm Perrin	8- Wm Whiteside
3- Joseph Long	9- James Whiteside
4- Richard Coats	10-Charles Matlock
5- John Sanders	11-Joseph Breeden
6- Nicholas Counts	12-Henry Ivey

    Who being elected tryed and sworn well and truly to try and the truth
to speak in this issue joined in this case do say they find the Defendant
not guilty of the trespass as mentioned in the plaintiffs Declaration. It is
therefore considered by the Court that the Defendant Jesse & William do recover from the plaintiff George, the costs in and about prosecuting said
suit in this behalf expended and the plaintiff in mercy &c. From which Judgment the said plaintiff hath prayed for and obtained an appeal to the next
Circuit Court of Grainger County to be holden for said County at the Court-
House in Rutledge on the second Monday in April, files his reasons in writing for said appeal and enters into Bond together with John F.Jack and Jas.
Conn, his securities in the sum of three hundred Dollars for the prosecution of said appeal -whereupon said appeal is granted by the Court.

William Hix)
    vs)
David Abernathy) Justices present, James Brown, George Moody, John Moffett & Moses Hodges, Esquires. Whereupon came the parties by their Attornies and Jury, towit-

1- John Vinyard	7- David Counts
2- Wm Perrin	8- Wm Whiteside
3- Joseph Long	9- Thomas Whiteside
4- Richard Coats	10-Chas. Matlock
5- John Snodgrass	11-Joseph Breeden
6- Nicholas Counts	12-Thomas Ivey

    Who being elected tryed and sworn well and truly to try and the truth
to speak in this issue joined in this case do say they find the

(p 361)   February Term 1811
Defendant did assume and take upon himself as the plaintiff hath complained
against him and assess the plaintiffs damage do recover of the Defendant the
damages aforesaid assessed together with his costs in and about prosecuting
said suit in this behalf expended and the Defendant in mercy &c.

    George Moody, Esquire was appointed to take in lists of polls and tax-
able property for the year 1810, returns his lists for said year, to Court.

    Thomas Gill and Etheldred Williams Executors of the last Will and testament of Wm Copeland Deceased exhibits to Court an Inventory of said Estate to Court, which is received by the Court and ordered to be recorded.

Wm Keith, Esquire, who was appointed to take in list of polls and taxable property for the year 1811, returns his list to Court.
William Keith, Rainger of Grainger County returns a list of Strays to Court in the following words, towit- A list of strays remaining on my books not proven away according to Law.
Jacob Showman - one hogg------------$1.00
Wm McPhetridge -1 black horse --   20.00
Miller W.Easley - 1 ---   1.25

William McNeill)
    vs)
James Conn -Sheriff)   Justices present, George Moody, Noah Jarnagin,Jas. Brown, Isaiah Midkiff, Joseph Cobb, David Tate and John Moffett. The motion which was made in this case at the last Term of this Court to enter up a Judgment against the said James Conn for the sum of $12.90 was taken up and after argument heard as well in support of said motion as against it the Court are equally Divided in opinion on this case.

Ordered by the Court that from Stephen Johnson down the river to the mouth of Clarkson's branch thence down the river including James Harrises and John Noe and all hands living in that bent thence down the river to Coulters Island and all the hands on Coulters plantation from thence to Benj. Shipley's from thence to Stephen Johnson, so as to include John Alford and Stephen Miller and Richard Grantham to work under Hugh Taylor overseer.

James Brown, Esqr. who was appointed to take in lists of Polls and taxable property for the year 1811 return his list to Court.

Court adjourns till tomorrow morning 9 o'clock.
        Wednesday morning February 20th 1811- Court met according to adjournment. Justices present, David Tate, Chas.McAnally and Henry Boatman.Es.

Ordered by the Court that Wm McPhetridge be released from the payment of the amount due for one stray horse which has been by him posted and which has been proven away according to Law.

George Evans)
    vs)
Jesse Cheek)   Justices present, Henry Boatman, Joseph Cobb and David Tate Esquires- Whereupon came the parties by their Attornies and a Jury, towit-
1 Richard Coats- 8- Francis Daniel - 9- John Carrothers

(p 362)
2- John Arwine Jr.   6- Robt.Massengill
3- Daniel Robertson   7- Thomas Sharp
4- William Bryant   8- Thomas Reece Sr.

10- Andrew Stone - Elijah Griffits and 12- Stephen Smith

Who being elected tryed and sworn well and truly to try and the truth to speak in the issue joined in this case do say they find the Defendant not guilty of the trespass as mentioned in the plaintiffs Declaration. It is therefore considered by the Court that the Defendant recover of the plaintiff the costs in and about prosecuting said suit in that behalf expended and the plaintiff in mercy &c.from which Judgment the said George Evans hath prayed for and obtained an appeal to the next Circuit Court of Grainger County to be held for said County in the Court House in Rutledge on the second Monday of April next and enters into bond together with John Williams and John F.Jack his securities in the sum of five hundred Dollars for the prosecution of his said appeal files his reasons in writing for his said appeal, whereupon said appeal granted by the Court.

Charles McAnally Esqr. who was appointed to take in list of polls and taxable property for the year 1811 in the bounds of Capt. D.McAnally Company returns his list to Court.

William Rankins Esqr. who was appointed to take in lists of polls & taxable property for the year 1811 returns his list to Court.

Ordered by the Court that Joseph Long be excused from further attendance at the present term as a Juror.

Thomas Brown Esquire, who was appointed to take in lists of polls and taxable property for the year 1811 return the lists to Court.

Peter Harris Esqr. who was appointed to take in lists of polls and taxable property for the year 1811 returns his list to Court.

James Moore Esqr. who was appointed to take in lists of polls and taxable property for the year 1811 returns his list to Court.

Ordered by the Court that Charles McAnally -David McAnally and WmClay Esqr. be appointed to settle with Robert Nall and Philip Sigler Admrs. of the Estate of Wm Nall Deceased and make report to next Court.

Ordered by the Court a majority of the acting Justices being present that Edward Tate and Thomas Gill be allowed the sum of four dollars each for two days by them spent in setting with the Collector and Trustee of this County for the last year. Issd. in full.

Ordered by the Court that Philip Sigler- David McAnally and William Clay Esqr. be appointed to settle with Sarah Shelton, widow and relict of Wm Shelton Deceased and that they make report of said settlement to next Court.

(p 363)   February Term A.D. 1811
    Ordered by the Court a majority of the acting Justices being present that the taxes for the year 1811 be the same as for the year 1810 -except that an additional tax be laid for the purpose of praying Jurors, towit-

On each white poll ——6¼¢— On each black poll —— 12½¢
"   " hundred acres of land - 6¼¢ - On each town lott- 12½¢
On each Stud horse for covering mares - $1.00- Each retail store -$2.50

Ordered by the Court that Samuel Davis of the age of fourteen years and six months be bound by Indenture to Henry Boatman until he shall attain the age of twenty one years.

Ordered by the Court that John Smith be appointed a Constable in the bounds of Capt. Thomas Morrises Company and the said John Smith enters into bond together with Wm Robertson and Woolry Beeler his securities in the sum of $500 for the faithful discharge of his said appointment.

Ordered by the Court that John Campbell be appointed overseer of the road in the room of John McElhaney removed and that he have the same bounds for hands to work under him on said road that said McElhaney had.

Ordered by the Court that the following be appointed Jurors to May term—1811, towit—

1- William Dodson
2- David Elkins
3- James Alsup
4- Samuel West
5- Major Lea
6- Abner Lowe
7- David Proffitt
8- Thomas Gill
9- William Kirk
10-Joseph Noe Jr.
11-Andrew Elder
12-Thomas Kenn
13-John Kidwell
14-John McPheters and
15-David Watson

Ordered by the Court that David McAnally, Ryal Jinnings,———Dodson Sr. Henry Hipsher, David McCoy, Andrew Elder, Edward McGinnis,& Robert McGinnis be appointed a Jury to view and lay off a publick road to leave the turnpike road near Beans Plantation running thence up Copper Valley to the County Line so as to meet the road extending over said valley through Hawkins County.

Ordered by the Court that Francis Daniel, Caleb Howell, Henry Ivey, Henry Howell, Henry Mays, Isaac Mitchell, Malakiah Howell, Sherod Mays, John Daniel be appointed a Jury to lay off a road the nearest and best way from Mayes ford on Holston river to intersect the road leading from Cheeks Xroads Mossy Creek Iron works at or near the house of Caleb Howell.

Ordered by the Court that Ambrose Hodges be appointed overseer of the road in the room and stead of George Boatman and that he have the same bounds for hands to work under him that said Boatman had. Issued.

(p 364)   February Term A.D. 1811
Ordered by the Court that Stephen Willis Senter be overseer of the road from the double white oak above the widow Hendersons to Beans Station in the room and stead of Stephen Smith and that he be allowed the same bounds for hands that said Smith had and all the hands from Col.Hendersons down to Thos. Whitesides bounds. Issued.

Court adjourns till tomorrow morning 9 o'clock.

Thursday February 21st. 1811— Court met according to adjournment. Justices present, Thomas Brown, Thomas Henderson, Isaiah Midkiff & David Tate, Henry Boatman, David McAnally, Joseph Cobb and Charles McAnally.

Frederick Miller   )
            vs   )
Christopher Bradshaw   )   Justices present, Thomas Brown, Isaiah Midkiff, Thomas Henderson & David McAnally, Esqrs.

Motion in arrest of Judgment the reason in arrest of Judgment which were
filed in this case came on now to be argued and after arguments heard, in
support of said motion as against it. It is considered by the Court that
the Judgment heretofore rendered in this case be reversed and that said motion be confirmed.

Ordered by the Court that the Jurors be released from further attendance at this Term.

Peter Lowe   )
      vs   )
James Fowler)   Justices present, Charles McAnally, David Tate, Henry Boatman, Joseph Cobb, Esquires. Rule to take the Deposition of Vincent Coe &
and John Hickey in this case before Charles McAnally and David McAnally Esqrs
ten days notice to be given the plaintiff by the Defendant before Deposition taken which depositions when taken to read in evidence in this case.

Edmund Bean   )
      vs   )
Myrtle Smith)   Justices present, Charles McAnally, David McAnally, David Tate
Henry Boatman and Joseph Cobb, Esqrs. the rule heretofore made to quash the
proceedings in this case came on now to be argued and after arguments heard
of Council as well in support of said motion as against it. It is considered
by the Court that said motion be overruled.

John C. Haley)
      vs   )
Warham Easley)   Justices present, Thomas Brown, Thomas Henderson, Henry
Boatman & Peter Harris, Esqrs.

John C. Haley by John Williams Esqr. his Attorney makes a motion to
Court to enter up a Judgment against Warham Easley Deputy Sheriff of Grainger County for the sum of $22.50 together with the further sum of fifty
cents for costs and charges being the amount of an Execution issued by David McAnally against John Sanders –Solomon Massengill and Dudley Cox which
is alledged to have come to the hands of the said Deputy Sheriff and which
he has as alledged failed to act on and return according to Law and after
argument heard as well in support of said motion or against it –It is considered by the Court that Judgment be entered against the said Warham.Easley,

(p 365)   February Term 1811
Sheriff of Grainger County for the sum of $22.50 Debt together with the fur-
ther sum of fifty cents costs &c.and also the costs attending the motion &
also the costs attending the motion and the Defendant in Mercy &c. –ordered
by pltff. that no execution issue for nine months.

John Holt   )
      vs   )
Wm Reece   )   Justices present, Henry Boatman, Thos. Henderson,
Elisha Williamson &)   Thomas Brown & Peter Harris,Esquires.
Wm McGill   )
        A motion which was heretofore made in arrest of Judgment in this
case wherein reasons were filed on now to be argued before the Court and after arguments heard as well in support of said motion as against – It is considered by the Court that said motion be overruled and that the said plaintiff have his Judgment.

William Keith)
    vs   )
Peter Woodin) Justices present, Thomas Brown, Thomas Anderson, and Henry
Boatman, Esqrs. the plaintiff in this case having appeared by Jacob Peck his
Attorney and having filed his Declaration against the said Peter Woodin &
the said Peter Woodin having failed to attend and defend his second suit it
is considered by the Court that Judgment by default be entered up against
the said Woodin cont'd on enquiry.

William McNeill   )
    vs   ) Motion - the question coming on whether this cause on
James Conn,Sheriff) which the Justices on tuesday last divided was consequence of the Division Dismissed after argument heard as well in support of
said motion or against it was determined it was not and that the cause stand
continued for further argument on the original motion against the Defendant
at the next Term.

On motion of John Cooke Esqr. Atto. for Stephen W.Senter to award an
order of sale to sell 3 lotts in the town of Rutledge which has been attached as the property of Peter Woodin on which attachment a Judgment has been
ordered &c. It is ordered by the Court that an order of sale do issue to the
Sheriff of this County commanding him to sell three lotts in the town of
Rutledge at the suit of Stephen W.Senter against Peter Woodin agreeably to
an attachment returned by James Conn Sheriff &c.to Isaiah Midkiff Esquire
on which Judgment was entered for the sum of fourteen dollars twenty two
cents and all costs &c.

Isaac Campbell Deputy Sheriff has attended four days on the Court at
the present term.

James Conn Esqr. collector of taxes for the County of Grainger reported to Court the following tracts of land as not having bee given in as taxable property for the year 1810, towit-
Hugh Cain 100 acres of land- Robert Long 100 acres of land -John or Henry
Tanner 100 acres of land -Stephan Shelton 100 acres of land- David Hitts
100 acres of land-Dawson Cheek 200 acres of land -Tarlton Carrell 100
acres of land -Joseph Collins 100 acres of land -Griffe Collins 100 acres
of land.
(p 366)   February Session 1811

Daniel Collins 100 acres of land -Bull 100 acres of land-Valentine Dodson
100 acres of land- Daniel James 100 acres of land-Samuel Blyth 10,000
acres of land North of Clinch Mountain -Esa Johnston 500 acres of land South
of Richland Knobbs and that the owner thereof have no goods or chattels that
he knows of within his County that he knows of on which he can distress -
towit-
Hugh Cain 100 acres of Land -double tax for the year 1810 62¢-Clerk &
printer $2.35 - Robert Long 100 acres of Land double tax for the year 1810
62¢ Clerk & printer $2.35- John or Henry Tanner - 100 acres of land- double
tax for the year 1810 -62¢ Clerk & printer $2.35 - Stephan Shelton 100
acres of land double tax for the year 1810 -62¢-Clerk & printer $2.35 -
David Hitts 100 acres of land double tax for the year 1810 62¢- Clerk &
printer $2.35 -Dawson Cheek 200 acres of land double tax for the year 1811
62¢ Clerk & printer $2.35 -Tarlton Carrell 100 acres of land double tax for
the year 1810 62¢-

Clerk & printer $2.35 -Joseph Collins 100 acres of land double tax for the year 1810 62¢ Clerk & printer $2.35- Griffe Collins 100 acres of land double tax for the year 1810 62¢- Clerk & printer $2.35 -Dowell Collins 100 acres of land double tax for the year 1810 62¢- Clerk & printer $2.35 - George Bull 100 acres of land double tax for the year 1810 62¢ -Clerk & printer $2.35 - Valentine Dodson 100 acres of land double tax for the year 1810 - 62¢ - Clerk & printer $2.35 -Daniel James 100 acres of land double tax for the year 1810 62¢- Clerk & printer $2.35 -Samuel Blyth 10,000 acres of Land North of Clinch Mountain double tax for the year 1810 -62¢- Clerk & printer $2.35 -Esa Johnston - 500 acres of land double tax for the year 1810 $3.70½ - Clerk & printer $2.35 - Therefore it is considered by the Court that Judgment be entered up against the said tracts of land for the amount of the taxes due thereon together with the costs and charges thereto respectively annexed and that the said tracts of land be sold or so much thereof respectively on the first Monday in November next and the succeeding day as will be sufficient to satisfy the above taxes costs and charges unless the same be previously satisfied and it is ordered by the Court that of Grainger County carry this Judgment into execution according to Law.

James Conn Esqr. collector of taxes for the County of Grainger reported to Court that the taxes remained unpaid on the following tracts of land for the year 1810 and that the overseer thereof have no goods or (p 367) chattels within his County on which he can distress for the said taxes, towit David Erwine 100 acres of land taxes & costs $2.66 - Wm Reece 55 acres of Land taxes & costs $2.41 3/4 - John Rodgers Sr. 100 acres of land taxes & costs (knox road) $2.66 - Jesse Riggs 156 acres of land taxes and costs $2.84 - Richard Granthem 185 acres of land taxes & costs $2.92 3/4 -Stephen Johnston 150 acres taxes & costs $2.82½- Samuel Riggs 156 acres taxes and costs $2.83½ - therefore it is considered by the Court that Judgment be entered up against the said tracts of land for the taxes severally due thereon together with the costs and charges thereto respectively annexed and that the said tracts of Land be sold or so much thereof respectively as will be sufficient to satisfy the above taxes costs and charges on the first Monday in November next and the succeeding day unless said taxes costs and charges be previously satisfied and it is ordered by the Court that the Sheriff of Grainger County carry this Judgment into execution according to Law.

James Conn Esqr. collector of taxes for the County of Grainger Exhibited to Court a list of Insolvents for the year 1810 amounting to ten dollars eighty five cents - it is considered by the Court that said Collector for the said year of 1810 be released from the payment of the taxes due on said insolvents for said year and that he have a credit for five dollars eight and one half cents in his settlement with the treasurer of the Districts of Washington and Hamilton it being the amount due the State on said insolvents and that he have a credit for five dollars thirty seven cents in his settlement with the County Trustee it being the amount due the County on said insolvents.

James Conn Esqr. collector of taxes for the County of Grainger for the year 1810 by Isaac Campbell his lawful Deputy exhibits to Court a list of Insolvents in said County for said year amounting to two.

Court adjourns till Court in Course.
(p 368) May Sessions A.D. 1811

At a Court of Pleas & Quarter Sessions began and holden for the County of Grainger at the Court House in Rutledge on the third Monday in May A.D. 1811 and on the 20th day of said month. Present, David Tate, James Brown and Thomas Henderson Esqrs.

James Conn Esqr. high Sheriff of Grainger County makes report to Court that he has Executed the Venire facias on the following persons, towit- Except James Alsup.

1- William Dodson
2- David Elkins
3- James Alsup
4- Samuel West
5- John McPheters
6- Major Lea
7- Abner Lowe
8- David Proffitt
9- David Watson
10-Thomas Gill
11-William Kirk
12-Joe Hoe Jr.
13-Andrew Elder
14-Thomas Mann &
15-John Kidwell

A Deed of conveyance from Joseph Cobb to Nathaniel Taylor which has heretofore been probated before Judge Roane is Exhibited in open Court and State Tax paid.

Ordered by the Court that Andrew Elder be Excused from further attendance as a Juror at the present term.

Ordered by the Court that William Dodson be appointed a Constable for the County of Grainger in the bounds of Captain George Manns Company and the said William Dodson enters into bond together with Thomas Dennis and John Kitchen in the sum of five hundred Dollars for the prosecution and faithful discharge of the duties of Constable in said Company.

Ordered by the Court that John McPheters have leave to record his ear mark towit-one hole crop in the right ear and a swallow fork in the left ear.

On motion of Jesse Cheek by his Attorney Jacob Peck a rule is entered to shew cause why the said Jesse should have an order for a ferry on the South side of Clinch river on his own Land in Bristows bend in the County of Grainger.

Luke Lea)
  vs)
Jesse Higgs &)   On motion of the plaintiff by Jacob Peck his Atto.and
Bartly Marshal)   it appearing to the Court that on the 23rd. day of Feb.
1810 a Judgment was entered at the suit of Luke Lea in this Court against the Defendant Jesse for the sum of $107.50 besides costs- ten dollars twenty six and one fourth cents and it also appearing that fi-fa- issued.

(p 389)   Monday May 20th 1811

To the County of Jefferson on which a Stray Bond for twelve months was taken by the Sheriff of Jefferson County with Bartly Marshal Security dated the 20th day of March 1810 which term hath now Expired - It was therefore considered by the Court that the said Luke Lea recover against the said

Defendants Jesse and Bartlet the sum of one hundred and sixteen dollars sixty three cents the original principle and interest thereon from the said 20th day of February 1810 up to the present term of this Court and also the costs of this motion and the Defendant in mercy &c.

The Court enters a rule that hereafter they will take up causes for trial and proved to try causes on the first day of the term when caused are in a State for trial.

Ordered by the Court that Elijah Sims an orphan Boy of the age of twelve years be bound by Indenture to Martin Stubblefield until he arrives to the age of twenty one years.

Ordered by the Court that John Boyd —James Brown and David Tate be Judges on an ensuing Election to Elect a Governor—Members to assembly & representatives to Congress.

James Conn)
   vs   )   John Stiffey the Defendant appears as Bail in this case sur-
Wm Wilson)   renders him in open Court in Discharge of himself and the sd.
Defendant gives Jacob Peck —Thomas Wilson and William Hankins Esqr. as Bail for his appearance in the State of the said John Stiffey who appeared in open Court and acknowledged themselves indebted to the plaintiff in the sum of $200 conditioned that the said William shall perform the Decision of the Court or that they shall surrender his body in discharge of themselves or that he will do it for him.

Ordered by the Court that John Hall have leave to return his list of taxable property towit- 120 acres of Land and one white poll for the year 1811.
   Ordered by the Court, a majority of the acting Justices being present that James Conn Sheriff of Grainger County be allowed the sum of Eighty Dollars as full compensation for his Ex officio services from May. Issd.

Ordered by the Court a majority of the acting Justices being present that Sterling Cocke Clerk of Grainger County be allowed the sum of fifty Dollars as a compensation for his Ex officio services from May term of this Court. Issued.

Ordered by the Court, a majority of the acting Justices being present

(p 370)   Monday May 20th 1811
that Isaiah Midkiff be allowed $25 for compensation three months since his last allowance for keeping and maintaining Jeremiah Midkiff - one of the poor of this County, towit-$25 from November term 1810 & $25 from Feb. term 1811. Issued in full. to the present term of this Court.

Ordered by the Court, a majority of the acting Justices being present that Daniel Chandler be allowed the sum of twelve dollars for keeping and maintaining Ann Roane, one of the poor of this County from Feb. term 1811 till the present term and it is further ordered by the Justices aforesaid that the Chandler be allowed the further sum of twelve dollars for keeping Ann Roane one of the poor of this County from May term 1811 till August term 1811 with condition that if the said Ann Roane should die before the next term of this Court then there is to be a Deduction for the time that he has not kept her.

Ordered by the Court, a majority of the acting Justices being present that Samuel Perry Register of Grainger County be allowed the sum of twelve dollars and fifty cents for the purpose of purchasing a Register's book for said Court. .

Ordered by the Court a majority of the acting Justices being present that Samuel Peery Register of Grainger County be allowed the sum of twenty five cents for each Deed by him recorded previous to his getting a bound Book for the use of the County in which he has bee expected to record or transcribe from other books, Deeds heretofore registered by him in said Bound Book, the number of Deeds transcribed being ascertained amount to sixty eight for which he is allowed seventeen dollars.

Ordered by the Court that Solomon Massengill be appointed overseer of the road from the Owl hole gap in the Richland Knobbs at Crows old place to Moores old ferry in the room and stead of Abner Lowe and that he have the same bounds for hands to work under him on said Roads that said Abner Lowe had.   Issd.

Ordered by the Court that Adam Petree be appointed overseer of the road from Clinch river opposite Adam Petree and that the said Petree be allowed the same bounds for hands that was formerly allowed Alexander Cabbage.Isd.

Ordered by the Court that Samuel Dodson be appointed overseer of the road from opposite David Bunches to the Kentucky road and that he have the hands in the following bounds, towit-from Clinch mountain to Clinch River and below the Kentucky road down to opposite Ralph Sheltons thence across so as to include said Bunches to work under him as overseer of said road in the room and stead of Thomas Ogles -Overseer resigned.

(p 371)   Monday May 20th 1811

Ordered by the Court that James Parker be appointed overseer of the road in the room and stead of Abel Dale and that he have the same hands to work under him on said road that said Abel Dale had.Issued.

Wm Keith,Ranger of Grainger County makes the following return to Court. A list of Strays remaining on my books not proven away according to Law.
Joseph Noe Jr. - one horse ------ $12.12
Wm Clay Esqr. one mare ------------ 13.00
Wm Lane 6 head of hogs -------   9.?0
Wm Clay Esqr. 1 shoat--------   ?6 2/3
                                    $ 22.73 3/4
Wm Keith -Ranger of Grainger County.

The Jury, who were appointed to view and lay off a road the nearest & best way from Mayes ford on Clinch river to intersect the road leading from Cheeks X road to Mossy Creek Iron works at or near the house of Caleb Howell make their report to Court in the following words, towit- We the undersigned being duly sworn to view a road to near C.Howells -Beginning at Mayes ford thence along said road thence to John Daniels from thence to Malekiah Howells sugar camp from thence a straight line to M.Dowells ------thence along said road that leads from Mossy Creek Iron works to Cheeks X roads so as to

meet said road at the dwelling house of Caleb Howell.
Given under our hands the 14th day of May 1811.
Report ordered to be filed.

> Caleb Howell —Seal
> John Daniel —Seal
> Sherod Mays —Seal
> Henry Howell —Seal
> Malakiah Howell—Seal
> Henry Ivey ——— Seal
> Francis Daniel— Seal
> Jack Mitchell— Seal

Court adjourns till tomorrow morning 9 o'clock —

Tuesday May 21st. 1811— Court met according to adjournment.
Justices present, Thomas Henderson, Wm Keith and Isaiah Middiff, Esqrs.

Ordered by the Court that Benjamin Hudson by Henry Widener have leave
to return acres of land for taxes for the year 1811 which has not heretofore bee returned for said year.

On motion of Henry Boatman by John Cocke Esquire, his Attorney to enter up a Judgment against Caleb Reece, Thomas Reece and Wm Williams for the
sum of $195.40 for that sum of money which the said Henry Boatman suggests
he has paid as security for them the said Caleb Reece, Thomas Reece and Wm
Williams and because the Court are not satisfied that the said Henry Boatman is security as aforesaid —whereupon came a Jury, towit—

1— Wm Dodson	7— Henry Widener
2— David Elkins	8— Samuel Bunch
3— Samuel West	9— John C.Haley
4— Henry Howell	10—Rubin Crowe
5— Wm Robertson	11—Jesse Cheek
6— Edmund Bean	12—Enoch Moore

(p 372)   Tuesday May 21st. 1811
Who being elected tryed and sworn well and truly to inquire whether
Henry Boatman was security for the said Caleb Reece,Thomas Reece and Wm
Williams by him said Henry alledged and the Court being satisfied that
Henry has paid the sum of money as aforesaid — It is therefore considered
by the Court that the said Henry Boatman recover against the said Caleb
Reece, Thomas Reece and Wm Williams the aforesaid sum of $195.40 together
with his costs by him and about prosecuting his suit in that behalf Expend-
ed and the Defendants in mercy &c. Ex.Ised.

Thomas Gill, one of the Executors of Wm Copeland Deceased—exhibits to
Court an account of the sales of the Estate of said Deceased which is received by the Court and ordered to be recorded.

Ordered by the Court that Mary Copeland and Etheldred Williams be appointed Guardians of Cynthia Copeland,Ann F.Copeland, Samuel Copeland,and
Henry Copeland minor heirs of Wm Copeland Deceased for the special purpose
of attending to the interest of said minors, in a petition which it is stated to the Court will be presented to the next term of this Court by Henry
Howell for the purpose of obtaining a partition and division of the tracts

of land which it is suggested was held as tennants in common by the said Henry Howell and the said Wm Copeland in his lifetime.

Mathew Campbell Executor of the last Will and testament of Joseph Douglass Deceased returns to Court a list of the household and kitchen furniture of said Deceased as sold by him which is ordered to be recorded.

Ordered by the Court that Henry Rice be released from the pay of a polltax for 1811 by reason of his being exempted by Law on account of his age & it is ordered by the Court that the Sheriff refund to said Henry his poll tax if he has collected it and that he have a credit for the amount due the State on one poll in his settlement with the treasurer of the Districts of Washington & Hamilton and also a credit for the amount due the County in his settlement with the County Trustee.Jasi.

Ordered by the Court that Thomas Henderson, George Moody and Henry Boatman, Esquires be appointed to settle with Mathew Campbell Executor of Joseph Douglass Deceased and make report to the present term of this Court.

Edmund Bean)
  vs   )
Wyett Smith)   Justices present, Mathew Campbell, George Moody, David Tate and Noah Jernagin,Esquires.
    Whereupon came a Jury, towit-

(p 373)   Tuesday May 21st. 1811
1- Wm Dodson   7- Egrilla Mitchell
2- David Elkins   8- Therod Hays
3- Samuel Tact   9- Jesse Cheek
4- Major Lea   10-Malcalch Powell
5- Abner Lowe   11-Nicholas Counts
6- David Proffitt   12-John Cuddits

Who being elected tryed and sworn well and truly to try and the truth to speak on the matter in dispute in this case do say they find for the plaintiff and assess his damages to forty five dollars besides his costs. Whereupon Edmund Bean by John Cocke Esquire his Atto. moves the Court to enter up a Judgment against Felps Reed and Alex. Thompson securities of the said Wyett Smith for the aforesaid sum of forty five dollars and costs. It is therefore considered by the Court that the said Edmund Bean recover against the said Wyett Smith and Felps Reed and Alex.Thompson his securities the damages aforesaid in form aforesaid assessed together with his costs by him in and about prosecuting his said suit in this behalf expended from which Judgments the said Defendants pray an appeal to the next Circuit Court to be held for the County of Grainger at the Court House in Rutledge on the second Monday in October next -Bond executed -reasons filed and appeal Granted by the Court.
Alexander W.Sanders)
    vs   )
John C.Haley   )   Justices present, towit-George Moody, David Tate Thomas Henderson & Wm Keith,Esqrs. Whereupon came a Jury, towit-

1- Joseph Lea Jr. 3- Lazrol Brunson 5- John McFheeters 7-Therod Hays
2- Thomas Thurn   4- Abner Lowe   6- David Watson   8-Henry Whitener

9- Samuel Bunch - 10-Rubin Grove-11-Enoch Moore - 12- Jesse Harris

Who being elected tryed and sworn well and truly to try and the truth
to speak in this issue in this case do say they find the Defendant did not
assume in manner and form as the plaintiff in his Declaration against him
hath complained. It is therefore considered by the Court that the said John
Chaley recover against the said Harmon H.Sanders his costs by him in and
about prosecuting said suit in this behalf expended and the plaintiff in
mercy &c.

James Conn)
    vs)
William Wilson)   The plaintiff in this case by Chas.F.Keith Esquire his
Atto. with leave to the Court enters a rule to shew cause why the original
writ in this case should be amended by amending the plea of the writ.

John Smith)
    vs)
Noah Jarnagin) Justices present, James Moore, David Tate,John Moffett
and Wm Keith, Esqrs. Whereupon came a Jury, towit-

(p 374)   Tuesday May 21st. 1811

1- Wm Dodson	7- Aquilla Mitchell
2- David Elkins	8- John Kidwell
3- Samuel West	9- Jesse Cheek
4- John Hodge	10-Malichiah Harrell
5- Jeremiah Selvage	11-Thomas Gill &
6- David Proffett	12-John Griffetts

Who being elected tried and sworn well and truly & the truth to speak
on the issue found &c. Whereupon John Cocke Attorney for Plaintiff directs
a non suit to be entered.

John Smith)
    vs)
Noah Jarnagin) In this case the Jury impannelled & sworn & John McElhiney
who was legally subpoened to attend as a witness in this case & give evidence on behalf of John Smith the Plaintiff being solemnly called to come
into Court & give testimony in this case, came not but altogether failed
& made default. It is therefore considered by the Court that said John Mc
Elhaney for each his default do forfeit the sum of one hundred & twenty five
Dollars according to act of Assembly in such case made and provided & that
a Sci.fa. do issue to the said John McElhaney to shew cause if any he has or
can why Judgment final may not be awarded against him.

Ordered by the Court that Israel McBee be appointed overseer of the road
leading from the ford of Dodsons Creek to Robert Huddleston in the room of
Mathew Talley and that he have the same bounds for hands that said Talleys
had.
Mathew Campbell Executor of the Will and Testament of Joseph Douglass
deceased Exhibits to Court a supplemental account of the sales of said Estate which is received by the Court and ordered to be recorded.

Thomas Henderson, James Moore and Henry Boatman Esqrs. who were

appointed at the present Term to settle with Campbell Executor of the estate
of Joseph Douglass deceased returns an account of said settlement to Court
which is received and ordered to be recorded.

Mathew Campbell Executor of the Estate of Joseph Douglass deceased is
appointed by the Court Guardian of the estate of Samuel Douglass -Fanny
Douglass and Nancy Douglass and younger Douglass minor heirs of Joseph Douglass deceased and the said Mathew Campbell appointed in open Court together
with Wm Mitchell and Samuel Peery, who gave Bond with the above securities
to David Tate, Noah Jarnagin & Wm Keith Justices of Grainger County in the
sum of seven hundred and ninety two dollars for his faithful Guardianship

Court adjourns till tomorrow morning 9 o'clock.

(p 375)   Wednesday May 22nd. 1811 -Court met according to adjournment,
Justices present, Thomas Henderson, James Moore and Philip Sigler Esqrs.

Ordered by the Court that Godfrey Cariger have leave to return his lists
of taxable property for the year 1811, towit- 500 acres of Land on Richland
Creek.
Jesse Cheek)
    vs   )
George Evans)   Justices present, Thomas Henderson, Joseph Cobb, Henry Boatman and James Moore, Esqrs. Thereupon come the parties by their Attorneys &
a Jury, towit-
1- William Dodson   7- John Breeden
2- David Elkins   8- Thomas Brown
3- Samuel West   9- Thomas Jones
4- Abner Love   10-Richard Shelton
5- Thomas Gill   11-John McBroon
6- Henry Hamill   12-James Simpson

Who being elected tried and sworn well & truly to try and the truth to
speak in this case, having retired from the Barr for the purpose of consid-
ering of their opinion in this case.

Wednesday May the 22nd. 1811
    Returned into Court and having agreed on their Verdict the Court by con-
sent of the Parties suffered Jury to be discharged and a mistrial by Consent.

The issues on which the above impannelled Jurors were sworn to try are
the following towit- was Jesse Cheek, the Caveator settled down and in ac-
tual possession of the Land included in the defendants George Evans Survey
on or before the first day of January one thousand eight hundred and nine.
Issues tendered by the Plaintiff - Has the Plaintiff or defendant the legal
right of Survey.
                J.Cooke &
                J.Peck Attorneys
    Ordered by the Court that the following persons be Jurors to attend the
next Circuit Court to be holden of the Court House in Rutledge the second
Monday in Oct. next, towit- Carried over.

(p 376)   Wednesday May the 22nd. 1811

1- David Tate Esqr.	21- Joseph Long
2- James Brown	22-Robert Dixon
3- John Arwine	23-Edmond Churchman
4- Edward Tate	24-Henry Widener
5- McNess Moore	25-Abel Dale
6- John Noe	26-Wm McPhetridge
7- Henry Boatman	27-David McAnally Sr.
8- James Carmichael	28-Royal Jinnings
9- John Moffitt	29-Thomas Sharp
10-Peter Harris	30-Robert Blair
11-Daniel Taylor	31-Robert Caines
12-Henry Howell	32- Henry Ivey
13-Caleb Howell	33- Joseph Cobb
14-John Moody	34- Phelps Reed
15-Joseph Beeler	35- James Simpson
16-Samuel McBee	36- Thomas Bunch
17-Wm Hamilton	37- Daniel Robertson
18-John Hayes	38- Nicholas Counts
19-Samuel Peery	
20-George Sparkman	

Ordered by the Court that the following persons be appointed to attend as Jurors at the next Term of this Court, towit-

1- Thomas Bunch	7- James Hill
2- Andrew McPheeters	8- Robert D.Eaton
3- Wm Kirkham	9- Nicholas Counts
4- Martin Albert	10-Samuel Peery
5- Henry Howell	11-Reubin Dalton
6- Abel Hill	12-David Holt
	13-Samuel Dodson
	14-George Noe
	15-Henry Crawley

Ordered by the Court that Samuel Blyth have leave to return his list of taxable property for the year 1811, towit-12,734 acres of Land in 13 tracts adjoining or nearly adjoining each other on the South East side

(p 377)   Wednesday May the 22nd. 1811
of Clinch River and also that Robert Snook have leave to return his lists of taxable property for the year 1811, towit- 17,212 acres in 18 tracts adjoining or nearly adjoining each other on the waters above mentioned, or at least principal part on said waters and further that John Leonard have leave to return his list of Taxable property for said year of 1811-towit, 4880 acres of Land in 37 tracts adjoining or nearly adjoining each other & that Samuel Nicholson have leave to return his list of taxable property for the year 1811, towit-3370 acres of Land in 113 tracts among the above motion and on the waters of Bull Run and Black Fox Creek and that John Woodward have leave to return his list of Taxable property towit- 1120 and in 13 tracts adjoining the Lands of Samuel Blyth -Robert & John Leonards Note & other Grants and former sales in the above division which fill up its bounds making in all about 70,000 acres.   A list of Lands in the County of Grainger first in Kings big Survey which survey lies in the Counties of Grainger & Claiborne-& Hawkins on both sides of Clinch River, extending from Clinch Mountain to Powell's Mt.and from black waters Creek to Indian Creek-Granted to James King -Samuel Blyth, 10,000 acres between the waters of Indian Creek

and German Creek.

Samuel Nicholson, 200 acres of Land in 5 tracts among branches of Clinch
River- Robert Snock - 100 acres of Land in tracts near the heads of Indian
Creek and German Creek. The foregoing Lists returned in open Court by Sam-
uel Nicholson.

James Charles motion)
    vs   )   Charles F.Keith Atto. for the plaintiff in this
Stephen W.Senter &   )   case directs in open Court that this suit go off
Tandy Senter   )   the docket. It is considered by the Court that
the defendants recover of the plaintiff the cost in & about prosecuting the
said motion in this behalf expended and the plaintiff in mercy & —Justices
present, Thomas Henderson,James Moore and Henry Boatman, Esquires.

David Proffitt   )
    vs   )
Thomas Whitesides)   Thereupon came the parties by their Attornies and a
Jury, towit-
1- John McWhetern   7- George Owens
2- Major Lea   8- Nicholas Counts
3- David Jobson   9- Joel Martin
4- Joseph Moe   10-Balser Sherley
5- Thomas Mann   11-William Dyer
6- John Kilwell   12-Dudley Hayes

(p 378)   Wednesday May the 22nd. 1811
Who being elected tried and sworn well and truly to try and the truth
to speak in this issue joined in this case -

William Clay, Charles McAnally and David McAnally Esqrs. Commissioners
appointed by the Court to settle with Philip Sigler and Robert Hall Admrs.
of William Hall deceased, exhibits an account of said settlement to Court
which is received by the Court and ordered to be recorded.

William Clay, David McAnally and Philip Sigler Esqrs. who were appointed at the last Term of the Court to settle with Sarah Shelton Administratrix
of the estate of Wm Shelton deceased exhibits to Court an account of said
settlement which is received by the Court and ordered to be recorded.

Court adjourned till tomorrow morning 7 o'clock.
Court met according to adjournment -
              Thursday May the 23th 1811
Justices present, Thomas Henderson, Charles McAnally and James Moore-Wm
Keith, Esqrs.

David Proffitt   )
    vs -No. 652)
Thomas Whitesides) this day came here again as well the said David Proffitt
as the said Thomas Whitesides and their Attornies and the Jurors aforesaid
who having been elected tried and sworn as aforesaid &c.

Court adjourns for twenty minutes- Court met according to adjournment
Justices present, Thomas Henderson, Henry Boatman and James Moore.

David Proffitt)
      vs)
Thomas Whitesides) This day come here again their said parties by their attornies & the Jurors aforesaid who having been elected tried and sworn as
aforesaid to do say the Defendant is guilty of the trespass &c in manner &
form as the plaintiff in his declaration against him hath complained & that
he is not justified as in pleading he hath alledged & assess the plaintiffs
damages by reason of said trespass to twenty dollars besides his costs— It
is therefore considered by the Court that plaintiff David do recover against
the defendant Thomas his damages aforesaid in form aforesaid assessed and
the defendant in mercy &c — from which Judgment the said Thomas hath prayed
an appeal to the next Circuit Court to be held for the County of Grainger
at the Court House in Rutledge on the second Monday   (p 379)   in

                 Thursday May the 23rd. 1911

October next files reasons in writing for his said appeal and enters into
bond together with James Kennedy and Wm Whitesides in the sum of two hundred fifty dollars for the prosecution of his said appeal —whereupon said
appeal is granted by the Court.

      The Jury who were appointed at the last term of this Court to view &
lay off a public road to leave the Turnpike road near Beans old plantation
running up Copper Valley to the County line so as to meet the Road extending over said Valley through Hawkins County makes their report to Court and
in as much as there is not a sufficient number of Justices present to act
on said report it is ordered by the Court that said report stand continued
over to be acted upon at the next Term of this Court.

      Ordered by the Court that Caleb Howell be appointed overseer over that
part of the road leading from Mayes ford on Holston River to Caleb Howell's
on the County line and that said Howell have the following hands to work on
said road, towit— all the hands in the bounds of Capt. Howell's Company.

      Ordered by the Court that Wm Snodgrass be appointed overseer of the
road from Coxes old plantation to the Knox County line in the room and stead
of James Elkins that the said William have the same bounds for hands to
work on said road that James Elkins had.

      Ordered by the Court that James Davis an orphan now of the age of nine
years be bound after the manner of an apprentice to Henry Boatman until he
shall attain the age of 21 years and the said James Davis is bound by Indenture according to the directions of the Act of Assembly in that case made
and provided to the said Henry Boatman.

John Hall   )
    vs Covenant)   Issue & Demurrer
David Stuart   )   Issue of covenant performed only submitted to the Jury
Justices present, Joseph Cobb, David Tate, Isiah Midtiff & Wm Keith.
Thereupon came a Jury, towit—

1- Wm Dodson	7- Henry Howell
2- David Elkins	8- Edward Strange
3- Samuel West	9- Thomas James
4- Abner Lowe	10-John Campbell
5- David Proffitt	11-John Humphreys
6- Thomas Gill	12-John Bull

Tho being elected tried and sworn well and truly to try and the truth
to speak on the issue joined in this case do say the defendant hath not kept

Thursday May the 23rd. 1811
(p 390)   and performed his covenant in pleading he hath alledged & assess
the plaintiffs damages occasioned by reason of the non-performance thereof
to three thousand and sixty four Dollars and costs.

   I, John Hall do hereby vest the interest of the above Judgment in John
Cocke but am in no wise to be responsible for any deficiency if the same or
any part should not be collected.
                    John Hall
   Ordered by the Jury be released from further attendance at the present
Term.
   Court adjourned till tomorrow morning 7 o'clock.
                Friday May the 24th 1811-

   Court met according to adjournment -Justices present, Thomas Henderson
James Moore and David Tate, Esqrs.

   A Bill of sale from Joseph Cooper -Mary Cooper,Mary Cooper, Jacob Meyer
Mary Meyer, Benj.Crowe, Polley Crowe, Benj.Horton, Villey Horton,John Jarnagin Sr. Mary Jarnagin of the County of Highland and State of Ohio to John
Cocke of the town of Rutledge County of Grainger of Tennessee for five negro
slaves, to wit- Dolly Thomas, Jeff James and John was presented to the Court
and authentication thereon from the State of Ohio being read on motion it is
ordered by the Court that said Bill of sale be committed to record-Let it
be Registered.

John Hall.   )
No.651 - App.)
David Stewart)   Justices present, Joseph Cobb, Wm Keith, Henry Roabrum,
James Moore, Thomas Henderson & David Tate,Esqrs.

   David Stewart the defendant by Jacob Peck,Esqr. his Atto.this day
comes here into Court & tenders a Bill of Exceptions to the opinion of the
Court yesterday, which the Court refuses to sign, because it was not in the
opinion of the Court tendered in due time.

John Hall   )
651 vs   )
David Stewart)   This day comes the defendant David Stewart, Jacob Peck
Esqrs. Attorney and moves in arrest of Judgment and files his reasons in
writing in arrest of Judgment.

(p 391)   Friday May the 24th 1811

Andrew Stone)
     vs   )
David Proffitt) This day here the defendant by John Williams Esqr. his Atto.
and presents a petition to the Court praying a petition to the Court, praying
that writs of Certiorari and Super orders may issue in this case which being
read & considered of the Court. It is ordered by the Court that writs do issue agreeably to the prayer of the petition.

William McNeill)
   vs   )   Motion
James Conn,Sheriff)   Justices present, David Tate, Wm Keith, Henry Boatman,
Isaiah Midkiff, James Moore & Noah Jarnagin,Esqrs.

      The motion which was heretofore made in this case to enter up a Judg-
ment against the said James Conn Sheriff for the sum of twelve dollars &
ninety nine cents, this day came on to be argued and after a Judgment of
Council being heard as well in support of said motion as against it- It is
therefore considered by the Court that the said Wm McNeill do recover against
the said sum of twelve dollars and ninety nine cents together with his costs
by him in and about prosecuting his said motion in this behalf expended and
the defendnt in mercy &c. from which Judgment the said James Conn prays an
appeal to the next Circuit Court of Law and Equity to be held for the County
of Grainger at the Court House in Rutledge on the second Monday of October
next and the said James Conn enters into Bond together with Henry Howell &
Thomas Cocke his securities in the sum of $100 for the prosecution of his sd.
appeal & files his reasons in writing for his said appeal -whereupon said
appeal is granted by the Court.

      Isaac Campbell constable has attended on the Court five days, at the
present Term.

John Baker   )
   vs   )
Robert Massengill &)   This day comes here the defendant by John Cocke
James Alsup   )   Esqr. their Atto. and moves the Court to non pross
the plaintiff for want of replication to the first plea of the Defendant.
After argument it is ordered by the Court that the plaintiff be non pross-
ed to which opinion of the Court the said plaintiff by Jacob Peck & Clement
C.Clay Esqrs. his attorneys tenders a Bill of exceptions, which is signed &
sealed by Isaiah Midkiff, Henry Boatman & Noah Jarnagin, Esqrs. whereupon
the said John Baker by Jacob Peck and Clement C.Clay Esqrs. his attornies
move the Court for a writ of errors to remove the proceedings in this cause
to the next Circuit Court, of Law to be held for Grainger County at the Court-
House in Rutledge on the second Monday in Oct. next and enters into Bond with
Jacob Peck, James Moore and Clement C.Clay his securities for the prosecution
of said writ of Error and the

(p 382)   Friday May the 24th 1811-
said Plaintiff by his Attorney files an assignment of Errors is granted by
the Court.

John Hall   )
   vs   )
David Stewart)   Justices present, David Tate, Thomas Henderson -Henry
Boatman & Isaiah Midkiff- This day came therefore said parties by their Attornies. The demurrers filed in this cause came on to be argued and after
arguments of Council being heard thereon. It is ordered by the Court, that
the demurrers be sustained, the reasons in arrest of Judgment filed in this
case, this day came on to be argued and after arguments of Council being
had thereon it is therefore ordered by the Court that the reasons in arrest
of Judgment be over ruled. It is therefore considered by the Court that the
Plaintiff John Hall do recover against the Defendant David Stewart the sum
of three thousand and sixty four Dollars the damages by the Jurors in this

case assessed by reasons of the non performance of the Covenant of said Defendant, together with his costs by him in and about prosecuting his said suit in this behalf expended and the defendant in mercy &c.

Ordered by the Court that Wm Snodgrass be appointed overseer of the road in the room and stead of James Elkins and that he have the hands and same bounds for work that Elkins had.

Elizabeth Short)
vs)
Isaiah Midkiff) Justices present, Joseph Cobb, Henry Boatman, Noah Jarnagin & James Moore- This day came here the said Elizabeth Short by Pleasant M.Miller Esqr.her Attorney and with leave of the Court enters a motion to set aside the writ of Super cedeas issued in this case and after arguments of Council being had thereon it is considered by the Court that the Certiorari in this case be dismissed.

May Term 1811.

Ordered by the Court that James Gill be appointed a Judge of the General Election which is the first thursday and Friday in August next in the room and place of John Boyd appointed the first day of the Term.

May Term 1811

James Conn, Sheriff and collector for the years 1810 and eleven reports to Court, the following Tracts of Land as not having bee given in for the years 1810 and 1811, towit-

Friday May the 24th 1811

(p 383)
William Hunt, Panther Creek, 170 acres for the years 1810 and 1811.
Samuel Minet - 9000 acres North of Holston River for the years 1810 and 1811, therefore it is considered by the Court that Judgment be rendered against the owners of said tracts of Land for a double tax & the costs thereon.

Court adjourned till Court in Course.

Thomas Henderson.

Monday August Sessions 1811

At a Court of pleas and quarter sessions began and holden for the County of Grainger at the court house of Rutledge on the third Monday in August in the year of our Lord one thousand eight hundred and eleven and on the 19th day of said month Justices present, George Moody, David Tate and Mathew Campbell, Esqrs.

James Conn, Esquire high sheriff of said County makes report to Court that he has executed the Venire facias on the following persons, towit-

1- Thomas Bunch
2- Wm Kirkham
3- Henry Howell
4- Abel Hill x
John Hill Excused
6- Robert D.Eaton excused
7- Nicholas Counts
8- Samuel Peery
9- Rubin Dalton
10-David Holt
11-Samuel Dodson
12-George Noe excused
13-Henry Crawley x
14-Martin Albert

James Conn comes into Court and appoints Isaac Campbell to attend on the Court at the present term.

Henry Howell)
   vs) Justices present, David Tate, Philip Sigler, George Moody
Robert Yancey), and Thomas Brown, Esqrs. On motion of Henry Howell by John Cocke, Esqr. his Atto. to enter up a Judgment against Robert Yancey for the sum of six dollars together with the sum of three dollars and six cents interest &c. which sum the said Henry Howell alledged he has been compelled to pay as one of the securities of the said Robert Yancey and it appearing to the satisfaction of the Court that the said Henry Howell has been compelled to pay the said sum of six dollars as one of the securities

Monday August Sessions 1811

(p 384) of the said Robert Yancey - It is therefore considered by the Court that Judgment be entered up against the said Robert Yancey for the sum of six dollars principal together with the sum of three dollars and six cents Interest and also the costs attending the motion and the Defendant in mercy.

Henry Howell)
   vs)
Robert Yancey) Justices present, Mathew Campbell, David Tate & Philip Sigler.

   On motion of Henry Howell by John Cocke Esqr. his Atto. to enter up a Judgment against Robert Yancey for the sum of Twenty one dollars principal together with the sum of seven dollars and thirty five cents interest which sum of twenty one dollars the said Henry Howell alledged he has been compelled to pay for said Robert Yancey as one of his securities and it appearing to the satisfaction of the Court that the said Henry has been compelled to pay said sum of twenty one dollars as one of the securities of the said Robert Yancey. It is ordered by the Court that Judgment be entered against the said Robert Yancey for the sum of twenty one dollars principal together with the sum of seven dollars thirty five cents Interest &c. and also the costs attending this motion the aforesaid in mercy &c.

Ordered by the Court that Nimrod Cyrus have leave to alter his Ear mark from a crop in the right Ear and a swallow fork in the Left Ear.

Ordered by the Court that Henry Hawkins be appointed a constable in the bounds of Thomas Sharp's Company militia and the said Henry Hawkins comes into Court with Mathew Campbell his securities and enters into Bond in the sum of five hundred dollars for the performance of the said appointment - whereupon the said Henry Hawkins is appointed as aforesaid.

Henry Howell)
   vs)
Robert Yancey) Justices present, Mathew Campbell -David Tate & Philip Sigler, Esqrs.

   On motion of Henry Howell by John Cocke, Esqr. his Atto. to enter up a Judgment against Robert Yancey for the sum of six dollars and thirty cents which he, the said Henry Howell alledged he has been compelled to pay as one of the securities of the said Robert Yancey, together with the sum of two dollars and seventy cents Interest &c and it appearing to the satisfaction of the (p 385) Court that the said Henry Howell has been compelled

to pay the said sum of six dollars and thirty cents as security for the sd.
Robert Yancey &c. It is therefore considered by the Court that Judgment be
entered against the said Robert Yancey for the sum of six dollars principal
together with the sum of two dollars and seventy cents Interest &c and also
the costs attending this motion and Defendant in mercy &c.

John Hall)
    vs)
David Stewart)   Justices present, David Tate, Mathew Campbell, George Moody
& Philip Sigler, Esqrs. In this case a writ of fieri facias having issue
directed to the Sheriff of Cocke County and came to the hands of Thomas Mitchell Sheriff of said County and he returns to Court that he did on the 13th.
day of July 1811-Levy on one Bay mare and other property she ——— in his
return and said Sheriff for their endorsee on said Execution that the sale
was stopped by a Replevy -whereupon Thomas George Esqr. Atto. for the said
John Hall makes a motion to Court to set aside said return & that the Court
may award an alias writ of fieri facias to the Sheriff of Cocke County, after
arguments of Council being heard as well in support of said motion as against
It is ordered by the Court that return be set aside and that an alias writ of
Fieri Facias do issue &c. and it was further ordered by the Court that the
Clerk do return the replevy Bond taken by him in this case, from which Judg-
ment the said David Stewart by Jacob Peck, Esqr. his Atto. prays an appeal to
the next Circuit Court of Law and Equity to be holden for the County of
Grainger at the Court house in Rutledge on the second Monday of October next.

    Ordered by the Court that Isaiah McBee be appointed overseer of the road
leading from Dodsons Creek to Robert Huddlestons— Beginning at the fork of
the road half a mile from said Huddlston to the fork of said Huddleston to
the fork North of Wm Haines plantation and the McBee be allowed the same
bounds for hands that Mathew Talley had.

    Ordered by the Court that Joseph Dennis be appointed overseer of the
road from the ford of Flat Creek at Nalls meeting house to the fork of the
road near Robert Fields and that he have Lewis Atkins, Richard Atkins, Adam
Hinchey, Martin Thornberry and Robert Fields original Bounds for hands to
work on said Road.

    Ordered by the Court that Thomas Dennis be appointed overseer of the
road in the room and stead of Wm Dodson and that he have the same bounds
for hands to work under him on said road that said Wm Dodson had.

    Ordered by the Court that Alex. Hume be appointed overseer of the road
in the room and stead of John Richardson and that he have the same bounds
for hands that said Richardson had to work under him on said road.

(p 386)   Monday August the 19th 1811

    Ordered by the Court that Royal Jinnings have all the hands in the
bounds heretofore allowed him that Wm Kirby have all the hands in the bounds
heretofore allowed him and Samuel Dodson's have all the residue of the hands
heretofore -Thomas Ogle to work under them respectively as overseer of their
respective roads.

    Ordered by the Court that Abner Trogden be appointed overseer of the road in the room and stead of Meredith Coffee and that the same bounds for hands that the said Coffee had.

A Bill of Sale from Milton Senter to John F. Jack for a negro slave named Billy was proven in open Court by the oaths of Sterling Cocke and John Cocke subscribing witnesses thereto and admitted to record. Let it be registered.

Court adjourned till tomorrow morning 9 o'clock.

Court met according to adjournment- Justices present, David Tate, Mathew Campbell and Philip Sigler, Esqrs.

On application John Cocke Esqr. has leave to administer on all and singular the goods and chattels rights and credits of Zackfield Macklin deceased not administered on and the said John Cocke enters into Bond in the sum of fifteen hundred dollars with John F. Jack and Sterling Cocke his securities whereupon the said John Cocke was qualified according to Law.

Ordered by the Court that John Smith be released from the payment of the taxes Due on one Stud horse it appearing to the satisfaction of the Court that the said horse has been returned as taxable property for the year 1811 in Claiborne County and that said Smith has prayed said tax due on said horse in said County of Claiborne- and it is further ordered that James Conn Shff. and collector of the publick and the County taxes for the said year be released from the payment of one dollar and fifty cents the amount of the State tax due on said horse for said year and the said James Conn be released from the Jury and all other County tax due for the year 1811 on said horse.

(p 387)   Tuesday August the 20th 1811

Thomas Bunch }
   vs   }
Robert Yancey }   Justices present, David Tate, Mathew Campbell & Philip Sigler, Esqrs. On motion of Thomas Bunch by John Cocke Esqr. his Atto. to enter up a Judgment against Robert Yancey for the sum of thirty dollars which sum the said Thomas Bunch alledged he has been compelled to pay as one of the securities of said Robert Yancey together with the further sum of twelve dollars and sixty cents Interest &c. and it appearing to the satisfaction of the Court that said Thomas Bunch has been compelled to pay said sum of money as security of said Robert. It is therefore considered by the Court that Judgment be entered against the said Robert Yancey for the sum of thirty dollars together with the further sum of twelve dollars and sixty cents Interest &c. and also the costs attending this motion and the Defendant in mercy &c.

Ordered by the Court that Philip Sigler Esqr. be allowed the sum of thirty dollars and fifty cents for services by him performed as administrater of the Estate of William Hall deceased.

Ordered by the Court that William Hutcheson be appointed a constable in the bounds of James Brown's Company and the Wm Hutcheson comes into Court together with Thomas James & George Coffman his securities and enters into Bond in the sum of five hundred dollars for the faithful discharge of his said appointment and the said William is qualified.

according to Law.

William Keith Rainger of Grainger County returns the following Lists to Court. A list of Strays remaining on my Book not proven away according to Law, towit- Wm Kirby- one horse appraised ——————————————————$40.00
Henry Crawley - one Bay horse appraised to ———————————— 25.00
William Clay Esqr. - one Sorrel mare appraised to ———————— 19.00
William Keith -Rainger for Grainger County.

Joseph M.Anderson)
    vs   )
Robert Yancey   )   Justices present, David McAnally, Wm Keith,George Moody & Philip Sigler, Esqrs.

On motion of Joseph M.Anderson by John Cocke Esqr. his Atto. to enter up a judgment against Robert Yancey for the sum of one hundred dollars with interest which sum the said Joseph M.Anderson alledged he has been compelled to pay for the said Robert Yancey whereupon the Court Directs the following

(p 388)   to be impannelled to enquire whether the said Joseph M.Anderson was security of said Robert Yancey & where upon said Joseph M.Anderson was compelled to pay as security aforesaid whereupon came a jury to enquire of the above facts towit-

1- Thomas Bunch
2- William Kirkham
3- Henry Howell
4- Nicholas Counts
5- Samuel Peery
6- Reubin Dalton
7- David Holt
8- Samuel Dodson
9- Jas.Richardson
10-Wm Robinson
11-William Stone
12-Andrew Stone

Who being elected tried and sworn well and truly to enquire & the truth to speak in this case do say they find the said Joseph M.Anderson was security of the said Robert Yancey & that he has paid one hundred dollars about five years ago as security of said Robert Yancey to John Moffitt whereupon the said plaintiff by his said Attorney moves to enter up a judgment against said defendant for the sum of one hundred dollars with interest for five years. It is therefore considered by the Court that said plaintiff do recover against said Defendant the aforesaid sum of one hundred dollars and also the further sum of thirty dollars his damages occasioned by reason of the detention of that Debt & also the costs attending this motion and the said plaintiff comes into Court and acknowledges to have received sixteen dollars about twelve months ago, which sum he directs to be credited on the above judgment.

Ordered by the Court that James Moore, Noah Jarnagin & Wm Keith Esqrs. be commissioners to settle with Margaret Hall guardian of the minor heirs of James Hall deceased and make report to the present Term of this Court.

Court adjourns for half an hour- Court met according to adjournment. Justices present, David Tate, Mathew Campbell & George Moody,Esqrs.

Ordered by the Court that Jane Adkins be bound by Indenture to Jacob Noe until she be eighteen years old.

Ordered by the Court that the following persons be a jury to view &

lay off a road the nearest and best way from Blackwells Branch to James Rich-
ardsons below Buffalow Creek & make report to next Court, towit-David Tate Jr.
William James, John Gallion, Samuel West, Henry Howell, Jas.Richardson &
John Humphreys.

(p 389)   Tuesday August the 20th 1811

Ambrose Yancey)
     vs   )
Robert Yancey)   Justices present, David McAnally,George Moody, David Tate
& Joseph Cobb.

     Ambrose Yancey by John Cooke Esqr. his Atto. makes a motion to Court to
enter up a judgment against said Robert Yancey for money which he alledged
he has been compelled to pay as security of said Robert Yancey and because
the Court is not satisfied that said Ambrose Yancey was security of said
Robert and what sum he has paid as security whereupon came a jury to enquire of said facts, towit-

1- Thomas Bunch   7- David Holt
2- William Kirkham   8- Samuel Dodson
3- Balsar Sherley   9- Joseph Rich
4- Nicholas Counts   10-Wm Robison
5- Samuel Peary   11-Wm Stone
6- Reuben Dalton   12-Daniel Robison

     Who being elected tried and sworn well and truly to enquire and the truth
to speak on the above facts do say they find that the above Ambrose Yancey
was security of said Robert & that he has been compelled to pay one hundred
and sixty four dollars and eighty two cents -whereupon it is ordered by the
Court that said Ambrose do recover against the said Robert the sum of one hundred sixty four dollars and eighty two cents damage occasioned by reason of
the detention of the Debt and also the costs attending this motion & the Defendant in mercy will ever &c.

Heirs and Legal representatives of)
William Henderson   )
     vs   )
Robert Yancey   ) Justices present, David Tate, Mathew
Campbell and Philip Sigler, Esqrs.

     On motion of the heirs and Legal representatives of Wm Henderson by Thos.
Gray, Esqr. their Attorney to enter up a Judgment against Robert Yancey for
the sum of eleven Dollars & seventy five cents together with interest &c which
sum of eleven Dollars seventy five cents the said representatives of the sd.
Wm Henderson alledges they have been compelled to pay as security of Robert
Yancey and it appearing to the satisfaction of the Court that the said representatives or those whom they represent have been compelled to pay the sd.
sum of Eleven Dollars seventy five cents. It is therefore considered by the
Court that the heirs of and Legal representatives of the said Wm Henderson
do recover against the said Robert Yancey the sum of Eleven Dollars seventy
five cents principal together with the further sum of —— dollars and seventy five cents interest &c. and also the costs attending this motion and
the Defendant in mercy will ever &c.

(p 390)   Tuesday August the 20th 1811

Charles McAnally)
  vs   )
Robert Yancey   )   Justices present, Wm Clay, David Tate and Joseph Cobb
Esqrs. On motion of Charles McAnally by John Cocke, Esqrs. his attorney to
enter up a Judgment against Robert Yancey for the sum of four dollars together with the further sum of one dollar and twenty eight cents for Interest
on said sum of four Dollars, which said sum of four Dollars the said Charles
McAnally alledges he has been compelled to pay as one of the securities of
said Robert Yancey and it appearing to the satisfaction of the Court that the
said Charles McAnally had been compelled to pay the said sum of four Dollars
as one of the securities of the said Robert. It is therfore considered by
the Court that Judgment be entered up against the said Robert Yancey in favour of plaintiff Charles for the sum of four Dollars principal together with
the further sum of one dollar and eighty cents Interest and also the costs
attending this motion and the Defendant in mercy &c.

George Noe   )
  vs   )
Robert Yancey)   Justices present, David Tate, Philip Sigler and George
Moody. On motion of George Noe by John Cocke, Esqr. his Atto. to enter up
a Judgment against Robert Yancey for the sum of $28 which the said George
Noe alledged he has been compelled to pay for said Robert Yancey as one of
the securities and it appearing to the satisfaction of the Court that the
said George Noe has been compelled to pay the said sum of $28 as security
for said Robert. It is therefore considered by the Court that Judgment be
entered up against the said Robert Yancey for the sum of $28 and princi-
pal together with the further sum of eight dollars and sixty one cents Int.
&c and also the costs attending this motion and the Defendant in mercy &c.

    Ordered by the Court that Henry Crawley be released from the papayment
of $25 due a stray mare by him taken and posted, it appearing to the satis-
faction of the Court that said Stray has been proven away according to Law.

John Nicely)
  vs   ) Lease
John Smith)

(p 391)   Tuesday August the 20th 1811

    John Smith the Defendant in proper person comes into Court and surren-
ders himself in discharge of his Bail in the above case, whereupon Wm Robison and Jacob Fack comes into Court and undertake that the said Defendant
will pay the condemnation money surrenders himself into prison in their discharge or that they will do it for him.

    On motion of James Richardson and John Richardson by John Cocke Esqrs.
their Atto. to award a Subpoena and direct the same to issue to Margaret Hall
requiring of his guardian of the minor heirs of her late husband to render
an account of his guardianship at the next Term of this Court. It is considered by the Court that a Subpoena do issue to the Margaret Hall, guardian of
the minor heirs of her said late husband requiring of her as guardian of sd.
minor heirs to appear at the next Term of this Court and render an account
of her guardianship.
    Ordered by the Court that the following Jury be appointed to attend

at November Term of this Court A.D.1811-Viz.

1- James Hodges   7- Robert D.Eaton
2- Thomas Parker   8- Abner Lowe
3- John Hill   9- Thomas Bunch
4- Gilbert Vandergtiff   10-Robert McGinnis
5- Wm Haynes   11-John Vineyard Sr.
6- Wm James   12-David Coats
                             13-Samuel Moffitt

Ambrose Yancey)
       vs   )
Robert Yancey) Justices present, David Tate, Mathew Campbell & Philip
Sigler, Esqr. - On motion of Ambrose Yancey by John Cocke Esqr. his Atto.
& enter up a Judgment against Robert Yancey for the sum of ten dollars prin.
together with interest &c which sum of ten dollars the said Ambrose Yancey
alledges he has been compelled to pay as security of said Robert Yancey and
it appearing to the satisfaction of the Court that the said Ambrose Yancey
has been compelled to pay the said sum of ten dollars as security of said
Yancey - It is therefore considered by the Court that the said Ambrose Yancey do recover against the said Robert Yancey the sum of ten dollars principal together with the sum of three dollars and forty two cents interest
and also the costs.

     Ordered by the Court that Henry Hipsher be appointed overseer of the
road from the Kentucky road up the Copper Valley to the Hawkins County Line
and that he be allowed all the hands from the road West of the Hawkins line
East to the top of Clinch Mountain South to Clinch River North to work under him as overseer on said road.

(p 392)   Tuesday August the 20th 1811
     Court adjourned till Court in Course.
                                 D.McAnally   )
                                 James Brown) Esqrs.

               Monday November 18th A.D. 1811
     At a Court of pleas and quarter Sessions began and holden for the County
of Grainger at the Court house in Rutledge on the third Monday of November
of the year of our land one thousand eight hundred and eleven being the 18
day of said month.
                 Justices present, David Tate- Isaiah Midkiff
                                 George Moody.
(p 393)   Monday November 18th A.D. 1811

     James Conn, Esqr. high Sheriff of said County returns to Court that he
has executed the Venire facias on the following persons except Thomas Parker
and David Counts- Viz.

1- James Hodges   8- Thomas Bunch
2- Thomas Parker   9- Robert McGinnis
3- John Hill   10-John Vinyard Sr.
4- Gilbert Vandegriff   11-David Counts
5- William James   12-Samuel Moffitt
6- William Haynes   13-Abner Lowe
7- Robert D.Eaton

The Court appointed Edward Tate Constable to attend on the Court at present term.

James Conn & his wife)
Jenny Conn late)
Jenny Henderson, Thomas Henderson)
Sarah Hunter, son &Polly Henderson)
heirs of Wm Henderson --dec'd)
     vs)
Robert Yancey)

The plaintiffs in this case by Chas.F.Keith Esqr. their Atto. makes a motion to enter up a Judgment against the said Robert Yancey for so much as the said Wm Henderson --Dec'd. was compleated to pay as one of the securities of said Robert Yancey & late Sheriff it appearing to the satisfaction of the Court from the examination on oath of Col. John Lea that the said Wm Henderson Dec'd was compelled to pay one hundred and one dollars as security of the said Robert Yancey. It is therefore considered by the Court that the said plaintiff did recover against the said Defendant the aforesaid sum of one hundred and one Dollars.

George Taylor assignee)
of Jesse Riggs)
     vs)
John Duke Admr. of)
Pleasant Duke --Dec'd &)
Joseph Noe)

Alexander Thompson one of the securities of Joseph Noe surrenders him in open Court in discharge of himself. Whereupon Henry Howell & Edward Tate came into open Court & undertake that if the Defendant Joseph Noe be cast in this action that they will pay the cost and condemnation money, surrenders him into prison for the same.

Ordered by the Court that Frankey Thomason an orphan Girl now of the age of Eleven years Eleven months and two days be Bound unto James Exell untill she shall attain the age of eighteen years & Indentures are Executed accordingly.

On motion of Jenney Coulter & Gabriel Mc Crow by John Williams Esqr. their Atto. they have leave to administer on all and singular the goods and chattels of John Coulter Deceased and the said Jenney Coulter & Gabriel Mc Crow enter into Bond John Howell, John Boyd, Thomas Coulter, Thomas Murphy John Alfred, Robert Yancey & James Blair, their securities in the sum of

(p 394°   Monday November 18th 1811

Eight thousand dollars, whereupon the said Jenney Coulter & Gabriel McCrow were qualified as administrators of said Estate and the said Jenney Coulter & Gabriel McCrow Returns to Court an Inventory of said Estate.

On motion of John Williams Esqr. It is ordered by the Court that Jenny Coulter Administratrix & Gabriel McCrow administrator of all and singular the goods and chattels rights and credits of John Coulter --Deceased have leave to sell all the perishable property together with the negroes belonging to said Estate.

On facts disclosed by affidavit of Abel Hill who was summoned to attend as a Juror at the term of this Court that the said Abel Hill be released from the forfeiture incurred by reason of his non attendance.

By order of the Court Edward Tate is appointed Constable in this County and the said Edward Tate enters into Bond in the sum of $500 together with

David Tate & Henry Rowell his securities, whereupon the said Edward Tate took an oath to support the Constitution of the United States, the Constitution of the State of Tennessee and also the oath prescribed by Law for Constables.

The Court proceeded to Ballot for a Constable - John Blackburn & Robert Huddleston being candidates & on counting the Ballots John Blackburn entered into Bond in the sum of $500 together with Samuel McBee and Thomas James his securities, whereupon the said John Blackburn took and oath to support the Constitution of the United States, the Constitution of the State of Tennessee & also the oath prescribed by Law for Constables.

Ordered by the Court that John Long be appointed overseer of the road from the top of Clinch mountain at the Powder Spring Gap to Crows old place in the nickle and knobbs at the Owl hole gap in the room & stead of James King and that he have the same hands and same bounds for hands that Peery had.
(p 395)   Monday November 18th A.D. 1811

Alexander Thompson)
& Phelps Reed   )
    vs   )   Execution
Wyett Smith   )   Justices present, David Tate, Isaiah Midkiff
and George Moody, Esqrs.
        Alexander Thompson & Fess Reed by Charles F. Keith Esqr. their Atto. makes a motion to the Court to enter up a judgment against Wyett Smith for the sum of sixty dollars and fifty four cents which sum they alledge they have been compelled to pay as securities for the said Wyett Smith and it appearing to the satisfaction of the Court that the said Wlex. Thompson & Felps Reed have paid the aforesaid sum as security for the said Wyett Smith, it is therefore considered by the Court that the said Alex. Thompson and Felps Reed do recover the aforesaid sum of sixty dollars and fifty four cents together with the costs and charges by them expended in prosecuting this motion & the Defendant in mercy &c.

        Court adjourned till tomorrow morning 8 o'clock.
            Tuesday November 19th A.D. 1811
        Court met according to adjournment- Justices present, David Tate, Isaiah Midkiff & Mathew Campbell.

James Conn & his wife   )
Jenney Conn late Jenny Henderson   )   In this case the Defendant Robert
Thomas Henderson, Sarah Henderson)   Ivey, John Williams Esqrs. his Atto.
Polly Henderson -Heirs of   )   with leave of the Court enters a
William Henderson -Dec'd   )   rule to shew cause why the Judgment
    vs   )   entered in this cause yesterday
Robert Yancey   )   should not be set aside.

George Taylor, Assignees &c)
    vs   )
John Duke ADMR. of   )   On argument it is ordered by the Court that
Pleasant Duke & Joseph Noe)   the Demurrer to the Second and third pleas
                                in this case be sustained.

William Trigg surviving Executor&c)
N.658   vs   )
Abraham Pruit   )   Justices present, David Tate, Isaiah
Midkiff & Mathew Campbell,Esqrs. Whereupon came a Jury, towit- James Hodges
John Hill, Wm James, Abner Lowe, Thomas Bunch, Samuel Bunch, John McBroom
Robert Blair, Henry Hawkins, Samuel Williams Francis Daniel & Joseph Alsup
(p 396)   Tuesday November the 18th A.D. 1811
& John Alsup who being elected tried and sworn well & truly to try and the
truth to speak on the issue joined in this case do say the defendant hath
not paid the Debt in the Declaration mentioned as in pleading he hath alledged they find for the plaintiff one hundred and fifty eight dollars the
Debt in the Declaration mentioned and assess the damages occasioned by reason
of the detention thereof to twenty dollars and sixty two cents besides his
costs. It is therefore considered by the Court that the said Wm Trigg, surviving Executor, do recover against the said Abraham Pruit the sum of one
hundred and fifty eight dollars, the sum mentioned in the declaration and
the damages aforesaid in form aforesaid assessed & also the cost in and about
prosecuting said suit in that behalf expended and the Defendant in mercy &c.
     In the above case Abraham Pruit -Defendant comes into Court & surrend-
ers himself in discharge of his Bail -whereupon Chas.F.Keith,Esqr. Atto.
for plaintiff prays the said Abraham Pruit in custody of the Sheriff.

George Taylor Assignee &c)
     vs   )
John Duke Admr.   )
& Joseph Noe   )   Justices present, David Tate, Mathew Campbell
Isaiah Midkiff & George Moody, Esqrs.
     John Duke, one of the Defendanrs in this case being solemnly called
came not & -whereupon came a Jury, towit-the same Jury as in the above suit
No. 658. Who being elected, tried and sworn well and truly to enquire & the
truth to speak on the issue joined in this case do say the Defendant Joseph
Noe, hath not paid the debt in the Declaration mentioned in this case as in
pleading he hath alledged and find for the plaintiff $300 the debt in the
declaration mentioned and assess the Plaintiffs damages occasioned by the
detention of that debt to one hundred & sixteen dollars & eighty five cents
& costs. It is therefore considered by the Court that the said George Taylor
recover against the said Joseph Noe the sum of $300 the debt in the decla-
ration mentioned together with the Damages aforesaid in form aforesaid assessed together with the costs of said suit in that behalf expended and the
Defendant in mercy &c.

William Keith   )
No. 671 vs-Attachment-)
Peter Woodin   )   Justices present, Philip Sigler, James Moore
David Tate, Isaiah Midkiff & Mathew Campbell,Esqrs.

(p 397)   Tuesday November 18th 1811
Whereupon came a Jury, towit-the same Jury as in No. 658, who being elected
tried and sworn, well and truly to enquire qhat damages the Plaintiff hath
sustained in this case do say they assess the plaintiffs damages to $100
besides his costs. It is therefore considered by the Court that the said Wm
Keith do recover against the said Defendant Peter, his damages aforesaid in
form aforesaid assessed together with his costs in and about prosecuting his
said writ in that behalf expended and the Defendant in mercy &c.

On application the Court discharge the Jury from further attendance at the present Term.

Elizabeth Short)
    vs
Isaiah Midkiff) Justices present, James Moore, Mathew Campbell and Henry Boatman,Esqr. This case, it having appeared to the satisfaction of the Court that the said Elizabeth Short hath heretofore obtained a judgment against the said Isaiah Midkiff on which judgment the said Isaiah Midkiff obtained writs of Certiorari and Supercedeas and removed the said suit into the County Court of Grainger and at May Term 1811 of said Court the said suit having gone off the Docket at the costs of said Midkiff. On motion of the said Elizabeth Short by John Williams Esqr. his Attorney towards a writ of prosecendo directed to Thomas Henderson,Esqr. commanding him to proceed to issue an Execution on said judgment and after argument the Court do award a writ of prosedendo directed to Thomas Henderson,Esqr. requiring him to issue an execution against the said Midkiff in favor of the said Elizabeth Short and the said Elizabeth recover against the said Isaiah -the costs.

On motion of Robert Yancey by John Williams Esqr. his Atto. to set aside a judgment which was entered yesterday against him, the said Robert Yanceyin favour of the heirs & representatives of Wm Henderson Dec'd and after argument heard as well in support of said motion as against it. It is considered by the Court that the motion be made absolute and that the judgment obtained yesterday by the heirs of Wm Henderson -Dec'd. be set aside and reversed.

Ordered by the Court that Thomas Henderson Jr. be appointed Guardian of Sarah Henderson & Polly Henderson minor heirs of Wm Henderson Dec'd for the purpose of defanding a petition about to be filed relative to the dividing of the land of John Coulter -Dec'd in which they hold an Interest.

(p 398)   Tuesday November the 18th A.D. 1811

James Conn,Esqr. high Sheriff and collector of the Taxes for the County of Gringer returned to Court a list of Insolvents for the years 1810 & 1811 amounting to 11 in number for the year 1810 & 1811 in number for the year 1811, wherefore it is considered by the Court that the aforesaid Collector be released from the payment of the Taxes due the State on twenty one - White polls & that said Sheriff have a credit for that amount in his settlement with the Treasurer of the Districts of Washington and Hamilton & that he have a credit for three Dollars & twenty nine cents the amount due the County &c in his settlement with the County Trustee.

Wm Keith,Ranger of Grainger County returns to Court the following List of Strays remaining on his Book, not proven away according to Law. Returnable to November Term 1811,towit-
Edward Tate - one Boar hog appraised to ———————— .75
Jeremiah Selvage - one black Steer ———————— 3.33¼
Nicholas Counts - 4 hogs ———————— 14.50
Miller Easley one Red Barrow ———————— 1.25
    William Keith -Ranger of
    Grainger County.
Ordered by the Court that Joseph Cobb- one of the members of this Court be appointed to examine Rachel Moody separate and apart from the husband whether she had executed a Deed Conveyance from her and others heirs of John

Moody- Deceased to Joseph Grubb and make known the purpose of such examination to this Court at the present, term.

Joseph Cobb, one of the members of this Court to examine Rachel Moody separate and apart from her husband whether she had executed a Deed from her and others heirs of John Moody Dec'd to Jesse Grubb -freely, voluntarily and without any threats, compulsion restraint of her said Husband returns to the bar and Declars to the Court that he has made the above examination and Explained the said writing to her that she did sign and seal the said Deed of Conveyance from her and others heirs of John Moody Dec'd to Jesse Grubb of her own will and choice and without any threats restraint or compulsion of her said Husband and wishes not to retract it and the said Rachel Moody & issue the said Court the said writing being again to her shewn and explained acknowledged the deed Executor thereof as her act and   (p 399)

                    Tuesday November the 18th 1811

Deed for the purpose therein Expressed -George Moody one of the parties to said Deed of Conveyance likewise appeared in open Court and acknowledged the same as his act and Deed.

Ordered by the Court that Joseph Cobb, Esquire be appointed to Examine Rachel Moody separate and apart from her husband whether she had executed a Deed from her and other heirs of John Moody Dec'd to Philip Raley of Bulford County in the State of Virginia.

Joseph Cobb, one of the members of this Court who was appointed by the Court take the examination of Rachel Moody separate and apart from her husband whether she has executed a Deed from her and other heirs of John Moody Dec'd to Philip Raley freely voluntarily and without threats, compulsion or restraint of her said Husband returns to the Court and declares that he has made the above examination and explained the said writing to her that she did sign and seal the said Deed freely voluntarily and without any threats, restraints or compulsion of her said husband and wishes not to retract it and the said Rachel Moody comes into Court and the said writing being again to her explained acknowledges the one execution of the same as her act and Deed for the purpose therein Expressed-George Moody, likewise one of the parties to the said written Indenture appeared in open Court & acknowledged the due execution as the same as his act and Deed.

Ordered by the Court that Joseph Cobb, Esquire be appointed to examine Rachel Moody, separate and apart from her husband whether she had executed a Conveyance from her and other heirs of John Moody-Deceased to Julius Saunders, freely, voluntarily and without any threats, compulsion or Constraint of her husband, returns to the bar and Declares to the Court that he has made the above Examination and that the said Rachel Moody did sign and seal the said Deed freely, voluntarily and without any threats and of her own free will and choice and without any threats, compulsion or restraint of her said husband and wishes not to tetract it and the said Rachel Moody appeared   (p 400)   in open Court and the said written Indenture

                    Tuesday November 18th 1812-

in open Court being again to her Explained acknowledged the due Execution thereof as her act and Deed for the taxes and purposes therein Expressed . George Moody one of the parties to the said written Indenture likewise appeared if open Court and the said written Indenture being again to her explained acknowledged the due execution thereof as her act and Deed for

the taxes and purposes therein Expressed -George Moody one of the parties
to the said written Indenture likewise appeared in open Court and acknowledged the Execution of the same as his act and Deed.

Ordered by the Court that Joseph Cobb,Esquire be appointed to Examine
Rachel Moody separate and apart from her husband whether she had executed
a Deed from her and other heirs of John Moody-Dec'd to John Moody, freely
voluntarily and without any threats -compulsion or constraint of her husband and make known said Examination to this Court.

Joseph Cobb, one of the members of this Court who was to examine Rachel Moody, separate and apart from her husband whether she had executed
a Deed from her and other heirs of John Moody,deceased to John Moody comes
into Court and Declares to the Court that he has made the above Examination
and explained the said Indenture to her that she did sign and seal and Execute the same of her own free will and choice and without any threats, com-
lulsion or constraint of her said husband and wishes not to retract it and
the said Rachel Moody comes into Court and the said written Indenture being
again to her explained acknowledged the Executor of the same as he act and
Deed for the purposes therein expressed.

George Moody, one of the parties to the said written Indenture likewise appeared in open Court and acknowledged the Examination thereof as his
act and Deed.

Ordered by the Court that the following persons be appointed jurors to
attend the next County Court,towit-

1- Henry Howell	7- James Parker
2- Thomas Bunch	8- Jas.Richardson
3- Nicholas Counts	9- John Erwine Jr.
4- Stephen Smith	10-Joseph Rich
5- Joel Perrin	11-Joseph Noe Jr.
6- William Harmon	12-John Hall Sr.
	13-Francis Daniel

Ordered by the Court that the following persons be appointed jurors to
attend the Circuit Court of Grainger County on the second Monday in April
next, towit-
(p 401)   Tuesday November 18th 1811

1- James Moore	15- Wm Mitchell	29- Henry Balser
2- David Tate	16-Robert Harris	30- Joseph Cobb
3- Isaiah Midkiff	17-Peter Hamilton	31- McNess Moore
4- Mathew Campbell	18-Thomas Brown	32- David Holt
5- Philip Sigler	19-John Hill	33- John Griffitts
6- Thomas Bunch	20-Henry Widener	34- Daniel Taylor
7- John Moody	21-Chas.Matlock	35- Felps Reed
8- Daniel Robertson	22-John Arwine	36- John Kidwell
9- Jas.Carmichael	23-Balser Sherley	37- Thomas Gill
10-Henry Howell	24-Noah Jarnagin	38- Henry Ivey
11-Jas.Simpson	25-Samuel Bunch	39- Sherod Mays
12-Peter Harris	26-Martin Albert	
13-John Moffit	27- David McAnally	
14-James Harris	28-David Counts	

James Conn, Esqr. high Sheriff of Grainger County reports to Court the following tracts of land as having been returned as taxable property in the County of Grainger for the year 1811 and that the owners thereof have no goods nor chattels that he know in his County on which he can Distress for the taxes one for said year towit-

Samuel Blyth, 10,000 acres of land between Indian and German Creek in one tract - taxes ————————————————$57.25
Clerk and Printer ————————————— 2.35
Samuel Blyth - 13,754 acres South of
Clinch river ———— taxes ———— 51.06½
Clerk and printer ————————————— 2.35
John Leonard - 4880 acres South of
Clinch river in 37 tracts -taxes ———— 15.17 3/4
Clerk and printer ————————————— 2.35
Samuel Nicholson - 3370 acres Bull Run
Potson and Black Fox Creek in 43 tracts 12.59 3/4
Clerk and printer ————————————— 2.35
Samuel Nicholson - 200 acres Clinch river
& Indian Creek in 5 tracts - taxes ———— .74½
Clerk and printer ————————————— 2.35
Robert Smock - 17,212 acres S.Clinch river
18 tracts - taxes ————————————— 64.29½
Clerk and printer ————————————— 2.35
Robert Smock - 100 acres on the head of
Indian Creek & German Creek - in 2 tracts 37½
Clerk and printer ————————————— 2.35
John Woodward 1120 acres adjoining the
lands of Blyth Smock -Leonard &c in 15
tracts taxes ————————————— 4.17½
Clerk and printer ————————————— 2.35

(p 402)   Tuesday November the 18th 1811

It is therefore considered by the Court that Judgment be entered up against the said tracts of Land for the taxes due thereon together with the costs and charges thereto, respectively annexed and that the said tracts of Land be sold or so much thereof respectively on the first Monday in November next and the succeeding day as will be sufficient to satisfy the above taxes, costs and charges and that the Sheriff of Grainger County, carry this Judgment into Execution according to Law.

James Conn, Esquire high Sheriff of Grainger County returned to Court the following tracts of Land on not having been given in as taxable property in the County of Grainger for the year 1810 and 1811, towit- George Guss 150 acres of Land lying on the head of German Creek - Double tax for 1810 and 1811 ———— $1.34½
Clerk and printer ————————————— 2.35
Thomas & John Kelland or heirs or assigns 22,000 acres of Land Southside of Clinch River Grainger County held by Grant No.517 Issued to Thomas Blount and John G.Blount Double tax for 1810 & 1811, towit-Double tax for 1810 ————————————— 123.10

Clerk and printer ————————————————$2.35
Double tax for 1811 ———— 158.30
Clerk and printer ———— 2.35

It is therefore considered by the Court that judgment be entered up against the above tracts of Land for the double tax due thereon for said years and that the said tracts of Land be sold or so much thereof respectively on the first Monday in November next and the succeeding Day as will be sufficient to satisfy the taxes costs and charges thereto, respectively annexed.

Court adjourned till tomorrow morning 9 o'clock -

Wednesday morning November the 19th 1811- Court met according to adjournment. Justices present -David Tate, Isaiah Midkiff and James Moore Esqrs.

David Deadrick)
vs)
Charles Mayberry) In this case the plaintiff by his Attorney makes a motion to Court to set aside the petition for Certiorari in this case. It is considered by the Court that the plaintiff David Deadrick recover against the Defendant Charles Mayberry and George Coffman and Thomas James his securities the sum of forty six Dollars and eighty cents and also the costs in and about prosecuting said suit in this behalf expended and the Defendant in mercy &c.

Ordered by the Court that Etheldred Williams and   (p 403)   at a Court of Pleas and Quarter Sessions began and held for the County of Grainger at the Court House in Rutledge on the third Monday of February 1812 & on the seventh day of said month. Justices present, Noah Jarnagin, George Moody, James Moore and Joseph Cobb, Esqrs.

James Conn, Esqr. high Sheriff of said County makes return to Court that he has executed the Venire facias on the following persons, towit-

1- Henry Howell
2- Thomas Bunch
3- Nicholas Counts
4- Stephen Smith
5- Joel Perrin
6- Wm Harmon

7- James Parker
8- Jas. Richardson
9- John Erwine
10- John Holt Sr.
11- Joseph Rich
12- Joseph Noe Jr.
13- Francis Daniel

Henry Stephens, Esqr. produces to Court a license signed by the Honourable William Cocke and Archabald Roane -Judges of the Circuit of Law in the State of Tennessee, authorizing the said Stephen to practice law in the several Counties in this State and the said Stephens took the necessary oaths and was admitted a practicing Attorney of this Court.

The last Will and testament of William James Deceased was produced to Court the Execution thereof proven by the oaths of John Dennis and Sarah Dennis subscribing witnesses thereto -whereupon the same is ordered to be recorded.

Henry Howell)
vs)
Jesse Riggs) Abraham Wilson and Elisha Riggs comes into Court and replevies

the property levied or attached in this suit and obligate themselves to pay the condemnation money or surrender the said Jesse Riggs in prison in discharge of the same.

Ordered by the Court that Gabriel McClallan and Jenny Coulter Administrators of the Estate of John Coulter Deceased have leave to return to Court the mount of the sales of said Estate which is received by the Court and ordered to be recorded.

Jacob Hackney of Grainger County presents to Court a petition praying
(p 404)   Monday February 17th 1812
to have leave to keep an Ordinary or house of public entertainment in said County, who enters into bond in the sum of $1000 together with John Cocke his security and it appearing to the satisfaction of the Court that the sd. Jacob Hackney is of sufficient property to keep an Ordinary or house of intertainment; it is ordered by the Court that the prayer of the petition be granted and that a license issue the said Jacob therefore for one year.

A commission signed by Willie Blount, Governor of the State of Tennessee appointing Thomas James -William Lane, Samuel McBee, Robert Gaines and William Mays Justices of the peace for Grainger County, who came into Court, took the necessary oaths and were qualified as Justices of the peace for Grainger County, who took their Treaty as such.

Joshua Hickey presented a petition to Court praying leave to keep an Ordinary or house of public entertainment in the town of Rutledge and the Court being satisfied that the said Joshua Hickey is of sufficient property to keep said Ordinary do grant the said petition to be granted -whereupon the said Joshua Hickey enters into bond in the sum of $1000 together with Henry Henry his security, whereupon the Court direct a license to issue to the said Joshua Hickey for one year.

Ordered by the Court that Daniel Robison, Frederick Moyers, Thomas Mc Broom, Martin Albert, Miller Easley, Balser Shirley and John Hall, be appointed a Jury to view and lay off a road leading down the Richland Valley leaving the present road at or near where two pines now stands near the edge of road on the right hand side a little beyond where said road crosses Pattersons Creek and passing through John Bunches field falling in again into the present between the stone house and stable of John Bunch and make report at the present term of this Court.

(p 405)   Monday February 17th 1812

Ordered by the Court that Younger Douglass now of the age of nine yrs. be bound by Indenture to Claiborne Hailey until he attain the age of twenty one years.

John Sherley presented a petition to the Court praying a license to keep an Ordinary or house of entertainment in the town of Rutledge for the term of one year and the Court being satisfied that the said John Sherley is of sufficient property to keep said Ordinary. Order the prayer of the petition to be granted, whereupon the said John Sherley enters into bond together with John Cocke his security in the sum of $1000 for the faithful performance of his said bond, whereupon the Court directs a license to the issue to the said Sherley therefore.

William Stephenson having preferred a petition to the Court praying a license to keep an Ordinary or house of publick entertainment at Beans Station for the year and the Court being satisfied that the said Wm Stephenson is a man sufficient property to keep an Ordinary; It is therefore ordered by the Court that the prayer of the said petition be granted, whereupon the said Wm Stephenson enters into bond together with John Boyd his security in the sum of $1000 for the faithful performance of his duty as Ordinary keeper, therefore the Court is to issue to said Wm Stephenson, a License.

Ordered by the Court a majority of the acting Justices present, that Sterling Cocke, Clerk of Grainger County be allowed the sum of fifteen dollars for making out the tax list for the year 1810 and further that the sd. Sterling Cocke be allowed the further sum of $20 for his services in making out the tax list for the year 1811.

Ordered by the Court a majority of the acting Justices being present that the report of the Jury at the last term of this Court, who were appointed to view and lay off a road the nearest and best way from Blackwell's branch to James Richardson's be confirmed.

(p 406)   Monday February 17th 1812

Joseph Noe   )
       vs   )
Thomas Warren   )   Justices present, Isaiah Midkiff, Noah Jarnagin and Wm Lane, Esquires on motion of Joseph Noe, John Cocke, Esqr. his Attorney to enter up a judgment against Thomas Warren for the sum of $208.35, which he alledged he has been compelled to pay as the security of the said Thomas Warren and in as much as the Court are not satisfied that the said Joseph Noe has paid the said sum as security of the said Thomas, direct the following Jury to be impannelled to enquire whether the said Noe has paid said sum of money as security &c. whereupon came the following Jury, towit-

1- Thomas Bunch	7- John Moody
2- William Harmon	8- Warham Easley
3- James Parker	9- ------
4- John Arwine Jr.	10-David Counts
5- James Richardson	11-George Evans
6- James Alsup	12-Gabriel McCraw

Who being elected tryed and sworn well and truly to enquire whether the said Joseph Noe was security of the said Thomas Warren &c. do say they find the said Joseph Noe was security of the said Thomas Warren and that he has paid the sum of $208.35 for him.

John Duke- Admr. of)
Pleasant Duke -Dec'd)
       vs   )   Justices present, David Tate, Isaiah Midkiff &
Thomas Warren   )   George Moody, Esqrs.

On motion of John Duke, Admr. of Pleasant Duke Deceased by John Cocke his Atto. to enter up a judgment against Thomas Warren for the sum of $208.35 which he has been compelled to pay as has been Admr. of Pleasant Duke Dec'd.

wherein Pleasant Duke was security in his lifetime of the said Thomas Warren and in as much as the Court are not satisfied that the said Pleasant was security of the said Thomas and that the said John Duke has paid said sum of money as Admr. of said Pleasant the Court directs the same Jury as in the last case to be impannelled, (p 407) who being elected tryed & sworn well and truly to enquire what money the said plaintiff as Admr. of Pleasant Duke -Dec'd has paid or whether Pleasant Duke was security of Thos. Warren do say they find Pleasant Duke was security of Thomas Warren and that John Duke Admr. of Pleasant Duke has been compelled to pay the sum of $208.35

Ordered by the Court that Jacob Showman be appointed Constable in the bounds of Capt. Robert D.Eaton's Company who came into Court, took the oath (necessary) and entered into Bond together with Frederick Moyers and James Brown his securities in the sum of $500 for the faithful discharge of his said appointment.
Justices present, David Tate, Joseph Cobb, Thomas Brown, William Lane Mathew Campbell, and Samuel McBee, Esqrs.

William Bunch having exhibited to Court the scalp of a wolf, which he the said William swears he has killed in the County and the Court being satisfied the said wolf was more than four months old, allow the said Wm Bunch $3.00 for said scalp and direct the same to be burned.

Ordered by the Court that Janet Norris be added to the list of hands working under George Norris overseer of the road.

James Blair Admr. of James Blair Dec'd- returns to Court the amount of sales of the estate of said Deceased which is received by the Court and ordered to be recorded.

Ordered by the Court that a majority of the acting Justices being present that James Conn Sheriff of Grainger County be allowed the sum of $63.43 and 3/4 for taking Joseph York to Sullivan Joal and for expences in taking care of said York while prisoner in his custody.

(p 408)   Monday February 17th 1812

Ordered by the Court that Frederick Moyers be allowed the sum of $17 for keeping the Court house from May term 1811 till the present term, a majority of the acting Justices being present, the order is allowed.

John Blair, minor heir of John Blair-Dec'd comes into open Court and chose John Cocke his Guardian.

The Court provided to ballot for a Constable John Boyd and John Hodge candidates and on counting the votes it appeared the John Hodge had twelve votes and John Boyd nine votes., it is therefore ordered by the Court that John Hodge be appointed Constable in the bounds of Capt. John Campbell's Company who came into Court and entered into Bond together with James Conn Henry Howell, Wm Rayl and Thomas Hurry his securities, in the sum of $500 took the necessary oaths prescribed by law for Constables to take.

Ordered by the Court, a majority of the acting Justices being present that Isaiah Midkiff be allowed the sum of $25 for keeping and maintaining Jeremiah Midkiff, one of the poor of this County from May term 1811 till

August term 1811.

Ordered by the Court, a majority of the acting Justices being present that Isaiah Midkiff be allowed the sum of $25 for keeping and maintaining Jeremiah Midkiff, one of the poor of this County from August term 1811 till November term 1811.

Ordered by the Court that Isaiah Midkiff be allowed the sum of $25 for keeping and maintaining Jeremiah Midkiff one of the poor of this County from November term 1811 till the present term, a majority of the acting Justices being present.

Ordered by the Court, a majority of the acting Justices being present that William Rayl Jr. now an orphan of the age   (p 409)   of sixteen years and three months be bound to William Rayl Sr. until he attain the age of twenty one years.

Ordered by the Court that the Sheriff of Grainger County be required & directed to bring into Court Thomas Craig, Chas.Craige, Rebeccah Craige, Wm Craige at the present term.

Ordered by the Court that Thomas Henderson Esqr. be appointed to take in a list of polls and taxable property in the bounds of Capt. John Campbell Company for the year 1812 and also that he be appointed to take the enumeration of the free taxable inhabitance in said Company and return the same to next term.

Ordered by the Court that George Moody, Esqr. be appointed to take in a list og polls and taxable property in the bounds of Capt. John Howells Company for the year 1812 and further that he be appointed to take the enumeration of the free taxable inhabitance in said Company and return the same to next Court.

Ordered by the Court that Thomas Brown Esqr. be appointed to take in a list of the polls and taxable property in the bounds of Capt. Monrow's Comp. for the year 1812 and further that he be appointed to take the enumeration of the free taxable inhabitants in said Company and return the same to next Court.

Ordered by the Court that Philip Sigler Esqr. be appointed to take a list of polls and taxable property in the bounds of Capt. Thomas Browns Company for the year 1812 and also that he be appointed to take the enumeration of the free taxable inhabitants in said Company and return the same to next Court.

Ordered by the Court that Philip Sigler, Esqr. be appointed to take a list of polls and taxable property in the bounds of Capt. Thomas Brown's Company for the year 1812 and also that he be appointed to take the enumeration of the free taxable inhabitants in the bounds of said Company and return the same to the next Court.

Ordered by the Court that David Tate Esqr. be appointed to take a list of the polls and taxable property in the bounds of Capt. Samuel Richardson's Company for the year 1812 and also that he be appointed to take the enumeration of the free taxable inhabitants in the bounds of said Company and return the same to the next Court.

Ordered by the Court that Isaiah Midkigg Esqr. be appointed to
(p 410) take a list of polls and taxable property in the bounds of Capt.
Joseph Rich's Company for the year 1812 and also that he be appointed to
the enumeration of the free taxable inhabitants in said Company and return
the same to the next Court.

Ordered by the Court that Noah Jarnagin Esqr. be appointed to take a
list of the polls and taxable property in the bounds of Capt. Robert D. Eaton
Company for the year 1812 and also that he be appointed to take the Enumeration of the free taxable inhabitants in said Company and return the same to
the next Court.

Ordered by the Court that Mathew Campbell Esqr. be appointed to take in
a list of the polls and taxable property in the bounds of Capt. Thomas Sharp
Company for the year 1812 and also that he be appointed to take the enumeration of the free taxable inhabitants in said Company and return the same
to the next Court.

Ordered by the Court that Samuel McBee Esqr. be appointed to take in a
list of the polls and taxable property in the bounds of Capt. Odneil Sanders
Company for the year 1812 and also that he be appointed to take the enumeration of the free taxable inhabitants in said Company and return the same
to next Court.

Ordered by the Court that John Moffitt Esqr. be appointed to take in a
list of the polls and taxable property in the bounds of Capt. Thomas Mann's
Company for the year 1812 and also that he be appointed to the enumeration
of the free taxable Inhabitants in the bounds of said Company and returns
the same to the next Court.

Ordered by the Court that David McAnally be appointed to take in a list
of polls and taxable property in the bounds of Capt. David McAnally's Company for the year 1812,

(p 411)   Monday February 17th 1812
and also that he be appointed to take the enumeration of the free taxable
inhabitants in said Company and return the same to the next Court.

Ordered by the Court, a majority of the acting Justices present that
Daniel Taylor, Hugh Larimore, John Alfred, John Harris, Wm Harris, Peter
Harris Esqrs. Hughs Taylor, be a Jury to view the nearest and best way from
Marshall's ford to intersect the present road between Robert Longs and Pe-
ter Harris and make report to next Court.

Ordered by the Court that George Dyer be appointed overseer of the
road in the place of Wm Harmon and have the same hands and same bounds for
hands that said Harmon had.

Ordered by the Court that Thomas Gill be appointed overseer of the road
in the room and stead of Wm Syephenson and to have the same hands and bounds
for hands that said Stephenson had together with his own hands in addition.

Ordered by the Court that Robert Munrow be appointed overseer of the road leading from John Salley's to where said road intersects to road leading from Wm Hamilton's on Gap Creek and also that Samuel McBee Esqr. make a division of the hands between Wm Hamilton and said Munrow.

Ordered by the Court, a majority of the acting Justices being present that Thomas Henderson Jr. Thomas Johnson, James Blair Sr. Henry Bowen, John Bowen, Capt. John Campbell's and Thomas Gill be appointed a Jury to view & lay off a road the best way from Oansville to the head of the lane near Bean Station and make report to the next Court.

Ordered by the Court that Levi Clark be appointed overseer of the road in the room of Charles Matlock and that he have the same hands and same bounds for hands that said Matlock had.

(p 412)   Monday February 17th 1812

A Commission was produced to Court signed by his Excellency Willie Blount Governor of the State of Tennessee appoining James G.Harris and other Justices of the peace for Grainger County and the said James G.Harris came into Court & took the necessary oaths as prescribed for Justices to take and he took his seat on the bench.

Thomas Dennis and Joseph Fields Executors of the last Will and testament of William James came into Court & took upon themselves the Execution of said Will and were qualified as Executors of the last Will and testament of said William James -Deceased.

Henry Clear, who is bound in recognisance to appear at the present term under a charge of having begotten a bastard child by a certain Milly Minett appeared in Court, entered into Bond together with Mathew Campbell, Robert Blair and Wm Hutcheson his securities in the penal sum of $500 for maintenance of said child.

Ordered by the Court that John Griffitts be appointed a constable, who enters into bond in the sum of $500 together with Rial Jinnings and George Evans his securities for the faithful discharge of said appointment.

Court adjourned till tomorrow morning 9 o'clock.

Court met according to adjournment- Tuesday Feby. 18th 1812- Justices present, George Moody, Thomas Brown and Henry Boatman, Esqrs.

Ordered by the Court that Jacob Hackney be required to take charge of the Court House until otherwise directed.

Ordered by the Court that David McAnally, Noah Jarnagin and Mathew Campbell Esqrs. be appointed to settle with Joseph Cobb Admr. of John Blair Deceased and also as Guardian of the minor heirs of said Deceased and make report to the present term of this Court, the above to be settled as Admr. and Guardian in behalf of his wife Administratrix and Guardian of the said minor heirs of said Deceased.

(p 413)   Tuesday February 18th 1812

Ordered by the Court that Richard Harris be released from the payment of a poll tax for himself, it appearing to the satisfaction of the Court, that he is above the age of fifty years and that the Sheriff have a credit in the settlement of his amount for the sum of thirty four and one fourth cents, towit- $0.122 in the above tax and the residue in the County tax for the year 1811.

Peter Lowe)
    vs
James Fowler) Justices present, Thomas James, Henry Boatman and Wm Mays whereupon came the parties by their Attornies and a Jury, towit-

1- Thomas Bunch   7- David Tate
2- Nicholas Counts   8- John Hall
3- Wm Harmon   9- Joseph Alsup
4- James Parker   10-John Boyd
5- John Arwine Jr.   11-Thomas ----
6- Joseph Rich   12-Isaac Mitchell

Who being elected tryed and sworn well and truly and the truth to speak in this issue joined in this case do say they find the defendant James Fowler was not directed by the plaintiff Peter to stay away as in pleading he hath alledged. It is therefore considered by the Court that the plaintiff Peter Lowe recover against the defendant Jems Fowler the sum of one hundred and twenty five dollars, the sum in the writ of sine facias mentioned final together with his costs in and about prosecuting said suit in that behalf expended and the defendant in mercy &c.

Ordered by the Court a majority of the acting Justices being present that William Harris be allowed the sum of six dollars and twenty five cents for his trouble in taking Daniel L---- to a Justice of the peace in Claiborne County charged with horse stealing.

Ordered by the Court a majority of the acting Justices being present that Daniel Chandler be allowed the sum of $12 for each three months since his last allowance -towit, $12 from August term 1811 and $12 from Nov.term 1811 till the present term of this Court, for keeping and maintaining Ann Roane one of the poor of this County.

(p 414)   Tuesday February 18th 1812

John Cocke Admr. of the Bonis non of Zackfield Macklin Deceased returns in open Court an Inventory of the estate of said Deceased which is received by the Court and ordered to be recorded.

Ordered by the Court that Wm Kirby be released from the payment of $40 the price of a horse heretofore posted - it appearing to the satisfaction of the Court that the said stray horse has been heretofore proven away from the said William and the probate thereof last term.

Robert Blair having preferred a petition for a license to keep a house of publick intertainment and it appearing to the satisfaction of the Court an examination that the said Blair was a man of sufficient property as required by Act of Assembly - the Court orders a license to Issue authorising the said Robert Blair to keep an Ordinary or house of intertainment, who came into Court and together with Henry Hawkins his security entered into bond in the sum of $1000 for the faithful discharge of the duties enjoined on him as Ordinary keeper, whereupon a license issue for one year.

Justices present be ing a majority

1- John Cocke	7- David McAnally
2- David Tate	8- George Moody
3- Mathew Campbell	9- James G.Harris
4- James Moore	10-Isaiah Midkiff
5- Noah Jarnagin	11-William Hayes
6- John Moffitt	12-Joseph Cobb

Ordered by the Court that the tax be laid for the present year 1812 the same as for the year 1811.

Ordered by the Court that John Ferguson be appointed overseer of the road in the room and stead of Wm Quinn and that he have the same hands and same bounds for hands that said Guinn had.

The Jury who were appointed at the present term of this Court to view and lay off a road leading through John Bunches field intersecting the Richland Valley road near the house of   (p 415)

Sunday February 18th 1812

John Bunches making their report to Court in writing which is received by the Court, a majority of the acting Justices being present confirmed and ordered to be recorded, which is in the following words, towit-

We, the Jurors appointed to lay out a road by order of the Court have attended and do say from the corner of the right hand fence on the other side of Patterson's creek and a straight line between John Bunches store house and the old road.

Feby. 18th 1812

Martin Albert	Miller Fosley
Frederick Moyers	Daniel Robertson
John Hall	Balsar Sherley

Ordered by the Court that Thomas Key be appointed overseer of the road from Clinch River to that part of the road opposite Adam Petrees and that the said Thomas Key be allowed the same hands and bounds for hands formerly allowed said Petree.

William Keith, Ranger of Grainger County returns to Court the following list and in the following words and figures towit- Edward Churchman - one

Bull yearling appraised ---------------------------------$2.50
John Hall one heifer appraised to ------------------- 3.33
John Ivey one cow appraised to ---------------------- 7.00
Tandy Senter one heifer appraised to --------------- 3.00

Wm Keith Rainger of Grainger County

Ordered by theCourt that James Bryan be appointed an overseer of the road in room of Absolem Roach and that he have the same hands and same bounds for hands that said Roach had.

Ordered by the Court that Joseph Swan be appointed overseer of the road in the room and stead of Fial Jinnings and that he be allowed the same hands and same bounds that Jinnings had.

Ordered by the Court that Henry Boatman be appointed overseer of the road in the room and stead of Ambrose   (p 416)   Hodge and have the same hands and same bounds for hands that said Hodge had.

John Cocke and George Moody were appointed at the last Term of this Court to settle with David Tate Admr. of Samuel Wilson Dec'd exhibit and accountof said settlement to Court which is received by the Court and ordered to be recorded.

Ordered by the Court that Thomas Henderson be appointed Guardian of Sarah Henderson and May Henderson minor heirs of Wm Henderson Deceased and the said Thomas Henderson together with Henry Howell and James Conn his security enters into bond in the sum of $4000 to Isaiah Midkiff –James Harris and Henry Boatman Justices of the Court of Pleas and Quarter Sessions for the performance of his said Guardianship.

Ordered by the Court that Etheldred Williams be appointed Guardian of Cynthia Copeland, Nancy Copeland, Samuel Copeland and Henry Copeland, minor heirs of Wm Copeland Deceased– and the said Etheldred Williams comes into Court and enters into bond together with Thomas Gill and John F. Jack his securities to David Tate, George Moody and James G. Harris, Justices of the Court of Pleas and Quarter Sessions who undertake in behalf of the said minors in sum of $10,000 for the due performance of his said Guardianship.

William Clay by Jacob Peck Esqr. his Atto. exhibited to Court a petition praying to keep an Ordinary or house of Publick entertainment for one year and thereupon John Cocke Esqr. moved the Court to postpone the examination of said petition until tomorrow – alledged that he could establish by respectable testimony, towit–Reubin Dixon, John Justice Hall and Balsar Sherley   (p 417)   that said William was not a man of probity but on the contrary was dishonest, having committed offence which would exclude him from the indulgence prayed for and further moved the Court for process of Subpoena to issue to force the attendance of said Reubin Dixon, Balsar Sherley and John Justice Hall and Balsar Sherley which motion was approved by Jacob Peck Atto. of said William and after argument had the Court directed the prayer of the petition to be granted without examination into the probity of said William and the said William Clay comes into Court together with Noah Jarnagin his security and enters into bond in the sum of $1000 for the performance of his duties as ordinary keeper, whereupon the Court direct a license to issue to the William authorising him to keep said ordinary or house of publick entertainment for one year.

Noah Jarnagin, Mathew Campbell and David Tate Esqrs. who were appointed at the present term of this Court to settle with Joseph Cobb Admr. of John Blair Deceased, exhibited the account of said settlement to Court which is received by the Court and ordered to be recorded.

Jane Coulter, widow and relict of John Coulter Deceased– having prefered her petition to Court praying her dower to be laid to the lands her said husband died seized and possessed and it appearing to the satisfaction of the Court the representatives of said John Coulter Deceased had notice of said petition therefore it is ordered by the Court, a majority of the acting

Justices being present that   7- Thomas Johnson
1- Henry Hays   8- Henry Bowen
2- McNess Moore   9- Henry Boatman
3- Stephen W.Senter   10-David Tate Esqrs.
4- George Moody   11-Wm Mays and
5- Nicholas Counts Sr.   12-Sherod Hays
6- Thomas Bunch

be a Jury to lay off the dower of Jenny Coulter, widow and relict of John
Coulter Deceased of the lands which the said John Coulter died seized and
possessed of and further it is ordered   (p 418)   that Joseph Cobb
be the surveyor for said Davison and make report to the next term of this
Court.

     Gabriel McGraw Admr. of the Estate of John Coulter Deceased who has been
summoned on Guarnashee to declare what effects of Robert Yancey he has in
his hands on the following executions which has shortly issued against the
said Robert Yancey, makes the following return, towit-
A memorandum of the Executions against Robert Yancey-
One in favor of Wm Windham
1 in favor of Henry Howell
1 in favor of Joseph M.Anderson
1 in favor of the heirs of William Henderson
1 in favor of William Howell
1 in favor of Chas.McAnally
1 in favor of Richard Reynolds
1 in favor of George Noe
1 in favor of Wm Jones
1 in favor of Ambrose Yancey
1 in favor of Henry Howell
1 in favor of the heirs of Wm Henderson
1 in favor of Henry Howell
At November Sessions 1811 letters of Administration were granted to me on
the Estate of John Coulter Dec'd the proceeds of the sale of the personal
property of said Coulter amounted to $3174.70 out of the amount said Yancey
was entitled to - one 7th part after paying all just claims against said Estate being Verbally Guarnashed to declare what property or money I have in
my hands of the said Yancey do say on oath that I have nothing in my hands
of the said Yancey that he can legally claim that all his Interest in said
Estate was conveyed to me by said Yancey previous to my being Guarnashed on
the above Execution for   (p 419)   a valuable consideration towit,
in October last and if here after anything should become due said Yancey
I am advised that I have sometime to settle and adjust the affairs of said
Estate and pay out portions as the letters of Administration were Granted
at Nov. Sessions of Grainger County Court 1811. It is to be however understood that the foregoing conveyance executed in October 1811 was to indemnify me from any damage I might sustain by being said Yancey's security in a
Bill of injunction filed against Thomas Bunch injoining about the sum of
$140 with Interest and costs of suit and after being discharged from said
securityship and all other claims that I against said Yancey if there should
be any left in my hands to be applyed to use of said Yancey's creditors, the
claim of one Judgment - Joseph M.Anderson which judgment I have a right to
retain by Verbal agreement with said Anderson - A Note I hold for the sum
of $100 Given to John Williams in October last and assigned to me on 26th
of Nov. last, I further state I know of some Judgements which has been

rendered prior to the assignment, the information came to me through Robert Yancey, the Judgment of Henry Howells, Joseph N.Anderson, Ambrose Yancey, George Noe, Chas.McAnally, Wm Windham - he informed me of a Judgment he had obtained, I did not know of the Judgment Wm Henderson heir against said Yancey until the day the above Note was assigned but whether before or after the assignment I can not seem to recollect, I think it was after I was served notice in these cases. Gabriel McGraw, Thomas Murry, John Alfred, Eli Coulter, Thomas Coulter, Elizabeth McIlhatton, Thomas Henderson for himself and as Guardian and James Conn having prefered to Court a petition praying a Division of the lands of John Coulter Dec'd as Heirs, and (p 420) legal representatives of said Coulter Dec'd and Henry Howell, claiming under some one of the heirs of said Dec'd having acknowledged Notice of said petition whereupon the Court direct the following commissioners to be appointed to lay off the said Land in lotts to the several legatees of said Dec'd -towit, Henry Mays, McNess Moore, Stephen W.Senter, George Moody and Nicholas Counts to lay off the lands as aforesaid to the several legatees of said Dec'd and to those claiming under them according to Law and make report to next Court and that Joseph Cobb be the surveyore for the purpose of surveying and lay off lotts to the several legatees and representatives of said Dec'd when making said Division.

Court adjourned till tomorrow morning 9 o'clock.

Court met according to adjournment. Justices present, James Moore, David Tate, Mathew Campbell and Philip Sigler Esqrs.

(p 420)
George B by George Beeler his next friend)
    vs)
William Dyer) Justices present, Philip Sigler, James Moore, Mathew Campbell, Joseph Cobb and David Tate, Esqrs.
    Whereupon came the parties by their Attornies and a Jury, towit-
1- Henry Howell
2- Thomas Bunch
3- Nicholas Counts
4- William Harmon
5- James Parker
6- Jas.Richardson
7- John Arwine Jr.
8- Andrew Seabolt
9- Joseph Alsup
10-John Hall
11-Charles Matlock &
12-Reuben Groves
    Who being elected tryed and sworn well and truly to try and the truth to speak in this issue in this case, having returned to the bar do say they are not agreed in their Verdict. Whereupon the Court direct by consent.

Dudley Cox)
    vs)
Thomas Alsup) Justices present, Thomas Henderson, Noah Jarnagin and Isaiah Midkiff.
    David Tate, who was summoned to act as Guarnashee at the present term of this Court, makes an oath of the following statements, towit-
that he is indebted to Thomas N.Alsup in the sum of $9.50 or thereabouts and that of his own knowledge he knows of no (p 421) other person
              Wednesday Feby. 19th 1812
that is indebted to or has any of the effects of said Thomas in their hands

it is considered by the Court that the said sum be denied the hands of the said David on his Garnishment.

John Boyd having preferred a petition to Court praying a license to keep an Ordinary or house of entertainment and it appearing to the satisfaction of the Court on examination the was a person of sufficient property as required by Act of Assembly, the Court ordered that a license be granted authorizing the said John Boyd to keep a house of entertainment who came into Court and entered into bond together with Samuel Bunch and Thomas Whitesides his security to the State in the sum of $1000 for the faithful discharge of the duties enjoined on him as Ordinary keeper.

Ordered by the Court that John Satyrfield be appointed overseer of the road leading from Mayes ford to John Bulls beginning at the foot of the hill near said Satyrfield and ending at Henry Beatman's and that the said Satyrfield is to have all the hands who are convenient and not engaged on any other road.

Henry Howell prefers his petition to Court praying that Commissioners may be appointed to make partition of two tracts of Land between him and the heirs of Wm Copeland Dec'd which he and the said William held in fee simple as tenants in common in his lifetime, one tract laying in the County of Grainger on waters of German Creek surveyed March the twenty fourth 1810. Beginning at a stake on David Holts North East corner &c. the other tract of land containing 133 acres lying in the County of Grainger on the waters of German Creek adjoining a tract of land granted to David Holt at Fowler's Gap Beginning at the three white oaks &c and it appearing to the Court that the Guardian of the minor heirs of Wm Copeland together with Etheldred Williams who entermarried with Mary Copeland Daughter of said William and

Wednesday February 19th 1812

(p 422)   Mary Copeland widow and relict of said Dec'd had notice of said petition – It is ordered by the Court that 1- Joseph Rich – 2- Daniel Taylor 3- Thomas Bunch- 4- George Moody and 5- Sherod Mays be appointed Commissioners to make partition of the two above described tracts of land which the said Henry and said William in his lifetime held as tenants in common, ordered that Joseph Cobb be surveyor to attend said Commissioners in laying off said partition and that said Commissioners make report of the Davison or partition by them made to the term of this Court.

Anthony Street Sr.)
    vs   )
Jesse Cheek   )   In this case an Execution having Issued signed by Isaiah Midkiff, Esqrs. one of the Justices of the peace for Grainger County for the sum of Eleven Dollars thirty eight cents last which Execution came to the hands of Richard Shelton one of the Constables of Grainger County who made the following return in the following words, towit- came to hand Feby. 27th 1812 levied the same day upon the tract of land, towit- one tract of 73 acres also 47 others also 30 acres lying and being in the County of Grainger on Indian Creek including the Mill field when Charles Giliton formerly lived as the property of Jesse Cheek by one Richard Shelton Constable.

On motion of John Cocke Attorney for plaintiff to award an order of sale to sell the tracts of land levied on by Virtue of said Execution, (p 423)   Wednesday February 19th 1812

Joseph Cobb   )
    vs   )
Richard Malone   )   Whereas Thomas Henderson, Esqr. issued an attachment in favour of Joseph Cobb against Richard Malone for the sum of four dollars with costs &c which came to the hands of James Conn Sheriff of Grainger County who returns the same to Court with the following indorsement or return, towit- came to hand February 7th 1812 James Conn Sheriff levied the within attachment on two tracts of land on the Natches Creek waters of Clinch containing about 25 acres, the other on the waters of Clinch containing 100 acres, the property of Richard Mason, James Conn Sheriff - 7th Feby. 1812- It is considered by the Court that order of sale issue to the Sheriff of Grainger County commanding him to proceed to sell the land levied on as aforesaid & the defendant in mercy &c.

    Court adjourned till tomorrow morning 9 o'clock.

              Thursday February 20th 1812 - Court met according to adjournment.   Justices present - Isaiah Midkiff, John Cocke, Esqrs.

    Ordered by the Court that James Conn Sheriff &c be released from the payment of Double Tax on 10,000 acres of land for the year 1809, is not being collected by him by reason of said land not being sold according to law and that he have a credit in his settlement with the Treasurer in the districts of Washington and Hamilton for the amount due the State and also the amount due the County in his settlement with the County Trustee.

Joseph Noe Sr.)
    vs   )
Elijah Clark   )   Justices present, David Tate, Isaiah Midkiff and Thomas
Henderson, Esqrs.
    His Attorney makes a motion to Court to grant him a process directed to George Moody, Esqrs. directing him to issue and Execution in his favour against Elijah Clark for the sum of $50 debt, one month interest, fifty cents costs.

(p 424)   Thursday Ferbuary 20th 1812

    Moses Hodges, Esqr. having heretofore issued an Execution for said sum dated the 10th April 1810, which was levied on 100 acres of land and returned to Court. The Court ordered an order of sale to issue to sell said land which land was sold for $7.00 which being applied to costs left only thirty two cents to be applied to the extinguishment of the aforesaid Judgment of $50 Debt &c.

Stephen W. Senter)
    vs Covenant)
John Boyd   )   John Boyd Covenantee by Jacob Peck Esqr. his Attorney moves the Court for to shew cause why the Court in this case should be dismissed and after argument of Council being had it is considered by the Court that said Rule shall not be enetered.

    Ordered by the Court that it be certified that Sterling Cocke has attained to the age of twenty one years that he is a man of good moral Character and has resided a number of years in this County.

Ordered by the Court that it be certified that Wm Hamilton has attained the age of twenty one years that he has resided a number of years in this County and that he is a man of good moral character.

On application it is ordered by the Court that James Conn Sheriff and collector of the publick and County Tax have a temporary credit in his settlement with the Trustee of this County and also with the State Treasurer for the taxes due for the year 1811 on the following tracts of land, towit Blyth Samuel, 13,734 acres - Blyth Samuel 10,000 acres, Hall John 120 acres Henderson Benjamin by Henry Widener 200 acres, Lenard John 4880 acres Nicholson Samuel 3370 acres - Smock Robert, 100 acres - Woodward John, 1120 acres - Nathaniel Taylor, 150 acres - the County tax amounting to --- the Tax amounting to ------ He, the said James Conn not having had time to expose said lands to sale agreeable to law.

(p 425)   Thursday February 20th 1812

John C. Hall   )
   vs   )
John Sanders and)
John Cocke   )   John C. Haley by Thomas Gray Esqr. his Atto. makes a motion to Court to enter up a Judgment against said John Sanders and John Cocke his security on a stay bond entered into by them to said John C. Halsey dated the 19th day of Feby. 1811 which said Bond is for the penal sum of $279.96 conditioned for the payment of the Debt specified in an Execution issued from the Clerks Office of Grainger County in favour of said John C. Hailey against John Sanders &c. after argument of Council being heard as well in favour of said motion as against it, it is considered by the Court that said plaintiff John C. Haley do recover against the defendants John Sanders and John Cocke the sum of one hundred and twenty three dollars twenty four cents Damages together with all costs.

Ordered by the Court that Isaac Mitchell have leave to administer on all and singular the goods and chattels rights and credits of James Mitchell supposed to be Deceased, who enters into Bond together with George Moody and Henry Howell, his securities in the sum of $1000 for his said administration and was qualified accordingly.

Wm McNeill   )
  vs   Appeal)
Henry Howell) Justices present, Moody, Thomas Henderson and Noah Jarnagin Esqrs. Whereupon come the parties by their Atto. and a Jury, towit-

1- Nicholas Counts	7- Daniel Robinson
2- Wm Harmon	8- Isaac Mitchell
3- James Parker	9- David Proffitt
4- Jas. Rochardson	10-David Tate Jr.
5- Joseph Rich	11-Jonathan Williams
6- Warham Easley	12-John Campbell

Who being elected tryed and sworn well and truly to speak the truth in

this issue on matter of dispute in this case do say they find for the defendant - It is therefore considered by the Court that the defendant. It is therefore considered by the Court that the defendant Henry Howell recover against
the said plaintiff Wm McNeill his costs in and about prosecuting and defendant said suit in this behalf expended and the plaintiff in mercy &c.

(p 426)   Thursday February 20th 1812

John Cooke, who was chose by John Blair as his Guardian at the present
term of this Court, comes into Court and enters into Bond to Thomas Henderson, Noah Jarnagin and George Moody in the sum of six hundred Dollars
interest for the said minor heirs together with Henry Howell and John F.
Jack his securities for the faithful discharge of his said Guardianship.

Ordered by the Court that the account of money returned by David Tate
on yesterday as Guarnashee in the suit of Dulley Cox against Thomas H.
Alsup and Judicial attachment issued by the said plaintiff be condemned in
the hands of the said David Tate until a Decision can be had in the suit
Thomas H. Alsup.

Ordered by the Court that William Blair, James Blair, Thomas Henderson
Thomas Johnson, McNess Moore, Master Moore, John Boyd, Martin Stubblefield
Stephen Johnston & Jonathan Hunpower or any five of them be a Jury to view
and lay out a road from the County line near Stubblefields meeting house
through Blairs Gap and into the main post road near the head of German
Creek and make report to next Court of the conveniency or inconveniency
of the way.

William McNeill   )
    vs   appeal   )
Jonathan Williams) Justices present, Noah Jarnagin, James Moore and Isaiah
Midkiff, Esqrs. Whereupon came the parties by their Atto. and a Jury, towit-

1- Henry Howell   7- David Robinson
2- Thomas Bunch   8- Warham Easley
3- John Arwine Jr.   9- David Tate Jr.
4- Nicholas Counts   10-John Campbell
5- Wm Hanson   11-David Proffitt
6- Isaac Mitchell   12-Andrew Seabolt

Who being elected tryed and sworn well and truly to try and the truth
to speak in this matter in Dispute do say they find for the plaintiff the sum
(p 427)   Thursday February 20th 1812
of $25.86 besides costs. It is therefore considered by the Court that the
said Wm McNeill recover against the said Jonathan Williams the sum of $25.86
besides his costs in and about prosecuting said suit in this behalf expended
and the Defendant in mercy &c.

Ordered by the Court that James Parker be discharged from further attendance and that Daniel Taylor also be discharged from further attendance
as Jurors at the present term.

Ordered by the Court that the following persons -towit, be appointed
to attend as Jurors at the next term of this Court, towit-

1- Edward Churchman
2- John Bowen
3- John Peters
4- Peter Gilmore
5- Henry Danewood
6- Thomas Ball
7- Zera McGee
8- Jacob Noe
9- John Webster
10- Thomas Mann
11- Nicholas Counts
12- Archabald Hopper
13- Alex.Hamilton
14- Jonathan Williams
15- John Ivey
16- Thomas Sharp   and that Venire facias isshe &c.

Ordered by the Court that Asa Jarnagin be overseer of the road from the first big spring above Chesley Jarnagin's to the first big hollow below Robert D.Eaton's in the room and stead of William Hinds and that he have the same bounds for hands that said Hinds had to open the road agreeable to State Act of Assembly respecting the Stage road-.

Ordered by the Court that James Conn collector of the publick and County taxes for the years 1810 and 1811 be released from the taxes due on the following tracts of land, towit- for the year 1810 and on the following taxable property for the year 1810- Stephen Johnston - one white poll and

Thursday February 20th 1812
(p 428)   2 black polls taxes $1.87½- William Kirkham, 200 acres land -
1 white poll taxes $1.30 for the year 1810- Richard Shelton 123 acres of
land - 1 white poll $0.653 3/4 for 1811- Charles Matlock 300 acres- 1
black poll taxes $2.34½ and that the said collector have a credit for the
amount due the State on the above taxable property and also that the said
collector have a credit for the amount due the County &c, towit-
Credit in his settlement with the Treasurer of the District of Washington
and Hamilton and also in his settlement with the County Trustee for the
amount due each said taxable property for said year. It appearing to the
Court that the said land has been twice returned on the tax list for the
above years and that in conveyance thereof the Sheriff did not proceed to
the collections of the taxes but once.

John Griffitt, who was appointed a Constable at the present term of
this Court and Give bond for the performance of his said appointment came
into Court and was qualified according to Law.

Ordered by the Court that Susannah Denson, now of the age of thirteen
years be bound by indenture to Henry Howell until she attain the age of
Eighteen years.
Court adjourned till tomorrow morning 9 o'clock.

Friday February 21st. 1812
Court met according to adjournment. Justices present, David Tate,Isaiah
Midkiff and George Moody, Esqrs.

Parker Adkins)
   vs   )
Philip Sword) On motion of John F. Jack Atto. for for Defendant to enter a nol pros in this case and it appearing to the Court that Notices having issued to the plaintiff and each returned not found and the plaintiff failing to attend after being called to prosecute his said suit, It is ordered by the Court that the plaintiff in this case be non suited.

(p 429)   Friday February 21st. 1812

    Ordered by the Court that Clerk issue a Certificate to Daniel Taylor for four days, it appearing that he has attended as a Juror that number of days, at the present term.

Dudley Cox   )
   vs   )
Thomas H. Alsup) James Alsup and Jacob Peck comes into Court and replevies the property attached in the hands of David Tate in this case and undertake that the plaintiff will pay the condemnation money if he be case in this action or that he will do it for him or render his body in prison in discharge of themselves.

    Justices present, David Tate, Isaiah Midkiff, George Moody and James Moore, Esqrs.

    Thomas Gray, Atto. for the several plaintiffs mentioned in the Guarnishmants of Gabriel McCraw taken at the present Term, makes a motion to Court to condemn Robert Yanceys rateable portion of the personal Estate of John Coulter Deceased— amounting as appears from a statement in the Guarnishments to three thousand one hundred and seventy four dollars and seventy cents in the hands of Gabriel McCraw Admr. of the Estate of said John Coulter Deceased— for the benefit of the several plaintiffs Creditors who has sued out Executions on which said Gabriel McCraw was summoned as Guarnashee Except what expences said McCraw may have expended in recovering letters of administration to issue to him by the Court on his final settlement for his trouble and expences incurred in managing said Estate as administrator. It is therefore considered by the Court after argument had of Council that the said Robert Yanceys rateable part of the amount of sales of the personal property of John Coulter Deceased be condemned in the hands of the said Gabriel McCraw Admr. for the benefit of the   (p 430)
Friday February 21st. 1812
several plaintiff Creditors who has sued out Execution on which said Gabriel McCraw was summoned as Guarnashee except what expences said McCraw may have expended in procuring letters of administration to issue to him on said Estate and also what may hereafter be allowed him by the Court on his final settlement for his trouble and expences incurred in managing said Estate as administrator and further that no execution issue until the time limited by law, expences for the settlement of his accounts as Admr.

    Ordered by the Court that hereafter the minutes of the Court shall be sealed and signed by the Court present on each morning after the Session of the Court begins and on the evening of the last day of the Term.
    Court adjourned till Court in Course.
                                    Thomas Henderson.
            THE END

www.ingramcontent.com/pod-product-compliance
Lightning Source LLC
Chambersburg PA
CBHW080242030426

42334CB00023BA/2674